AMERICAN GOVERNMENT

Roots and Reform

2016 Presidential Election Edition, Thirteenth Edition

AP® Edition

Karen O'Connor

Jonathan N. Helfat Distinguished
Professor of Political Science, American University

Larry J. Sabato

University Professor and Robert Kent
Gooch Professor of Politics, University of Virginia

 Pearson

330 Hudson Street, New York, NY 10013

Portfolio Manager: Jeff Marshall
Content Producer: Kimberly Dunworth
Content Developers: Angela Kao and Melissa Mashburn, Ohlinger Publishing Services
Portfolio Manager Assistant: Laura Hernandez
Product Marketer: Jeremy Intal
Field Marketer: Brittany Pogue-Mohammed
Content Producer Manager: Melissa Feimer
Content Development Manager: Beth Jacobson, Ohlinger Publishing Services

Content Developer, Learning Tools: Claudine Bellanton
Art/Designer: Kathryn Foot
Digital Studio Course Producer: Tina Gagliostro
Full-Service Project Management: Valerie Iglar-Mobley, Integra Software Services, Inc.
Compositor: Integra Software Services, Inc.
Printer/Binder: LSC Roanoke
Cover Printer: Phoenix Color
Cover Design: Lumina Datamatics, Inc.
Cover Credit: Mina De La O/Getty Images
Text Font: Adobe Caslon Pro 10.5/13

Acknowledgments of third-party content appear on the appropriate page within text or on page 465, which constitutes an extension of this copyright page.

Library of Congress Cataloging-in-Publication Data
Names: O'Connor, Karen, 1952- author. | Sabato, Larry, author.
Title: American government: roots and reform/Karen O'Connor and Larry J. Sabato.
Description: 13th edition. | Hoboken, N.J.: Pearson Higher Education, 2018.
Identifiers: LCCN 2016028572| ISBN 9780134535678 | ISBN 0134535677
Subjects: LCSH: United States—Politics and government—Textbooks.
Classification: LCC JK276 .A5475 2018 | DDC 320.473—dc23
LC record available at https://lccn.loc.gov/2016028572

3   17

Pearson

www.PearsonSchool.com/Advanced

AP Edition:
ISBN 10:   0-13-461164-0 (High School Binding)
ISBN 13: 978-0-13-461164-8 (High School Binding)

Dedications

To Dolly, who at 86 followed politics, an addiction she bequeathed to me.

Karen O'Connor

To my Government 101 students over the years, who all know that "politics is a good thing."

Larry J. Sabato

PART IV Public Policy

Detailed Contents

PART II Institutions of Government

As you open this book, you may be asking yourself, "What possible impact could the Framers of the Constitution—long gone—have on my life in the twenty-first century?" Why is learning about history important to the study of politics today? And how are the ideas of the Framers relevant for understanding modern political issues such as health care, immigration, and abortion rights? We believe that without knowing the history—the roots—of our government, we won't understand how movements for political change—or reform—came to pass.

As students of the American political process, it can be challenging to identify what is really important and how government truly affects your lives. It is tempting to get caught up in key terms and definitions and miss the major themes that prevail—not only in the American political system, but also around the world.

People like you are still the cornerstone of the political process, something we may forget from time to time. But your vote counts, and executing your rights as a citizen of the United States by taking the time to vote is an important facet of American life that has changed over time to include nearly all citizens, regardless of gender or race.

We hope you will challenge prevailing notions about politics, ideas that suggest government is bloated, inefficient, wasteful, and only for old people. We hope you will come to see that politics can be a good thing, and that government is only able to represent the interests of those who actively pursue their own voice. To this end, we challenge you to identify the issues that affect your everyday lives—education, health care, the economy, just to name a few—and take every opportunity to make your voices heard. Just as the Framers' decisions in crafting a constitution live on in American political institutions, every decision made by policy makers today will have a lasting impact on your lives tomorrow.

MEET YOUR AUTHORS

Karen O'Connor is the Jonathan N. Helfat Distinguished Professor of Political Science and the Founder and Director Emerita of the Women & Politics Institute at American University. Before coming to American University, Professor O'Connor taught political science for seventeen years at Emory University in Atlanta, Georgia, where she was the first woman to receive the university's highest teaching award. She has been recognized by several associations as the most outstanding woman in political science and public administration as well as by the Southern Political Science Association (SPSA) for her contributions to the discipline. She has served on the American Political Science Association (APSA) and SPSA councils and as chair of the Law and Courts and Women and Politics Research sections of the APSA.

Larry J. Sabato is the founder and director of the University of Virginia Center for Politics. A Rhodes Scholar, Professor Sabato has taught more than tens of thousands of students in his career at Oxford University, Cambridge University, and the University of Virginia. At the University of Virginia, he has received every major teaching award, including the university's highest honor, the Thomas Jefferson Award. In 2013, Professor Sabato won an Emmy award for the documentary *Out of Order*, which he produced to highlight the dysfunctional U.S. Senate, and in 2014, he received a second Emmy award for the PBS documentary based on his *New York Times* bestseller *The Kennedy Half-Century*. Professor Sabato directs the Crystal Ball Web site, which has an unparalleled record of accuracy in predicting U.S. elections. For more information, visit http://www.centerforpolitics.org.

- This country was founded with the express purpose of welcoming immigrants with open arms, providing safe haven from persecution in native lands. Could the Framers have foreseen tough immigration laws like those considered by the Court in *Arizona* v. *United States* (2012)?
- The Framers saw Congress as a body with limited powers. But modern members of Congress balance the roles of lawmaker, budgeter, and policy maker while also acting as representatives of their district, state, party, and sometimes their race, ethnicity, or gender. How does this affect their behavior?
- The Twenty-Sixth Amendment lowered the voting age to 18. Today, young people are becoming increasingly civically aware and engaged. Could the Framers ever have anticipated how demographic changes would affect public policy?

American Government: Roots and Reform provides students with a historical context for understanding modern-day events and legislation. By drawing on more than 250 years of the American political experience, the text aids instructors and students in making comparisons between past and present. In so doing, it helps students realize that some of the challenges we face in American politics today are not new—they are simply new to us. Further, it emphasizes that by learning from the experiences of our predecessors, we may be better able to address these problems efficiently and effectively.

As instructors of American government and politics, we are faced with an increasingly challenging dilemma—persuading students to invest in the American political system at a time when trust in government is at all-time lows, and disillusionment is the norm. But as we well know, this task is perhaps more important than ever. Our students live in a rapidly changing political landscape, in which both the identity of America and its role in the world are dramatically challenged and altered. We explore issues the Framers could never have envisioned and how the basic institutions of governments have changed in responding to these new demands.

Our philosophy remains the same as always—roots and reform. By providing students with information about the roots of government and by explaining why it is important, they come to understand how their participation influences policy reforms today. And, we hope students will come to see that politics can be, and most often is, a good thing.

MYPOLISCILAB™

MyPoliSciLab with Pearson eText is an online homework, tutorial, and assessment system that improves results by helping students better master concepts and by providing educators with a dynamic set of tools for gauging individual and class performance. Its immersive experiences truly engage students in learning, helping them to understand course material, and improve their performance.

- **News clips and historical videos** bring to life chapter content and key moments in American government. For example, to augment coverage of gerrymandering, students can watch a short Associated Press report that explains the 2010 Republican redistricting plan known as RedMap. And when reading about the civil rights movement, students can watch an historical newsreel from the 1960s. Icons appear within the eText where links to these videos are located.

- **Interactive figures and maps** feature Social Explorer technology that allows updates with the latest data, toggles to illustrate movement over time, and clickable hot spots with pop-ups of images and captions. For example, when learning about the 2016 presidential campaigns and election results, students can examine a map that shows the phenomenon of frontloading, or explore an interactive map of the United States that details voting laws and voter turnout by state. Icons appear within the eText where links to these interactive figures and maps are located.

- *American Government: Roots and Reform*, AP Edition, includes **primary sources**, giving students historical context relevant to the study of American government, and helping them develop critical thinking skills.

- **Study Plan**—Practice tests help students achieve this book's learning objectives. For each chapter, there is a diagnostic pretest, a post-test, and a chapter exam that allow instructors to keep track of student mastery of the topics covered in the chapters.

- **The Pearson eText with Chapter Audio** offers a fully digital version of the print book and is readable on Apple iPad and Android tablets with the Pearson eText app. Students can highlight relevant passages and add notes.

MyPoliSciLab Preview and Adoption Access

Upon textbook purchase, students and teachers are granted access to MyPoliSciLab with Pearson eText. High school teachers can obtain preview or adoption access to MyPoliSciLab in one of the following ways:

Preview Access
- Teachers can request preview access online by visiting www.PearsonSchool.com/Access_Request. Select Social Studies, choose Initial Access, and complete the form under Option 2. Preview Access information will be sent to the teacher via e-mail.

Adoption Access
- With the purchase of this program, a Pearson Adoption Access Card with Instructor Manual will be delivered with your textbook purchase. (ISBN: 978-0-13-354087-1)

- Ask your sales representative for a Pearson Adoption Access Card with Instructor Manual. (ISBN: 978-0-13-354087-1)

  OR

- Visit PearsonSchool.com/Access_Request, select Social Studies, choose Initial Access, and complete the form under Option 3—MyLab/Mastering Class Adoption Access. Teacher and Student access information will be sent to the teacher via e-mail.

Students, ask your teacher for access.

Pearson reserves the right to change and/or update technology platforms, including possible edition updates to customers during the term of access. This will allow Pearson to continue to deliver the most up-to-date content and technology to customers. Customer will be notified of any change prior to the beginning of the new school year.

STRUCTURAL CHANGES AND COVERAGE UPDATES

While the 2016 election edition stays true to its historical approach and emphasis on currency, the overall content of the book has been significantly streamlined and shortened for greater readability and ease of comprehension. Instead of 18 chapters, the book is now 16 chapters long.

- In this edition, **Chapter 12** on **Campaigns, Elections, and Voting** combines the coverage of Chapters 12 and 13 from the previous edition.
- Also in this edition, **Chapter 15** on **Social and Economic Policy** combines the coverage of Chapters 15 and 16 from the previous edition.
- To maintain greater focus on the core content and narrative, "The Living Constitution" and "Take a Closer Look" boxed features have been incorporated in the main text or dropped. One feature appears in every chapter—**"American Politics in Comparative Perspective"**—as a window into other systems of government around the world.

As always, we strive to present a currency unparalleled by any other book in the market. *American Government: Roots and Reform* includes updated examples, figures, and tables that draw on experiences in American government in the here and now that are relevant to students' lives. At the same time, the book's historical approach has been strengthened with new opening vignettes and key examples. A better understanding of how American government has developed over time is a critical dimension that makes the content interesting to students.

- The entire book has been updated with examples and data from the **2016 presidential election results** as well as decisions from the **2015–2016 term of the Supreme Court.**
- **Chapter 1** has been significantly shortened. Coverage of ideology has been moved to Chapter 10 on Public Opinion and Political Socialization, and coverage of the types of government has been moved to Chapter 3 on the Federal System.
- **Chapter 2** opens with a vignette about the Twenty-Sixth Amendment and includes a new table that lists the twenty-seven amendments by number, year, historical era, main topic, and main area of impact.
- **Chapter 3** opens with a new vignette about the Iroquois Confederacy. Coverage of different types of government (from Chapter 1) now appears in this chapter.
- **Chapter 4** opens with a new vignette about the *Crown v. Zenger* (1735) case that set the standard for civil liberties and freedom of the press. It also includes updates of cases such as *Whole Woman's Health* v. *Hellerstedt* (2016) and the current state of *Roe v. Wade* in 2016.
- **Chapter 5** opens with a new vignette and photo about Harriet Tubman. Updates include coverage of cases such as *Obergefell* v. *Hodges* (2015) and developments that have expanded the rights of same-sex couples and transgender people serving in the military.
- **Chapter 6** opens with a new vignette about the 1865 incident between Representative Preston Brooks and Senator Charles Sumner and includes the latest results from the 2016 elections.
- **Chapter 7** includes the results of the 2016 presidential election with a revised section titled "Presidential Spouses" instead of "First Ladies." General updates focus on the modern aspects of the presidency and the Supreme Court decision in *United States* v. *Texas* (2016) about President Obama's use of executive agreements as it relates to immigration.
- **Chapter 8** opens with a new vignette about George Washington's first cabinet appointees: Alexander Hamilton, Thomas Jefferson, Henry Knox, and

Edmund Randolph. The chapter includes a new section on how the bureaucracy is staffed.

- **Chapter 9** opens with a new vignette about John Adams and the Judiciary Act of 1801. Updates include coverage of cases heard in 2015–2016 and President Obama's stalled nomination choice to replace Justice Antonin Scalia, Judge Merrick Garland.

- **Chapter 10** includes the latest data from the 2016 election coverage and coverage of political ideology (moved from Chapter 1).

- **Chapter 11** opens with a new vignette about the results of the 2016 presidential election and the role of partisan polarization in the divided electorate. The rest of the chapter has been updated to reflect party development in the 2016 election.

- **Chapter 12** opens with a new vignette that highlights similarities between the campaigns of Theodore Roosevelt and Donald Trump and also illustrates how campaigns have changed over time or (in many ways) have stayed the same. In this edition, Chapter 12 combines coverage of campaigns, elections, and voting into a single chapter that reflects the latest results and data from the 2016 election.

- **Chapter 13** has been updated to include new coverage that reflects the major presence of the Internet and social media influence in political news coverage, and several new figures show where different age groups obtain their news coverage; how media coverage of the 2016 presidential candidates might have influenced election outcomes; and how media outlets align with party affiliation.

- **Chapter 14** opens with a new vignette that hearkens back to James Madison's cautions over the dangers of factions in *Federalist No. 10*.

- **Chapter 15** is thoroughly revised and updated and combines coverage of social and economic policy into a single chapter. It begins with a new vignette about the Affordable Care Act and includes overviews of the following topics: the policy-making process, fiscal policy, monetary policy, health policy, education policy, and social welfare policy.

- **Chapter 16** opens with a new vignette that charts U.S. foreign policy between the Cold War and 9/11. The rest of the chapter has been streamlined and updated to include coverage of the continued existence of the prison at Guantanamo Bay and the continuing threats by terrorist groups like ISIS.

CONTENT HIGHLIGHTS

Every chapter in this text uses history to serve three purposes: first, to show how institutions and processes have evolved to their present states; second, to provide some of the color that makes information memorable; and third, to provide students with a more thorough appreciation of the fact that our government was born amid burning issues of representation and power—issues that continue to smolder today. A richer historical texture helps to explain the present.

With roots and reform providing the foundation from which all topics and concepts in this book are discussed, the text is divided into four parts. Part I, Foundations of Government, covers the American government's roots, context, and culture. Through a discussion of the Constitution, it considers those broad concepts associated with government in the United States: the federal system, civil liberties, and civil rights. Part I sets the stage for the coverage in Part II, Institutions of Government, which introduces students to the institutions of government through its discussion of Congress, the presidency, the executive branch and the federal bureaucracy, and the judiciary. Political Behavior, Part III, delves into the ideas and processes that make democracy what it is: public opinion and political socialization, political parties, elections and voting, the campaign process, the news media, and interest groups. Part IV, Public Policy, rounds out the coverage with detailed discussions of domestic policy, economic policy, and foreign and defense policy. Coverage in these chapters makes use of the most current data and debates to frame discussions of health care, energy and the environment, education, and the United States' role on the global political stage.

Each chapter also includes the following pedagogical features:

- **Roots of and Toward Reform** sections highlight the text's emphasis on the importance of the history of American government as well as the dynamic cycle of reassessment and reform that allows the United States to continue to evolve. Every chapter begins with a "Roots of" section that gives a historical overview of the topic at hand and ends with a "Toward Reform" section devoted to a particularly contentious aspect of the topic discussed.

ROOTS OF CIVIL LIBERTIES: THE BILL OF RIGHTS

4.1 Explain the roots of civil liberties in the Constitution and their development in the Bill of Rights.

In 1787, most state constitutions explicitly protected a variety of personal liberties, such as freedoms of speech and religion, freedom from unreasonable searches and seizures, and trial by jury. The new federal system established by the Constitution would redistribute power between the national government and the states. Without an explicit guarantee of specific civil liberties, could the national government be trusted to uphold the freedoms already granted to citizens by their states?

Recognition of the increased power of the new national government led Anti-Federalists to stress the need for a bill of rights. Anti-Federalists and many others were confident they could control the actions of their own state legislators, but they did not trust the national government to protect civil liberties.

The notion of including a bill of rights in the Constitution was not popular at the Constitutional Convention. When George Mason of Virginia suggested adding such a bill to the preface of the proposed Constitution, representatives unanimously defeated his resolution.[1] In subsequent ratification debates, Federalists argued that a bill of rights was unnecessary, putting forward three main arguments in opposition.

TOWARD REFORM: CIVIL LIBERTIES AND COMBATING TERRORISM

4.7 Evaluate how reforms to combat terrorism have affected civil liberties.

The brilliance of the civil liberties codified by the First Congress is that the Bill of Rights remains a relatively stable statement of our natural rights as Americans, even as technology has evolved. Judicial interpretation ensures that the sentiments expressed more than 200 years ago still apply to the modern world. After the terrorist attacks of **September 11**, 2001, however, some critics charged that the U.S. government began to operate in "an alternate reality," in which Bill of Rights guarantees were suspended just as they had been during the Civil War and World Wars I and II.[99] The difference in this modern era, critics claim, is that the "war" has no direct enemy, and its timeline for completion is ever-changing. Here, we detail the provisions of laws such as the USA PATRIOT Act and the Military Commissions Act, as well as subsequent actions by the National Security Agency under Barack Obama's administration, and explain how they have affected the civil liberties discussed in this chapter.

- **American Politics in Comparative Perspective** is a new visual feature meant to expose readers to other systems of government around the world. Each feature includes a photo essay, table, figure, or map that compares some aspect of U.S. government to two or more countries. For example, in Chapter 2, the feature highlights the relative brevity of the U.S. Constitution as compared to similar documents in fifteen other countries. In Chapter 6, the feature examines three different types of legislature: unicameral, asymmetric bicameral, and symmetric bicameral houses. In Chapter 11, the feature compares the U.S. Electoral College system to others in Afghanistan, Israel, Brazil, and France. Each box concludes with critical thinking questions that challenge readers to consider the similarities and differences of each system, analyze relative advantages and disadvantages, and better understand America's system as it compares with the rest of the world.

AMERICAN POLITICS IN COMPARATIVE PERSPECTIVE

How Many Legislative Houses? One, Two, or One-and-a-Half?

In the United States, the two houses of Congress that make up the national legislature have robust powers. The House of Representatives and Senate have authority over legislation, budget authorizations, constitutional amendments, and oversight of the bureaucracy. "Symmetric bicameralism" is the term used by political scientists to describe a legislature like the U.S. Congress or Mexico's Congress of the Union that consists of two houses with an even balance of powers. This is not the only model used among democracies in the world, however. "Unicameralism" refers to legislative systems such as Israel's Knesset that consist of a single chamber. "Asymmetric bicameralism" refers to legislative systems with two unequal chambers like India's national legislature. These structural differences can have a major impact on how, and even whether, legislation can be enacted in different systems.

The national legislature of Israel, the Knesset, is a single chamber with 120 members. Israel is a parliamentary system in which most majorities are coalitions of several different parties.

India's national legislature has a lower house directly elected by voters and an upper house indirectly elected by state legislatures. The lower house may bypass the upper house on most issues.

Mexico has a bicameral legislature with two equal houses. Mexico's president is elected separately and constitutes a distinct executive branch of government equal to Congress.

- **New photos** capture major events from the last few years, of course, but also illustrate politics' relevancy; they show political actors and processes as well as people affected by politics, creating a visual narrative that enhances rather than repeats the text. Historical photos further illustrate how the past informs the present.

- **Key terms** related to the chapter content are defined throughout the text to help students identify new and important concepts and again in a comprehensive glossary.

- A focus on **qualitative literacy** helps students analyze, interpret, synthesize, and apply visual information—skills essential in today's world. We receive information from the written and spoken word, but knowledge also comes in visual forms. We are used to thinking about reading text critically, but we do not always think about "reading" visuals in this way. A focus on qualitative literacy encourages students to think about the images and informational graphics they will encounter throughout this text as well as those they see every day in the newspaper, in magazines, on the Web, on television, and in books. Critical thinking questions assist students in learning how to analyze visuals.

  - **Tables** consist of textual information and/or numerical data arranged in tabular form in columns and rows. Tables are frequently used when exact information is required and when orderly arrangement is necessary to locate and, in many cases, to compare the information. All tables in this edition include questions and encourage critical thinking.

  - **Charts, graphs, and maps** depict numerical data in visual forms. Examples that students will encounter throughout this text are line graphs, pie charts, and bar graphs. Line graphs show a progression, usually over time (as in how the U.S. population has grown over time). Pie charts (such as ones showing population demographics) demonstrate how a whole (total American population) is divided into its parts (different racial and ethnic groups). Bar graphs compare values across categories, showing how proportions are related to each other (as in how much money each party raised in presidential election years). Bar graphs can present data either horizontally or vertically. All charts and graphs in this edition are based on questions that encourage critical thinking.

  - Some of the most interesting commentary on American politics takes place in the form of **political cartoons**. The cartoonist's goal is to comment on and/or criticize political figures, policies, or events. The cartoonist uses several techniques to accomplish this goal, including exaggeration, irony, and juxtaposition. For example, the cartoonist may point out how the results of governmental policies are the opposite of their intended effects (irony). In other cartoons, two people, ideas, or events that do not belong together may be joined to make a point (juxtaposition). Knowledge of current events is helpful in interpreting political cartoons.

SUPPLEMENTS

For the Instructor

Most of the teacher supplements and resources for this text are also available electronically to qualified adopters on the Instructor Resource Center (IRC). Upon adoption or to preview, please go to www.pearsonschool.com/Access_Request and select Instructor Resource Center. You will be required to complete a brief one-time registration subject to verification of educator status. Upon verification, access information and instructions will be sent to you via e-mail. Once logged into the IRC, enter ISBN 0-13-461164-0 in the "Search Our Catalog" box to locate resources.

Instructor's Resources includes Instructor's Manual, Test Bank, MyTest, and PowerPoints.

INSTRUCTOR'S MANUAL   Create a comprehensive roadmap for teaching classroom, online, or hybrid courses. Designed for both new and experienced instructors, the Instructor's Manual includes a sample syllabus, lecture and discussion suggestions, activities for in or out of class, and essays on teaching American Government. Available within MyPoliSciLab or on the IRC for download.

TEST BANK   Evaluate learning at every level. Reviewed for clarity and accuracy, the Test Bank measures this material's learning objectives with multiple choice, true/false, fill-in-the-blank, short answer, and essay questions. You can easily customize the assessment to work in any major learning management system and to match what is covered in your course. Available within MyPoliSciLab or on the IRC for download.

PEARSON MYTEST   This powerful assessment generation program includes all of the questions in the Test Bank. Quizzes and exams can be easily authored and saved online and then printed for classroom use, giving you ultimate flexibility to manage assessments anytime and anywhere. To learn more, visit www.pearsonhighered.com/mytest.

POWERPOINT PRESENTATION WITH CLASSROOM RESPONSE SYSTEM (CRS)   Make lectures more enriching for students. The PowerPoint Presentation includes a full lecture script, discussion questions, and photos and figures from the material, and links to MyPoliSciLab multimedia. With integrated clicker questions, get immediate feedback on what your students are learning during a lecture. Available within MyPoliSciLab or on the IRC for download.

CORRELATION GUIDE FOR AP GOVERNMENT AND POLITICS: UNITED STATES

AP Topics	American Government: Roots and Reform, 13/e, AP Edition
Big Idea 1: Constitutional Democracy	
Enduring Understanding 1.A: A balance between governmental power and individual rights has been a hallmark of American political development.	pp. 5, 31, 36, 64–67, 149
Enduring Understanding 1.B: The writing and ratification of the Constitution emerged from the debate about weaknesses in the Articles of Confederation and was the product of important compromises.	Chapter 2; pp. 21–22, 40, 44–45
Enduring Understanding 1.C: The Constitution creates a complex and competitive policymaking process to ensure the people's will is accurately represented and that freedom is preserved.	Chapters 2, 15 & 16; pp. 169–171, 217–219, 361, 362–367
Enduring Understanding 1.D: Federalism reflects the dynamic distribution of power between national and state governments.	Chapter 3; pp. 28, 37, 197, 195, 222
Big Idea 2: Civil Liberties, Civil Rights	
Enduring Understanding 2.A: Provisions of the Bill of Rights are continually being interpreted to balance the power of government and the civil liberties of individuals.	Chapters 4 & 5; pp. 36
Enduring Understanding 2.B: The due process clause of the 14th Amendment has been interpreted to prevent the states from infringing upon basic liberties.	Chapters 4 & 5; pp. 65, 77, 97
Enduring Understanding 2.C: The 14th Amendment's "equal protection clause" has often been used to support the advancement of equality.	Chapters 4 & 5; pp. 92-93, 96, 98–99
Big Idea 3: American Political Culture and Beliefs	
Enduring Understanding 3.A: Citizen beliefs about government are shaped by the intersection of demographics, political culture, and dynamic social change.	Chapter 10; pp. 20, 107–115, 233–237
Enduring Understanding 3.B: Widely held political ideologies shape policy debates and choices in American politics.	Chapters 10 & 12; pp. 235, 295–299

CORRELATION GUIDE FOR AP GOVERNMENT AND POLITICS: UNITED STATES (CONTINUED)

AP Topics	*American Government: Roots and Reform, 13/e, AP Edition*
Big Idea 4: Political Participation	
Enduring Understanding 4.A: Public opinion is measured through scientific polling and the results of public opinion polls influence public policies and institutions.	pp. 221–225, 227–229, 230, 238–239
Enduring Understanding 4.B: The various forms of media provide citizens with political information and influence the ways in which they participate politically.	Chapter 13; pp. 168, 287–289, 315–317
Enduring Understanding 4.C: Political parties, interest groups, and social movements provide opportunities for participation and influence how people relate to government.	Chapters 11 & 14; pp. 146–148, 159, 254, 295–296, 345–346
Enduring Understanding 4.D: Although laws and amendments have expanded voting rights in the U.S., voting participation varies widely from election to election.	Chapters 10 & 12; pp. 15, 37, 97, 273, 283, 296–299, 301–303
Enduring Understanding 4.E: The impact of federal policies on campaigning and electoral rules continues to be contested by both sides of the political spectrum.	Chapter 12; pp. 27, 276, 299–303
Big Idea 5: Interaction Among Branches	
Enduring Understanding 5.A: The republican ideal in the U.S. is manifested in the structure and operation of the legislative branch.	Chapters 6, 15 & 16; pp. 26, 29, 31, 122, 126
Enduring Understanding 5.B: The presidency has been enhanced beyond its expressed constitutional powers.	Chapters 7 & 8; pp. 29, 31, 161–162, 170–171, 190–191, 346–347, 353–354
Enduring Understanding 5.C: The design of the judicial branch protects the court's independence as a branch of government, and the emergence and use of judicial review remains a powerful judicial practice.	Chapter 9; pp. 29, 31, 196–200, 347, 354, 400
Enduring Understanding 5.D: The federal bureaucracy is a powerful institution implementing federal policies with sometimes questionable accountability.	Chapter 8

Acknowledgments

The authors would like to thank those who reviewed the text at the various stages of revision; they gave generously of their time and expertise and we are, as always, in their debt.

Karen O'Connor thanks the thousands of students in her American Government courses at Emory and American Universities who, over the years, have pushed her to learn more about American government and to have fun in the process. She especially thanks Jonathan and Robin Helfat for their generous support of her scholarly work. Her former students, too, have contributed in various ways to this project, especially Linda Mancillas at Georgia Gwinnett College, John R. Hermann at Trinity University, Sue Davis at Denison University, and Laura van Assendelft at Mary Baldwin College. She also thanks Professor Kent Miller for his ongoing review of the text.

For the past seven editions, Alixandra B. Yanus of High Point University offered invaluable assistance, unflagging support, friendship, and a keen eye to the latest trends in footwear—a must in a profession known for sensible shoes. First, as a student at American University, where she won the President's Award for Outstanding Research, and next at the University of North Carolina at Chapel Hill, her fresh perspectives on politics and ideas about things of interest to students, as well as her keen eye for the typo, her research abilities, and her unbelievably hard work, have continually made this a much better book. As a co-author on the last three editions, she stepped up to be an invaluable contributor, bringing enthusiasm and the viewpoint of a newly minted PhD and an outstanding, devoted classroom teacher to the book. She remains a dear friend.

Karen further acknowledges the help and encouragement of Steve Gilbert, Beth Mutha, Jerry Share, Christina Stayeas, and Armistead Williams III. She also is appreciative of the constant companionship of Penny Louise, who asks for nothing more than any dog would, and keeps Karen (and often "Aunt Ali") from going crazy as we work to keep this book current and student-friendly; and her brother, TR, who starts her Sundays with a Starbucks mixture of soy that actually doesn't taste that bad.

Last, but certainly not least, Karen needs to recognize the support of her daughter, Meghan O'Connor McDonogh. She grew up with this book and considers Eric Stano, our editor during her college and doctoral studies, to be a quasi big brother, which sometimes frightens Karen. And, despite her vow never to teach or coach, she does both at The Catholic University of America, proving that old adage that the apple sometimes does not fall far from the tree.

Particular thanks goes to Ray Smith at Columbia University and New York University, who tackled the revisions of the chapters on domestic and economic policy as well as the rapidly shifting landscape of foreign and defense policy for this edition. Our continued thanks go to Christopher Simon at the University of Utah, Glenn Hastedt of James Madison University, Steven Koven at the University of Louisville, Daniel S. Papp of Kennesaw State University, and Kiki Caruson of the University of South Florida, whose earlier work on policy content continues to serve as a strong foundation.

Larry J. Sabato would like to acknowledge the 15,000-plus students from his University of Virginia Introduction to American Politics classes over thirty-five years and the many student interns at the UVA Center for Politics who have offered valuable suggestions and an abundance of thoughtful feedback. A massive textbook project like this one needs the very best assistance an author can find, and this author was lucky enough to find some marvelously talented people. Carah Ong

Whaley worked tirelessly to research the new edition and weave together beautifully constructed sections on recent American politics. Her attention to detail and editor's eye have refined many chapters and improved the overall flow. As always, the staff of the University of Virginia Center for Politics and a team of extraordinary interns contributed in many important ways toward the successful completion of this volume, including chief of staff Ken Stroupe and communications director Kyle Kondik. Their commitment to excellence is also obvious in their work for the Center's Crystal Ball website (www.centerforpolitics.org/crystalball)—a very useful resource in completing this volume.

In the now many years we have been writing and rewriting this book, we have been blessed to have been helped by many people at Pearson Education. For this edition, our editor, Jeff Marshall, has responded to our fiery personalities and endless ideas with a few tricks—and a whole lot of enthusiasm—of his own. We were lucky to have two development editors for this edition: Angela Kao brought a quiet efficiency to the process; she has demonstrated great flexibility, advising us on content, developing facets of the digital edition, and doing all the behind-the-scenes work that too often goes underappreciated; Melissa Mashburn brought her editorial know-how, good humor, patience, enthusiasm, and careful eye to our updates and new features. Our thanks also go to the team at Ohlinger Publishing Services for their work on the interactive aspects of this revision: Debbie Coniglio, Kim Norbuta, and Natalee Sperry. And, we would be remiss not to thank our former editor, Eric Stano, who guided this book for more than ten years. We would also like to acknowledge the tireless efforts of the Pearson Education sales force. In the end, we hope all of these talented people see how much their work and support have helped us to write a better book.

Finally, the authors wish to thank the many professors and researchers who provided detailed feedback on how to improve content, especially John Kincaid at Lafayette College. Additionally, we thank many other colleagues for their invaluable input during professional conferences and Pearson-sponsored events. They gave generously of their time and expertise and we are, as always, in their debt.

Test Bank Advisory Board: Paul Benson, Texas Woman's University; Fred Gordon, Columbus State University; Natalie Johnson, Francis Marion University; Clarissa Peterson, DePauw University; Tony Wohlers, Cameron University; and Jason Wojcik, SUNY Alfred State.

APSA 2015: Brian Califano, Missouri State University; David A. Caputo, Pace University; Lori Cox Han, Chapman University; Joshua Dyck, University of Massachusetts, Lowell; Maurice Eisenstein, Purdue University Calumet; Bryan Gervais, UTSA; Ben Gonzalez, Highline College; Mel Hailey, Abilene Christian University; Kerstin Hamann, University of Central Florida; Meredith Heiser, Foothill College; Erika Herrera, Lone Star College; Judith Hurtado Ortiz, Peralta; Gabe Jolivet, Ashford University; Ryan Krog, George Washington University; Jessica Lavariega Monforti, Pace University; Liz Lebron, LSU; Andrew Levin, Harper College; Stephen Meinhold, UNC-W; Keesha Middlemass, Trinity University; Samantha Mosier, Missouri State University; Jason Myers, CSU Stanislaus; Todd Myers, Grossmont Community College; Sharon Navarro, University of Texas at San Antonio; John Payne, Ivy Tech Community College; Anne C. Pluta, Rowan; Dan Ponder, Drury University; David Ramsey, UWF; Jason Robles, Colorado State University; John David Rausch, Jr., West Texas A&M University; Jon Ross, Aurora College; Erich Saphir, Pima College; Justin Vaughn, Boise State University; Peter Wielhouwer, Western Michigan University; Patrick Wohlfarth, University of Maryland, College Park; Chris Wolfe, Dallas County Community College; Youngtae Shin, University of Central Oklahoma.

APSA 2016: Cathy Andrews, Austin Community College; Sara Angevine, Whittier College; Benjamin Arah, Bowie State University; Yan Bai, Grand Rapids Community College; Michael Bailey, Georgetown University; Karen L. Baird, Purchase College, SUNY; Richard Bilsker, College of Southern Maryland; Russell Brooker, Alverno College; Christopher M. Brown, Georgia Southern University; Jonathan Buckstead, Austin Community College; Camille Burge, Villanova University; Isaac M. Castellano, Boise State University; Stefanie Chambers, Trinity College; Anne Marie Choup, University of Alabama, Huntsville; Nick Clark, Susquehanna University; Mary Anne Clarke, RI College; Carlos Cunha, Dowling College; John Diehl, Bucks County Community College; Joseph DiSarro, Washington and Jefferson University; Margaret Dwyer, Milwaukee School of Engineering; Laurel Elder, Hardwick College; Melinda Frederick, Prince George's Community College; Amanda Friesen, IUPUI; Jason Giersch, UNC, Charlotte; Mauro Gilli, ETH; Margaret Gray, Adelphi University; Mark Grzegorzewski, Joint Special Operations University; John Hanley, Duquesne University; Jacqueline Holland, Lorain County Community College; Jack Hunt, University of Southern Maine; Clinton Jenkins, George Washington University; Nadia Jilani-Hyler, Augusta University; Christopher N. Lawrence, Middle Georgia State University; Daniel Lewis, Siena College; Joel Lieske, Cleveland State; Nancy Lind, Illinois State University; Matt Lindstrom, College of St. Benedict / St. John's University; Eric D. Loepp, UW-Whitewater; Kevin Lorentz, Wayne State University; Gregory Love, University of Mississippi; Abbie Luoma, Saint Leo University; Linda K. Mancillas, Georgia Gwinnett College; Buba Misawa, Washington and Jefferson College; Martha Musgrove, Tarrant County College – South Campus; Steven Nawara, Lewis University; Tatishe Nteta, University of Massachusetts, Amherst; Dr. Mjahid Nyahuma, Community College of Philadelphia; Matthew Platt, Morehouse College; Marcus Pohlmann, Rhodes College; Adriane M. Raff Corwin, Bergen & Brookdale Community Colleges; Lauren Ratliff, The Ohio State University; Dr. Keith Reeves, Swarthmore College; Ted Ritter, Virginia Union University; Joseph W. Roberts, Roger Williams University; Amanda Rosen, Webster University; Scot Schraufnagel, Northern Illinois University; John Seymour, El Paso Community College; Ginger Silvera, Cal State, Dominguez Hills; Kyla Stepp, Central Michigan University; Ryane Straus, College of Saint Rose; Maryam Stevenson, Troy University; Tressa Tabares, American River College; Bernard Tamas, Valdosta State University; Lee Trepanier, Saginaw Valley State University; Kevin Wallsten, California State University, Long Beach; Richard Waterman, University of Kentucky; Joe Weinberg, University of Southern Mississippi; Jonathan Whatron, Southern Connecticut State University; Elizabeth G. Williams, PhD, Santa Fe College.

2016 WebEx Meetings for REVEL: Maria Albo, University of North Georgia; Hendel Cerphy, Palm Beach State College; Karl Clark, Coastal Bend College; Amy Colon, SUNY Sullivan; Lishan Desta, Collin College; Agber Dimah, Chicago State University; Dr. Barbara Warner, Arkansas State University; Kathleen Ferraiolo, James Madison University; Terri Susan Fine, University of Central Florida; Maria Gonzalez, Miami Dade College; Joe Gaziano, Lewis University; Dion George, Atlanta Metropolitan State College; Colin Glennon, East Tennessee State University; Mike Green, Southern New Hampshire University; Jan Hardt, University of Central Oklahoma; Kathryn Hendricks, MCC – Longview; Julie Hershenberg, Collin College; Jeneen Hobby, Cleveland State University; Andy Howard, Rio Hondo College; Nikki Isemann, Southeast Community College; Nicole Kalaf-Hughes, Bowling Green State University; Frederick M. Kalisz, Bridgewater State University; Lance Kelley, NWTC; Eric Loepp, University of Wisconsin, Whitewater; Benjamin Melusky, Franklin and Marshall College; David Monda, Mt. San Jacinto College; Laura Pellegrini, LBCC; Dave Price, Santa Fe College; Jennifer Sacco, Quinnipiac University; Larry W. Smith, Amarillo College; J. Joel Tovanche, Tarrant County College.

Spring 2016 WebEx Meetings: Cathy Andrews, Austin Community College; Yan Bai, Grand Rapids Community College; Richard Bilsker, College of Southern Maryland; Jonathan Buckstead, Austin Community College; Adriane M. Raff Corwin, Bergen & Brookdale Community Colleges; Carlos Cunha, Dowling College; Margaret Dwyer, Milwaukee School of Engineering; Jacqueline Holland, Lorain County Community College; Nadia Jilani-Hyler, Augusta University; Nancy Lind, Illinois State University; Eric D. Loepp, UW-Whitewater; Abbie Luoma, Saint Leo University; Martha Musgrove, Tarrant County College – South College; Steven Nawara, Lewis University; Maryam Stevenson, Troy University; Lee Trepanier, Saginaw Valley State University; Elizabeth G. Williams, PhD, Santa Fe College.

2016 Texas WebEx Meetings: Ralph Angeles, Lone Star College; Delina Barrera, University of Texas Pan American; Jennifer Boggs, Angelo State University; Bryan Calvin, Tarrant County College Northwest; William Carroll, Sam Houston State University; Anita Chadha, University of Houston-Downtown; Jennifer Danley-Scott, Texas Woman's University; Bianca Easterly, Lamar University; Reynaldo Flores, Richland College; Katie Fogle Deering, North Central Texas University; Sylvia Gonzalez-Gorman, Texas Tech; Peyton Gooch, Stephen F. Austin; Donald Gooch, Stephen F. Austin; Cheri Hobbs, Blinn College; Cynthia Hunter-Summerlin, Tarrant County College Trinity River; Joe Ialenti, North Central Texas College; Dominique Lewis, Blinn College; Eric Lundin, Lonestar College; Sharon Manna, North Lake College; Holly Mulholland, San Jacinto College Central; Hillel Ofek, University of Texas at Austin; Lisa Palton, San Jacinto Community College; William Parent, San Jacinto College Central; Cecil Pool, El Centro College; Jennifer Ross, Brookhaven College DCCCD; Lane Seever, Austin Community College; Max Seymour, West Texas A&M University; Les Stanaland, North Central Texas College; Dustin Tarver, Blinn College; James Tate, Richland College; Blake Tritico, Sam Houston State University; Karen Webb, Texas Woman's University.

May 2016 Hoboken / Boston Focus Groups: Flannery Amdahl, Hunter College; Thomas Arndt, Rowan University; Ben Christ, Harrisburg Area Community College; Mary Anne Clarke, RI College; Ken Cosgrove, Suffolk University; Melissa Gaeke, Marist College; Todd M. Galante, Rutgers University-Newark; Jack Hunt, University of Southern Maine; Ed Johnson, Brookdale Community College; Frederick M. Kalisz, Jr., Bridgewater State University; M. Victoria Perez-Rios, John Jay College of Criminal Justice, CUNY; Francois Pierre-Louis, Queens College, CUNY; John Seymour, El Paso Community College; Ursula C. Tafe, University of Massachusetts Boston; Anh Tran, Baruch College; John Trujillo, Borough of Manhattan Community College; Aaron Zack, John Jay College.

WHAT HAPPENED WHEN EUROPEANS REACHED THE AMERICAS?

Attitudes in the United States towards explorers such as Christopher Columbus have shifted sharply in recent decades. Columbus once was heralded for "discovering" the Americas and a federal holiday still honors him each October. However, emphasis has been placed increasingly on explorers' negative impacts on native peoples and broader critiques of European colonialism.

AMERICAN GOVERNMENT: ROOTS, CONTEXT, AND CULTURE

LEARNING OBJECTIVES

1.1 Trace the origins of American government.

1.2 Explain the functions of American government.

1.3 Analyze the changing characteristics of the American public.

1.4 Characterize changes in Americans' attitudes toward and expectations of government.

government
The formal vehicle through which policies are made and affairs of state are conducted.

n 1492, Christopher Columbus, with the support of the king and queen of Spain, landed in the Bahamas in the "New World" on his journey to find a quicker water route to India and its riches. Believing he had landed in India, he named the native peoples Indians. After the news of Columbus's expedition, other explorers sponsored by Spain, such as Hernando de Soto and Juan Ponce de Leon, traveled west looking for gold, furs, and rich soil. Adventurers such as John Cabot and Sir Frances Drake from England and Giovanni da Verrazano, an Italian sponsored by France, soon launched their own expeditions.

These explorers were not interested in establishing permanent residences. The monarchies supporting them wanted to claim native lands for themselves. Spain, France, and England more than welcomed the gold, furs, and new agricultural riches, which greatly enlarged their national treasuries.

As nations began to compete for lands, Pope Alexander VI, who claimed all lands for God and thus the Roman Catholic Church, issued a proclamation in 1494 that drew a north/south line through the Western Hemisphere, giving the west to Spain and the east to Portugal. Spain occupied settlements in Florida and eventually the entire Southwest and what later became known as the Louisiana Purchase.

By the mid-1500s, France, Holland, and Great Britain were engaged in exploring North America. French fur trappers moved throughout what is now the eastern parts of Canada and established a settlement in Quebec. To facilitate trade, trappers knew that they must establish good working relationships with several Indian tribes. In sharp contrast, the Spanish enslaved American Indians and treated them with brutality. It wasn't to be too long before France, Holland, and Great Britain recognized the potential offered by the New World and sought to seek land previously claimed by Spain.

● ● ●

In this text, we explore the American political system through a historical lens. This perspective allows us to analyze the ways that the ideas and actions of a host of different Americans—from European explorers, to Indians, to colonists, to the Framers of the Constitution as well as the global citizens of today—have affected how our **government**—the formal vehicle through which policies are made and affairs of state are conducted—works.

ROOTS OF AMERICAN GOVERNMENT: WE THE PEOPLE

1.1 Trace the origins of American government.

Much has changed since the earliest explorers and settlers came to the New World. The people who live in America today differ greatly from those early inhabitants. In this section, we lay the groundwork for the study of the United States today by looking at the earliest inhabitants of the Americas, their initial and ongoing interactions with European colonists, and how new Americans continually built on the experiences of the past to create a new future.

The Earliest Inhabitants of the Americas

By the time the first colonists arrived in what is now known as the United States, indigenous peoples had been living in the area for more than 30,000 years. Most historians and archaeologists believe that these peoples migrated from present-day Russia through the Bering Strait into North America and then dispersed throughout the American continents. Some debate continues, however, about where they first appeared and whether they crossed an ice bridge from Siberia or arrived on boats from across the Pacific. Other peoples came from the Southern Hemisphere and settled in the Southwest.

FIGURE 1.1   WHAT DID TRIBAL DISTRIBUTION LOOK LIKE BEFORE EUROPEAN SETTLEMENT?

The first peoples of North America were extremely diverse, with hundreds of different cultures, languages, and traditions dispersed across North America before the arrival of European settlers.

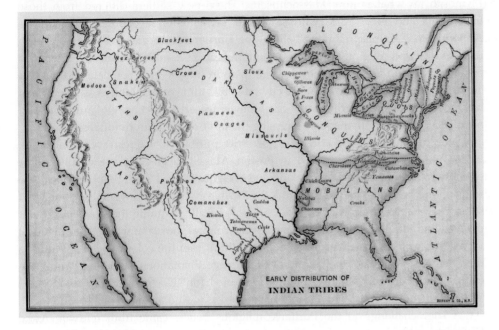

The indigenous peoples were not a homogeneous group; their cultures, customs, and values varied widely, as did their political systems. The number of these indigenous peoples, who lived in all parts of what is now the United States, is impossible to know for certain. Estimates by scholars, however, range from 100 million people to many more. These numbers quickly diminished as colonists brought with them to the New World a range of diseases to which the indigenous peoples had not been exposed. In addition, warfare with the European settlers as well as within tribes not only killed many American Indians but also disrupted previously established ways of life. And, the European settlers displaced Indians, repeatedly pushing them westward as they created settlements and, later, colonies.

The First Colonists

Colonists journeyed to North America for a variety of reasons. Many wealthy Englishmen and other Europeans left home seeking to enhance their fortunes. With them came a host of laborers who hoped to find their own opportunities for riches. In fact, commerce was the most common initial reason for settlement in North America.

The first permanent English settlement was established in Jamestown, Virginia, in 1607 by a joint stock company seeking riches in the New World. In 1619, the first slaves arrived there. In 1609, the Dutch New Netherland Company settled along the Hudson and lower Delaware Rivers, calling the area New Netherlands. Later, in 1626, the Dutch West India Company purchased Manhattan Island from an Indian tribe and established trading posts on the Hudson River. Both Fort Orange, in what is now Albany, New York, and New Amsterdam, New York City's Manhattan Island, were populated not by colonists but by salaried employees. Among those who flocked to New Amsterdam (renamed New York in 1664) were settlers from Finland, Germany, and Sweden. The varied immigrants also included free blacks. This ethnic and racial mix created its own system of cultural inclusiveness that continues to make New York City and its citizenry unique today (see Figure 1.2).

FIGURE 1.2   WHAT DID COLONIAL SETTLEMENT LOOK LIKE BEFORE 1700?

Prior to 1700, pockets of colonial settlement existed along the east coast of what became the United States, from present-day Virginia to what is now Maine. These settlements were divided among a number of colonial powers, including the English in the northeast and around the Chesapeake Bay, the Dutch in what is present-day New York, and the Swedes, largely in present-day Delaware.

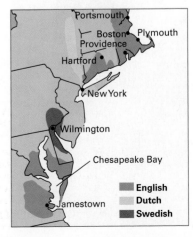

Mayflower
The ship carrying Pilgrim settlers from England whose arrival in Massachusetts in 1620 is considering a founding moment for the nation.

Roger Williams
Seventeenth century religious and political leader who was expelled by Puritans in Massachusetts and then established the colony of Providence Plantations that later became Rhode Island.

Anne Hutchinson
Seventeenth century political leader and thinker who supported religious liberty.

Thomas Hooker
Colonial-era politician who supported expanded voting rights.

William Penn
Quaker leader and supporter of religious tolerance who founded Pennsylvania.

WHO WAS ANNE HUTCHINSON?
Anne Hutchinson was a midwife and minister who challenged the prevailing religious thinking of the Massachusetts Bay Colony. She was expelled from the colony and went on to found a new settlement at Portsmouth, Rhode Island, attracting many women to her views on Christianity.

A Religious Tradition Takes Root

In 1620, a group of Protestants known as Puritans left Europe aboard the *Mayflower*. Destined for Virginia, they found themselves off course and landed instead in Plymouth, in what is now Massachusetts. These new settlers differed from those in Virginia and New York, who saw their settlements as commercial ventures. Adhering to Calvinist religious beliefs, the Puritans (also called Pilgrims, a term used to describe religious travellers) came instead as families bound together by a common belief in the powerful role of religion in their lives. They believed the Old Testament charged them to create "a city on a hill" that would shine as an example of righteousness. To help achieve this goal, they enforced a strict code of authority and obedience, while simultaneously stressing the importance of individualism.

Soon, the ideas at the core of these strict puritanical values faced challenges. In 1631, **Roger Williams** arrived in Boston, Massachusetts. He preached extreme separation from the Church of England and even questioned the right of Europeans to settle on Indian lands. He believed that the Puritans went too far when they punished settlers who deviated from their strict code of morality, arguing that it was God, not people, who should punish individuals for their moral shortcomings. These "heretical views" prompted local magistrates to banish him from the colony in 1635. Williams then helped to establish the colony of Providence Plantations. Providence, now the capital of present-day Rhode Island, was named for "God's merciful Providence," which Williams believed had allowed his followers to find a place to settle.

A later challenge to the Puritans' religious beliefs came from midwife **Anne Hutchinson**. She began to share her view that the churches established in Massachusetts had lost touch with the Holy Spirit. Many of her followers were women who were attracted to her progressive ideas on the importance of religious tolerance, as well as on the equality and rights of women. Authorities in Massachusetts tried Hutchinson for blasphemy for her views and banished her from the colony. She and her followers eventually settled in Portsmouth, Rhode Island, which became a beacon for those seeking religious toleration and popular—as opposed to religious—sovereignty.

Thomas Hooker, too, soon found himself at odds with the Calvinist Puritans in the Massachusetts Bay Colony. Hooker believed they were too narrow-minded; in his view, all men should have the right to vote regardless of religious views or property qualifications. He and his supporters thus relocated to the new colony of Connecticut, where they developed a settlement at Hartford. Hooker's words inspired the drafting of the Connecticut constitution, thought to be the first to establish a representative government.

Later colonies in the New World were established with religious tolerance in mind. In 1632, King Charles I granted a well-known English Catholic, George Calvert, the first Lord Baltimore, a charter to establish the Catholic colony of Maryland in the New World. In 1681, King Charles II bestowed upon **William Penn** a charter giving him sole ownership of a vast area of land just north of Maryland. The king called the land Pennsylvania, or Penn's Woods. Penn, a Quaker, eventually also purchased the land that is present-day Delaware. In this area, Penn launched what he called "the holy experiment," attracting other persecuted Europeans, including German Mennonites and Lutherans, and French Huguenots. The survival of Penn's colony is largely attributable to its ethnic and religious diversity.

FUNCTIONS OF AMERICAN GOVERNMENT

1.2 Explain the functions of American government.

The people who settled in colonial America were a diverse lot. They were driven to settle in the New World for a variety of reasons, including religious freedom and economic gain. Thus, when the colonists declared independence from Great Britain in 1776, it was no easy task to devise a system of government that served all of these citizens' interests.

Eventually, leaders fashioned a political system with the people at the center of power. Many citizens, however, were uncomfortable with calling this new system a **democracy** because it conjured up fears of the people and mob rule. They instead preferred the term **republic**, which implied a system of government in which the interests of the people were represented by more educated or wealthier citizens who were responsible to those who elected them. Today, the words democracy and republic often are used interchangeably. Yet, in the United States, we still pledge allegiance to our "republic," not our democracy.

The first words of the new Constitution—"We, the People"—left little doubt about the source of power in the new political system. In attempting "to form a more perfect Union," the Framers, through the Constitution, set forth several key functions of American government, as well as governmental guarantees to the people, which have continuing relevance today. These principal functions of government and the guarantees they provide to citizens permeate our lives. Whether it is your ability to obtain a low-interest student loan, health insurance, or be licensed to drive a car at a particular age, government plays a major role.

Establishing Justice

One of the first tasks expected of any government is the creation of a system of laws allowing individuals to abide by a common set of principles. Societies adhering to the rule of law allow for the rational dispensing of justice by acknowledged legal authorities. Thus, the Constitution authorizes Congress to create a federal judicial system to dispense justice. The Bill of Rights contains several amendments geared toward the administration of justice including the right to a trial by jury, the right for those charged with crimes to be informed of the charges against them, and the right to be tried in a courtroom presided over by an impartial judge and a jury of one's peers.

Ensuring Domestic Tranquility

As we discuss throughout this text, the role of governments in ensuring domestic tranquility is a subject of much debate and has been since the period between 1715 and 1789 known as the **Enlightenment**. In crises, the federal government, as well as state and local governments, can take extraordinary measures to contain the threat of terrorism from abroad as well as within the United States. Governments also maintain many agencies designed to ensure our safety. Local governments have police forces, states have national guards, and the federal government has both the armed services and the ability to call up state militias to quell any threats to order.

Providing for the Common Defense

The Framers recognized that a major purpose of government is to provide defense for its citizens against threats of foreign aggression. In fact, in the early years of the republic, many believed that the major function of government was to protect the nation from foreign threats, such as the British invasion of the United States in the War of 1812 and the continued problem of piracy on the high seas. Thus, the Constitution calls for the president to be commander in chief of the armed forces, and Congress has the authority to raise an army. The defense budget continues to be a considerable and often controversial proportion of all federal outlays.

Promoting the General Welfare

When the Framers added "promoting the general Welfare" to their list of key governmental functions, they never envisioned how governmental involvement at all levels would expand so tremendously. In fact, promoting the general welfare was more of an ideal than a mandate for the new national government. Over time, though, our notions of what governments should do have expanded along with governmental size to

democracy
A system of government that gives power to the people, whether directly or through elected representatives.

republic
A government rooted in the consent of the governed; a representative or indirect democracy.

Enlightenment
A philosophical movement in eighteenth-century Europe; its adherents advocated liberty and tolerance of individual differences, decried religious and political abuses, and rejected the notion of an absolute monarch.

AMERICAN POLITICS IN COMPARATIVE PERSPECTIVE

How Much of the World Is "Free"?

The international nongovernmental organization Freedom House produces an annual map of "Freedom in the World" that evaluates the overall level of political rights and civil liberties in 195 countries. The group creates a composite score for each country based on 25 different indicators related to areas such as voting, freedom of expression, and minority rights. Each country is then assigned an overall status of "Free," "Partly Free," or "Not Free." The methodology, which is derived from the United Nation's Universal Declaration of Human Rights, assesses the real-world rights and freedoms enjoyed by individuals, rather than governments or government performance per se. The 2016 map scored 86 countries as "Free," 50 countries as "Not Free," and 59 countries with mixed records were rated as "Partly Free." As reflected in the map, most of Europe and the Americas are rated as "Free," alongside other important outposts of freedom in southern Africa, India, and Oceania. However, large swathes of Africa, Asia, and the Middle East contain repressive countries whose abuse of political rights and civil liberties led them to be scored as "Not Free."

FIGURE 1.3　HOW DOES FREEDOM COMPARE AROUND THE WORLD?

Free　Partly Free　Not Free

CRITICAL THINKING QUESTIONS

1. What broad geographic patterns do you note in this map? How would you explain them?

2. What outliers do you note within regions, such a countries that are "not free" in otherwise "free" areas, or vice versa? How might you account for these?

3. What other values could be measured that you believe to be of equal or nearly equal importance to freedom?

include Social Security, federal interstate highways, and funding for local public schools. As we discuss throughout this text, however, the proper scope of government is a source of much disagreement and debate among Americans and their elected representatives.

Securing the Blessings of Liberty

Americans enjoy a wide range of liberties and opportunities to prosper. They are able to criticize the government and to petition it when they disagree with its policies or have a grievance. People can act as they wish so long as their actions don't infringe on the rights of others. This freedom to criticize and to petition is perhaps the best way to "secure the Blessings of Liberty."

THE CHANGING AMERICAN PEOPLE

1.3 Analyze the changing characteristics of the American public.

One year after ratification of the U.S. Constitution, fewer than 4 million people lived in the thirteen states. Most of those people shared a single language and a Protestant-Christian heritage, and those who voted were white male property owners. The Constitution mandated that the number of members of the House of Representatives should not exceed one for every 30,000 people and set the size of the first House at sixty-five members.

As the nation grew westward, hundreds of thousands of new immigrants came to America, often in waves, fleeing war or famine or simply in search of a better life. Although the geographic size of the United States has remained stable since the addition of Alaska and Hawaii as states in 1959, the population has grown to over 323 million inhabitants. As a result of this population growth, most people today feel far removed from the national government and their elected representatives (see Figure 1.4).

FIGURE 1.4   HOW DOES POPULATION CORRELATE WITH REPRESENTATION?

The population of the United States has grown dramatically since the nation's founding. Larger geographic area, immigration, and living longer have contributed to this trend. The size of the House of Representatives, however, has not kept pace with this expansion.

SOURCE: U.S. Census Bureau Population Projections, www.census.gov.

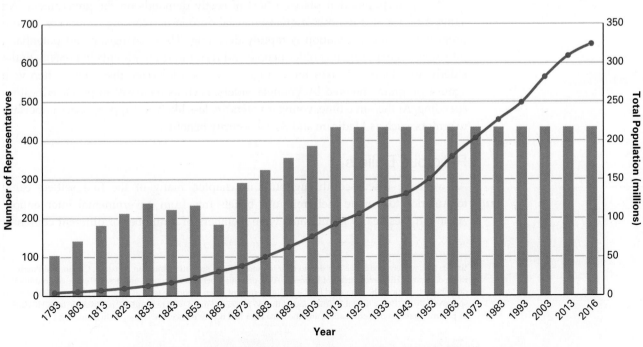

Racial and Ethnic Composition

The American population, originally settled by immigrants, has changed constantly as new people arrived from various regions—Western Europeans fleeing religious persecution in the 1600s to early 1700s; slaves brought in chains from Africa in the mid to late 1700s; Chinese laborers arriving in California to work on the railroads following the Gold Rush in 1848; Irish Catholics settling in the Northeast to escape the potato famine in the 1850s; Northern and Eastern Europeans from the 1880s to 1910s; and, most recently, South and Southeast Asians, Cubans, and Mexicans, among others. Today, almost 15 percent of Americans can be classified as immigrants.

Immigration has led to significant alterations in American racial and ethnic composition. The balance in America has changed dramatically over the past fifty years, with the proportion of Hispanics* overtaking African Americans as the second largest racial or ethnic group. The Asian American population, moreover, is now the fastest growing minority group in the United States. The majority of babies born in the United States are now members of a minority group, a fact that will have a significant impact not only on the demographics of the American polity but also on how America "looks."

In states such as California, Hawaii, New Mexico, and Texas, members of minority groups already are the majority of residents. Nevada, Maryland, and Georgia are soon to follow. In a generation, minorities are likely to be the majority in America.

Aging

Just as the racial and ethnic composition of the American population is shifting, so too is the average age. "For decades, the U.S. was described as a nation of the young because the number of persons under the age of twenty greatly outnumber[ed] those sixty-five and older," but this is no longer the case.[1] Because of changes in patterns of fertility, life expectancy, and immigration, the nation's age profile has altered drastically. At the founding of the United States, the average life expectancy was thirty-five years; today, it is nearly eighty years, although studies show that whites aged 45 to 54 have experienced a 22 percent increase in death rates, making them the only group to experience declines in longevity. Explanations include rapidly rising suicide rates and illnesses and deaths related to drug addiction and alcohol abuse.[2] Whites in other democracies are not part of this trend.

An aging population places a host of costly demands on the government. An aging America also imposes a great financial burden on working Americans, whose proportion in the population is rapidly declining. These changes could potentially pit younger people against older people and result in dramatic cuts in benefits to the elderly and increased taxes for younger workers. Moreover, the elderly often vote against programs favored by younger voters, such as increases to public education spending. At the same time, younger voters are less likely to support issues important to seniors, such as Medicare and Social Security benefits.

Religious Beliefs

As we have discussed throughout this chapter, many of the first settlers came to America to pursue their religious beliefs free from governmental intervention. Although these early immigrants were members of a number of different churches,

---

*In this text, we have made the decision to refer to those of Spanish, Latin American, Mexican, Cuban, and Puerto Rican descent as Hispanic instead of Latino/a. Although this label is not accepted universally by the community it describes, Hispanic is the term used by the U.S. government when reporting federal data. In addition, a 2008 survey sponsored by the Pew Charitable Trusts found that 36 percent of those who responded preferred the term Hispanic, 21 percent preferred the term Latino, and the remainder had no preference. See www.pewhispanic.org.

nearly all identified with Christian sects. Moreover, they viewed the Indians' belief systems, which included multiple gods, to be savage and unholy. Records exist of early Jewish colonists as well as Muslims from Africa brought to the New World as slaves, but the numbers of early Americans practicing these faiths were small in comparison to Christian settlers.[3] Thus, references to Christianity and Christian values permeate American social and political systems.

While many citizens view the United States as a Christian nation, a great number of religious groups—including Jews, Buddhists, Hindus, and Muslims—have established roots in this country. With this growth have come different political and social demands. For example, some American Jews continually work to ensure that America's policies in the Middle East favor Israel, while some Muslims demand more support for a Palestinian state.

Regional Growth and Expansion

Regional sectionalism emerged almost immediately in the United States. Settlers from the Virginia Colony southward largely focused on commerce. Those seeking various forms of religious freedom populated many of the settlements from the mid-Atlantic and Northeast. That search for religious freedom also came with puritanical values, so that New England evolved differently from the South in many aspects of culture.

Sectional differences continued to emerge as the United States developed into a major industrial nation and waves of immigrants with various religious traditions and customs entered the country, often settling in areas where other immigrants from their homeland already lived. For example, thousands of Scandinavians flocked to Minnesota, and many Irish settled in the urban centers of the Northeast, as did many Italians and Jews. All brought with them unique views about numerous issues and varying demands on government as well as different ideas about the role of government. Subsequent generations have often handed down these political views, and many regional differences continue to affect public opinion today.

One of the most long-standing and dramatic regional differences in the United States is that between the South and the North. During the Constitutional Convention, most Southerners staunchly advocated for a weak national government. The Civil War was later fought in part because of basic philosophical differences about government as well as slavery, which many Northerners opposed. As we know from modern political polling, the South continues to lag behind the rest of the nation in supporting civil rights, while still favoring return of power to the states and downsizing the national government.

The West, too, has always appeared unique compared with the rest of the United States. Populated first by those seeking free land and then by many chasing dreams of gold, the American West has often been characterized as "wild." Its population today is a study in contrasts. Some people have moved there to avoid city life and have an anti-government bias. Other Westerners are attracted to the region's abundant sunshine and natural resources and seek governmental solutions to problems like drought and environmental degradation.

Significant differences in attitude also arise in rural versus urban areas. Those who live in rural areas are much more conservative than those in large cities.[4] One need only look at a map of the vote distribution in recent presidential elections to see stark differences in candidate appeal. Democratic candidates have carried almost every large city in America; Republicans have carried most rural voters as well as most of America's heartland.[5]

WHAT DOES THE TYPICAL AMERICAN FAMILY LOOK LIKE?

WHAT DOES THE TYPICAL AMERICAN FAMILY LOOK LIKE?
As the demographics of American society change over time, the composition of American families has become increasingly heterogeneous. Here, the characters from the first season of the sitcom *Modern Family* exemplify the age, ethnic, and sexual diversity in families today, making the "typical American family" difficult to describe.

politics
The study of who gets what, when, and how—or how policy decisions are made.

Family and Family Size

In the past, familial gender roles were clearly defined. Women did housework and men worked in the fields. Large families were imperative; children were a source of cheap farm labor. Industrialization and knowledge of birth control methods, however, began to put a dent in the size of American families by the early 1900s. No longer needing children to work for survival of the household, couples began to limit family size.

In 1949, 49 percent of those polled thought that four or more children constituted the "ideal" family size; today, most Americans believe that having no children or two children at most is "best." In 1940, nine of ten households were traditional family households. Today, 35 percent of children under eighteen live with just one of their parents; the majority of those live with their mother. Moreover, nearly one-third of all households consist of a single person, a trend that reflects, in part, the aging American population and declining marriage rate.[6] Nearly half of Americans have never been married.

Even the institution of marriage has undergone tremendous change. Since the U.S. Supreme Court's decision *Obergefell* v. *Hodges* (2015), same-sex marriage is legal in all states.[7] These changes in composition of households, lower birthrates, marriage, and the prevalence of single-parent families affect the kinds of demands people place on government. Single-parent families, for example, may be more likely to support government-subsidized day care or after-school programs.

TOWARD REFORM: PEOPLE AND POLITICS

1.4 Characterize changes in Americans' attitudes toward and expectations of government.

As the American population has changed over time, so has the American political process. **Politics** is the study of who gets what, when, and how—the process by which policy decisions are made. The evolving nature of the American citizenry deeply affects this process. Competing demands often lead to political struggles, which create winners and losers within the system. A loser today, however, may be a winner tomorrow in the ever-changing world of politics. The political ideologies of those in control of Congress, the executive, and state houses also have a huge impact on who gets what, when, and how.

Nevertheless, shared American values continue to bind citizens together. Many Americans share the common goal of achieving the **American Dream**—an American ideal of a happy and successful life in which education, freedom, and home ownership are core elements. Although manifestations of the American Dream have changed over time, it often includes wealth, a house, a better life for one's children, and, for some, the opportunity to grow up to be president. Many voters for President **Donald J. Trump** saw the American Dream falling from their or their children's grasp.

In roughly the first 150 years of our nation's history, the federal government had few responsibilities, and citizens had few expectations of it beyond national defense, printing money, and collecting tariffs and taxes. The state governments were generally far more powerful than the federal government in matters affecting the everyday lives of Americans. As the nation and its economy grew in size and complexity, the federal government took on more responsibilities, such as regulating some businesses, providing poverty relief, and inspecting food. With these new roles come greater demands on government.

Today, many Americans lack faith in the country's institutions (see Figure 1.5). These concerns make it even easier for citizens to blame the government for all kinds of woes—personal as well as societal—or to fail to credit it for those things it does well. Many Americans, for example, enjoy a remarkably high standard of living, and much of it is due to governmental programs and protections.

The current frustration and dissatisfaction with politics and government may be just another phase, as the changing American body politic seeks to redefine its ideas about and expectations of government and how to reform it. This process is likely to define politics well into the future, but the individualistic nature of the American system will have long-lasting effects on how to accomplish that redefinition. Many Americans say they want less government, but as they get older, they don't want

American Dream
An American ideal of a happy, successful life, which often assumes wealth, a house, and a better life for one's children.

Donald J. Trump
The forty-fifth president, a Republican, elected in 2016; first president elected without prior political or military experience; an experienced businessman.

FIGURE 1.5 DO AMERICANS HAVE CONFIDENCE IN AMERICAN INSTITUTIONS?

The line graph below shows the percentages of Americans declaring they have a "great deal" of confidence in American institutions. Note the declining trend of trust in all political institutions, as well as Americans' record low levels of trust in Congress.

SOURCE: Gallup.

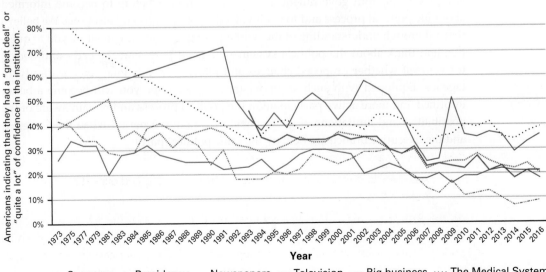

--- Congress — Presidency ⋯⋯ Newspapers — Television — Big business ⋯⋯ The Medical System

WHAT IS THE ROLE OF AMERICAN GOVERNMENT?

The most important responsibility of American government is to protect its citizens. Thus, despite their disillusionment with the government, citizens in a time of need often turn to political leaders for support. Here, President Barack Obama comforts victims of Superstorm Sandy in New Jersey, just days before the 2012 election.

less Social Security. They want lower taxes and better roads, but they don't want to pay road tolls. They want better education for their children, but lower expenditures on schools. They want greater security at airports, but low fares and quick boarding. Some clearly want less for others but not themselves—a demand that puts politicians in the position of nearly always disappointing some voters.

In this text, we present you with the tools needed to understand how our political system has evolved and to understand changes yet to come. Approaching the study of American government and politics with an open mind should help you become a better citizen. We hope that you learn to ask questions, to comprehend how various issues have come to be important, and to see why a particular law was enacted, how it was implemented, and if it needs reform. We further hope that you will learn not to accept at face value everything you see on the TV news, hear on the radio, or read on social media, especially in the blogosphere and Twitterverse. Work to understand your government, and use your vote and other forms of participation to help ensure that your government works for you.

We recognize that the discourse of politics has changed dramatically, most notably in the unprecedented events surrounding the 2016 presidential election. We hope that Americans will pay increasing attention to our democracy and consider carefully what we want from government. It is easier than ever before to become informed about the political process and to get involved in campaigns and elections. We believe that a thorough understanding of the workings of government will allow you to question and think about the political system—the good parts and the bad—and decide for yourself whether proposed changes and reforms are advantageous or disadvantageous. Equipped with such an understanding, we hope you will become a better informed and more active participant in the political process and remain aware of the possibilities and limitations of government as we enter a period when the Congress and the Executive branch are held by the same political party.

REVIEW THE CHAPTER

Roots of American Government: We the People

1.1 Trace the origins of American government.

American government is rooted in the cultures and experiences of early European colonists as well as interactions with the indigenous populations of the New World. The first colonists sought wealth. Later pilgrims came for religious freedom. The colonies set up systems of government that differed widely in terms of form, role, and function. As the colonies developed, they sought more independence from the British monarchy.

Functions of American Government

1.2 Explain the functions of American government.

The functions of American government include establishing justice, ensuring domestic tranquility, providing for the common defense, promoting the general welfare, and securing the blessings of liberty.

The Changing American Public

1.3 Analyze the changing characteristics of the American public.

Several characteristics of the American electorate can help us understand how the system continues to evolve and change. Among these are changes in size and population, racial and ethnic composition, age, religious beliefs, regional growth and expansion, and family and family size.

Toward Reform: People and Politics

1.4 Characterize changes in Americans' attitudes toward and expectations of government.

Shifts in population have created controversy in the American electorate throughout America's history. Americans have high and often unrealistic expectations of government, yet often fail to appreciate how much their government actually does for them. Americans' failing trust in institutions also explains some of the dissatisfaction among the American electorate.

LEARN THE TERMS

American Dream
Anne Hutchinson
democracy
Donald J. Trump

Enlightenment
government
Mayflower
politics

republic
Roger Williams
Thomas Hooker
William Penn

HOW MANY CONSTITUTIONAL AMENDMENTS HAVE ADDRESSED VOTING?

Many constitutional amendments have addressed voting rights. Above, President Richard M. Nixon signs the Twenty-Sixth Amendment, which guaranteed eighteen-year-olds the right to vote in all elections. Robert Kunzig, the General Services Administrator, waits to certify the document, and members of the singing group "Young Americans" also signed the amendment.

THE CONSTITUTION

LEARNING OBJECTIVES

2.1 Identify the causes of the American Revolution and the ideals on which the United States and the Constitution are based.

2.2 Identify the components of the Articles of Confederation and the reasons for their failure.

2.3 Outline the issues resolved by the compromise during the writing of the Constitution.

2.4 Describe the framework for government expressed in the Constitution.

2.5 Outline the arguments for and against ratification of the Constitution.

2.6 Describe the processes by which the Constitution can be amended.

At age eighteen, all American citizens are eligible to vote in state and national elections. This has not always been the case. It took an amendment to the U.S. Constitution—one of only seventeen that have been added since ratification of the Bill of Rights in 1791—to guarantee the vote in national elections to those younger than twenty-one years of age.

In 1942, during World War II, Representative Jennings Randolph (D–WV) proposed a constitutional amendment that would lower the voting age to eighteen, believing that since young men were old enough to be drafted, go to war, and fight and die for their country, they also should be allowed to vote. He continued to reintroduce his proposal during every session of Congress and in 1954 President Dwight D. Eisenhower endorsed the idea in his State of the Union Address. Presidents Lyndon B. Johnson and Richard M. Nixon—men who had also called upon the nation's young men to fight on foreign shores—echoed his appeal.[1]

During the 1960s, the campaign to lower the voting age took on a new sense of urgency as the draft sent hundreds of thousands of young men to fight in the unpopular war in Vietnam, and thousands of men and women were killed in action. "Old Enough to Fight, Old Enough to Vote" was one popular slogan of the day. By 1970, four states—the U.S. Constitution allows states to set the eligibility requirements for their voters—had lowered their voting ages to eighteen. Later that year, Congress passed legislation lowering the voting age in national, state, and local elections to eighteen.

The state of Oregon, however, challenged the constitutionality of the law in court, arguing that the Constitution did not give Congress the authority to establish a uniform voting age in state and local government elections. The U.S. Supreme Court agreed.[2] The decision from the divided Court meant that those under age twenty-one could vote in national elections but that the states were free to prohibit them from voting in state and local elections. The decision presented the states with a logistical nightmare. States setting the voting age at twenty-one would be forced to keep two sets of registration books: one for voters twenty-one and over and one for voters under twenty-one.

Jennings Randolph, by then a senator from West Virginia, reintroduced his proposed amendment to lower the national voting age to eighteen.[3] Within three months of the Supreme Court's decision, Congress sent the proposed Twenty-Sixth Amendment to the states for their ratification. The required three-fourths of the states approved the amendment within three months—making its adoption on June 30, 1971, the quickest in the history of the constitutional amending process.

• • •

The Framers never intended the U.S. Constitution to be easily changed. They made the amendment process time consuming and difficult. Over the years, thousands of amendments—including those to prohibit child labor, provide equal rights for women, grant statehood to the District of Columbia, balance the federal budget, and ban flag burning—have been debated or sent to the states for approval, only to die slow deaths. Only twenty seven amendments have made their way into the Constitution. What the Framers wrote in Philadelphia has continued to work, in spite of increasing demands on and dissatisfaction with our national government. Although Americans often clamor for reform, perhaps they are happier with the system of government created by the Framers than they realize. The ideas that went into the making of the Constitution and the ways it has evolved to address the problems of a growing and changing nation form the core of our discussion in this chapter.

New World
The Western Hemisphere of Earth, also called The Americas, which was unknown to Europeans before 1492.

Benjamin Franklin
A brilliant inventor and senior statesman at the Constitutional Convention who urged colonial unity as early as 1754, twenty-two years before the Declaration of Independence.

French and Indian War
The American phase of what was called the Seven Years War, fought from 1754 to 1763 between Britain and France with Indian allies.

mercantilism
An economic theory designed to increase a nation's wealth through the development of commercial industry and a favorable balance of trade.

ROOTS OF THE U.S. CONSTITUTION

2.1   Identify the causes of the American Revolution and the ideals on which the United States and the Constitution are based.

Beginning in the early seventeenth century, colonists came to the **New World** for a variety of reasons. Often, they sought a new start on a continent where land was plentiful or saw business opportunities to be gained in the New World. Others wished to escape religious persecution. The independence and diversity of the settlers in the New World complicated the question of how best to rule the new colonies. Almost all of the colonists agreed that the king ruled by divine right, but British monarchs allowed the colonists significant liberties in terms of self-government, religious practices, and economic organization. For 140 years, this system worked fairly well.[4] By the early 1750s, however, after a century and a half of physical separation, development of colonial industry and relative self-governance by the colonies led to weakening ties with—and loyalties to—the Crown.

As early as 1754, at the urgings of **Benjamin Franklin**, more than twenty representatives from the Mid-Atlantic and Northern colonies met in Albany, New York. Their chief concern was their role in the **French and Indian War** being fought in the colonies between the French and English. The resultant Albany Plan of Union, however, was rejected by the states but bits found their way into the Articles of Confederation.

By the early 1760s, each of the thirteen colonies had drafted its own constitution, which provided the fundamental rules or laws by which it operated. Moreover, many of the most oppressive British traditions—feudalism, a rigid class system, and the absolute authority of the king—were absent in the colonies. Land was abundant. The guild and craft systems that severely limited entry into many skilled professions in Great Britain were not part of life in the colonies because individuals could freely pursue skilled crafts. And, although religion was central to the lives of most colonists, no single state church existed, so the colonists did not follow the British practice of compulsory tithing (giving a fixed percentage of one's earnings to the state-sanctioned and state-supported church).

Trade and Taxation

Mercantilism, an economic theory designed to increase a nation's wealth through the development of commercial industry and a favorable balance of trade, justified Britain's maintenance of strict import/export controls on the colonies. From 1650 until well into the 1700s, Britain tried to control colonial imports and exports, believing it critical to export more goods than it imported as a way of increasing the gold and silver in its treasury. Britain found it difficult to enforce these policies, however, and the colonists, seeing little self-benefit in their operation, widely ignored them.

This fragile arrangement was soon put to the test. The French and Indian War, fought from 1754 to 1763 on the western frontier of the colonies and in Canada, was part of a global war initiated by the British—then the greatest power in the world. This American phase of what was called the Seven Years War was fought between Britain and France with American Indians as French allies. To raise money to pay for the war as well as the expenses of administering the colonies, Parliament enacted the Sugar Act in 1764. This act placed taxes on sugar, wine, coffee, and other products commonly exported to the colonies. A postwar colonial depression heightened resentment of the tax. Major protest, however, failed to materialize until imposition of the Stamp Act by the British Parliament in 1765. This law required that all paper items—from playing cards to books—bought and sold in the colonies carry a stamp mandated by the Crown. The colonists feared this act would establish a precedent for the British Parliament not only to control commerce in the colonies but also to raise revenues from the colonists without approval of the colonial governments. The political cry "no taxation without representation" rang out across the colonies. To add insult to injury, in 1765, Parliament passed the Quartering Act, which required colonists to furnish barracks or provide living quarters within their own homes for British troops.

Most colonists, especially those in New England, where these acts hit merchants hardest, were outraged. Men throughout the colonies organized the Sons of Liberty and women formed the Daughters of Liberty. Protests against the Stamp Act were violent and loud. Riots, often led by the Sons of Liberty, broke out. These were especially violent in Boston, where an angry mob burned the colonial governor's home and protesters threatened British stamp agents charged with collecting the tax. The outraged colonists also organized a boycott of goods needing the stamps as well as a boycott of British imports.

First Steps Toward Independence

In 1765, at the urging of **Samuel Adams**, nine of the thirteen colonies sent representatives to a meeting in New York City where they drafted a detailed list of Crown violations of the colonists' fundamental rights. Known as the **Stamp Act Congress**, this gathering was the first official meeting of the colonies and the first step toward creating a unified nation. Attendees defined what they thought to be the proper relationship between colonial governments and the British Parliament; they ardently believed Parliament had no authority to tax them without colonial representation in that body, yet they still remained loyal to the king. In contrast, the British believed that direct representation of the colonists was impractical and that members of Parliament represented the best interests of all the British, including the colonists who were British subjects.

The Stamp Act Congress and its petitions to the Crown did little to stop the onslaught of taxing measures. Parliament did, however, repeal the Stamp Act and revise the Sugar Act in 1766, largely because of the uproar made by British merchants who were losing large sums of money as a result of the boycotts. Rather than appeasing the colonists, however, these actions emboldened them to increase their resistance. In 1767, Parliament enacted the Townshend Acts, which imposed duties on all kinds of colonial imports, including tea. Responses from the **Sons and Daughters of Liberty** was immediate. Protesters announced another boycott of tea, and almost all colonists gave up their favorite drink in a united show of resistance to the tax and British authority.[5] Tensions continued to run high, especially after the British sent 4,000 troops to Boston. On March 5, 1770, British troops opened fire on an unruly mob that included disgruntled dockworkers, whose jobs had been taken by British soldiers, and members of the Sons of Liberty, who were taunting the soldiers and throwing objects at British sentries stationed in front of the Boston Customs House where taxes were collected. The troops killed five colonists, including **Crispus Attucks**, an African American and the first American to die in the early days of unrest before the Revolution, in what became known as the Boston Massacre. The Massacre and Revere's print are credited with transforming public opinion. Following this confrontation, the British Parliament lifted all duties except those on tea. The tea tax, however, continued to be a symbolic irritant. To keep this revolutionary fervor going, in 1772, at the suggestion of Samuel Adams, colonists created the Committees of Correspondence to keep each other abreast of developments with the British.

Meanwhile, despite dissent in Britain over treatment of the colonies, Parliament passed another tea tax designed to shore up the sagging sales of the East India

Samuel Adams
Cousin of President John Adams and an early leader against the British and loyalist oppressors; he played a key role in developing the Committees of Correspondence and was active in Massachusetts and colonial politics.

Stamp Act Congress
A gathering of nine colonial representatives in 1765 in New York City where a detailed list of Crown violations was drafted; first official meeting of the colonies and the first official step toward creating a unified nation.

Sons and Daughters of Liberty
Loosely organized groups of patriotic American colonists who were early revolutionaries.

Crispus Attucks
An African American and first American to die in what became known as the Boston Massacre in 1770.

WHY WAS SAMUEL ADAMS IMPORTANT?

Samuel Adams (1722–1803), cousin of President John Adams, was an early leader against the British and loyalist oppressors. He played a key role in developing the Committees of Correspondence and was active in Massachusetts and colonial politics. Today, he is known for the beer that bears his name, which is ironic, considering he bankrupted his family's brewery business.

WHAT REALLY HAPPENED AT THE BOSTON MASSACRE?

Paul Revere's famous engraving of the Boston Massacre played fast and loose with the facts. While the event occurred on a cold winter's night, the engraving features a clear sky and no ice or snow. Crispus Attucks, the revolution's first martyr, was African American, although the engraving depicts him as a white man seen lying on the ground closest to the British soldiers. Popular propaganda such as this engraving—and even dubbing the incident a "massacre"—did much to stoke anti-British sentiment in the years leading up to the Revolutionary War.

Company, a British exporter of tea. The colonists' boycott had left that trading company with more than 18 million pounds of tea in its warehouses. To rescue British merchants from disaster, in 1773, Parliament passed the Tea Act, which granted a monopoly to the financially strapped East India Company to sell tea imported from Britain. This act allowed the company to funnel business to American merchants loyal to the Crown, thereby undercutting dissident colonial merchants who could sell only tea imported from other nations. This practice drove down the price of tea and hurt colonial merchants who were forced to buy tea at higher prices from other sources.

When the next shipment of tea from Britain arrived in Boston, the colonists responded by throwing the Boston Tea Party; other colonies held similar tea parties up and down the eastern coast. King George III flew into a rage upon hearing of the actions of his disloyal subjects. "The die is now cast," the king told his prime minister. "The colonies must either submit or triumph."

King George III's first act of retaliation was to persuade Parliament to pass the Coercive Acts of 1774. Known in the colonies as the Intolerable Acts, they contained a key provision calling for a total blockade of Boston Harbor, cutting off Bostonians' access to many foodstuffs until restitution was made for the tea. Another provision reinforced the Quartering Act. It gave Massachusetts's royal governor the authority to house British soldiers in the homes of Boston citizens, allowing Britain to send an additional 4,000 soldiers in a show of force.

The First and Second Continental Congresses

The British could never have guessed how the cumulative impact of these actions would unite the colonists. The Committees of Correspondence spread the word, and the people of Boston received food and money from all over the thirteen colonies. The tax itself was no longer the key issue; now the extent of British authority over the colonies presented the far more important question. At the request of the colonial assemblies of Massachusetts and Virginia, all but Georgia's colonial assembly agreed to select a group of delegates to attend a continental congress authorized to communicate with the king on behalf of the now-united colonies.

The **First Continental Congress**, comprising fifty-six delegates, met in Philadelphia from September 5 to October 26, 1774. The colonists had yet to think of breaking with Great Britain; at this point, they simply wanted to iron out their differences with the king. By October, they had agreed on a series of resolutions to oppose the Coercive Acts and to establish a formal organization to boycott British goods. The Congress also drafted a Declaration of Rights and Resolves, which called for colonial rights of petition and assembly, trial by peers, freedom from a standing army, and the selection of representative councils to levy taxes. The Congress further agreed that if the King did not capitulate to its demands, it would meet again in Philadelphia in May 1775.

King George III refused to yield, tensions continued to rise, and a Second Continental Congress was deemed necessary. Before it could meet, fighting broke out on April 19, 1775, at **Lexington and Concord**, Massachusetts, with what was later called "the shot heard 'round the world." Eight colonial soldiers, called Minutemen, were killed, and 16,000 British troops besieged Boston.

When the **Second Continental Congress** convened in Philadelphia on May 10, 1775, delegates were united by their increased hostility to Great Britain. In a final attempt to avert conflict, the Second Continental Congress adopted the Olive Branch Petition on July 5, 1775, asking the king to end hostilities. King George III rejected the petition and sent an additional 20,000 troops to quell the rebellion; he labeled all in attendance traitors to the king and subject to death.

In January 1776, **Thomas Paine** issued (at first anonymously) *Common Sense*, a pamphlet paid for by statesman Benjamin Franklin of Pennsylvania, forcefully arguing for independence from Great Britain. In frank, easy-to-understand language, Paine denounced the corrupt British monarchy and offered reasons to break with Great Britain. "The blood of the slain, the weeping voice of nature cries 'Tis Time to Part,'" wrote Paine. *Common Sense*, widely read throughout the colonies, helped to change minds in a very short time. In its first three months of publication, *Common Sense* sold 120,000 copies—one for every thirteen people in the colonies.

Common Sense galvanized the American public against reconciliation. On May 15, 1776, Virginia became the first colony to call for independence. On June 7, 1776, Richard Henry Lee of Virginia rose to move "that these United Colonies are, and of right ought to be, free and independent States, and that all connection between them and the State of Great Britain is, and ought to be, dissolved." His three-part resolution—which called for independence, the formation of foreign alliances, and preparation of a plan of confederation—triggered hot debate among the delegates. A proclamation of independence from Great Britain constituted treason, a crime punishable by death. Although six of the thirteen colonies had already instructed their delegates to vote for independence, the Second Continental Congress was suspended to allow its delegates to return home to their respective colonial legislatures for final instructions. Independence was not a move the colonists took lightly.

The Declaration of Independence

The Congress set up committees to consider each point of Richard Henry Lee of Virginia's proposal. The Committee of Five (Chair **Thomas Jefferson**, John Adams, Benjamin Franklin, Robert Livingston, and Roger Sherman) began work on the **Declaration of Independence**, which drew heavily on the works of the Enlightenment period. On July 2, 1776, twelve of the thirteen colonies (with New York abstaining) voted for independence. Two days later, on July 4th, the Second Continental Congress voted to adopt the Declaration of Independence. On July 9, 1776, the document, now with the approval of New York, was read aloud in Philadelphia.[6]

First Continental Congress
Meeting held in Philadelphia from September 5 to October 26, 1774, in which fifty-six delegates (from every colony except Georgia) adopted a resolution in opposition to the Coercive Acts.

Lexington and Concord
The first sites of armed conflict between revolutionaries and British soldiers, remembered for the "shot heard round the world" in 1775.

Second Continental Congress
Meeting that convened in Philadelphia on May 10, 1775, at which it was decided that an army should be raised and George Washington of Virginia was named commander in chief.

Thomas Paine
The influential writer of *Common Sense*, a pamphlet that advocated for independence from Great Britain.

Common Sense
A pamphlet written by Thomas Paine that challenged the authority of the British government to govern the colonies.

Thomas Jefferson
Principle drafter of the Declaration of Independence; second vice president of the United States; third president of the United States from 1801 to 1809. Co-founder of the Democratic-Republican Party created to oppose Federalists.

Declaration of Independence
Document drafted largely by Thomas Jefferson in 1776 that proclaimed the right of the American colonies to separate from Great Britain.

social contract theory
The belief that governments exist based on the consent of the governed.

political culture
Commonly shared attitudes, behaviors, and core values about how government should operate.

In simple but eloquent language, the Declaration set out the reasons for separation of the colonies from Great Britain. Most of its stirring rhetoric drew heavily on the works of seventeenth- and eighteenth-century political philosophers, particularly the French Enlightenment theorist Jean-Jacques Rousseau and the English philosopher John Locke. Locke's (as well as Rousseau's) theory of natural liberty and equality and his advocacy of **social contract theory**, which holds that governments exist based on the consent of the governed, heavily influenced Jefferson who was credited with primary authorship of the Declaration. According to Locke, people agree to set up a government largely for the protection of property rights, to preserve life and liberty, and to establish justice. Furthermore, argued Locke, individuals who give their consent to be governed have the right to resist or remove rulers who deviate from those purposes. Such a government exists for the good of its subjects and not for the benefit of those who govern. Thus, rebellion is the ultimate sanction against a government that violates the rights of its citizens.

It is easy to see the colonists' debt to John Locke. In Jefferson's stirring language, the Declaration of Independence proclaims:

> We hold these truths to be self-evident, that all men are created equal, that they are endowed by their Creator with certain unalienable Rights, that among these are Life, Liberty and the pursuit of Happiness.

Jefferson and others in attendance at the Second Continental Congress wanted to have a document that would stand for all time, justifying their break with Great Britain and clarifying their notions of the proper form of government. So, the Declaration continued:

> That to secure these rights, Governments are instituted among Men, deriving their just powers from the consent of the governed. That whenever any Form of Government becomes destructive of these ends, it is the Right of the People to alter or abolish it, and to institute new Government, laying its foundation on such Principles and organizing its Powers in such form, as to them shall seem most likely to effect their Safety and Happiness.

After its stirring preamble, the enumeration of the wrongs suffered by the colonists under British rule, its final words are apt. All pertain to the denial of personal rights and liberties, many of which would later be guaranteed by the U.S. Constitution through the Bill of Rights.

The Basic Tenets of American Democracy

The British had no written constitution. Delegates to the Second Continental Congress were attempting to codify many arrangements that had never before been expressed in legal terminology. Thus, a second committee of delegates sat down to draft a document creating a new government necessary to wage war and to reflect the unique **political culture** of the colonies. We define political culture as commonly shared attitudes, behaviors, and core values about how government should operate. American political culture emphasizes several key values.

Liberty and equality, borrowed from the French, who were to come to the colonists' aid in the Revolutionary War, are the most important characteristics of the American republican form of government. Popular consent, the principle that governments must draw their powers from the consent of the governed, is another distinguishing element of American political culture. So, too, is majority rule. This principle means that election of officials and transformation of policies into law will take place only if the majority (normally 50 percent of the total votes cast plus one) of citizens in any political unit support such changes. American democracy also places heavy importance on the individual. In the U.S. system, all individuals are deemed rational and fair and endowed "with certain unalienable rights." This is quite different from many European democracies and Canada to the north. Their respective governments are founded on the idea of group rights, minimizing those of individuals for the greater good.

AN ATTEMPT AT A NATIONAL GOVERNMENT: THE ARTICLES OF CONFEDERATION

2.2 Identify the components of the Articles of Confederation and the reasons for their failure.

In late 1777, the Second Continental Congress adopted the **Articles of Confederation**, creating a loose "league of friendship" between the thirteen sovereign, or independent, colonies (some that even called themselves separate countries), and presented the Articles to the colonies for ratification. The Articles created a type of government called a confederation or confederacy, one quite common among the Indian tribes. The national government in a confederacy is weaker than the sum of its parts, and the states often consider themselves independent nation-states linked together only for limited purposes, such as national defense. The Articles of Confederation included the following:

- A national government with a Congress empowered to make peace, coin money, appoint officers for an army, control the post office, and negotiate with Indian tribes.
- Each state's retention of its independence and sovereignty, or ultimate authority, to govern within its territories.
- One vote in the legislature, the Congress of the Confederation, for each state regardless of size.
- The vote of nine states to pass any measure (a unanimous vote for any amendment).
- The selection and payment of delegates to the Congress by the states.

The Articles, finally ratified by all thirteen states in March 1781, fashioned a government that reflected the political culture and philosophy of the times.[7] Although it had its flaws, the government under the Articles of Confederation saw the nation through the Revolutionary War. However, once the British surrendered in 1781, and the new nation found itself no longer united by the war effort, the national government quickly fell into chaos.

Problems Under the Articles of Confederation

Historians refer to the chaotic period from 1781 to 1789, when the former colonies were governed under the Articles, as the **Critical Period**.[8] The Congress of the Confederation rarely could assemble the required quorum of nine states to conduct

Articles of Confederation
The compact between the thirteen original colonies that created a loose league of friendship, with the national government drawing its powers from the states.

Critical Period
The chaotic period from 1781 to 1789 after the American Revolution during which the former colonies were governed under the Articles of Confederation.

business. Even when it did meet, states found it difficult to agree on any policies. To raise revenue to pay off war debts and run the government, Congress proposed various land, poll, and liquor taxes. But, since it had no specific power to tax, all these proposals were rejected. At one point, Congress was even driven out of Philadelphia (then the capital of the new national government) by its own unpaid army.

Although the national government could coin money, it had no resources to back up the value of its currency. Continental dollars were worth little, and trade between states grew chaotic as some of them began to coin their own money. Another weakness was that the Articles of Confederation did not allow Congress to regulate commerce among the states or with foreign nations. As a result, individual states attempted to enter into agreements with other countries, and foreign nations were suspicious of trade agreements made with the Congress of the Confederation.

Fearful of a chief executive who would rule tyrannically, the drafters of the Articles made no provision for an executive branch of government that would be responsible for executing, or implementing, laws passed by the legislative branch. Instead, the president was merely the presiding officer at meetings. The Articles of Confederation, moreover, had no provision for a judicial system to handle the growing number of economic conflicts and boundary disputes among the individual states. Several states claimed the same lands to the west, and Pennsylvania and Virginia went to war with each other.

The Articles' greatest weakness, however, was its failure to provide for a strong central government. Although states had operated independently before the war, during the war they acceded to the national government's authority to wage armed conflict. Once the war was over, however, each state resumed its sovereign status and was unwilling to give up rights, such as the power to tax, to an untested national government. Consequently, the government could not force states to abide by the provisions of the second Treaty of Paris, signed in 1783, which officially ended the Revolutionary War. For example, states passed laws to allow debtors who owed money to Great Britain to postpone payment. These actions violated the treaty. Still, the Articles did foster some successes. Improvements were made in transportation and communication. The establishment of a national postal service also helped foster a sense of some nationality that went beyond state borders.

Rebellion in the States

Before concerned states and individuals could take action to strengthen the government, new unrest broke out in America. In 1780, Massachusetts adopted a constitution that appeared to favor the interests of the wealthy. Property-owning requirements barred the lower and middle classes from voting and office holding. And, as the economy of Massachusetts declined, banks foreclosed on the farms of many Massachusetts Continental Army veterans who were still waiting for promised bonuses that the national government had no funds to pay. The last straw came in 1786, when the Massachusetts legislature enacted a new law requiring the payment of all debts in cash. Frustration and outrage at the new law incited Daniel Shays, a former Continental Army captain, and 1,500 armed, disgruntled farmers to march to the government arsenal in Springfield, Massachusetts. This group obstructed the entrance to the state court located there, thus preventing the court from foreclosing on the mortgages on their farms.

The Congress of the Confederation immediately authorized the secretary of war to call for a new national militia. Congress made a $530,000 appropriation for this purpose, but every state except Virginia refused to pay. The governor of Massachusetts then tried to raise a state militia, but because of the poor economy, the commonwealth's treasury lacked the necessary funds to support his action. A militia finally was assembled after frantic attempts to collect private financial support. By February 4, 1787, this privately

WHAT WAS THE RESULT OF SHAYS'S REBELLION?

With Daniel Shays in the lead, a group of farmers who had served in the Continental Army marched to Springfield, Massachusetts, to stop the state court from foreclosing on the veterans' farms. The rebellion illustrated many of the problems of the national government under the Articles of Confederation and is widely thought to have influenced the proceedings of the Constitutional Convention.

paid force ended what was called **Shays's Rebellion**. The failure of the Congress to muster an army and quell the rebellion provided a dramatic example of the weaknesses inherent in the Articles of Confederation and shocked the nation's leaders into recognizing the new national government's inadequacies. It finally prompted several states to join together and call for a convention in Philadelphia in 1787.

WRITING THE U.S. CONSTITUTION

2.3 Outline the issues resolved by compromise during the writing of the Constitution.

On February 21, 1787, in the throes of economic turmoil and with domestic tranquility gone haywire, the Congress called for a **Constitutional Convention** in Philadelphia for "the sole and express purpose of revising the Articles of Confederation." However, many delegates who gathered in sweltering Philadelphia on May 25, 1787, were prepared to take potentially treasonous steps to preserve the union. On the first day of the convention, delegates from Virginia proposed fifteen resolutions creating an entirely new government (later known as the Virginia Plan). Their enthusiasm, however, was not universal. Many delegates considered these resolutions to be in violation of the convention's charter. They proposed the New Jersey Plan, which took greater steps to preserve the Articles.

These proposals met heated debate on the convention's floor. Eventually, the Virginia Plan triumphed. Although the delegates had established the basic structure of the new government, the work of the Constitutional Convention was not complete. Remaining differences were resolved through a series of compromises, and less than one hundred days after the meeting convened, the Framers had created a new constitution to submit to the electorate for its approval.

Shays's Rebellion
A rebellion in which an army of 1,500 disgruntled and angry farmers led by Daniel Shays marched to Springfield, Massachusetts, and forcibly restrained the state court from foreclosing mortgages on their farms.

Constitutional Convention
The meeting in Philadelphia in 1787 that was first intended to revise the Articles of Confederation but produced an entirely new document, the U.S. Constitution.

George Washington
Widely considered the "Father of the Nation," he was the commander of the revolutionary armies; served as the presiding officer of the Constitutional Convention; and as the United States' first president from 1789 to 1797.

constitution
A document establishing the structure, functions, and limitations of a government.

The Characteristics and Motives of the Framers

The fifty-five delegates who attended the Constitutional Convention labored long and hard that summer. Owing to the high stakes of their actions, they conducted all of the convention's work behind closed doors. **George Washington** of Virginia, who commanded the U.S. army during the Revolutionary War, was unanimously elected the convention's presiding officer. He cautioned delegates not to reveal details of the convention even to family members. The delegates agreed to accompany Benjamin Franklin of Pennsylvania to all of his meals. They feared that the normally gregarious gentleman might get carried away with the mood or by liquor and inadvertently let news of the proceedings slip from his tongue.

All of the delegates to the Constitutional Convention were men; hence, they often are called the "Founding Fathers." This text generally refers to them as the Framers because their work provided the framework for the new government of the United States. The Framers brought with them a vast amount of political, educational, legal, and business experience. Clearly, they were an exceptional lot who ultimately produced a brilliant **constitution**, or document establishing the structure, functions, and limitations of a government.

Debate about the Framers' motives filled the air during the ratification struggle and has provided grist for the mill of historians and political scientists over the years. In his *Economic Interpretation of the Constitution of the United States* (1913), Charles A. Beard argued that the 1780s were a critical period not for the nation as a whole, but rather for business owners who feared that a weak, decentralized government could harm their economic interests.[9] Beard argued that merchants wanted a strong national government to promote industry and trade, to protect private property, and to ensure payment of

FIGURE 2.1   WHO WERE THE FRAMERS?

The Framers of the Constitution spent a summer in Philadelphia in nearly complete secrecy, drafting our nation's supreme code of laws. But, who really were these men? They came from varied jobs, cultures, and viewpoints; some men were slaveholders, many were lawyers, and others had little political experience. These differences influenced many of the compromises seen in the final version of the Constitution.

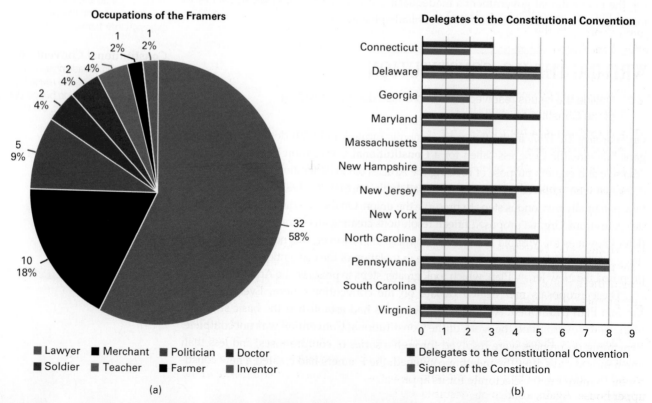

(a)   (b)

the public debt—much of which was owed to them. Therefore, according to Beard, the Constitution represents "an economic document drawn with superb skill by men whose property interests were immediately at stake."[10] Many would say the same today.

By the 1950s, Beard's view had fallen into disfavor when other historians were unable to find direct links between wealth and the Framers' motives for establishing the Constitution. Others faulted Beard's failure to consider the impact of religion and individual views about government.[11] In the 1960s, however, another group of historians began to argue that social and economic factors were, in fact, important motives for supporting the Constitution. In 1969, Gordon S. Wood's *The Creation of the American Republic* resurrected this debate. Wood deemphasized economics to argue that major social divisions explained different groups' support for (or opposition to) the new Constitution. He concluded that the Framers were representative of a class that favored order and stability over some of the more radical ideas that had inspired the American Revolutionary War and the break with Britain.[12]

The Virginia and New Jersey Plans

The less populous states were concerned with being lost in any new system of government in which states were not treated as equals regardless of population. It is not surprising, therefore, that a large state and then a small one, Virginia and New Jersey, respectively, weighed in with ideas about how the new government should operate.

The **Virginia Plan** called for a national system based heavily on the European nation-state model, wherein the national government derives its powers from the people and not from the member states.

Its key features included:

- Creation of a powerful central government with three branches—legislative, executive, and judicial.
- A two-house legislature with one house elected directly by the people, the other chosen from among persons nominated by the state legislatures.
- A legislature with the power to select the executive and the judiciary.
- An executive selected by the legislature to execute the laws passed by Congress.

In general, delegates from smaller states such as New Jersey and Connecticut were comfortable with the arrangements under the Articles of Confederation. These states offered another model of government, the **New Jersey Plan**. Its key features included:

- Strengthening the Articles, not replacing them.
- Creating a one-house legislature with one vote for each state and with representatives chosen by state legislatures.
- Giving Congress the power to raise revenue from duties on imports and from postal service fees.
- Creating an executive branch of multiple persons elected by Congress.
- Creating a national Supreme Court with members appointed for life by the executive.

Constitutional Compromises

The Virginia and New Jersey Plans necessitated serious compromise. Three of these were particularly important. Below, we discuss the Great Compromise, which concerned the form of the new government, the issue of slavery, and the Three-Fifths Compromise, which dealt with representation.

THE GREAT COMPROMISE   The most serious disagreement between the Virginia and New Jersey Plans concerned state representation in Congress. When a deadlock loomed, Connecticut offered its own compromise. Representation in the lower house would be determined by population, and each state would have an equal vote in the upper house. Again, a stalemate occurred.

Virginia Plan
A proposed framework for the Constitution favoring large states. It called for a bicameral legislature, which would appoint executive and judicial officers.

New Jersey Plan
A framework for the Constitution proposed by a group of small states; it called for a one-house legislature with one vote for each state, a Congress with the ability to raise revenue, and a Supreme Court appointed for life.

Great Compromise

The final decision of the Constitutional Convention to create a two-house legislature, with the lower house elected by the people and powers divided between the two houses; also made national law supreme.

A committee to work out an agreement soon reported back what became known as the **Great Compromise**. Taking ideas from both the Virginia and New Jersey Plans, it recommended:

- A two-house, or bicameral, legislature.
- In one house of the legislature (later called the House of Representatives), representatives would number fifty-six—no more than one representative for every 30,000 inhabitants. The people would directly elect those representatives.
- That house would have the power to originate all bills for raising and spending money.
- In the second house of the legislature (later called the Senate), each state would have an equal vote, and state legislatures would select the representatives.
- In dividing power between the national and state governments, national power would be supreme.[13]

The Great Compromise ultimately met with the approval of all states in attendance. The smaller states were pleased because they received equal representation in the Senate; the larger states were satisfied with the proportional representation in the House of Representatives. The small states then would dominate the Senate, while the large states would control the House. But, because both houses had to pass any legislation, neither body could dominate the other.

THE ISSUE OF SLAVERY Slavery, which formed the basis of much of the southern states' cotton economy, was one of the thorniest issues for the Framers to tackle. To reach an agreement on the Constitution, the Framers had to craft a compromise that balanced southern commercial interests with comparable northern concerns about the evils of slavery. Eventually, the Framers agreed that Northerners would support continuation of the slave trade for twenty more years, as well as a twenty-year ban on taxing exports to protect the cotton trade, while Southerners consented to a provision requiring only a majority vote on navigation laws. The Framers also gave the national government the authority to regulate foreign commerce and agreed that the Senate would have the power to ratify treaties by a two-thirds majority, which assuaged the fears of southern states, which made up more than one-third of the nation.

WHY WAS SLAVERY SUCH AN IMPORTANT ISSUE AT THE CONSTITUTIONAL CONVENTION?

Even a the time of the writing of the Constitution, many Americans struggled to reconcile moral, legal, and economic views on the institution of slavery. Some of the Framers, like Alexander Hamilton, Benjamin Franklin, and John Jay, became supporters of abolition. Other Framers, especially those living in the South, objected to efforts to abolish slavery. Although the importation of slaves was banned in 1808, the institution was allowed to continue well into the nineteenth century.

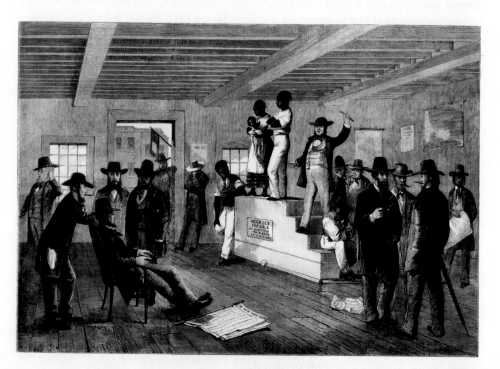

One major conflict had yet to be resolved: how to determine state population with regard to representation in the House of Representatives. Slaves could not vote, but the southern states wanted them included in the determination of population numbers. After considerable dissension, the delegates decided that population for purposes of representation and the apportionment of direct taxes would be calculated by adding the "whole Number of Free Persons" to "three-fifths of all other Persons." "All other Persons" was the delegates' euphemistic way of referring to slaves. Known as the **Three-Fifths Compromise**, this highly political deal ensured that the South would hold 47 percent of the House—enough to prevent attacks on slavery but not so much as to foster the spread of slavery northward.

Unfinished Business: Selection of the President

The Framers next turned to fashioning an executive branch. While they agreed on the idea of a one-person executive, they could not settle on the length of the term of office or on the procedure for choosing the chief executive. With Shays's Rebellion still fresh in their minds, the delegates feared putting too much power, including selection of a president, into the hands of the lower classes. At the same time, representatives from the smaller states feared that selection of the chief executive by the legislature would put additional power into the hands of the large states.

Amid these fears, the Committee on Unfinished Portions conducted its sole task: ironing out problems and disagreements concerning the office of chief executive. The committee recommended that the presidential term of office be fixed at four years instead of seven, as had been proposed earlier. The committee also made it possible for a president to serve more than one term.

In addition, the Framers created the **Electoral College** as a mechanism for selecting the chief executive of the new nation. The Electoral College system gave individual states a key role because each state would choose electors equal to the number of representatives it had in the House and Senate. This step was a vague compromise that removed election of the president and vice president from both the Congress and the people and placed it in the hands of electors whose method of selection would be left to the states. As **Alexander Hamilton** noted in *Federalist No. 68*, the Framers fashioned the Electoral College to avoid the "tumult and disorder" they feared could result if the masses were allowed to vote directly for president.

In drafting the new Constitution, the Framers also took care to provide for removal of the chief executive. The House of Representatives assumed the sole responsibility of investigating and charging a president or vice president with "Treason, Bribery, or other high Crimes and Misdemeanors." A majority vote then would result in issuing articles of impeachment against the president or vice president. In turn, the Senate took on the sole responsibility of trying the president or vice president on the charges issued by the House. To convict and remove the president or vice president from office required a two-thirds vote of the Senate. The chief justice of the United States was to preside over the Senate proceedings in place of the vice president (that body's constitutional leader) to prevent any conflict of interest on the vice president's part.

THE U.S. CONSTITUTION

2.4 Describe the framework for government expressed in the Constitution.

The U.S. Constitution's opening line, "We the People," ended, at least for the time being, the question of the source of the government's power: it came directly from the people. The Constitution then explained the need for the new outline of government: "in Order to form a more perfect Union" indirectly acknowledged the weaknesses of the Articles of Confederation in governing a growing nation. Next, the optimistic

Three-Fifths Compromise
Agreement reached at the Constitutional Convention stipulating that three-fifths of the total slave population of each state was to be for purposes of determining population for representation in the U.S. House of Representatives.

Electoral College
The system established by the Constitution through which the president is chosen by electors from each state, which has as many electoral votes as it has members of Congress.

Alexander Hamilton
A key Framer who envisioned a powerful central government, co-authored *The Federalist Papers*, and served as the first Secretary of the Treasury.

Montesquieu
The French baron and political theorist who first articulated the concept of separation of powers with checks and balances.

federalism
The distribution of constitutional authority between state governments and the national government, with different powers and functions exercised by both.

separation of powers
A way of dividing the power of government among the legislative, executive, and judicial branches, each staffed separately, with equality and independence of each branch ensured by the Constitution.

goals of the Framers for the new nation were set out: to "establish Justice, insure domestic Tranquility, provide for the common defence, promote the general Welfare, and secure the Blessings of Liberty to ourselves and our Posterity," followed by the formal creation of a new government: "do ordain and establish this Constitution for the United States of America."

On September 17, 1787, the delegates approved the Constitution. While the completed document did not satisfy all delegates, of the fifty-five delegates who attended some portion of the meetings, thirty-nine ultimately signed it. The sentiments uttered by Benjamin Franklin probably well reflected those of many others: "Thus, I consent, Sir, to this Constitution because I expect no better, and because I am not sure that it is not the best."[14]

The Basic Principles of the Constitution

The structure of the proposed new national government owed much to the writings of the French philosopher **Montesquieu** (1689–1755), who advocated distinct functions for each branch of government, called *separation of powers,* with a system of *checks and balances* between each branch. The Constitution's concern with the distribution of power between states and the national government also reveals the heavy influence of political philosophers as well as the colonists' experience under the Articles of Confederation.[15]

FEDERALISM   The question before and during the convention concerned how much power states would give up to the national government. Given the nation's experiences under the Articles of Confederation, the Framers believed that a strong national government was necessary for the new nation's survival. However, they were reluctant to create a powerful government after the model of Great Britain, the country from which they had just won their independence. The colonists did not even consider Great Britain's unitary system. Instead, they fashioned a way, now known as a federal system, to divide the power of government between a strong national government and the individual states, with national power being supreme. **Federalism** was based on the principle that the federal, or national, government derived its power from the citizens, not the states, as the national government had done under the Articles of Confederation.

Opponents of this system feared that a strong national government would infringe on their liberty. But, supporters of a federal system argued that a strong national government with distinct state governments could, if properly directed by constitutional arrangements, actually be a source of expanded liberties and national unity. The Framers viewed the division of governmental authority between the national government and the states as a means of checking power with power, and providing the people with double security against governmental tyranny. Later, the passage of the Tenth Amendment, which stated that powers not given to the national government were reserved by the states or the people, further clarified the federal structure.

SEPARATION OF POWERS   **Separation of powers** is simply a way of parceling out power among the three branches of government. Its three key features are:

1. Three distinct branches of government: the legislative, the executive, and the judicial.
2. Three separately staffed branches of government to exercise these functions.
3. Constitutional equality and independence of each branch.

As illustrated in Figure 2.2, the Framers carefully created a system in which law-making, law-enforcing, and law-interpreting functions were assigned to independent branches of government. Only the legislature has the authority to make laws; the

FIGURE 2.2 WHAT ARE THE SEPARATION OF POWERS AND HOW DO CHECKS AND BALANCES WORK UNDER THE U.S. CONSTITUTION?

Drawing inspiration from Montesquieu, the Framers crafted a political system of checks and balances and separation of powers. Each of the three branches—executive, legislative, and judicial—has distinct powers, and each branch has powers that intersect with the powers of each of the other branches. This system prevents any one branch from becoming too powerful.

Legislative Checks on the Executive
Impeach the president
Reject legislation or funding the president wants
Refuse to confirm nominees or approve treaties*
Override the president's veto by a two-thirds vote

Executive Checks on the Legislative
Veto legislation
Call Congress into special session
Implement (or fail to implement) laws
   passed by Congress

Judicial Checks on the Legislative
Rule federal and state laws
   unconstitutional

Judicial Checks on the Executive
Declare executive branch actions
   unconstitutional
Chief justice presides over
   impeachment trials

Legislative Checks on the Judicial
Change the number and
   jurisdiction of federal courts
Impeach federal judges
Propose constitutional amendments to
   override judicial decisions

Executive Checks on the Judicial
Appoint federal judges
Refuse to implement decisions

* This power belongs to the Senate only.

chief executive enforces laws; and the judiciary interprets them. Moreover, initially, members of the House of Representatives, members of the Senate, the president, and members of the federal courts were selected by, and therefore responsible to, different constituencies.

The Framers could not have foreseen the intermingling of governmental functions that has since evolved. In Article I of the Constitution, the legislative power is vested in Congress. But, the president also has a role in the legislative process; for a bill to become law, he must sign the legislation. If he disagrees with the content of a bill, he may also veto the legislation, although a two-thirds vote in Congress can override his veto. Judicial interpretation also helps to clarify the language or implementation of legislation enacted through this process.

So, instead of a pure system of separation of powers, a symbiotic, or interdependent, relationship among the three branches of government has existed from the beginning. Or, as one scholar has explained, there are "separated institutions sharing powers."[16] While Congress still is entrusted with making the laws, the president, as a single person who can easily capture the attention of the media and the electorate, retains tremendous power in setting the agenda and proposing legislation. And, although the Supreme Court's major function is to interpret the Constitution, its decisions affecting criminal procedure, reproductive rights, health care, and other issues have led many critics to charge that it has surpassed its constitutional authority and become, in effect, a law-making body.

CHECKS AND BALANCES   The separation of powers among the three branches of the national government is not complete. The powers of each branch (as well as

checks and balances
A constitutionally mandated structure that gives each of the three branches of government some degree of oversight and control over the actions of the others.

the powers of the two houses of the national legislature and the powers between the states and the national government) are also used to check those of the other two governmental branches. The power of each branch of government is checked, or limited, and balanced because the legislative, executive, and judicial branches share some authority, and no branch has exclusive domain over any single activity. The creation of this system, **checks and balances**, allowed the Framers to minimize the threat of tyranny from any one branch. Thus, for almost every power granted to one branch, the Framers established an equal control in the other two branches.

The Structure of the Constitution

The document finally signed by the Framers condensed numerous resolutions into a Preamble and seven separate articles remedying many of the deficiencies within the Articles of Confederation (see Table 2.1). The first three articles established the three branches of government, defined their internal operations, and clarified their relationships with one another. The Framers technically considered all branches of government equal, yet some initially appeared more powerful than others. The order of the articles, as well as the detail contained in the first three, reflects

TABLE 2.1 HOW DO THE ARTICLES OF CONFEDERATION AND THE U.S. CONSTITUTION COMPARE TO ONE ANOTHER?

	Articles of Confederation	Constitution
Formal name of the nation	The United States of America	Not specified, but referred to in the Preamble as "the United States of America"
Legislature	Unicameral, called Congress	Bicameral, called Congress, divided into the House of Representatives and the Senate
Members of Congress	A delegation between two and seven members per state	Two senators per state, representatives apportioned according to population of each state
Voting in Congress	One vote per state delegation	One vote per representative or senator
Appointment of members	All appointed by state legislatures in the manner each legislature directed	Representatives elected by popular vote; senators appointed by state legislatures (which was switched to direct election by the Seventeenth Amendment of 1913)
Term of legislative office	One year	Two years for representatives; six years for senators
Term limit for legislative office	No more than three of every six years	None
When Congress is not in session	A Committee of States had the full powers of Congress	The president of the United States can call on Congress to assemble
Chair of legislature	President of Congress	Speaker of the House of Representatives; vice president is president of the Senate
Executive	None; the "president" was simply presiding officer of Congress	President
National judiciary	Maritime judiciary established—other courts left to states	Supreme Court established as well as other federal courts Congress deems necessary
Adjudicator of disputes between states	Congress	Supreme Court
New states	Admitted upon agreement of nine states (special exemption provided for Canada)	Admitted upon agreement of majority of Congress
Amendment	When agreed upon by all states	When agreed upon by two-thirds of Congress and three-fourths of the states
Navy	Congress authorized to build a navy; states authorized to equip warships to counter piracy	Congress authorized to build a navy; states not allowed to keep ships of war
Army	Congress to decide on size of force and to requisition troops from each state according to population	Congress authorized to raise and support armies
Power to coin money	United States and the states	United States only
Taxes	Apportioned by Congress, collected by the states	Levied and collected by Congress
Ratification	Unanimous consent required	Consent of nine states required

the Framers' concern that these branches of government might abuse their powers. The four remaining articles define the relationships between the states, declare national law to be supreme, and set out methods of amending and ratifying the Constitution.

ARTICLE I: THE LEGISLATIVE BRANCH **Article I** vests all legislative powers in the Congress and establishes a bicameral legislature, consisting of the Senate and the House of Representatives. It also sets out the qualifications for holding office in each house, the terms of office, the methods of selection of representatives and senators, and the system of apportionment among the states to determine membership in the House of Representatives.

One of the most important sections of Article I is section 8. It carefully lists those powers the Framers wished the new Congress to possess. These specified, or **enumerated powers** contain many key provisions that had been denied to the Continental Congress under the Articles of Confederation. A final, general clause authorizing Congress to "make all Laws which shall be necessary and proper for carrying into Execution the foregoing Powers" completes Article I. The **necessary and proper clause** is the basis for the **implied powers** that Congress uses to execute its other powers.

ARTICLE II: THE EXECUTIVE BRANCH **Article II** vests the executive power, that is, the authority to execute the laws of the nation, in a president of the United States. Section 1 sets the president's term of office at four years and explains the Electoral College. It also states the qualifications for office and describes a mechanism to replace the president in case of death, disability, or removal from office. Article II also limits the presidency to natural-born citizens. The powers and duties of the president are set out in section 3. Among the most important of these are the president's role as commander in chief of the armed forces, the authority to make treaties with the consent of the Senate, and the authority to "appoint Ambassadors, other public Ministers and Consuls, the Judges of the Supreme Court, and all other Officers of the United States." From these powers presidents have claimed **inherent powers**, allowing them to take broad reaching authority not specified in the Constitution from using the National Guard to integrate state schools over the deviance of state governors or sending immediate aid to states or nations in need.

ARTICLE III: THE JUDICIAL BRANCH **Article III** establishes a Supreme Court and defines its jurisdiction. During the Philadelphia meeting, the smaller states feared that a strong unelected judiciary would trample on their liberties. Thus, the Framers permitted Congress to establish lower national courts but did not require it. State courts and the national court system would exist side by side with distinct areas of authority. Federal courts had authority to decide cases arising under federal law and the U.S. Constitution. The U.S. Supreme Court also assumed the power to settle disputes between states or between a state and the national government. Ultimately, it was up to the Supreme Court to determine what the provisions of the Constitution actually meant.

ARTICLES IV THROUGH VII The remainder of the articles in the Constitution attempted to anticipate problems that might occur in the operation of the new national government as well as its relations to the states. **Article IV** begins with what is called the **full faith and credit clause**, which mandates that states honor the laws and judicial proceedings of other states. Article IV also includes the mechanisms for admitting new states to the union.

Article V specifies how amendments can be added to the Constitution. The Bill of Rights, which added ten amendments to the Constitution in 1791, was one of the first items of business when the First Congress met in 1789.

Article I
Vests all legislative powers in the Congress and establishes a bicameral legislature, consisting of the Senate and the House of Representatives; it also sets out the qualifications for holding office in each house, the terms of office, the methods of selection of representatives and senators, and the system of apportionment among the states to determine membership in the House of Representatives.

enumerated powers
The powers of the national government specifically granted to Congress in Article I, section 8 of the Constitution.

necessary and proper clause
The final paragraph of Article I, section 8, of the Constitution, which gives Congress the authority to pass all laws "necessary and proper" to carry out the enumerated powers specified in the Constitution; also called the elastic clause.

implied powers
The powers of the national government derived from the enumerated powers and the necessary and proper clause.

Article II
Vests the executive power, that is, the authority to execute the laws of the nation, in a president of the United States; section 1 sets the president's term of office at four years and explains the Electoral College and states the qualifications for office and describes a mechanism to replace the president in case of death, disability, or removal from office.

inherent powers
Powers that belong to the president because they can be inferred from the Constitution.

Article III
Establishes a Supreme Court and defines its jurisdiction.

Article IV
Mandates that states honor the laws and judicial proceedings of other states. Article IV also includes the mechanisms for admitting new states to the union. *See also* "full faith and credit clause".

full faith and credit clause
Section of Article IV of the Constitution that ensures judicial decrees and contracts made in one state will be binding and enforceable in any other state.

Article V
Specifies how amendments can be added to the Constitution.

WHY DOES THE PRESIDENT DELIVER A STATE OF THE UNION ADDRESS?

In Article II of the Constitution, the Framers required the president to report directly to Congress "from time to time" about the affairs of the state. Today, the speech has become a media event; the president's Address is carried live on television, radio, and social media.

Article VI
Contains the supremacy clause, which asserts the basic primacy of the Constitution and national law over state laws and constitutions. *See also* "supremacy clause."

supremacy clause
Portion of Article VI of the Constitution mandating that national law is supreme over (that is, supersedes) all other laws passed by the states or by any other subdivision of government.

Article VI contains the supremacy clause, which asserts the basic primacy of the Constitution and national law over state laws and constitutions. The **supremacy clause** provides that the "Constitution, and the laws of the United States" as well as all treaties are to be the supreme law of the land. Without the supremacy clause and the federal courts' ability to invoke it, the national government would have little actual enforceable power; thus, many commentators call the supremacy clause the linchpin of the entire federal system.

Mindful of the potential problems that could occur if church and state were too enmeshed, the Framers specified in Article VI that no religious test shall be required for holding any office. This mandate is strengthened by the separation of church and state guarantee that became part of the Constitution when the First Amendment was ratified.

The seventh and final article of the Constitution concerns the procedures for ratifying the new Constitution: nine of the thirteen states would have to agree to, or ratify, its new provisions before it would become the supreme law of the land.

RATIFYING THE U.S. CONSTITUTION

2.5 Outline the arguments for and against ratification of the Constitution.

While delegates to the Constitutional Convention labored in Philadelphia, the Congress of the Confederation continued to govern the former colonies under the Articles of Confederation. The day after the delegates signed the Constitution, the secretary of the Convention left for New York City, then the nation's capital, to deliver the official copy of the document to the Congress. He also took with him a resolution of the delegates

AMERICAN POLITICS IN COMPARATIVE PERSPECTIVE

How Does the U.S. Constitution Compare?

Although nearly every country has a formal written constitution, America's stands out in two major ways. First, it is the oldest and longest continuously-operating written constitution. Second, it is one of the shortest and least detailed. The original text written in 1787 was less than 5,000 words, and even with the twenty-seven amendments, the document remains less than 8,000 words.

Combined together, these two features mean that many aspects of American government and politics originated from outside the constitutional framework itself. For instance, little or nothing is laid out about the role of political parties, the conducting of elections, the congressional committee system, or the organization of the federal government. These have evolved organically and somewhat haphazardly over time, rather than as part of an overarching, interlocking system. The brevity of the document also leaves a major role for the courts in sorting out the meaning of the Constitution—even though the power of the judiciary is not clearly delineated.

The U.S. Constitution also includes some anachronistic elements that may have made sense at the time of the founding but are less defensible today. Consider the Electoral College, which was an important compromise in 1787 but contains many ambiguities and potential sources of complication every four years during presidential elections. At the same time, the very antiquity of the Constitution and its continuity over centuries lends it an aura of legitimacy, even reverence, that enhances political stability.

In many other countries, the national constitution resembles a detailed law code covering nearly all aspects of the government and the political system. In contrast, the U.S. Constitution remains more of a "citizens' charter" to promote self-governance. Below are how some selected democracies compare in regard to the year of adoption of that the country's current constitution and the length of its constitutional text.

FIGURE 2.3   AMERICAN GOVERNMENT IN COMPARATIVE PERSPECTIVE: HOW DOES THE U.S. CONSTITUTION COMPARE

This chart lists fifteen democracies in the chronological order of the enactment of their current constitutions; it also indicates the word lengths of these documents. Note that, by comparison, the U.S. Constitution is quite old and also rather short. This word count includes both the original text enacted in 1789 as well as the 27 amendments that were adopted between 1791 and 1992.

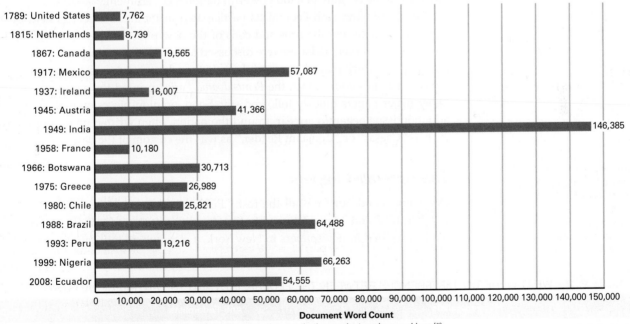

	Document Word Count
1789: United States	7,762
1815: Netherlands	8,739
1867: Canada	19,565
1917: Mexico	57,087
1937: Ireland	16,007
1945: Austria	41,366
1949: India	146,385
1958: France	10,180
1966: Botswana	30,713
1975: Greece	26,989
1980: Chile	25,821
1988: Brazil	64,488
1993: Peru	19,216
1999: Nigeria	66,263
2008: Ecuador	54,555

DATA SOURCE Comparative Constitutions Project (http://comparativeconstitutionsproject.org/ccp-rankings/#)

CRITICAL THINKING QUESTIONS

1. The brevity and ambiguity of the U.S. Constitution leave it open to a wide range of interpretations and differing understandings over time. Would you consider that a strength or a weakness. If so, why?

2. Most Americans consider the constitutional system as almost synonymous with the American state itself. In many other countries, however, the national constitution has been changed much more often. How do you think this would influence how citizens in those countries think about their constitutions?

3. Would the United States benefit from the writing of a new, much more detailed constitution? What would be the major arguments for and against such a major change?

Federalists
Those who favored a stronger national government and supported the proposed U.S. Constitution; later became the first U.S. political party.

Anti-Federalists
Those who favored strong state governments and a weak national government; opposed ratification of the U.S. Constitution.

calling upon each of the states to vote on the new Constitution. Anticipating resistance from representatives in the state legislatures, however, the Framers required the states to call special ratifying conventions to consider the proposed Constitution.

The Congress of the Confederation immediately accepted the work of the convention and forwarded the proposed Constitution to the states for their votes. It was by no means certain, however, that the states would adopt the new Constitution. From the fall of 1787 to the summer of 1788, debate over the proposed Constitution raged around the nation. State politicians understandably feared a strong central government. Farmers and other working-class people feared a distant national government. And, those who had accrued substantial debts during the economic chaos following the Revolutionary War feared that a new government with a new financial policy would plunge them into even greater debt. The public in general was very leery of taxes—these were the same people who had revolted against the king's taxes. At the heart of many of their concerns lay an underlying apprehension of the massive changes that a new system would create. Favoring the Constitution were wealthy merchants, lawyers, bankers, and those who believed that the new nation could not continue to exist under the Articles of Confederation.

Federalists versus Anti-Federalists

During the debate over whether to ratify the Constitution, those who favored the new strong national government chose to call themselves **Federalists**. They were well aware that many people still generally opposed the notion of a strong national government. They did not want to risk being labeled nationalists, so they tried to get the upper hand in the debate by nicknaming their opponents **Anti-Federalists**. As noted in Table 2.2, Anti-Federalists argued that they simply wanted to protect state governments from the tyranny of a too powerful national government.[17]

Federalists and Anti-Federalists participated in the mass meetings held in state legislatures to discuss the pros and cons of the new plan. Tempers ran high at these meetings, and fervent debates were discussed at town hall meetings and published in newspapers, which played a powerful role in the adoption process. Just two days after the convention's end, in fact, the *Pennsylvania Packet* printed the entire Constitution. Other major papers quickly followed suit. Soon, opinion pieces on both sides of the adoption issue began to appear around the nation, often written under pseudonyms such as "Caesar" or "Constant Reader," as was the custom of the day.

The Federalist Papers

One name stood out from all the rest: "Publius" (Latin for "the people"). Between October 1787 and May 1788, eighty-five essays written under that pen name routinely appeared in newspapers in New York, a state where ratification was in doubt.

TABLE 2.2   WHAT WERE THE DIFFERENCES BETWEEN THE FEDERALISTS AND THE ANTI-FEDERALISTS?

	Federalists	Anti-Federalists
Who were they?	Property owners, landed rich, merchants of Northeast and Mid-Atlantic	Small farmers, shopkeepers, laborers
Political philosophy	Elitist; saw themselves and those of their class as most fit to govern (others were to be governed)	Believed in the decency of "the common man" and in participatory democracy; viewed elites as corrupt; sought greater protection of individual rights
Type of government favored	Powerful central government; two-house legislature; upper house (six-year term) further removed from the people, whom they distrusted	Wanted stronger state governments (closer to the people) at the expense of the powers of the national government; sought smaller electoral districts, frequent elections, referendum and recall, and a large unicameral legislature to provide for greater class and occupational representation
Alliances	Pro-British, anti-French	Anti-British, pro-French

Alexander Hamilton and **James Madison** wrote most of them. Hamilton, a young, fiery New Yorker born in the British West Indies, wrote fifty-one; Madison, a Virginian who later served as the fourth president, authored twenty-six; jointly, they penned another three. **John Jay**, also of New York, and later the first chief justice of the United States, wrote five of the pieces. These eighty-five essays became known as ***The Federalist Papers***.

Today, *The Federalist Papers* are considered masterful explanations of the Framers' intentions as they drafted the new Constitution. At the time, although they were reprinted widely, they were far too theoretical to have much impact on those who would ultimately vote on the proposed Constitution. Dry and scholarly, they lacked the fervor of much of the political rhetoric then in use. *The Federalist Papers* did, however, highlight the reasons for the new government's structure and its benefits. These musings of Madison, Hamilton, and Jay continue to stand as the clearest articulation of the political theories and philosophies that lie at the heart of our Constitution.

Forced on the defensive, the Anti-Federalists responded to *The Federalist Papers* with their own series of letters written under the pen names "Brutus" and "Cato," two ancient Romans famous for their intolerance of tyranny. These letters (actually essays) undertook a line-by-line critique of the Constitution, as did other works.

Anti-Federalists argued that a strong central government would render the states powerless.[18] They stressed the strengths granted to the government under the Articles of Confederation and maintained that the Articles, not the proposed Constitution, created a true federal system. Moreover, they believed that the strong national government would tax heavily, that the U.S. Supreme Court would overwhelm the states by invalidating state laws, and that the president eventually would have too much power as commander in chief of a large and powerful army.[19]

In particular, Anti-Federalists feared the power of the national government to run roughshod over the liberties of the people. They proposed that the taxing power of Congress be limited, that the executive be curbed by a council, that the military consist of state militias rather than a national force, and that the jurisdiction of the Supreme Court be limited to prevent it from reviewing and potentially overturning the decisions of state courts. But, their most effective argument concerned the absence of a bill of rights in the Constitution. James Madison answered these criticisms in *Federalist Nos. 10* and *51*. In *Federalist No. 10*, Madison pointed out that the voters would not always succeed in electing "enlightened statesmen" as their representatives. The greatest threat to individual liberties would therefore come from factions within the government that might place narrow interests above broader national interests and the rights of citizens. While recognizing that no form of government could protect the country from unscrupulous politicians, Madison argued that the organization of the new government would minimize the effects of political factions. The great advantage of a federal system, Madison maintained, was that it created the "happy combination" of a national government too large for any single faction to control and several state governments that would be smaller and more responsive to local needs. Moreover, he argued in *Federalist No. 51* that the proposed federal government's separation of powers would prohibit any one branch from either dominating the national government or violating the rights of citizens.

Winning Support for the Constitution

Debate continued in the thirteen states as votes were taken from December 1787 to June 1788, in accordance with the ratifying process laid out in Article VII of the proposed Constitution. Three states acted quickly to ratify the new Constitution. Two small states, Delaware and New Jersey, voted to ratify before the large states could rethink the notion of equal representation of the states in the Senate. Pennsylvania, where Federalists were well organized, was also one of the first three states to ratify. Massachusetts assented to the new government but tempered its support by calling for an immediate addition of amendments, including one protecting personal rights.

James Madison
A key Framer often called the "Father of the Constitution" for his role in conceptualizing the federal government. Co-authored *The Federalist Papers*; served as secretary of state; served as the fourth U.S. president from 1809 to 1817.

John Jay
A member of the Founding generation who was the first Chief Justice of the United States. A diplomat and co-author of the *Federalist Papers*.

The Federalist Papers
A series of eighty-five political essays written by Alexander Hamilton, James Madison, and John Jay in support of ratification of the U.S. Constitution.

New Hampshire became the crucial ninth state to ratify on June 21, 1788. This action completed the ratification process outlined in Article VII of the Constitution and marked the beginning of a new nation. But, New York and Virginia, which at that time accounted for more than 40 percent of the new nation's population, had not yet ratified the Constitution. Thus, the practical future of the new nation remained in doubt.

Hamilton in New York and Madison in Virginia worked feverishly to convince delegates to their state conventions to vote for the new government. In New York, sentiment against the Constitution ran high. In Albany, fighting broke out over ratification and resulted in injuries and death. When news of Virginia's acceptance of the Constitution reached the New York convention, Hamilton was able to convince a majority of those present to follow suit by a margin of three votes. Both states also recommended the addition of a series of structural amendments and a bill of rights.

North Carolina and Rhode Island continued to hold out against ratification. Both had recently printed new currencies and feared that values would plummet in a federal system that authorized the Congress to coin money. On August 2, 1788, North Carolina became the first state to reject the Constitution on the grounds that no Anti-Federalist amendments were included. Soon after, in September 1789, owing much to the Anti-Federalist pressure for additional protections from the national government, the first Congress submitted the Bill of Rights to the states for their ratification. North Carolina then ratified the Constitution by a vote of 194–77. Rhode Island, the only state that had not sent representatives to Philadelphia, remained out of the new nation until 1790. Finally, under threats from its largest cities to secede from the state, the legislature called a convention that ratified the Constitution by only two votes (34–32)—one year after George Washington became the first president of the United States.

The Bill of Rights

Once the Constitution was ratified, elections took place. When Congress convened, it immediately sent a set of amendments to the states for ratification. An amendment authorizing the enlargement of the House of Representatives and another to prevent members of the House from raising their own salaries failed to garner favorable votes in the necessary three-fourths of the states. The remaining ten amendments, known as the **Bill of Rights**, were ratified by 1791 in accordance with the procedures set out in the Constitution. Sought by Anti-Federalists as a protection for individual liberties, they offered numerous specific limitations on the national government's ability to interfere with a wide variety of personal liberties, some of which many state constitutions had already guaranteed. These include freedom of expression, speech, press, religion, and assembly, guaranteed by the First Amendment. The Bill of Rights also contains numerous safeguards for those accused of crimes. The Ninth Amendment notes that these enumerated rights are not inclusive, meaning they are not the only rights to be enjoyed by the people, and the Tenth Amendment states that powers not given to the national government are reserved by the states or the people.

TOWARD REFORM: METHODS OF AMENDING THE U.S. CONSTITUTION

2.6 Describe the processes by which the Constitution can be amended.

The Framers did not want to fashion a government subject to the whims of the people. Therefore, they made the formal amendment process a slow one to guard against impulsive amendment of the Constitution. In keeping with this intent, only seventeen amendments have been added since the Bill of Rights were ratified in 1791 (see Table 2.3). However, informal amendments, prompted by judicial interpretation, cultural and social change, and technological change, have had a tremendous impact on the Constitution.

TABLE 2.3 WHAT ARE THE AMENDMENTS TO THE U.S. CONSTITUTION?

Constitutional amendments have mostly been enacted during four distinct historical periods, often separated by decades and associated with major upheavals in American history. Amendments also mostly deal with four major themes: federalism and states' rights; the role and powers of Congress or the presidency; civil liberties or civil rights; or voting and elections. (Only two amendments have ever directly created public policy, one by establishing Prohibition and the other repealing it.) The amendments have also had widely varying levels of historical significance.

Number and Year	Historical Era	Main Topic of Amendment	Main Area of Impact
1 (1791)	**Founding Era (1791–1804)**	Free expression and religion	Civil liberties
2 (1791)		Right to bear arms	Civil liberties
3 (1791)		Quartering of troops	Civil liberties
4 (1791)		Unreasonable search and seizure	Civil liberties
5 (1791)		Rights of the accused	Civil liberties
6 (1791)		Rights of the accused	Civil liberties
7 (1791)		Rights of the accused	Civil liberties
8 (1791)		Cruel and unusual punishment	Civil liberties
9 (1791)		Other rights of the people	Civil liberties
10 (1791)		Rights of the states	Federalism
11 (1795)		Immunity of states to lawsuits	Federalism
12 (1804)		Electoral College	Voting and elections
13 (1865)	**Civil War Era (1865–1870)**	Ending slavery	Civil rights
14 (1868)		Equal protection of the law	Civil rights
15 (1870)		Voting on the basis of race	Voting and elections
16 (1913)	**Progressive Era (1913–20)**	Federal income tax	Federalism
17 (1913)		Direct election of senators	Voting and elections
18 (1919)		Prohibition on sale of alcohol	Public policy
19 (1920)		Voting on the basis of sex	Voting and elections
20 (1933)	***Outliers (1933–51)***	Repeal of prohibition	Public policy
21 (1933)		Start of presidential and congressional terms	Congress and presidency
22 (1951)		Two-term limit for presidents	Voting and elections
23 (1961)	**Civil Rights Era (1961-71)**	Electoral votes for Washington, DC	Voting and elections
24 (1964)		Ban on poll taxes	Voting and elections
25 (1967)		VP as acting president	Congress and presidency
26 (1971)		Voting for 18-year-olds	Voting and elections
27 (1992)	***Outlier (1992)***	Congressional pay raises	Congress and presidency

Formal Methods of Amending the Constitution

Article V of the Constitution creates a two-stage amendment process: proposal and ratification. The Constitution specifies two ways to accomplish each stage. As explained in Table 2.4, amendments to the Constitution can be proposed by: (1) a vote of two-thirds of the members in both houses of Congress; or, (2) a vote of two-thirds of the state legislatures specifically requesting Congress to call a national convention to propose amendments. The second method has never been used.

The ratification process is fairly straightforward. When Congress votes to propose an amendment, the Constitution specifies that the ratification process must occur in one of two ways: (1) a favorable vote in three-fourths of the state legislatures; or, (2) a favorable vote in specially called ratifying conventions in three-fourths of the states. Since ratification of the Constitution, however, only one ratifying convention has been called.

The intensity of efforts to amend the Constitution has varied considerably, depending on the nature of the change proposed. Whereas the Twenty-First Amendment took only ten months to ratify, the Equal Rights Amendment (ERA) was introduced

TABLE 2.4 WHAT ARE THE CONSTITUTIONAL AND POLITICAL DIMENSIONS OF ENACTING A CONSTITUTIONAL AMENDMENT?

Although Article V provides a number of options for amending the Constitution, one main route is generally used. The constitutional requirements and political realities of this usual route are presented here.

How are the parts of government involved?	What constitutional support is required?	What are the political implications?
House	Proposal by a vote of ⅔ of all members	This is a supermajority of 288 out of 435 members, requiring at least some bipartisan support.
Senate	Proposal by a vote of ⅔ of all members	This is a supermajority of 67 out of 100 members, requiring at least some bipartisan support.
States	Ratification by a vote of ¾ of the state legislatures	This is a supermajority of at least 38 out of 50 states. A simple majority must vote for ratification in each of the state's legislative chambers. This requires at least some bipartisan support across multiple parts of the country.
Presidents and Governors	Presidents and governors play no formal institutional role.	Presidents and governors may offer their political support or opposition. They may also influence how the provisions of an amendment are later applied in practice.
Federal and State Courts	The courts may not review or strike down an amendment.	In any future rulings, all courts are bound by the provisions of an amendment. They may be called on to later interpret an amendment's legal meaning and impact.

in every session of Congress from 1923 until 1972, when Congress finally voted favorably for it. Even then, years of lobbying by women's groups were insufficient to garner necessary state support. By 1982, the congressionally mandated date for ratification, only thirty-five states—three short of the number required—had voted favorably on the amendment.[20] Yet, it has been reintroduced every session of Congress in a somewhat symbolic move.

The failed battles for the ERA as well as other amendments, including one to prohibit child labor and another to grant statehood to the District of Columbia, underscore how difficult it is to amend the Constitution. Thus, unlike the constitutions of individual states or many other nations, the U.S. Constitution rarely has been amended.

WHICH IS THE ONLY CONSTITUTIONAL AMENDMENT TO BE REPEALED?

For all its moral support from groups such as the Women's Christian Temperance Union (WCTU), whose members invaded bars to protest the sale of alcoholic beverages, the Eighteenth Amendment (Prohibition) was a disaster. Among its side effects was the rise of powerful crime organizations responsible for illegal sales of alcoholic beverages. Once proposed, it took only ten months to ratify the Twentieth Amendment, which repealed Prohibition.

Informal Methods of Amending the Constitution

The formal amendment process is not the only way the Constitution has been altered over time. Judicial interpretation, cultural and social change, and the growth of technology also have had a major impact on how the Constitution has evolved.

JUDICIAL INTERPRETATION As early as 1803, the Supreme Court declared in *Marbury* v. *Madison* that federal courts had the power to nullify acts of the nation's government when the courts found such acts to conflict with the Constitution.[21] Over the years, this check on the other branches of government and on the states has increased the authority of the Court and significantly altered the meaning of various provisions of the Constitution. This fact prompted President Woodrow Wilson to call the Supreme Court "a constitutional convention in continuous session," a role demonstrated by recent decisions in civil liberties, civil rights, and economic regulation.

Today, some analysts argue that the original intent of the Framers—as evidenced in *The Federalist Papers*, as well as in private notes taken by James Madison at the Constitutional Convention—should govern judicial interpretation of the Constitution.[22] Others argue that the Framers knew a changing society needed an elastic, flexible document that could adapt to the ages.[23] In all likelihood, the vagueness of the document was purposeful. Those in attendance in Philadelphia recognized that they could not agree on everything and that it was wiser to leave interpretation to future generations.

SOCIAL AND CULTURAL CHANGE Even the most far-sighted of those in attendance at the Constitutional Convention could not have anticipated the vast changes that have occurred in the United States. For example, none could have imagined that an African American would one day become president of the United States. Likewise, few of the Framers could have anticipated the diverse roles that women now play in American society. The Constitution has evolved to accommodate such social and cultural changes. As a candidate for president in 2016, Donald J. Trump supported many policies that do not align with traditional interpretations of the Constitution, most particularly with regard to freedom of the press and religious freedom guarantees. Americans will likely see an escalation in social and cultural changes supported by those who voted for President Trump and Republicans in Congress, given the powers available to the executive and legislative branches of government under single party control.

TECHNOLOGICAL CHANGE Ongoing technological advances continue to create new questions related to privacy and free speech rights under the Constitution. To what extent can private companies regulate Internet access and traffic speeds? Under what circumstances should online speech be regulated?

Government access to private online communication and personal electronic devices is another issue testing the flexibility of the Constitution. In 2014, the U.S. Supreme Court addressed the scope of protection for digital information seized from a cell phone. A unanimous Court found that a warrant was needed before the phone could be searched.[24] Additional cases on these and other issues related to technology will continue to arise.

REVIEW THE CHAPTER

Roots of the U.S. Constitution

2.1 Identify the causes of the American Revolution and the ideals on which the United States and the Constitution are based.

Settlers came to the New World for a variety of reasons, but most of these early inhabitants remained loyal to Great Britain and considered themselves subjects of the king. Over the years, as new generations of Americans were born on colonial soil, those ties weakened. A series of taxes levied by the British Crown ultimately led colonists to convene the Second Continental Congress and to declare their independence. American political culture emphasizes several key values, including liberty, equality, majority rule, and individualism.

An Attempt at a National Government: The Articles of Confederation

2.2 Identify the key components of the Articles of Confederation and the reasons for their failure.

The Articles of Confederation (1781) created a loose league of friendship between the new national government and the states. Numerous weaknesses in the new government quickly became apparent. Among the major flaws were Congress's inability to tax or regulate commerce, the absence of an executive to administer the government, the lack of a strong central government, and no judiciary.

Writing the U.S. Constitution

2.3 Outline the issues resolved by compromise during the writing of the Constitution.

When weaknesses of the Articles of Confederation became apparent, the states called for a meeting to reform them. The Constitutional Convention (1787) threw out the Articles of Confederation and fashioned a new, more workable form of government. The U.S. Constitution resulted from a series of compromises, including those over representation, issues involving large and small states, slavery, and how to determine population. The delegates also made compromises on how members of each branch of government were to be selected. They created the Electoral College to give states a key role in the selection of the president.

The U.S. Constitution

2.4 Describe the framework for government expressed in the Constitution.

The proposed U.S. Constitution created a federal system that drew heavily on Montesquieu's ideas about separation of powers. These ideas concerned a way of parceling out power among the three branches of government. A system of checks and balances also prevented any one branch from having too much power.

Ratifying the U.S. Constitution

2.5 Outline the arguments for and against ratification of the Constitution.

The drive for ratification became a fierce fight between Federalists and Anti-Federalists. Federalists lobbied for the strong national government created by the Constitution; Anti-Federalists favored greater state power.

Toward Reform: Methods of Amending the U.S. Constitution

2.6 Describe the processes by which the Constitution can be amended.

The Framers did not want the whims of the people to sway the government unduly. Therefore, they designed a deliberate two-stage, formal amendment process that required approval on both federal and state levels; this process has rarely been used. However, informal amendments, prompted by judicial interpretation, cultural and social changes, and technological change, have had a tremendous impact on the Constitution.

LEARN THE TERMS

Alexander Hamilton
Anti-Federalists
Article I
Article II
Article III

Article IV
Article V
Article VI
Articles of Confederation
Benjamin Franklin

Bill of Rights
checks and balances
Common Sense
constitution
Constitutional Convention

Crispus Attucks
Critical Period
Declaration of Independence
Electoral College
enumerated powers
federalism
Federalists
The Federalist Papers
First Continental Congress
French and Indian War
full faith and credit clause
George Washington

Great Compromise
implied powers
inherent powers
James Madison
John Jay
Lexington and Concord
mercantilism
Montesquieu
necessary and proper clause
New Jersey Plan
New World
political culture

Samuel Adams
Second Continental Congress
separation of powers
Shays's Rebellion
social contract theory
Sons and Daughters of Liberty
Stamp Act Congress
supremacy clause
Thomas Jefferson
Thomas Paine
Three-Fifths Compromise
Virginia Plan

HOW DID NATIVE AMERICANS GOVERN THEMSELVES?

The governing structure of the Iroquois Confederacy, which was located mainly in what is today's New York State, has been acknowledged as one of a number of sources for the Articles of Confederation and the U.S. Constitution. Above, at an exhibition at the Smithsonian Institution, visitors view a 1794 treaty between the United States and the Iroquois Confederacy.

THE FEDERAL SYSTEM

LEARNING OBJECTIVES

3.1 Trace the roots of the federal system and distinguish it from other types of government.

3.2 Explain the constitutional foundations for federalism.

3.3 Trace the evolution of federalism, from ratification to the present.

3.4 Analyze the impact of federalism on the relationships among national, states, and local levels of government.

The millions of Indians living throughout most parts of what is now the United States during colonial times were divided into as many as 600 tribes. Tribe members shared a common ancestry, language, culture, and support for political authority. Each tribe believed in its sovereignty, which bound its members to its ideals and authority. Similar to the principles that found their way into the Constitution of the United States of America, the power of elected officials came directly from the people.

Unlike the United States, however, tribes operated by consensus. Principles of majority rule were foreign to Indians. All decisions made by those in authority were based on political and religious beliefs with no differentiation between the two—another difference from the United States government, which forbade government establishment of an official religion.

American Indian men and women were routinely allowed to vote. Female citizens of the United States were forced to wait until the ratification of the Nineteenth Amendment in 1920 to vote in national elections.

Common troubles and the need to create a united front to prevent Europeans from taking their lands led a group of tribes on the East Coast to create a **confederation**, a political structure in which power is granted to a central authority by its individual components—in this case, each sovereign tribe or nation. Called the **Iroquois Confederacy**, the Mohawk, Oneida, Onondaga, Cayuga, and Seneca created this structure to protect themselves from outside threats.

The Iroquois Confederacy's constitution, the "Great Binding Law," included a Council of Fifty with seats apportioned by population and status. While women could not vote, in many tribes the oldest woman held the key position of selecting those who would represent her tribe at the Council. The Great Binding Law also created a system of checks and balances, an approach to governing that is a key feature in how the U.S. government is structured.

• • •

Like the Great Binding Law of the Iroquois Confederacy, the U.S. Constitution binds a diverse array of governments at the national, state, and local levels. The Constitution lays out the duties, obligations, and powers of national and state governments; states establish and charter local governments. Throughout history, crises, historical evolution, public opinion, and judicial interpretation continually have reshaped these relationships. All of these forces have had a tremendous influence on policy decisions affecting your daily life. Because there is only one national government, for example, you do not need a passport to travel from Texas to Oklahoma. Only one national currency exists, as does a national minimum wage, although states may set higher hourly wages. But, the laws of various states exhibit many differences. The age at which you may marry is a state issue, as are laws governing divorce, child custody, and criminal justice, including how—or if—the death penalty may be applied. Local governments often set liquor or smoking laws. Other policies and programs, such as waging war and air traffic regulation, lie solely within the province of the national government. In areas such as education, however, the national, state, and local governments work together in a system of shared powers.

confederation
Type of government in which the national government derives its powers from the states; a league of independent states.

Iroquois Confederacy
A political alliance of American Indian tribes established in the seventeenth century that featured aspects of the federal system of government adapted by the Framers.

ROOTS OF THE FEDERAL SYSTEM

3.1 Trace the roots of the federal system and distinguish it from other types of government.

The Framers wrote the U.S. Constitution at a time when many citizens and political theorists were beginning to question the source of government's power. They drew upon their struggles under the British crown to fashion a new system of government,

TABLE 3.1 HOW DID ARISTOTLE CLASSIFY THE TYPES OF GOVERNMENTS?

Rule by	In Whose Interest	
	Public	**Self**
One	Monarchy	Tyranny
The Few	Aristocracy	Oligarchy
The Many	Polity	Democracy

SOURCE: Aristotle, *Politics* 3, 7.

monarchy
A form of government in which power is vested in hereditary kings and queens who govern the entire society.

totalitarianism
A form of government in which power resides in leaders who rule by force in their own self-interest and without regard to rights and liberties.

oligarchy
A form of government in which the right to participate depends on the possession of wealth, social status, military position, or achievement.

democracy
A system of government that gives power to the people, whether directly or through elected representatives.

federal system
System of government in which the national government and state governments share power and derive all authority from the people.

where power was divided between sovereign state and national governments, and the ultimate source of power lay with the people. Creating a strong national government, but maintaining a role for the states and the people, was important to the Framers because state and local governments pre-dated the existence of the national government in every one of the thirteen colonies. Even the earliest settlers in the New World realized that rules or laws were necessary to keep order within a community.

Choosing a Type of Government

Early Greek theorists such as Plato and Aristotle tried to categorize governments by who participates, who governs, and how much authority those who govern enjoy. As Table 3.1 shows, a **monarchy**, the form of government in Great Britain from which the colonists fled, is defined by the rule of one hereditary king or queen in the interest of all of his or her subjects. Another form, an aristocracy, is government by the few in the service of the many. **Totalitarianism** is a type of government that Aristotle considered rule by "tyranny." Tyrants, such as Adolph Hitler, rule their countries to benefit themselves. In tyrannical or totalitarian systems, the leader exercises unlimited power, and individuals have no personal rights or liberties. Generally, the rule of these systems tends to be based on a particular religion or orthodoxy, an ideology, or a personality cult organized around a supreme leader. An **oligarchy**, in contrast, occurs when a few people rule in their own interest. In an oligarchy, wealth, social status, military position, or achievement dictates participation in government. Many commentators refer to Vladimir Putin's leadership in Russia as an example of this type of government.

Aristotle called rule of the many for the benefit of all citizens a "polity" and rule of the many to benefit themselves a "democracy." The term **democracy** derives from the Greek words *demos* ("the people") and *kratia* ("power" or "authority") and may apply to any system of government that gives power to the people, either directly, or indirectly through elected representatives. Of the more than 190 countries in the world today, 123 are democracies.

Devising a Federal System

American colonists rejected a system with a strong ruler, such as the British monarchy, when they declared their independence. They feared replicating the landed and titled system of the British aristocracy and viewed the formation of a republican form of government as far more in keeping with their values.

The United States became the first country to adopt a **federal system** of government (although the word "federal" never appears in the U.S. Constitution). The Framers designed this system, wherein the national and state governments share power and derive all authority from the people, to remedy many of the problems experienced under the Articles of Confederation. Under the Articles, the national government derived all of its powers from the states, similar to the Iroquois Confederacy, where the central government derived its powers from individual Indian nations. This arrangement led to a weak national government often unable to respond to even localized crises, such as Shays's Rebellion.

FIGURE 3.1 WHAT IS THE SOURCE OF GOVERNMENTAL AUTHORITY?

The source of governmental authority varies between federal, unitary, and confederate systems. Having experienced the challenges of both unitary and confederate systems, the Framers of the Constitution chose a federal system, in which the power of both state and national governments derives from the people.

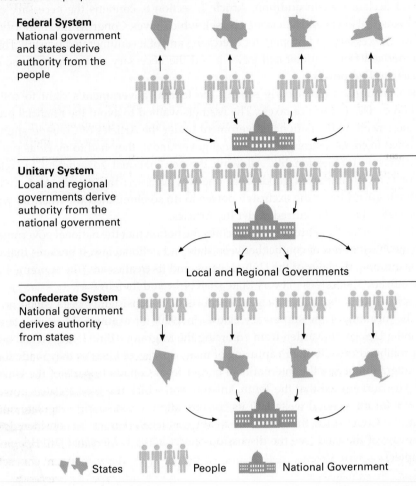

Federal System
National government and states derive authority from the people

Unitary System
Local and regional governments derive authority from the national government

Local and Regional Governments

Confederate System
National government derives authority from states

States   People   National Government

The new system of government also had to be different from the **unitary system** found in Great Britain, where local and regional governments derived all of their power from a strong national government (see Figure 3.1). Having been under the rule of British kings, whom they considered tyrants, the Framers feared centralizing power in one government or institution. Therefore, they made both the state and the federal governments accountable to the people. While the governments shared some powers, each government was supreme in some spheres, as described in the following section.

unitary system
System of government in which the local and regional governments derive all authority from a strong national government.

FEDERALISM: DIVIDING POWER UNDER THE CONSTITUTION

3.2 Explain the constitutional foundations for federalism.

The U.S. Constitution spells out a division of power between the national and state governments. Some powers are expressly assigned to the national government, while others are given to the states. The two governments share some powers, while others are denied to both the national and state governments. No powers, however, are given to local governments. Local governments lack sovereign authority and must be chartered by the state governments.

enumerated powers
The powers of the national government specifically granted to Congress in Article I, section 8 of the Constitution.

implied powers
The powers of the national government derived from the enumerated powers and the necessary and proper clause.

Tenth Amendment
The final part of the Bill of Rights that defines the basic principle of American federalism in stating that the powers not delegated to the national government are reserved to the states or to the people.

reserved powers
Powers reserved to the states by the Tenth Amendment that lie at the foundation of a state's right to legislate for the public health and welfare of its citizens.

National Powers Under the Constitution

All of the powers specifically stated in Article I, section 8, of the Constitution are called **enumerated powers**. Chief among these exclusive powers of the national government are the authorities to coin money, conduct foreign relations, provide for an army and navy, and declare war. In addition, Article I, section 8, contains the necessary and proper clause (also called the elastic clause), which gives Congress the authority to enact laws "necessary and proper" for exercising any of its enumerated powers. These powers derived from enumerated powers and the necessary and proper clause are known as **implied powers**.

The Constitution also clearly set out the federal government's right to collect duties and excises (a form of taxes). The Framers wanted to avoid the financial problems experienced by the national government under the Articles of Confederation. If they wished to create a strong new national government, they had to make its power to raise revenue unquestionable. Allowing the new national government to collect tariffs, or taxes on imported goods, was one way to assert this power. And, giving the national government the exclusive power to do so eliminated the financial wars between states that had occurred under the Articles.

Article VI of the Constitution underscores the notion that the national government is supreme in situations of conflict between state and national law. It declares that the U.S. Constitution, the laws of the United States, and its treaties are "the supreme Law of the Land; and the Judges in every State shall be bound thereby."

In spite of this explicit language, the courts have consistently been called on to clarify the meaning of the supremacy clause. In 1920, for example, Missouri sought to prevent a U.S. game warden from enforcing the Migratory Bird Treaty Act of 1918, which prohibited the killing or capturing of many species of birds as they made their annual migration across the international border from Canada to parts of the United States.[1] Missouri argued that the Tenth Amendment, which reserved a state's powers to legislate for the general welfare of its citizens, allowed Missouri to regulate hunting. But, the Court ruled that since the treaty was legal, it must be considered the supreme law of the land (see the discussion of *McCulloch* v. *Maryland* [1819] later in this chapter).

State Powers Under the Constitution

Because states held all the power at the time the Constitution was written, the Framers felt no need, as they did for the new national government, to list and restate all of the powers of the states, although some are specified throughout the Constitution. Article I of the U.S. Constitution notes that each state is entitled to two senators, and it leaves to the states the times, places, and manner of national elections. Thus, the states may enact their own restrictions on who can and cannot vote so long as those restrictions are constitutional. Article II requires that each state appoint electors to vote for president. And, Article IV guarantees each state a "Republican Form of Government," meaning one that represents the citizens of the state.

Not until the **Tenth Amendment**, the final part of the Bill of Rights, were the states' powers described in greater detail: "The powers not delegated to the United States by the Constitution, nor prohibited by it to the States, are reserved to the States respectively, or to the people." These powers, often called the states' **reserved powers**, include the ability to legislate for the public health, safety, and morals of their citizens. Today, the states' rights to legislate under their reserved powers provide the rationale for laws passed regarding access to bathrooms for transgendered persons and restrictions on abortion providers, to give but two examples. Reserved powers also form the basis for state criminal laws, including those concerning the death penalty. As long as the U.S. Supreme Court continues to find the death penalty not in violation of the

The Federal System 47

FIGURE 3.2   HOW IS GOVERNMENTAL POWER DISTRIBUTED IN THE FEDERAL SYSTEM?

The Constitution divides power between the national and state governments. It gives the national government a list of enumerated powers, while many state powers are captured in the reserved powers clause of the Tenth Amendment. The national and state governments also share some powers, known as concurrent powers.

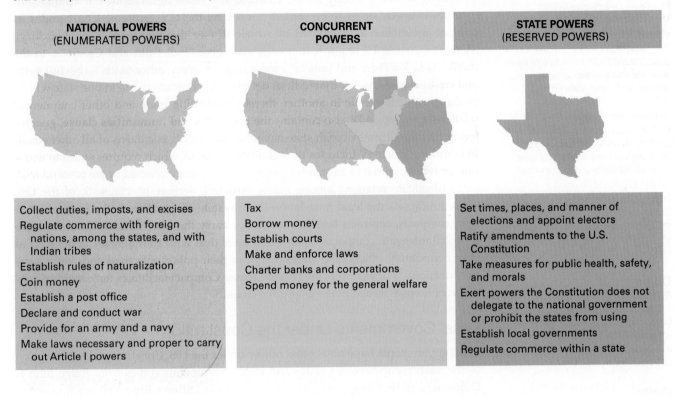

NATIONAL POWERS (ENUMERATED POWERS)	CONCURRENT POWERS	STATE POWERS (RESERVED POWERS)
Collect duties, imposts, and excises Regulate commerce with foreign nations, among the states, and with Indian tribes Establish rules of naturalization Coin money Establish a post office Declare and conduct war Provide for an army and a navy Make laws necessary and proper to carry out Article I powers	Tax Borrow money Establish courts Make and enforce laws Charter banks and corporations Spend money for the general welfare	Set times, places, and manner of elections and appoint electors Ratify amendments to the U.S. Constitution Take measures for public health, safety, and morals Exert powers the Constitution does not delegate to the national government or prohibit the states from using Establish local governments Regulate commerce within a state

U.S. Constitution, the states may impose it, whether by lethal injection, gas chamber, electric chair, hanging, or firing squad.

Concurrent Powers Under the Constitution

As revealed in Figure 3.2, national and state powers overlap. The area in which the systems overlap represents **concurrent powers**—powers shared by the national and state governments. States already had the power to tax; the Constitution extended this power to the national government as well. Other important concurrent powers include the rights to borrow money, establish courts, charter banks, and spend money for the general welfare. Due to concurrent powers, most individuals must file both state and federal tax returns.

Powers Denied Under the Constitution

Article I of the Constitution explicitly denies some powers to the national government or states. Congress, for example, is barred from favoring one state over another in regulating commerce, and it cannot lay duties on items exported from any state. Article I also prohibits the national government from granting titles of nobility, and government employees may not accept salaries or gifts from foreign heads of state.

State governments (as well as the national government) are denied the authority to take arbitrary actions affecting constitutional rights and liberties. Neither national nor state governments may pass a **bill of attainder**, a law declaring an act illegal without a judicial trial. The Constitution also bars national and state governments from passing *ex post facto* **laws**, those that make an act punishable as a crime even if the action was legal at the time it was committed.

concurrent powers
Powers shared by the national and state governments.

bill of attainder
A law declaring an act illegal without a judicial trial.

ex post facto **law**
Law that makes an act punishable as a crime, even if the action was legal at the time it was committed.

full faith and credit clause
Section of Article IV of the Constitution that ensures judicial decrees and contracts made in one state will be binding and enforceable in any other state.

privileges and immunities clause
Part of Article IV of the Constitution guaranteeing that the citizens of each state are afforded the same rights as citizens of all other states.

extradition clause
Part of Article IV of the Constitution that requires states to extradite, or return, criminals to states where they have been convicted or are to stand trial.

interstate compacts
Contracts between states that carry the force of law; generally now used as a tool to address multistate policy concerns.

Dillon's Rule
A premise articulated by Judge John F. Dillon in 1868 which states that local governments do not have any inherent sovereignty and instead must be authorized by state governments that can create or abolish them.

charter
A document that, like a constitution, specifies the basic policies, procedures, and institutions of local government. Charters for local governments must be approved by state legislatures.

FIGURE 3.3 HOW MANY GOVERNMENTS EXIST IN THE UNITED STATES?

More than 90,000 governments exist in the United States. Most of these governments are at the local level and divided among municipal governments, towns, and special districts such as school districts. The most common form of government is the special district.

SOURCE: U.S. Census Bureau, www2.census.gov/govs/cog/g12_org.pdf

1	**U.S. government**
50	**State governments**
90,056	**Local governments**
3,031	County
19,519	Municipal (city)
16,360	Townships
12,880	School districts
38,266	Special districts
90,107	**TOTAL**

Interstate Relations Under the Constitution

In addition to delineating the relationship between states and the national government, the Constitution provides a mechanism for resolving interstate disputes and facilitating relations among states. To avoid any sense of favoritism, it arranges for disputes between states to be settled directly by the U.S. Supreme Court under its original jurisdiction as mandated by Article III (see the discussion of the judiciary). Moreover, Article IV requires that each state give "Full Faith and Credit ... to the public Acts, Records, and judicial Proceedings of every other State." The **full faith and credit clause** ensures that judicial decrees and contracts made in one state will be binding and enforceable in another, thereby facilitating trade and other commercial relationships. Article IV also contains the **privileges and immunities clause**, guaranteeing that the citizens of each state have the same rights as citizens of all other states. In addition, Article IV includes the **extradition clause**, which requires states to extradite, or return, criminals to states where they have been convicted or are to stand trial.

To facilitate relations among states, Article I, section 10, clause 3, of the U.S. Constitution sets the legal foundation for interstate cooperation in the form of **interstate compacts**, contracts between states that carry the force of law. Currently, more than 200 interstate compacts exist. While some deal with rudimentary items such as state boundaries, others help states carry out their policy objectives and administrative functions.[2] For example, the Driver License Compact facilitates nationwide recognition of licenses issued in the respective states.

Local Governments Under the Constitution

Local governments have no express power under the U.S. Constitution. A description of the relationship between states and local governments comes from Judge John F. Dillon, who in 1868 articulated a premise known as **Dillon's Rule**. Dillon's Rule states that all local governments—whether towns, villages, cities, or counties, or some other form—do not have any inherent sovereignty and instead must be authorized by state governments, which can create or abolish them.

Local governments, therefore, need a **charter**—a document that, like a constitution, specifies the basic policies, procedures, and institutions that are acceptable to the state legislature. States issue charters that establish the authority and procedures defining a municipality, and all amendments to these charters require approval by state governments. The responsibilities of local governments described in these charters vary widely and include public health and safety, education, jobs, zoning land, and assistance to those in need. Local governments are of several types, as highlighted in Figure 3.3.

COUNTIES   **Counties** are the basic administrative units of local government. Every state has counties, although in Louisiana they are called parishes, and in Alaska, boroughs. With few exceptions, counties have very broad responsibilities and are used by state governments for welfare and environmental programs, courts, and the registration of land, births, and deaths.

MUNICIPALITIES   **Municipalities** are city governments created in response to the emergence of relatively densely populated areas. Some of the most intense struggles among governments within the United States are over the boundaries, scope of authority, and sources of revenue for municipal governments. County and municipal boundaries may overlap. State actions have merged city and county into a consolidated government in several areas, including San Francisco, California; Denver, Colorado; Honolulu, Hawaii; and Jacksonville, Florida.

TOWNS   The term is used today to refer to smaller communities, often run by a mayor and town council. The definition of a town varies considerably from state to state. In some states, towns and municipalities may be virtually indistinguishable, while other states set specific restrictions on the size of each type of government.

SPECIAL DISTRICTS Among forms of government, special districts are the most numerous. A **special district** is a local government restricted to a particular function. These districts exist for services such as libraries, sewage, water, and parks and are governed through a variety of structures. One reason for the proliferation of special districts is the desire to avoid restrictions on funds faced by municipalities or other jurisdictions.

School districts, the most common form of special districts, exist to provide free public education to students. They frequently cross town lines for purposes of practicality. They have their own budgets and must persuade those without children in a district to agree to help fund schools and extracurricular programs. Most school districts also receive assistance from states or the federal government for some specialized programs.

THE EVOLUTION OF FEDERALISM

3.3 Trace the evolution of federalism, from ratification to the present.

The nature of federalism, including its allocation of power between the national government and the states, has changed dramatically over the past 200 years. Much of this change has resulted from rulings of the U.S. Supreme Court, which has played a major role in defining the nature of the federal system. Other changes have resulted from major crises throughout American history.

Federalism and the Marshall Court

Few Supreme Courts have had a greater impact on the federal–state relationship than the one headed by Chief Justice **John Marshall** from 1801–1835. In a series of decisions, he and his associates carved out an important role for the Court in defining the balance of power between the national government and the states. Three rulings in the early 1800s, *McCulloch v. Maryland* (1819), *Gibbons v. Ogden* (1824), and *Barron v. Baltimore* (1833), were particularly important.

DEFINING NATIONAL POWER: *MCCULLOCH V. MARYLAND* (1819) *McCulloch v. Maryland* **(1819)** was the first major Supreme Court decision to define the relationship between the national and state governments. In 1816, Congress chartered the Second Bank of the United States. (The charter of the First Bank had been allowed to expire.) In 1818, the Maryland state legislature levied a tax requiring all banks not chartered by Maryland (that is, the Second Bank of the United States) to: (1) buy stamped paper from the state on which their bank notes were to be issued; (2) pay the state $15,000 a year; or, (3) go out of business. James McCulloch, the head cashier of the Baltimore branch of the Bank of the United States, refused to pay the tax, and Maryland brought suit against him. After losing in a Maryland state court, McCulloch appealed the decision to the U.S. Supreme Court by order of the U.S. secretary of the treasury. In a unanimous opinion, the Court answered the two central questions presented to it: (1) Did Congress have the authority to charter a bank? and, (2) if it did, could a state tax it?

Chief Justice John Marshall's answer to the first question—whether Congress had the right to establish a bank or another type of corporation—continues to stand as the classic exposition of the doctrine of implied powers and as a statement of the authority of a strong national government. Although the word "bank" does not appear in the Constitution, the Constitution enumerates powers that give Congress the authority to levy and collect taxes, issue a currency, and borrow funds. From these enumerated

counties
The basic administrative units of local government.

municipalities
City governments created in response to the emergence of relatively densely populated areas.

special district
A local government that is restricted to a particular function.

John Marshall
The longest-serving Supreme Court Chief Justice, Marshall served from 1801 to 1835. Marshall's decision in *Marbury* v. *Madison* (1803) established the principle of judicial review in the United States.

McCulloch **v.** *Maryland* **(1819)**
The Supreme Court upheld the power of the national government and denied the right of a state to tax the federal bank, using the Constitution's supremacy clause. The Court's broad interpretation of the necessary and proper clause paved the way for later rulings upholding expansive federal powers.

Gibbons v. Ogden **(1824)**
The Supreme Court upheld broad congressional power to regulate interstate commerce. The Court's broad interpretation of the Constitution's commerce clause paved the way for later rulings upholding expansive federal powers.

Barron v. Baltimore **(1833)**
Supreme Court ruling that, before the Civil War, limited the applicability of the Bill of Rights to the federal government and not to the states.

Roger B. Taney
Supreme Court Chief Justice who served from 1835-1864. Taney supported slavery and states' rights in the pre-Civil War era.

dual federalism
The belief that having separate and equally powerful levels of government is the best arrangement, often referred to as layer-cake federalism.

powers, Marshall found, it was reasonable to imply that Congress had the power to charter a bank, which could be considered "necessary and proper" to the exercise of its aforementioned enumerated powers.

Marshall next addressed whether any state government could tax a federal bank. To Marshall, this was not a difficult question. The national government depended on the people, not the states, for its powers. In addition, Marshall noted, the Constitution specifically called for the national law to be supreme. "The power to tax involves the power to destroy," wrote the Chief Justice.[3] Thus, the state tax violated the supremacy clause because individual states cannot interfere with operations of the national government, whose laws are supreme.

AFFIRMING NATIONAL POWER: *GIBBONS V. OGDEN* (1824) Shortly after *McCulloch*, the Marshall Court had another opportunity to rule in favor of a broad interpretation of the scope of national power. *Gibbons v. Ogden* **(1824)** involved a dispute that arose after the New York state legislature granted to Robert Fulton the exclusive right to operate steamboats on the Hudson River.[4] Simultaneously, Congress licensed a ship to sail on the same waters. By the time the case reached the Supreme Court, it was complicated both factually and procedurally. Suffice it to say that both New York and New Jersey wanted to control shipping on the lower Hudson River. But, *Gibbons* actually addressed one simple, very important question: What was the scope of Congress's authority under the commerce clause? The states argued that "commerce," as mentioned in Article I, should be interpreted narrowly to include only direct dealings in products. In *Gibbons*, however, the Supreme Court ruled that Congress's power to regulate interstate commerce included the power to regulate commercial activity as well, and that the commerce power had no limits except those specifically found in the Constitution. Thus, New York had no constitutional authority to grant a monopoly to a single steamboat operator, an action that interfered with interstate commerce.[5]

LIMITING THE BILL OF RIGHTS: *BARRON V. BALTIMORE* (1833) In 1833, in one of Chief Justice Marshall's last major cases on the federal–state relationship, *Barron v. Baltimore* **(1833)**, the Court addressed the issue of whether the due process clause of the Fifth Amendment applied to actions of the states.[6] John Barron, a Baltimore businessman, ran a successful docking business off the city's wharf. As the city entered a period of extensive construction, dirt, sand, and silt drifted to his section of the wharf, making it unusable as a harbor. Barron sued the city and state for damages, arguing that the city took his lands "without just compensation," as guaranteed by the Fifth Amendment of the U.S. Constitution. The Marshall Court ruled that Barron had no federal claim because enumerated rights contained in the Bill of Rights applied only to the national government.[7]

The Civil War and Dual Federalism

In the early to mid-1800s, a national crisis began over the division of power between the states and the federal government. One major battleground in this struggle was the issue of slavery, which the pro-states' rights Southern states fought to maintain. In contrast, the Northern states, where commercial and manufacturing interests were more powerful, favored greater national power. Chief Justice **Roger B. Taney**, who succeeded John Marshall, saw the Court as an arbiter of those competing state and nationalist views. Chief Justice Taney and the Court also began to articulate further the notions of concurrent power and **dual federalism**. Dual federalism posits that having separate and equally powerful state and national governments is the best constitutional arrangement. Adherents of this theory typically believe the national government should not exceed its constitutionally enumerated powers, and, as stated in the Tenth Amendment, all other powers are—and should be—reserved to the states or to the people.

AMERICAN POLITICS IN COMPARATIVE PERSPECTIVE

How Widespread Are Federal Systems of Government?

The United States has a federal system of government in which national and subnational political units known as states share power. A number of other countries, including Canada, Switzerland, India, and Nigeria, also have federal systems of government. However, most of the world's nations, including Great Britain, France, China, Japan, and Iran, have unitary systems, with authority concentrated in the central government. Although federal systems are relatively few in number, they tend to be large and politically important. This world map illustrates countries with federal systems of government in green. Countries with other systems of government are shown in gray.

FIGURE 3.4   WHICH COUNTRIES HAVE FEDERAL SYSTEMS OF GOVERNMENT?

Since India's independence from Great Britain in 1947, its federal system has united citizens speaking thousands of languages and from a variety of diverse religions.

Russia, the world's largest country by landmass, has a federal system comprised of 83 subnational units. The government was formed in 1993 after the dissolution of the Soviet Union.

Some subnational units in Brazil are based on cultural boundaries that precede Portuguese colonization. Other subnational units have been created for economic or administrative purposes.

Malaysia has what is known as an asymmetric federation. Some subnational units have more power than others.

■ Federal system   ■ Not a federal country

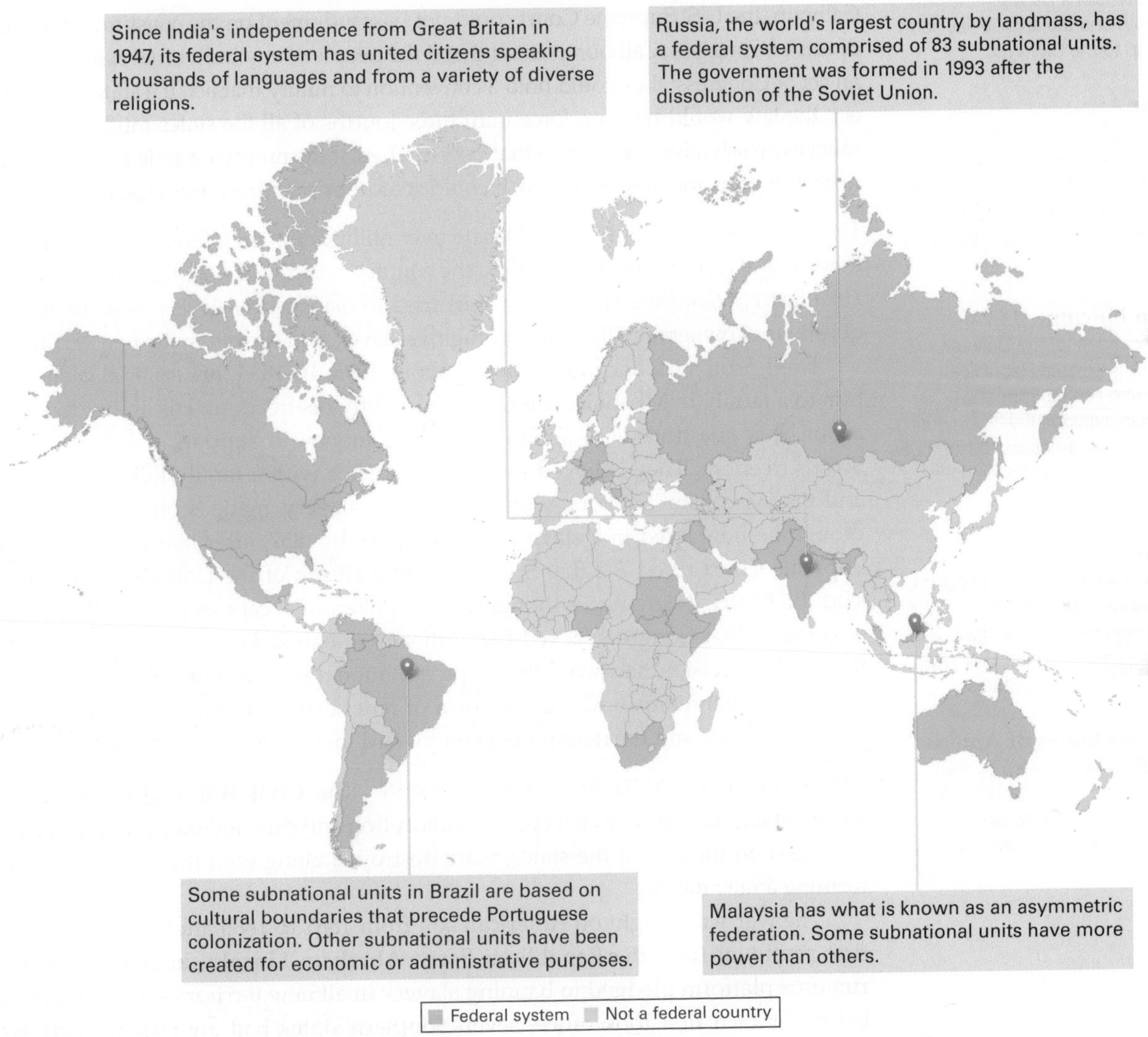

CRITICAL THINKING QUESTIONS

1. Study the map and then research what economic, cultural, and political characteristics the countries with federal systems have in common. Why might these characteristics have led to the adoption of federal systems?

2. Examine countries such as India, Nigeria, and Germany. What challenges might these countries face in maintaining a federal system in a region where most other countries choose a different form of government?

3. What other countries might be likely candidates for adopting federal systems in the future? Why do you think these countries are particularly good candidates?

nullification
The belief in the right of a state to declare void a federal law.

John C. Calhoun
A politician and political theorist from South Carolina who supported slavery and states' rights in the pre-Civil War era and served as vice president from 1825 to 1832.

***Dred Scott* v. *Sandford* (1857)**
A Supreme Court decision that ruled the Missouri Compromise unconstitutional and denied citizenship rights to enslaved African Americans. *Dred Scott* heightened tensions between the pro-slavery South and the abolitionist North in the run up to the Civil War.

Civil War
The military conflict from 1861 to 1865 in the United States between the Northern forces of the Union and the Southern forces of the Confederacy. Over 600,000 Americans lost their lives during this war.

Abraham Lincoln
Sixteenth president of the United States, the first elected Republican president, who served from 1861-1865. Lincoln, who led the Union during the Civil War, was assassinated in 1865 by a Confederate sympathizer, John Wilkes Booth.

secession
A unilateral assertion of independence by a geographic region within a country. The eleven Southern states making up the Confederacy during the Civil War seceded from the United States.

Confederate States of America
The political system created by the eleven states that seceded from the Union during the Civil War, which ceased to exist upon the Union victory.

NULLIFICATION   While the courts worked to carve out the appropriate roles for each level of government in the federal system, the political debate over states' rights swirled in large part over what is called **nullification**, the belief in the right of a state to declare a federal law void. The question of nullification arose in 1828, when the national government enacted a tariff act, most commonly referred to as the "Tariff of Abominations," that raised duties on raw materials, iron, hemp, and flax and reduced protections against imported woolen goods. Vice President **John C. Calhoun** opposed the bill because it badly affected his home state of South Carolina. Not only did South Carolinians have to pay more for raw materials because of the tariff bill, but it was also becoming increasingly difficult for them to sell their dwindling crops abroad for a profit.

Calhoun theorized that the federal government functioned merely as the agent of the states (the people and the individual state governments) and that the Constitution was simply a compact providing instructions on how the agent was to act. Thus, according to Calhoun, the U.S. Supreme Court could not pass judgment on the constitutional validity of acts of Congress. Calhoun posited that if the people of any individual state did not like an act of Congress, they could hold a convention to nullify that act. If a state contested an act, the law would have no force until three-fourths of all the states ratified an amendment expressly giving Congress that power. Then, if the nullifying state still did not wish to be bound by the new provision, it could secede, or withdraw, from the Union.

THE *DRED SCOTT* DECISION   Debate over nullification only forestalled debate on the inevitable slavery issue. By the 1850s, the country could wait no longer. In cases such as *Dred Scott* v. *Sandford* (1857), the Court tried to manage the slavery issue by resolving questions of ownership, the status of fugitive slaves, and slavery in the new territories.[8]

Dred Scott was born into slavery about 1795. In 1833, his original owners sold him to a family in Missouri. Later, he tried to buy his freedom. His ability to take this action was questioned, so abolitionists gave money to support a test case seeking Scott's freedom. They believed his prior residence with a family living in free states and the Wisconsin Territory, which prohibited slavery, made Scott a free man, even though he now lived in a slave state, Missouri. In 1857, after many delays, the U.S. Supreme Court ruled 7–2 that Scott was not a citizen of the United States. "Slaves," said the Court, "were never thought of or spoken of except as property." The Court also found that Congress lacked the authority to ban slavery in the territories. In so doing, this decision narrowed the scope of national power, while it enhanced that of the states. Eventually, however, no form of federalism could accommodate the existence of slavery, and the nation marched toward inevitable war with itself.

THE CIVIL WAR AND RECONSTRUCTION   The **Civil War** forever changed the nature of federalism. The concepts of nullification and dual federalism, as well as their emphasis on the role of the states, were destroyed along with the South's attempt at forming a new nation.

The war was fought on American soil from 1861 to 1865 after the election of the first president from the Republican Party, **Abraham Lincoln**, in 1860. Lincoln had run on a platform pledged to banning slavery in all new territories. By January 1861, before Lincoln first took office, seven Southern states had announced their **secession** from the United States to form the **Confederate States of America**. The first six states to secede had slave populations of nearly 50 percent. Eventually the new nation, never recognized as such by any other country, included eleven states with many men living in the southern parts of Union states also taking up arms for the Confederacy and against the Union.

The war had many causes, including slavery, which Southerners viewed as critical to the maintenance of their agricultural economy. The institution of slavery appalled Northerners. This chasm over slavery was a highlight of many of the cultural, social, and political differences that had grown between the North and South since the ratification of the Constitution and Bill of Rights.

The war left 620,000 dead, more wounded, and the South's decimation by battles and General William Tecumseh Sherman's famous March to the Sea in which the Union Army, beginning in Atlanta, Georgia, leveled fields, infrastructure, homes, and cities setting fire to all. The Civil War remains the bloodiest war ever fought by the United States. When the war ended, many Southerners bristled as a host of constraints were placed on those who had taken up arms against the Union or had helped in the Confederate war effort.

Most historians date the **Reconstruction** period as beginning at the end of the Civil War and lasting until 1877. President Lincoln had made it clear to his advisors that he wished a gentle way to deal with the vanquished states as did his successor, **Andrew Johnson**, who became president after the assassination of Lincoln. Their wishes were ignored. Former Confederate states were required to "reconstruct," or adopt new state constitutions approved by the nationalist Congress in Washington, D.C., and endure a range of punishments for their actions.

The elections of 1866, the first after the war, barred former Confederates from voting. Radical Republicans were able to win most key races vowing to set up a labor-dependent economy using the U.S. Army and freedmen, newly freed slaves, along with thousands of Northerners seeking new opportunities in the vanquished South. Called "carpet baggers," they came south as missionaries to minister to newly freed slaves, teachers, and even politicians since nearly all Southern men had taken up arms against the Union.

The actions of this new breed of politician helped facilitate passage of the Thirteenth, Fourteenth, and Fifteenth Amendments to the Constitution, creating a profound change in the reunited nation's concept of federalism.

After the Civil War, the Supreme Court often stepped in to limit state powers in favor of a stronger national government. The Court also recognized the need for national involvement in projects such as railroad construction, canal building, and the development of new technology, such as the telegraph.[9] And, beginning in the 1880s, the Court allowed Congress to regulate many aspects of economic relationships, such as outlawing monopolies, a type of regulation formerly considered to exist exclusively in the realm of the states. By the 1890s, passage of laws such as the Interstate Commerce Act and the Sherman Anti-Trust Act allowed Congress to establish itself as the supreme player in a growing national economy.

This role was enhanced by the ratification of the Sixteenth and Seventeenth Amendments during the early twentieth century. The **Sixteenth Amendment** gave Congress the power to levy and collect taxes on incomes without apportioning them among the states. The revenues taken in by the federal government through taxation of personal income "removed a major constraint on the federal government by giving it access to almost unlimited revenues."[10] The **Seventeenth Amendment**, ratified in 1913, similarly enhanced the power of the national government at the expense of the states. This amendment terminated the state legislatures' election of senators and placed their election in the hands of the people. With senators no longer directly accountable to the state legislatures, states lost their principal protectors in Congress.

Cooperative Federalism and the Growth of National Government

While the ratification of the Sixteenth and Seventeenth Amendments set the stage for expanded national government, the catalyst for dual federalism's demise was a series of economic events that ended in the cataclysm of the Great Depression:

- Throughout the 1920s, bank failures were common.
- In 1921, the nation experienced a severe slump in agricultural prices.
- In 1926, the construction industry went into decline.
- In the summer of 1929, inventories of consumer goods and automobiles were at an all-time high.

Reconstruction
The period from 1865–1877 after the Civil War, in which the U.S. militarily occupied and dominated the eleven former states of the Confederacy.

Andrew Johnson
Seventeenth president of the United States, a Republican, who served from 1865 to 1869. Johnson had served as Abraham Lincoln's vice president and became president after Lincoln's assassination.

Sixteenth Amendment
Amendment to the U.S. Constitution that authorized Congress to enact a national income tax.

Seventeenth Amendment
Amendment to the U.S. Constitution that made senators directly elected by the people, removing their selection by state legislatures.

HOW DID THE ROLE OF THE
NATIONAL GOVERNMENT CHANGE
AFTER THE CIVIL WAR?

Construction of a coast-to-coast trans-portation system like the transcon-tinental railroad, shown here, was a much celebrated event in nineteenth century America. Transportation lines and telecommunications systems that stretched across multiple state boundaries necessitated a greater role for the national government. Such changes helped to doom the system of dual federalism, which dominated for the first one hundred years of the nation's history.

Calvin Coolidge
Thirtieth president of the United States, a Republican, who served from 1923 to 1929.

Herbert Hoover
Thirty-first president of the United States, a Republican, who served from 1929 to 1933 during the start of the Great Depression.

Franklin D. Roosevelt (FDR)
Thirty-second president, a Democrat, who served from 1933 to 1945. FDR's leadership took the United States through the Great Depression and World War II.

New Deal
The name given to the program of "Relief, Recovery, Reform" begun by President Franklin D. Roosevelt in 1933 to bring the United States out of the Great Depression.

- On October 29, 1929, stock prices, which had risen steadily since 1926, crashed, taking with them the entire national economy.

Despite the severity of these indicators, Presidents **Calvin Coolidge** and **Herbert Hoover** took little action, believing that the national depression comprised an amalga-mation of economic crises better dealt with by state and local governments. It would take the election of President **Franklin D. Roosevelt (FDR)** in 1932 both to respond to this crisis and forever change the relationship between state and national govern-ments. To create these changes, Roosevelt proposed a program of relief, recovery, and reform known as the **New Deal**.

In the first few weeks of the legislative session after FDR's Inauguration, Congress passed a series of acts creating the new federal agencies and programs proposed by the president. These new agencies, often known by their initials, created what many termed an "alphabetocracy." Among the more significant New Deal programs were the Federal Housing Administration (FHA), which provided federal financing for new home construction; the Civilian Conservation Corps (CCC), a work relief pro-gram for farmers and homeowners; the Social Security Administration (SSA), which provided government support to retired wage earners; and the National Recovery Administration (NRA), which imposed restrictions on production in agriculture and many industries while also providing subsidies to farmers.

New Deal programs forced all levels of government to work cooperatively with one another. Local governments, especially those of cities, were embraced as equal partners in an intergovernmental system for the first time and became play-ers in the national political arena because many members of Congress wanted to bypass state legislatures, where urban interests usually were underrepresented. FDR also relied on big-city Democratic political machines to turn out voters to support his programs.

Those who feared these unprecedented changes in the federal system quickly challenged the constitutionality of the programs. And, at least initially, the U.S. Supreme Court often agreed with them. Through the mid-1930s, the Court contin-ued to rule that certain aspects of New Deal programs went beyond the authority of Congress to regulate commerce. FDR's frustration with the Court prompted him to suggest what ultimately was nicknamed his "Court-packing plan." Knowing he could

TRYING TO CHANGE THE UMPIRING

HOW DID FDR'S PUBLIC ACTIONS CHANGE CONCEPTIONS ABOUT FEDERALISM?

This cartoon illustrates FDR's difficulties garnering support from the Supreme Court for the economic and social programs he believed were necessary to end the Great Depression. To coerce support from the Court to transform the federal–state relationship, FDR proposed his Court-packing plan, which was met with great opposition. The plan, however, seemed to convince a majority of justices to overturn the Court's earlier decisions and to support the constitutionality of New Deal programs.

cooperative federalism
The intertwined relationship between national, state, and local governments that began with the New Deal; often referred to as marble-cake federalism.

do little to change the minds of those already on the Court, FDR suggested enlarging its size from nine to thirteen justices. This plan would have given him the opportunity to pack the Court with a majority of justices predisposed toward the constitutional validity of the New Deal.

Even though Roosevelt was popular, the Court-packing plan was not.[11] Congress and the public expressed outrage over even the suggestion of tampering with an institution of government. But, the Court appeared to respond to this threat. In 1937, it reversed its series of anti–New Deal decisions, concluding that Congress (and therefore the national government) had broad authority to legislate in any area as long as what was regulated affected commerce in any way. The Court also upheld the constitutionality of most of the massive New Deal relief programs, including the National Labor Relations Act of 1935, which authorized collective bargaining between unions and employees;[12] the Fair Labor Standards Act of 1938, which set a national minimum wage; and the Agricultural Adjustment Act of 1938, which provided crop subsidies to farmers.[13] Congress then used these newly recognized powers to legislate in a wide range of areas, including maximum hour laws and regulation of child labor.

The New Deal dramatically changed the federal system. Most political scientists likened the federal system before the 1930s to a layer cake: in most policy areas, each level or layer of government—national, state, and local—had clearly defined powers and responsibilities. By contrast, the metaphor of marble-cake federalism refers to what political scientists call **cooperative federalism**, a term that describes the intertwined relations among the national, state, and local governments that began during this period (see Figure 3.5). States began to take a secondary, albeit important, cooperative role in the scheme of governance, as did many cities.

FIGURE 3.5 HOW HAS THE FEDERAL-STATE RELATIONSHIP EVOLVED?

The balance of power between the national and state governments has evolved over time. In the early years of the new republic, the nation maintained a system of dual federalism, often referred to as layer cake federalism. This relationship transformed into a marble cake form of federalism known as cooperative federalism during the 1930s with the passage of FDR's New Deal program. This image illustrates the changing national–state relationship, building on the cake metaphor. It is too early to assess what type of federalism President Donald J. Trump will embrace.

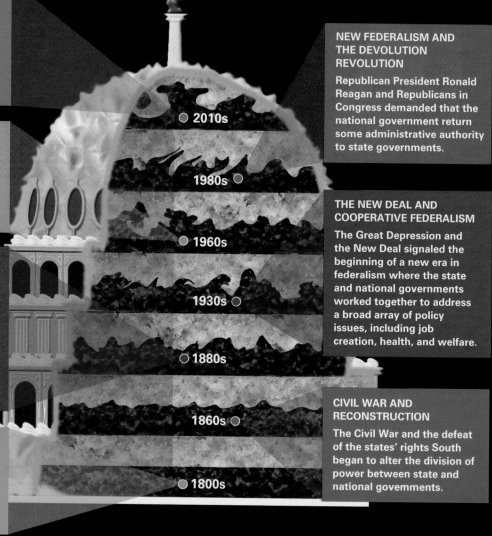

PROGRESSIVE FEDERALISM

The modern relationship between the states and federal government is both cooperative and coercive, depending on the issue area.

THE GREAT SOCIETY

One of the hallmarks of President Lyndon B. Johnson's Great Society program was offering federal financial aid to states in the form of grants-in-aid.

GROWING NATIONAL INTERVENTION IN THE ECONOMY

The needs of a growing and more technologically advanced nation required the intervention of the national government in economic affairs such as regulating business and constructing roads, railroads, and ports.

DUAL FEDERALISM

The division of national and state powers envisioned by the Framers; each government had separate spheres of authority dictated by the Constitution.

NEW FEDERALISM AND THE DEVOLUTION REVOLUTION

Republican President Ronald Reagan and Republicans in Congress demanded that the national government return some administrative authority to state governments.

THE NEW DEAL AND COOPERATIVE FEDERALISM

The Great Depression and the New Deal signaled the beginning of a new era in federalism where the state and national governments worked together to address a broad array of policy issues, including job creation, health, and welfare.

CIVIL WAR AND RECONSTRUCTION

The Civil War and the defeat of the states' rights South began to alter the division of power between state and national governments.

2010s
1980s
1960s
1930s
1880s
1860s
1800s

TOWARD REFORM: BALANCING NATIONAL AND STATE POWER

3.4 Analyze the impact of federalism on the relationships among national, state, and local levels of government.

As we have seen throughout this chapter, attempting to find equilibrium between the powers and responsibilities of national and state governments is one of the greatest challenges of a federal system. While the interdependent relationship of the state and national governments characterized by cooperative federalism can be an advantageous

FIGURE 3.6   WHAT ARE THE STATE AND LOCAL FISCAL CHALLENGES RELATED TO HEALTH CARE AND MEDICAID?

Spending on health care, due to the aging of the population and costly advances in medical technologies, is likely to drastically increase for state and local governments in coming decades. This may force a reduction in expenditures in other areas, such as education and public safety.

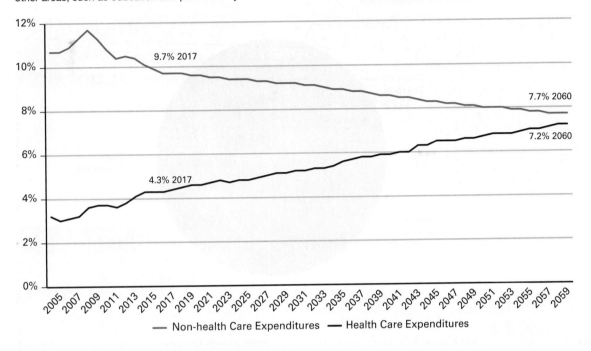

— Non-health Care Expenditures   — Health Care Expenditures

way of solving large-scale problems, it may also ask both the states and the national government to do things they are not necessarily equipped to do. State governments, for example, may struggle with redistributive policies such as health care exchanges or the testing associated with the "No Child Left Behind" Act (see Figure 3.6).

The relative strengths of the national and state governments continue to evolve today; finding a way to utilize these strengths is the aim of **progressive federalism**. Advocates of progressive federalism, such as former President **Barack Obama**, view the relationship between the states and the national government as both coercive and cooperative.[14] The form taken by the relationship depends chiefly on the political environment at each level of government. The best and first option is when the federal government is able to reach consensus and establish a national standard. However, failing the national government's ability to enact a particular proposal, national policy makers may embrace states' efforts to address that policy issue, particularly when those in power agree with the outcome of the state policy-making process. This approach allows policy makers to achieve their goals gradually and encourages states to act as what U.S. Supreme Court Justice Louis Brandeis called laboratories of democracy.[15]

Here, we explore two major factors that influence the relative balance of power between the state and national governments. First, we consider the role that finances play in creating and resolving national-state conflict and cooperation. We also consider the continuing role of the Supreme Court as the umpire of the federal system.

The Influence of Federal Grants

Until the 1960s, the national government constructed most federal grant programs in cooperation with the states, with emphasis on assisting the states in fulfilling their traditional responsibilities to protect the health, welfare, and safety of their citizens. Today, however, the national government provides grants from its general revenues to states, local governments, nonprofit organizations, and even individuals

progressive federalism
A pragmatic approach to federalism that views relations between national and state governments as both coercive and cooperative.

Barack Obama
The first African American president of the United States, a Democrat, who served as forty-fourth president from 2009 to 2017. Senator from Illinois from 2005 to 2008; member of the Illinois Senate from 1997 to 2004.

FIGURE 3.7 HOW DO FEDERAL GRANTS HELP STATE GOVERNMENTS?

Finances are one very important tool that the national government uses to influence state policy. On average, approximately one-third of state revenues come from the federal government, which means that states are highly dependent on the national government for financial solvency.

SOURCE: U.S. Census Bureau

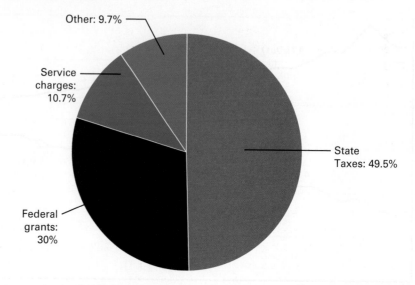

Other: 9.7%

Service charges: 10.7%

State Taxes: 49.5%

Federal grants: 30%

categorical grants
Grants that appropriate federal funds to states for a specific purpose.

Lyndon B. Johnson (LBJ)
Thirty-sixth president of the United States, a Democrat, who served from 1964 to 1969. LBJ led the nation during the Civil Rights era and the Vietnam War.

Great Society
Reform program begun in 1964 by President Lyndon B. Johnson that was a broad attempt to combat poverty and discrimination through urban renewal, education reform, and unemployment relief.

Ronald Reagan
Fortieth president of the United States, a Republican, who served from 1981 to 1989. Reagan led the nation through the end of the Cold War and his leadership led to a national shift toward political conservatism.

New Federalism
Federal–state relationship proposed by the Reagan administration during the 1980s; hallmark is returning administrative powers to the state governments.

block grant
A large grant given to a state by the federal government with only general spending guidelines.

(see Figure 3.7). These programs range from grants to support state programs that aid needy families to Pell grants that give college students help to fund their educations. These grants are given for a number of purposes, including: (1) providing state and local governments with additional funds; (2) setting national standards for national problems such as clean air and water; and, (3) attempting to financially equalize rich and poor states and localities. Federal grants are of three major types: (1) categorical grants; (2) block grants; and, (3) programmatic requests.

CATEGORICAL GRANTS **Categorical grants** are grants for which Congress appropriates funds for *specific* purposes. About 90 percent of federal aid monies go to categorical grants. These grants became more prominent in 1964, when President **Lyndon B. Johnson (LBJ)** launched his **Great Society** program, which included what LBJ called a "War on Poverty." Categorical grants allocate federal dollars by a precise formula, often based on population. They are subject to detailed conditions imposed by the national government. Often, they are made available on a matching basis; that is, states must contribute money to match federal funds, although the national government may pay as much as 90 percent of the total. Categorical grants may be used by the national government to alter states' policy priorities or to coerce states to adopt particular policy objectives. With large sums of money at stake, states will often neglect their own wants and needs to follow the leadership of the national government.

BLOCK GRANTS In 1980, former California Republican Governor **Ronald Reagan** became president, pledging to advance what he called **New Federalism** and a return of power to the states. The hallmark of this action was the consolidation of many categorical grants into fewer, less restrictive **block grants**—large amounts of money given to states with only general spending guidelines. Many of these went to education and health care.[16] Perhaps not surprisingly, block grants continue to be popular with governors, who often urge the consolidation of even more programs into block grants.

PROGRAMMATIC (EARMARK) REQUESTS Informally known as earmarks, **programmatic requests** are federal funds designated for special projects within a state or congressional district that direct specific exemptions from taxes or mandated fees. Federal funds have been provided for special projects since the first Congress, but the use of these grants has exploded in the past two decades. Programmatic requests are not competitively awarded, and have thus become very controversial owing to the use of paid political lobbyists who try to secure federal funds for their clients, be they states, cities, universities, or nonprofit groups. Members of Congress also attempt to secure these funds to bring programs and economic development back to their home districts. In 2016, Citizens Against Government Waste found over 123 programmatic requests in its *Congressional Pig Book*, an increase of 17.1 percent since 2015.[17]

programmatic requests
Federal funds designated for special projects within a state or congressional district; also called earmarks.

Federalism and the Supreme Court

The U.S. Supreme Court has always played an important role as the umpire of the federal system. When governmental powers, especially those of the state and national governments, come into conflict, it is the Court's job to determine which government is supreme. From the 1930s until the 1980s, the Court made its federalism decisions largely outside of the public eye. While the Court under Chief Justice Earl Warren in the 1950s and 1960s attracted a great deal of attention, it was largely for the justices' decisions on civil rights and liberties issues, not the Court's decisions on the balance of power between the state and national governments. Through the process of incorporation, which bound state governments to the provisions of the U.S. Constitution, however, many of these decisions had the result—intended or not—of expanding federal power at the expense of subnational units.

THE REHNQUIST COURT Beginning in the late 1980s, however, the Court's willingness to allow Congress to regulate in a variety of areas waned. According to one observer, the federalism decisions made by the Court under the Chief Justice William H. Rehnquist in the 1980s and 1990s were "a reexamination of the country's most basic constitutional arrangements."[18] The Court's decisions largely agreed with the Republican states' rights view supported by advocates of New Federalism.

THE ROBERTS COURT In 2005, following the death of Chief Justice Rehnquist, President George W. Bush appointed Chief Justice John Roberts to head the Supreme Court. In its early years, the Roberts Court appeared reluctant to address high-profile federalism cases. Today, the Court has become a willing participant in the federalism debate, deciding a series of visible cases related to the balance of national and state power. These cases considered issues such as immigration, redistricting, same-sex marriage, and the Affordable Care Act (Obamacare).[19] Much to the surprise of many Court-watchers, the Roberts Court has frequently sided with the power of the national government. Whether these decisions are a temporary departure from the norm or a harbinger of a new era in federalism remains to be seen, especially in light of President Donald J. Trump's intention to nominate states' rights conservatives to the bench and his stated intent to overturn *Roe* v. *Wade*.

REVIEW THE CHAPTER

Roots of the Federal System

3.1 Distinguish federalism from other forms of government.

Aristotle classifies the types of governments according to who rules, and in whose interest. Types of governments include monarchy, totalitarianism, aristocracy, oligarchy, polity, confederacy, and democracy. Fears about mob rule and the vast size of the United States led the Framers to create a republican democracy that relies on the role of representatives to filter citizens' viewpoints.

Federalism: Dividing Power Under the Constitution

3.2 Explain the constitutional foundations for federalism.

The national government has both enumerated and implied powers under the Constitution. National and state governments share an additional group of concurrent powers. Other powers are reserved to the states or the people, or expressly denied to both governments. The powers of the national government are ultimately declared supreme. Local governments are not expressly mentioned in the Constitution but are formed when state governments delegate their sovereign authority.

The Evolution of Federalism

3.3 Trace the evolution of federalism, from ratification to the present.

Dual federalism was characterized by a system of separate but equally powerful state and national governments. This system was exemplified by states' authority to regulate issues such as slavery, evident in the doctrine of nullification and the Supreme Court's decision in *Dred Scott* v. *Sanford* (1857). The Civil War changed forever the nature of federalism. The notion of equally powerful but separate national and state governments met its demise in the wake of the Great Depression. Franklin D. Roosevelt's New Deal ushered in an era of cooperative federalism, in which the powers of the national and state and local governments became more integrated, working together to solve shared problems.

Toward Reform: Balancing National and State Power

3.4 Analyze the impact of federalism on the relationships among national, state, and local levels of government.

The balance of power between the state and national governments may be affected by a number of factors. The federal government provides money to states in a number of ways, including categorical grants, block grants, and programmatic requests. The Supreme Court also plays an important role as the umpire of the federal system. The 1980s ushered in an era of New Federalism, in which President Ronald Reagan and Republican representatives in Congress sought to return power to the states. Progressive federalism, an approach that views the relationship between the states and the national government as both cooperative and coercive, gained ground during President Barack Obama's two terms in office. President Donald J. Trump's approach to federalism will likely depart from President Obama's.

LEARN THE TERMS

Abraham Lincoln
Andrew Johnson
Barack Obama
Barron v. *Baltimore* (1833)
bill of attainder
block grant
Calvin Coolidge

categorical grants
Civil War
charter
concurrent powers
Confederate States of America
confederation
cooperative federalism

counties
democracy
Dillon's Rule
Dred Scott v. *Sandford* (1857)
dual federalism
enumerated powers
ex post facto law

extradition clause
federal system
Franklin D. Roosevelt (FDR)
full faith and credit clause
Gibbons v. *Ogden* (1824)
Great Society
Herbert Hoover
implied powers
interstate compacts
Iroquois Confederacy
John C. Calhoun
John Marshall

Lyndon B. Johnson (LBJ)
McCulloch v. *Maryland* (1819)
monarchy
municipalities
New Deal
New Federalism
nullification
oligarchy
privileges and immunities
   clause
programmatic requests
progressive federalism

Reconstruction
reserved powers
Roger B. Taney
Ronald Reagan
secession
Seventeenth Amendment
Sixteenth Amendment
special district
Tenth Amendment
totalitarianism
unitary system

HOW DID THE *ZENGER* CASE EXPAND FREEDOM OF THE PRESS?

The 1734 case of *The Crown* v. *Zenger* strengthened the core principle of freedom of the press that information that is true may be published even if it insults those in power. In this illustration, the right of Zenger to make truthful accusations against the British governor of New York is defended in court.

CIVIL LIBERTIES

LEARNING OBJECTIVES

4.1   Explain the roots of civil liberties in the Constitution and their development in the Bill of Rights.

4.2   Distinguish between the establishment and the free exercise clauses of the First Amendment.

4.3   Outline the First Amendment liberties and limitations on the freedoms of speech, press, assembly, and petition.

4.4   Describe the Second Amendment right to bear arms.

4.5   Outline the constitutional rights of defendants and the issues involved in protecting defendants' liberties as guaranteed by the Bill of Rights.

4.6   Explain the origins and significance of the right to privacy.

4.7   Evaluate how reforms to combat terrorism have affected civil liberties.

On May 11, 1732, Colonel William Cosby arrived in what is now New York City to became the Province of New York's new royal governor. The Province of New York included what are now the states of New York, New Jersey, Vermont, Delaware, and parts of several other northeastern states. Nothing in the historical record indicates that Cosby was anything other than a power-hungry, corrupt fool. After watching the new governor's actions and petty politics, which included rigging elections and dismissing the Chief Justice of the New York Court and replacing him with an old crony, John Peter Zenger, a German immigrant, decided to begin publication of the *New York Weekly Journal* in autumn 1733. His goal? Spread the news of the governor's actions around the province.

Zenger, an expert printer, solicited columns and news articles from a stable of authors. At that time, however, it was a crime to write or publish criticisms of any public officials or government—even if the accusations were true. Upon publication of articles criticizing Cosby, the governor issued a proclamation condemning the "scandalous, virulent, false and seditious reflections" contained in the paper. On Cosby's orders, the sheriff jailed Zenger. Two grand juries refused to indict Zenger as requested by the province's attorney general. Stymied, Cosby instructed that Zenger be arrested by information, meaning a judge issued a warrant for Zenger's arrest charging him with seditious libel. It was yet another highly unpopular move by the governor. Zenger was sent to New York's Old City Jail, and bond was set so high that he was unable to make bail. Thus, he ended up staying in jail for nearly a year.

The tale gets worse for Zenger. During what became his first trial, both of his lawyers were disbarred at the direction of the governor. Thus, they could no longer represent Zenger. At his second trial, however, gasps were heard around the courtroom as his new lawyer, 38-year-old Andrew Hamilton, the most famous attorney in the colonies (no relation to Alexander Hamilton), rose to announce his representation of Zenger.

The presiding judge who saw that Zenger would not reveal the names of the authors of the "libelous" articles, thought the case was cut and dried. Zenger did not deny publishing the articles, and they definitely criticized Cosby. But, Hamilton had not earned his reputation for nothing.

Appealing directly to the twelve empaneled jurors, he argued that governments should not be allowed to punish those who published truthful criticism about public officials. How could public officials be held accountable if the hands of the press were tied, Hamilton asked the jury.

At the end of Hamilton 's closing, the judge directed the jury to find Zenger guilty. Within ten minutes after it retired, the jury came back and rendered a "not guilty" verdict, freeing Zenger. This decision, *The Crown* v. *Zenger* (1735) set an important standard for civil liberties that found its way into colonial and state constitutions and, eventually, the Bill of Rights. Early on, colonists realized how important freedom of the press was to a free flow of ideas in what was to become the new republic.

• • •

Civil liberties are the personal guarantees and freedoms that government cannot abridge, by law, constitution, or judicial interpretation. As guarantees of "freedom to" action, they place limitations on the power of the government to restrain or dictate an individual's actions. **Civil rights**, in contrast, provide freedom from arbitrary or discriminatory treatment by government or individuals.

Questions of civil liberties often present complex problems. We must decide how to determine the boundaries of speech and assembly and how much control over our personal liberties we give to police or other law enforcement officials. Moreover,

The Crown v. *Zenger* **(1735)**
Legal case in the colony of New York that is considered a precursor to free press provisions in the Constitution. The case did not set legal precedent, but did reflect a difference between British authorities and colonists with regard to press freedoms.

civil liberties
The personal guarantees and freedoms that the government cannot abridge by law, constitution, or judicial interpretation.

civil rights
The government-protected rights of individuals against arbitrary or discriminatory treatment by governments or individuals.

during times of war and social unrest, it is important to consider the liberties accorded to those who oppose war or are suspected of anti-government activities.

Resolution of civil liberties questions often falls to the judiciary, which must balance the competing interests of the government and the people. In this chapter, we explore the various dimensions of civil liberties guarantees contained in the U.S. Constitution and the Bill of Rights.

ROOTS OF CIVIL LIBERTIES: THE BILL OF RIGHTS

4.1 Explain the roots of civil liberties in the Constitution and their development in the Bill of Rights.

In 1787, most state constitutions explicitly protected a variety of personal liberties, such as freedoms of speech and religion, freedom from unreasonable searches and seizures, and trial by jury. The new federal system established by the Constitution would redistribute power between the national government and the states. Without an explicit guarantee of specific civil liberties, could the national government be trusted to uphold the freedoms already granted to citizens by their states?

Recognition of the increased power of the new national government led Anti-Federalists to stress the need for a bill of rights. Anti-Federalists and many others were confident they could control the actions of their own state legislators, but they did not trust the national government to protect civil liberties.

The notion of including a bill of rights in the Constitution was not popular at the Constitutional Convention. When George Mason of Virginia suggested adding such a bill to the preface of the proposed Constitution, representatives unanimously defeated his resolution.[1] In subsequent ratification debates, Federalists argued that a bill of rights was unnecessary, putting forward three main arguments in opposition.

1. A bill of rights was unnecessary in a constitutional republic founded on the idea of popular sovereignty and inalienable, natural rights. Moreover, most state constitutions contained bills of rights, so federal guarantees were unnecessary.

2. A bill of rights would be dangerous. According to Alexander Hamilton in *Federalist No. 84*, since the national government was one of enumerated powers (that is, it had only the powers listed in the Constitution), "Why declare that things shall not be done which there is no power to do?"

3. A national bill of rights would be impractical to enforce. Its validity would largely depend on public opinion and the spirit of the people and government.

Some Framers, however, came to support the idea. After the Philadelphia convention, James Madison conducted a lively correspondence with Thomas Jefferson about the need for a national bill of rights. Jefferson supported such guarantees far more quickly than did Madison. But, the reluctant Madison soon found himself in a close race against James Monroe for a seat in the House of Representatives in the First Congress. The district was largely Anti-Federalist. In an act of political expediency, Madison issued a new series of public letters similar to *The Federalist Papers*, in which he vowed to support a bill of rights. Once elected to the House, Madison made good on his promise and became the prime author of the Bill of Rights. Still, he considered Congress to have far more important matters to handle and viewed his work on the Bill of Rights as "a nauseous project."[2]

With fear of political instability running high, Congress worked quickly to approve Madison's draft. The proposed Bill of Rights with twelve amendments was sent to the states for ratification in 1789, the same year the first Congress convened. By 1791, the states had approved the first ten of its amendments.

The **Bill of Rights** contains numerous specific guarantees against encroachment by the national government, including those of free speech, press, and religion. The Ninth and Tenth Amendments, favored by the Federalists, note that the Bill of Rights is not exclusive.

The **Ninth Amendment** makes clear that the Bill of Rights' listing of rights does not mean that others do not exist. This amendment played a critical role when the Supreme Court began to address the constitutionality of state laws prohibiting contraceptives, surely nothing the Framers were thinking about as they neared completion of the Bill of Rights. The **Tenth Amendment** reiterates that powers not delegated to the national government are reserved to the states or to the people.

The Incorporation Doctrine: The Bill of Rights Made Applicable to the States

The Framers intended the Bill of Rights to limit the national government's power to infringe on the rights and liberties of the citizenry. Thus, in *Barron* v. *Baltimore* (1833), the Supreme Court ruled that the Bill of Rights limited only the actions of the U.S. government and not those of the states.[3] In 1868, however, the **Fourteenth Amendment** was added to the U.S. Constitution. Its language suggested that some or even all protections guaranteed in the Bill of Rights might be interpreted to prevent state infringement of those rights. Section 1 of the Fourteenth Amendment reads: "No State shall …. deprive any person of life, liberty, or property, without due process of law." Questions about the scope of "life" and "liberty" as well as the meaning of the phrase "due process of law" continue even today to engage legal scholars and jurists.

Until nearly the turn of the twentieth century, the Supreme Court steadfastly rejected numerous arguments for interpreting the Fourteenth Amendment's **due process clause** in such a way as to make various provisions in the Bill of Rights applicable to the states. In 1897, however, the Court began to increase its jurisdiction over the states by holding them to what was termed a **substantive due process** standard. This new standard required states to prove that their laws constituted a valid exercise of their power to regulate the health, welfare, or public morals of citizens.[4] Interference with state power, however, was rare, and states passed **sedition laws** that made it illegal to speak or write any political criticism that threatened to diminish respect for the government, its laws, or public officials. States anticipated that the U.S. Supreme Court would uphold the constitutionality of these laws. When Benjamin Gitlow, a member of the Socialist Party, printed a manifesto in which he urged workers to overthrow the U.S. government, he was convicted of violating a New York state law that prohibited such advocacy. Although his conviction was upheld, in *Gitlow* v. *New York* (1925), the justices noted that states were not completely free to limit forms of political expression, saying:

> For present purposes we may and do assume that freedom of speech and of the press—which are protected by the First Amendment from abridgement by Congress—are among the *fundamental personal rights and "liberties"* protected by the due process clause of the Fourteenth Amendment from impairment by the states [emphasis added].[5]

Gitlow, with its finding that states could not abridge free speech protections, was the first decision to clearly articulate the **incorporation doctrine**. It also enunciated the belief that some "personal rights" and "liberties" were so fundamental that they

Bill of Rights
The first ten amendments to the U.S. Constitution, which largely guarantee specific rights and liberties.

Ninth Amendment
Part of the Bill of Rights that makes it clear that enumerating rights in the Constitution or Bill of Rights does not mean that others do not exist.

Tenth Amendment
The final part of the Bill of Rights that defines the basic principle of American federalism in stating that the powers not delegated to the national government are reserved to the states or to the people.

Fourteenth Amendment
One of three major amendments enacted after the Civil War, extending "equal protection of the law" to all citizens.

due process clause
Clause contained in the Fifth and Fourteenth Amendments; over the years, it has been construed to guarantee a variety of rights to individuals.

substantive due process
Judicial interpretation of the Fifth and Fourteenth Amendments' due process clauses. Protects citizens from arbitrary or unjust state or federal laws.

sedition laws
Laws that make it illegal to speak or write any political criticism that threaten to diminish respect for the government, its laws, or public officials. State sedition laws were overturned as a result of the 1925 *Gitlow* Supreme Court decision.

***Gitlow* v. *New York* (1925)**
A Supreme Court case that extended the First Amendment's protections of freedom of speech and of the press to the state governments.

incorporation doctrine
An interpretation of the Constitution holding that the due process clause of the Fourteenth Amendment requires state and local governments to guarantee the rights stated in the Bill of Rights.

selective incorporation
A judicial doctrine whereby most, but not all, protections found in the Bill of Rights are made applicable to the states via the Fourteenth Amendment.

fundamental freedoms
Those rights defined by the Court as essential to order, liberty, and justice and therefore entitled to the highest standard of review.

Warren Court
The period in Supreme Court history during which Earl Warren served as Chief Justice (1953-1969), noted for its many rulings expanding civil liberties and civil rights.

Earl Warren
The fourteenth Chief Justice of the United States who served from 1953 to 1969 and led the Court through an important liberal phase; previously a Republican governor and vice presidential nominee.

required special protection from the states. This was clarified in *Near* v. *Minnesota* (1931), when the U.S. Supreme Court further developed this doctrine by holding that a state law violated the First Amendment's freedom of the press.[6]

Selective Incorporation and Fundamental Freedoms

The Supreme Court has not made all specific guarantees in the Bill of Rights applicable to the states through the due process clause of the Fourteenth Amendment as shown in Table 4.1. Instead, the Court has used the process of **selective incorporation** to limit the rights of states by protecting against abridgement of **fundamental freedoms**. These freedoms—defined by the Court as essential to order, liberty, and justice—are subject to the Court's most rigorous standard of review. The liberal **Warren Court** led by Chief Justice **Earl Warren**, was responsible for ten of the decisions listed in Table 4.1.

The Court set out the rationale for selective incorporation in *Palko* v. *Connecticut* (1937).[7] Frank Palko was charged with first-degree murder for killing two Connecticut police officers, found guilty of a lesser charge of second-degree murder, and sentenced to life imprisonment. Connecticut appealed. Palko was retried, found guilty of first-degree murder, and sentenced to death. Palko then appealed his second conviction, arguing that it violated the Fifth Amendment's prohibition against double jeopardy because the due process clause of the Fourteenth Amendment had made the Fifth Amendment applicable to the states.

The Supreme Court disagreed. It ruled that the due process clause bound states only to those rights that were "of the very essence of a scheme of ordered liberty." The Fifth Amendment's double jeopardy clause was not, in the Court's view, among these rights. The Court overruled that decision in 1969.[8]

Today, selective incorporation requires states to respect freedoms of press, speech, and assembly, among other liberties. The Court has not incorporated other guarantees, such as those contained in the Third and Seventh Amendments (housing of soldiers and jury trials in civil cases), because it has yet to consider them sufficiently fundamental to national notions of liberty and justice.

WHEN DID THE COURT FIRST ARTICULATE THE DOCTRINE OF SELECTIVE INCORPORATION?

Gitlow v. *New York* (1925) was a free speech case involving Benjamin Gitlow (shown on the right testifying before Congress), the executive secretary of the Socialist Party. Before *Gitlow* it generally was thought that, despite the Fourteenth Amendment, the limitations of the Bill of Rights did not apply to the states. After *Gitlow*, the Court gradually bound states to most of these provisions through a process known as selective incorporation.

TABLE 4.1 HOW HAS SELECTIVE INCORPORATION MADE THE BILL OF RIGHTS APPLICABLE TO THE STATES?

Amendment	Right	Date	Case Incorporated
I	Speech	1925	*Gitlow* v. *New York*
	Press	1931	*Near* v. *Minnesota*
	Assembly	1937	*DeJonge* v. *Oregon*
	Religion	1940	*Cantwell* v. *Connecticut*
II	Bear arms	2010	*D.C.* v. *Heller*/*McDonald* v. *City of Chicago*
III	No quartering of soldiers		Not incorporated
IV	No unreasonable searches or seizures	1949	*Wolf* v. *Colorado*
	Exclusionary rule	1961	*Mapp* v. *Ohio*
V	Just compensation	1897	*Chicago, B&O R.R. Co.* v. *Chicago*
	Self-incrimination	1964	*Malloy* v. *Hogan*
	Double jeopardy	1969	*Benton* v. *Maryland*
	Grand jury indictment		Not incorporated
VI	Public trial	1948	*In re Oliver*
	Right to counsel	1963	*Gideon* v. *Wainwright*
	Confrontation of witnesses	1965	*Pointer* v. *Texas*
	Impartial trial	1966	*Parker* v. *Gladden*
	Speedy trial	1967	*Klopfer* v. *North Carolina*
	Compulsory trial	1967	*Washington* v. *Texas*
	Criminal trial	1968	*Duncan* v. *Louisiana*
VII	Civil jury trial		Not incorporated
VIII	No cruel and unusual punishment	1962	*Robinson* v. *California*
	No excessive bail	1971	*Schilb* v. *Kuebel*

FIRST AMENDMENT GUARANTEES: FREEDOM OF RELIGION

4.2 Distinguish between the establishment and the free exercise clauses of the First Amendment.

The **First Amendment** to the Constitution begins, "Congress shall make no law respecting an establishment of religion, or prohibiting the free exercise thereof." This statement sets the boundaries of governmental action. The **establishment clause** directs the national government not to sanction an official religion. The **free exercise clause** ("or prohibiting the free exercise thereof") guarantees citizens that the national government will not interfere with practice of their religion. These guarantees, however, are not absolute and can come into conflict creating a difficult job for the courts. As the Supreme Court observed in 1940, the First Amendment "embraces two concepts—freedom to believe and freedom to act. The first is absolute. Thoughts cannot be regulated. In contrast, conduct remains subject to regulation by all levels of government."[9]

The Establishment Clause

The separation of church and state has always generated controversy in American politics. A majority of Americans clearly value the moral teachings of their respective religions. U.S. coins are embossed with "In God We Trust." The U.S. Supreme Court asks for God's blessing on the Court at the beginning of every session. Every session

First Amendment
Part of the Bill of Rights that imposes a number of restrictions on the federal government with respect to civil liberties, including freedom of religion, speech, press, assembly, and petition.

establishment clause
The first clause of the First Amendment; it directs the national government not to sanction an official religion.

free exercise clause
The second clause of the First Amendment; it prohibits the U.S. government from interfering with a citizen's right to practice his or her religion.

Lemon **test**
Three-part test created by the Supreme Court for examining the constitutionality of religious establishment issues.

of the U.S. House and Senate begins with a prayer, and both the House and Senate have their own chaplains. Through the years, the Court has been divided over the interpretation of the establishment clause. Does this clause erect a total wall between church and state, as favored by Thomas Jefferson, or does it allow some governmental accommodation of religion?

The Court's basic rule for dealing with church-state questions is known as the **Lemon** test. This three-part test is named for the 1971 case of *Lemon* v. *Kurtzman*. According to the *Lemon* test, a practice or policy is constitutional under the establishment clause if it:

1. has a legitimate secular purpose;
2. neither advances nor inhibits religion; and,
3. does not foster an excessive government entanglement with religion.[10]

One practice that clearly violates the *Lemon* test is prayer in public schools. In *Engel* v. *Vitale* (1962), for example, the Court ruled that the recitation of a brief non-denominational prayer drafted by the local school board in public school classrooms was unconstitutional.[11] One year later, in *Abington School District* v. *Schempp* (1963), the Court ruled that state-mandated Bible reading or recitation of the Lord's Prayer in public schools was also unconstitutional.[12] More recently, the Court has also prohibited prayer at other public school events, such as graduations and sporting events, although many public schools ignore that mandate.[13]

The Court, however, has allowed a wide variety of other church-state entanglements. For example, the use of public buildings for religious worship[14] and governments providing textbooks, computers, and other instructional materials to students at religious schools are allowed.[15] The Court also permits governments to offer students vouchers to attend private or religious schools.[16] And, student fees at public universities may be used to fund the activities of religious organizations, so long as those groups allow members of a variety of faiths.[17]

Establishment issues, however, do not always focus on education. The Court has used the *Lemon* test to rule that a privately donated courthouse display, which included the Ten Commandments and 300 other historical documents illustrating the

SHOULD CHILDREN BE REQUIRED TO PRAY IN PUBLIC SCHOOLS?

School prayer is just one of the thorny questions the Supreme Court has addressed under the establishment clause. While prayer in public schools was once quite common, since the 1960s the Court has usually decided against this practice, even when it is student-led. Despite Court rulings, many educational institutions maintain this practice.

evolution of American law, violated the First Amendment's establishment clause.[18] However, it has allowed the display of a white cross erected on a World War I memorial on federal lands. According to the Court, the cross "is not merely a reaffirmation of Christian beliefs" but a symbol "often used to honor and respect" heroism.[19]

The Free Exercise Clause

The free exercise clause of the First Amendment proclaims that "Congress shall make no law … prohibiting the free exercise [of religion]." Although the free exercise clause of the First Amendment guarantees individuals the right to be free from governmental interference in the exercise of their religion, this guarantee, like other First Amendment freedoms, is not absolute.

In the area of free exercise, the Court often has had to confront questions of "What is a god?" and "What is a religious faith?"—questions that theologians have grappled with for centuries. In 1965, for example, in a case involving three men who were denied conscientious objector deferments during the Vietnam War because they did not subscribe to "traditional" organized religions, the Court ruled unanimously that belief in a supreme being was not essential for recognition as a conscientious objector.[20] Thus, the men were entitled to the draft deferments because their views paralleled those who objected to war and who belonged to traditional faiths. In contrast, the Court has ruled that prisoners can be denied access to religious services provided the action was "reasonably related to penological interests."[21] Lawful free exercise curtailments by the government as a result of this 1987 ruling include denying Islamic prisoners access to religious services for security reasons. Thus, the U.S. Supreme Court has interpreted the Constitution to mean that governmental interests can outweigh free exercise rights in some situations.

Congress has objected to many of the Court's rulings curtailing religious freedom.[22] While the Court has limited some aspects of 1993's Religious Freedom Restoration Act (RFRA), the Act has been used to protect the use of hallucinogenic drugs in religious ceremonies.[23] More recently, RFRA successfully was used to challenge the constitutionality of the Affordable Care Act's provisions requiring employer-sponsored health plans to include coverage for contraceptives. Private employers may now opt out of coverage for their female employees if the employer has religious objections to the use of contraceptives.

FIRST AMENDMENT GUARANTEES: FREEDOMS OF SPEECH, PRESS, ASSEMBLY, AND PETITION

4.3 Outline the First Amendment liberties and limitations on the freedoms of speech, press, assembly, and petition.

The Supreme Court has, to varying degrees, scrutinized the remaining guarantees protected by the First Amendment. During times of war, for example, the Court generally has allowed Congress and the chief executive extraordinary leeway in limiting First Amendment liberties including the aforementioned free exercise and establishment clauses. Below, we provide historical background and current judicial interpretations of the liberties of speech, press, assembly, and petition.

Freedoms of Speech and the Press

A democracy depends on a free exchange of ideas, and the First Amendment shows that the Framers were well aware of this fact. Historically, one of the most volatile issues of constitutional interpretation has centered on the First Amendment's mandate that "Congress shall make no law … abridging the freedom of speech or of the press." As with the establishment and free exercise clauses of the First Amendment,

prior restraint
Constitutional doctrine that prevents the government from prohibiting speech or publication before the fact; generally held to be in violation of the First Amendment.

Alien and Sedition Acts
Laws passed in 1798 that allowed the imprisonment and deportation of aliens considered dangerous and criminalized false statements against the government.

abolitionist
A supporter, especially in the early nineteenth century, of an end to the institution of slavery.

Abraham Lincoln
Sixteenth president of the United States, the first elected Republican president, who served from 1861- 1865. Lincoln, who led the Union during the Civil War, was assassinated in 1865 by a Confederate sympathizer, John Wilkes Booth.

Espionage Act
A 1917 law that prohibited urging resistance to the draft or distributing anti-war leaflets; by the Supreme Court in *Schenck* v. *U.S.*

the Court has not interpreted speech and press clauses as absolute bans on government regulation. This leeway in interpretation has led to thousands of cases seeking both broader and narrower judicial interpretations of the scope of these clauses in the First Amendment. Over the years, the Court has employed a hierarchical approach in determining what governments can and cannot regulate, with some liberties getting greater protection than others. Generally, the Court has granted thoughts the greatest protection and actions or deeds the least. Words have fallen somewhere in the middle, depending on their content and purpose.

THE ALIEN AND SEDITION ACTS   When the states ratified the First Amendment in 1791, it was considered to protect against **prior restraint** of speech or expression—meaning to guard against the prohibition of speech or publication before the fact. Faced with increasing criticism of the Federalist government by Democratic-Republicans in 1798, the Federalist Congress, with President John Adams's blessing, enacted the **Alien and Sedition Acts**. These acts banned any criticism of the Federalist government by the growing numbers of Democratic-Republicans informally headed by Thomas Jefferson. Although the law clearly flew in the face of the First Amendment's ban on prior restraint, the Adams administration successfully prosecuted, and partisan Federalist judges imposed fines and jail terms on at least ten Democratic-Republican newspaper editors. The Alien and Sedition Acts became a major issue in the 1800 presidential election campaign, which led to the election of Jefferson, a vocal opponent of the acts. Upon taking office, Jefferson quickly pardoned all who had been convicted under their provisions. The newly-elected majority Democratic-Republican Congress allowed the acts to expire before the Federalist-controlled U.S. Supreme Court had an opportunity to rule on the constitutionality of these First Amendment infringements, although commentators then and now viewed them as unconstitutional.

SLAVERY, THE CIVIL WAR, AND RIGHTS CURTAILMENTS   After the public outcry over the Alien and Sedition Acts, the national government largely refrained from regulating speech. But, in its place, the states, which were not yet bound by the Bill of Rights through selective incorporation, began to prosecute those who published articles critical of governmental policies. In the 1830s, at the urging of **abolitionists**, those who sought an end to slavery, the publication or dissemination of any positive information about slavery became a punishable offense in the North. By contrast, in the South, supporters of slavery enacted laws to prohibit publication of any anti-slavery sentiments. Southern postmasters, for example, refused to deliver northern abolitionist newspapers, a step that amounted to censorship of the U.S. mail.

During the Civil War, President **Abraham Lincoln** took several steps that violated the First Amendment. He made it unlawful to print any criticisms of the national government or of the Civil War, effectively suspending the First Amendment's free press protections. Lincoln went so far as to order the arrest of several newspaper editors critical of his conduct of the war and ignored a decision written by Chief Justice Roger Taney, sitting as a circuit court judge, saying that jailing of editors indefinitely was unconstitutional.[24]

WORLD WAR I AND ANTI-GOVERNMENTAL SPEECH   The next major efforts to restrict freedom of speech and the press did not occur until Congress, at the urging of President Woodrow Wilson during World War I, passed the **Espionage Act** in 1917. The government convicted nearly 2,000 Americans of violating its various provisions, especially prohibitions on urging resistance to the draft or distributing anti-war leaflets. In *Schenck* v. *U.S.* (1919), the Supreme Court upheld the Espionage Act, ruling that Congress had a right to restrict speech "of such a nature as to create a clear and present danger that will bring about the substantive evils that Congress has a right to prevent."[25] Under this **clear and present danger test**, the circumstances surrounding an incident are important. Anti-war leaflets, for example, may be permissible during peacetime, but during World War I they were considered too dangerous because they posed the possibility of encouraging more opposition to the war.

Still, for decades, the Supreme Court wrestled with what constituted a danger. Finally, in *Brandenburg* v. *Ohio* (1969), the Court fashioned a new test for deciding whether the government could regulate certain kinds of speech: the **direct incitement test**. Now, the government could punish the advocacy of illegal action only if "such advocacy is directed to inciting or producing imminent lawless action and is likely to incite or produce such action."[26] The requirement of "imminent lawless action" makes it more difficult for the government to punish speech and publication and is consistent with the Framers' notion of the special role played by these elements in a democratic society.

Protected Speech and Press

The expression of ideas through speech and the press is a cornerstone of a free society. In line with this thinking, the U.S. Supreme Court has accorded constitutional protection to a number of aspects of speech and the press, even though the content of such expression may be objectionable to some citizens or the government. Here, we discuss the implications of these protections with respect to prior restraint, symbolic speech, and hate speech.

LIMITING PRIOR RESTRAINT   As was the case with the Alien and Sedition Acts, although Congress attempted to limit speech before the fact as early as 1798, the U.S. Supreme Court did not take a firm position on this issue until the 1970s. In *New York Times Co.* v. *U.S.* (1971), also called the Pentagon Papers case, the Court ruled that the U.S. government could not block the publication of secret Department of Defense documents illegally furnished to the *Times* by anti-war activists.[27] In 1976, the U.S. Supreme Court went even further, noting in *Nebraska Press Association* v. *Stuart*, a case that involved a challenge to the actions of a state court judge who barred press reports of an ongoing trial, that any attempt by the government to prevent expression carried "'a heavy presumption' against its constitutionality."[28]

SYMBOLIC SPEECH   In addition to the general protection accorded to pure speech, the Supreme Court has extended the reach of the First Amendment to **symbolic speech**, a means of expression that includes symbols or signs. In the words of Justice John Marshall Harlan, these kinds of speech are part of the "free trade in ideas."[29] Perhaps the most visible example of symbolic speech is the burning of the American flag as an expression of protest.

The Supreme Court first acknowledged that symbolic speech was entitled to First Amendment protection in *Stromberg* v. *California* (1931).[30] In that case, the Court overturned a communist youth camp director's conviction under a state statute prohibiting the display of a red flag, a symbol of support for Communism and opposition to the U.S. government. In a similar vein, the right of high school students to wear black armbands to protest the Vietnam War was upheld in *Tinker* v. *Des Moines Independent Community School District* (1969).[31]

In recent years, however, the Court has appeared less willing to support the standards established in *Tinker*. In a case commonly referred to as "Bong Hits 4 Jesus," the Court ruled that a student's free speech rights were not violated when a school suspended him for displaying what the Court characterized as a "sophomoric" banner at an Olympic torch relay parade.[32]

clear and present danger test
Test articulated by the Supreme Court in *Schenck* v. *U.S.* (1919) to draw the line between protected and unprotected speech; the Court looks to see "whether the words used" could "create a clear and present danger that they will bring about substantive evils" that Congress seeks "to prevent."

direct incitement test
Test articulated by the Supreme Court in *Brandenburg* v. *Ohio* (1969) holding that the First Amendment protects advocacy of illegal action unless imminent lawless action is intended and likely to occur.

New York Times Co. v. *U.S.* (1971)
The case in which the Supreme Court ruled that the U.S. government could not block the publication of secret Department of Defense documents illegally furnished to the *Times* by anti-war activists. Also called the *Pentagon Papers* case.

symbolic speech
Symbols, signs, and other methods of expression generally considered to be protected by the First Amendment.

hate speech
Communication that belittles a person or group on the basis of race, gender, ethnicity, or other characteristics.

HATE SPEECH   In the 1990s, a particularly thorny First Amendment issue emerged as cities and universities attempted to prohibit what they viewed as **hate speech**, or any communication that belittles a person or group on the basis of individual characteristics. In *R.A.V. v. City of St. Paul* (1992), a St. Paul, Minnesota, ordinance that made it a crime to engage in speech or action likely to arouse "anger," "alarm," or "resentment" on the basis of race, color, creed, religion, or gender was challenged. The Court ruled 5–4 that a white teenager who burned a cross on a black family's front lawn, thereby committing a hate crime under the ordinance, could not face charges under that law because the First Amendment prevents governments from "silencing speech on the basis of its content."[33] In 2003, after much criticism, the Court narrowed this definition, ruling that state governments could constitutionally restrict cross burning when it occurred with the intent of racial intimidation.[34]

AMERICAN POLITICS IN COMPARATIVE PERSPECTIVE

How do Governments Regulate Religious Clothing?

One of the most readily-identifiable manifestations of religious belief takes the form of attire that signals the religious observance of the wearer. The First Amendment in the United States guarantees "free exercise" of religion among civilians, but members of the military have long been subject to tighter regulation of their self expression. Other democratic countries, including France and Mexico, have also struggled with the issue of religious garb in the public sphere.

The United States: Religious Expression in the Army

For many years, the American military's strict code of appearance and dress prevented soldiers of the Sikh religion from wearing beards and turbans. However, in 2010, a Sikh soldier in the U.S. Army was allowed for the first time to retain these important outward expressions of his faith.

France: Muslim Hijabs in Schools

In 2004, France banned Muslims women and girls from wearing *hijabs* (headscarves) in public schools. The country claimed to be upholding its longstanding traditions of secularism, but many have viewed the move as a form of anti-Muslim bias in a historically majority-Christian country. A 2016 ban by some French mayors of burkinis, which cover a woman's hair and body but leave her face, hands, and feet exposed, is the most recent controversy over attire worn predominantly by Muslim women.

Mexico: Clerical Garb in Public

For most of the twentieth century, Mexico legally enforced a policy of "anti-clericalism" aimed at weakening the power of the Catholic Church. Priests were prohibited from wearing clerical garb outside the grounds of their churches and denied other civil rights. These laws were mostly repealed in the early 1990s.

CRITICAL THINKING QUESTIONS

1. Should there be limits on when and where people can wear articles of clothing that express their religious beliefs?
2. Why might some people have a problem with the wearing of religious garb in the army or schools?
3. Under what circumstances, if ever, would a government be justified in prohibiting the free expression of religious beliefs?

Occupy Wall Street
A recent social movement that promotes protests and political activism against income inequality and corporate greed.

Black Lives Matter (BLM)
A recent social movement focused on direct protest and political activism against police brutality, mass incarceration, and related offenses against African Americans.

libel
False written statement that defames a person's character.

slander
Untrue spoken statements that defame the character of a person.

***New York Times Co. v. Sullivan* (1964)**
Case in which the Supreme Court concluded that "actual malice" must be proven to support a finding of libel against a public figure.

fighting words
Words that "by their very utterance inflict injury or tend to incite an immediate breach of peace." Fighting words are not subject to the protections of the First Amendment.

***Miller v. California* (1973)**
Supreme Court case that created the "Miller test" to determine when sexually-explicit expression was obscene and therefore beyond the protection of the First Amendment.

While the actions of white supremacist groups have formed the basis of recent Court definitions of hate speech, charges by conservative commentators that young activists in the **Occupy Wall Street** and **Black Lives Matter (BLM)** movements are participating in hate speech suggest a new chapter in arguments over what constitutes problematic speech.

Three-quarters of colleges and universities, meanwhile, have banned speech or conduct that creates or fosters an intimidating, hostile, or offensive environment on campus.[35] To prevent disruption of university activities, some universities have even established "free speech zones," on campus. Critics, including the American Civil Liberties Union, charge that free speech zones imply the limitation of speech on other parts of the campus, which they see as a violation of the First Amendment. And, problematic speech remains a fact of campus life with anonymous postings on Yik Yak and other forms of social media.

Unprotected Speech and Press

Although the Supreme Court has allowed few governmental bans on most types of speech, some forms of expression lack protection. In 1942, the Supreme Court set forth the rationale by which it would distinguish between protected and unprotected speech. According to the Court, libel, slander, fighting words, and obscenity are not protected by the First Amendment because "such expressions are no essential part of any exposition of ideals, and are of such slight social value as a step to truth that any benefit that may be derived from them is clearly outweighed by the social interest in order and morality."[36]

LIBEL AND SLANDER   **Libel** is a false written statement that defames the character of a person. If the statement is spoken, it is **slander**. In many nations—such as Great Britain, for example—suing someone for libel is relatively easy. In the United States, however, the standards of proof reach much higher. A person who believes that he or she has been a victim of libel must show that the statements made were untrue. Truth is an absolute defense against the charge of libel, no matter how painful or embarrassing the revelations.

Individuals who the U.S. Supreme Court considers "public persons or public officials" often find it even more difficult to sue for libel or slander. *New York Times Co. v. Sullivan* (1964) was the first major libel case considered by the Supreme Court.[37] An Alabama state court found the *Times* guilty of libel for printing a full-page advertisement accusing Alabama officials of physically abusing African Americans during various civil rights protests. (Civil rights activists, including former First Lady Eleanor Roosevelt, paid for the ad.) The Supreme Court overturned the conviction and established that a finding of libel against a public official could stand only if "actual malice," or a knowing disregard for the truth, was shown. Later, the Court ruled that even intentional infliction of emotional distress was not sufficient grounds for proving libel.[38] Still, some have questioned whether or not tweets posted by various presidential campaigns in 2016 were libelous.

FIGHTING WORDS   In 1942, the Court stated that **fighting words**, or words that "by their very utterance inflict injury or tend to incite an immediate breach of peace," are not subject to the protections of the First Amendment.[39] Federal and state governments can therefore regulate fighting words, which include "profanity, obscenity, and threats."

OBSCENITY   In *Miller v. California* (1973), the U.S. Supreme Court set out a test that continues to form the modern basis for defining obscenity. The justices concluded that lower courts must ask, "whether the work depicts or describes, in a patently offensive way, sexual conduct specifically defined by state law" and "whether the work, taken as a whole, lacks serious literary, artistic, political, or scientific value." The Court also noted that local standards might affect its assessment of obscenity, under the rationale that what the citizens of New York City find acceptable might not be the case in Maine or Mississippi.[40]

Time and contexts clearly have altered the Court's and, indeed, much of America's perceptions of what works are obscene. But, the Supreme Court has allowed communities great leeway in drafting statutes to deal with obscenity and, even more importantly, other forms of questionable expression. The Court, for example, has allowed some states to ban totally nude erotic dancing, concluding that statutes of this nature furthered a substantial governmental interest in creating order in society and regulating morals and therefore did not violate the First Amendment.[41] Other states continue to allow this practice.

The Internet, however, poses a particular challenge to the *Miller* test. Applying local standards is almost impossible in this context, since users in one state may easily access information generated in another state. Congress and the Supreme Court have struggled, in particular, to regulate the transmission of obscene or "harmful" materials over the Internet to anyone under age eighteen. However, the Court has upheld the constitutionality of one piece of legislation regulating the transmission of obscene content over the Internet, the PROTECT Act, which outlawed the sale or transmission of child pornography.[42]

Freedoms of Assembly and Petition

"Peaceful assembly for lawful discussion cannot be made a crime," Chief Justice Charles Evans Hughes wrote in *DeJonge v. Oregon* (1937), which incorporated the First Amendment's freedom of assembly clause.[43] Despite this clear assertion, the fundamental freedoms of assembly and petition have been among the most controversial, especially in times of war. As with other First Amendment liberties, the Supreme Court often has become the arbiter between the freedom of the people to express dissent and government's authority to limit controversy in the name of national security, as discussed later in this chapter.

The freedoms of assembly and petition relate directly to those of speech and the press because the freedom to assemble hinges on peaceful conduct. If the words spoken or actions taken at any event cross the line of constitutionality, the First Amendment may no longer protect events such as parades or protests. Absent that

DeJonge v. _Oregon_ (1937)
Supreme Course case that applied the First Amendment's protections of freedom of assembly to the states.

HOW DO WE USE OUR RIGHT TO ASSEMBLE?

The First Amendment rights to assembly and petition are often seen in the form of protests, marches, and rallies. Here, protestors took to the streets in Cleveland, OH, the day after a local grand jury decided not to indict the officers who shot and killed 12-year-old Tamir Rice. Rice was playing in a public park with a toy gun. Since then, a number of high-profile killings by police of unarmed black teenagers and adults have sparked both lawful peaceful protests and unlawful riots in cities across the United States.

protection, leaders and attendees may be subject to governmental regulation and even arrest, incarceration, or civil fines.

The U.S. Supreme Court has rarely addressed the question of the right to petition the government. But, in 2010, the Court heard a case questioning the constitutionality of Washington State's Public Records Act. This law allowed the government to release the names of citizens who had signed a petition in support of a ballot initiative that would have banned gay couples from adopting children. The plaintiffs who signed the "Preserve Marriage, Protect Children" petition did not want their names released because they feared harassment. The Court, however, ruled that disclosure of these names did not violate the First Amendment.[44]

THE SECOND AMENDMENT: THE RIGHT TO KEEP AND BEAR ARMS

4.4 Describe the Second Amendment right to bear arms.

During colonial times, the colonists' distrust of standing armies was evident. Most colonies required all white men to keep and bear arms, and deputized these men to defend their settlements against Indians and European powers. The colonists viewed these local militias as the best way to keep order and protect liberty.

FIGURE 4.1 HOW DO STATES RESTRICT THE RIGHT TO BEAR ARMS?

The Law Center to Prevent Gun Violence, a liberal advocacy group, annually ranks the 50 states based on the strength of what it calls "smart gun laws". These include running background checks on all purchasers, limiting bulk firearms purchases, and requiring a permit for concealed weapons. In 2015, the group ranked California as maintaining the strongest gun laws and Kansas the weakest.

SOURCE: Data from the Law Center to Prevent Gun Violence, www.gunlawscorecard.org.

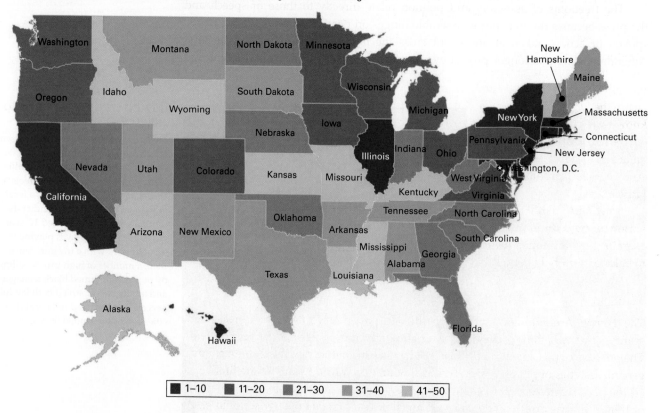

1–10   11–20   21–30   31–40   41–50

The Framers added the Second Amendment to the Constitution to ensure that Congress could not pass laws to disarm state militias. This amendment appeased Anti-Federalists, who feared that the new Constitution would abolish the right to "keep and bear arms." It also preserved an unstated right—the right to revolt against governmental tyranny. Through the early 1920s, few state statutes were passed to regulate firearms (and generally these laws dealt with banning possession of firearms by former slaves).

In 1934, Congress passed the National Firearms Act. This was in response to the explosion of organized crime in the 1920s and 1930s that occurred after the **Eighteenth Amendment** prohibited the sale of alcohol. Organized crime families became notorious for shooting anyone who tried to stop the profitable illegal sales of alcohol. To quell this dangerous unintended consequence of the amendment, the act imposed taxes on automatic weapons and sawed-off shotguns. In *U.S.* v. *Miller* (1939), a unanimous Court upheld the constitutionality of the act, stating that the Second Amendment was intended only to protect a citizen's right to own ordinary militia weapons, which did not include sawed-off shotguns.[45]

For nearly seventy years following *Miller*, the Court did not directly address the Second Amendment. Then, in *D.C.* v. *Heller* (2008), the Court offered some clarification, ruling that the Second Amendment protected an individual's right to own a firearm for personal use in Washington, D.C.[46] In light of the Court's ruling, the D.C. City Council adopted new gun control laws requiring gun registration and prohibiting assault weapons and large-capacity magazines. A U.S. District Court ruled that these laws were valid and within the scope of the *Heller* decision.[47] And, in 2010, in *McDonald* v. *City of Chicago*, the Supreme Court broadened the ownership rights in *Heller* to include citizens of all states. It also incorporated the Second Amendment.[48]

THE RIGHTS OF CRIMINAL DEFENDANTS

4.5   Outline the constitutional rights of defendants and the issues involved in protecting defendants' liberties as guaranteed by the Bill of Rights.

Article I, section 9 of the Constitution guarantees a number of rights and liberties for persons accused of federal crimes. Among those are **writs of** *habeas corpus*, or court orders in which a judge requires authorities to prove that they are holding a prisoner lawfully and that allow the prisoner to be freed if the government's case does not persuade the judge. In addition, *habeas corpus* rights imply that prisoners have a right to know what charges are being made against them.

Article I of the Constitution also prohibits *ex post facto* laws, those that make an act punishable as a crime even if the act was legal at the time it was committed. And, Article I prohibits **bills of attainder**, laws declaring an act illegal without a judicial trial.

The Fourth, Fifth, Sixth, and Eighth Amendments supplement these rights with a variety of procedural guarantees, often called **due process rights**. In this section, we examine how the courts have interpreted and applied these guarantees in an attempt to balance personal liberties and national safety and security.

The Fourth Amendment and Searches and Seizures

The **Fourth Amendment** to the Constitution protects people from unreasonable searches by the national government and, through incorporation, state governments. The purpose of this amendment was to deny national authorities the right to conduct general searches of private property. Thus, without a warrant searches are limited to: (1) the person arrested; (2) things in plain view of the accused person; and, (3) places or things that the arrested person could touch or reach or that otherwise could easily

Eighteenth Amendment
A 1913 amendment that created the nationwide prohibition on alcoholic beverages; it was repealed in 1933.

writs of *habeas corpus*
Petition requesting that a judge order authorities to prove that a prisoner is being held lawfully and that allows the prisoner to be freed if the government's case does not persuade the judge. *Habeas corpus* rights imply that prisoners have a right to know what charges are being made against them.

ex post facto **law**
Law that makes an act punishable as a crime even if the action was legal at the time it was committed.

bill of attainder
A law declaring an act illegal without a judicial trial.

due process rights
Protections drawn from the Fourth Amendment and the Bill of Rights. Due process may be procedural, ensuring fair treatment, or substantive, protecting fundamental rights.

Fourth Amendment
Part of the Bill of Rights that protects people from unreasonable searches and seizures of their persons, houses, papers, and effects without a warrant from a judge among other guarantees.

Fifth Amendment
Part of the Bill of Rights that imposes a number of restrictions on the federal government with respect to the rights of persons suspected of committing a crime. It provides for indictment by a grand jury and protection against self incrimination, and prevents the national government from denying a person life, liberty, or property without the due process of law. It also prevents the national government from taking property without just compensation.

grand jury
A group of citizens charged with determining whether enough evidence exists for a case to go to trial. Guaranteed by the Fifth Amendment.

WHY WAS ERNESTO MIRANDA IMPORTANT TO THE DEVELOPMENT OF DEFENDANTS' RIGHTS?

Even though Ernesto Miranda's confession was not admitted as evidence at his retrial, the testimony of his ex-girlfriend and the victim was enough to convince the jury of his guilt. He served nine years in prison before he was paroled. After his release, he routinely sold autographed cards inscribed with what are called the *Miranda* rights now read to all suspects. In 1976, four years after his release, Miranda was stabbed to death during a card game. Two *Miranda* cards were found on his body, and the person who killed him was read his *Miranda* rights upon his arrest.

be in the arrestee's immediate control. In situations where individuals would reasonably have some expectation of privacy—such as houses or offices—police must obtain a search warrant from a "neutral and detached magistrate" prior to conducting a more extensive search.[49] But, in 2014, the Court loosened requirements in deciding 6–3 that one person may give permission for a house search if the objector to the search is removed from the house.[50]

Cars, however, have proven problematic in relation to searches by the authorities. Although an individual has an expectation of privacy in their own vehicle, cars "can quickly be moved out of the locality or jurisdiction in which the warrant must be sought."[51] Border patrol agents, therefore, have great leeway in pulling over suspicious motorists.[52] And, courts do not require search warrants in possible drunk driving situations.[53] Police must also allow citizens access to their vehicles during a search,[54] and they may not implant GPS tracking devices on criminal suspects' vehicles without a warrant.[55]

Warrantless searches may occur under several other circumstances. No warrant is necessary if police suspect that someone is committing or is about to commit a crime. In these cases, "reasonable suspicion" presents sufficient justification for stopping a suspect—a much lower standard than probable cause.[56] Police, for example, use reasonable suspicion to justify so-called "stop-and-frisk" searches. In these searches, law enforcement agents stop pedestrians and search for weapons or contraband. Questions, however, have been raised about racial bias in these searches, which occur far more often to African Americans and Hispanics. Some judges have also ruled that police officers had no reasonable suspicion to apprehend individuals; in these cases, any evidence obtained in stop-and-frisk searches has been declared inadmissible in court.

In addition, if the police obtain consent for a search from an individual, no warrant is necessary. And, warrantless searches are permissible in places where citizens cannot reasonably expect privacy. For example, under the open fields doctrine first articulated by the Supreme Court in 1924, if you own a field, and even if you post "No Trespassing" signs, the police can search your field without a warrant to see if you are engaging in any type of illegal activity.[57] Similarly, firefighters can enter your home to fight a fire without a warrant. But, if they decide to investigate the cause of the fire, they must obtain a warrant before they reenter.[58]

The Fifth Amendment: Self-Incrimination and Double Jeopardy

The **Fifth Amendment** provides a variety of guarantees protecting those charged with a crime. It requires, for example, that persons accused in the most serious cases first be subject to a grand jury investigation. A **grand jury** is a group of citizens charged with determining whether enough evidence exists for a case to go to trial.

The Fifth Amendment also states that "No person shall be … compelled in any criminal case to be a witness against himself." "Taking the Fifth" is shorthand for exercising one's constitutional right not to self-incriminate. The Supreme Court has interpreted this guarantee to be "as broad as the mischief against which it seeks to guard," finding that criminal defendants do not have to take the stand at trial to answer questions, nor can a judge make mention of their failure to do so as evidence of guilt.[59] Moreover, prosecutors cannot imply that a defendant who refuses to take the stand must be guilty or have something to hide.

This right not to incriminate oneself also means that prosecutors cannot use as evidence in a trial any of a defendant's statements or confessions that were not made voluntarily or after a lawyer is requested. As is the case in many areas of law, however, judicial interpretation of the term "voluntary" has changed over time.

In earlier times, it was not unusual for police to beat defendants to obtain their confessions. In 1936, however, the Supreme Court ruled that convictions for murder based solely on confessions given after physical beatings were unconstitutional.[60]

Police then began to resort to other measures for forcing confessions. Defendants, for example, faced questioning for hours on end with no sleep or food, or threats of physical violence until they were mentally beaten into giving confessions. In other situations, police threatened family members. In one case, authorities told a young mother accused of marijuana possession that her welfare benefits would be terminated and her children taken away if she failed to talk.[61]

Miranda v. *Arizona* **(1966)** was the Supreme Court's first response to coercive efforts used to obtain confessions. On March 3, 1963, an eighteen-year-old girl was kidnapped and raped on the outskirts of Phoenix, Arizona. Ten days later, police arrested Ernesto Miranda, a poor, mentally disturbed man with a ninth-grade education. In a police-station lineup, the victim identified Miranda as her attacker. Police then took Miranda to a separate room and questioned him for two hours. At first, he denied guilt. Eventually, however, he confessed and wrote and signed a brief statement describing the crime and admitting his guilt. At no time did police tell him that he did not have to answer any questions or that he could have an attorney present.

After Miranda's conviction based on his admission of guilt, his case was appealed on the grounds that his Fifth Amendment right not to incriminate himself had been violated because the police had coerced his confession. Writing for the Court, Chief Justice Earl Warren, himself a former district attorney and a former California state attorney general, noted that because police have a tremendous advantage in any interrogation situation, the law must grant criminal suspects greater protections. A confession obtained in the manner of Miranda's was not truly voluntary; thus, the justices concluded it was inadmissible at trial.

To provide guidelines for police to implement *Miranda*, the Court mandated that: "Prior to any questioning, the person must be warned that he has a right to remain silent, that any statements he does make may be used as evidence against him, and that he has a right to the presence of an attorney, either retained or appointed."[62] In response to this mandate from the Court, police routinely began to read suspects what are now called their *Miranda* **rights**, a practice you undoubtedly have seen repeated over and over in movies and TV police dramas.

Although the **Burger Court** did not enforce the reading of *Miranda* rights as vehemently as had the Warren Court, Chief Justice **Warren E. Burger**, Warren's successor, acknowledged that they had become an integral part of established police procedures.[63] The more conservative Rehnquist and Roberts Courts, however, have been more willing to weaken *Miranda* rights, allowing coerced confessions and employing much more flexible standards for the admission of evidence.[64]

The Fifth Amendment also mandates: "nor shall any person be subject for the same offense to be twice put in jeopardy of life or limb." This **double jeopardy clause**, protects individuals from being tried twice for the same crime in the same jurisdiction. Thus, if a jury finds a defendant not guilty of a murder, the defendant cannot be retried in that jurisdiction for the murder even if new information supporting a guilty verdict is discovered. But, if a defendant was tried in a state court, he or she could still face charges in a federal court or vice versa. This provision is relatively clear and embedded in the law; the Court has heard little litigation on this issue in the past fifty years, but has slated argument on a double jeopardy case for its 2016–2017 term.

The Fourth and Fifth Amendments and the Exclusionary Rule

In *Weeks* v. *U.S.* (1914), the U.S. Supreme Court adopted the **exclusionary rule**, which bars the use of illegally seized evidence at trial. Thus, although the Fourth and Fifth Amendments do not prohibit the use of evidence obtained in violation of their provisions, the exclusionary rule is a judicially created remedy to deter constitutional violations. In *Weeks*, for example, the Court reasoned that allowing police

Miranda v. *Arizona* **(1966)**
A landmark Supreme Court ruling holding that the Fifth Amendment requires individuals arrested for a crime to be advised of their right to remain silent and to have counsel present.

Miranda **rights**
Statements required of police that inform a suspect of his or her constitutional rights protected by the Fifth Amendment, including the right to an attorney provided by a court if the suspect cannot afford one.

Burger Court
The period in Supreme Court history during which Warren Burger served as Chief Justice (1969–1986).

Warren E. Burger
The fifteenth Chief Justice of the United States who served from 1969 to 1986 and who led the Court in an increasingly conservative direction.

double jeopardy clause
Part of the Fifth Amendment that protects individuals from being tried twice for the same offense in the same jurisdiction.

exclusionary rule
Judicially created rule that prohibits police from using illegally seized evidence at trial.

Sixth Amendment
Part of the Bill of Rights that sets out the basic requirements of procedural due process for federal courts to follow in criminal trials. These include speedy and public trials, impartial juries, trials in the state where the crime was committed, notice of the charges, the right to confront and obtain favorable witnesses, and the right to counsel.

capital cases
Court cases in which a conviction may result in the application of the death penalty.

and prosecutors to use the "fruits of a poisonous tree" (evidence obtained in an illegal search) would only encourage that activity.[65]

In balancing the need to deter police misconduct against the possibility that guilty individuals could go free, the Warren Court decided that deterring police misconduct was more important. In *Mapp* v. *Ohio* (1961), the Warren Court ruled "all evidence obtained by searches and seizures in violation of the Constitution, is inadmissible in a state court."[66] This historic and controversial case put law enforcement officers on notice that if they violated any constitutional rights in the search for evidence, their efforts would be for naught because federal or state trials could not accept tainted evidence.

In 1976, the Court noted that the exclusionary rule "deflects the truth-finding process and often frees the guilty."[67] Since then, the Court has carved out a variety of limited "good faith exceptions" to the exclusionary rule, allowing the use of tainted evidence in a variety of situations, especially when police have a search warrant and, in good faith, conduct the search on the assumption that the warrant is valid. Since the purpose of the exclusionary rule is to deter police misconduct, and in this situation no police misconduct exists, the courts have permitted introduction of the seized evidence at trial. Another exception to the exclusionary rule is "inevitable discovery." Courts may allow illegally seized evidence if such evidence would likely have been discovered in the course of continuing investigation.

The Sixth Amendment and the Right to Counsel

The **Sixth Amendment** guarantees to an accused person "the Assistance of Counsel in his defense." In the past, this guarantee meant only that an individual could hire an attorney to represent him or her in court. Since most criminal defendants are too poor to hire private lawyers, this provision gave little assistance to many who found themselves on trial. Recognizing this, Congress required federal courts to provide an attorney for defendants who could not afford one. **Capital cases**, in which the death penalty is a possibility, were the first to require this provision;[68] eventually, in all federal criminal cases, the poor were guaranteed legal counsel.[69] The Court also began to expand the right to counsel to some state offenses but did so in a piecemeal fashion that gave the states little direction. Given the high cost of legal counsel, this ambiguity often made it cost-effective for the states not to provide counsel at all.

These ambiguities came to an end with the Court's decision in *Gideon* v. *Wainwright* (1963).[70] Clarence Earl Gideon, a fifty-one-year-old drifter, was charged with breaking into a Panama City, Florida, pool hall and stealing beer, wine, and some change from a vending machine. At his trial, he asked the judge to appoint a lawyer for him because he was too poor to hire one. The judge refused, and Gideon was convicted and given a five-year prison term for petty larceny. The case against Gideon had not been strong, but as a layperson unfamiliar with the law, trial practice, and procedure, he was unable to point out its weaknesses.

The apparent inequities in the system that had resulted in Gideon's conviction continued to bother him. Eventually, he requested some paper from a prison guard, consulted books in the prison library, and then drafted and mailed a writ of *certiorari* to the U.S. Supreme Court, asking it to overrule his conviction.

In a unanimous decision, the Supreme Court agreed with Gideon and his court-appointed lawyer, Abe Fortas, a future associate justice of the Court. Writing for the Court, Justice Hugo Black explained, "lawyers in criminal courts are necessities, not luxuries." Therefore, the Court concluded, the state must provide an attorney to indigent defendants in felony cases. Underscoring the importance of counsel, the jury acquitted Gideon when he was retried with a lawyer to argue his case.

The Burger and Rehnquist Courts gradually expanded the *Gideon* rule. The justices first applied this standard to cases that were not felonies[71] and, later, to many cases in which probation and future penalties were possibilities. In 2008, the Court also ruled that the right to counsel began at the accused's first appearance before a judge.[72]

The issue of legal representation also extends to questions of competence. Various courts have held that lawyers who fell asleep during trial, failed to put forth a defense, or were drunk during the proceedings were "adequate." In 2005, however, the Supreme Court ruled that the Sixth Amendment's guarantees required lawyers to take reasonable steps to prepare for their clients' trial and sentencing, including examination of their prior criminal history.[73]

The Sixth Amendment and Jury Trials

The Sixth Amendment (and, to a lesser extent, Article III of the Constitution) provides that a person accused of a crime shall enjoy the right to a speedy and public trial by an impartial jury—that is, a trial in which a group of the accused's peers act as a fact-finding, deliberative body to determine guilt or innocence. It also gives defendants the right to confront witnesses against them. The Supreme Court has held that jury trials must be available if a prison sentence of six or more months is possible.

Impartiality is a requirement of jury trials that has undergone significant change, with the method of jury selection being the most frequently challenged part of the process. Historically, lawyers had used peremptory challenges (those for which no cause needs to be given) to exclude women and minorities from juries, especially in certain types of cases. In 1954, however, the U.S. Supreme Court ruled that Hispanics were entitled to a jury trial that included other Hispanics.[74] And, in 1986, the Court ruled that the use of peremptory challenges specifically to exclude African American jurors violated the equal protection clause of the Fourteenth Amendment.[75] In 1994, the Court extended its ruling to discrimination in jury selection on the basis of gender.[76]

The right to confront witnesses at trial also is protected by the Sixth Amendment. However, this right is not absolute. The testimony of a six-year-old alleged child abuse victim via one-way closed-circuit TV, for example, is permissible.[77] In this case, the child was questioned out of the presence of the defendant, who was in communication with his defense and prosecuting attorneys. The defendant, along with the judge and jury, watched the testimony.

The Eighth Amendment and Cruel and Unusual Punishment

Among its protections, the **Eighth Amendment** prohibits "cruel and unusual punishments," a concept rooted in the English common-law tradition. Today, the United States is the only western nation to put people to death for committing crimes. Not surprisingly, tremendous state-by-state differences exist in the imposition of the death penalty. Texas leads the nation in the number of executions each year.

The death penalty was in use in all colonies at the time they adopted the U.S. Constitution, and its constitutionality went unquestioned. In fact, in two separate cases in the late 1800s, the Supreme Court ruled that deaths by public shooting[78] and electrocution were not "cruel and unusual" forms of punishment in the same category as "punishments which inflict torture, such as the rack, the thumbscrew, the iron boot, the stretching of limbs and the like."[79]

Recently, the Court has addressed the imposition of state laws in which juveniles may be sentenced to life imprisonment without any opportunity for parole. In 2016, by a 6–3 vote, the Court ruled that its 2012 decision limiting life sentences for juveniles was retroactive.[80] President Obama weighed in on cruel and unusual punishment by prohibiting federal prisons from putting juveniles in solitary confinement.

Eighth Amendment
Part of the Bill of Rights that states: "Excessive bail shall not be required, nor excessive fines imposed, nor cruel and unusual punishments inflicted."

HOW DO STATES VARY IN THEIR APPLICATION OF THE DEATH PENALTY?

A growing number of states have formally or informally objected to the use of the death penalty as a means of punishment for felony crimes. While many human rights activists praise these decisions, others—such as the families of victims of violent crime—are more hesitant to offer support. Here, Anthony Porter (far left), who had been wrongfully convicted and sentenced to death row, celebrates his release with some of the Northwestern University students whose research helped to set him free.

MODERN QUESTIONS OF CONSTITUTIONALITY   In the 1960s, the NAACP (National Association for the Advancement of Colored People) Legal Defense and Educational Fund (LDF), believing that African Americans received the death penalty more frequently than members of other groups, orchestrated a carefully designed legal attack on its constitutionality.[81] Public opinion polls revealed that in 1971, on the eve of the LDF's first major death sentence case to reach the Supreme Court, public support for the death penalty had fallen below 50 percent. With the timing just right, in *Furman* v. *Georgia* (1972), the Supreme Court effectively put an end to capital punishment, at least in the short run.[82] The Court ruled that because the death penalty often was imposed in an arbitrary manner, it constituted cruel and unusual punishment in violation of the Eighth and Fourteenth Amendments. Following *Furman*, several state legislatures enacted new laws designed to meet the Court's objections to the arbitrary nature of the sentence. In 1976, in *Gregg* v. *Georgia*, the Supreme Court in a 7–2 decision ruled that Georgia's rewritten death penalty statute was constitutional.[83]

This ruling did not deter the NAACP LDF from continuing to bring death penalty cases before the Court. In 1987, a 5–4 Court ruled that imposition of the death penalty—even when it appeared to discriminate against African Americans—did not violate the equal protection clause.[84] The Court noted that even if statistics show clear discrimination, reversal of an individual sentence required demonstration of racial discrimination in that particular case.

Four years later, a case involving the same defendant produced an equally important ruling on the death penalty and criminal procedure. In the second case, the Court held that new issues could not be raised on appeal, even if some state error existed. The case, *McCleskey* v. *Zant* (1991), produced new standards designed to make the filing of repeated appeals much more difficult for death-row inmates.[85] In 2016, voters in Nebraska and Oklahoma approved measures allowing the death penalty.

Although as recently as 2008 the Supreme Court has upheld the constitutionality of the death penalty by lethal injection,[86] it has made some exceptions. The Court, for example, has exempted two key classes of people from the death penalty: those who are what the law calls mentally retarded and those under the age of eighteen.[87]

PROTECTING THE WRONGFULLY CONVICTED   At the state level, some officials have publicly questioned the application of the death penalty. In 1999, a class project by Northwestern University students unearthed information that led to the release of thirteen men on Illinois' death row. Before leaving office in January 2003, that state's governor, George Ryan (R-IL), also commuted the sentences of 167 death-row inmates, giving them life in prison instead. This action constituted the single largest anti–death-penalty action since the Court's decision in *Gregg*, and it spurred national conversation on the death penalty, which, in recent polls, has seen its lowest levels of support since 1978. A growing number of states have followed Ryan's lead.

In another effort to verify that those on death row are not there in error, several states offer free DNA testing to death-row inmates. Inmates in other states may file a civil rights lawsuit seeking DNA testing. [88] The U.S. Supreme Court recognized the potential exculpatory power of DNA evidence in *House* v. *Bell* (2006). In this case, the Court ruled that a Tennessee death-row inmate who had exhausted other federal appeals was entitled to an exception to more stringent federal appeals rules because DNA and related evidence suggested his innocence.[89]

THE RIGHT TO PRIVACY

4.6 Explain the origins and significance of the right to privacy.

To this point, we have discussed rights and freedoms that have been derived from specific guarantees contained in the Bill of Rights. However, the U.S. Supreme Court also has given protection to rights not enumerated specifically in the Constitution. Although silent about the **right to privacy**, the Bill of Rights contains many indications that the Framers expected some areas of life to be off limits to governmental regulation. The liberty to practice one's religion guaranteed in the First Amendment implies the right to exercise private, personal beliefs. The guarantee against unreasonable searches and seizures contained in the Fourth Amendment similarly suggests that persons are to be secure in their homes and should not fear that police will show up at their doorsteps without cause. As early as 1928, Justice Louis Brandeis hailed privacy, an unenumerated right, as "the right to be left alone—the most comprehensive of rights and the right most valued by civilized men."[90] Not until 1965, however, did the Court attempt to explain the origins of this right.

right to privacy
The right to be left alone; a judicially created principle encompassing a variety of individual actions protected by the penumbras cast by several constitutional amendments, including the First, Third, Fourth, Ninth, and Fourteenth Amendments.

Birth Control

Today, most Americans take access to birth control for granted. Grocery stores sell condoms, most college health centers give them away, and TV stations air ads for them. Other forms of birth control from pills to implants to intrauterine devices also are advertised on TV, in magazines, and online. Acceptance of and easy access to birth control, however, was not always the case. Many states often barred the sale of contraceptives to minors, prohibited the display of contraceptives, or even banned their sale altogether, even to married couples. One of the last states to do away with these kinds of laws was Connecticut. It outlawed the sale of all forms of birth control and even prohibited physicians from discussing it with their married patients until the Supreme Court ruled its restrictive laws unconstitutional.

Griswold v. *Connecticut* (1965) involved a challenge to the constitutionality of an 1879 Connecticut law prohibiting the dissemination of information about and/or the sale of contraceptives.[91] In *Griswold*, seven justices decided that various portions of the Bill of Rights, including the First, Third, Fourth, Ninth, and Fourteenth Amendments, cast what the Court called "penumbras" (unstated liberties on the fringes or in the shadow of more explicitly stated rights), thereby creating zones of privacy, including a married couple's right to plan a family. Thus, the Connecticut statute was ruled unconstitutional because it violated marital privacy, a right the Court concluded could be read into the U.S. Constitution through interpreting several amendments.

Later, the Court expanded the right to privacy to include the right of unmarried individuals to have access to contraceptives. "If the right of privacy means anything," wrote Justice William J. Brennan Jr., "it is the right of the individual, married or single, to be free from unwarranted governmental intrusion into matters so fundamentally affecting a person as the decision to bear or beget a child."[92] This right to privacy formed the basis for later decisions from the Court, including the right to secure an abortion.

Abortion

In the early 1960s, two instances of birth-related tragedies occurred. European women who had taken the drug thalidomide while pregnant gave birth to severely deformed babies, and, in the United States, a nationwide measles epidemic resulted in the birth of babies with major health problems. The increasing medical safety of abortions and the growing women's rights movement combined with these tragedies to put pressure

WHAT WAS THE OUTCOME OF *GRISWOLD* V. *CONNECTICUT* (1965)?

In this photo, Estelle Griswold (left), executive director of the Planned Parenthood League of Connecticut, and Cornelia Jahncke, its president, celebrate the Supreme Court's ruling in *Griswold* v. *Connecticut* (1965). *Griswold* invalidated a Connecticut law that made selling contraceptives or disseminating information about contraception to married couples illegal.

Roe v. *Wade* (1973)

The Supreme Court found that a woman's right to an abortion was protected by the right to privacy that could be implied from specific guarantees found in the Bill of Rights applied to the states through the Fourteenth Amendment.

on the legal and medical establishments to support laws guaranteeing a woman's access to a safe and legal abortion.

By the late 1960s, fourteen states had voted to liberalize their abortion policies, and four states decriminalized abortion in the early stages of pregnancy. But, many women's rights activists wanted more. They argued that the decision to carry a pregnancy to term was a woman's fundamental right. In 1973, in one of the most controversial decisions ever handed down, seven members of the Court agreed with this position.

The woman whose case became the catalyst for pro-choice and pro-life groups was Norma McCorvey, an itinerant circus worker. The mother of a toddler she was unable to care for, McCorvey could not leave another child in her mother's care. So, she decided to terminate her second pregnancy. McCorvey turned to two young Texas lawyers who were aiming to challenge Texas's restrictive statute and were looking to bring a lawsuit with just such a plaintiff. McCorvey, who was unable to obtain a legal abortion, later gave birth and put the baby up for adoption. Nevertheless, she allowed her lawyers to proceed, with her as their plaintiff. Her lawyers used the pseudonym Jane Roe for McCorvey in their challenge of the Texas law as enforced by Henry Wade, the district attorney for Dallas County, Texas.

When the case finally came before the Supreme Court, Justice Harry A. Blackmun, a former lawyer at the Mayo Clinic, one of the best hospitals in America, relied heavily on medical evidence to rule that the Texas law violated a woman's constitutionally guaranteed right to privacy, which, he argued, included her decision to terminate a pregnancy. Writing for the majority in ***Roe* v. *Wade* (1973)**, Blackmun divided pregnancy into three stages. In the first trimester, a woman's right to privacy gave her an absolute right (in consultation with her physician), free from state interference, to terminate her pregnancy. In the second trimester, the state's interest in the health of the mother gave it the right to regulate abortions, but only to protect the woman's health. Only in the third trimester—when the fetus becomes potentially viable—did the Court find that the state's interest in potential life outweighed a woman's privacy interests. Even in the third trimester, however, the Court ruled that abortions to save the life or preserve the health of the mother were legal.[93]

Roe v. *Wade* unleashed a torrent of political controversy. Pro-life groups, caught off guard, scrambled to recoup their losses in Congress. Representative Henry Hyde (R–IL) persuaded Congress to ban the use of Medicaid funds for abortions for poor women, and the Supreme Court upheld the constitutionality of the Hyde Amendment in 1977 and again in 1980.[94] The issue soon became political—it was incorporated into the Republican Party's platform in 1980—and quickly polarized both major political parties.

Since that time, well-organized pro-life groups have attacked the right to an abortion and its constitutional underpinnings in the right to privacy. The administrations of Ronald Reagan and George Bush strongly opposed abortions, and their Justice Departments regularly urged the Court to overrule *Roe.* They came close to victory in *Webster* v. *Reproductive Health Services* (1989).[95] In *Webster,* the Court upheld state-required fetal viability tests in the second trimester, even though these tests increased the cost of an abortion considerably. The Court also upheld Missouri's refusal to allow abortions to be performed in state-supported hospitals or by state-funded doctors or nurses. Perhaps most noteworthy, however, was that four justices seemed willing to overrule *Roe* v. *Wade.*

After *Webster,* states began to enact more restrictive legislation. In ***Planned Parenthood of Southeastern Pennsylvania* v. *Casey* (1992)**, the Court wrote that Pennsylvania could limit abortions as long as its regulations did not pose "an undue burden" on pregnant women. The narrowly supported standard, by which the Court upheld a twenty-four-hour waiting period and parental consent requirements, did not overrule *Roe* but clearly limited its scope. *Casey* lowered the standard of review from strict scrutiny—used for fundamental freedoms—to a far lower **undue burden test**.[96]

In the 1990s, pro-choice Democratic President Bill Clinton and Republican-controlled Congresses repeatedly clashed on the issue of abortion rights. In 1996 and again in 1998, Congress passed and sent to President Clinton a bill to ban—for the first time—a specific procedure used in late-term abortions. The president repeatedly vetoed the federal Partial Birth Abortion Ban Act. In 2003, however, Republican control of the White House and both houses of Congress facilitated passage of the act. Pro-choice groups immediately filed lawsuits challenging the constitutionality of this law. In a 5–4 decision, *Gonzales* v. *Carhart* (2007), the Supreme Court upheld the federal act, even though it contained no exceptions for the health of the mother. Observers viewed this ruling as a significant step toward reversing *Roe* v. *Wade* altogether.

The Court's decision in *Gonzales* empowered states to enact abortion regulations with new gusto. In 2013, Texas enacted legislation that required clinic physicians to have admitting privileges to local hospitals and required clinics to meet the same standards as ambulatory surgical centers. With only eight justices on the Court, five members found that these provisions of the Texas law imposed an undue burden on women seeking an abortion and thus were unconstitutional. The majority noted that the closures of Texas clinics, which would have left no clinics in West Texas, an area larger than California, would mean "fewer doctors, longer waiting times, increased crowding, and significantly greater travel distances, all of which, when taken together, burden a woman's right to choose."[97] This ruling in ***Whole Woman's Health* v. *Hellerstedt* (2016)** calls into question similar laws in 26 states and the more than 250 restrictions enacted by state and local governments that currently are being litigated in the courts, putting it on a par with *Roe* and *Casey* in its impact on legal access to abortion.

LGBT Issues

Not until 2003 did the U.S. Supreme Court rule that an individual's constitutional right to privacy, which provided the basis for the *Griswold* (contraceptives) and *Roe* (abortion) decisions, prevents states from criminalizing private sexual behavior. This monumental decision invalidated the laws of fourteen states.

Planned Parenthood of Southeastern Pennsylvania v. *Casey* **(1992)**
The Supreme Court's decision in this abortion case replaced the strict scrutiny standard of *Roe* with the less stringent undue burden standard.

undue burden test
A standard set by the Supreme Court in the *Casey* case in 1992 that narrowed *Roe* v. *Wade* and allowed for greater regulation of abortion by the states.

Whole Woman's Health v. *Hellerstedt* **(2016)**
Supreme Court abortion ruling that struck down state law provisions in Texas as presenting an undue burden on women seeking abortions. This decision invalidated numerous state and local laws that imposed similar limitations on clinics.

WHICH CASE LED TO GREATER DISCUSSION OF GAY RIGHTS ISSUES?

Tyron Garner (left) and John Geddes Lawrence (center), the plaintiffs in *Lawrence* v. *Texas* (2003), are shown here with their attorney. The ruling in this case proved to be a huge victory for advocates of gay and lesbian rights, as it deemed anti-sodomy laws unconstitutional. Following this decision, states began to debate laws related to marriage and other rights for same-sex couples.

September 11ᵗʰ
A terrorist plot carried out on September 11, 2001 that used hijacked civilian aircraft to attack the World Trade Center in New York and the Pentagon near Washington, D.C.

In *Lawrence* v. *Texas* (2003), six members of the Court overruled its decision in *Bowers* v. *Hardwick* (1986), which had upheld anti-sodomy laws. They found the Texas law unconstitutional; five justices found it violated fundamental privacy rights.[98] Justice Sandra Day O'Connor agreed that the law was unconstitutional, but concluded it was an equal protection violation. Lesbian, bisexual, gay and transgender rights are discussed further in Chapter 5.

TOWARD REFORM: CIVIL LIBERTIES AND COMBATING TERRORISM

4.7 Evaluate how reforms to combat terrorism have affected civil liberties.

The brilliance of the civil liberties codified by the First Congress is that the Bill of Rights remains a relatively stable statement of our natural rights as Americans, even as technology has evolved. Judicial interpretation ensures that the sentiments expressed more than 200 years ago still apply to the modern world. After the terrorist attacks of **September 11**, 2001, however, some critics charged that the U.S. government began to operate in "an alternate reality," in which Bill of Rights guarantees were suspended just as they had been during the Civil War and World Wars I and II.[99] The difference in this modern era, critics claim, is that the "war" has no direct enemy, and its timeline for completion is ever-changing. Here, we detail the provisions of laws such as the USA PATRIOT Act and the Military Commissions Act, as well as subsequent actions by the National Security Agency under Barack Obama's administration, and explain how they have affected the civil liberties discussed in this chapter.

The First Amendment

Both the 2001 USA PATRIOT Act and the 2006 Military Commissions Act contain a variety of major and minor interferences with the civil liberties that Americans, as well as those visiting our shores, have come to expect. The USA PATRIOT Act, for example, violates the First Amendment's free speech guarantees by barring those who have been subject to search orders from telling anyone about those orders, even in situations in which no need for secrecy can be proven. It also authorizes the Federal Bureau of Investigation (FBI) to investigate citizens who choose to exercise their freedom of speech, without demonstrating that any parts of their speech might be labeled illegal.

In addition, respect for religious practices fell by the wayside in the wake of the war on terrorism. For example, many Muslim detainees captured in Iraq and Afghanistan were fed pork, a violation of basic Islamic dietary laws. Some were stripped naked in front of members of the opposite sex, another religious violation.

The Fourth Amendment

The USA PATRIOT Act enhances the ability of the government to curtail specific search and seizure restrictions in four areas: (1) It allows the government to examine an individual's private records held by third parties. This empowers the FBI to force anyone, including physicians, libraries, bookshops, colleges and universities, and phone and Internet service providers, to turn over all records on a particular individual. (2) It expands the government's right to search private property without notice to the owner. (3) According to the ACLU, the act "expands a narrow exception to the Fourth Amendment that had been created for the collection of foreign intelligence information."[100] (4) The act expands an exception for spying that collects "addressing information" about where and to whom communications are going, as opposed to what is contained in the documents. This fourth exception has been the subject of much controversy in the wake of revelations brought forth by former government employee Edward Snowden, who played a major role in revealing the broad scope of the National Security Agency's surveillance and data collection on the actions of private citizens. Each day, billions of pieces of information about individuals' activities—including phone calls, text messages, emails, and internet transmissions—were collected without probable cause and scanned by the government in an attempt to identify patterns of suspicious behavior that may be a threat to national security.

Judicial oversight of these governmental powers is virtually nonexistent. Proper governmental authorities need only certify to a judge, without any evidence, that the requested search meets the statute's broad criteria. Moreover, the legislation deprives judges of the authority to reject such applications.

Other Fourth Amendment violations include the ability to conduct searches without a warrant. The government also does not have to demonstrate probable cause that a person has, or might, commit a crime. Thus, the USA PATRIOT Act also goes against key elements of the due process rights guaranteed by the Fifth Amendment. Although more recent policies have attempted to scale back the scope of the program somewhat, government data collection and observation of citizen activity remains common.

Due Process Rights

The Military Commissions Act eliminated many due process rights, including the right to challenge "detention, transfer, treatment, trial, or conditions of confinement" of detainees. It allowed the government to declare permanent resident aliens to be enemy combatants and enabled the government to jail these people indefinitely without any opportunity to file a writ of *habeas corpus*. In 2008, however, the Roberts Court ruled this final provision unconstitutional, finding that any detainees could challenge their extended incarceration in federal court.[101]

Secret offshore prisons, known as black sites, have also held many suspected terrorists against their will. In September 2006, President George W. Bush acknowledged the existence of these facilities, moving fourteen such detainees to the detention facility at Guantanamo Bay, Cuba. The conditions of this facility sparked intense debate, as opponents cited numerous accusations of torture as well as possible violations of human rights. Those in support of the continued use of Guantanamo declared the detainees unlawful combatants and not war criminals subject to the provisions of the Geneva Convention. After President Barack Obama took office in 2009, he vowed to close Guantanamo by January 2010 and move detainees to a facility in Illinois. As of 2016, however, Guantanamo Bay remained open.

Federal activity has also curtailed the Sixth Amendment right to trial by jury. Those people detained as enemy combatants often do not have access to the evidence against them and are subject to coercion or torture in the gathering of additional evidence. Trials of enemy combatants are closed, and people tried in these courts do not have a right to an attorney of their choosing. The Supreme Court limited the federal government's activity in these tribunals, but the Military Commissions Act returned these powers to the executive branch.[102] The Obama administration, to the surprise of many observers, did little to restore the rights revoked by these acts and further limited some detainees' abilities to challenge their incarceration. These actions have been questioned by some federal court judges and continue to be the subject of litigation.[103]

Finally, significant controversy has surrounded the Eighth Amendment's prohibition on cruel and unusual punishment. The Department of Justice under President George W. Bush issued a secret memo endorsing harsh interrogation techniques to obtain evidence necessary to fight terrorism. Interrogation practices were not considered illegal unless they produced pain equivalent to that with organ failure or death.

WHAT ARE LIVING CONDITIONS LIKE FOR DETAINEES?

Prisoners of the war on terrorism live in maximum security prisons where their civil liberties are often compromised. Here, military police escort a detainee to his cell in Guantanamo Bay Detention Camp.

Among the techniques authorized by the government were combinations of "painful physical and psychological tactics, including head-slapping, simulated drowning, and frigid temperatures."[104] The most controversial of these techniques was waterboarding, which simulates drowning. Although the Obama administration harshly attacked the use of such tactics and techniques, it announced that those who committed these acts during the Bush administration would not be prosecuted.[105] As a candidate for president in 2016, President Donald J. Trump called for renewed use of a range of enhanced interrogation techniques. Talking about waterboarding at a summer 2016 rally in Ohio he said, "I like it a lot. I don't think it's tough enough."[106] Trump also stated on the campaign trail that he considered killing the families of Islamic State (ISIS) members a useful tactic to defeat the terrorist organization.[107] Critics have noted that such acts would violate the Geneva Conventions, a series of treaties regulating the treatment of civilians and prisoners of war agreed to in 1949 by 196 countries including the United States.[108] Given such statements during his campaign, observers assume the Trump administration's positions on civil liberties will bear similarities to the George W. Bush administration's positions.

Roots of Civil Liberties: The Bill of Rights

4.1 Explain the roots of civil liberties in the Constitution and their development in the Bill of Rights.

Most of the Framers originally opposed the Bill of Rights. Anti-Federalists, however, continued to stress the need for a bill of rights during the drive for ratification of the Constitution, and some states tried to make their ratification contingent on the addition of a bill of rights. Thus, during its first session, Congress sent the first ten amendments to the Constitution, the Bill of Rights, to the states for their ratification. Later, the addition of the Fourteenth Amendment allowed the Supreme Court to apply most of the amendments to the states through a process called selective incorporation.

First Amendment Guarantees: Freedom of Religion

4.2 Distinguish between the establishment and the free exercise clauses of the First Amendment.

The First Amendment guarantees freedom of religion. The establishment clause, which prohibits the national government from establishing a religion, does not generally allow prayer in schools. However, the Court has held that many forms of aid are constitutionally permissible. The Court has also allowed some governmental regulation of religious practices under the free exercise clause.

First Amendment Guarantees: Freedoms of Speech, Press, Assembly, and Petition

4.3 Outline the First Amendment liberties and limitations on the freedoms of speech, press, assembly, and petition.

Historically, one of the most volatile subjects of constitutional interpretation has been the First Amendment's mandate that "Congress shall make no law … abridging the freedom of speech or of the press." As with the establishment and free exercise clauses of the First Amendment, the Court has not interpreted the speech and press clauses as absolute bans against government regulation. The Supreme Court has ruled against prior restraint, thus protecting freedom of the press. The Court has also protected symbolic speech and hate speech. Areas of speech and publication unprotected by the First Amendment include libel, fighting words, and obscenity. The freedoms of peaceable assembly and petition are directly related to the freedoms of speech and the press.

The Second Amendment: The Right to Keep and Bear Arms

4.4 Describe the Second Amendment right to bear arms.

Initially, the right to bear arms was envisioned in terms of state militias. Over the years, states and Congress have enacted various gun ownership restrictions with little Supreme Court interpretation. However, the Court ruled in *D.C.* v. *Heller* (2008) and *McDonald* v. *City of Chicago* (2010) that the Second Amendment protects an individual's right to own a firearm.

The Rights of Criminal Defendants

4.5 Outline the constitutional rights of defendants and the issues involved in protecting defendants' liberties as guaranteed by the Bill of Rights.

The Fourth, Fifth, Sixth, and Eighth Amendments provide a variety of procedural guarantees to individuals accused of crimes. The Fourth Amendment prohibits unreasonable searches and seizures. The Fifth Amendment protects those who have been charged with crimes. It mandates the use of grand juries in cases of serious crimes. It also guarantees that "no person shall be compelled to be a witness against himself." Finally, the Fifth Amendment's double jeopardy clause protects individuals from being tried twice for the same crimes in the same jurisdiction. The Court's interpretation of the Sixth Amendment's guarantee of "assistance of counsel" stipulates that the government provide counsel to defendants unable to pay for it in cases subject to prison sentences. The Sixth Amendment also requires an impartial jury. The Court's current view is that the Eighth Amendment's ban against "cruel and unusual punishments" does not bar imposition of the death penalty.

The Right to Privacy

4.6 Explain the origins and significance of the right to privacy.

The right to privacy is a judicially created right carved from the penumbras (unstated liberties implied by more explicitly stated rights) of several amendments, including the First, Third, Fourth, Ninth, and Fourteenth Amendments. The Court has found statutes that limit access to birth control, prohibit abortion, and ban homosexual acts to be unconstitutional under this right. The Court has abandoned its use of privacy doctrine standards dealing with abortion and adopted an undue burden standard.

Toward Reform: Civil Liberties and Combating Terrorism

4.7 Evaluate how reforms to combat terrorism have affected civil liberties.

After the terrorist attacks of September 11, 2001, Congress and the executive branch enacted reforms that dramatically altered civil liberties in the United States. Critics charge that the changes have significantly compromised a host of constitutional guarantees, while supporters say that they are necessary to protect national security in a time of war.

LEARN THE TERMS

Abraham Lincoln
abolitionists
Alien and Sedition Acts
bill of attainder
Bill of Rights
Black Lives Matter (BLM)
Burger Court
capital cases
civil liberties
civil rights
clear and present danger test
DeJonge v. *Oregon* (1937)
direct incitement test
double jeopardy clause
due process clause
due process rights
Earl Warren
Eighth Amendment
Eighteenth Amendment
Espionage Act
establishment clause

exclusionary rule
ex post facto law
First Amendment
Fourth Amendment
Fourteenth Amendment
Fifth Amendment
fighting words
free exercise clause
fundamental freedoms
Gitlow v. *New York* (1925)
grand jury
hate speech
incorporation doctrine
Lemon test
libel
Miranda rights
Miranda v. *Arizona* (1966)
Miller v. *California* (1973)
New York Times Co. v. *Sullivan* (1964)
New York Times Co. v. *U.S.* (1971)
Ninth Amendment

Occupy Wall Street
Planned Parenthood of Southeastern Pennsylvania v. *Casey* (1992)
prior restraint
right to privacy
Roe v. *Wade* (1973)
sedition laws
selective incorporation
September 11th
Sixth Amendment
slander
substantive due process
symbolic speech
Tenth Amendment
The Crown v. *Zenger* (1735)
undue burden test
Warren Court
Warren E. Burger
Whole Woman's Health v. *Hellerstedt* (2016)
writ of *habeas corpus*

WHO CONDUCTED THE UNDERGROUND RAILROAD?
Harriet Tubman ran multiple missions to help enslaved African Americans in the South find freedom in the North via the Underground Railroad, a network of safe houses that extended into Canada. This photograph shows Tubman, far left, with a group of people she helped to escape to freedom.

CIVIL RIGHTS

LEARNING OBJECTIVES

5.1 Trace the roots of movements to guarantee rights to African Americans and women.

5.2 Outline developments in African Americans' and women's push for equality from 1890 to 1954.

5.3 Analyze the legal protections enacted for African Americans' and women's civil rights since 1955.

5.4 Summarize the struggles of other group-differentiated minorities for civil rights.

5.5 Evaluate the standards by which civil rights are protected today and analyze the reforms still necessary.

Harriet Tubman
Born a slave in Maryland in the early 1820s, Tubman escaped to freedom and became a conductor on the Underground Railroad. She led more than seventy people to freedom in the North, served in the Union during the Civil War, and championed women's suffrage.

abolitionist
A supporter, especially in the early nineteenth century, of ending the institution of slavery.

civil rights
The government-protected rights of individuals against arbitrary or discriminatory treatment by governments or individuals.

equal protection clause
Section of the Fourteenth Amendment that guarantees that all citizens receive "equal protection of the laws".

Slavery first made its ugly appearance at the Jamestown Colony in Virginia in 1619 when settlers brought 19 slaves with them as field laborers. The issue of slavery later found its way into constitutional debate and, ultimately, the U.S. Constitution included a ban on the importation of slaves from outside of the new nation.

The invention of the cotton gin in 1793 made it easier to process raw cotton, a highly profitable crop, and dramatically raised the demand for more enslaved labor. Slave owners subjected their slaves to a host of abuses, including beatings and sexual assault. Families were routinely separated when members were sold to other owners. As slaves desperate for freedom began escaping to free states in the North where slavery was illegal, the U.S. Congress enacted the Fugitive Slave Act in 1793 requiring the return of any escaped slaves to their owners.

The act did not deter the efforts of those united against slavery to create a series of safe houses and secret routes to help slaves escape to freedom in the North. This Underground Railroad is perhaps best embodied by **Harriet Tubman**.

Tubman was born into slavery on the Eastern Shore of Maryland in the early 1820s. In 1849, she escaped from the Maryland coast where her first job as a child was to keep her master's baby from crying. Tubman later reported that once she was whipped seven times before breakfast. Upon reaching freedom in Philadelphia in 1849, she immediately returned to Maryland and in a series of thirteen daring escapes led more than seventy relatives and friends to freedom—never losing a single man, woman, or child. Her actions are all the more noteworthy in that Congress passed an even more stringent Fugitive Slave Act in 1850. The act barred escaped slaves from becoming free anywhere in the United States or its territories. Flyers went up all over the nation offering huge rewards for the capture of the 5-foot-tall "conductor" on the Underground Railroad. Noted **abolitionist** William Lloyd Garrison began referring to Tubman as "Moses."

Tubman was much more than an abolitionist. When the Civil War began in 1861, she signed up as a Union cook and nurse. She then became an armed scout and spy for the Union forces serving throughout the war in dangerous situations. She also became the first woman to lead an armed expedition that resulted in the liberation of more than 700 slaves; many of the men she helped to free would join the Union Army.

After the war, Tubman continued her activism. She worked with noted suffragist Susan B. Anthony traveling to suffrage conventions in New York City, Boston, and Washington, D.C. Her efforts brought her many accolades from women's rights organizations for her lifetime service to the cause of humanity. It is thus fitting that her image will take the place of former president Andrew Jackson, a staunch supporter of slavery and foe of women's rights, on the front of the twenty dollar bill.

• • •

Since the founding era, concepts of **civil rights**—the government-protected rights of individuals against arbitrary or discriminatory treatment by governments or individuals based on categories such as race, sex, national origin, age, religion, or sexual orientation—have changed dramatically. As we will discuss in this chapter, the Fourteenth Amendment, one of three Civil War Amendments ratified from 1865 to 1870, was the first provision to introduce the notion of equality into the Constitution by specifying that a state could not deny "any person within its jurisdiction equal protection of the laws." Throughout history, this **equal protection clause**, which guarantees that no citizen shall be denied rights or privileges given to any other citizen by constitution or law, has been the linchpin of efforts to protect a variety of groups from discrimination. As a result, the Fourteenth Amendment has generated more litigation to determine and specify its meaning than any other provision of the Constitution. Within a few years of its ratification, women—and later African Americans and other minorities and disadvantaged groups—began to seek expanded civil rights in all walks of life. Throughout this chapter, we will explore how these litigation, lobbying, and social protest efforts have changed notions of equality and civil rights in the United States.

ROOTS OF CIVIL RIGHTS

5.1 Trace the roots of movements to guarantee rights to African Americans and women.

The U.S. Declaration of Independence states that, "all men are created equal." This simple language articulates a closely held American ideal: that of equality of opportunity. Though all people may not have the same skills, talents, or abilities, from the beginning, the United States has been built on the assumption that all citizens— "men"—should have the same chance to work hard and build a successful life for themselves and their families. Importantly, citizens are not guaranteed equality of result. In other words, there is no assumption that they will be guaranteed the same income, possessions, or outcomes, only that they will be able to pursue their goals equally, without interference on the basis of arbitrary personal characteristics.

Of course, the definition of "men" has broadened tremendously since the nation's inception. When the Framers wrote the Declaration, their language referred most directly to property-owning white men. Over time, that definition has grown to accommodate white men who did not own property, African American men, women, and citizens of a wide variety of races, creeds, colors, and ethnicities. Today, we expect that all American citizens, regardless of their economic, political, or social status, should have equal opportunity to pursue their goals and dreams.

Voting rights—or suffrage—of women and African Americans is considered a given in modern U.S. society, but that was not the case at the Founding. The period from 1800 to 1890 was one of tremendous change and upheaval in America. Despite the Civil War and the freeing of slaves, the promise of equality guaranteed to African Americans by the Civil War Amendments failed to become a reality. Women's rights activists also began to make claims for equality, often using the arguments enunciated for the abolition of slavery, but they, too, fell far short of their goals.

Slavery and Congress

Congress banned the slave trade in 1808, after expiration of the twenty-year period specified by the Constitution. In 1820, blacks made up 25 percent of the U.S. population and formed majorities or near majorities in states such as South Carolina, Mississippi, and Florida. By 1840, that figure had fallen to 20 percent of the total U.S. population. The South became increasingly dependent on agriculture, such as cotton, tobacco, and rice, with cheap slave labor as its economic base. At the same time, technological advances were turning the northern states into an increasingly industrialized region, which deepened the cultural and political differences as well as the animosity between North and South.

As the nation grew westward in the early 1800s, conflicts between northern and southern states intensified over the free versus slave status of new states admitted to the Union. The first major crisis occurred in 1820, when Missouri applied for admission as a slave state—that is, one in which slavery would be legal. Missouri's admission would have weighted the Senate in favor of slavery and therefore was opposed by northern senators. To resolve this conflict, Congress passed the Missouri Compromise of 1820. The Compromise prohibited slavery north of the geographical boundary at 36 degrees latitude. This act allowed the Union to admit Missouri as a slave state. To maintain the balance of slave and free states, Maine was carved out of a portion of Massachusetts.

Frederick Douglass
A former slave born in the early 1800s who became a leading abolitionist, writer, and suffragist.

Elizabeth Cady Stanton
Leading nineteenth-century feminist, suffragist, and abolitionist who, along with Lucretia Mott, organized the Seneca Falls Convention. Stanton later founded the National Woman Suffrage Association (NWSA) with Susan B. Anthony.

Lucretia Mott
Leading nineteenth-century feminist, suffragist, and abolitionist who, along with Elizabeth Cady Stanton, organized the Seneca Falls Convention.

Seneca Falls Convention
The first major feminist meeting, held in New York State in 1848, which produced the historic "Declaration of Sentiments" calling for equal rights for women.

Dred Scott v. Sandford (1857)
A Supreme Court decision that ruled the Missouri Compromise unconstitutional and denied citizenship rights to enslaved African Americans. *Dred Scott* heightened tensions between the pro-slavery South and the abolitionist North in the run up to the Civil War.

The First Civil Rights Movements: Abolition and Women's Rights

The Missouri Compromise solidified the South in its determination to keep slavery legal, but it also fueled the fervor of those opposing it. William Lloyd Garrison, a white New Englander, galvanized the abolitionist movement in the early 1830s with publication of the weekly anti-slavery newspaper *The Liberator*. Garrison co-founded the American Anti-Slavery Society in 1833; by 1838, it had more than 250,000 members.

Slavery was not the only practice that people began to question in the decades following the Missouri Compromise. In 1840, for example, Garrison and **Frederick Douglass**, a well-known black abolitionist writer, left the Anti-Slavery Society when it refused to accept demands that women be allowed to participate equally in all its activities. Custom dictated that women not speak out in public, and most laws explicitly made women second-class citizens. In most states, for example, women could not divorce their husbands or keep their own wages and inheritances. And, of course, they could not vote.

Elizabeth Cady Stanton and **Lucretia Mott**, founders of the first women's rights movement, attended the 1840 meeting of the World Anti-Slavery Society in London with their husbands. In spite of their long journey, they were not permitted to participate in the convention because they were women. As they sat in a mandated area apart from the male delegates, they compared their status to that of the slaves they sought to free. They concluded that women were not much better off than slaves, and they resolved to address this issue. In 1848, they finally sent out a call for the first women's rights convention. Three hundred women and men, including Frederick Douglass, attended the first meeting for women's rights, held in Seneca Falls, New York.

The **Seneca Falls Convention** passed resolutions demanding the abolition of legal, economic, and social discrimination against women. All of the resolutions reflected the attendees' dissatisfaction with contemporary moral codes; divorce and criminal laws; and the limited opportunities for women in education, the church, medicine, law, and politics. Ironically, only the call for "woman suffrage"—a call to give women the right to vote—failed to win unanimous approval. Similar conventions took place later across the Northeast and Midwest. At an 1851 meeting in Akron, Ohio, for example, former slave Sojourner Truth delivered her famous "Ain't I a Woman?" speech, calling on women to recognize the plight of their black sisters. For the most part, however, white women's rights activists were quite racist.

The 1850s: The Calm Before the Storm

By 1850, much had changed in America: the Gold Rush had spurred westward migration, cities grew as people were lured from their farms, railroads and the telegraph increased mobility and communication, and immigrants flooded into the United States. The women's movement gained momentum, and slavery continued to tear the nation apart. Harriet Beecher Stowe's *Uncle Tom's Cabin*, a widely circulated novel that depicted the evils of slavery, further inflamed the country.

The tremendous national reaction to *Uncle Tom's Cabin*, which later prompted President Abraham Lincoln to call Stowe "the little woman who started the big war," had not yet faded when a new controversy over the Missouri Compromise became the lightning rod for the first major civil rights case addressed by the U.S. Supreme Court. In **Dred Scott v. Sandford (1857)**, the Court ruled that the Missouri Compromise, which prohibited slavery north of a set geographical boundary, was unconstitutional. Furthermore, the Court added that slaves were not U.S. citizens and, as a consequence, could not bring suits in federal court.

The Civil War and Its Aftermath: Civil Rights Laws and Constitutional Amendments

The Civil War had many causes, but slavery was clearly a key issue. During the war, which lasted from 1861 to 1865, abolitionists continued to press for an end to slavery. They were partially rewarded when President Abraham Lincoln issued the **Emancipation Proclamation**, which provided that all slaves in states still in active rebellion against the United States would be freed automatically on January 1, 1863. Designed as a measure to gain favor for the war in the North, the Emancipation Proclamation did not free all slaves—it freed only those who lived in the Confederacy. Complete abolition of slavery did not occur until congressional passage and ultimate ratification of the Thirteenth Amendment in 1865.

The **Thirteenth Amendment** was the first of the three Civil War Amendments. It banned all forms of "slavery [and] involuntary servitude." Although the federal government required the southern states to ratify the Thirteenth Amendment as a condition of readmission to the Union after the war, most former Confederate states passed laws designed to restrict opportunities for newly freed slaves. These Black Codes denied most legal rights to newly freed slaves by prohibiting African Americans from voting, sitting on juries, or even appearing in public places. The Black Codes laid the groundwork for Jim Crow laws, which later would institute segregation in all walks of life in the South.

An outraged Congress enacted the Civil Rights Act of 1866 to invalidate some state Black Codes. President Andrew Johnson vetoed the legislation, but—for the first time in history—Congress overrode a presidential veto. The Civil Rights Act formally made African Americans citizens of the United States and gave Congress and the federal courts the power to intervene when states attempted to restrict the citizenship rights of male African Americans in matters such as voting. Congress reasoned that African Americans were unlikely to succeed if they had to file discrimination complaints in state courts, where most judges were elected. Passage of a federal law allowed African Americans to challenge discriminatory state practices in federal courts, where the president appointed judges for life.

Because controversy remained over the constitutionality of the act (since the Constitution gives states the right to determine qualifications of voters in Article I), Congress proposed the **Fourteenth Amendment** simultaneously with the Civil Rights Act to guarantee, among other things, citizenship to all freed slaves. Other key provisions of the Fourteenth Amendment barred states from abridging "the privileges or immunities of citizenship" or depriving "any person of life, liberty, or property, without due process of law." As previously discussed, the Fourteenth Amendment also includes the equal protection clause, which prohibits states from denying "any person within its jurisdiction the equal protection of the laws."

Unlike the Thirteenth Amendment, which had near-unanimous support in the North, the Fourteenth Amendment faced opposition from many women because it failed to guarantee them suffrage. During the Civil War, women's rights activists put aside their claims for expanded rights for women, most notably the right to vote, and threw their energies into the war effort. They were convinced that once the

WHO WAS SOJOURNER TRUTH?

Sojourner Truth was an abolitionist and women's rights activist. She was born into slavery, but escaped around her thirtieth birthday. For more than fifty years after her escape, she travelled the country, speaking passionately for civil rights for all. Her most notable speech, "Ain't I a Woman?" played an important role in highlighting the underrepresentation of African American women in the 1840's women's rights movement.

Emancipation Proclamation
President Abraham Lincoln issued this proclamation on January 1, 1863, in the third year of the Civil War. It freed all slaves in states that were in active rebellion against the United States.

Thirteenth Amendment
One of three major amendments ratified after the Civil War; specifically bans slavery in the United States.

Fourteenth Amendment
One of three major amendments ratified after the Civil War; guarantees equal protection and due process of the law to all U.S. citizens.

Fifteenth Amendment
One of three major amendments ratified after the Civil War; specifically enfranchised newly freed male slaves.

Susan B. Anthony
Nineteenth-century feminist, suffragist, and founder of the National Woman Suffrage Association with Elizabeth Cady Stanton. Anthony later formed the National American Woman Suffrage Association (NAWSA), which along with the National Woman's Party (NWP) helped to ensure ratification of the Nineteenth Amendment.

Civil Rights Act of 1875
Passed by Congress to enforce the Fourteenth Amendment's guarantees of equal protection to African Americans. Granted equal access to public accommodations among other provisions.

Jim Crow laws
Laws enacted by southern states that required segregation in public schools, theaters, hotels, and other public accommodations.

government freed the slaves and gave them the right to vote, women would receive this same right. They were wrong.

In early 1869, after ratification of the Fourteenth Amendment (which specifically added the word "male" to the Constitution for the first time), women's rights activists met in Washington, D.C., to oppose any new amendment that would extend suffrage to black males and not to women. Many of the women used racist arguments to state their case. Ending slavery was one thing, in their opinion, but extending voting rights to African American males and not white women was another. Nevertheless, Congress passed the **Fifteenth Amendment** in early 1869. It guaranteed the "right of citizens" to vote regardless of their "race, color or previous condition of servitude." Sex was not mentioned.

Women's rights activists were shocked. Abolitionists' continued support of the Fifteenth Amendment prompted many women's rights supporters to leave the abolition movement and to work solely for the cause of women's rights. Twice burned, **Susan B. Anthony** (who had joined the women's movement in 1852) and Elizabeth Cady Stanton decided to form their own group, the National Woman Suffrage Association (NWSA), to achieve that goal and other women's rights. Another more conservative group, the American Woman Suffrage Association was founded at the same time to pursue the sole goal of suffrage. In spite of the NWSA's opposition, however, the states ratified the Fifteenth Amendment in 1870.

Civil Rights, Congress, and the Supreme Court

Continued Southern resistance to African American equality led Congress to pass the **Civil Rights Act of 1875**, designed to grant equal access to public accommodations such as theaters, restaurants, and transportation. The act also prohibited the exclusion of African Americans from jury service. By 1877, however, national interest in the legal condition of African Americans waned. Most white Southerners and even some Northerners never had believed in true equality for "freedmen," as former slaves were called. Any rights that freedmen received had been contingent on federal enforcement. And, federal occupation of the South (known as Reconstruction) ended in 1877. National troops were no longer available to guard polling places and to prevent whites from excluding black voters, and southern states quickly moved to limit African Americans' access to the ballot. Other forms of discrimination also came about as state judicial decisions upheld **Jim Crow laws**, which required segregation in public schools and facilities, including railroads, restaurants, and theaters. Some Jim Crow laws, specifically known as miscegenation laws, barred interracial marriage.

All these laws, at first glance, appeared to conflict with the Civil Rights Act of 1875. In 1883, however, a series of cases decided by the Supreme Court severely damaged the vitality of the 1875 act. The *Civil Rights Cases (1883)* were five separate cases involving convictions of private individuals found to have violated the Civil Rights Act by refusing to extend accommodations to African Americans in theaters, a hotel, and a railroad.[1] In deciding these cases, the Supreme Court ruled that Congress could prohibit state or governmental action but not private acts of discrimination. The Court thus concluded that Congress had no authority to outlaw private discrimination in public accommodations. The Court's opinion in the *Civil Rights Cases* provided a moral reinforcement for the Jim Crow system. Southern states viewed the Court's ruling as an invitation to gut the reach and intent of the Thirteenth, Fourteenth, and Fifteenth Amendments.

In devising ways to make certain that African Americans did not vote, southern states had to sidestep the intent of the Fifteenth Amendment. This amendment did not guarantee suffrage; it simply said that states could not deny anyone the right to

WHAT DID JIM CROW LAWS DO?
Throughout the South, examples of Jim Crow laws abounded. There were Jim Crow schools, restaurants, hotels, and businesses. Some buildings even had separate "white" and "colored" facilities, such as the public drinking fountains shown here. The Supreme Court would later rule that the creation of such distinctions relegated African-Americans to a form of second-class citizenship that was injurious to their "hearts and minds," and, as such, unconstitutional.

vote on the basis of race or color. To exclude African Americans in a way that seemed racially neutral, southern states used three devices before the 1890s: (1) **poll taxes**, small taxes on the right to vote that often came due when poor African American sharecroppers had the least amount of money on hand; (2) some form of property-owning qualifications; and, (3) "literacy" or "understanding" tests, which allowed local voter registration officials to administer difficult reading-comprehension tests to potential voters whom they did not know. For example, some potential voters were asked to rewrite entire sections of the Constitution by hand as the registrar dictated its text.

These voting restrictions had an immediate impact. By the late 1890s, black voting fell by 62 percent from the Reconstruction period, while white voting fell by only 26 percent. To make certain these laws did not further reduce the numbers of poor or uneducated white voters, many southern states added a **grandfather clause** to their voting qualification provisions, granting voting privileges to those citizens who failed to pass a wealth or literacy test only if their grandfathers had voted before Reconstruction. Grandfather clauses effectively denied the descendants of slaves the right to vote.

THE PUSH FOR EQUALITY, 1890–1954

5.2 Outline developments in African Americans' and women's push for equality from 1890 to 1954.

The **Progressive Era (1890–1920)** was characterized by a concerted effort to reform political, economic, and social affairs. Evils such as child labor, the concentration of economic power in the hands of a few industrialists, limited suffrage, political corruption, business monopolies, and prejudice against African Americans all were targets of progressive reform. Distress over the inferior legal status of African Americans increased with the U.S. Supreme Court's decision in *Plessy v. Ferguson* (1896), a case that some commentators point to as the Court's worst hour.[2]

poll taxes
Taxes levied in many southern states and localities that had to be paid before an eligible voter could cast a ballot.

grandfather clause
Voter qualification provision in many southern states that allowed only those citizens whose grandfathers had voted before Reconstruction to vote unless they passed a wealth or literacy test.

Progressive Era (1890–1920)
A period of widespread activism to reform political, economic, and social ills in the United States.

Plessy v. Ferguson **(1896)**
Supreme Court case that challenged a Louisiana statute requiring that railroads provide separate accommodations for blacks and whites; the Court found that separate-but-equal accommodations did not violate the equal protection clause of the Fourteenth Amendment.

separate-but-equal doctrine
The central tenet of the *Plessy* v. *Ferguson* decision that claimed that separate accommodations for blacks and whites did not violate the Constitution. This doctrine was used by southern states to pass widespread discriminatory legislation at the end of the nineteenth century.

National Association for the Advancement of Colored People (NAACP)
An important rights organization founded in 1909 to oppose segregation, racism, and voting rights violations targeted against African Americans.

National American Woman Suffrage Association (NAWSA)
Organization created by joining the National and American Woman Suffrage Associations.

WHY WAS THE NIAGARA MOVEMENT FOUNDED?
W.E.B. Du Bois (third from left in the second row, facing left) is pictured with the other original leaders of the Niagara Movement in this 1905 photo. The meeting detailed a list of injustices suffered by African Americans.

In 1892, a group of African Americans in Louisiana decided to test the constitutionality of a Louisiana law mandating racial segregation on all public trains. This meant that certain undesirable cars at the rear of the train were reserved for blacks. They convinced Homer Plessy, a man who was one-eighth black and who easily "passed" for white, to board a train in New Orleans and proceed to the "whites only" car.[3] The authorities were alerted, and Plessy was arrested when he refused to take a seat in the car reserved for African Americans, as required by state law. Plessy challenged the law, arguing that the Fourteenth Amendment prohibited racial segregation.

The Supreme Court disagreed. After analyzing the history of African Americans in the United States, the majority concluded that the Louisiana law was constitutional. The justices based the decision on their belief that separate facilities for blacks and whites provided equal protection of the laws. After all, they reasoned, the Louisiana statute did not prevent Plessy from riding the train; it required only that the races travel separately. Justice John Marshall Harlan was the lone dissenter. He argued that "the Constitution is colorblind" and that it was senseless to hold constitutional a law "which, practically, puts the badge of servitude and degradation upon a large class of our fellow citizens."

Not surprisingly, the **separate-but-equal doctrine** enunciated in *Plessy v. Ferguson* soon came to mean only separate, as new legal avenues to discriminate against African Americans made their way into law. The Jim Crow system soon expanded and became a way of life and a rigid social code throughout the American South. By 1900, equality for African Americans was far from the promise first offered by the Civil War Amendments. Again and again, the Supreme Court nullified the intent of the amendments and sanctioned racial segregation; southern states avidly followed its lead.[4]

The Founding of the National Association for the Advancement of Colored People

In 1909, a handful of individuals active in a variety of progressive causes, including woman suffrage and the fight for better working conditions for women and children, met to discuss the idea of a group devoted to addressing the problems of the "Negro." Major race riots had occurred in several American cities, and progressive reformers were concerned about these outbreaks of violence and the possibility of others. Oswald Garrison Villard, the influential publisher of the *New York Evening Post*—and the grandson of William Lloyd Garrison—called a conference to discuss the matter. This group soon evolved into the **National Association for the Advancement of Colored People (NAACP)**. Along with Villard, its first leaders included W.E.B. Du Bois, a founder in 1905 of the Niagara Movement, a group of African American intellectuals who took their name from their first meeting place in Niagara Falls, Ontario, Canada.

The Suffrage Movement

The struggle for women's rights was revitalized in 1890, when the National and American Woman Suffrage Associations merged. The new organization, the **National American Woman Suffrage Association (NAWSA)**, was headed by Susan B. Anthony. Unlike NWSA, which had sought a wide variety of expanded rights for women, this new association largely devoted itself to securing women's suffrage. The proliferation of women's groups during the Progressive Era greatly facilitated its task. In addition to the rapidly growing temperance movement whose members pressed to ban the sale of alcohol, which many women blamed for a variety of social ills, women's groups sprang up to seek goals such as maximum hour or minimum wage laws for women, improved sanitation, public morals, and education.

NAWSA based its claim to the right to vote largely on the fact that women, as mothers, should be enfranchised. The new women's movement—called the **suffrage movement** because of its focus on voting rights—soon took on racist and nativist overtones. Suffragists argued that if undereducated African American men and immigrants could vote, why couldn't women?

By 1917, the new women's movement had more than 2 million members. Its growth was aided by the formation of the more radical **National Woman's Party (NWP)** in 1915. Members of the National Woman's Party gained publicity for the cause of women's suffrage through daily arrests in front of the White House as well as the force-feeding in prison of members staging a hunger strike. In 1920, a coalition of women's groups, led by NAWSA and the more militant NWP, was able to secure ratification of the **Nineteenth Amendment** to the Constitution through rallies, protest marches, and the support of President Woodrow Wilson. The Nineteenth Amendment guaranteed all women the right to vote—fifty years after the Fifteenth Amendment had enfranchised African American males.

After passage of the suffrage amendment in 1920, the fragile alliance of diverse women's groups that had come together to fight for the vote quickly disintegrated. Women returned to their home groups to pursue their individualized goals. In fact, after the tumult of the suffrage movement, organized activity on behalf of women's rights did not reemerge in national politics until the 1960s. In the meantime, the NAACP continued to fight racism and racial segregation. Its activities and those of others in the civil rights movement would later give impetus to a new women's movement.

suffrage movement
The drive for voting rights for women that took place in the United States in the nineteenth and early twentieth centuries until ratification of the Nineteenth Amendment in 1920.

National Woman's Party (NWP)
A militant suffrage organization founded in the early twentieth century. Members of the NWP were arrested, jailed, and even force-fed by authorities when they went on hunger strikes to secure voting rights for women.

Nineteenth Amendment
Amendment to the Constitution passed in 1920 that guaranteed women the right to vote.

Litigating for Equality

During the 1930s, leaders of the NAACP began to sense that the time was right to launch a full-scale challenge to the constitutionality of *Plessy*'s separate-but-equal doctrine. Traditional legislative channels were unlikely to work, given African Americans' limited political power. Thus, the federal courts and a litigation strategy were the NAACP's only hopes. The NAACP mapped out a long-range plan that would first target segregation in professional and graduate education.

TEST CASES The NAACP opted first to challenge the constitutionality of Jim Crow laws in higher education test cases. In 1935, all southern states maintained fully segregated elementary and secondary schools. Colleges and universities also were segregated, and most states did not provide for postgraduate education for African Americans. NAACP lawyers chose to target law schools because they were institutions that judges could well understand, and integration at the graduate level would prove less threatening to most whites.

Lloyd Gaines, a graduate of Missouri's all-black Lincoln University, sought admission to the all-white University of Missouri Law School in 1936. The school immediately rejected him. In the separate-but-equal spirit, the state offered to build a law school at Lincoln (although no funds were allocated for the project) or, if he did not want to wait, to pay his tuition at an out-of-state law school. Gaines rejected the offer, sued, lost in the lower courts, and appealed to the U.S. Supreme Court.

MR. PRESIDENT, HOW LONG MUST WOMEN WAIT FOR LIBERTY?

Members of the National Woman's Party (NWP) and other women's rights organizations used marches, protests, and rallies to mobilize for political change. Here, NWP members are shown protesting in front of the White House. Women engaging in these activities were routinely arrested, jailed, and even force-fed in an attempt to end their activism on behalf of women's suffrage.

NAACP Legal Defense and Educational Fund (LDF)

The legal arm of the NAACP that successfully litigated the landmark case of *Brown* v. *Board of Education* and a host of other key civil rights cases.

Thurgood Marshall

A leading civil rights lawyer and the first head of the NAACP's Legal Defense and Educational Fund. Marshall was the first African American appointed to the Supreme Court and served on the Court from 1967 until 1991.

The attorneys filed Gaines's case at a promising time. A constitutional revolution of sorts occurred in Supreme Court decision making in 1937. Prior to this, the Court was most receptive to, and interested in, the protection of economic liberties. In 1937, however, the Court began to regard the protection of individual freedoms and personal liberties as important issues. Thus, in 1938, Gaines's lawyers pleaded his appeal to a far more sympathetic Supreme Court. NAACP attorneys argued that the creation of a separate law school of a laughable lesser caliber than that of the University of Missouri would not and could not afford Gaines an equal education. The justices agreed and ruled that Missouri had failed to meet the separate-but-equal requirements of *Plessy*. The Court ordered Missouri either to admit Gaines to the school or to set up a law school for him.[5]

Recognizing the importance of the Court's ruling, the NAACP, in 1939, created a separate, tax-exempt legal defense fund to devise a strategy that would build on the Missouri case and bring about equal educational opportunities for all African American children. The first head of the **NAACP Legal Defense and Educational Fund (LDF)**, was **Thurgood Marshall**, who later became the first African American to serve on the U.S. Supreme Court. Sensing that the Court would be more amenable to the NAACP's broader goals if it were first forced to address a variety of less threatening claims to educational opportunity, Marshall and the LDF brought a series of carefully crafted test cases to the Court. These cases attracted attention across the United States and helped to raise the visibility of civil rights issues.

The first case involved H.M. Sweatt, a forty-six-year-old African American mail carrier who applied for admission to the all-white University of Texas Law School in 1946. Rejected on racial grounds, Sweatt sued. The judge gave the state six months to establish a law school or to admit Sweatt to the university. The state legislature then authorized $3 million for the creation of the Texas State University for Negroes. One hundred thousand dollars of that money was allotted for a new law school in Austin across the street from the state capitol building. It consisted of three small basement rooms, a library of 10,000 books, access to the state law library, and three part-time first-year instructors as the faculty. Sweatt declined the opportunity to attend the substandard university and instead chose to continue his legal challenge.

While working on the Texas case in the late 1940s, the LDF also decided to pursue a case involving George McLaurin, a retired university professor who had been denied admission to the doctoral program in education at the University of Oklahoma. Marshall reasoned that McLaurin, at age sixty-eight, would be immune from the charges that African Americans wanted integration so they could intermarry with whites, an act that was illegal in most southern states. After a lower court ordered McLaurin's admission, the university reserved a dingy alcove in the cafeteria for him to eat in during off-hours, gave him his own table in the library behind a shelf of newspapers, and created a separate bathroom for him. In what surely "was Oklahoma's most inventive contribution to legalized bigotry since the adoption of the 'grandfather clause,'" McLaurin was forced to sit outside classrooms while lectures and seminars were conducted inside.[6]

The Supreme Court handled these two cases together.[7] The eleven southern states filed an *amicus curiae* (friend of the court) brief, in which they argued that *Plessy* should govern both cases. The LDF received assistance, however, from an unexpected source—the U.S. government. In a dramatic departure from the past, President **Harry S Truman** directed his Department of Justice to file an *amicus* brief urging the Court to overrule *Plessy*. Earlier, Truman had issued an executive order desegregating the military. President Truman believed that because so many African Americans had fought and died for their country in World War II, these kinds of executive actions were not only proper but honorable as well.

Although the Court did not overrule *Plessy*, the justices found that measures taken by the states in each case failed to live up to the strictures of the separate-but-equal doctrine. The Court unanimously ruled that the remedies to each situation were inadequate to afford a sound education. In the *Sweatt* case, for example, the Court declared that the intangible characteristics of a law school—including such things as faculty reputation and alumni networks—made it impossible for the state to provide an equal education in a segregated setting.[8]

In 1950, after the Court had handed down these decisions, the LDF concluded that the time had come to launch a full-scale attack on the separate-but-equal doctrine.

Harry S Truman
The thirty-third president, a Democrat, who served from 1945 until 1953. Truman became president when Franklin D. Roosevelt died in office; he led the United States through the end of World War II and the start of the Cold War.

WHAT DID "SEPARATE BUT EQUAL" LOOK LIKE?

Here, George McLaurin, the plaintiff in one of the NAACP LDF's challenges to the separate-but-equal-doctrine is shown outside his classroom. This was the university's shameful accommodation when a federal district court ordered his admission into the University of Oklahoma's doctoral program.

**Brown v. Board of Education
(1954)**
U.S. Supreme Court decision holding
that school segregation is inherently
unconstitutional because it violates the
Fourteenth Amendment's guarantee of
equal protection of the law.

The Court's decisions were encouraging, and the position of the U.S. government and the population in general (especially outside the South) appeared more receptive to an outright overruling of *Plessy.*

BROWN v. BOARD OF EDUCATION   *Brown v. Board of Education* (1954) actually was five cases brought from different areas of the South and border states involving public elementary or high school systems that mandated separate schools for blacks and whites.[9] In *Brown*, LDF lawyers, again led by Thurgood Marshall, argued that the equal protection clause of the Fourteenth Amendment made *Plessy's* separate-but-equal doctrine unconstitutional, and that if the Court was still reluctant to overrule *Plessy*, the only way to equalize the schools was to integrate them. A major component of the LDF's strategy was to prove that the intellectual, psychological, and financial damage done to African Americans as a result of segregation prevented any court from finding that the separate-but-equal policy was consistent with the intent of the Fourteenth Amendment's equal protection clause.

In *Brown*, the LDF presented the Supreme Court with evidence of the harmful consequences of state-imposed racial discrimination. To buttress its claims, the LDF introduced the now-famous doll study, conducted by Kenneth and Mamie Clark, two prominent African American sociologists at the University of Chicago who had long studied the negative effects of segregation on African American children. Their research revealed that black children not only preferred white dolls when shown black dolls and white dolls but that many added that the black doll looked "bad." The LDF attorneys used this information to illustrate the negative impact of racial segregation and bias on an African American child's self-image.

The LDF supported its legal arguments with important *amicus curiae* briefs submitted by the U.S. government, major civil rights groups, labor unions, and religious groups decrying racial segregation. On May 17, 1954, Chief Justice Earl Warren delivered the fourth opinion of the day, *Brown v. Board of Education.* Writing for the unanimous Court, Warren stated:

> To separate [some school children] from others...solely because of their race generates a feeling of inferiority as to their status in the community that may affect their hearts and minds in a way very unlikely ever to be undone. We conclude, unanimously, that in the field of public education the doctrine of "separate but equal" has no place.

Brown was, without doubt, the most important civil rights case decided in the twentieth century.[10] It immediately evoked an uproar that shook the nation. Some segregationists gave the name Black Monday to the day the decision was handed down. The governor of South Carolina denounced the decision, saying, "Ending segregation would mark the beginning of the end of civilization in the South as we know it."[11] The LDF lawyers who had argued these cases, as well as the cases leading to *Brown*, however, were jubilant.

STATUTORY PROTECTIONS FOR CIVIL RIGHTS, 1955–PRESENT

5.3   Analyze the legal protections for African Americans' and women's civil rights enacted since 1955.

Although it did not create immediate legal change, *Brown* served as a catalyst for a civil rights movement across the United States, and especially in the South. The decision emboldened activists and gave them faith that the government might one day change its segregationist policies in all areas of the law.[12] Subsequent successes in the civil rights movement also inspired a 1960s women's rights movement. This movement focused much of its effort on establishing protections for women in employment and education and attempting to enact an Equal Rights Amendment to the Constitution.

School Desegregation After *Brown*

One year after *Brown*, in a case referred to as *Brown* v. *Board of Education II* (1955), the Court ruled that racially segregated systems must be dismantled "with all deliberate speed."[13] To facilitate implementation, the Court placed enforcement of *Brown* in the hands of appointed federal district court judges, whom it considered more immune to local political pressures than elected state court judges.

The NAACP and its LDF continued looking to the courts for implementation of *Brown*, while the South entered into a near conspiracy to avoid the mandates of *Brown II*. In Arkansas, for example, Governor Orval Faubus, who was facing a reelection bid, announced that he would not "be a party to any attempt to force acceptance of change to which people are overwhelmingly opposed."[14] The day before school was to begin, he declared that National Guardsmen would surround Little Rock's Central High School to prevent African American students from entering. While the federal courts in Arkansas continued to order desegregation, the governor remained adamant. Finally, President **Dwight D. Eisenhower** sent federal troops to Little Rock to protect the rights of the nine African American students attending Central High.

In reaction to the governor's illegal conduct, the Court broke with tradition and issued a unanimous decision in *Cooper* v. *Aaron (1958)*, which was filed by the Little Rock School Board and asked the federal district court for a delay of two and one-half years in implementing desegregation plans. Each justice signed the opinion individually, underscoring his own support for the notion that "no state legislator or executive or judicial officer can war against the Constitution without violating his undertaking to support it."[15] The state's actions thus were ruled unconstitutional and its "evasive schemes" illegal.

A New Move for African American Rights

In 1955, soon after *Brown II*, the civil rights movement took another step forward—this time in Montgomery, Alabama. **Rosa Parks**, the local NAACP's Youth Council adviser, decided to challenge the constitutionality of the segregated bus system. First, Parks and other NAACP officials began to raise money for litigation and made speeches around town to garner public support. Then, on December 1, 1955, Rosa Parks made history when she refused to leave her seat in the front of the colored section of the bus to make room for a white male passenger without a seat. Police arrested her for violating an Alabama law banning integration of public facilities, including buses. After being freed on bond, Parks and the NAACP decided to enlist city clergy to help her cause. At the same time, they distributed 35,000 handbills calling for African Americans to boycott the Montgomery bus system on the day of Parks's trial. Black ministers used Sunday services to urge their members to support the boycott. On Monday morning, African Americans walked, carpooled, or used black-owned taxicabs. That night, local ministers decided the boycott should continue. A new, twenty-six-year-old minister, the Reverend **Martin Luther King Jr.**, was selected to lead the newly formed Montgomery Improvement Association.

As the boycott dragged on, Montgomery officials and local business owners, who were suffering negative economic consequences, began to harass the city's African American citizens. The black residents held out, despite suffering personal hardship for their actions, ranging from threats to job loss to bankruptcy. In 1956, a federal court ruled that the segregated bus system violated the equal protection clause of the Fourteenth Amendment. After a year-long boycott, African

Dwight D. Eisenhower
The thirty-fourth president, a Republican, who served from 1953 to 1961. Eisenhower commanded Allied Forces during World War II.

Rosa Parks
A leading civil rights activist of the twentieth century. Parks was most notably involved with the Montgomery Bus Boycott.

Martin Luther King Jr.
A Baptist minister, proponent of nonviolence, and the most prominent leader of the civil rights movement of the 1950s and 1960s. He was assassinated on April 4, 1968.

**WHAT ROLE DID CIVIL DISOBEDI-
ENCE PLAY IN THE CIVIL RIGHTS
MOVEMENT?**

Here, Rosa Parks is fingerprinted by a
Montgomery, Alabama, police officer
after her arrest for violating a city law
requiring segregation on public buses.
Parks refused to give up her seat to
accommodate a white man, starting
a city-wide bus boycott. Parks is just
one of many citizens who engaged in
these nonviolent acts of resistance to
unjust laws.

American Montgomery residents ended their protest when city officials ordered
the public transit system to integrate. The first effort at nonviolent protest had
been successful. Organized boycotts and other forms of nonviolent protest were
to follow.

Formation of New Groups

The recognition and respect earned by the Reverend Martin Luther King Jr.
within the African American community helped him launch the Southern Christian
Leadership Conference (SCLC) in 1957, soon after the end of the Montgomery Bus
Boycott. Unlike the NAACP, which had northern origins and had come to rely
largely on litigation as a means of achieving expanded equality, the SCLC had a
southern base and was rooted more closely in black religious culture. The SCLC's
philosophy reflected King's growing belief in the importance of nonviolent protest
and civil disobedience.

On February 1, 1960, a few students from the all-black North Carolina Agricultural
and Technical College in Greensboro participated in the first sit-in for civil rights. The
students went to a local lunch counter, sat down, and ordered cups of coffee. They
were not served, but stayed until closing. After the national wire services picked up
the story, over the next several days, the students were joined by hundreds of others
from the Greensboro area. When the students refused to leave, the police arrested and
jailed them, rather than their white tormentors. Soon thereafter, African American college students around the South did the same. The national media extensively covered
their actions.

Over spring break 1960, with the assistance of an $800 grant from the SCLC, 200
student delegates—black and white—met at the historically black Shaw University
in Raleigh, North Carolina, to consider recent sit-in actions and to plan for the future.
Later that year, the Student Nonviolent Coordinating Committee (SNCC) was formed.
Whereas the SCLC generally worked with church leaders in a community, SNCC
was much more of a grassroots organization. Always perceived as more radical than
the SCLC, SNCC tended to focus its organizing activities on the young, both black
and white.

In addition to joining the sit-in bandwagon, SNCC also came to lead what were called freedom rides, designed to shine the spotlight on segregated public accommodations. Bands of college students and other civil rights activists traveled by bus throughout the South in an effort to force bus stations to desegregate. Often these protesters faced angry mobs of segregationists and brutal violence, as local police chose not to defend the protesters' basic constitutional rights to free speech and peaceful assembly. African Americans were not the only ones to participate in freedom rides; increasingly, white college students from the North began to play an important role in SNCC.

While SNCC continued to sponsor sit-ins and freedom rides, in 1963 King launched a series of massive nonviolent demonstrations in Birmingham, Alabama, long considered a major stronghold of segregation. Thousands of blacks and whites marched to Birmingham in a show of solidarity. Peaceful marchers were met there by the Birmingham police commissioner, who ordered his officers to use dogs, clubs, and fire hoses on the marchers. Americans across the nation were horrified as they witnessed on television the brutality and abuse heaped on the protesters. As the marchers had hoped, the shocking scenes helped convince President **John F. Kennedy** to propose important civil rights legislation.

The Civil Rights Act of 1964

In 1963, President John F. Kennedy requested that Congress pass a law banning discrimination in public accommodations. Seizing the moment, the Reverend Martin Luther King Jr. called for a monumental march on Washington, D.C., in August 1963 to demonstrate widespread support for far-ranging anti-discrimination legislation. It was clear that national legislation outlawing discrimination was the only answer: southern legislators would never vote to repeal Jim Crow laws. At the March on Washington for Jobs and Freedom, more than 250,000 people heard King deliver his famous "I Have a Dream" speech from the Lincoln Memorial. Before Congress had the opportunity to vote on any legislation, however, President Kennedy was assassinated on November 22, 1963, in Dallas, Texas.

When Vice President Lyndon B. Johnson, a southern-born, former Senate majority leader, succeeded Kennedy as president, he put civil rights reform at the top of his legislative priority list, and civil rights activists gained a critical ally. Changes in public opinion also helped the push for civil rights legislation in the halls of Congress. Between 1959 and 1965, southern attitudes toward integrated schools changed enormously. The proportion of Southerners who responded that they would not mind their child's attendance at a racially balanced school doubled.

In spite of strong presidential support and the sway of public opinion, the **Civil Rights Act of 1964** did not sail through Congress. Southern senators, led by South Carolina's Strom Thurmond, a Democrat who later switched to the Republican Party, conducted the longest filibuster in the history of the Senate. For eight weeks, Thurmond led the effort to hold up voting on the civil rights bill. Once passed, the act:

- Outlawed arbitrary discrimination in voter registration and expedited voting rights lawsuits.
- Barred discrimination in public accommodations engaged in interstate commerce.
- Authorized the Department of Justice to initiate lawsuits to desegregate public facilities and schools.
- Provided for the withholding of federal funds from discriminatory state and local programs.
- Prohibited discrimination in employment on grounds of race, creed, color, religion, national origin, or sex.
- Created the Equal Employment Opportunity Commission (EEOC) to monitor and enforce the bans on employment discrimination.

John F. Kennedy
The thirty-fifth president, a Democrat, who served from 1961 to 1963 and marked a generational shift in U.S. politics at the height of the Cold War. He was assassinated November 22, 1963.

Civil Rights Act of 1964
Wide-ranging legislation passed by Congress to outlaw segregation in public facilities and discrimination in employment, education, and voting; created the Equal Employment Opportunity Commission.

National Organization for Women (NOW)
The leading activist group of the women's rights movement, especially in the 1960s and 1970s.

Eleanor Roosevelt
First Lady of the United States from 1933 to 1945. Roosevelt championed human rights throughout her life and served as the U.S.'s first delegate to the United Nations General Assembly and later chaired the UN's Commission on Human Rights.

Many Southerners adamantly believed that the Civil Rights Act of 1964 was unconstitutional because it went beyond the scope of Congress's authority to legislate under the Constitution, and they quickly brought lawsuits to challenge its scope. In 1964, on expedited review, the Supreme Court upheld its constitutionality, finding that Congress had operated within the legitimate scope of its commerce power as outlined in Article I.[16]

Still, tensions continued to grow in the aftermath of the new law. African Americans in the North, who believed their brothers and sisters in the South were making progress against discrimination, found themselves frustrated. Northern blacks, too, were experiencing high unemployment, poverty, and discrimination, and had little political clout. Some, including African American leader Malcolm X, even argued that to survive, African Americans must separate themselves from white culture in every way. These increased frustrations resulted in violent race riots in many major cities from 1964 to 1968, when many African Americans in the North took to the streets, burning and looting to vent their rage. The assassination of the Reverend Martin Luther King Jr. in 1968 triggered a new epidemic of race riots. The full implementation of "equality" as defined under the Civil Rights Act of 1964 continues today, as we discuss later in this chapter.

A New Movement for Women's Rights

As in the abolition movement of the 1800s, women from all walks of life participated in the civil rights movement. Women were important members of groups such as SNCC and the SCLC, as well as more traditional groups such as the NAACP, yet they often found themselves treated as second-class citizens. At one point during an SNCC national meeting, its male chair proclaimed: "The only position for women in SNCC is prone."[17] Statements and attitudes such as these led some women to found early women's liberation groups that generally were quite radical but small in membership. Others established more traditional groups, such as the **National Organization for Women (NOW)**. Modeled closely after the NAACP, the founders of NOW sought to work within the political system to prevent discrimination.

Three key events helped to forge a new movement for women's rights in the early 1960s. In 1961, soon after his election, President John F. Kennedy created the President's Commission on the Status of Women, headed by former First Lady **Eleanor Roosevelt**. The commission's report, *American Women*, released in 1963, documented pervasive discrimination against women in all areas of life. In addition, the civil rights movement and the publication of Betty Friedan's *The Feminine Mystique* (1963), which led some women to question their lives and status in society.[18] Soon after, the Civil Rights Act of 1964 prohibited discrimination based not only on race but also on sex. Ironically, southern Democrats had added that provision to Title VII of the act. These senators saw a prohibition against sex discrimination in employment as a joke, and viewed its addition as a means to discredit the entire act and ensure its defeat. Thus, it was added at the last minute, and female members of Congress seized the opportunity to garner additional support for the measure.

Key victories for women's rights under Title VII of the Civil Rights Act of 1964 include:

- Consideration of sexual harassment as sex discrimination.[19]
- Inclusion of law firms, which many argued were private partnerships, in the coverage of the act.[20]
- A broad definition of what can be considered sexual harassment, including same-sex harassment.[21]

- Allowance of voluntary programs to redress historical discrimination against women.[22]

Ironically, NOW was formed in 1966 after the Equal Employment Opportunity Commission, created by the CRA of 1964, refused to investigate claims of sex discrimination concluding that race-based charges deserved precedence.

Other Statutory Remedies for Sex Discrimination

The Civil Rights Act of 1964—and a 1978 amendment that prohibited discrimination on the basis of pregnancy—is not the only piece of legislation that provides statutory protection for women. The **Equal Pay Act of 1963**, for example, requires employers to pay women and men equal pay for equal work. Although women have won important victories under the act, and subsequent legislation such as the Lilly Ledbetter Fair Pay Act has been passed, a large wage gap between women and men continues to exist. Young male college graduates earn an average hourly rate of $20.94 compared to $16.58 for women.[23]

Another important piece of legislation is **Title IX** of the Education Amendments of 1972. This act bars educational institutions that receive federal funds from discriminating against female students. Title IX greatly expanded the opportunities for women in elementary, secondary, and postsecondary institutions. Most of today's college students do not go through school being excluded from home economics or technology education classes because of their sex. Nor, probably, do many attend schools that have no team sports for females. Yet, this was commonly the case in the United States prior to passage of Title IX.[24] Major rulings by the U.S. Supreme Court that uphold the provisions of Title IX include:

- Holding school boards or districts responsible for both student-on-student harassment and harassment of students by teachers.[25]
- Allowing retaliatory lawsuits by coaches on behalf of their sports teams denied equal treatment by school boards.[26]

Work remains before equality under Title IX is achieved, however. A recent study found a huge difference in money spent on men's athletics in comparison to women's athletics in Division I colleges and universities.[27] Protection from sexual harassment and sexual violence is another key provision of Title IX. In the wake of highly publicized cases of sexual assault on college campuses and reports of discriminatory treatment of assault victims, the Department of Education has stepped up Title IX enforcement efforts. Colleges and universities are required to report allegations of sexual assault to the Department of Education and to investigate all charges fully.

The Equal Rights Amendment

Having achieved success in broadening statutory protections for women's civil rights, activists turned their efforts to lobbying Congress and the state legislatures to enact an **Equal Rights Amendment (ERA)**. The amendment, which had been proposed in every Congress since 1923, provides that:

- Equality of rights under the law shall not be denied or abridged by the United States or by any state on account of sex.
- The Congress shall have the power to enforce, by appropriate legislation, the provisions of this article.

Equal Pay Act of 1963
Legislation that requires employers to pay men and women equal pay for equal work.

Title IX
Provision of the Education Amendments of 1972 that bars educational institutions that receive federal funds from discriminating against female students.

Equal Rights Amendment (ERA)
Proposed amendment to the Constitution that states "Equality of rights under the law shall not be denied or abridged by the United States or any state on account of sex."

League of United Latin American Citizens (LULAC)
An activist group founded in 1929 to combat discrimination against, and promote assimilation among, Americans of Hispanic origin.

In 1972, in response to pressure from NOW, the National Women's Political Caucus, and a wide variety of other feminist groups, Congress voted in favor of the ERA by overwhelming majorities (84–8 in the Senate; 354–24 in the House). Within a year, twenty-two states ratified the amendment, most by overwhelming margins, but the tide soon turned. In *Roe* v. *Wade* (1973), the Supreme Court decided that women had a constitutionally protected right to privacy that included the right to terminate a pregnancy. Almost overnight, *Roe* provided the ERA's opponents with political fuel. Although privacy rights and the ERA have nothing to do with each other, opponents effectively persuaded many people in states that had yet to ratify the amendment that the two were linked. They also claimed that the ERA and feminists were anti-family and that the ERA would force women out of their homes and into the workforce because husbands would no longer be responsible for supporting their wives financially.

These arguments and the amendment's potential to make women eligible for the unpopular military draft brought the ratification effort to a near standstill. In 1974 and 1975, the amendment only squeaked through the Montana and North Dakota legislatures, and two states—Nebraska and Tennessee—voted to rescind their earlier ratifications. By 1978, one year before the expiration deadline for ratification, thirty-five states had voted for the amendment—three short of the three-fourths necessary for ratification. Efforts in key states such as Illinois and Florida failed as opposition to the ERA intensified. Faced with the prospect of defeat, ERA supporters heavily lobbied Congress to extend the deadline for ratification. Congress extended the ratification period by three years, but to no avail. No additional states ratified the amendment, and three more rescinded their votes. The proposed amendment died without ratification on June 30, 1982.

OTHER GROUPS MOBILIZE FOR RIGHTS

5.4 Summarize the struggles of other group-differentiated minorities for civil rights.

African Americans and women are not the only groups that have suffered unequal treatment under the law. Denial of civil rights has led other disadvantaged groups to mobilize. Their efforts parallel in many ways the efforts made by African Americans and women. Many groups recognized that litigation and the use of test-case strategies would be key to further civil rights gains. Others have opted for more direct, traditional forms of activism.

Hispanic Americans

Hispanics are the largest minority group in the United States. But, Hispanic population growth in the United States is not a new phenomenon. In 1910, the Mexican Revolution forced Mexicans seeking safety and employment into the United States. And, in 1916, New Mexico entered the union officially as a bilingual state—the only one in the United States.

Early Hispanic immigrants, many of whom were from families who had owned land when parts of the Southwest were still under Mexico's control, formed the **League of United Latin American Citizens (LULAC)** in 1929. LULAC continues to be the largest Hispanic organization in the United States, with local councils in every state and Puerto Rico. Hispanics returning home from fighting in World War II also formed the American G.I. Forum in Texas to fight discrimination and improve their legal status.

As large numbers of immigrants from Mexico and Puerto Rico entered the United States, they quickly became a source of cheap labor, with Mexicans initially tending to settle in the Southwest, where they most frequently found employment as migratory farm workers, and Puerto Ricans mainly moving to New York City. Both groups gravitated to their own neighborhoods, where life revolved around the Roman Catholic Church and the customs of their homeland, and both groups largely lived in poverty. Still, in 1954, the same year as *Brown*, Hispanics won a major victory when, in *Hernandez v. Texas*, the Supreme Court struck down discrimination based on race and ethnicity.[28] In *Hernandez*, the Court ruled unanimously that Mexican Americans had the right to a jury that included other Mexican Americans.

A push for greater Hispanic rights began in the mid-1960s, just as a wave of Cuban immigrants started to establish homes in Florida, dramatically altering the political and social climate of Miami and neighboring towns and cities in South Florida. This new movement, marked by the establishment of the National Council of La Raza in 1968, incorporated many tactics drawn from the African American civil rights movement, including sit-ins, boycotts, marches, and other activities designed to heighten publicity for their cause. In one earlier example, in 1965, **Cesar Chavez** and **Dolores Huerta** organized migrant workers into the United Farm Workers Union, which would become the largest such union in the nation, and led them in a strike against produce growers in California. Organizers eventually coupled this strike with a national boycott of various farm products, including lettuce and grapes. After several years, declining sales led producers to give in to some of the workers' demands.

Hispanics also have relied heavily on litigation to secure legal change. The **Mexican American Legal Defense and Educational Fund (MALDEF)** began its life in 1968 after members of LULAC met with NAACP LDF leaders and with their assistance secured a $2.2 million start-up grant from the Ford Foundation. The founders of MALDEF originally created it to bring test cases before the Supreme Court with the intent to force school districts to allocate more funds to schools with predominantly low-income minority populations, to implement bilingual education programs, to require employers to hire Hispanics, and to challenge election rules and apportionment plans that undercount or dilute Hispanic voting power.

MALDEF has been successful in expanding voting rights and electoral opportunities to Hispanic Americans. In 1973, for example, it won a major victory when the Supreme Court ruled that multimember electoral districts (in which more than one person represents a single district) in Texas discriminated against African Americans and Hispanics.[29] In multimember systems, legislatures generally add members to larger districts instead of drawing smaller districts in which a minority candidate could garner a majority of the votes necessary to win.

The organization's success in educational equity cases came more slowly. In 1973, for example, in *San Antonio Independent School District v. Rodriguez*, the Supreme Court refused to find that a Texas law under which the state appropriated a set dollar amount to each school district per pupil, while allowing wealthier districts to enrich educational programs from other funds, violated the equal protection clause of the Fourteenth Amendment.[30] In 1989, however, MALDEF won a case in which a state district judge elected by the voters of only a single county declared the state's entire method of financing public schools to be unconstitutional under the state constitution.[31] And, in 2004, it entered into a settlement with the state of California in a case brought four years earlier to address, in MALDEF's words, "the shocking inequities facing public school children across the state."[32]

MALDEF continues to litigate and lobby in a wide range of areas of concern to Hispanics. High on its agenda today are equal access to education, affirmative action, health care for undocumented immigrants, workers' rights and challenging restrictive drivers' license and voter ID laws. To ensure that Hispanics are adequately represented, it also continues to challenge state redistricting plans that dilute Hispanic voting impact.

Cesar Chavez
Labor organizer who, with Dolores Huerta, founded the United Farm Workers Union (UFW) in the 1960s.

Dolores Huerta
Labor organizer who, with Cesar Chavez, founded the United Farm Workers Union (UFW) in the 1960s.

Mexican American Legal Defense and Educational Fund (MALDEF)
An organization modeled on the NAACP Legal Defense and Educational Fund that works to protect the civil rights of Americans of Mexican and other Hispanic heritage.

HOW ARE HISPANIC AMERICANS FIGHTING IMMIGRATION RESTRICTIONS?

Here, hundreds of Hispanic residents gather near the battleship USS Iowa, a museum in Los Angeles Harbor, to protest against U.S. Republican presidential candidate Donald J. Trump, as he delivers a speech on national security aboard the ship. Many Mexican Americans were upset by Trump's assertions as a presidential candidate that Mexican immigrants were "rapists" and "drug runners."

The National Hispanic Leadership Agenda (NHLA), meanwhile, is a coalition of 40 major Hispanic groups. Established in 1991, its broad agenda includes immigration reform, access to healthcare, raising the minimum wage, and protecting voting rights and educational opportunity. NHLA also works closely with members of the Congressional Hispanic Caucus.

Today, nearly all Hispanic groups are fighting immigration restrictions and policies aimed at restricting new immigration and returning undocumented immigrants to Mexico. Unequal treatment and racial profiling of Hispanics by law enforcement are also high on groups' lists of priorities.

American Indians

American Indians are the first true Americans, and their status under U.S. law is unique. The U.S. Constitution considers Indian tribes distinct governments, a situation that has affected the treatment of these Americans by Congress and the Supreme Court.

For years, Congress and the courts manipulated the law to promote westward expansion of the United States. The Northwest Ordinance of 1787, passed by the Continental Congress, specified that "good faith should always be observed toward the Indians; their lands and property shall never be taken from them without their consent, and their property rights, and liberty, they shall never be invaded or disturbed, unless in just and lawful wars authorized by Congress." The federal government did not follow this pledge. During the eighteenth and nineteenth centuries, it isolated American Indians on reservations as it confiscated their lands and denied them basic political rights. The U.S. government administered Indian reservations, and American Indians often lived in squalid conditions.

With passage of the Dawes Act in 1887, however, the government switched policies, promoting assimilation over separation. This act gave each American Indian family land within the reservation; the rest was sold to whites, thus reducing Indian lands from about 140 million acres to about 47 million. Moreover, to encourage American Indians to assimilate, the act mandated sending Indian children to boarding schools off the reservation. It also banned native languages and rituals. American Indians did not become U.S. citizens, nor were they given the right to vote, until 1924.

WHEN DID AMERICAN INDIANS GAIN THE RIGHT TO VOTE?
American Indians were not given the right to vote in federal elections until 1924. However, some state constitutions prevented American Indians from voting for even longer. New Mexico, where these citizens are seen registering to vote for the first time in 1948, was one such state.

At least in part because tribes were small and scattered (and the number of members declining), American Indians did not begin to mobilize until the 1960s. During this time, American Indian activists, many trained by the American Indian Law Center at the University of New Mexico, began to file hundreds of test cases in the federal courts involving tribal fishing rights, tribal land claims, and taxation of tribal profits. The Native American Rights Fund (NARF), founded in 1970, became the NAACP LDF of the American Indian rights movement.

American Indians have won some very important victories concerning hunting, fishing, and use of their lands. And, tribes all over the country have sued to reclaim lands they maintain the United States stole from them. Tribal sovereignty allows American Indians to host gambling casinos across the country, frequently on lands abutting cities and in states where gambling is illegal. This phenomenon has resulted in billions of dollars of revenue for Indian tribes.

Asian and Pacific Island Americans

Today, Asian and Pacific Island Americans are the fastest-growing minority group in the United States. But, one of the most significant difficulties for Asian and Pacific Island Americans has been finding a Pan-Asian identity. Originally, Asian

Chinese Exclusion Act
A law passed by Congress in 1882 that prohibited all new immigration into the U.S. from China.

Korematsu **v.** *U.S.* **(1944)**
A Supreme Court ruling that upheld the authority of the U.S. government to require mass internment of people of Japanese ancestry in the United States during World War II.

and Pacific Island Americans were far more likely to identify with their individual Japanese, Chinese, Korean, or Filipino heritage.[33] Not until 1977 did the U.S. government decide to use "Asian and Pacific Island" for all of those with these origins. Some subgroups have challenged this identity; in the 1990s, native Hawaiians unsuccessfully requested to be categorized with American Indians, with whom they felt greater affinity.

Discrimination against Asian and Pacific Island immigrants developed over time in the United States. In 1868, Congress passed a law allowing free migration from China, because workers were needed to complete building the western extension of the transcontinental railroad. But in 1882, Congress passed the **Chinese Exclusion Act**, which was the first act to restrict the immigration of any identifiable nationality. This legislation implicitly invited more discriminatory laws against the Chinese, which closely paralleled the Jim Crow laws affecting African Americans.

Several Supreme Court cases also slowed the progress of Asian and Pacific Island Americans. This began to change in 1886, when the Court decided the case of *Yick Wo* v. *Hopkins*. A number of events precipitated this decision. Discriminatory provisions in the California Constitution prevented Chinese people from practicing many professions. However, the Chinese in California were allowed to open laundries. And, many immigrants did. In response to this growing trend, the city of San Francisco passed a ban on laundries operating in wooden buildings, two-thirds of which were owned by persons of Chinese ancestry. The Court in *Yick Wo* found that the law violated the Constitution because one ethnic group was being targeted.[34]

In 1922, the Court took a step backward, ruling that Asian and Pacific Island Americans were not white and therefore not entitled to full citizenship rights.[35] Conditions became even worse, especially for those of Japanese descent, after the Japanese attack on Pearl Harbor in 1941. In response to the attack, President Franklin D. Roosevelt issued Executive Order 9066, which led to the internment of over 130,000 Japanese Americans, Italian Americans, and German Americans, some of whom were Jewish refugees. More than two-thirds of those confined to internment camps were U.S. citizens. The Supreme Court upheld the constitutionality of these camps in *Korematsu* **v.** *U.S.* **(1944).** In sharp contrast, as a goodwill gesture to an ally,

HOW WERE JAPANESE AMERICANS TREATED DURING WORLD WAR II?

The internment of Japanese Americans during World War II was a low point in American history. In *Korematsu* v. *U.S.* (1944), the U.S. Supreme Court upheld the constitutionality of this action. Here, children wait to be relocated from their homes to an internment camp.

the U.S. government offered Chinese immigrants the opportunity to apply for U.S. citizenship. At the end of the war, President Harry S Truman extended the same privilege to Filipino immigrants, many of whom had aided in the war effort.

During the 1960s and 1970s, Asian and Pacific Island Americans, like many other groups discussed in this chapter, began to organize for equal rights. Filipino farm workers, for example, joined with Mexican immigrants to form the United Farm Workers Union. In 1973, the Movement for a Free Philippines emerged to oppose the government of Ferdinand Marcos, the president of the Philippines. Soon, it joined forces with the Friends of Filipino People, also founded in 1973. These groups worked with the Free Legal Assistance Group (FLAG) to openly oppose the Vietnam War and, with the aid of the Roman Catholic Church, established relief organizations for Filipinos in the United States and around the world.

In the 1970s and 1980s, Japanese Americans also mobilized, lobbying the courts and Congress for reparations for their treatment during World War II. In 1988, Congress passed the Civil Liberties Act, which apologized to the interned and their descendants and offered reparations to them and their families.

The Lesbian, Gay, Bisexual, and Transgender (LGBT) Community

Until very recently, members of the **LGBT community** have experienced many challenges in achieving anything approximating equal rights.[36] However, gays and lesbians have, on average, far higher household incomes and educational levels than other minority groups, and they are converting these advantages into political clout. Like African Americans and women, members of the LGBT community have worked through the courts to achieve incremental legal change. In the late 1970s, gay and lesbian activists dedicated to ending legal restrictions on the civil rights of homosexuals founded Lambda Legal, the National Center for Lesbian Rights, and Gay and Lesbian Advocates and Defenders (GLAAD).[37] These groups won important legal victories concerning HIV/AIDS discrimination, insurance policy survivor benefits, and even some employment issues. However, progress in other areas has relied on changing voters' and policy makers' hearts and minds.[38]

In 1993, for example, President Bill Clinton tried to ban discrimination against homosexuals in the armed services. Eventually, Clinton compromised with congressional and military leaders on what was called the "Don't Ask, Don't Tell" (DADT) policy. The military would no longer ask gays and lesbians if they were homosexual, but it barred them from revealing their sexual orientation under threat of discharge. Despite the compromise, the armed services discharged thousands on the basis of their sexual orientation. Government officials called the policy into question as the wars in Iraq and Afghanistan increased America's need for active-duty military personnel. In 2010, Congress passed and President Barack Obama signed into law a formal repeal of DADT. In September 2011, the policy officially ended, paving the way for many military members to openly acknowledge their homosexuality. In June of 2016, Defense Secretary Ashton Carter announced an end to a longstanding ban on transgender people serving in the military.

Changes in public opinion have also opened the door for greater legal and constitutional protection for LGBT rights.[39] These changes were reflected in the Court's decision in *Lawrence* v. *Texas* (2003). In this case, the Court reversed an earlier ruling, finding a Texas statute banning sodomy to be unconstitutional. Following the Court's ruling in *Lawrence*, many Americans were quick to call for additional rights for homosexuals. A good number of corporations responded to this amplified call. For example, Walmart announced it would ban job discrimination based on sexual

LGBT community
A minority group based on sexual orientation and gender identity that includes lesbian, gay, bisexual, and transgender (LGBT) people.

Lawrence **v.** *Texas* **(2003)**
A 2003 Supreme Court ruling that anti-sodomy laws violated the constitutional right to privacy.

WHY IS SAME-SEX MARRIAGE CONTROVERSIAL?

The legalization of same-sex marriage in California in 2008 allowed gay couples committed to one another for decades to tie the knot. Here, lesbian activists Del Martin (age 87) and Phyllis Lyon (age 83)—partners for more than 50 years—are married by San Francisco Mayor Gavin Newsom. Unions such as this face opposition by many religious conservatives, who believe homosexuality is a sin and support only the rights of heterosexual couples to marry. Martin died in August 2008, only a few months after her wedding.

***United States* v. *Windsor* (2013)**
A Supreme Court ruling striking down the 1996 Defense of Marriage Act (DOMA), which prohibited federal recognition of same-sex marriages.

***Obergefell* v. *Hodges* (2015)**
Supreme Court ruling that held that same-sex couples have a fundamental right to marry under the Constitution.

Americans with Disabilities Act (ADA)
A law enacted by Congress in 1990 designed to guarantee accommodation and access for people with a wide range of disabilities.

orientation. In addition, editorial pages across the country praised the Court's ruling, arguing that the national view toward homosexuality had changed.[40] In ***United States* v. *Windsor* (2013)**, the Supreme Court declared the 1996 Defense of Marriage Act (DOMA), a federal law defining marriage as between one man and one woman, unconstitutional.[41] This decision paved the way for same-sex marriages in all fifty states, which was mandated by the 2015 Supreme Court ruling in ***Obergefell* v. *Hodges***. President Trump vowed to appoint a justice to the Court to override this decision while campaigning, but softened his stance in a television interview shortly after his election.

Discrimination toward the LGBT community continues, however. Recent state-level legislation banning transgendered people from using the bathroom of their self-identified gender and "religious freedom" laws allowing individuals to choose not to provide goods and services to gay couples based on the religious beliefs of the individuals have been characterized as a backlash by rights advocates. And, in June 2016, a lone gunman espousing hatred of the LGBT community and allegiance to the ISIS terrorist group murdered 49 people and injured more than 50 others at a gay nightclub in Orlando, Florida.

Americans with Disabilities

Americans with disabilities have lobbied hard for anti-discrimination legislation as well as equal protection under the Constitution. In the aftermath of World War II, many veterans returned to a nation unequipped to handle their disabilities. The Korean and Vietnam Wars made the problems of disabled veterans all the more clear. These veterans saw the successes of African Americans, women, and other minorities, and they too began to lobby for greater protection against discrimination.[42] In 1990, in coalition with other disabled people, veterans finally convinced Congress to pass the **Americans with Disabilities Act (ADA)**. The statute defines a disabled person as someone with a physical or mental impairment that limits one or more "life activities," or who has a record of such impairment. It thus extends the protections of the Civil Rights Act of 1964 to all citizens with physical or mental disabilities. It guarantees access to public facilities, employment, and communication services. Furthermore, it requires employers to acquire or modify work equipment, adjust work schedules, and make existing facilities accessible to those with disabilities. For example, people in wheelchairs must have ready access to buildings, and deaf employees must have telecommunication devices made available to them.

The largest national nonprofit organization lobbying for expanded civil rights for the disabled is the American Association of People with Disabilities (AAPD). Acting on behalf of more than 56 million Americans who suffer from some form of disability, it works in coalition with other disability organizations to make certain that the ADA is implemented fully. The activists who founded AAPD lobbied for the ADA and recognized that "beyond national unity for ADA and our civil rights, people with disabilities did not have a venue or vehicle for working together for common goals."[43]

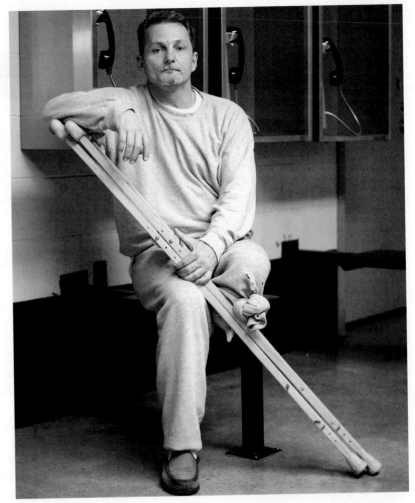

TOWARD REFORM: PROTECTING CIVIL RIGHTS

5.5 Evaluate the standards by which civil rights are protected today.

The definition of equality, as well as conceptions of who deserves equal protection of the laws, has changed dramatically over the course of American history. No provision has done more to change Americans' conceptions of equality than the Fourteenth Amendment. However, as we will discuss below, different types of discrimination are subject to different standards of review under the Amendment's equal protection clause.

The Equal Protection Clause and Constitutional Standards of Review

The Fourteenth Amendment protects all U.S. citizens from state action that violates "equal protection of the laws." The question of what constitutes equal protection has been the subject of much litigation; to make judgments on this issue more straightforward, the Supreme Court has applied three **standards of review**, or the level of deference the Court gives other governments in crafting policies that make distinctions on the basis of personal characteristics, such as race, gender, or sexual orientation. As shown in Table 5.1, most laws are subject to what is called the rational basis or minimum rationality test. This lowest level of scrutiny means that governments must show a rational foundation for any distinctions they make. As early as 1937 and as discussed in Chapter 4, however, the Supreme Court recognized that certain freedoms were so fundamental that a very heavy burden would fall on any government seeking to restrict those rights. When fundamental freedoms such as those guaranteed by the First Amendment or **suspect classifications** such as race are involved, the Court

WHOM DOES THE AMERICANS WITH DISABILITIES ACT PROTECT?

George Lane was the appellant in *Tennessee* v. *Lane* (2004), concerning the scope of the Americans with Disabilities Act, which guarantees the disabled access to public buildings, among other protections. Lane was forced to crawl up two flights of stairs to attend a state court hearing on a misdemeanor charge. Had he not, he could have been jailed.

standards of review
The levels of deference the Court gives governments to craft policies that make distinctions on the basis of personal characteristics. These standards stem from the Court's need to ensure that laws do not undermine the Fourteenth Amendment's equal protection clause.

suspect classifications
Category or class, such as race or a fundamental freedom, that triggers the highest standard of scrutiny from the Supreme Court.

TABLE 5.1 WHAT ARE THE STANDARDS OF REVIEW FASHIONED BY THE COURT UNDER THE EQUAL PROTECTION CLAUSE?

Type of Classification: *What kind of statutory classification is at issue?*	Standard of Review: *What standard of review will be used?*	Test: *What does the Court ask?*	Example: *How does the Court apply the test?*
Fundamental freedoms (including religion, speech, assembly, press, marriage); suspect classifications (including race, alienage, and national origin)	Strict scrutiny or heightened standard	Is the classification necessary to the accomplishment of a permissible state goal? Is it the least restrictive way to reach that goal?	*Brown* v. *Board of Education* (1954): Racial segregation was not necessary to accomplish the state's goal of educating its students.
Gender	Intermediate standard	Does the classification serve an important governmental objective, and is it substantially related to those ends?	*Craig* v. *Boren* (1976): Allowing 18 to 21-year-old women to drink alcohol while prohibiting men of the same age from doing the same is not substantially related to the goal of preventing drunk driving.
Others (including age, wealth, and mental capacity)	Minimum rationality standard	Are the government's actions "rationally" related to a "legitimate" government interest?	*Nebbia* v. *New York*: It was rational for the state to set prices of milk for dairy farmers, dealers, and retailers.

strict scrutiny

A heightened standard of review used by the Supreme Court to determine the constitutional validity of a challenged practice. Legislation affecting the fundamental freedoms of speech, assembly, religion, and the press as well as suspect classifications are automatically accorded this level of review.

affirmative action

Policies designed to give special attention or compensatory treatment to members of a previously disadvantaged group.

uses a heightened standard of review called **strict scrutiny** to determine the constitutional validity of the challenged practices. In legal terms, this means that if a statute or governmental practice makes a classification based on one of these suspect classifications, the statute is presumed to be unconstitutional unless the state can provide "compelling affirmative justifications"—that is, (1) unless the state can prove that the law in question is necessary to accomplish a permissible goal and (2) that it is the least restrictive means of accomplishing that goal.

This strict scrutiny standard was most clearly articulated in *Korematsu* v. *U.S.* (1944), which involved a constitutional challenge to the internment of Japanese Americans as security risks during World War II. In the Court's opinion, Justice Hugo Black noted that "all legal restrictions which curtail the civil rights of a single racial group are immediately suspect" and should be given "the most rigid scrutiny."[44] Despite this, in *Korematsu*, the Court ruled that these internments served a compelling governmental objective and were not discriminatory on their face. In other words, the national security risks posed by Japanese Americans in a time of war were sufficient to justify their internment. During the 2016 presidential primary campaign, Donald Trump announced he would ban Muslim immigrants from entering the United States, relying on *Korematsu*.

Since the 1970s, the Court has applied the strict scrutiny standard in cases involving **affirmative action**, or policies designed to give special attention or compensatory treatment to members of a previously disadvantaged group. In a series of cases involving admissions policies at the University of Michigan, the Court allowed universities to give preference to minority applicants.[45] However, the Court struck down Michigan's undergraduate point system, which gave minority applicants twenty automatic points simply because they were minorities.[46]

In 2016, the Court upheld by a 4-3 ruling a University of Texas affirmative action plan noting that courts must give substantial leeway to colleges to design their admissions programs. Many hailed this decision, *Fisher* v. *University of Texas*, as the most important education discrimination case since *Brown*.[47]

Treatment of gender under the equal protection clause came under scrutiny in a case argued in 1971 by Ruth Bader Ginsburg (later an associate justice of the Supreme Court) as director of the Women's Rights Project of the ACLU. In this case, the Supreme Court ruled that an Idaho law granting a male parent automatic preference over a female parent as the administrator of their deceased child's estate violated the equal protection clause of the Fourteenth Amendment. *Reed* v. *Reed* (1971), the Idaho

AMERICAN POLITICS IN COMPARATIVE PERSPECTIVE

How do Barriers between Nations Compare?

A major theme of Donald J. Trump's 2016 presidential campaign was that he would construct an impenetrable wall all the way along the U.S.-Mexico border. Erecting such walls has a long history but has been associated with closed, authoritarian societies rather than modern democracies. Beginning in the seventh century B.C., for example, China fortified its borders by constructing the its Great Wall. And, following World War II, the repressive East German regime built the Berlin Wall to divide that city into East (communist) and West (democratic) areas. Such historical episodes are repeated today in calls for the construction of a "fence" or a "wall" between the United States and Mexico to stem illegal immigration and drug trafficking. Building a fence, however, poses a dilemma; although it may increase domestic security, it may also strain relations with neighbors and allies around the world. Cost is also an issue.

Construction on the Great Wall of China began as early as 700 B.C. It extends for more than 13,000 miles along the border of China and Mongolia and can be seen from space.

This photo of the Berlin Wall, taken after the reunification of East and West Germany but before the wall was completely demolished, illustrates the effects of the division of the German capital. Note the contrast between the vibrancy of the West and the desertion of the East.

This photo illustrates a small section of the fence between the United States and Mexico in the American Southwest. The fence remains an ongoing debate; hundreds of miles of fence have been constructed in California, Arizona, and New Mexico. Work continues in these states and Texas.

CRITICAL THINKING QUESTIONS

1. What similarities do you see between the walls or fences depicted here? What differences do you observe?
2. Do each of these walls have the same implications for domestic and foreign policy? Why or why not?
3. Do you believe that a border fence is constitutional? What combination of physical boundaries and legal constraints should the United States use to protect its borders from illegal immigrants?

intermediate standard of review
A standard of review in which the Court determines whether classifications serve an important governmental objective and are substantially related to serving that objective. Gender-related legislation automatically accorded this level of review.

rational basis standard of review
A standard of review in which the Court determines whether any rational foundation for the discrimination exists. Legislation affecting individuals based on age, wealth, mental capacity are generally given this level of review.

case, turned the tide in terms of constitutional litigation. Although the Court did not rule that sex was a suspect classification, for the first time it concluded that the equal protection clause of the Fourteenth Amendment prohibited unreasonable classifications based on sex.[48]

In 1976, the Court ruled that sex discrimination complaints would be judged according to a new, judicially created intermediate standard of review a step below strict scrutiny.[49] In *Craig* v. *Boren* (1976), the Court carved out a new test for examining claims of sex discrimination alleged to violate the U.S. Constitution: "to withstand constitutional challenge, . . . classifications by gender must serve important governmental objectives and must be substantially related to achievement of those objectives." According to the Court, it created an **intermediate standard of review** within what previously was a two-tier distinction—strict scrutiny and rational basis.

The level of review used by the Court has a crucial impact on the status of civil rights in the United States. Clearly, a statute excluding African Americans from draft registration would be unconstitutional. But, because gender is not subject to the same higher standard of review used in racial discrimination cases, the Court has ruled the exclusion of women from requirements of the Military Selective Service Act permissible because the policy serves "important governmental objectives."[50] Still, because women now can be placed in all military positions, including combat roles, the Congress in 2016 began deliberating a requirement for women to register for the draft.

Standards for review of statutes involving sexual orientation remain undecided in some areas but not all. The Court has long held that marriage is a fundamental right but its decision in *Windsor* left commentators unsure of the standard of review used by the Court for same-sex marriage. In *Obergefell* v. *Hodges* (2015), the Court narrowly ruled that marriage is a fundamental freedom. Thus, restrictions on same-sex marriage are to be treated with strict scrutiny.

The **rational basis standard of review**, which the Court first clearly enunciated in *Nebbia* v. *New York* (1934) is fairly clear cut.[51] Basically, if the Court finds no fundamental liberty interest or a suspect classification, the Court will allow the law to stand as constitutional as long as it is rationally related to a legitimate government interest. Thus, in *Nebbia*, New York's desire to set prices on milk was deemed within it constitutional authority to regulate for the health and welfare of its citizens. Categories dealing with wealth and age still fall under this standard of review. Many decisions giving heightened scrutiny to some groups, such as members of the LGBT community, were decided by 5-4 or 5-3 decisions. As such, the appointment of a conservative justice by President Donald J. Trump could lead the Court to reverse itself, limiting rights for affected groups.

REVIEW THE CHAPTER

Roots of Civil Rights

5.1 Trace the roots of movements to guarantee rights to African Americans and women.

When the Framers tried to compromise on the issue of slavery, they only postponed dealing with a volatile question that eventually would rip the nation apart. Southern states with large populations of slaves feared the loss of the cheap labor that made their agricultural economy so profitable. Ultimately, the Civil War brought an end to slavery. Among its results were the triumph of the abolitionist position and the adoption of the Thirteenth, Fourteenth, and Fifteenth Amendments. During this period, women also sought expanded rights, especially the right to vote, to no avail.

The Push for Equality, 1890–1954

5.2 Outline developments in African Americans' and women's push for equality from 1890 to 1954.

Although the Civil War Amendments became part of the Constitution, the Supreme Court limited their application. As legislatures throughout the South passed Jim Crow laws, the NAACP was founded in the early 1900s to press for equal rights for African Americans. Women's groups also were active during this period, successfully lobbying for passage of the Nineteenth Amendment, which ensured them the right to vote.

Statutory Protections for Civil Rights, 1955–Present

5.3 Analyze the legal protections enacted for African Americans' and women's civil rights since 1955.

African Americans used bus boycotts, sit-ins, freedom rides, pressure for voting rights enforcement, and massive nonviolent demonstrations to win greater protection for their civil rights. These efforts culminated in passage of the Civil Rights Act of 1964. Women's rights activists won passage of the Equal Pay Act of 1963 and the Civil Rights Act of 1964. However, the new women's rights movement was unsuccessful in achieving passage of the Equal Rights Amendment.

Other Groups Mobilize for Rights

5.4 Summarize the struggles of other group-differentiated minorities for civil rights.

Building on the successes of African Americans and women, other groups, including Hispanics, American Indians, Asian and Pacific Island Americans, the LGBT community, and those with disabilities, organized to litigate for expanded civil rights and to lobby for anti-discrimination laws.

Toward Reform: Protecting Civil Rights

5.5 Evaluate the standards by which civil rights are protected today.

No provision has done more to change Americans' conceptions of equality than the Fourteenth Amendment's equal protection clause. Claims brought under this clause are evaluated using three standards of review. In general, strict scrutiny, the most stringent standard, is applied to race-based claims and cases involving fundamental freedoms. The Court developed an intermediate standard of review to assess the constitutionality of sex discrimination claims. All other claims are subject to the rational basis test.

LEARN THE TERMS

abolitionist
affirmative action
Americans with Disabilities Act (ADA)
Brown v. *Board of Education* (1954)
Cesar Chavez

civil rights
Chinese Exclusion Act
Civil Rights Act of 1875
Civil Rights Act of 1964
Dolores Huerta
Dred Scott v. *Sandford* (1857)

Dwight D. Eisenhower
Eleanor Roosevelt
Elizabeth Cady Stanton
Emancipation Proclamation
Equal Pay Act of 1963
equal protection clause

Equal Rights Amendment (ERA)
Fifteenth Amendment
Fourteenth Amendment
Frederick Douglass
grandfather clause
Harriet Tubman
Harry S Truman
intermediate standard of review
Jim Crow laws
John F. Kennedy
Korematsu v. *U.S.* (1944)
Lawrence v. *Texas* (2003)
League of United Latin American
    Citizens (LULAC)
LGBT community

Lucretia Mott
Martin Luther King Jr.
Mexican American Legal Defense and
    Educational Fund (MALDEF)
National American Woman Suffrage
    Association (NAWSA)
National Association for the Advance-
    ment of Colored People (NAACP)
NAACP Legal Defense and Educa-
    tional Fund (LDF)
National Organization for Women (NOW)
National Woman's Party (NWP)
Nineteenth Amendment
Obergefell v. *Hodges* (2015)
Plessy v. *Ferguson* (1896)

poll tax
Progressive Era (1890-1920)
rational basis standard of review
Rosa Parks
Seneca Falls Convention
separate-but-equal doctrine
standards of review
strict scrutiny
suffrage movement
Susan B. Anthony
suspect classifications
Thirteenth Amendment
Title IX
Thurgood Marshall
United States v. *Windsor* (2013)

SOUTHERN CHIVALRY — ARGUMENT VERSUS CLUB'S.

IS PARTISANSHIP IN CONGRESS NEW?

This 1856 lithograph shows South Carolina Representative Preston Brooks beating abolitionist Massachusetts Senator Charles Sumner in the United States Senate chamber. This is a Northern depiction condemning the violence against Sumner; whereas in the South, Preston Brooks was honored for his actions.

SOURCE: Lithograph by J.L. Magee. (Photo by New York Historical Society/Getty Images)

CONGRESS

LEARNING OBJECTIVES

6.1 Describe the constitutional provisions that define Congress.

6.2 Analyze the ability of members of Congress to represent their constituents.

6.3 Describe how incumbency and redistricting help members of Congress to stay in office.

6.4 Assess the roles of leaders, political parties, and committees in Congress.

6.5 Describe the powers of Congress.

6.6 Describe the factors that influence how members of Congress make decisions.

6.7 Evaluate the strategic interactions between Congress, the president, the courts, and the people.

bicameral legislature
A two-house legislature.

I n the 1830s through the 1850s, heated arguments about slavery often lead to violence on the floor of Congress. In a fight on the floor of the House in 1836, members were observed with pistols brandished. Later in the year, a House committee meeting was dissolved when a member, distraught by the testimony of a witness, drew his pistol. The meeting was cancelled and the member was charged with contempt of Congress.

In 1842, after Representative Thomas Arnold of Tennessee, a member of the House who belonged to the Whig Party, publicly criticized a fellow Whig for his support of slavery, two Southern Democrats, one brandishing a bowie knife, called Arnold a "damned coward," and threatened to cut him from ear to ear. Arnold held his own; just ten years before he had stopped an armed assassin as he tried to enter the Capitol.

These examples of the lack of civility evident in the halls of Congress are far from a complete record. Reporters often did not report these types of incidents because they were also subject to similar threats or violence for their writings.

In 1856, emotions came to a peak when Representative Preston Brooks (D–SC) went to the Senate floor and beat Senator Charles Sumner (R–MA), an ardent abolitionist, with a gold-headed cane in retaliation for a speech Sumner had made against slavery two days earlier. Sumner was so badly injured that he had to be carried off the floor and was unable to resume his duties for three years due to the grievous nature of his injuries. Brooks was declared a hero by the South, and Sumner was declared a martyr by the North—further inflaming tensions over slavery.

● ● ●

The Framers' original conception of Congress's authority was much narrower than it is today. Those in attendance at the Constitutional Convention wished to create a legislative body that would be able to make laws as well as raise and spend revenues. Over time, Congress has attempted to maintain these roles, but changes in demands made on the national government have allowed the executive and judicial branches to gain powers at the expense of the legislative branch. Moreover, the power and the importance of individual members have grown.

Today, members of Congress must combine and balance the roles of lawmaker, budgeter, and policy maker with acting as a representative of their district, state, party, and sometimes race, ethnicity, or gender. Not surprisingly, this balancing act often results in role conflict.

In this chapter, we analyze the powers of Congress and the competing roles members play as they represent the interests of their constituents, make laws, and oversee actions of the other two branches of government. We also show that as these functions have changed throughout U.S. history, so has Congress itself.

ROOTS OF THE U.S. CONGRESS

6.1 Describe the constitutional provisions that define Congress.

Article I of the Constitution describes the structure of the legislative branch of government. The Great Compromise at the Constitutional Convention resulted in the creation of a lower house, the House of Representatives, and an upper house, the Senate. Any two-house legislature, such as the one created by the Framers, is called a **bicameral legislature**. The population of each state determines the number of representatives that state sends to the House of Representatives. In contrast, two senators represent each state in the Senate, regardless of the state's population.

Article I of the U.S. Constitution sets forth the formal, or legal, requirements for membership in the House and Senate. As agreed to at the Constitutional Convention, House members must be at least twenty-five years of age; senators, thirty. Members of the House must be citizens of the United States for at least seven years; those elected to the Senate, at least nine years. Both representatives and senators must be legal residents of the states from which they are elected.

Today, many members of Congress find the job exciting and fulfilling in spite of public criticism of the institution. But, it wasn't always so. Until Washington, D.C., got air-conditioning and drained its swamps, it was a miserable town. Most representatives spent as little time there as possible, viewing Congress, especially the House, as a stepping stone to other political positions back home. Only after World War I did most House members become congressional careerists who viewed their work in Washington as long term.[1]

The eligible electorate in each congressional district votes to elect members of the House of Representatives to two-year terms. The Framers expected that House members would be more responsible to the people, both because they were elected directly by them and because they were up for reelection every two years. The U.S. Constitution requires that a census, which entails the counting of all Americans, be conducted every ten years. Until the first census could be taken, the Constitution fixed the number of representatives in the House of Representatives at sixty-five. In 1790, one member represented about 30,000 people. But, as the population of the new nation grew and states were added to the union, the House became larger and larger. In 1910, it expanded to 435 members, and in 1929, its size was fixed at that number by statute. When Alaska and Hawaii became states in the 1950s, however, the number of seats increased to 437. The number reverted to 435 in 1963.

Each state is granted its share of these 435 representatives on the basis of its population. After each U.S. Census, a constitutionally mandated process called **apportionment** adjusts the number of seats allotted to each state. After seats are apportioned, state legislatures must redraw congressional districts to reflect population shifts, thereby ensuring that each member in Congress represents approximately the same number of residents. This process of redrawing congressional districts to reflect increases or decreases in the number of seats allotted to a state, as well as population shifts within a state, is called redistricting. It is discussed in greater detail later in this chapter.

Senators are elected to six-year terms, and originally state legislatures chose them because the Framers intended senators to represent their states' interests in

apportionment
The process of allotting congressional seats to each state according to its proportion of the population, following the decennial census.

HOW LONG ARE MEMBERS' TERMS?

Members of the Senate serve six-year terms, while members of the House of Representatives serve for two years. There are no term limits, so members may run for reelection for an unlimited number of terms. The advantages of incumbency make turnover in Congress very low; new members such as Elise Stefanik (R-NY), the youngest woman ever elected to the institution, constitute only a small percentage of representatives. She chairs the House's Millennial Task Force.

TABLE 6.1 WHAT ARE THE POWERS OF CONGRESS?

The powers of Congress, found in Article I, section 8, of the Constitution, include the powers to:
Lay and collect taxes and duties.
Borrow money.
Regulate commerce with foreign nations and among the states.
Establish rules for naturalization (the process of becoming a citizen) and bankruptcy.
Coin money, set its value, and fix the standard of weights and measures.
Punish counterfeiting.
Establish a post office and post roads.
Issue patents and copyrights.
Define and punish piracies, felonies on the high seas, and crimes against the law of nations.
Create courts inferior to (below) the U.S. Supreme Court.
Declare war.
Raise and support an army and navy and make rules for their governance.
Provide for a militia (reserving to the states the right to appoint militia officers and to train militias under congressional rules).
Exercise legislative powers over the seat of government (the District of Columbia) and over places purchased to be federal facilities (forts, arsenals, dockyards, and "other needful buildings").
"Make all Laws which shall be necessary and proper for carrying into Execution the foregoing Powers, and all other Powers vested by this Constitution in the government of the United States."

bill
A proposed law.

impeachment
The power delegated to the House of Representatives in the Constitution to charge the president, vice president, or other "civil officers," including federal judges, with "Treason, Bribery, or other high Crimes and Misdemeanors." This is the first step in the constitutional process of removing government officials from office.

the Senate. State legislators lost this influence over the Senate with the ratification of the Seventeenth Amendment in 1913, which provides for the direct election of senators by voters. Then, as now, one-third of all senators are up for reelection every two years.

The Constitution specifically gives Congress its most important powers: the authorities to make laws and raise and spend revenues. No **bill**, or proposed law, can become law without the consent of both houses. Examples of other powers shared by both houses include the power to declare war, raise an army and navy, coin money, regulate commerce, establish the federal courts and their jurisdiction, set forth rules of immigration and naturalization, and "make all Laws which shall be necessary and proper for carrying into Execution the foregoing Powers." As interpreted by the U.S. Supreme Court, the necessary and proper clause, found at the end of Article I, section 8, when coupled with one or more of the specific powers enumerated in Article I, section 8, has allowed Congress to increase the scope of its authority, often at the expense of the states and into areas not necessarily envisioned by the Framers (see Table 6.1).

The Constitution gives formal law-making powers to Congress alone. But, it is important to remember that presidents issue proclamations, executive orders, and executive agreements with the force of law; bureaucrats issue quasi-legislative rules and are charged with enforcing laws, rules, and regulations; and the Supreme Court and lower federal courts render opinions that generate principles also having the force of law.

Reflecting the different constituencies and size of each house of Congress (as well as the Framers' intentions), Article I gives special, exclusive powers to each house in addition to their shared role in law-making. For example, as noted in Table 6.2, the Constitution specifies that all revenue bills must originate in the House of Representatives.

Over the years, however, this mandate has become less clear, and it is not unusual to see budget bills being considered simultaneously in both houses. Ultimately, each house must approve all bills in their exact wording. The House also has the power of **impeachment**, or to charge the president, vice president, or other

TABLE 6.2 WHAT ARE THE KEY CONSTITUTIONAL DIFFERENCES BETWEEN THE HOUSE OF REPRESENTATIVES AND THE SENATE?

House	Senate
435 voting members (apportioned by population)	100 voting members (two from each state)
Two-year terms	Six-year terms (one-third up for reelection every two years)
Initiates all revenue bills	Offers "advice and consent" on many major presidential appointments
Initiates impeachment procedures and passes articles of impeachment	Tries impeached officials
	Approves treaties

"civil officers," including federal judges, with "Treason, Bribery, or other high Crimes and Misdemeanors." But, only the Senate has authority to conduct impeachment trials, with a two-thirds "yea" vote being necessary to remove a federal official, such as the president or a judge, from office.

AMERICAN POLITICS IN COMPARATIVE PERSPECTIVE

How Many Legislative Houses? One, Two, or One-and-a-Half?

In the United States, the two houses of Congress that make up the national legislature have robust powers. The House of Representatives and Senate have authority over legislation, budget authorizations, constitutional amendments, and oversight of the bureaucracy. "Symmetric bicameralism" is the term used by political scientists to describe a legislature like the U.S. Congress or Mexico's Congress of the Union that consists of two houses with an even balance of powers. This is not the only model used among democracies in the world, however. "Unicameralism" refers to legislative systems such as Israel's Knesset that consist of a single chamber. "Asymmetric bicameralism" refers to legislative systems with two unequal chambers like India's national legislature. These structural differences can have a major impact on how, and even whether, legislation can be enacted in different systems.

The national legislature of Israel, the Knesset, is a single chamber with 120 members. Israel is a parliamentary system in which most majorities are coalitions of several different parties.

India's national legislature has a lower house directly elected by voters and an upper house indirectly elected by state legislatures. The lower house may bypass the upper house on most issues.

Mexico has a bicameral legislature with two equal houses. Mexico's president is elected separately and constitutes a distinct executive branch of government equal to Congress.

CRITICAL THINKING QUESTIONS

1. Would it be more or less difficult to enact legislation under unicameralism, asymmetric bicameralism, or symmetric bicameralism? How might legislative structure have a positive or negative influence on a country's governance?

2. Is it important for geographic and other minorities to have an enhanced political voice through an upper house? What might be lost under a unicameral system?

3. How would Congress be different if it had only a single chamber? Who would be the "winners and losers" under such an institutional configuration?

The Senate also has the sole authority to approve major presidential appointments, including federal judges, ambassadors, and Cabinet- and sub–Cabinet-level positions by a simple majority vote. The Senate, too, must approve all presidential treaties by a two-thirds vote.

REPRESENTING THE AMERICAN PEOPLE

6.2 Analyze the ability of members of Congress to represent their constituents.

Members must attempt to represent varied constituencies—party leaders, colleagues, and lobbyists in Washington, D.C., and voters at home.[2] In attempting to do so, members spend full days in their home districts as well as in D.C. (see Table 6.3). According to one study of House members, average representatives made about forty trips back home to their districts each year.[3] One member from a safe district, however, admitted spending no more than 180 days in his district…the minimum for legal residency in the state.[4] One journalist has aptly described a member's days as a

> …kaleidoscopic jumble: breakfast with reporters, morning staff meetings, simultaneous committee hearings to juggle, back-to-back sessions with lobbyists and constituents, phone calls, briefings, constant buzzers interrupting office work to make quorum calls and votes on the run, afternoon speeches, evening meetings, receptions, fund-raisers, all crammed into four days so they can race home for a weekend gauntlet of campaigning. It's a rat race.[5]

One research report on Congress found that members worked an average of seventy hours per week while in Washington and fifty-nine hours per week when Congress was not in session.[6] While this report found that members' political and campaign work took up less than 20 percent of their time, another source revealed that a slide presentation for incoming Democratic freshmen assumed a 9- to 10-hour workday, with four hours per day set aside for "call time" (telephone fundraising conducted outside the members' office per federal election law) and an hour set aside for tasks such as meet and greets and media outreach.[7]

TABLE 6.3   WHAT IS A TYPICAL DAY LIKE FOR A MEMBER OF CONGRESS?

5:00 a.m.	Arrive at office.
7:00 a.m.	Give a tour of the U.S. Capitol to high donor constituents.
8:00 a.m.	Eat breakfast with the House Shipbuilding Caucus.
9:00 a.m.	Meet with Speaker of the House and other members of Congress.
10:00 a.m.	Attend House Armed Services Committee hearing.
11:00 a.m.	Prepare for afternoon press conference, return phone calls, and sign constituent mail.
12:00 p.m.	Meet with constituents who want the member to join a caucus that may benefit the district.
1:00 p.m.	Glance at several local and national newspapers to keep track of current events.
2:00 p.m.	Attend Homeland Security Subcommittee hearing.
3:00 p.m.	Attend floor vote.
3:30 p.m.	Meet with group of high school students on front steps of Capitol.
4:15 p.m.	Return to office to sign more constituent mail and to meet with representatives of the American Heart Association.
5:00 p.m.	Attend Sustainable Energy and Environment Caucus meeting.
6:00 p.m.	Fundraising Call Time—Party HQ
7:00 p.m.	Attend fundraiser.
9:00 p.m.	Return to office to sign more constituent mail and read more newspapers.
11:00 p.m.	Leave office to go home.

SOURCE: Adapted from Bob Clark, "A Day in the Life …" *Evening Tribune* (October 7, 2009), www.eveningtribune.com (accessed October 20, 2010).

**WHO ARE THE NONVOTING
MEMBERS REPRESENTING
WASHINGTON, D.C.?**
Shadow Senators Paul Strauss (rear)
and Michael Brown (left) and Delegate
Eleanor Holmes Norton (center), all
Democrats, represent Washington,
D.C., in the Senate and the House,
respectively. When Democrats held
the House, Norton was allowed to cast
votes in committee, a privilege she
lost in 2011 when Republicans gained
control of the House. D.C.'s two
shadow senators have no voting rights
or legal standing and their offices are
paid for by the people of the District of
Columbia.

Congressional Demographics

One measure of the representativeness of Congress is how well members' demographic characteristics reflect those of the American public. A cursory examination of these characteristics reveals that Congress is better educated, richer, more male, and whiter than the general population. More than two-thirds of the members of the House and Senate also hold advanced degrees.[8]

Many members of both houses have significant inherited wealth, but given their educational attainment, which is far higher than the average American's, it is not surprising to find so many wealthy members of Congress. More than half of all members of Congress are millionaires. The Senate, in fact, is often called the Millionaires Club. The average net worth of a House member today is nearly $7 million, while the average net worth of a senator is more than $12.5 million.

The average member of Congress is also older than the American public. Members of the House average 57 years of age; senators average 62 years of age.

Members of Congress are more religious than the general public. The highest percentage of House members identify as Protestants and are overrepresented in comparison to their percentage of the population, as are Roman Catholics and Jews. In contrast, nonreligious Americans and minority religious groups, such as Muslims and members of Eastern religions, are significantly underrepresented (see Figure 6.1).

The 2016 elections produced many new faces, with almost 50 new members slated to join the 115th Congress. The elections posted few gains for minority groups. While three of the four women elected to the Senate were racial or ethnic minorities, the overall number of women in the House remained static. Nine new women of color were elected to the House bringing their total number to 33, however. The number of African Americans grew by two overall, while the number of Asian Pacific Islanders and American Indians in the 115th Congress remained the same. So, too, did the number of openly LGBT incumbents (a total of six), although none of the thirteen members of the LGBT community seeking new seats won election. Collectively, the 115th Congress looks quite a bit like the 114th, with Republicans retaining control of both houses.

FIGURE 6.1 HOW WELL DOES THE HOUSE OF REPRESENTATIVES REFLECT THE AMERICAN PEOPLE?

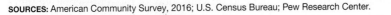

Membership in the House of Representatives is more diverse than ever before, but ethnic and racial minorities and women remain significantly underrepresented relative to their proportions of the population. Non-Hispanic whites are 62 percent of the American population but still make up 80 percent of House members; likewise, men are a bit less than half the population but hold more than 80 percent of House seats. These pie charts reflect the demographics of the 435 members of the 114th Congress (2015–2017) and do not include non-voting delegates from American Samoa, the District of Columbia, Guam, the U.S. Virgin Islands, the Northern Mariana Islands, and Puerto Rico.

SOURCES: American Community Survey, 2016; U.S. Census Bureau; Pew Research Center.

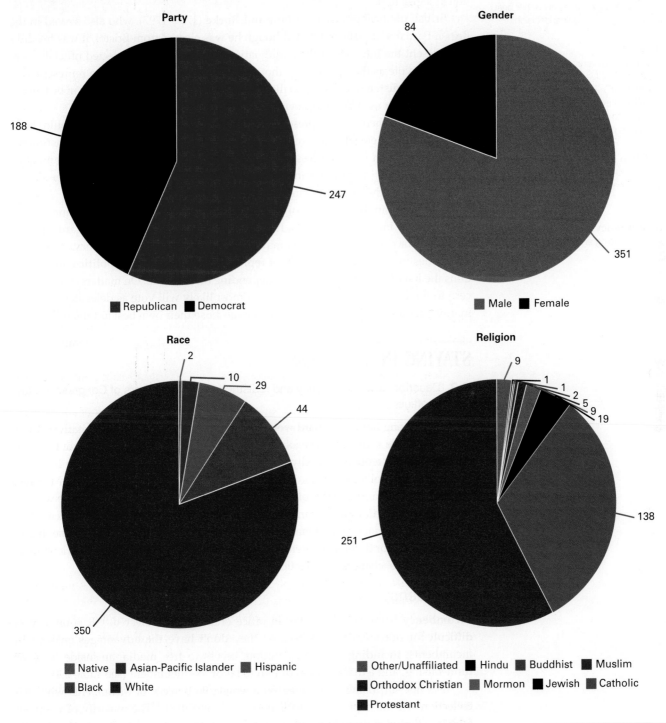

Edmund Burke
Conservative British political philosopher of the eighteenth century who articulated the view that elected representatives should act as "trustees" and use their own best judgement when voting.

trustee
Role played by an elected representative who listens to constituents' opinions and then uses his or her best judgment to make a final decision.

delegate
Role played by a representative who votes the way his or her constituents would want, regardless of personal opinions; may refer to an elected representative to Congress or a representative to the party convention.

politico
An elected representative who acts as a trustee or as a delegate, depending on the issue.

incumbency
Already holding an office.

Representational Strategies

In addition to acting as physical representatives of their constituents, members of Congress must also represent their constituents' substantive policy interests. Over the years, political theorists have offered various ideas about how any legislative body can best achieve these goals. Are members of Congress, for example, bound to vote the way their constituents expect them to vote, even if they personally favor another policy? Your answer to these questions may depend on your view of the representative function of legislators.

British political philosopher **Edmund Burke** (1729–1797), who also served in the British Parliament, believed that although he was elected from Bristol, it was his duty to represent the interests of the entire nation. He reasoned that elected officials were obliged to vote as they personally thought best. According to Burke, a representative should be a **trustee** who listens to the opinions of constituents and then can be trusted to use his or her own best judgment to make final decisions.

A second theory of representation holds that a representative should be a **delegate**. True delegates are representatives who vote the way their constituents would want them to, regardless of their own opinions. Delegates, therefore, must be ready and willing to vote against their conscience or personal policy preferences if they know how their constituents feel about a particular issue.

Not surprisingly, members of Congress and other legislative bodies generally do not fall neatly into either category. It is often unclear how constituents regard a particular issue, or conflicting opinions may arise within a single constituency. With these difficulties in mind, a third theory of representation holds that a **politico** alternately dons the hat of a trustee or delegate, depending on the issue. On matters of great concern to their constituents, representatives most likely will vote as delegates; on other matters, representatives will act as trustees and use their own best judgment.[9]

STAYING IN CONGRESS

6.3 Describe how incumbency and redistricting help members of Congress to stay in office.

Despite the long hours and hard work required of senators and representatives, thousands of people aspire to these jobs every year. Yet, only 535 men and women (plus six nonvoting members) actually serve in the U.S. Congress. Membership in one of the two major political parties is almost always a prerequisite for election because election laws in various states often discriminate against independents (those without party affiliation) and minor-party candidates. The ability to raise money often is key to any member's victory, and many members spend nearly all of their free time on the phone, dialing for dollars, or attending fundraisers. Incumbency and redistricting also affect members' chances at reelection.

Incumbency

Incumbency helps members stay in office once they are elected.[10] It is often very difficult for outsiders to win because they don't have the advantages enjoyed by incumbents, including name recognition, access to free media, an inside track on fund-raising, and a district often drawn to favor the incumbent (see Table 6.4).

It is not surprising, then, that, on average, 96 percent of incumbents who seek reelection win their primary and general election races.[11] The majority of members who lose their reelection bids are affected by redistricting.

In 2016, incumbents were re-elected in record numbers. While forty-three members did not seek re-election, only eight incumbents lost their re-election bids. All but one loss was a Democrat to a Republican. In the Senate, only one incumbent, Kelly Ayotte (R-NH) lost her seat in a close race against Democratic Governor Maggie Hassan.

TABLE 6.4   WHAT ARE THE ADVANTAGES OF INCUMBENCY?

Name recognition. Members' names have been on the ballot before, and voters may associate their names with programs or social services they have brought to the district.

Credit claiming. Members may claim to be responsible for federal money brought to the district.

Casework. Members and their staffs help constituents solve problems with the government, including navigating red tape and tracking down federal aid.

Franking privilege. Members may send mail or newsletters for free by using their signature in place of a stamp.

Access to media. Members and their staffs may have relationships with reporters and may find it easy to spin stories or give quotes.

Ease in fund-raising. Incumbents' high reelection rates make them a safe bet for individuals or groups wanting to give donations in exchange for access.

Experience in running a campaign. Members have already put together a campaign staff, made speeches, and come to understand constituent concerns.

Redistricting. In the House, a member's district may be drawn to enhance electability.

Redistricting

The process of redrawing congressional districts to reflect increases or decreases in seats allotted to the states, as well as population shifts within a state, is called **redistricting**. Redistricting is a largely political process. In most states, partisan state legislatures draw district lines. As a result, the majority party in the state legislature uses the redistricting process as an opportunity to ensure formation of voting districts that protect their majority. The process of drawing congressional districts can therefore become highly contentious. In recent years, redistricting battles in many states have become increasingly personal, with members of some state legislatures even walking out during the process. Hoping to avoid this sort of political high theater, some states, including Iowa and Arizona, appoint nonpartisan committees or use some other independent means of drawing district lines. Although the processes vary in detail, most states require legislative approval of redistricting plans.

The redistricting process often involves **gerrymandering**—the drawing of congressional districts to produce a particular electoral outcome without regard to the shape of the district (see Figure 6.2). Because of enormous population growth, the partisan implications of redistricting, and the requirement under the Voting Rights Act of 1965 for minorities to have an equal chance to elect candidates of their choice, legislators end up drawing oddly shaped districts to elect more members of their party.[12] Redistricting plans routinely meet with court challenges across the country. In its 2016–2017 term the Court will hear a case involving the use of race in redistricting. The outcome of that decision is likely to be determined when the 2016 vacancy on the Court is filled by President Donald J. Trump.[13]

For a long time, the U.S. Supreme Court considered redistricting based on partisan considerations to be a political question not within the scope of constitutional law but rather one worked out through the regular political process.[14] But, in recent years, the Supreme Court has involved itself in some such cases and has ruled as follows:

- Congressional and state legislative districts may be apportioned on the basis of population.[15]
- District lines must be contiguous; one must be able to draw the boundaries of the district with a single unbroken line.[16]
- Purposeful gerrymandering of a congressional district to dilute minority strength is illegal under the Voting Rights Act of 1965.[17]
- Redrawing districts to enhance minority representation is constitutional if race is not the "predominant" factor.[18]
- States may redistrict more frequently than every ten years.[19]

redistricting
The process of redrawing congressional districts to reflect increases or decreases in seats allotted to the states, as well as population shifts within a state.

gerrymandering
The drawing of congressional districts to produce a particular electoral outcome without regard to the shape of the district.

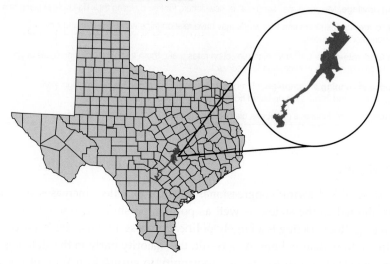

FIGURE 6.2   WHAT IS GERRYMANDERING?

This map of a Texas congressional district created after the 2010 Census illustrates the bizarre geographical contortions that result from gerrymandering. The term was coined by combining the last name of the Massachusetts governor first credited with politicizing the redistricting process, Elbridge Gerry, and the word "salamander," which looked like the oddly shaped district that Gerry created.

Texas 35th District, 2012

majority party
The political party in each house of Congress with the most members.

minority party
The political party in each house of Congress with the second most members.

party caucus (or conference)
A formal gathering of all party members.

Redistricting decisions may have significant consequences for members of Congress. The boundaries of a member's district determine the demographic and partisan makeup of their constituency. In districts that heavily favor members of one party over another, it may be hard to have competitive elections, and voters from the minority party may feel alienated from the political process. Some commentators suggest that increasingly partisan congressional redistricting is a major contributor to the high levels of partisanship exhibited in recent Congresses.

HOW CONGRESS IS ORGANIZED

6.4 Assess the role of leaders, political parties, and committees in Congress.

As demonstrated in Figure 6.3, the organization of both houses of Congress is closely tied to political parties and their strength in each house. The basic division in Congress is between majority and minority parties. The **majority party** in each house is the party with the most members. The **minority party** in each house is the party with the second most members (see Figure 6.3).

At the beginning of each new Congress, the members of each party formally gather in their **party caucus (or conference)** (see Figure 6.4 for the partisan composition of Congress). Historically, these caucuses have enjoyed varied powers, but today the party caucuses have several roles, including nominating or electing party officers, reviewing committee assignments, discussing party policy, imposing party discipline, setting party themes, and coordinating media. Conference and caucus chairs are recognized party leaders who work with other leaders in the House or Senate.[20]

Each caucus or conference has specialized committees that fulfill certain tasks. House Republicans, for example, have a Committee on Committees that makes committee assignments.

The Democrats' Steering Committee performs this function. Each party also has congressional campaign committees to assist members in their reelection bids.

FIGURE 6.3 HOW ARE THE HOUSE OF REPRESENTATIVES AND THE SENATE ORGANIZED?

Parties play a very important role in organizing both the House and Senate. The majority and minority leaders are chosen by the party caucus or conference, as are other key leaders in the party hierarchy. This structure helps to organize operations and conflict in each of the institutions.

SOURCE: Walter H. Davidson, et al., *Congress and Its Members*, 14th ed. (Washington, DC: CQ Press, 2014.)

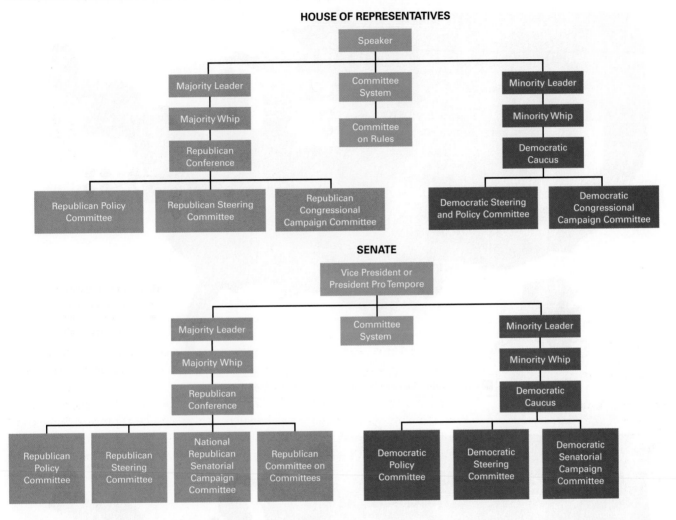

Leadership in the House of Representatives

Even in the first Congress in 1789, the House of Representatives was almost three times larger than the Senate. It is not surprising, then, that from the beginning the House has shown tighter organization, more elaborate structure, and governance by stricter rules. Traditionally, loyalty to party leadership and voting along party lines have been more common in the House than in the Senate. House leaders also play a key role in moving the business of the House along. Historically, the Speaker of the House, the majority and minority leaders, and the Republican and Democratic House whips have made up the party leadership that runs the institution.

THE SPEAKER OF THE HOUSE The **Speaker of the House**, the chamber's most powerful position, is the only officer of the House of Representatives specifically mentioned in the Constitution. The office follows a model similar to the British Parliament—the Speaker was the one who spoke to the king and conveyed the wishes of the House of Commons to the monarch.[21]

The entire House of Representatives elects the Speaker at the beginning of each new Congress, or in the case of death or resignation of the Speaker, soon after the vacancy occurs. Traditionally, the Speaker is a member of the majority party. Although typically not the member with the longest service, the Speaker generally has served in

Speaker of the House
The only officer of the House of Representatives specifically mentioned in the Constitution; the chamber's most powerful position; traditionally a member of the majority party.

FIGURE 6.4   WHAT IS THE PARTISAN COMPOSITION OF THE 115TH CONGRESS?

The partisan composition of the 115th Congress is quite similar to the 114th Congress, with Republicans holding the majority in the House of Representatives and the Senate. Democrats made small gains in each of the houses, but it was not enough to switch overall control.

SOURCE: CNN Races and Results, www.cnn.com/election/2016/results/race/house and www.cnn.com/election/2016/results/race/senate

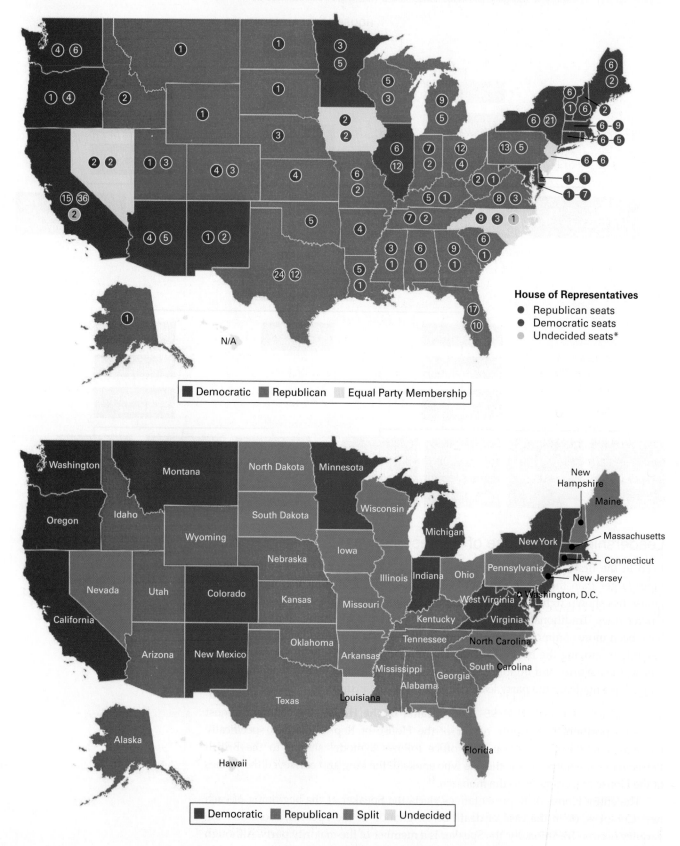

House of Representatives
- Republican seats
- Democratic seats
- Undecided seats*

Democratic   Republican   Equal Party Membership

Democratic   Republican   Split   Undecided

WHO WAS THE FIRST FEMALE SPEAKER OF THE HOUSE?

Nancy Pelosi was the first woman Speaker, and served in that role between January 2007 and January 2011. A strong Speaker, she was known for her ability to count votes before allowing any bill on the floor, resulting in the highest levels of party unity in recent history.

the House for a long time and in other House leadership positions as an apprentice. Speaker Paul Ryan (R–WI) was in office sixteen years before being elected to the position in 2015. Ryan accepted the position somewhat reluctantly because the ideological diversity of Republicans in the House makes governing difficult. The stakes are high for him to produce a more cohesive party with new legislation to show. The House in the 114th Congress through the end of 2016 was one of the least productive in history. Ryan was also challenged in his efforts to unite his party behind presidential candidate Donald Trump. Ryan's support for Trump was itself guarded and how well the two can work together is something to watch.

The Speaker presides over the House of Representatives, oversees House business, serves as the official spokesperson for the House, and is second in the line of presidential succession (after the vice president). The Speaker is also expected to smooth the passage of party-backed legislation through the House. To aid in this process, the Speaker generally has great political influence within the chamber and in policy negotiations with the president.

LEADERSHIP TEAMS   After the Speaker, the next most powerful people in the House are the majority and minority leaders, who are elected in their individual party caucuses or conferences. The **majority leader** is the head of the party controlling the most seats in the House; his or her counterpart in the party with the second highest number of seats is the **minority leader**. The majority leader helps the Speaker schedule proposed legislation for debate on the House floor.

The Republican and Democratic **whips**, who are elected by party members in caucuses, assist the Speaker and majority and minority leaders in their leadership efforts. The position of whip originated in the British House of Commons, where it was named after the "whipper in," the rider who keeps the hounds together in a fox hunt. Party whips—first designated in the U.S. House of Representatives in 1899—do, as their name suggests, try to whip fellow Democrats or Republicans into line on partisan issues. They try to maintain close contact with all members on important votes, prepare summaries of content and implications of bills, take vote counts during debates and votes, and in general persuade members to toe the party line. Whips and their deputy whips also serve as communications links, distributing word of the party line from leaders to rank-and-file members and alerting leaders to concerns in the ranks. These tasks are more difficult today, especially within the Republican Party.

majority leader
The head of the party controlling the most seats in the House of Representatives or the Senate; is second in authority to the Speaker of the House and in the Senate is regarded as its most powerful member.

minority leader
The head of the party with the second highest number of elected representatives in the House of Representatives or the Senate.

whip
Party leader who keeps close contact with all members of his or her party, takes vote counts on key legislation, prepares summaries of bills, and acts as a communications link within a party.

president pro tempore
The official chair of the Senate; usually the most senior member of the majority party.

Leadership in the Senate

Organization and formal rules never have played the same role in the Senate as in the House. Through the 1960s, the Senate was a gentlemen's club whose folkways—unwritten rules of behavior—governed its operation. One such folkway, for example, stipulated that political disagreements not become personal criticisms. A senator who disliked another referred to that senator as "the able, learned, and distinguished senator." A member who really could not stand another called that senator "my very able, learned, and distinguished colleague."

In the 1960s and 1970s, senators became increasingly active on a variety of issues on and off the Senate floor, and extended debates often occurred on the floor without the rigid rules of courtesy that had once prevailed. These changes have made the majority leader's role as coalition-builder extraordinarily challenging, mirroring problems facing the Speaker.[22]

PRESIDING OFFICER The Constitution specifies that the presiding officer of the Senate is the vice president of the United States. Because he is not a member of the Senate, he votes only in the case of a tie.

The official chair of the Senate is the **president pro tempore**, or pro tem, whom the majority party selects and who presides over the Senate in the absence of the vice president. The position of pro tem today is primarily an honorific office generally awarded to the most senior senator of the majority party. Once elected, the pro tem stays in that office until the majority party in the Senate changes. Since presiding over the Senate can be a rather perfunctory duty, neither the vice president nor the president pro tempore actually performs the task very often. Instead, this particular duty rotates among junior members of the majority party of the chamber, allowing more senior members to attend meetings of greater importance.

MAJORITY LEADER The true leader of the Senate is the majority leader, elected to the position by the majority party. Because the Senate is a smaller and more collegial body, the majority leader is not nearly as powerful as the Speaker of the House.

LEADERSHIP TEAMS The minority leader and the Republican and Democratic whips round out the leadership positions in the Senate and perform functions similar to those of their House counterparts. But, leading and whipping in the Senate can be quite a challenge. Senate rules always have given tremendous power to individual senators; in most cases, senators can offer any kind of amendments to legislation on the floor, and an individual senator can bring all work on the floor to a halt indefinitely through a filibuster unless three-fifths of the senators vote to cut him or her off.[23]

The Committee System

The saying "Congress in session is Congress on exhibition, whilst Congress in its committee rooms is Congress at work" may not be as true today as it was when Woodrow Wilson wrote it in 1885.[24] Still, "the work that takes place in the committee and subcommittee rooms of Capitol Hill is critical to the productivity and effectiveness of Congress."[25] Standing committees are the first and last places to which most bills go. Usually, committee members play key roles in floor debate about the merits of bills that have been introduced. When the House and Senate pass different versions of a bill, a conference committee with members of both houses meets to iron out the differences. Committee organization and specialization are especially important in the House of Representatives because of its size. The establishment of subcommittees allows for even greater specialization.

TYPES OF COMMITTEES   Congressional committees are of four types: (1) standing; (2) joint; (3) conference; and, (4) select (or special).[26]

1.   **Standing committees** are those to which bills are referred for consideration; they are so called because they continue from one Congress to the next. They consider issues roughly parallel to those of the departments represented in the president's Cabinet. For example, there are standing committees on agriculture, education, the judiciary, veterans' affairs, transportation, and commerce.

2.   **Joint committees** are standing committees that include members from both houses of Congress and are set up to conduct investigations or special studies. They focus public attention on major matters such as the economy, taxation, or scandals.

3.   **Conference committees** are special joint committees created to reconcile differences in bills passed by the House and Senate. A conference committee comprises members from the House and Senate committees that originally considered the bill.

4.   **Select (or special) committees** are temporary committees appointed for specific purposes, such as investigating the September 11, 2001, terrorist attacks or examining Secretary of State **Hillary Clinton's** actions on Benghazi or her use of a private email server. These committees can be very partisan.

In the 114th Congress, the House had twenty standing committees, as shown in Table 6.5, each with an average of thirty-one members. Together, these standing committees had roughly ninety subcommittees that collectively acted as the eyes, ears, and hands of the House. The Senate had sixteen standing committees ranging in size from fifteen to twenty-nine members. It also had roughly seventy subcommittees, which allowed all majority party senators to chair at least one.

Although most committees in one house parallel those in the other, the **House Committee on Rules,** for which no counterpart in the Senate exists, plays a major role in the House's law-making process. As an indication of this committee's importance, the Speaker directly appoints its chair and majority party members. This committee reviews most bills after they come from a committee and before they go to the full chamber for consideration. Performing a traffic cop function, the Committee on Rules gives each bill what is called a rule, which contains the date the bill will come up for debate and the time that will be allotted for discussion, and often specifies what kinds of amendments can be offered. Bills considered under a closed rule cannot be amended.

Standing committees have considerable power. They can kill bills, amend them radically, or hurry them through the process. In the words of former President Woodrow Wilson, once a bill is referred to a committee, it "crosses a parliamentary bridge of sighs to dim dungeons of silence whence it never will return."[27] Committees report out to the full House or Senate only a small fraction of the bills assigned to them. A **discharge petition** signed by a majority (218) of the House membership can force bills out of a House committee.

In contrast to members of the House, who hold few committee assignments (an average of 1.8 standing and three subcommittees), senators each serve on an average of three to four committees and seven subcommittees. Whereas the committee system allows House members to become policy or issue specialists, Senate members often are generalists who must prioritize the importance of their committee work.

Senate committees have the same power over framing legislation as House committees, but the Senate, as an institution more open to individual input than the House, gives less deference to the work done in committees. In the Senate, legislation is more likely to be rewritten on the floor, where all senators can generally participate and add amendments.

standing committee
Committee to which proposed bills are referred; continues from one Congress to the next.

joint committee
Standing committee that includes members from both houses of Congress set up to conduct investigations or special studies.

conference committee
Special joint committee created to reconcile differences in bills passed by the House and Senate.

select (or special) committee
Temporary committee appointed for a specific purpose.

Hillary Clinton
First female major party candidate for president of the United States, a Democrat, who ran against President Donald J. Trump in 2016. Secretary of State from 2009 to 2013; New York senator from 2001 to 2009; former first lady.

House Committee on Rules
The influential "Rules Committee" determines the scheduling and conditions, such as length of debate and type of allowable amendments, for all bills in the House of Representatives (but not in the Senate, where debate is less regulated).

discharge petition
Petition that gives a majority of the House of Representatives the authority to bring an issue to the floor in the face of committee inaction.

TABLE 6.5 WHAT WERE THE COMMITTEES OF THE 114TH CONGRESS?

Standing Committees	
House	**Senate**
Agriculture	Agriculture, Nutrition, and Forestry
Appropriations	Appropriations
Armed Services	Armed Services
Budget	Budget
Education and the Workforce	Health, Education, Labor, and Pensions
Energy and Commerce	Commerce, Science, and Transportation
Financial Services	Finance
Foreign Affairs	Foreign Relations
Homeland Security	Homeland Security and Governmental Affairs
Judiciary*	Judiciary*
Constitution and Civil Justice	*The Constitution*
Courts, Intellectual Property, and the Internet	*Antitrust, Competition Policy, and Consumer Rights*
Crime, Terrorism, Homeland Security, and Investigations	*Crime and Terrorism*
Immigration and Border Security	*Immigration and the National Interest*
Regulatory Reform, Commercial and Antitrust Law	*Oversight, Agency Action, Federal Rights and Federal Courts*
	Privacy, Technology and the Law
Veterans' Affairs	Veterans' Affairs
Natural Resources	Energy and Natural Resources
House Administration	Rules and Administration
Small Business	Small Business and Entrepreneurship
Science, Space, and Technology	Banking, Housing, and Urban Affairs
Ethics	Environment and Public Works
Oversight and Government Reform	
Rules	
Transportation and Infrastructure	
Ways and Means	

Select, Special, and Other Committees		
House	**Senate**	**Joint Committees**
Select Permanent Committee on Intelligence	Select Ethics	Economics
Select Committee on the Events Surrounding the 2012 Terrorist Attack in Benghazi	Select Intelligence	Taxation
	Special Aging	Library
	Indian Affairs	Printing

*****NOTE:** The subcommittees of the House and Senate Judiciary Committees during the 114th Congress are listed in italics.

seniority
Time of continuous service on a committee.

COMMITTEE CHAIRS Committee chairs enjoy tremendous power and prestige, with authorization to select all subcommittee chairs, call meetings, and recommend majority members to sit on conference committees. Committee chairs may even opt to kill a bill by refusing to schedule hearings on it. They also have a large committee staff at their disposal and are often recipients of favors from lobbyists, who recognize the chair's unique position of power. Interpersonal skills, influence, and expertise are a chair's best resources.

Historically, committee chairs were the majority party members with the longest continuous service on the committee. Committee chairs in the House, unlike the Senate, are no longer selected by **seniority**, or time of continuous service on the committee. Instead, to ensure that candidates demonstrate party loyalty, party leaders interview potential chairs. Six years of service on a particular committee is the limit on all committee chairs.

COMMITTEE MEMBERSHIP   Some committees, such as Energy and Commerce, facilitate reelection by giving House members influence over decisions that affect large campaign contributors. Other committees, such as Education and the Workforce or Judiciary, attract members eager to work on the policy responsibilities assigned to the committee even if the appointment does them little good at the ballot box. Another motivator for certain committee assignments is the desire to have power and influence within the chamber. The Appropriations and Budget Committees provide that kind of reward for some members, given the monetary impact on bills that come from other committees. Congress can approve programs, but unless money for them is appropriated in the budget, they are largely symbolic.

In both the House and the Senate, committee membership generally reflects party distribution within that chamber. On committees more critical to the operation of the House or to the setting of national policy, the majority often takes a disproportionate share of the slots. Since the Committee on Rules regulates access to the floor for legislation approved by other standing committees, control by the majority party is essential for it to manage the flow of legislation. For this reason, no matter how narrow its margin in the chamber, the majority party makes up more than two-thirds of the Committee on Rules's membership.

POWERS OF CONGRESS

6.5   Describe the powers of Congress.

The Framers wished to ensure that the national government had sufficient power to govern the states. Thus, Article I, section 7, of the Constitution details the procedures by which Congress can make laws and raise revenues. Article I, section 8, also details Congress's power to tax, spend, regulate commerce, coin money, and make "all Laws which shall be necessary and proper for carrying into Execution" those powers.

Today, Congress not only makes laws dealing with substantive policy but also spends significant time negotiating and trying to pass the nation's budget. In addition, in accordance with the system of checks and balances, it has a key oversight role. Through the War Powers Resolution, congressional review, approval of nominations, and impeachment, Congress can check the power of the executive and judicial branches.

The Law-Making Function

Congress's law-making power allows it to affect the day-to-day lives of all Americans and set policy for the future. Although proposals for legislation—be they about immigration, terrorism, Medicare, or tax policy—can come from the president, executive agencies, committee staffs, interest groups, or even private individuals, only members of the House or Senate can formally submit a bill for congressional consideration. Once a member of Congress introduces a bill, it usually reaches a dead end.

One or more standing committees and both chambers must approve each piece of legislation, and if House and Senate versions differ, each house must accept a conference report resolving those differences. Multiple stopping points provide many opportunities for legislation to die or members to revise the content of legislation and may lead representatives to alter their views on a particular piece of legislation several times over. Thus, it is much easier to defeat a bill than to pass one (see Figure 6.5). Of the approximately 10,600 bills introduced during the 113th Congress, the House and Senate voted fewer than 300 into law and critics noted that few dealt with important policy or substantive issues. More common were laws naming public buildings.

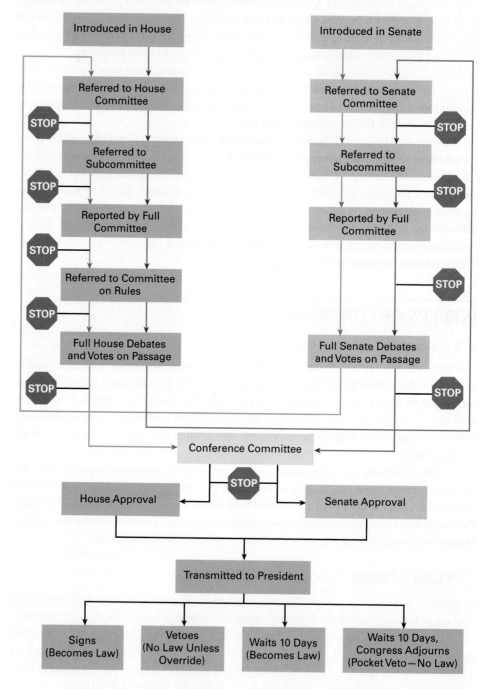

FIGURE 6.5 HOW DOES A BILL BECOME A LAW?

A bill must go through a carefully prescribed process in both the House of Representatives and the Senate in order to be enacted into law. After a bill has passed both houses, differences must be reconciled and the proposed legislation must meet with the president's approval. As a result, though many bills are introduced, few actually become law.

President Barack Obama vetoed nine bills passed by the 114th Congress. One of those vetoes was overridden by Congress in September of 2016.

COMMITTEE REFERRAL   The House and Senate have parallel processes, and often the same bill is introduced in each chamber at the same time. One member of Congress must introduce a bill, but several other members (called co-sponsors) often sponsor a bill, in an attempt to show support for its aims. Once introduced, the bill is sent to the clerk of the chamber, who gives it a number (for example, HR 1 or S 1—indicating

House or Senate bill number one, respectively). The bill is then printed, distributed, and sent to the appropriate committee or committees for consideration.

The committee usually refers the bill to one of its subcommittees, whose staff researches the proposed legislation, and then the chair decides whether or not to hold hearings on the bill. The subcommittee hearings provide an opportunity for those on both sides of the issue to voice their opinions. Since the 1970s, most hearings have been open to the public. After the hearings, the subcommittee revises the bill and then votes to approve or defeat it. If the subcommittee votes in favor of the bill, it is returned to the full committee. There, it goes through **markup**, a session during which committee members can offer changes to a bill before it goes to the floor. The full committee may also reject the bill before it goes to the floor in either house.

FLOOR DEBATE   The second stage of action takes place on the House or Senate floor. As previously discussed, in the House, before a bill may be debated on the floor, the Committee on Rules must approve it and give it a rule and a place on the calendar, or schedule. (House budget bills, however, do not go to the Committee on Rules.) In the House, the rule given to a bill determines limits on the floor debate and specifies what types of amendments, if any, may be attached to the bill. Once the Committee on Rules considers the bill, it is added to the calendar.

When the day arrives for floor debate, the House may choose to form a **Committee of the Whole**. This procedure allows the House to deliberate with only one hundred members present to expedite consideration of the bill. During this time, members may offer amendments, and the full House ultimately takes a vote. If the bill survives, it goes to the Senate for consideration if that body did not consider it simultaneously.

Unlike the House, whose size necessarily limits debate, the Senate may hold up bills by a hold or a filibuster. A **hold** is a procedure by which a senator asks to be informed before a particular bill (or nomination) is brought to the floor. This request signals the Senate leadership and the sponsors of the bill that a colleague may have objections to the bill (or nomination) and should be consulted before further action is taken. A hold may be anonymous or public and can be placed for any reason—including reviewing, negotiating changes, or attempting to kill a bill. Holds can be lifted by a senator at any time or stand as permanent blocks to specific legislation or judicial and diplomatic nominations.

Filibusters, a formal way of halting Senate action on a bill by means of long speeches or unlimited debate, grew out of the absence of rules to restrict speech in the Senate. The content of a filibuster has no limits as long as a senator keeps talking. A senator may read from a phone book, recite poetry, or read cookbooks to delay a vote. Often, a team of senators takes turns speaking to continue the filibuster in the hope of tabling or killing a bill. The use of filibusters has increased in recent years. Moreover, simply the threat of a filibuster can be quite potent; in the modern Senate, it often takes the assured votes of sixty senators for a bill to come to a final vote because of the threat of a filibuster.

Unless Senate rules are altered to require only a simple majority to end a filibuster—a step referred to as the nuclear option that was taken by Senate Democrats in 2013 to advance votes on President Obama's judicial nominees—senators may forcibly end a filibuster in only one way. Sixty of them must sign a motion for **cloture**. After a cloture motion passes the Senate floor, members may spend no more than thirty additional hours debating the legislation at issue.

FINAL APPROVAL   The third stage of action takes place when the two chambers of Congress approve different versions of the same bill. When this happens, they establish a conference committee to iron out the differences between the two versions. The conference committee, whose members are from the original House and Senate committees, hammers out a compromise, which is returned to each chamber for a final vote. Sometimes, the conference committee fails to agree and the bill dies there.

markup
A session in which committee members offer changes to a bill before it goes to the floor.

Committee of the Whole
A procedure that allows the House of Representatives to deliberate with a lower quorum and to expedite consideration and amendment of a bill.

hold
A procedure by which a senator asks to be informed before a particular bill or nomination is brought to the floor. This request signals leadership that a member may have objections to the bill (or nomination) and should be consulted before further action is taken.

filibuster
A formal way of halting Senate action on a bill by means of long speeches or unlimited debate.

cloture
Mechanism requiring the vote of sixty senators to cut off debate.

WHAT IS THE PRESIDENT'S ROLE IN LAW-MAKING?

After a bill has won the approval of both houses of Congress, the president has the final opportunity to approve the law or veto it, sending it back to Congress for a potential veto override. Here, President Barack Obama, surrounded by Vice President Joe Biden and legislative leaders, signs into law the Patient Protection and Affordable Care Act of 2010 (Obamacare), which reformed health care in the United States.

veto
The formal, constitutional authority of the president to reject bills passed by both houses of Congress, thus preventing them from becoming law without further congressional action.

pocket veto
If Congress adjourns during the ten days the president has to consider a bill passed by both houses of Congress, the bill is considered vetoed without the president's signature.

No changes or amendments to the compromise version are allowed. If the bill does not pass in both houses, it dies. If the bill passes, it is sent to the president, who has ten days to consider a bill. He has four options:

1. The president can sign the bill, at which point it becomes law.

2. The president can **veto** the bill, which is more likely to occur when the president is of a different party from the majority in Congress; Congress may override the president's veto with a two-thirds vote in each chamber, a very difficult task.

3. The president can wait the full ten days, at the end of which time the bill becomes law without his signature if Congress is still in session.

4. If Congress adjourns before the ten days are up, the president can choose not to sign the bill, which is called a **pocket veto**. To become law, the bill then has only one path: to be reintroduced in the next session of Congress and put through the process all over again.

The Budgetary Function

Since the writing of the Constitution, Congress has enjoyed significant authority over the budgetary process. For much of American history, however, congressional budgets were piecemeal and made without an eye toward setting the course of public policy. By the 1920s, as a result of growing federal regulation and the bureaucracy, many policy makers sensed a need for greater centralization and order in the budgetary process. Thus, Congress passed and President Warren G. Harding signed into law the Budget and Accounting Act of 1921. This legislation required the president—for the first time—to submit a budget to Congress. The president's proposal would include the prior year's spending, projections, and proposals for the next year. Congress, in turn, could alter the allocation of appropriations but could not increase the total level of spending proposed by the president. To aid the executive branch in this role, the act also created the Bureau of the Budget. In 1970, the name of this agency was changed to the Office of Management and Budget.

This process continued relatively unfettered until the early 1970s, when tension between a Democratic-controlled Congress and a Republican president,

Richard M. Nixon, exposed several shortcomings in the system. For example, although Congress authorized the expenditure of funds for many social problems, President Nixon refused to spend appropriated money on them. Angered and frustrated by Nixon's flagrant use of executive power, Congress solidified its role in the budgetary process by passing the Congressional Budget Act of 1974.

CONGRESSIONAL BUDGET ACT OF 1974 The **Congressional Budget Act of 1974** established the congressional budgetary process in use today. The act also created the Congressional Budget Office (CBO), a nonpartisan agency to help members make accurate estimations of revenues and expenditures and to lay out a plan for congressional action on the annual budget resolution, appropriations, reconciliation, and any other revenue bills. In general, these bills and resolutions establish levels of spending for the federal government and its agencies during the next fiscal year. (The federal government's fiscal year runs from October 1 of one year to September 30 of the next.) Although these levels rarely change dramatically from year to year, the programs and policies that receive increases and decreases in federal spending make a powerful statement about the goals of Congress and the president.

One special process detailed by the Congressional Budget Act of 1974 is **reconciliation**. The reconciliation procedure allows consideration of controversial issues affecting the budget by limiting debate to twenty hours, thereby ending the threat of a filibuster in the Senate. This process received a great deal of attention in 2010, when members of Congress used it to pass the health care reform bill.

The Congressional Budget Act of 1974 also includes a timetable intended to make sure that action on the budget occurs without unnecessary delay (see Table 6.6). Under this constraint, Congress must complete initial action on the budget resolution by April 15 of the preceding fiscal year. The budget resolution—or one or more continuing resolutions allowing the government to spend money at the same rates as the previous fiscal year—must receive approval by the start of the new fiscal year on October 1. When this does not occur, the federal government may shut down.

PORK AND PROGRAMMATIC REQUESTS Representatives often seek to win appropriations known as **pork**, legislation that allows representatives to bring money and jobs to their districts in the form of public works programs, military bases, or other programs. Many of these programs, once called earmarks but now called **programmatic requests**, are funds that an appropriations bill designates for specific projects within a state or congressional district. Legislators who bring jobs and new public works programs back to their districts are hard to defeat when up for reelection. But, ironically, these programs also attract much of the public criticism directed at the federal government in general and Congress in particular.

HON CLINTON

Richard M. Nixon
The thirty-seventh president, a Republican, who served from 1969 through 1974. Nixon advocated détente during the Cold War and resigned rather than face impeachment and likely removal from office due to the Watergate scandal.

Congressional Budget Act of 1974
Act that established the congressional budgetary process by laying out a plan for congressional action on the annual budget resolution, appropriations, reconciliation, and any other revenue bills.

reconciliation
A procedure that allows consideration of controversial issues affecting the budget by limiting debate to twenty hours, thereby ending threat of a filibuster.

pork
Legislation that allows representatives to bring money and jobs to their districts in the form of public works programs, military bases, or other programs.

programmatic requests
Federal funds designated for special projects within a state or congressional district. Also referred to as earmarks.

HOW ARE CONGRESSIONAL OVERSIGHT HEARINGS CONDUCTED?

On June 28, 2016, the House Select Committee on Benghazi issued its final report on the 2012 attack on the U.S. embassy that cost the lives of four Americans, including the U. S. Ambassador to Libya. The 800-page report was the culmination of two years of investigation and hearings that cost more than seven million taxpayer dollars. Viewed by Republicans as an important fact-finding mission and by Democrats as a partisan witch hunt, the theatrical aspects of this sort of congressional oversight were clearly illustrated by the nearly 11 hours of questions directed at former Secretary of State and Democratic presidential candidate Hillary Clinton on October 22, 2015, shown here.

TABLE 6.6 WHAT IS THE TIMELINE FOR THE CONGRESSIONAL BUDGETARY PROCESS?

Date	Action
First Monday in February	**President submits budget to Congress**—President's budget is prepared by the Office of Management and Budget; includes requested levels of spending for the next fiscal year.
February 15	**Budget outlooks**—Congressional Budget Office submits economic projections to the House and Senate Budget Committees.
April 15	**Budget resolution**—Congress must complete action on the initial version of a budget resolution.
May 15	**Appropriation begins**—House begins to consider appropriations bills.
June 10	**Appropriations Committee**—House Appropriations Committee should conclude consideration of appropriations issues.
June 15	**Reconciliation ends**—House must handle any reconciliation bills by this date.
June 30	**Appropriation ends**—Full House should conclude consideration of all appropriations bills.
October 1	**Fiscal year begins**—Government's fiscal year runs from October 1 to September 30.

divided government
The political condition in which different political parties control the presidency and at least one house of Congress.

War Powers Resolution
Passed by Congress in 1973; the president is limited in the deployment of troops overseas to a sixty-day period in peacetime (which can be extended for an extra thirty days to permit withdrawal) unless Congress explicitly gives its approval for a longer period.

The Oversight Function

Historically, Congress has performed its oversight function by holding committee hearings in which members question bureaucrats to determine if they are enforcing and interpreting the laws as intended by Congress. These hearings, now routinely televised, are among Congress's most visible and dramatic actions, especially in times of **divided government**, that is, when the executive and legislative branches are controlled by different parties. Congress uses hearings not only to gather information but also to focus on particular executive-branch actions. They often signal that Congress believes an agency needs to make changes in policy or performance before it next comes before the committee to justify its budget or actions. Congress also uses hearings to improve program administration. They can also be used for partisan reasons.

Congress may also exercise its oversight powers in a number of other ways. It may, for example, use its powers under the War Powers Resolution or the Congressional Review Act of 1996 to examine actions taken by the president. The Senate also has the authority to offer advice and consent on executive and judicial branch nominees or may refuse to consider them at all. Congress's ultimate oversight power, however, is the power to impeach other federal officials and remove them from office.

THE WAR POWERS RESOLUTION   In a delayed response to Lyndon B. Johnson's conduct of the Vietnam War, in 1973 Congress passed the **War Powers Resolution** over President Nixon's veto. The resolution permits the president to send troops into action only with the authorization of Congress or if the United States, its territories, or the armed forces are attacked. It also requires the president to notify Congress within forty-eight hours of committing troops to foreign soil. In addition, the president must withdraw troops within sixty days unless Congress votes to declare war. The president also must consult with Congress, if at all possible, prior to committing troops.

The War Powers Resolution, however, has had limited effectiveness in claiming an oversight role for Congress in international crisis situations. Presidents Gerald R. Ford, Jimmy Carter, and Ronald Reagan never consulted Congress in advance of committing troops, citing the need for secrecy and swift movement, although each president did notify Congress shortly after the deployment of troops abroad. They contended that the War Powers Resolution was probably unconstitutional because it limits presidential prerogatives as commander in chief.

CONGRESSIONAL REVIEW   The Congressional Review Act of 1996 allows Congress to exercise its oversight powers by nullifying agency regulations. Under the home rule charter of the District of Columbia, the House and Senate may also nullify actions of the Washington, D.C. City Council. This process is called **congressional review**.[28] If using this oversight power, Congress has sixty days after the implementation of an administrative action or, in the case of the District of Columbia any laws, resolutions or ballot measures, to pass a joint resolution of legislative disapproval. The president must also approve the resolution. If the president vetoes the resolution of disapproval, Congress needs a two-thirds majority to override the president's veto.

Historically, congressional review has been used with success only once.[29] In 2001, Congress and President George W. Bush reversed Clinton administration ergonomics regulations, which were intended to prevent job-related repetitive stress injuries. In the only other use of congressional review to reach the president's desk, President Barack Obama vetoed a joint resolution against the implementation of regulations offered by the National Labor Relations Board and no further actions were taken against the new regulations.[30]

CONFIRMATION OF PRESIDENTIAL APPOINTEES   The Senate plays a special oversight function through its ability to confirm key members of the executive branch as well as presidential nominations to the federal courts. Although the Senate generally confirms most presidential nominees, it does not always do so. A wise president considers senatorial reaction before nominating potentially controversial individuals to his administration or to the federal courts.

In the case of federal district court appointments, senators often have considerable say in the nomination of judges from their states through **senatorial courtesy**, a process by which presidents generally defer to the senators who represent the state where the vacancy occurs. Through the "blue slip" process, senators may submit a favorable or unfavorable review of a nominee; they may also choose not to comment. Despite this procedure, the judicial nominees of recent presidents have encountered particularly hostile Senates. "Appointments have always been the battleground for policy disputes," says one political scientist. But now, "what's new is the rawness of it—all of the veneer is off."[31] Senate Majority Leader Mitch McConnell's refusal to hold hearings or vote on President Barack Obama's Supreme Court nominee Merrick Garland, who was tapped to replace Justice Antonin Scalia after Scalia's death in office on February 13, 2016, is an obvious illustration of this new approach.

IMPEACHMENT   The impeachment process is Congress's ultimate oversight of the U.S. president and federal court judges. The U.S. Constitution is quite vague about the impeachment process, and much debate over it concerns what constitutes an impeachable offense. The Constitution specifies that Congress can impeach a president for treason, bribery, or other "high crimes and misdemeanors." Most commentators agree that the Framers intended this phrase to mean significant abuses of power.

House and Senate rules control how the impeachment process operates. Yet, because Congress uses the process so rarely, and under such disparate circumstances, few hard and fast rules exist. The U.S. House of Representatives has voted to impeach only seventeen federal officials. Of those, seven were convicted and removed from office, and three resigned before the process was completed.

Only four resolutions against presidents have resulted in further action: (1) John Tyler, charged with corruption and misconduct in 1843; (2) Andrew Johnson, charged with serious misconduct in 1868; (3) Richard M. Nixon, charged with obstruction of justice and the abuse of power in 1974; and, (4) Bill Clinton, charged with perjury and obstruction of justice in 1998. The House rejected the charges against Tyler; the Senate acquitted Johnson by a one-vote margin; Nixon resigned before the full House voted on several articles of impeachment; and the Senate acquitted Clinton by a vote of 55–45 after the House voted for impeachment.

congressional review
A process whereby Congress can nullify agency regulations within a 60-day window by passing a joint resolution of legislative disapproval. The president's approval of the resolution or a two-thirds majority vote in both houses to overrule a presidential veto is also required.

senatorial courtesy
A process by which presidents generally allow senators from the state in which a judicial vacancy occurs to block a nomination by simply registering their objection.

unified government
The political condition in which the same political party controls the presidency and Congress.

HOW MEMBERS OF CONGRESS MAKE DECISIONS

6.6 Describe the factors that influence how members of Congress make decisions.

Members of Congress consider a number of factors when deciding how to vote on a piece of legislation. Among these are political parties; constituents; colleagues and caucuses; interest groups, lobbyists and political action committees; and staff and support agencies.

Political Parties

The influence of political parties on members' votes cannot be overstated. In fact, congressional party unity, a measure of the solidarity of the members of a political party, has reached historically high levels in recent years. Members of both the Democratic and Republican Parties in the House and Senate vote together on approximately 90 percent of all legislation considered by those bodies.

The incentives for members to vote with their party also rarely have been higher—or more creative. In addition to lending members campaign support through party organizations or member-to-member political action committees (PACs), leadership in both houses may also offer committee assignments or chairs as rewards to members who toe the party line.

The president may also act as chief of the party and attempt to coerce members to support his legislative package. This is particularly true in times of **unified government**, when the presidency and Congress are controlled by members of the same party and share a similar policy agenda. Divided government, however, often helps the party that controls the Congress, to the frustration of presidents or the opposition party.

Constituents

When they are voting, members of Congress always have in mind their constituents—the people who live and vote in a representative's home district or state. Studies by political scientists show that members vote in conformity with prevailing opinion in their districts about two-thirds of the time. On average, Congress passes laws that reflect national public opinion at about the same rate.[32] It is rare for a legislator to vote against the wishes of his or her constituents regularly, particularly on issues of social welfare, domestic policy, or other highly publicized issues.

HOW DO MEMBERS OF CONGRESS LEARN ABOUT THEIR CONSTITUENTS' OPINIONS ON POLITICAL ISSUES?

Members and their staffs spend a substantial portion of their time meeting with constituents in Washington, D.C., and in their district offices; they also monitor calls, letters, e-mail, and social media. Failure to remain in touch with their constituents at home may decrease a member's likelihood of winning another term in Congress. Here, Senator Chuck Schumer (D-NY) and New York City Mayor Bill DeBlasio speak to commuters in a Brooklyn, New York, subway station.

Gauging how voters regard any particular issue often is not easy. Because it is virtually impossible to know how the people back home feel on all matters, a representative's perception of his or her constituents' preferences is important. Even when voters have opinions, legislators may receive little guidance if they come from a narrowly divided district. Abortion is an issue about which many voters feel passionate, but a legislator whose district has roughly equal numbers of pro-choice and pro-life advocates can satisfy only a portion of his or her constituents.

In short, legislators tend to act on their own preferences as trustees when dealing with topics that have come through the committees on which they serve or with issues they know about as a result of experience in other contexts, such as their vocation. On items of little concern in their district or when they have limited first-hand knowledge, legislators tend to turn to other sources for voting cues. But, members are always keenly aware of the consequences of voting against their constituents' views on "wedge issues"—topics such as insurance coverage for contraceptives, immigration and moving jobs abroad—that tend to divide voters.

Colleagues and Caucuses

The range and complexity of issues confronting Congress means that no one can be up to speed on more than a few topics. When members must vote on bills concerning issues about which they know very little, they often turn for advice to colleagues who have served on the committee that handled the legislation. On issues that are of little interest to a legislator, **logrolling**, or vote trading, often occurs. Logrolling often takes place on specialized bills targeting money or projects to selected congressional districts. An unaffected member may exchange a yea vote now for the promise of a future yea vote on a similar piece of specialized legislation.

Members may also look to other representatives who share common interests. Special-interest caucuses created around issues, home states, regions, congressional class, or other commonalities facilitate this communication. Although all caucuses are informal in nature, some, such as the Black and Hispanic Caucuses, are far more organized than others. The House Congressional Caucus for Women's Issues, for example, has formal elections of its Republican and Democratic co-chairs and vice chairs, its members provide staff to work on issues of common concern to caucus members, and staffers meet regularly to facilitate support for legislation of interest to women.

Interest Groups, Lobbyists, and Political Action Committees

A primary function of most lobbyists, whether they work for interest groups, trade associations, or large corporations, is to provide information to supportive or potentially supportive legislators, committees, and their staffs. It is likely, for example, that a representative knows the National Rifle Association's (NRA's) position on gun control legislation. What the legislator needs from the NRA is information and substantial research on the feasibility and impact of such legislation. How could the states implement such legislation? Is it constitutional? Will it really have an impact on violent crime or crime in schools? Organized interests can persuade undecided legislators or confirm the support of their friends by providing information that legislators use to justify the position they have embraced. They also can supply direct campaign contributions, volunteers, and publicity to members seeking reelection.

The high cost of campaigning has made members of Congress, especially those without huge personal fortunes, attentive to those who help pay the tab for such expenses. Political action committees (PACs) organized by interest groups are an important source of most members' campaign funding. When an issue arises that is of little consequence to a member's constituents, that member, not surprisingly, tends to support the positions of those interests who helped pay for their last campaign. After all, who wants to bite the hand that feeds him or her?

logrolling
Vote trading; voting to support a colleague's bill in return for a promise of future support.

Congressional Research Service (CRS)

Created in 1914, the non-partisan CRS provides information, studies, and research in support of the work of Congress, and prepares summaries and tracks the progress of all bill.

Government Accountability Office (GAO)

Established in 1921, the GAO is an independent regulatory agency for the purpose of auditing the financial expenditures of the executive branch and federal agencies; until 2004, the GAO was known as the General Accounting Office..

Congressional Budget Office (CBO)

Created in 1974, the CBO provides Congress with evaluations of the potential economic effects of proposed spending policies and also analyzes the president's budget and economic projections.

Interest groups also use grassroots appeals to pressure legislators by urging their members in a particular state or district to call, write, fax, e-mail, text, or tweet their senators or representatives. Lobbyists cannot vote, but constituents back home can and do.

Staff and Support Agencies

Members of Congress rely heavily on their staffs for information on pending legislation.[33] House members have an average of fifteen staffers; senators, an average of thirty-five. Staff is divided between D.C. and district offices. When a bill is nonideological or one on which the member has no real position, staff members can be very influential. In many offices, they are the greatest influence on their boss's votes, and lobbyists are just as likely to contact key staffers as they are members. Congressional committees and subcommittees also have their own dedicated staff to assist committee members.

Additional help for members comes from support personnel at the **Congressional Research Service (CRS)** at the Library of Congress, the **Government Accountability Office (GAO)**, and the **Congressional Budget Office (CBO)**.

Created in 1914, the CRS is administered by the Library of Congress. It responds to more than a quarter-million congressional requests for information each year. Its staff conducts nonpartisan studies of public issues, as well as major research projects for committees at the request of members. The CRS also prepares summaries and tracks the progress of all bills introduced.

The GAO was established in 1921 as an independent regulatory agency for the purpose of auditing the financial expenditures of the executive branch and federal agencies. The GAO performs four additional functions: it sets government standards for accounting; it provides legal opinions; it settles claims against the government; and it conducts studies upon congressional request.

The CBO was created in 1974 to evaluate the economic effect of different spending programs and to provide information on the cost of proposed policies. It is responsible for analyzing the president's budget and economic projections. The CBO provides Congress and individual members with a valuable second opinion to use in budget debates.

TOWARD REFORM: BALANCING INSTITUTIONAL POWER

6.7 Evaluate the strategic interactions between Congress, the president, the courts, and the people.

The Framers envisioned that the Congress, the president, and the judiciary would have discrete powers, and that one branch would be able to hold the others in check. These checks and balances would also allow citizens to influence their government but temper the will of the people. Especially since the 1930s, the president often has held the upper hand in institutional power. In times of crisis or simply when it was unable to meet public demands for solutions, Congress has willingly handed over its authority to the chief executive. Even though the inherent powers of the chief executive give the president greater latitude, Congress does, of course, retain ultimate legislative authority to question executive actions and to halt administration activities by cutting off funds for programs a president wants. Similar checks and balances affect relations between Congress and the courts.

Congress and the Executive

The balance of power between Congress and the president has fluctuated over time. The post–Civil War Congress tried to regain control of the vast executive powers that the recently slain President Abraham Lincoln had assumed. Angered at the refusal of Lincoln's successor, Andrew Johnson, to go along with its radical Reconstruction of the South, Congress passed the Tenure of Office Act, which prevented the president, under threat of civil penalty, from removing any Cabinet-level appointees of the previous administration. Johnson accepted the challenge and fired Lincoln's secretary of war, who many believed guilty of heinous war crimes. The House voted to impeach Johnson, but the desertion of a handful of Republican senators prevented him from being removed from office. (The effort fell short by one vote.) Nonetheless, this attempt to remove the president greatly weakened his power, and the Congress again became the center of power and authority in the federal government.

Beginning in the early 1900s, however, a series of strong presidents acted at the expense of congressional power. Theodore Roosevelt, Franklin D. Roosevelt, and Lyndon B. Johnson viewed the presidency as carrying with it enormous powers. Especially since the presidency of Franklin D. Roosevelt, Congress has ceded to the president a major role in the legislative process.

Congress and the Judiciary

As part of our system of checks and balances, the power of judicial review gives the Supreme Court of the United States the ability to review the constitutionality of acts of Congress. Historically, the Court has used this power very carefully. From 1787 to 2015, the Supreme Court struck down only 177 federal laws.

Congress also interacts with the judiciary in a number of other ways. It is ultimately up to Congress to determine the number of judges on each court, as well as the boundaries of judicial districts and circuits. Congress also sets the jurisdiction of the federal courts. During recent Congresses, for example, several members, unhappy with Supreme Court actions on abortion and LGBT rights, pushed for a bill to prevent federal courts from hearing challenges related to these civil liberties issues. When Congress threatens the Court's jurisdiction, it is signaling its belief that federal judges have gone too far.

Congress and the People

Congress, at least conceptually, is the people's branch of government. Elected members are assumed to serve in the citizens' best interest. In recent years, however, citizens have increasingly questioned members' dedication to their representational role. In August of 2016, as shown in Figure 6.6, the congressional approval rate was a dismal 18 percent. This compares to a 54 percent approval rating of individual members of Congress by their constituents in 2014, the last year for which polling data on this issue exists. These low approval numbers mirror the frustrations of the American people over the increasing partisanship and unproductivity of the institution.

FIGURE 6.6 WHAT DO AMERICANS THINK ABOUT CONGRESS?

This graph shows the American public's views on Congress as an institution from October 1990 to August 2016. Approval of Congress has been below 50% since late August 2000 and below 20% since August 2010.

SOURCE: www.gallup.com/poll/156662/congress-approval-ties-time-low.aspx

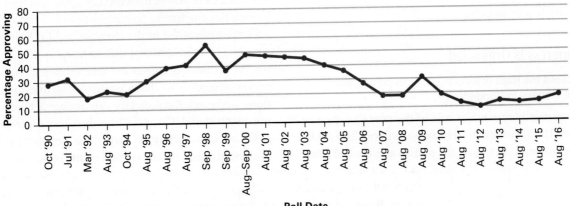

REVIEW THE CHAPTER

Roots of the U.S. Congress

6.1 Describe the constitutional provisions that define the Congress.

The Constitution created a bicameral legislature with members of each body to be elected differently and thus to represent different constituencies. Article I of the Constitution sets forth qualifications for office, states age minimums, and specifies how legislators are to be distributed among the states. In addition, the Constitution also provides a vast array of enumerated and implied powers to Congress. Both houses of Congress share some, such as law-making and oversight, but not others, such as confirmation of presidential appointees.

Representing the American People

6.2 Analyze the ability of members of Congress to represent their constituents.

Congress is the representative branch of the American national government. Representation can be measured in several ways. In general, members of Congress are better educated, richer, more likely to be male, more likely to be white and more likely to be religious than the general population. How well members represent their constituents' beliefs also varies with how they view their representational role—as trustees, delegates, or politicos.

Staying in Congress

6.3 Describe how incumbency and redistricting help members of Congress to stay in office.

Members of Congress are elected by their constituents to two-year terms in the House of Representatives and six-year terms in the Senate. Once elected, incumbency is a powerful advantage. Redistricting may also affect a member's ability to stay in Congress.

How Congress Is Organized

6.4 Assess the roles of leaders, political parties, and committees in Congress.

Political parties play a major role in the way Congress is organized. The Speaker of the House is traditionally a member of the majority party, and the parties also control other leadership roles, such as majority and minority leaders and whips. In addition to the party leaders, Congress has a labyrinth of committees and subcommittees that cover the entire range of government policies. In these environments, many policies take shape and members make their primary contributions to solving public problems.

Powers of Congress

6.5 Describe the powers of Congress.

The three most significant powers of Congress are its law-making, budgetary, and oversight functions. The road to enacting a bill into law is long and strewn with obstacles, and only a small share of the proposals introduced become law. The Congressional Budget Act of 1974 solidified Congress's role in the budgetary process. Congress conducts oversight in a number of ways, including through hearings. Congress also offers advice and consent on executive and judicial branch nominees and has the power to impeach federal officials and remove them from office.

How Members of Congress Make Decisions

6.6 Describe the factors that influence how members of Congress make decisions

A number of factors, including political party; constituents; colleagues and caucuses; staff and support agencies; and interest groups, lobbyists, and political action committees may influence a members' decisions. In modern Congresses, political party is a particularly influential factor.

Toward Reform: Balancing Institutional Power

6.7 Evaluate the strategic interactions between Congress, the president, the courts, and the people.

The balance of power between Congress and the executive branch has fluctuated tremendously over time. Congress was most powerful in the early years of U.S. history, but since the New Deal, the president has played an important role in proposing legislation and spending. An ongoing power struggle also characterizes legislative–judicial relations. Although the judiciary can declare acts of Congress unconstitutional, Congress also exercises control over the judiciary in a variety of ways. The people also hold an important check on all political institutions.

LEARN THE TERMS

apportionment
bicameral legislature
bill
cloture
Committee of the Whole
conference committee
Congressional Budget Act
    of 1974
Congressional Budget Office (CBO)
Congressional Research
    Service (CRS)
congressional review
delegate
discharge petition
divided government
Edmund Burke
filibuster

gerrymandering
Government Accountability
    Office (GAO)
Hillary Clinton
hold
House Committee on Rules
impeachment
incumbency
joint committee
logrolling
majority leader
majority party
markup
minority leader
minority party
party caucus (or conference)
pocket veto

politico
pork
president pro tempore
programmatic requests
reconciliation
redistricting
Richard M. Nixon
select (or special) committee
senatorial courtesy
seniority
Speaker of the House
standing committee
trustee
unified government
veto
War Powers Resolution
whip

WHY ARE PRESIDENTIAL FUNERALS OCCASIONS FOR NATIONAL MOURNING?

Presidents are leaders who unite the American public—in life and in death. Former presidents and vice presidents and their spouses attend the funeral service for President Ronald Reagan in the National Cathedral in Washington, D.C., prior to his interment in California.

THE PRESIDENCY

LEARNING OBJECTIVES

7.1 Describe the constitutional provisions that provide the roots of the American presidency.

7.2 Identify the roles and responsibilities of the president under the Constitution.

7.3 Trace the expansion of presidential power.

7.4 Describe the organization and functions of the Executive Office of the President.

7.5 Describe the relationship between the president and the public.

7.6 Describe the relationship between the president and the Congress.

When Ronald Reagan died on June 5, 2004, many Americans, first in California and then in Washington, D.C., lined up for hours to pay their respects to the man who had been the fortieth president of the United States. Many people could see, for the first time in recent memory, the grandeur of a presidential state funeral. The first president to lie in state in the Rotunda of the Capitol since Lyndon B. Johnson died in January 1973, Reagan was one of only nine American presidents to receive that honor. Presidential funerals underscore the esteem that most Americans accord the office of the president, regardless of its occupant. Just before the first president, George Washington, died, he made it known that he wanted his burial to be a quiet one, "without parade or funeral oration." He also requested a three-day delay of his burial—a common request at the time because of the fear of being buried alive. Despite these requests, Washington's funeral was a state occasion as hundreds of soldiers, with their rifles held backward, marched to Mount Vernon, Virginia, where he was interred. Across the nation, imitation funerals took place, and the military wore black armbands for six months.[1] When President Abraham Lincoln was assassinated in 1865, his funeral became a nationwide event. He lay in state in the East Room of the White House, where more than 25,000 mourners came to pay their respects. Black cloth draped the room, and two dozen Union soldiers formed an honor guard. Following the funeral, a parade to the Capitol was held in Washington, D.C. Thousands of free blacks escorted Lincoln to the Rotunda, where he lay in state for another day. The body of the deceased president then embarked on a national train tour to his burial site in Springfield, Illinois, allowing Americans across the country an opportunity to grieve.

Today, one of the first things a president does upon leaving office is to consider funeral plans. The military has a 138-page book devoted to the kind of ceremony and traditions so evident in the Reagan funeral: a horse-drawn caisson, a riderless horse with boots hung backward in the stirrups to indicate that the deceased will ride no more, a twenty-one-gun salute, and a flyover by military aircraft. Each president's family, however, has personalized their private, yet also public, opportunity to mourn. The Reagan family, for example, filed a 300-page plan for the funeral in 1989 and updated it regularly. President Gerald R. Ford filed a plan that was implemented after his death in 2006. Presidents Jimmy Carter and George Bush have also filed formal plans; Bill Clinton, George W. Bush, Barack Obama, and Donald J. Trump have yet to do so.

The Reagan funeral also created a national time-out from the news of war, and even presidential campaigns halted in respect for the deceased president. One historian commented that the event gave Americans the opportunity to "rediscover … what holds us together instead of what pulls us apart."[2] This is often the role of presidents—in life or in death.

• • •

The authority granted to the **president** by the U.S. Constitution and through subsequent congressional legislation makes it a position with awesome power and responsibility. Not only did the Framers not envision such a powerful role for the president, but they also could not have foreseen the skepticism with which the modern media greet many presidential actions. The modern media, used by successful presidents to help advance their agendas, have brought us closer to our presidents and made them seem more human, a mixed blessing for those trying to lead. Only two photographs exist of President Franklin D. Roosevelt in a wheelchair, his paralysis kept a closely guarded secret. Seven decades later, presidential candidate Mitt Romney was asked on national TV what he wore to bed.

Public opinion and confidence greatly affect a president's ability to get programs adopted and implemented. As one political scientist has noted, the president's power often rests on the power to persuade.[3] To persuade, a president must have the capacity to forge links with members of Congress as well as gain the support of the American people and the respect of foreign leaders. The tension between public expectations

president
The chief executive officer of the United States, as established by Article II of the U.S. Constitution.

vice president
An officer created by Article II of the U.S. Constitution to preside over the U.S. Senate and to fill any vacancy in the office of president due to death, resignation, removal, or (since 1967) disability.

about the presidency and the formal powers of the president permeates our discussion of how the office has evolved from its humble origins in Article II of the Constitution to its current stature.

ROOTS OF THE OFFICE OF PRESIDENT OF THE UNITED STATES

7.1 Describe the constitutional provisions that provide the roots of the American presidency.

The earliest example of executive power in the colonies was the position of royal governor. The king of England appointed a royal governor to each British colony and normally entrusted them with the "powers of appointment, military command, expenditure, and—within limitations—pardon, as well as with large powers in connection with the powers of law making."[4] Royal governors often found themselves at odds with the colonists and especially with elected colonial legislatures. The people, many of whom had fled from Great Britain to escape royal domination, distrusted and disdained the governors as representatives of the Crown. Other colonists, generations removed from England, no longer felt strong ties to the king and his power over them.

When the colonists declared their independence from Great Britain in 1776, their distrust of a strong chief executive remained. Most state constitutions reduced the once-powerful office of governor to a symbolic post elected annually by the legislature. However, some states did entrust wider powers to their chief executives. In New York, the people directly elected the governor. Perhaps because the people could then hold him accountable, they gave him the power to pardon, the duty to faithfully execute the laws, and the power to act as commander in chief of the state militia.

Under the Articles of Confederation, no executive branch of government existed; the eighteen different men who served as the president of the Continental Congress of the United States of America were president in name only—they held no actual authority or power in the new nation. When the delegates to the Constitutional Convention met in Philadelphia to fashion a new government, the need for an executive branch to implement the laws made by Congress created little dissent. Although some delegates suggested that multiple executives would be preferable, the Framers eventually agreed that executive authority should be vested in one person. This agreement was relatively easy because the Framers felt certain that George Washington—whom they had trusted with their lives during the Revolutionary War—would become the first president of the new nation.

The Framers also concurred on a title for the new office. Borrowing from the title used at several American colleges and universities, the Framers called the new chief executive "the president." How the president was to be chosen and by whom created a major stumbling block. James Wilson of Philadelphia suggested that the people should elect the president, who should remain "independent of the legislature." Wilson also suggested giving the executive an absolute veto over the acts of Congress. "Without such a defense," he wrote, "the legislature can at any moment sink it [the executive] into non-existence."[5]

The manner of the president's election troubled the Framers for some time. Their solution to the dilemma was the creation of the Electoral College. We leave the resolution of that issue aside for now and turn instead to details of the issues the Framers resolved quickly.

Presidential Qualifications and Terms of Office

The Constitution requires the president (and the **vice president**, whose major function is to succeed the president in the event of his death or disability) to be a natural-born citizen of the United States, at least thirty-five years old, and a resident of the

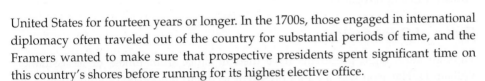

United States for fourteen years or longer. In the 1700s, those engaged in international diplomacy often traveled out of the country for substantial periods of time, and the Framers wanted to make sure that prospective presidents spent significant time on this country's shores before running for its highest elective office.

Although only two of the last six presidents failed to win a second term, at one time the length of a president's term created controversy. Various delegates to the Constitutional Convention suggested four-, seven-, and eleven-year terms with no eligibility for reelection. The Framers ultimately reached agreement on a four-year term with eligibility for reelection.

The first president, George Washington (1789–1797), sought reelection only once, and a two-term limit for presidents became traditional. Although Ulysses S. Grant unsuccessfully sought a third term, the two terms established by Washington remained the standard for 150 years, avoiding the Framers' much-feared "constitutional monarch," a perpetually reelected tyrant. In the 1930s and 1940s, however, Franklin D. Roosevelt ran successfully in four elections as Americans fought first the Great Depression and then World War II. Despite Roosevelt's popularity, negative reaction to his long tenure in office led to passage (and ratification in 1951) of the **Twenty-Second Amendment**. It limits presidents to two four-year terms. A vice president who succeeds a president due to death, resignation, or impeachment is eligible for a maximum of ten years in office: two years of a president's remaining term and two elected terms or more than two years of a president's term followed by one elected term.

The Framers paid little attention to the office of vice president beyond the need to have an immediate official stand-in for the president. Initially, for example, the vice president's only function was to assume the office of president in the case of the president's death or some other emergency. After further debate, the delegates made the vice president the presiding officer of the Senate (except in cases of presidential impeachment). The delegates gave the vice president authority to vote in that body only in the event of a tie.

During the Constitutional Convention, Benjamin Franklin staunchly supported inclusion of a provision allowing for impeachment, the first step in a formal process to remove a specified official from office. Each house of Congress was given a role in the impeachment process to ensure that the chief executive could be removed

Twenty-Second Amendment
Adopted in 1951; prevents presidents from serving more than two terms, or more than ten years if they came to office via the death, resignation, or removal of their predecessor.

Watergate
A scandal in the early 1970s involving a break-in at the Democratic National Committee offices in the Watergate office complex. The involvement of members of the Nixon administration and subsequent cover-up attempts led to President Richard Nixon's resignation from office and jail sentences for some members of his administration.

executive privilege
An implied presidential power that allows the president to refuse to disclose information regarding confidential conversations or national security to Congress or the judiciary.

U.S. v. Nixon (1974)
Supreme Court ruling on power of the president, holding that no absolute constitutional executive privilege allows a president to refuse to comply with a court order to produce information needed in a criminal trial.

Presidential Succession Act
A 1947 law enacted by Congress that provides for the filling of any simultaneous vacancy of the presidency and vice presidency.

Twenty-Fifth Amendment
Adopted in 1967 to establish procedures for filling vacancies in the office of president and vice president as well as providing for procedures to deal with the disability of a president.

only for "Treason, Bribery, or other high Crimes and Misdemeanors." The Framers empowered the House to impeach the president by a simple majority vote. The Senate then acts as a court of law and tries the president for the charged offenses, with the chief justice of the U.S. Supreme Court presiding. A two-thirds majority vote in the Senate on any count contained in the articles of impeachment is necessary to remove the president from office. The House of Representatives has impeached only two presidents, Andrew Johnson and Bill Clinton. The Senate removed neither man, however, from office.

In 1974, President Richard M. Nixon resigned from office rather than face the certainty of impeachment, trial, and removal from office for his role in covering up details about a break-in at the Democratic Party's national headquarters in the Watergate office complex. What came to be known simply as **Watergate** also produced a major decision from the Supreme Court on the scope of what is termed **executive privilege**. In *U.S. v. Nixon* **(1974)**, the Supreme Court ruled unanimously that no overriding executive privilege sanctioned the president's refusal to comply with a court order to produce information for use in the trial of the Watergate defendants. Since then, presidents have varied widely in their claim to executive privilege. President Bill Clinton asserted it several times, especially during the impeachment proceedings against him. President George W. Bush made such claims less frequently, instead often arguing that he and the vice president had what he called "constitutional prerogatives."[6]

Rules of Succession

Through 2016, eight presidents have died in office from illness or assassination. William H. Harrison was the first president to die in office—he caught a cold at his Inauguration in 1841 and died one month later. John Tyler thus became the first vice president to succeed to the presidency. In 1865, Abraham Lincoln became the first assassinated president.

Knowing that a system of orderly transfer of power was necessary, the Framers created the office of the vice president. To further clarify presidential succession, in 1947, Congress passed the **Presidential Succession Act**, which lists—in order—those in line to succeed the president (see Table 7.1).

The Succession Act has never been used because a vice president has always been available to take over when a president died in office. To ensure this will continue to be the case, the **Twenty-Fifth Amendment** became part of the Constitution in 1967 as a response to the assassination of President John F. Kennedy. Should a vacancy occur in the office of the vice president, the Twenty-Fifth Amendment directs the president to appoint a new vice president, subject to the approval (by a simple majority) of both houses of Congress.

The Twenty-Fifth Amendment also contains a section that allows the vice president and a majority of the Cabinet (or some other body determined by Congress) to

TABLE 7.1 WHAT IS THE PRESIDENTIAL LINE OF SUCCESSION?

1. Vice President	10. Secretary of Commerce
2. Speaker of the House	11. Secretary of Labor
3. President Pro Tempore of the Senate	12. Secretary of Health and Human Services
4. Secretary of State	13. Secretary of Housing and Urban Development
5. Secretary of the Treasury	14. Secretary of Transportation
6. Secretary of Defense	15. Secretary of Energy
7. Attorney General	16. Secretary of Education
8. Secretary of the Interior	17. Secretary of Veterans Affairs
9. Secretary of Agriculture	18. Secretary of Homeland Security

deem a president unable to fulfill his duties. It sets up a procedure to permit the vice president to become acting president if the president is incapacitated. The president also can voluntarily relinquish his power.

THE CONSTITUTIONAL POWERS OF THE PRESIDENT

7.2 Identify the roles and responsibilities of the president under the Constitution.

In contrast to Article I's laundry list of enumerated powers for the Congress, Article II details few specific presidential powers. Perhaps the most important section of Article II is its first sentence: "The executive Power shall be vested in a President of the United States of America." Nonetheless, presidents' combined powers, discussed below, make them major players in the policy process.

The Appointment Power

To help the president enforce laws passed by Congress, the Constitution authorizes him to appoint, with the advice and consent of the Senate, "Ambassadors, other public Ministers and Consuls, judges of the supreme Court, and all other Officers of the United States, whose Appointments are not herein otherwise provided for, and which shall be established by Law." Although this section of the Constitution deals only with appointments, behind that language lies a powerful policy-making tool. The president has the authority to make nearly 3,500 appointments to his administration (of which about 1,125 require Senate confirmation).[7] He also holds the power to remove many of his appointees at will. In addition, he technically appoints all military personnel subject to Senate approval, although often by voice vote. Many of these appointees are in positions to wield substantial authority over the course and direction of public policy. And, especially in the context of a president's ability to make appointments to the federal courts, presidential influence can last far past terms in office. President Obama's policy initiatives suffered because so many of his nominations stalled in the Republican-controlled Congress during his last two years in office.

In the past, when a president forwarded nominations to the Senate for its approval, the Senate traditionally gave his selections great respect—especially those for the **Cabinet**, an advisory group chosen by the president to help him make decisions and execute laws. In fact, until the 1990s, the Senate confirmed the vast majority of all presidential nominations.[8] This is no longer the case, as investigations into nominees' pasts and political wrangling in the Senate can delay the approval of nominees for months. Many appointees end up withdrawing from consideration as hearings often are not held within 18 months or more of a nomination.

Delay or rejection of nominees can have a major impact on the course of an administration. Rejections leave a president without first choices, affect a president's relationship with the Senate, and influence how the public perceives the president. Although the Senate in the 115th Congress is controlled by Republicans, some Democrats have pledged to block President Donald J. Trump's nominations using the filibuster.

The Power to Convene Congress

The Constitution requires the president to inform the Congress periodically of "the State of the Union" and authorizes the president to convene either one or both houses of Congress on "extraordinary Occasions." The power to convene Congress had more importance when Congress did not sit in nearly year-round sessions, although it may still be significant in times of national crisis.

UNDER WHAT CIRCUMSTANCES DOES A PRESIDENT REMOVE AN APPOINTEE?

Presidents have a large number of aides who help them craft policy. These aides are often held accountable for a president's policy-making failures. Here, President George W. Bush quite literally shows Secretary of Defense Donald Rumsfeld the door following Republican losses in the 2006 midterm elections. These defeats were at least in part attributable to Rumsfeld's failures in the conduct of wars in Afghanistan and Iraq.

Cabinet
The formal body of presidential advisers who head the fifteen executive departments. Presidents often add others to this body of formal advisers.

League of Nations
A multilateral diplomatic organization that existed from 1920-1946 that sought, unsuccessfully, to prevent future wars; the United States never joined.

executive agreements
Formal international agreements entered into by the president that do not require the advice and consent of the U.S. Senate.

veto
The formal, constitutional authority of the president to reject bills passed by both houses of Congress, thus preventing them from becoming law without further congressional action.

The Power to Make Treaties

The president's power to make treaties with foreign nations is checked by the Constitution's stipulation that at least two-thirds of the members of the Senate must approve all treaties. The chief executive can also "receive ambassadors," wording that has been interpreted to allow the president to recognize the existence of other nations.

Historically, the Senate ratifies about 90 percent of the treaties submitted by the president.[9] Perhaps the most notable example of a rejected treaty was the Senate's defeat of the Treaty of Versailles submitted by President Woodrow Wilson in 1919. The treaty was an agreement among the major nations to end World War I. At Wilson's insistence, it also called for the creation of the **League of Nations**—a precursor of the United Nations—to foster continued peace and international disarmament. In struggling to gain international acceptance for the League, Wilson had taken American support for granted. This was a dramatic miscalculation. Isolationists, led by Senator Henry Cabot Lodge (R–MA), opposed U.S. participation in the League on the grounds that the League would place the United States in the center of every major international conflict. Proponents countered that, League or no League, the United States had emerged from World War I as a world power and that membership in the League of Nations would enhance its new role. The vote in the Senate for ratification was very close, but the isolationists prevailed—the United States stayed out of the League, and Wilson was devastated.

The Senate also may require substantial amendment of a treaty prior to its approval. When President Jimmy Carter proposed the controversial Panama Canal Treaty in 1977 to turn the canal over to Panama, for example, the Senate demanded settlement of several conditions before approving the canal's return.

As a result, presidents may try to use **executive agreements** to form secret and highly sensitive arrangements with foreign nations without Senate approval. Presidents have used these agreements since the days of George Washington, and the courts have upheld their use. Since 1900, many presidents have favored executive agreements over treaties. They are not binding on subsequent administrations and can be undone immediately by successors, however.

The Veto Power

During the Constitutional Convention, proponents of a strong executive argued that the president should have an absolute and final **veto** over acts of Congress. Opponents of this idea, including Benjamin Franklin, countered that in their home states, the executive veto "was constantly made use of to extort money" from legislators. James Madison, however, argued that an executive veto was necessary to maintain the system of checks and balances.

Thus, the Framers gave the president veto power, but only as a "qualified negative." Although the president has the authority to veto any act of Congress (with the exception of joint resolutions that propose constitutional amendments), the Framers gave Congress the authority to override an executive veto by a two-thirds vote in each house. Congress, however, rarely can muster enough votes to override a veto. A notable exception occurred in September 2016 when Congress overrode President Obama's veto of a bill allowing the families of those killed in the September 11 terrorist attacks to sue Saudi Arabia for any involvement in the plot.

Even the threat of a presidential veto has become a powerful way for a president to influence law-making. Such a threat often prompts members of Congress to fashion legislation they know will receive presidential acquiescence, if not support.[10] In situations where the Congress and president are of the same party, vetoes are rare.

HOW HAVE PAST PRESIDENTS FULFILLED THE POWERS OF THE OFFICE?

The president of the United States is asked to wear many hats. A good number of these roles extend from the powers the Framers enumerated in Article II of the U.S. Constitution. Others have evolved out of necessity over time. Examine the examples of recent presidents (below) as they fulfilled these roles.

CHIEF LAW ENFORCER:
Troops sent by President Dwight D. Eisenhower enforce a federal court decision ordering the integration of public schools in Little Rock, Arkansas.

LEADER OF THE PARTY:
President Ronald Reagan mobilizes conservatives at the Republican National Convention, changing the nature of the party.

COMMANDER IN CHIEF:
President Barack Obama meets with members of the armed forces.

SHAPER OF PUBLIC POLICY:
President Richard M. Nixon cheers on the efforts of Apollo 11 astronauts as he celebrates U.S. space policy.

KEY PLAYER IN THE LEGISLATIVE PROCESS:
President Bill Clinton celebrates newly passed legislation at a bill-signing ceremony.

CHIEF OF STATE:
President John F. Kennedy and his wife, Jacqueline, pose for cameras with the president of France and his wife during the Kennedy's widely publicized 1961 trip to that nation.

The Power to Preside over the Military as Commander in Chief

One of the most important executive powers is that over the military. Article II states that the president is "Commander in Chief of the Army and Navy of the United States." While the Constitution specifically grants Congress the authority to declare war, presidents since Abraham Lincoln have used the commander in chief clause in conjunction with the chief executive's duty to "take Care that the Laws be faithfully executed" to wage war (and to broaden various presidential powers).

Modern presidents continually clash with Congress over the ability to declare war. The Vietnam War, in which 58,000 American soldiers were killed and 300,000 were wounded, was conducted (at a cost of $150 billion) without a congressional declaration of war.

During that highly controversial war, Presidents Johnson and Richard M. Nixon routinely assured members of Congress that victory was near. In 1971, however,

pardon
An executive grant providing restoration of all rights and privileges of citizenship to a specific individual charged with or convicted of a crime.

publication of what were called *The Pentagon Papers* revealed what many people had suspected all along: the Johnson administration had systematically altered casualty figures and distorted key facts to place the progress of the war in a more positive light. Angered that this misinformation had led Congress to defer to the executive in the conduct of the Vietnam War, in 1973, Congress passed the War Powers Resolution to limit the president's authority to introduce American troops into hostile foreign lands without congressional approval. President Nixon vetoed the resolution, but both houses of Congress overrode it by a two-thirds majority.

Presidents since Nixon have continued to insist that the War Powers Resolution is an unconstitutional infringement on their executive power. Still, in 2001, President George W. Bush complied with the resolution when he sought, and both houses of Congress approved, a joint resolution authorizing the use of force against "those responsible for the recent [September 11] attacks launched against the United States." In October 2002, after President Bush declared Iraq to be a "grave threat to peace," the House (296–133) and Senate (77–23) also voted overwhelmingly to allow the president to use force in Iraq "as he determines to be necessary and appropriate," thereby conferring tremendous authority on Bush and future presidents to wage war.

The Pardoning Power

Presidents can exercise a check on judicial power through their constitutional authority to grant reprieves or pardons. A **pardon** is an executive grant releasing an individual from the punishment or legal consequences of a crime before or after conviction, and restores all rights and privileges of citizenship. Presidents exercise complete pardoning power for federal offenses except in cases of impeachment, which cannot be pardoned. President Gerald R. Ford gave the most famous presidential pardon of all to former President Richard M. Nixon—who had not been formally charged with any crime—"for any offenses against the United States, which he, Richard Nixon, has committed or may have committed while in office." This unilateral, absolute pardon unleashed a torrent of public criticism against Ford and raised questions about whether Nixon had discussed the pardon with Ford before resigning. Many analysts attribute Ford's defeat in the 1976 election to that pardon.

Even though pardons generally apply to a specific individual, presidents have also used them to offer general amnesties. President Jimmy Carter, for example, incurred the wrath of many veterans' groups when he made an offer of unconditional amnesty to approximately 10,000 men who had fled the United States or gone into hiding to avoid the draft for military service in the Vietnam War.

Presidents may also use their pardoning power to make a policy statement. During his presidency, Barack Obama used his clemency power to commute the sentences of hundreds in federal prison for nonviolent drug offenses, sending a clear message to Congress that they ought to vote on legislation to reduce incarceration levels for such offenses. Obama has said of his use of the pardoning power, "I believe that at its heart, America is a nation of second chances, and I believe these folks deserve their second chance."[11]

THE DEVELOPMENT AND EXPANSION OF PRESIDENTIAL POWER

7.3 Trace the expansion of presidential power.

Every president brings to the position not only a vision of America but also expectations about how to use presidential authority. But, most presidents find accomplishing their goals much more difficult than they envisioned. As he was leaving office, for example, President Harry S Truman mused about what surprises awaited his successor, Dwight D. Eisenhower, a former general: "He'll sit here and he'll say, 'Do this! Do that!'

And nothing will happen. Poor Ike—it won't be a bit like the army. He'll find it very frustrating."[12]

inherent powers
Powers that belong to the president because they can be inferred from the Constitution.

The formal powers enumerated in Article II of the Constitution and the Supreme Court's interpretation of those constitutional provisions limit a president's authority. The times in which the president serves, his confidantes and advisers, and his personality and leadership abilities all affect how he wields these powers. Furthermore, not only do different times call for different kinds of leaders; they also often provide limits or, conversely, wide opportunities for whomever serves as president at the time. Crises, in particular, trigger expansions of presidential power.

Establishing Presidential Authority: The First Presidents

When President George Washington was sworn in on a cold, blustery day in New York City on April 30, 1789, he took over an office and a government yet to be created. Eventually, the government hired a few hundred postal workers and Washington appointed a small group of Cabinet advisers and clerks. George Washington set several important precedents for future presidents:

- He took every opportunity to establish the primacy of the national government. In 1794, for example, Washington used the militia of four states to put down the Whiskey Rebellion, an uprising of 3,000 western Pennsylvania farmers opposed to a federal excise tax on liquor. To emphasize the significance of the action, Washington, along with Secretary of the Treasury Alexander Hamilton, led the 15,000 troops into battle himself. Washington's action helped establish the idea of federal supremacy and the authority of the executive branch to collect taxes levied by Congress.

- He began the practice of regular meetings with his advisers, thus establishing the Cabinet system.

- He asserted the chief executive's prominent role in the conduct of foreign affairs. He sent envoys to negotiate the Jay Treaty to end continued hostilities with Great Britain. Then, over senatorial objection, he continued to wield his authority first to negotiate treaties and then simply to submit them to the Senate for approval. Washington made it clear that the Senate's function was limited to approval of treaties and did not include negotiation with foreign powers.

- He claimed the powers of the presidency as the basis for establishing a policy of strict neutrality when the British and French were at war. Although the Constitution is silent about a president's authority to declare neutrality, Washington's supporters argued that the Constitution granted the president **inherent powers**—that is, powers belonging to the president because they can be inferred from the Constitution, such as that authorizing him to conduct diplomatic relations.

Like Washington, the next two presidents, John Adams and Thomas Jefferson, acted in ways critical to the development of the presidency as well as to the president's role in the political system. Adams's poor leadership skills, for example, heightened the divisions between Federalists and Anti-Federalists and probably hastened the development of political parties. Jefferson took critical steps to expand the role of the president in the legislative process. Like Washington, he claimed that certain presidential powers were inherent and used such powers to justify nearly doubling the size of the nation through the Louisiana Purchase in 1803.

Incremental Expansion of Presidential Powers: 1809–1933

Although the first three presidents made enormous contributions to the office of the chief executive, the way government functioned in its formative years caused the balance of power to be heavily weighted in favor of a strong Congress. Americans routinely had close contacts with their representatives in Congress, while to most citizens the president seemed a remote figure. By the end of Jefferson's first term, it was clear that the Framers' initial fear of an all-powerful, monarchical president was unfounded. The strength of Congress and the relatively weak presidents who came after Jefferson allowed Congress quickly to assert itself as the most powerful branch of government.

President Andrew Jackson was the first strong national leader who represented more than just a landed, propertied elite. By the time Jackson ran for president in 1828, eleven new states had been added to the union, and the number of white males eligible to vote had increased dramatically, as nearly all states had removed property requirements for voting. The election of Jackson from Tennessee, as the seventh president, signaled the end of an era: he was the first president to be neither a Virginian nor an Adams. Jackson personified the western, frontier, egalitarian spirit, and his election launched the beginning of Jacksonian democracy. The masses loved him, and legends arose around his down-to-earth image. Jackson, for example, once was asked to give a position to a soldier who had lost his leg on the battlefield and needed the job to support his family. When told that the man hadn't voted for him, Jackson responded: "If he lost his leg fighting for his country, that is vote enough for me."[13]

Jackson used his image and personal power to buttress the developing party system by rewarding loyal followers of his Democratic Party with presidential appointments. Frequently at odds with Congress, he made use of the veto power against twelve bills, surpassing the combined total of ten vetoes used by his six predecessors. Jackson also reasserted the supremacy of the national government (and the presidency) by facing down South Carolina's nullification of a federal tariff law.

Abraham Lincoln's approach to the presidency was similar to Jackson's. To combat the unprecedented emergency of the Civil War, Lincoln assumed powers that no president before him had claimed. Because Lincoln believed he needed to act quickly for the very survival of the nation, he frequently took action without first obtaining the approval of Congress. Among many of Lincoln's legally questionable acts were:

- He suspended the writ of *habeas corpus*, which allows those in prison to petition for release, citing the need to jail persons suspected of disloyal practices.
- He expanded the size of the U.S. Army above congressionally mandated ceilings.
- He ordered a blockade of southern ports without the approval of Congress.
- He closed the U.S. mail to treasonable correspondence.

Lincoln argued that the inherent powers of his office allowed him to circumvent the Constitution in a time of war or national crisis. Since the Constitution confers on the president the duty to make sure that the laws of the United States are faithfully executed, reasoned Lincoln, these acts were constitutional. He simply refused to allow the nation to crumble because of what he viewed as technical requirements of the Constitution.

Creating the Modern Presidency

Since the 1930s, the general trend has been for presidential—as opposed to congressional—decision making to assume greater importance. The start of this trend can be traced to the four-term presidency of Franklin D. Roosevelt (FDR), who led the nation through several crises. Many now criticize this growth of presidential power as well as of the federal government and its programs. To understand the basis for a large number of today's calls for reform of the political system, it is critical to learn how the government and the role of the president grew.[14]

FDR took office in 1933 in the midst of the Great Depression, a major economic crisis in which a substantial portion of the U.S. workforce was unemployed. Noting the sorry state of the national economy in his Inaugural Address, FDR concluded: "This nation asks for action and action now." To jump-start the American economy, FDR asked Congress for and was given "broad executive powers to wage a war

HOW DID ABRAHAM LINCOLN EXPAND PRESIDENTIAL POWER?
During the Civil War, Lincoln assumed inherent powers that no president before him had claimed. He argued that these actions were necessary for the preservation of the Union. After the war, the president's powers never returned to their previous levels. Here, Lincoln is shown meeting with military leaders following the battle of Antietam, one of the bloodiest battles of the Civil War.

against the emergency, as great as the power that would be given to me if we were in fact invaded by a foreign foe."[15]

Just as Abraham Lincoln had taken bold steps upon his Inauguration, Roosevelt also acted quickly. He immediately fashioned a plan for national recovery called the New Deal, a package of bold and controversial programs designed to invigorate the failing American economy.

Roosevelt served an unprecedented twelve years in office; he was elected to four terms but died shortly after the beginning of the fourth. During his years in office, the nation went from the economic war of the Great Depression to the real international conflict of World War II. The institution of the presidency changed profoundly and permanently with the creation of new federal agencies to implement the New Deal.

FDR also personalized the presidency by establishing a new relationship between the president and the people. In his radio addresses, or fireside chats, as he called them, he spoke directly to the public in a relaxed and informal manner about serious issues.

To his successors, FDR left the modern presidency. This included a burgeoning federal bureaucracy, an active and usually leading role for the president in both domestic and foreign policy and legislation, and a nationalized executive office that used technology—first radio, then TV, and now the Internet and social media—to bring the president closer to the public than ever before.

THE PRESIDENTIAL ESTABLISHMENT

7.4 Describe the organization and functions of the Executive Office of the President.

As the responsibilities and scope of presidential authority grew over the years, so did the executive branch, including the number of people working directly for the president in the White House. The presidential establishment includes the vice president and the vice president's staff, the Cabinet, the president's spouse and the spouse's

first lady
The designation provided to the wife of a president or, at the state level, of a governor; no specific analogue exists for a male spouse.

staff, the Executive Office of the President, and the White House staff. All help presidents fulfill their duties as chief executive.

The Vice President

For many years, political observers considered the vice presidency a sure place for a public official to disappear into obscurity. When John Adams wrote to his wife, Abigail, about his position as America's first vice president, he said it was "the most insignificant office that was the invention of man … or his imagination conceived."[16]

Historically, presidents have selected their vice presidents largely to balance—politically, geographically, or otherwise—the presidential ticket, with little thought given to the possibility that the vice president could become president. Franklin D. Roosevelt, or example, a liberal New Yorker, selected John Nance Garner, a conservative Texan, to be his running mate in 1932. After serving two terms, Garner—who openly disagreed with Roosevelt over many policies, including Roosevelt's decision to seek a third term—unsuccessfully sought the 1940 presidential nomination himself.

How much power a vice president has depends on how much the president is willing to give. Jimmy Carter was the first president to grant his vice president, Walter Mondale, more than ceremonial duties. In fact, Mondale was the first vice president to have an office in the White House. More recent vice presidents, including Joe Biden, attained significant powers and access to the president, elevating the office to new heights. How much power President Trump will transfer to Vice President Mike Pence is still an open question.

The Cabinet

The Cabinet, which has no official basis in the Constitution but is implied by Article II, section 2, is an informal institution based on practice and precedent whose membership is determined by tradition and presidential discretion. By custom, this advisory group selected by the president includes the heads of major executive departments. Presidents today also include their vice presidents in Cabinet meetings as well as any other agency heads or officials to whom they would like to accord Cabinet-level status.

As a body, the Cabinet's major function is to assist the president in executing the laws and in making decisions. Although the Framers discussed the idea of some form of national executive council, they did not include a provision for one in the Constitution. They did recognize, however, the need for departments of government and departmental heads.

Over the years, the Cabinet has grown alongside the responsibilities of the national government. As interest groups, in particular, pressured Congress and the president to recognize their demands for services and governmental action, they often were rewarded by the creation of an executive department. Since a secretary heading an executive department automatically became a member of the president's Cabinet, powerful clientele groups, including farmers (Agriculture), business people (Commerce), workers (Labor), and teachers (Education), saw the creation of a department as a way to expand their access to the national government.

While the size of the president's Cabinet has increased over the years, the reliance of most presidents on their Cabinet secretaries has decreased. Some individual members of a president's Cabinet, however, may be very influential.

Presidential Spouses

From the time of Martha Washington, the spouses of U.S. presidents (formally called the **first lady**, a term coined in 1849) have assisted presidents as informal advisers while making other, more public, and significant contributions to American society. Abigail Adams, for example, was a constant sounding board for her husband, John. An early feminist, in 1776 she cautioned him "to Remember the Ladies" in any new code of laws.

Edith Bolling Galt Wilson was probably the most powerful first lady. When President Woodrow Wilson collapsed and was left partly paralyzed in 1919, she became his surrogate and decided whom and what the stricken president saw. Her detractors dubbed her "Acting First Man."

Eleanor Roosevelt also played a powerful and much criticized role in national affairs. Not only did she write a nationally syndicated daily newspaper column, but also she traveled and lectured widely, worked tirelessly on countless Democratic Party matters, and raised six children. After FDR's death, she shone in her own right as U.S. delegate to the United Nations, where she headed the commission that drafted the covenant on human rights. Later, she headed President John F. Kennedy's Commission on the Status of Women.

Michelle Obama not only led efforts to encourage healthy eating and to combat childhood obesity, but also took an active role in the 2016 presidential campaign. She spoke at the Democratic National Convention and served as a popular surrogate for Hillary Clinton.

Melania Trump played a limited role in her husband's campaign. As only the second first lady not to be born in the United States, she is expected to emulate former First Lady Jacqueline Kennedy and focus on the social aspects of the White House. She plans to make an end to cyberbullying a major project as first lady.

The Executive Office of the President (EOP)

Executive Office of the President (EOP)
A mini-bureaucracy created in 1939 to help the president oversee the executive branch bureaucracy.

In 1939, FDR established the **Executive Office of the President (EOP)** to oversee his New Deal programs. Its purpose was to provide the president with a general staff to help him direct the diverse activities of the executive branch. In fact, it is a mini-bureaucracy of advisers, many of whom are located in the ornate Eisenhower Executive Office Building next to the White House on Pennsylvania Avenue as well as in the White House itself.

The EOP has expanded to include several advisory and policy-making agencies and task forces. Over time, the units of the EOP have become the prime policy makers in their fields of expertise, as they play key roles in advancing the president's policy preferences. Among the EOP's most important members are the Council of Economic Advisers, the Office of Management and Budget, the Office of the Vice President, the Office of the U.S. Trade Representative, and the National Security Council. The NSC is

AMERICAN POLITICS IN COMPARATIVE PERSPECTIVE

How Does the Role of U.S. President Differ from Other Heads of State?

The American presidency fuses together a number of important constitutional roles. These include the powerful positions of commander in chief, chief diplomat, and head of the federal government, alongside the more ceremonial position of head of state.

However, in democracies with parliamentary systems, these roles are organized quite differently. In such countries, final executive authority resides with the prime minister, who is the head of government. The prime minister is chosen by the legislature, leads the Cabinet, and sets the overall direction of government policy.

Parliamentary systems designate a different person, however, to act as ceremonial head of state. This role can be filled by a hereditary king or queen, as in the Scandinavian countries and Japan, or by a "nonexecutive" or "figurehead" president, as in Germany and Italy.

These heads of state fulfill many of the same ceremonial functions that are carried out by the U.S. president, including hosting visiting dignitaries, bestowing honors and awards, formally addressing the nation, and conducting goodwill trips abroad.

Splitting the roles of head of state and head of government alters the nature of both. In particular, this division makes it very clear that the prime minister is "just another politician" who happens to be wielding power at the moment. The prime minister may be highly influential, but she or he is clearly *not* the symbolic "leader of the nation" as is the U.S. president.

BUCKINGHAM PALACE, LONDON:
Home of the British queen, who is head of state.

THE WHITE HOUSE, WASHINGTON DC:
Home of the U.S. president, who is head of government and head of state.

NUMBER 10 DOWNING STREET, LONDON:
Home of the British prime minister, who is head of government.

CRITICAL THINKING QUESTIONS

1. What does the relative size and opulence of these three buildings suggest about the status of each of their respective residents?
2. What would change about the U.S. presidency if some other government official were designated to be the symbolic head of state?
3. What areas of domestic or foreign policy would be impacted if the United States were to split the head of state and head of government roles?

headed by a national security adviser, and comprises the president; the vice president; and the secretaries of state, defense, and treasury. The chair of the Joint Chiefs of Staff and the director of the Central Intelligence Agency also participate.

The White House Staff

Often more directly responsible to the president are the several hundred members of the White House staff: the personal assistants to the president, including senior aides, their deputies, assistants with professional duties, and clerical and administrative aides. As personal assistants, these advisers are not subject to Senate confirmation, nor do they have divided loyalties. Their power derives from their personal relationship with the president, and they have no independent legal authority.

Although presidents organize the White House staff in different ways, they typically have a chief of staff whose job is to facilitate the smooth running of the executive branch of government. Successful chiefs of staff also have protected the president from mistakes and helped implement policies to obtain the maximum political advantage for the president. Other important White House aides include domestic, foreign, and economic policy strategists; the communications staff; the White House counsel; and a liaison between the president and Congress.

PRESIDENTIAL LEADERSHIP AND THE IMPORTANCE OF PUBLIC OPINION

7.5 Describe the relationship between the president and the public.

A president's success in having preferred programs adopted or implemented depends on many factors, including individual leadership capabilities, personality and powers of persuasion, the president's ability to mobilize public opinion, the public's perception of the president's performance, and Congress's perception of the president's public support.

Presidential Leadership and Personality

Leadership is not easy to exercise, and it remains an elusive concept for scholars to identify and measure, but it is important to all presidents seeking support for their programs and policies. Frequently, the difference between great and mediocre presidents centers on their ability to grasp the importance of leadership style. Truly great presidents, such as Lincoln and FDR, understood that the White House was a seat of power from which decisions could flow to shape the national destiny. They recognized that their day-to-day activities and how they went about them should be designed to bolster support for their policies and to secure congressional and popular backing that could translate their intuitive judgment into meaningful action. Mediocre presidents, on the other hand, have tended to regard the White House as "a stage for the presentation of performances to the public" or a fitting honor to cap a career.[17]

Political scientist Richard E. Neustadt calls the president's ability to influence members of Congress and the public "the power to persuade." Neustadt believes this power is crucial to presidential leadership because it enables presidents to get their policy goals enacted and win support for their policies in the electorate.[18] Persuasion may come from a variety of sources, including a president's natural charisma or ability to make people do things they would not ordinarily do.

Going Public

Even before radio, TV, and the Internet, presidents tried to reach out to the public to gain support for their programs through what President Theodore Roosevelt called

bully pulpit
The view that a major power of the presidency, albeit not one prescribed by the Constitution, is to draw attention to and generate support for particular positions.

the **bully pulpit**. The development of commercial air travel, radio, TV, computers, cell phones, and social media has made direct communication to larger numbers of voters much easier. Presidents, their spouses and family members, and other presidential advisers travel the world over to publicize their views and to build support on a personal level as well for administration programs.

Direct presidential appeals to the electorate, such as those often made by recent presidents, are referred to as "going public."[19] Going public means that a president bypasses the heads of members of Congress to gain support from the people, who can then place pressure on their elected officials in Washington. President Bill Clinton, for example, was keenly aware of the importance of maintaining his connection with the public. At a black-tie dinner honoring radio and TV correspondents, Clinton responded to criticisms leveled against him for not holding traditional press conferences by pointing out how clever he was to ignore the traditional press. "You know why I can stiff you on the press conferences? Because Larry King [then on CNN] liberated me from you by giving me to the American people directly."[20]

The President and Public Opinion

Presidents and other public figures often use approval ratings as tacit measures of their political capital: their ability to enact public policy simply because of their name and their office.[21] People assume that presidents who have high approval ratings—as President George W. Bush did in the immediate aftermath of the September 11, 2001, terrorist attacks—are more powerful leaders with a mandate for action that comes largely by virtue of high levels of public support. These presidents are often able to use their clout to push controversial legislation, such as the USA PATRIOT Act, through Congress. A public appearance from a popular president can even deliver a hotly contested congressional seat or gubernatorial contest to the president's party.

In sharp contrast, low approval ratings often cripple presidents in the policy arena. Their low ratings can actually prevent favored policies from being enacted on Capitol Hill, even when their party controls the Congress, as many of their partisans locked in close elections shy away from being seen or affiliated with an unpopular president.

Presidential popularity, though, generally follows a cyclical pattern. These cycles have been recorded since 1938, when pollsters first began to track presidential

WHY DO PRESIDENTS "GO PUBLIC"?

Modern presidents often excel at carefully scripted media events that allow them to reach out directly to supporters and place their critics on the hot seat. Here, President Barack Obama marks his final appearance at the White House Correspondent's Dinner in 2016 with a literal mic drop and the words "Obama Out."

popularity. Typically, presidents enjoy their highest level of public approval at the beginning of their terms and try to take advantage of this honeymoon period to get their programs passed by Congress as soon as possible. Each action a president takes, however, is divisive—some people will approve, and others will disapprove. Disapproval tends to have a negative cumulative effect on a president's approval rating. Since Lyndon B. Johnson's presidency, only five presidents have left office with approval ratings of more than 50 percent. President Donald J. Trump assumed the presidency with the highest negatives ever received by an incoming president and strained relationships with House and Senate leaders.

TOWARD REFORM: THE PRESIDENT AS POLICY MAKER

7.6 Describe the relationship between the president and the Congress.

When President Franklin D. Roosevelt sent his first legislative package to Congress, he broke the traditional model of law making.[22] As envisioned by the Framers, the responsibility of making laws fell to Congress. Now FDR was claiming a leadership role for the president in the legislative process. Said the president of this new relationship: "It is the duty of the President to propose and it is the privilege of the Congress to dispose."[23] With those words and the actions that followed, FDR shifted the presidency into a law- and policy-making role. Now the president and the executive branch not only executed the laws but generally suggested them and proposed budgets to Congress to fund those proposals.

The President's Role in Proposing and Facilitating Legislation

Modern presidents play a major role in setting the legislative agenda, especially in an era when the House and Senate are narrowly divided along partisan lines. Without working majorities, "merely placing a program before Congress is not enough," as President Lyndon B. Johnson once explained. "Without constant attention from the administration, most legislation moves through the congressional process at the speed of a glacier."[24]

However, presidents have a hard time persuading Congress to pass their programs. Recent research by political scientists shows that presidents are much more likely to win on bills central to their announced agendas than to secure passage of legislation proposed by others.[25]

Because presidents generally experience declining support for policies they advocate throughout their terms, it is important for presidents to propose key plans early in their administrations. Even President Lyndon B. Johnson, who was able to push nearly 60 percent of his programs through Congress, noted: "You've got to give it all you can, that first year … before they start worrying about themselves… . You can't put anything through when half the Congress is thinking how to beat you."[26]

Presidents can also bolster support for legislative packages by calling on their political party. As the informal leader of their party, presidents should build coalitions in Congress, where party loyalty is very important. This strategy works best when the president has helped to carry party members into office as well as when the president's party has a majority in the legislature.

The Budgetary Process and Legislative Implementation

Closely associated with the presidential ability to have legislation passed is a president's capacity to secure funding for new and existing programs. A president sets national policy and priorities through budget proposals and continued insistence on their congressional passage. The budget proposal not only outlines the programs the

Office of Management and Budget (OMB)
The office that prepares the president's annual budget proposal, reviews the budget and programs of the executive departments, supplies economic forecasts, and conducts detailed analyses of proposed bills and agency rules.

executive order
Rule or regulation issued by the president that has the effect of law. All executive orders must be published in the *Federal Register*.

president wants but also indicates the importance of each program by the amount of funding requested for each and for its associated agency or department.

Because the Framers gave Congress the power of the purse, Congress had primary responsibility for the budgetary process until 1930. The economic disaster set off by the stock market crash of 1929, however, gave FDR the opportunity to involve himself in the congressional budget process, just as he inserted himself into the legislative process. In 1939, the Bureau of the Budget, which had been created in 1921 to help the president inform Congress of the amount of money needed to run the executive branch of government, was made part of the newly created Executive Office of the President. In 1970, President Nixon changed its name to the **Office of Management and Budget (OMB)** to clarify its function in the executive branch.

The OMB works exclusively for the president and employs hundreds of budget and policy experts. Major OMB responsibilities include preparing the president's annual budget proposal; assessing the costs of the president's proposals; and reviewing the progress, budget, and program proposals of the executive department agencies. It also supplies economic forecasts to the president and conducts detailed analyses of proposed bills and agency rules. OMB reports allow presidents to attach price tags to their legislative proposals and defend their budgets.

Policy Making Through Executive Order

Proposing legislation and using the budget to advance policy priorities are not the only ways that presidents can affect the policy process, especially in times of highly divided government when the policies of the president and Congress may differ. Presidents may institute major policy changes by issuing an **executive order**, a rule or regulation set forth by the president that has the effect of law without congressional approval. Presidents Franklin D. Roosevelt and Harry S Truman used executive orders to seize mills, mines, and factories whose production was crucial to World War II and Korean War efforts. Roosevelt and Truman argued that these actions were necessary to preserve national security. The Supreme Court, however, eventually disagreed with the Truman administration in *Youngstown Sheet and Tube* v. *Sawyer* (1952). In that case,

HOW IMPORTANT IS A BALANCED BUDGET?

President Bill Clinton and Vice President Al Gore celebrate the first balanced budget in years, a feat not likely to be repeated soon.

the Court unequivocally stated that Truman had overstepped the boundaries of his office as provided by the Constitution.[27]

While many executive orders help clarify or implement legislation enacted by Congress, others have the effect of making new policy. President Truman also used an executive order to end segregation in the military, and affirmative action was institutionalized as national policy through Executive Order 11246, issued by Lyndon B. Johnson in 1966. These orders may be retracted by future presidents.

Presidents may also issue **signing statements**, occasional written comments attached to a bill, when signing legislation. Often, these written statements merely comment on the bill signed, but they sometimes include controversial claims by the president that some part of the legislation is unconstitutional and that the president intends to disregard it or to implement it in other ways. For example, President George W. Bush used signing statements to express his belief that portions of more than 1,200 laws were unconstitutional. "Among the laws Bush said he [could] ignore [were] military rules and regulations, affirmative action provisions, requirements that Congress be told about immigration services problems, 'whistle-blower' protections for nuclear regulator officials, and safeguards against political interference in federally funded research."[28]

Signing statements, thus, have become another way for presidents to use informal powers to make and influence public policy. These statements invite litigation and may delay policy implementation. Because signing statements happen at the end of the legislative process, they also represent a largely unchecked way for presidents to assert themselves in the ongoing power struggle with Congress.

signing statements
Occasional written comments attached to a bill signed by the president.

REVIEW THE CHAPTER

Roots of the Office of President of the United States

7.1 Describe the constitutional provisions that provide the roots of the American presidency.

To keep any one president from becoming too powerful, the Framers created an executive office with limited powers. They mandated that a president be at least thirty-five years old, a natural-born citizen, and a resident of the United States for fourteen years or more, and they opted not to limit the president's term of office. To further guard against tyranny, they made provisions for the removal of the president.

The Constitutional Powers of the President

7.2 Identify the roles and responsibilities of the president under the Constitution.

The Framers gave the president a variety of specific constitutional powers in Article II, including the powers to appoint, to convene Congress, and to make treaties. The Constitution also gives the president the capacity to grant pardons and to veto acts of Congress. In addition, the president derives considerable power from being commander in chief of the military.

The Development and Expansion of Presidential Power

7.3 Trace the expansion of presidential power.

The development of presidential power has depended on the personal force of those who have held the office. George Washington, in particular, took several actions to establish the primacy of the president in national affairs and as chief executive of a strong national government. With only a few exceptions, subsequent presidents often let Congress dominate in national affairs. Franklin D. Roosevelt (FDR), however, took more power for the office of

the president, and made more decisions in national and foreign affairs.

The Presidential Establishment

7.4 Describe the organization and functions of the Executive Office of the President.

As the responsibilities of the president have grown, so has the executive branch of government. Perhaps the most important policy advisers are those closest to the president: the vice president, the White House staff, some members of the Executive Office of the President, and the president's spouse.

Presidential Leadership and the Importance of Public Opinion

7.5 Describe the relationship between the president and the public.

To gain support for their programs or proposed budgets, presidents use a variety of skills, including personal leadership and direct appeals to the public. The leadership abilities and personal style of each president determines how they go about winning support. Since the 1970s, however, the American public has been increasingly skeptical of presidential actions, and few presidents have enjoyed the extended periods of popularity needed to help win support for programmatic change.

Toward Reform: The President as Policy Maker

7.6 Describe the relationship between the president and the Congress.

Since FDR, the public has looked to the president to propose legislation to Congress. Through proposing legislation, advancing budgets, involvement in the regulatory process, and executive orders and agreements, presidents make policy.

LEARN THE TERMS

bully pulpit
Cabinet
executive agreements
Executive Office of the President (EOP)
executive order
executive privilege
first lady

inherent powers
League of Nations
Office of Management and
    Budget (OMB)
pardon
president
Presidential Succession Act

signing statements
Twenty-Fifth Amendment
Twenty-Second Amendment
U.S. v. *Nixon* (1974)
veto
vice president
Watergate

WHAT IS THE ROLE OF THE PRESIDENT'S CABINET?

President George Washington sits with the first Cabinet in this undated lithograph by Currier and Ives. Shown from left to right: Washington; Henry Knox, Secretary of War; Alexander Hamilton, Secretary of the Treasury; Thomas Jefferson, Secretary of State; and Edmund Randolph, Attorney General.

THE EXECUTIVE BRANCH AND THE FEDERAL BUREAUCRACY

LEARNING OBJECTIVES

8.1   Outline the development of the federal bureaucracy.

8.2   Describe how the federal bureaucracy is organized.

8.3   Describe how the federal bureaucracy is staffed.

8.4   Identify the roles and responsibilities of the federal bureaucracy.

8.5   Identify the means of controlling the federal bureaucracy

federal bureaucracy
The thousands of federal government agencies and institutions that implement and administer federal laws and programs.

Max Weber
German sociologist active in the late nineteenth and early twentieth centuries who articulated the hierarchical structure and near-mechanical functioning of bureaucracies in complex societies.

When General George Washington took office as the first President of the United States, he vowed to hire only those "as shall be the best qualified." While Washington's first Cabinet appointee, Alexander Hamilton, the first Secretary of the Treasury, advocated for a strong national government, Washington's Secretary of State, Thomas Jefferson, believed that the states should retain the lion's share of power in the new nation. Washington appointed Jefferson, knowing that he and Hamilton would clash on many fundamental ideas about the role and scope of government. Later, Jefferson recalled his term of service alongside Hamilton: "Hamilton and myself were daily pitted. Like two fighting cocks." Washington, however, relished this conflict, believing diverse political views could lead him to make the best decisions.

But, when Thomas Jefferson took office as the third president of the United States of America, he fired most of President John Adams's Federalist appointees. He replaced them with men who agreed with his philosophy of a more limited national government. So began the principle of political patronage, which was to reach its apex with the election of Andrew Jackson in 1828.

• • •

The **federal bureaucracy**, or the thousands of federal government agencies and institutions that implement and administer federal laws and programs, is frequently called the "fourth branch of government." Critics often charge that the bureaucracy is too large, too powerful, and too unaccountable to the people or even to elected officials. Many politicians, elected officials, and voters complain that the federal bureaucracy is too wasteful. However, few critics discuss the fact that state and local bureaucracies and bureaucrats, whose numbers are proportionately far larger, also implement laws and policies and are often far less accountable than those working for the federal government.

Many Americans are uncomfortable with the prominent role of the federal government in their lives. Nevertheless, recent studies show that most users of federal agencies rate quite favorably the agencies and services they receive. Most of those polled drew sharp distinctions between particular agencies and the government as a whole. For example, only 20 percent of Americans in one poll expressed positive views toward federal agencies, whereas 61 percent of respondents voiced satisfaction with the agencies with which they have dealt.[1]

Harold D. Lasswell once defined political science as the "study of who gets what, when, and how."[2] Those questions of "what, when, and how" can perhaps best be answered by examining what the bureaucracy is, how it works, and how it is controlled—the topics in this chapter.

ROOTS OF THE FEDERAL BUREAUCRACY

8.1 Outline the development of the federal bureaucracy.

The term "bureaucracy" is French in origin taking the word bureau (a desk or office) and combining it with the Greek word *kratos*, meaning political power or rule. The word did not find its way into English usage until 1818, nearly thirty years after the new federal government began organizing into bureaus, or, more commonly, departments. German sociologist **Max Weber** defined bureaucracy as any system of administration conducted by trained professionals

In 1789, the federal bureaucracy consisted of three departments: Foreign Affairs, War, and Treasury. President George Washington inherited these departments from the government under the Articles of Confederation. A secretary headed each department, and the Department of State almost immediately became the new name for what was called Foreign Affairs in the Articles. To provide the president with legal advice, Congress also created the office of attorney general, a part-time position for one "learned in the law" to represent the interests of the United States government before the Supreme Court and to provide legal advice to the president.

From the beginning, individuals appointed as Cabinet secretaries (as well as the attorney general) were subject to approval by the U.S. Senate, but the president alone could remove them from office. Even the first Congress realized how important it was for a president to be surrounded by those in whom he had complete confidence and trust.

From 1816 to 1861, the size of the federal executive branch and the bureaucracy grew as existing departments faced increased demands and new departments were created. The Post Office, for example, which Article I constitutionally authorized Congress to create, was enlarged to meet the needs of a growing and westward-expanding population. President Andrew Jackson removed the Post Office from the jurisdiction of the Department of the Treasury in 1829 and promoted the postmaster general to Cabinet rank.

The Post Office quickly became a major source of jobs President Jackson could fill by presidential appointment, as every small town and village in the United States had its own postmaster. In commenting on Jackson's wide use of political positions to reward friends and loyalists, one fellow Jacksonian Democrat commented: "to the victors belong the spoils." From that statement came the term **spoils system**, which describes an executive's ability to fire public-office holders of the defeated political party and replace them with party loyalists. The spoils system was a form of **patronage**—jobs, grants, or other special favors given as rewards to friends and political allies for their support.

spoils system
The firing of public-office holders of a defeated political party to replace them with loyalists of the newly elected party.

patronage
Jobs, grants, or other special favors that are given as rewards to friends and political allies for their support.

The Civil War and the Growth of Government

The Civil War (1861–1865) permanently changed the nature of the federal bureaucracy. As the nation geared up for war, President Abraham Lincoln authorized the addition of thousands of new employees to existing departments. The Civil War also spawned the need for new government agencies in response to a series of poor harvests and distribution problems. President Lincoln (who understood that well-fed troops are necessary to conduct a war) created the Department of Agriculture in 1862, although it was not given full Cabinet-level status until more than twenty years later.

Congress also created the Pension Office in 1866 to pay benefits to the thousands of Union veterans who had fought in the war (more than 127,000 veterans initially were eligible for benefits). Overwhelmed with post–Civil War litigation and the high cost of outsourcing government litigation to private attorneys, Congress also created the Department of Justice as a Cabinet department in 1870. Congress and the president added other departments through 1900. Agriculture became a full-fledged department in 1889 and began to play an important part in informing farmers about the latest developments in soil conservation, livestock breeding, and planting.

WHICH U.S. PRESIDENT POPULARIZED THE SPOILS SYSTEM?

Here, a political cartoonist depicts how President Andrew Jackson might have been immortalized for his use of the spoils system. Note that President Jackson is shown riding a pig, rather than a horse. Words written in the ground below the animal include "fraud," "bribery," and "plunder."

From the Spoils System to the Merit System

By the time James A. Garfield, a distinguished Civil War officer, was elected president in 1880, many reformers were calling for changes in the patronage system. Garfield's

merit system
A system of employment based on qualifications, test scores, and ability, rather than party loyalty.

Pendleton Act
Reform measure that established the principle of federal employment on the basis of open, competitive exams and created the Civil Service Commission.

civil service system
The merit system by which many federal bureaucrats are selected.

Sixteenth Amendment
Amendment to the U.S. Constitution that authorized Congress to enact a national income tax.

immediate predecessor, Rutherford B. Hayes, had favored the idea of replacing the spoils system with a **merit system**, a system of employment based on qualifications, test scores, and ability rather than loyalty. Congress, however, failed to pass the legislation he proposed. Possibly because potential job seekers wanted to secure positions before Congress had the opportunity to act on an overhauled civil service system, thousands pressed Garfield for positions. Garfield's life was cut short by the bullets of an assassin who was a frustrated job seeker.

Public reaction to Garfield's death and increasing criticism of the spoils system prompted Congress to pass the Civil Service Reform Act in 1883, more commonly known as the **Pendleton Act**. It established a merit system of federal employment on the basis of open, competitive exams and created a bipartisan three-member Civil Service Commission, which operated until 1978. Initially, the law covered only about 10 percent of positions in the federal **civil service system**, but later laws and executive orders extended coverage of the act to more than 90 percent of all federal employees.

Regulating Commerce

As the nation grew, so did the bureaucracy (see Figure 8.1). In the wake of the tremendous growth of big business (especially railroads), widespread price fixing, and other unfair business practices that occurred after the Civil War, Congress created the Interstate Commerce Commission (ICC) in 1887. In doing so, Congress was reacting to public outcries over exorbitant rates charged by railroad companies for hauling freight. It became the first independent regulatory commission, an entity outside a major executive department. Congress creates independent regulatory commissions such as the ICC, which generally focus on particular aspects of the economy. Commission members are appointed by the president and hold their jobs for fixed terms, but the president cannot remove commissioners unless they fail to uphold their oaths of office. The creation of the ICC also marked a shift in the focus of the bureaucracy from service to regulation, giving the government—in the shape of the bureaucracy—vast powers over individual and property rights.

Theodore Roosevelt, a progressive Republican, became president in 1901. Immediately, he strengthened the movement toward governmental regulation of the economic sphere. When he asked Congress to establish and oversee employer-employee relations, Congress agreed—and the size of the bureaucracy grew further. At that time, many workers toiled long hours for low wages in substandard conditions. Many employers refused to recognize the rights of workers to join unions, and many businesses had grown so large and powerful they could force workers to accept substandard conditions and wages. Progressives wanted new government regulations to cure some of the ills suffered by workers and to control the power of increasingly monopolistic corporations.

In 1913, when it became clear that one agency could not represent the interests of both employers and employees, President Woodrow Wilson divided the Department of Commerce and Labor, creating two separate departments. One year later, Congress created the Federal Trade Commission (FTC) to protect small businesses and the public from unfair competition, especially from big business.

The ratification of the **Sixteenth Amendment** to the Constitution in 1913 also affected the size and growth potential of government. It gave Congress the authority to implement a federal income tax to supplement the national treasury and provided a huge infusion of funds to support new federal agencies, services, and programs.

FIGURE 8.1 HOW MANY EMPLOYEES WORK IN THE FEDERAL EXECUTIVE BRANCH?

The size of the federal executive branch has fluctuated with the needs of the nation. The line graph below tracks these changes from the country's creation to the twenty-first century. Notice the overall growth marked by periods of decline. What events may have caused these fluctuations?

SOURCE: Office of Personnel Management; U.S. Census Bureau.

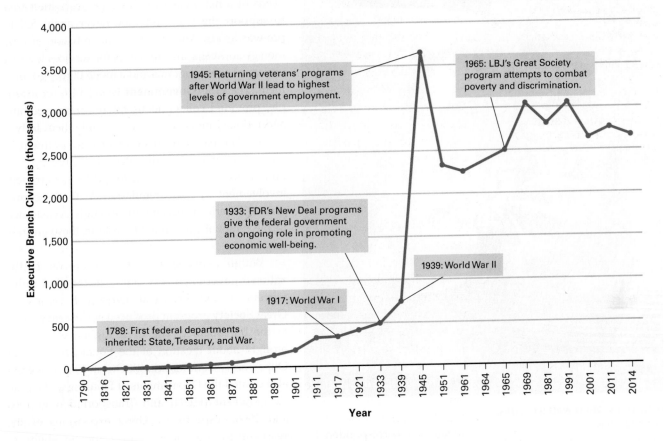

The World Wars and the Growth of Government

The economy appeared to boom as U.S. involvement in **World War I** caused an increase in manufacturing, but ominous events loomed just over the horizon. Farmers were in trouble after a series of bad harvests, the nation experienced a severe slump in agricultural prices, the construction industry went into decline, and bank failures became common throughout the 1920s. After stock prices crashed in 1929, the nation plunged into the **Great Depression**. To combat the resultant high unemployment and weak financial markets, President Franklin D. Roosevelt (who was first elected in 1932) created hundreds of new government agencies to regulate business practices and various aspects of the national economy. Roosevelt believed that a national economic depression called for national intervention. Thus, the president proposed, and the Congress enacted, far-ranging economic legislation. The desperate mood of the nation supported these moves, as most Americans began to reconsider their ideas about the proper role of government and the provision of governmental services. Formerly, most Americans had believed in a hands-off approach; now they considered it the federal government's job to get the economy going and get Americans back to work.

As the nation struggled to recover from the Great Depression, the Japanese attack on U.S. ships at Pearl Harbor, Hawaii, on December 7, 1941, forced the United States into **World War II**. The war immediately affected the economy: healthy, eligible men went to war, and women went to work at factories or in other jobs to replace the men.

World War I
A global military conflict that took place from 1914–1918 across Europe and its overseas territories. The United States militarily intervened from 1917–1918.

Great Depression
A severe global economic downturn marked by mass unemployment and poverty that began in the United States in 1929 and persisted to some degree until the end of the 1930s.

World War II
A global military conflict that took place from 1939–1945 in Europe, Africa, Asia, and the Pacific region. The United States was formally involved in the war from 1941-1945.

WAR PRODUCTION CO-ORDINATING COMMITTEE

HOW DID WORLD WAR II CHANGE GOVERNMENT?

During World War II, the size of the federal government grew dramatically. Men went off to war, and women were encouraged to work in factories at home in order to help the war effort, as exemplified by this famous poster of the fictional Rosie the Riveter. When the war ended, veterans returned to their jobs forcing many women out of work and back into the home.

G.I. (Government Issue) Bill
Federal legislation enacted in 1944 that provided college loans for returning veterans and reduced mortgage rates to enable them to buy homes.

Great Society
Reform program begun in 1964 by President Lyndon B. Johnson that was a broad attempt to combat poverty and discrimination through urban renewal, education reform, and unemployment relief.

Department of Homeland Security
Cabinet department created after the September 11, 2001, terrorist attacks to coordinate domestic security efforts.

Factories operated around the clock to produce the armaments, material, and clothes necessary to equip, shelter, and dress an army.

During World War II, the federal government also continued to grow tremendously to meet the needs of a nation at war. Tax rates were increased to support the war, and they never again fell to pre-war levels. After the war, this infusion of new monies and veterans' demands for services led to a variety of new programs and a much bigger government. The **G.I. (Government Issue) Bill**, for example, provided college loans for returning veterans and reduced mortgage rates to enable them to buy homes. The national government's involvement in these programs not only affected a large proportion of citizens, but also led to greater government involvement in more regulation. With these programs, Americans became increasingly accustomed to the national government's role in these entirely new areas.

Within two decades after World War II, the national government's response to the civil rights movement and President Lyndon B. Johnson's **Great Society** program produced additional growth in the bureaucracy. The Civil Rights Act of 1964 brought about creation of the Equal Employment Opportunity Commission (EEOC) in 1965. Congress also created the Departments of Housing and Urban Development (HUD) and Transportation in 1965 and 1966, respectively. These expansions of the bureaucracy corresponded to increases in the president's power and his ability to persuade Congress that new commissions and departments would prove an effective way to solve pressing social problems.

FORMAL ORGANIZATION OF THE BUREAUCRACY

8.2 Describe how the federal bureaucracy is organized.

The modern federal bureaucracy is comprised of fifteen Cabinet departments and countless other agencies. These agencies are so varied and diverse that even experts cannot agree on the exact number of separate governmental agencies, commissions, and departments that make up the federal bureaucracy.[3] The bureaucracy has grown so large and politically significant that many observers refer to it as the "fourth branch" of government.

Formal Organization

Federal agencies are classified based on their area of specialization, method of appointing officials, and accountability to the president and Congress. For example, the Occupational Safety and Health Administration (OSHA), a non-Cabinet level office, handles occupational safety, while the Department of State specializes in foreign affairs. It is normal, however, for more than one agency to be involved in a particular issue or for one agency to be involved in many issues. The largest department, the **Department of Homeland Security,** is probably the best example of this

FIGURE 8.2   WHAT ARE THE CABINET DEPARTMENTS?

Cabinet departments reflect the government's permanent interest in a particular issue area. The modern Cabinet includes fifteen agencies focusing on issues ranging from commerce and foreign affairs to education and health.

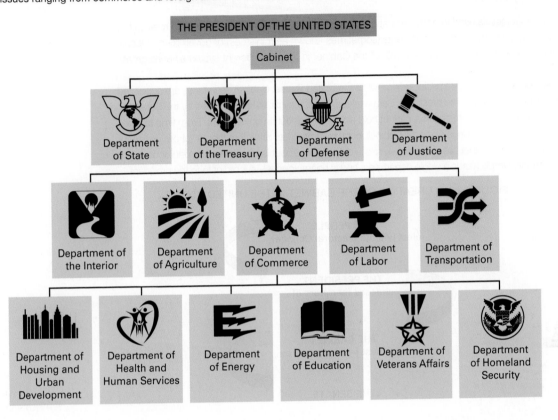

phenomenon. In fact, numerous agencies often have authority in the same issue areas, making administration even more difficult.

Agencies fall into four general categories: (1) Cabinet departments; (2) government corporations; (3) independent executive agencies; and, (4) independent regulatory commissions.

CABINET DEPARTMENTS   The fifteen **Cabinet departments** are major administrative units that have responsibility for conducting broad areas of government operations (see Figure 8.2). Cabinet departments account for about 60 percent of the federal workforce. The vice president, the heads of all the departments, and, depending on the president, additional appointees and staff make up the formal Cabinet. President Barack Obama included the U.S. Ambassador to the United Nations, the U.S. Trade Representative, the president's chief of staff, and the heads of the Environmental Protection Agency (EPA), Office of Management and Budget (OMB), and the Council of Economic Advisors in his Cabinet, for example.

Cabinet members called secretaries head the executive branch departments (except the Department of Justice, which the attorney general leads). Cabinet secretaries are responsible for establishing their department's general policy and overseeing operations. They are directly responsible to the president but are often viewed as having two masters—the president and citizens affected by the business of their departments.[4] Cabinet secretaries also are tied to Congress through the appropriations, or budgetary, process and their role in implementing legislation and making rules and policy.

Usually three to four undersecretaries or deputies assist the secretary by taking part of the administrative burden off his or her shoulders, and several assistant secretaries lend support by directing major programs within the department. In addition,

Cabinet departments
Major administrative units with responsibility for a broad area of government operations. Departmental status usually indicates a permanent national interest in a particular governmental function, such as defense, commerce, or agriculture.

AMERICAN POLITICS IN COMPARATIVE PERSPECTIVE

How Do U.S. Cabinets Compare to Parliamentary System Cabinets?

The term "Cabinet" is used in both separation-of-powers and parliamentary systems to refer to the heads of the most important departments (sometimes known as ministries) of government. Despite the use of the same word, the nature and role of the Cabinet in the two different systems varies greatly.

In separation-of-powers systems, including that of the United States, Cabinet secretaries are appointed by and are accountable to the president. Before taking office, they must be confirmed by the Senate and, during the time that they are in office, cannot hold any other position in government. From time to time, presidents convene meetings of the full Cabinet, but this is often just little more than a "photo op." In the United States, the Cabinet has no collective role in deliberating about issues or making decisions as a group; each secretary simply heads a single department and is unambiguously subordinate to the president.

FIGURE 8.3   CREATION OF THE CABINET IN THE UNITED STATES

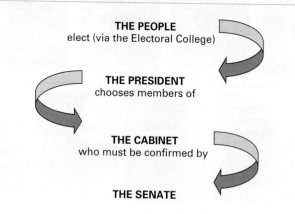

THE PEOPLE
elect (via the Electoral College)

THE PRESIDENT
chooses members of

THE CABINET
who must be confirmed by

THE SENATE

In parliamentary systems such as Canada, Cabinet ministers are selected by the prime minister from among other sitting members of the parliament. The prime minister serves as a "first among equals" and directs the work of the Cabinet, but they all derive their authority from the support of a majority in parliament. The Cabinet meets as often as weekly to reach collective decisions about the direction of policy. Along with the prime minister, they share collective responsibility for the work of government and are accountable to parliament, which can remove them from office.

FIGURE 8.4   CREATION OF THE CABINET IN PARLIAMENTARY SYSTEMS

THE PEOPLE
elect members of parliament who select

THE PRIME MINISTER
who chooses

THE CABINET
from among the members of parliament

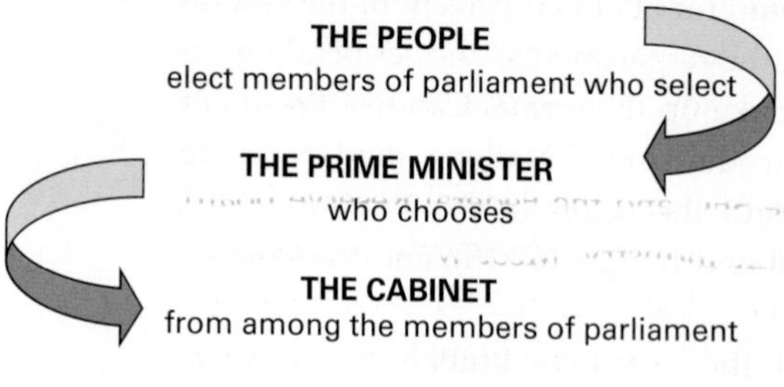

CRITICAL THINKING

1. How does the relationship between the Cabinet members and the chief executive differ in parliamentary systems from that relationship in the U.S.? How might this be good or bad for democracy?
2. In parliamentary systems, both the prime minister and the Cabinet are ultimately accountable to parliament. In the U.S. the executive and legislative branches are separate and co-equal. What are the major advantages and disadvantages of each system?
3. How might a parliamentary system in the United States affect the background and experience of the people who are chosen as Cabinet secretaries?

each secretary has numerous assistants who help with planning, budgeting, personnel, legal services, public relations, and key staff functions. Some of these individuals are political appointees while others are career civil servants.

Most departments are subdivided into bureaus, divisions, sections, or other smaller units, and the real work of each agency is done at this level. Subdivision usually takes place along functional lines, but the basis for division may be geography, work processes (for example, the Transportation Security Administration is housed in the Department of Homeland Security), or clientele (such as the Bureau of Indian Affairs in the Department of the Interior). Clientele agencies representing clearly defined interests, such as labor, large corporations, banks, or defense contractors, are particularly subject to outside lobbying. These organized interests are also active at the regional level, where the agencies conduct most of their program implementation.

INDEPENDENT EXECUTIVE AGENCIES **Independent executive agencies** closely resemble Cabinet departments but have narrower areas of responsibility. Generally speaking, independent agencies perform services rather than regulatory functions. The president appoints the heads of these agencies, and they serve, like Cabinet secretaries, at his pleasure.

Independent agencies exist apart from executive departments for practical or symbolic reasons. The National Aeronautics and Space Administration (NASA), for example, could have been placed within the Department of Defense. Such positioning, however, might have conjured up thoughts of a space program dedicated solely to military purposes, rather than to civilian satellite communication or scientific exploration. Similarly, the Department of the Interior could have been home to the Environmental Protection Agency (EPA); instead, Congress created the EPA as an independent agency in 1970 to administer federal programs aimed at controlling pollution and protecting the nation's environment. As an independent agency, the EPA is less indebted to the president on a day-to-day basis than if it were within a Cabinet department.

INDEPENDENT REGULATORY COMMISSIONS **Independent regulatory commissions** are agencies created by Congress to exist outside the major departments and regulate a specific economic activity or interest. Because of the complexity of modern economic issues, Congress sought to create commissions that could develop expertise and provide continuity of policy with respect to economic issues because neither Congress nor the courts have the time or specific talents to do so. Examples include the National Labor Relations Board (NLRB), the Federal Reserve Board (the "Fed"), the Federal Communications Commission (FCC), and the Securities and Exchange Commission (SEC).[5]

Older boards and commissions, such as the SEC and the Federal Reserve Board, generally are charged with overseeing a certain industry. Most were created specifically to be free from partisan political pressure. Each has five to seven members (always an odd number, to avoid tie votes) selected by the president, and confirmed by the Senate, for fixed, staggered terms to increase the chances of a bipartisan board. Unlike the case of executive department heads, the president cannot easily remove them. In 1935, the U.S. Supreme Court ruled that in creating independent commissions, Congress had intended them to be independent panels of experts sequestered, as far as possible, from immediate political pressures.[6]

Regulatory boards established since the 1960s concern themselves with how the business sector relates to public health and safety. The Occupational Safety and Health Administration (OSHA), for example, promotes job safety. These boards and commissions often lack autonomy and freedom from political pressures; a single administrator who is subject to removal by the president generally heads them.

independent executive agencies
Governmental units that closely resemble a Cabinet department but have narrower areas of responsibility and perform services rather than regulatory functions.

independent regulatory commission
An entity created by Congress outside a major executive department that regulates a specified interest or economic activity.

WHAT DO GOVERNMENT CORPORATIONS DO?

Amtrak provides train service across the United States. Its most profitable line runs through the Northeast Corridor from Boston to Washington, D.C. Thousands of travelers use these train lines to navigate the important business centers and congested airspace of the Northeast. Vice President Joe Biden was among these commuters; he frequently took the train from the nation's capital to his home in Wilmington, Delaware.

government corporations
Businesses established by Congress to perform functions that private businesses could provide, such as the U.S. Postal Service and Amtrak. Often established when the financial incentives for private industry to provide services are minimal.

Hatch Act
The 1939 act to prohibit civil servants from taking activist roles in partisan campaigns. This act prohibited federal employees from making political contributions, working for a particular party, or campaigning for a particular candidate.

Thus, they are far more susceptible to the political wishes of the president who appoints them.[7]

GOVERNMENT CORPORATIONS **Government corporations** date from the early 1930s. They are businesses established by Congress to perform functions that private businesses could provide. Some of the better-known government corporations include the U.S. Postal Service (removed from Cabinet status in 1971), Amtrak, and the Federal Deposit Insurance Corporation (FDIC). Unlike other governmental agencies, government corporations charge a fee for their services. The Tennessee Valley Authority (TVA), for example, provides electricity at reduced rates to millions of Americans in Appalachia.

The government often forms corporations when the financial incentives for private industry to provide services are minimal. The area served by the TVA demonstrates this point; it was a poor region of Appalachia that had failed to attract private electric companies. In other cases, Congress intervenes to salvage valuable public assets. For example, when passenger rail service in the United States became unprofitable, Congress stepped in to create Amtrak, nationalizing the passenger-train industry to keep passenger trains running, especially along the Northeast Corridor.

Government Workers and Political Involvement

As the number of federal employees and agencies grew during the 1930s, many Americans began to fear that members of the civil service would play major roles not only in implementing public policy but also in electing members of Congress and even the president. Consequently, Congress enacted the Political Activities Act of 1939, commonly known as the **Hatch Act**. It prohibited federal employees from becoming directly involved in working for political candidates. Although this act allayed many critics' fears, other people argued that the Hatch Act was too extreme.

In 1993, the Hatch Act was liberalized to allow employees to run for public office in nonpartisan elections, contribute money to political organizations, and campaign for or against candidates in partisan elections. Federal employees still, however, are prohibited from engaging in political activity while on duty, soliciting contributions

TABLE 8.1 WHAT DOES THE LIBERALIZED HATCH ACT STIPULATE?

Federal Employees May	Federal Employees May Not
Be candidates for public office in nonpartisan elections	Use their official authority or influence to interfere with an election
Assist in voter registration drives	Collect political contributions unless both individuals are members of the same federal labor organization or employee organization and the one solicited is not a subordinate employee
Express opinions about candidates and issues	Knowingly solicit or discourage the political activity of any person who has business before the agency
Contribute money to political organizations	Engage in political activity while on duty
Attend political fund-raising functions	Engage in political activity in any government office
Attend and be active at political rallies and meetings	Engage in political activity while wearing an official uniform
Join and be active members of a political party or club	Engage in political activity while using a government vehicle
Sign nominating petitions	Solicit political contributions from the general public
Campaign for or against referendum questions, constitutional amendments, and municipal ordinances	Be candidates for public office in partisan elections
Campaign for or against candidates in partisan elections	
Make campaign speeches for candidates in partisan elections	
Distribute campaign literature in partisan elections	
Hold office in political clubs or parties	

SOURCE: U.S. Special Counsel's Office

from the general public, and running for office in partisan elections (see Table 8.1). The act, however, has proved difficult to enforce. For example, government employees are not allowed to display photos of themselves with elected officials, unless it is an official photo. However, even if it is an official photo, it must be in its original, unaltered state, with no modifications such as horns or halos.[8]

WHO ARE BUREAUCRATS?

8.3 Describe how the federal bureaucracy is staffed.

The national government differs from private business in numerous ways. Governments exist for the public good, not to make money. Businesses are driven by a profit motive; many government leaders are driven by reelection. Businesses earn their money from customers; the national government raises revenue from taxpayers. Bureaucracies also differ from businesses because it is difficult to determine to whom bureaucracies are responsible. Is it the president? Congress? The people?

The different natures of government and business have a tremendous impact on the way the bureaucracy operates. Because all of the incentive in government "is in the direction of not making mistakes," public employees view risks and rewards very differently from their private-sector counterparts.[9] Government employees have little reason to take risks or go beyond their assigned job tasks. In contrast, private employers are far more likely to reward ambition. One key to understanding the modern bureaucracy is to learn who bureaucrats are, how the bureaucracy is organized, how organization and personnel affect each other, and how bureaucrats act within the political process. It also is important to recognize that government cannot be run entirely like a business. An understanding of these facts and factors can help in the search for ways to motivate positive change in the bureaucracy.

Who Are Bureaucrats?

Most federal bureaucrats are career government employees who work in the Cabinet-level departments and independent agencies that comprise more than 2,000 bureaus, divisions, branches, offices, services, and other subunits of the federal government. Federal workers number less than 2.6 million, the lowest number since 1966. The U.S. Postal Service employs over 617,000 persons, making it the nation's second largest employer behind Walmart. Small percentages work as legislative and judicial staff. The remaining federal civilian workers are spread out among the various executive departments and agencies throughout the United States. Most of these federal employees are paid according to what is called the "General Schedule" (GS). They advance within fifteen GS grades (as well as steps within those grades), moving into higher GS levels and salaries as their careers progress (see Figure 8.5).

At the lower levels of the U.S. Civil Service, competitive examinations are used to fill most positions. These usually involve a written test. Veterans automatically get points added to their scores. Mid-level to upper ranges of federal positions do not normally require tests; instead, applicants submit résumés online. Personnel departments then evaluate potential candidates and rank them according to how well they fit a particular job opening. The personnel department then forwards to the agency filling the vacancy only the names of those deemed "qualified." This can be a time-consuming process; it often takes six to nine months to fill a position in this manner.

Persons not covered by the civil service system make up the remaining 10 percent of the federal workforce. Their positions generally fall into three categories:

1. *Appointive policy-making positions.* Nearly 3,500 people are presidential appointees. Some of these, including Cabinet secretaries and under- and assistant secretaries,

---

FIGURE 8.5 WHO ARE FEDERAL WORKERS?

The federal government employs 2.6 million people in a diverse range of jobs, from administrative assistant to scientist. But, bureaucrats do not necessarily match the demographics of America. Older Americans and men are overrepresented at the highest levels of the federal workforce, while other groups, such as Hispanics and African Americans, are underrepresented. Women notably hold far fewer of the highest paying positions.

SOURCE: EEOC Annual Report on the Federal Work Force Part II, Workforce Statistics, Fiscal Year 2011 (EEOC Annual Report FY 2011).

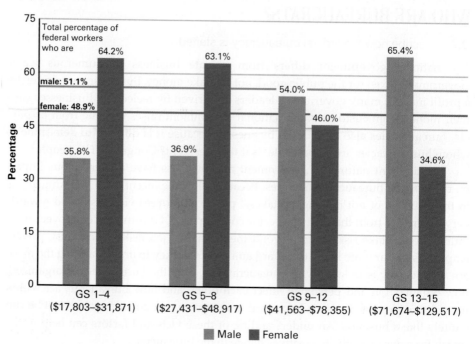

are subject to Senate confirmation. These appointees, in turn, are responsible for appointing high-level policy-making assistants who form the top of the bureaucratic hierarchy. These are called "Schedule C" political appointees.[10]

2. *Independent regulatory commissioners.* Although each president has the authority to appoint as many as one hundred commissioners, they become independent of the president's direct political influence as soon as they take office.

3. *Low-level, nonpolicy patronage positions.* These types of positions generally concern administrative assistants to policy makers.

More than 15,000 job skills are represented in the federal government. Government employees, whose average age is approximately fifty years old, have a length of service averaging between fifteen and twenty years. They include forest rangers, FBI agents, foreign service officers, computer programmers, security guards, librarians, administrators, engineers, plumbers, lawyers, doctors, postal carriers, and zoologists, among others. The diversity of jobs in the government mirrors that in the private sector. The federal workforce, itself, is also diverse but underrepresents Hispanics, in particular, and the overall employment of women lags behind that of men.[11]

About 15 percent of federal workers are found in or around the nation's capital; the rest are located in regional, state, and local offices scattered throughout the country. To enhance the efficiency of the bureaucracy, the United States is divided into ten regions, with most agencies having regional offices in at least one city in that region (see Figure 8.6). The decentralization of the bureaucracy facilitates accessibility to the public. The Social Security Administration, for example, has numerous offices so that its clients can have a place nearby to take their paperwork, questions, and problems. Decentralization also helps distribute jobs and incomes across the country.

FIGURE 8.6 WHAT ARE THE FEDERAL AGENCY REGIONS AND WHERE ARE THEIR HEADQUARTERS LOCATED?

To bring the federal bureaucracy closer to citizens and increase the efficiency of providing government services, the federal agencies maintain an office in Washington, D.C. and in ten other regional locations across the country. These cities are shown on the map below. Departments and agencies also often have offices in large cities in addition to regional headquarter locations.

SOURCE: Department of Health and Human Services, www.hhs.gov

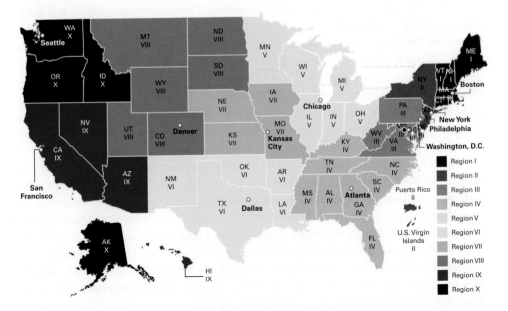

implementation
The process by which a law or policy is put into operation.

iron triangles
The relatively ironclad relationships and patterns of interaction that occur among agencies, interest groups, and congressional committees or subcommittees.

A major concern about the federal workforce is the high rate of turnover in many of the most important positions. At the Department of State, which once boasted many of the most highly coveted jobs in the federal bureaucracy, the dangers associated with postings throughout parts of the Middle East and Africa are making it harder to find well-qualified people to staff critical positions.[12] Consequently, the military has enlisted private contractors at unprecedented rates to fill many bureaucratic positions in these potentially dangerous sites. Many of these private contractors are former government employees who can make almost twice the amount of money working for private companies.[13]

The graying of the federal workforce is another concern. More than one-third are eligible for retirement.[14] Many in government hope that the Presidential Management Fellows Program, which began in 1977 to hire and train future managers and executives, will be enhanced to make up for the shortfall in experienced managers that the federal government now faces. Agencies even are contemplating ways to pay the college loans of prospective recruits, while at the same time trying to improve benefits to attract older workers.[15]

HOW THE BUREAUCRACY WORKS

8.4 Identify the roles and responsibilities of the federal bureaucracy.

Max Weber believed bureaucracies were a rational way for complex societies to organize themselves. Model bureaucracies, said Weber, exhibit certain features, including:

1. A chain of command in which authority flows from top to bottom.
2. A division of labor whereby work is apportioned among specialized workers to increase productivity.
3. Clear lines of authority among workers and their superiors.
4. A goal orientation that determines structure, authority, and rules.
5. Impersonality, whereby all employees are treated fairly based on merit and all clients are served equally, without discrimination, according to established rules.
6. Productivity, whereby all work and actions are evaluated according to established rules.[16]

Clearly, this Weberian idea is somewhat idealistic, and even the best run government agencies do not always work this way, but most try.

When Congress creates any kind of department, agency, or commission, it is actually delegating some of its powers listed in Article I, section 8, of the U.S. Constitution. Therefore, the laws creating departments, agencies, corporations, or commissions carefully describe their purpose and give them the authority to make numerous policy decisions, which have the effect of law. Congress recognizes that it does not have the time, expertise, or ability to involve itself in every detail of every program; therefore, it sets general guidelines for agency action and then allows the agency to work out the details. How agencies execute congressional wishes is called **implementation**, the process by which a law or policy is put into operation.

Historically, in attempting to study how the bureaucracy made policy, political scientists investigated what they termed **iron triangles**, the relatively ironclad relationships and patterns of interaction that occur among federal workers in agencies or departments, interest groups, and relevant congressional committees and subcommittees. Today, iron triangles no longer dominate most policy processes. Some do persist, however, such as the relationships between career employees at the Department of Veterans Affairs, staffers and members of the House Committee on Veterans Affairs, and members and lobbyists for the American Legion and the Veterans of Foreign Wars, the two largest veterans groups (see Figure 8.7).

FIGURE 8.7 WHAT CONSTITUTES AN IRON TRIANGLE?

Iron triangles are the relatively stable relationships formed among bureaucratic agencies, congressional committees, and interest groups. Cooperation between these three policy actors may make policy making in some issue areas, such as veterans' affairs, an insular process confined to a small clientele.

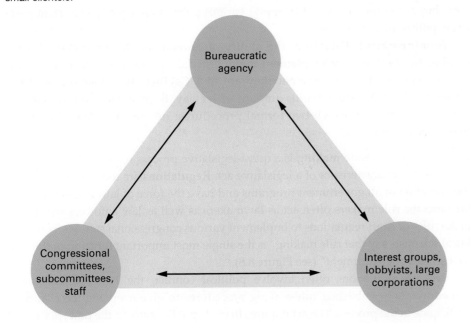

Many political scientists who examine external influences on the modern bureaucracy prefer to study **issue networks**. In general, issue networks, like iron triangles, include agency officials, members of Congress (and committee staffers), and interest group lobbyists. But, they also include lawyers, consultants, academics, public relations specialists, and sometimes even the courts. Unlike iron triangles, issue networks constantly are changing as members with technical expertise or newly interested parties become involved in issue areas and others phase out.

As a result of the increasing complexity of many policy domains, a number of alliances have also arisen within the bureaucracy. One such example is **interagency councils**, working groups established to facilitate the coordination of policy making and implementation across a host of agencies. Depending on the amount of funding these councils receive, they can be the prime movers of administration policy in any area where an interagency council exists. President George W. Bush formed an interagency council to address the economic crisis resulting from the September 11, 2001, terrorist attacks.

In areas marked by extraordinarily complex policy problems, recent presidential administrations have set up **policy coordinating committees (PCCs)** to facilitate interaction among agencies and departments at the sub-Cabinet level. For example, the Homeland Security Council PCC (the HSC-PCC) is composed of representatives from various executive departments as well as the FBI, CIA, Federal Emergency Management Agency (FEMA), and the vice president's office, among others. It oversees multiple agencies and executive departments to ensure the creation and implementation of consistent, effective homeland security policies.

Making Policy

The main purpose of all of these decision-making bodies is policy making. Policy making and implementation take place on both informal and formal levels. From a practical standpoint, many decisions are left to individual government employees on a day-to-day basis. Department of Justice lawyers, for example, make daily

issue networks
The loose and informal relationships that exist among a large number of actors who work in broad policy areas.

interagency councils
Working groups created to facilitate coordination of policy making and implementation across a host of governmental agencies.

policy coordinating committees (PCCs)
Committees created at the sub-Cabinet level to facilitate interactions between agencies and departments to handle complex policy problems.

administrative discretion
The ability of bureaucrats to make choices concerning the best way to implement congressional or executive intentions.

rule making
A quasi-legislative process resulting in regulations that have the characteristics of a legislative act.

regulations
Rules governing the operation of all government programs that have the force of law.

Federal Register
The official journal of the U.S. government, including all federal rules and public notices so that citizens and organization can follow proposed changes and comply with rule changes.

administrative adjudication
A quasi-judicial process in which a bureaucratic agency settles disputes between two parties similar to the way courts resolve disputes.

decisions about whether or not to prosecute suspects. Similarly, street-level Internal Revenue Service agents make many decisions during personal audits. These street-level bureaucrats make policy on two levels. First, they exercise broad judgment in decisions concerning citizens with whom they interact. Second, taken together, their individual actions add up to agency behavior.[17] Thus, how bureaucrats interpret and how they apply (or choose not to apply) various policies are equally important parts of the policy-making process.

Administrative discretion, the ability of bureaucrats to make choices concerning the best way to implement congressional or executive intentions, also allows decision makers (whether they are in a Cabinet-level position or at the lowest GS levels) a tremendous amount of leeway. Bureaucrats exercise administrative discretion through two formal procedures: rule making and administrative adjudication.

RULE MAKING   **Rule making** is a quasi-legislative process resulting in regulations that have the characteristics of a legislative act. **Regulations** are the rules that govern the operation of all government programs and have the force of law. In essence, then, bureaucratic rule makers often act as lawmakers as well as law enforcers when they make rules or draft regulations to implement various congressional statutes. Some political scientists say that rule making "is the single most important function performed by agencies of government" (see Figure 8.8).[18]

Because regulations often involve political conflict, the 1946 Administrative Procedures Act established rule-making procedures to give everyone the chance to participate in the process. The act requires that: (1) public notice of the time, place, and nature of the rule-making proceedings be provided in the *Federal Register*; (2) interested parties be given the opportunity to submit written arguments and facts relevant to the rule; and, (3) the statutory purpose and basis of the rule be stated. After rules are published, thirty days generally must elapse before they take effect.

Sometimes the law requires an agency to conduct a formal hearing before issuing rules. Staffers collect evidence and call interested parties and interest groups to testify on the issue. The process can take weeks, months, or even years, at the end of which agency administrators must review the entire record and then justify the new rules. Although cumbersome, the process has reduced criticism of some rules and bolstered the deference given by the courts to agency decisions.

Many Americans are unaware of their opportunity to influence government through the rule-making process. All private citizens with interest in potential rules have the right to submit comments. Recent presidents have taken efforts to make commenting easier for citizens by using the government's regulations.gov portal. As a result, the average rule receives about eighty comments, but some rules may receive thousands of comments from citizens.

ADMINISTRATIVE ADJUDICATION   Agencies regularly find that persons or businesses are not in compliance with the federal laws the agencies are charged with enforcing or that they are in violation of an agency rule or regulation. To force compliance, some agencies resort to **administrative adjudication**, a quasi-judicial process in which a bureaucratic agency settles disputes between two parties in a manner similar to the way courts resolve disputes. Administrative adjudication is referred to as quasi-judicial because adjudication by any body other than the judiciary would be a violation of the constitutional principle of separation of powers.

Several agencies and boards employ administrative law judges to conduct hearings. Although employed by the agencies, these judges are strictly independent and cannot be removed except for gross misconduct. Their actions, however, are reviewable in the federal courts, as are the findings of judges in agencies such as the Equal Employment Opportunity Commission and Social Security Administration.

FIGURE 8.8   HOW IS A REGULATION MADE?

The 1946 Administrative Procedures Act spells out a specific process for rule making in the federal bureaucracy. Similar to the process of making legislation, a proposed rule has many opportunities to fail to be implemented. Affected citizens also have a number of opportunities to offer their opinions of a proposed rule.

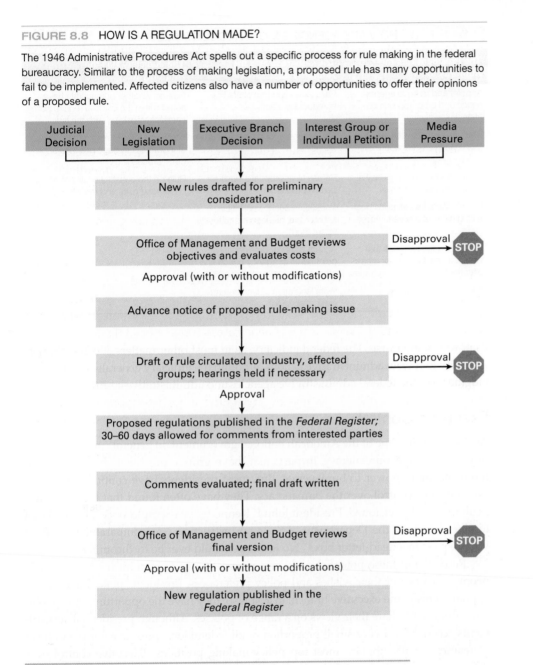

TOWARD REFORM: MAKING THE BUREAUCRACY ACCOUNTABLE

8.5 Identify the means of controlling the federal bureaucracy.

Although many critics of the bureaucracy argue that federal employees should be responsive to the public interest, the public interest is difficult to define. As it turns out, several factors control the power of the bureaucracy, and to some degree, the same kinds of checks and balances that operate among the three branches of government serve to rein in the bureaucracy (see Table 8.2).

Many political scientists argue that presidents should take charge of the bureaucracy because it is their responsibility to see that popular ideas and expectations are translated into administrative action. But, under our constitutional system, the president is not the only actor in the policy process. Congress creates the agencies, funds them, and establishes the broad rules of their operation. Moreover, Congress continually reviews the various agencies through oversight committee investigations, hearings, and

TABLE 8.2   HOW ARE AGENCIES MADE ACCOUNTABLE?

The President Has the Authority to:	The Congress Has the Authority to:	The Judiciary Has the Authority to:
Appoint and remove agency heads and other top bureaucrats.	Pass legislation that alters the bureaucracy's activities.	Rule on whether bureaucrats have acted within the law and require policy changes to comply with the law.
Reorganize the bureaucracy (with congressional approval).	Abolish or create programs and agencies.	Force agencies to respect the rights of individuals through hearings and other proceedings.
Make changes in an agency's annual budget proposals.	Refuse to appropriate funds for certain programs.	Rule on the constitutionality of all challenged rules and regulations.
Ignore legislative initiatives originating within the bureaucracy.	Investigate agency activities and compel bureaucrats to testify about them.	
Initiate or adjust policies that would, if enacted by Congress, alter the bureaucracy's activities.	Accept or reject presidential appointments of agency heads and other top bureaucratic officials.	
Issue executive orders.	Write legislation to limit bureaucratic discretion.	

its power of the purse. The federal judiciary, as in most other matters, has the ultimate authority to review administrative actions although the judiciary generally defers to the judgments of the federal administrative agencies and administrative courts.

Executive Control

As the size and scope of the American national government, in general, and of the executive branch and bureaucracy, in particular, have grown, presidents have delegated more and more power to bureaucrats. But, most presidents have continued to try to exercise some control over the bureaucracy. They have often found that task more difficult than first envisioned. President John F. Kennedy, for example, once lamented that to give anyone at the Department of State an instruction was comparable to putting your request in a dead-letter box.[19] No response would ever be forthcoming.

Recognizing these potential problems, presidents try to appoint the best possible people to carry out their wishes and policy preferences. Presidents make hundreds of appointments to the executive branch; in doing so, they have the opportunity to appoint individuals who share their views on a range of policies. Although presidential appointments account for a very small proportion of all federal jobs, presidents or the Cabinet secretaries usually appoint most top policy-making positions. Executive control over these positions can be severely hampered when Congress refuses to approve nominees.

With the approval of Congress, presidents can reorganize the bureaucracy. They also can make changes in an agency's annual budget requests and ignore legislative initiatives originating within the bureaucracy. Several presidents have made a priority of trying to tame the bureaucracy to increase its accountability. Thomas Jefferson, the first president to address the issue of accountability, attempted to cut waste and bring about a "wise and frugal government." The government began to seriously consider calls for reform during the Progressive era (1890–1920). Later, President Calvin Coolidge urged spending cuts and other reforms. His Correspondence Club aimed to reduce bureaucratic letter writing by 30 percent.[20]

Presidents also can shape policy and provide direction to bureaucrats by issuing executive orders.[21] Executive orders are rules or regulations issued by the president that have the effect of law; the *Federal Register* must publish all executive orders. A president can direct an agency to act, but it may take some time to carry out the order. Few presidents can ensure that the government will implement all their orders or will like all the rules that have been made. For example, even before Congress acted to protect women from discrimination by the federal government, the National

Organization for Women convinced President Lyndon B. Johnson to sign a 1967 executive order that added the category of "gender" to an earlier order prohibiting discrimination on the basis of race, color, religion, or national origin in the awarding of federal contracts. The president signed the order, but guidelines for implementation were not drafted until several years later.[22]

Republican candidates for president often promise to reduce the size or authority of the bureaucracy. President Donald J. Trump, a climate change skeptic, vowed to replace Environmental Protection Agency leadership and roll back regulations on the coal and gas industry while campaigning. Given disagreements with Obama administration policy, President Trump's signature line on reality TV—"you're fired"—captures his intention to significantly reshape many aspects of the federal bureaucracy.

Congressional Control

Congress can confirm (or reject) nominees to top bureaucratic positions and has also played an important role in checking the power of the bureaucracy. Constitutionally, it possesses the authority to create or abolish departments and agencies. It may also transfer agency functions and expand or contract bureaucratic discretion.

Congress can also use its investigatory powers to conduct program evaluations or hold oversight hearings. It can also call sitting and even former government officials to testify as was the case when Hillary Clinton testified for nearly eleven hours before a House Select Committee investigating her response as Secretary of State to the attack on the U.S. embassy in Benghazi, Libya.

Political scientists distinguish between two different forms of congressional oversight. One is proactive and allows Congress to set its own agenda for programs or agencies to review. For example, bureaucrats appear before congressional committees on a regular basis to inform members about agency activities, ongoing investigations, and budget requests. A second kind of oversight is reactive and generally involves a congressional response to a complaint filed by a constituent, a politically significant actor, or the media. It is not at all unusual for a congressional committee or subcommittee to conduct hearings on a particular problem and then direct the relevant agency to study the problem or find ways to remedy it. For example, when the Aliso Canyon natural gas storage facility owned by the Southern California Gas Company began leaking gas in late 2015, residents of the affected Porter Ranch neighborhood as well as local and state officials called for a response. Congressman Brad Sherman (D-CA) wrote a letter to the Environmental Protection Agency requesting an investigation into the leak, which the agency began almost immediately. While the leak was officially declared sealed in February of 2016, long-term consequences to the residents and environment remain unclear.

Congress also has the power of the purse. To control the bureaucracy, it can use its abilities to authorize spending and appropriate funds for an agency's activities. Money can be a powerful tool to coerce bureaucrats into making particular policies.

The first step in the funding process is authorization. Budget authorization originates in the various legislative committees that oversee particular agencies (such as Agriculture, Veterans Affairs, Education, and Labor) and sets the maximum amounts that agencies can spend on particular programs. While some authorizations, such as those for Social Security, are permanent, others, including Departments of State and Defense procurements, are watched closely and are subject to annual authorizations.

Once Congress authorizes programs, it requires specific allocation, or appropriation, of funds before they can be spent. Such appropriations originate with the House Appropriations Committee, not the specialized legislative committees. Thus, the House Appropriations Committee routinely holds hearings to allow agency heads to justify their budget requests.

To help Congress oversee the bureaucracy's financial affairs, in 1921 Congress created the General Accounting Office, now called the Government Accountability Office (GAO). The GAO is Congress's watchdog over executive branch spending. The GAO, the Congressional Research Service (CRS), and the Congressional Budget Office (CBO) provide Congress with its own bureaucracy to research and monitor what the executive branch and bureaucracy are doing. Today, the GAO not only tracks how money is spent by the executive branch but also monitors how policies are implemented. If the GAO uncovers problems with an agency's work, it notifies Congress immediately.

Legislators also augment their formal oversight of the executive branch by allowing citizens to appeal adverse bureaucratic decisions to agencies, Congress, and even the courts. Congressional review, a procedure by which joint resolutions of legislative disapproval can nullify agency regulations, is another method of exercising congressional oversight. This form of oversight is discussed in greater detail in our discussion of Congress.

Judicial Control

Whereas the president and Congress have direct ongoing control over the actions of the bureaucracy, the judiciary's oversight function is less apparent, but equally important. Federal judges can issue injunctions or orders to an executive agency even before a rule is publicized, giving the federal judiciary a potent check on the bureaucracy.

The courts also have ruled that agencies must give all affected individuals their due process rights guaranteed by the U.S. Constitution. The Social Security Administration cannot stop a recipient's checks, for example, unless that individual receives reasonable notice and an opportunity for a hearing. These types of cases make up the largest proportion of cases filed in federal district courts.

On a more informal, indirect level, litigation, or even the threat of litigation, often exerts a strong influence on bureaucrats. Injured parties can bring suit against agencies for their failure to enforce a law and can challenge agency interpretations of any law. In general, however, the courts give great weight to the opinions of bureaucrats and usually defer to their expertise.[23]

Roots of the Federal Bureaucracy

8.1 Outline the development of the federal bureaucracy.

The federal bureaucracy has changed dramatically since President George Washington's time, when the executive branch had only three departments—State, War, and Treasury. The size of the federal bureaucracy increased significantly following the Civil War. As employment opportunities within the federal government expanded, a civil service system was created to ensure that more and more jobs were filled according to merit and not by patronage. By the late 1800s, reform efforts led to further growth of the bureaucracy, as independent regulatory commissions came into existence. In the wake of the Great Depression, President Franklin D. Roosevelt's New Deal created many new agencies to get the national economy back on course.

Formal Organization of the Bureaucracy

8.2 Describe how the federal bureaucracy is organized.

The federal bureaucracy is comprised of fifteen Cabinet departments and countless other agencies. Federal agencies are classified based on their area of specialization, method of appointing officials, and accountability to the president and Congress. In general, bureaucratic agencies fall into four categories: departments, independent agencies, independent regulatory commissions, and government corporations. The Hatch Act regulates the political activity of employees in the federal government.

Who Are Bureaucrats?

8.3 Describe how the federal bureaucracy is staffed.

The modern bureaucracy has approximately 2.6 million civilian workers from all walks of life. Most of these federal employees are paid according to what is called the "General Schedule" (GS). They advance within fifteen GS grades (as well as steps within those grades), moving into higher GS levels and salaries as their careers progress.

How the Bureaucracy Works

8.4 Identify the roles and responsibilities of the federal bureaucracy.

The bureaucracy is responsible for implementing many laws passed by Congress. A variety of formal and informal mechanisms, such as rule making and administrative adjudication, help bureaucrats make policy.

Toward Reform: Making the Bureaucracy Accountable

8.5 Identify the means of controlling the federal bureaucracy.

Agencies enjoy considerable discretion, but they are also subject to many formal controls that help make them more accountable. The president, Congress, and the judiciary all exercise various degrees of control over the bureaucracy through oversight, funding, or litigation.

administrative adjudication
administrative discretion
Cabinet departments
civil service system
Department of Homeland Security
federal bureaucracy
Federal Register
government corporations
G.I. (Government Issue) Bill
Government corporations

Great Depression
Great Society
Hatch Act
implementation
independent executive agencies
independent regulatory commission
interagency councils
iron triangles
issue networks
Max Weber

merit system
patronage
Pendleton Act
policy coordinating committees (PCCs)
regulations
rule making
Sixteenth Amendment
spoils system
World War I
World War II

HAS THE MODERN SUPREME COURT BECOME TOO POWERFUL?

When the Framers created the Supreme Court in 1787, they thought it little more than a theoretical necessity. However, over the course of history, the "least dangerous branch" has gained significant power, both as a political institution and as a policy maker. The Supreme Court chamber pictured here is in the Capitol and was the Court's home from 1819 until 1935. This chamber served as a storeroom from 1960 until 1972, when Congress voted to restore it to its nineteenth-century appearance.

THE JUDICIARY

LEARNING OBJECTIVES

9.1 Describe the constitutional foundations of the federal judiciary and judicial review.

9.2 Describe the structure of the federal judiciary.

9.3 Outline the criteria for nominating and the process of approving federal judges and Supreme Court justices.

9.4 Outline the process by which the Supreme Court makes decisions and the factors that influence judicial decision making.

9.5 Evaluate the role of the Supreme Court in national policy making.

The debate between Federalists and Anti-Federalists that had fueled many of the conflicts surrounding ratification of the Constitution found new life as the Federalist-dominated Sixth Congress passed the Judiciary Act of 1801, which gave Federalists the opportunity to pack the courts with Federalist judges with lifetime appointments. Thomas Jefferson, a Democratic-Republican, beat John Adams, a Federalist, in Adams's failed bid for a second term in office. The election was decided on February 17, 1801. However, President-elect Jefferson had to wait until March 4, 1801, to assume office. Adams, referred to as a **lame duck** president because it was assumed that little could be done in the period between the election and the incoming president's Inauguration, surprised and angered Democratic-Republicans by convincing the also lame-duck Federalists in Congress to pass the Judiciary Act.

While the Judiciary Act of 1789 set out the general framework of the federal judiciary, the 1801 act went further. It reduced the size of the Supreme Court from six to five and created sixteen additional federal judgeships. And, it created new circuit courts to relieve Supreme Court justices from dreaded circuit court duties, which required considerable travel and personal inconvenience. By March 3, 1801, the Senate had confirmed all fifty-eight nominations made by Adams to fill judicial positions created by the new act. Once Adams received notice of the confirmations, he stayed on the job until midnight March 3, his last day in office, to execute the official commissions of the fifty-eight nominees. All were Federalists. Adams's Federalist secretary of state sealed all of the commissions and gave them to his brother to deliver. When Jefferson heard the news the next day before his inauguration, he was livid. All of those who had commissions in hand were duly sworn in guaranteeing a Federalist Supreme Court for years to come. Some commissions, however, remained undelivered and eventually culminated in one of the U.S. Supreme Court's most seminal decisions, *Marbury* v. *Madison*.

• • •

In 1787, when writing *The Federalist Papers*, Alexander Hamilton urged support for the U.S. Constitution. He firmly believed the judiciary would prove to be "the least dangerous" branch of government. The judicial branch seemed so inconsequential that when the young national government made its move to the District of Columbia in 1800, Congress actually forgot to include any space to house the justices of the Supreme Court. Last-minute conferences with Capitol architects led to the allocation of a small area in the basement of the Senate wing of the Capitol building for a courtroom. Noted one commentator, "A stranger might traverse the dark avenues of the Capitol for a week, without finding the remote corner in which justice is administered to the American Republic."[1]

Today, the role of the courts, particularly the Supreme Court of the United States, differs significantly from what the Framers envisioned. The "least dangerous branch" now is perceived by many people as having too much power.

Historically, Americans have remained unaware of the political power held by the courts. As part of their upbringing, they learned to regard the federal courts as above the fray of politics. That, however, has never been the case. Elected presidents nominate judges to the federal courts and justices to the Supreme Court, and elected senators ultimately confirm (or decline to confirm) presidential nominees to the federal bench. The process by which cases ultimately get heard—if they are heard at all—by the Supreme Court often is political as well. Interest groups routinely seek out good test cases to advance their policy positions. Even the U.S. government, generally through the Department of Justice and the U.S. solicitor general (a political appointee in that department), seeks to advance its position in court. Interest groups then often line up on opposing sides to advance their positions, much in the same way lobbyists do in Congress.

lame duck
An executive or legislature during the period just before the end of a term of office, when its power and influence are considered to be diminished.

jurisdiction
Authority vested in a particular court to hear and decide the issues in a particular case.

original jurisdiction
The jurisdiction of courts that hear a case first, usually in a trial. These courts determine the facts of a case.

appellate jurisdiction
The power vested in particular courts to review and/or revise the decision of a lower court.

We offer a note on terminology: in referring to the "Supreme Court," the "Court," or the "high Court" here, we always mean the U.S. Supreme Court, which sits at the pinnacle of the federal and state court systems. The Supreme Court is referred to by the name of the chief justice who presided over it during a particular period. For example, the Marshall Court is the Court presided over by John Marshall from 1801 to 1835, and the Roberts Court is the current Court that began in 2005. When we use the term "courts," we refer to all federal or state courts unless otherwise noted.

ROOTS OF THE FEDERAL JUDICIARY

9.1 Describe the constitutional foundations of the federal judiciary and judicial review.

The detailed notes James Madison took at the Constitutional Convention in Philadelphia make it clear that the Framers devoted little time to writing Article III, which created the judicial branch of government. The Framers believed that a federal judiciary posed little threat of tyranny; in *The Federalist Papers*, Alexander Hamilton even referred to the courts as "the least dangerous branch." One scholar, thus, has suggested that, for at least some delegates to the Constitutional Convention, "provision for a national judiciary was a matter of theoretical necessity…more in deference to the maxim of separation [of powers] than in response to clearly formulated ideas about the role of a national judicial system and its indispensability."[2]

The Framers also debated the need for any federal courts below the Supreme Court. Some argued in favor of deciding all cases in state courts, with only appeals going before the Supreme Court. Others argued for a system of federal courts. A compromise left the final choice to Congress, and Article III, section 1, begins simply by vesting "The judicial Power of the United States…in one supreme Court, and in such inferior Courts as the Congress may from time to time ordain and establish."

Article III, section 2, specifies the judicial power of the Supreme Court. It also discusses the types of cases the Court can hear, or its **jurisdiction** (see Table 9.1). Courts have two types of jurisdiction: original and appellate. **Original jurisdiction** refers to a court's authority to hear disputes as a trial court; these courts determine the facts of a case. The Supreme Court has original jurisdiction in cases involving a conflict between two or more state governments or public officials. **Appellate jurisdiction** refers to a court's ability to review and/or revise cases already decided by a trial court. The Supreme Court has appellate jurisdiction in all other cases. Article III, section 2, also specifies that all federal crimes, except those involving impeachment, shall be tried by jury in the state in which the crime was committed. The third section of the article defines treason and mandates that at least two witnesses appear in such cases.

TABLE 9.1 WHAT KINDS OF CASES DOES THE U.S. SUPREME COURT HEAR?

The following are the types of cases the Supreme Court was given the jurisdiction to hear as initially specified in Article III, section 2, of the Constitution:
All cases arising under the Constitution and laws or treaties of the United States
All cases of admiralty or maritime jurisdiction
Cases in which the United States is a party
Controversies between a state and citizens of another state (later modified by the Eleventh Amendment)
Controversies between two or more states
Controversies between citizens of different states
Controversies between citizens of the same state claiming lands under grants in different states
Controversies between a state, or the citizens thereof, and foreign states or citizens thereof
All cases affecting ambassadors or other public ministers

Had the Framers viewed the Supreme Court as the potential policy maker it is today, they most likely would not have provided for life tenure with "good behavior" for all federal judges in Article III. The Framers agreed on this feature because they did not want the justices (or any federal judges) subject to the whims of politics, the public, or politicians. Moreover, Alexander Hamilton argued in *Federalist No. 78* that the "independence of judges" was needed "to guard the Constitution and the rights of individuals."

The Constitution nonetheless did include some checks on the power of the judiciary. One such check gives Congress the authority to alter the Court's ability to hear certain kinds of cases. Congress can also propose constitutional amendments that, if ratified, can effectively reverse judicial decisions, and it can impeach and remove federal judges. In one further check, it is the president who, with the "advice and consent" of the Senate, appoints all federal judges.

The Court can, in turn, check the presidency by presiding over presidential impeachment. Article I, section 3, notes in discussing impeachment, "When the President of the United States is tried, the Chief Justice shall preside."

The Judiciary Act of 1789 and the Creation of the Federal Judicial System

In spite of the Framers' intentions, the pervasive role of politics in the judicial branch quickly became evident with the passage of the Judiciary Act of 1789. Congress spent nearly the entire second half of its first session deliberating the various provisions of the act to give form and substance to the federal judiciary. As one early observer noted, "The convention has only crayoned in the outlines. It left it to Congress to fill up and colour the canvas."[3]

The Judiciary Act of 1789 established the basic three-tiered structure of the federal court system. At the bottom were the federal district courts—at least one in each state. If people participating in a lawsuit (called litigants) were unhappy with the district court's verdict, they could appeal their case to the circuit courts, constituting the second tier. Each circuit court, initially created to function as a trial court for important cases, originally comprised one district court judge and two Supreme Court justices who met as a circuit court twice a year. Not until 1891 did circuit courts (or, as we know them today, courts of appeals) take on their exclusively appellate function and begin to focus solely on reviewing the findings of lower courts. The third tier of the federal judicial system defined by the Judiciary Act of 1789 was the Supreme Court of the United States. Although the Constitution mentions "the supreme Court," it did not designate its size. In the Judiciary Act, Congress set the size of the Supreme Court at six—the chief justice plus five associate justices. After being reduced to five members by the Judiciary Act of 1801, Congress expanded and contracted the Court's size until it was fixed at nine in 1869.

Article III, section 1, guarantees that the salaries of all federal judges will not be reduced during their service on the bench. At the Constitutional Convention, considerable debate raged over how to treat the payment of federal judges. Some believed Congress should have an extra check on the judiciary by being able to reduce their salaries. This provision was a compromise after James Madison suggested that Congress have the authority to bar increases and decreases in the salaries of these unelected jurists. The delegates recognized that decreases—as well as no opportunity for raises—could negatively affect the perks associated with life tenure.

John Jay was appointed chief justice of the Supreme Court of the United States by President George Washington. From this time onward, Courts were known by the name of the Chief Justice. Thus, the first Supreme Court was known as the Jay Court. When the justices met in their first public session in New York City in 1790, they were garbed magnificently in black and scarlet robes in the English fashion. The elegance

Federalist No. 78
A *Federalist Papers* essay authored by Alexander Hamilton that covers the role of the federal judiciary, including the power of judicial review.

Judiciary Act of 1789
Legislative act that established the basic three-tiered structure of the federal court system.

John Jay
A member of the Founding generation who was the first Chief Justice of the United States. A diplomat and a co-author of *The Federalist Papers*.

Whiskey Rebellion
A civil insurrection in 1794 that was put down by military force by President George Washington, thereby confirming the power of the new national government.

Chisholm v. *Georgia* (1793)
A Supreme Court case that allowed U.S. citizens to bring a lawsuit against states in which they did not reside; overturned by the Eleventh Amendment in 1789.

Eleventh Amendment
An amendment adopted in 1789 protecting states from being sued in federal court by a citizen of a different state or country.

WHY IS JOHN MARSHALL IMPORTANT TO THE DEVELOPMENT OF JUDICIAL AUTHORITY?

A single person can make a major difference in the development of an institution. Such was the case with John Marshall (1755–1835), who served thirty-four years as chief justice. More of a politician than a lawyer, Marshall served as a delegate to the Virginia legislature and played an instrumental role in Virginia's ratification of the U.S. Constitution in 1787. He became secretary of state in 1800 under John Adams. When Oliver Ellsworth resigned as chief justice of the United States in 1800, Adams nominated Marshall. Marshall served on the Court until the day he died, participating in more than 1,000 decisions and authoring more than 500 opinions.

of their attire, however, could not compensate for the relative ineffectiveness of the Court. Its first session initially had to be adjourned when fewer than half the justices attended. Later, once a sufficient number of justices assembled, the Court decided only one major case. Moreover, as an indication of its lowly status, one associate justice left the Court to become chief justice of the South Carolina Supreme Court. (Although today we might consider such a move as a step down, keep in mind that in the early years of the United States, many people viewed the states, and thus their courts, as more important than the national government.)

Hampered by frequent changes in personnel, limited space for its operations, no clerical support, and no system of reporting its decisions, the early Court did not impress many people. From the beginning, the circuit court duties of the Supreme Court justices presented problems for the prestige of the Court. Few good lawyers were willing to accept nominations to the Court because circuit court duties entailed a substantial amount of travel—most of it on horseback over poorly maintained roads. Southern justices often rode as many as 10,000 miles a year on horseback. President George Washington tried to prevail on several friends and supporters to fill vacancies on the Court, but most refused the "honor." John Adams, the second president of the United States, ran into similar problems. When Adams asked John Jay to resume the position of chief justice after Jay resigned to become governor of New York, Jay declined the offer.

In spite of these problems, in its first decade, the Court took several actions to mold the new nation. First, by declining to give George Washington advice on the legality of some of his actions, the justices attempted to establish the Supreme Court as an independent, nonpolitical branch of government. Although John Jay frequently gave the president private advice, the Court refused to answer questions President Washington posed to it concerning the construction of international laws and treaties.

The early Court also tried to advance principles of nationalism and to maintain the national government's supremacy over the states. As circuit court jurists, the justices rendered numerous decisions on such matters as national suppression of the **Whiskey Rebellion**, which occurred in 1794 after imposition of a national excise tax on whiskey, and the constitutionality of the Alien and Sedition Acts, which made it a crime to criticize national governmental officials or their actions.

During the ratification debates, Anti-Federalists had warned that Article III extended federal judicial power to controversies "between a State and Citizens of another State"— meaning that a citizen of one state could sue any other state in federal court, a prospect unthinkable to defenders of state sovereignty. Although Federalists, including Alexander Hamilton and James Madison, had scoffed at the idea, the nationalist Supreme Court quickly proved them wrong in *Chisholm v. Georgia* (1793). In *Chisholm*, the justices interpreted the Court's jurisdiction under Article III, section 2, to include the right to hear suits brought by a citizen against a state in which he did not reside. Writing in *Chisholm*, Associate Justice James Wilson denounced the "haughty notions of state independence, state sovereignty, and state supremacy."[4] The states' reaction to this perceived attack on their authority led to passage and ratification in 1798 of the **Eleventh Amendment** to the Constitution, which specifically limited judicial power by stipulating that the authority of the federal courts could not "extend to any suit…commenced or prosecuted against one of the United States by citizens of another State."

The Marshall Court: *Marbury* v. *Madison* (1803) and Judicial Review

The actions of **John Marshall**, who headed the Court from 1801 to 1835, brought much needed respect and prestige to the Court. President John Adams appointed Marshall chief justice in 1800, three years after he declined to accept a nomination as associate justice. An ardent Federalist, Marshall is considered the most important justice to serve on the Court. Part of his reputation results from the duration of his service and the historical significance of this period in our nation's history.

As chief justice, Marshall helped to establish the role and power of the Court. The Marshall Court, for example, discontinued the practice of *seriatim* (Latin for "in a series") opinions, which was the custom of the King's Bench in Great Britain. Prior to the Marshall Court, the justices delivered their individual opinions in order of seniority. For the Court to take its place as an equal branch of government, Marshall believed the justices needed to speak as a Court and not as six individuals. In fact, during Marshall's first four years in office, the Court routinely spoke as one, and the chief justice wrote twenty-four of its twenty-six opinions.

The Marshall Court also established the authority of the Supreme Court over the judiciaries of the various states.[5] In addition, the Court established the supremacy of the federal government and Congress over state governments through a broad interpretation of the necessary and proper clause in *McCulloch* v. *Maryland* (1819).[6]

Finally, the Marshall Court claimed the right of **judicial review**, the power of the courts to review acts of other branches of government and of the states. The Supreme Court derives much of its day-to-day power and impact on the policy process from this right. This claim established the Court as the final arbiter of constitutional questions, with the right to declare congressional acts void.[7]

Alexander Hamilton first publicly endorsed the idea of judicial review in *Federalist No. 78*, noting, "Whenever a particular statute contravenes the Constitution, it will be the duty of the judicial tribunals to adhere to the latter and disregard the former." Nonetheless, because the U.S. Constitution does not mention judicial review, the actual authority of the Supreme Court to review the constitutionality of acts of Congress was an unsettled question. But, in *Marbury v. Madison* (1803), Chief Justice John Marshall claimed this sweeping authority for the Court by asserting that the Constitution's supremacy clause implies the right of judicial review.[8]

Marbury v. *Madison* arose amid a sea of political controversy. In the final hours of his administration, John Adams appointed William Marbury as the justice of the peace for the District of Columbia. But, in the confusion of winding up matters, Adams's secretary of state failed to deliver Marbury's commission. Marbury then asked James Madison, Thomas Jefferson's secretary of state, for the commission. Under direct orders from Jefferson, who was irate over the Adams administration's last-minute appointment of Federalist judges (quickly confirmed by the Federalist Senate), Madison refused to turn over the commission. Marbury and three other Adams appointees who were in the same situation then filed a writ of *mandamus* (a legal motion) asking the Supreme Court to order Madison to deliver their commissions.

Political tensions ran high as the Court met to hear the case. Jefferson distrusted and detested Marshall, who was his cousin, and threatened to ignore any order of the Court. Marshall realized that a refusal of the executive branch to comply with the decision could devastate both him and the prestige of the Court. Responding to this challenge, in a brilliant opinion that in many sections reads more like a lecture to Jefferson than a discussion of the merits of Marbury's claim, Marshall concluded that although Marbury and the others were entitled to their commissions, the Court lacked the power to issue the writ sought by Marbury. In *Marbury* v. *Madison*, Marshall further ruled that those parts of the Judiciary Act of 1789 that extended the original jurisdiction of the

WHAT IS THE CONSTITUTIONAL BASIS FOR JUDICIAL REVIEW?

Although Article III of the Constitution is ambiguous about the nature and scope of judicial review, major thinkers of the time—including Alexander Hamilton, pictured here—believed that a written constitution required careful oversight by the judiciary.

John Marshall
The longest-serving Supreme Court chief justice, Marshall served from 1801 to 1835. Marshall's decision in *Marbury* v. *Madison* (1803) established the principle of judicial review in the United States.

judicial review
Power of the courts to review acts of other branches of government and the states.

***Marbury* v. *Madison* (1803)**
Case in which the Supreme Court first asserted the power of judicial review by finding that part of the congressional statute extending the Court's original jurisdiction was unconstitutional.

trial court
Court of original jurisdiction where cases begin.

appellate court
Court that generally reviews only findings of law made by lower courts.

constitutional (or Article III) courts
Federal courts specifically created by the U.S. Constitution or by Congress pursuant to its authority in Article III.

legislative courts
Courts established by Congress for specialized purposes, such as the Court of Appeals for Veterans Claims.

Court to allow it to issue writs of *mandamus* were inconsistent with the Constitution and therefore unconstitutional.

Although the immediate effect of the decision was to deny power to the Court, its long-term effect was to establish the implied power of judicial review. Said Marshall, writing for the Court, "it is emphatically the province and duty of the judicial department to say what the law is." Since *Marbury*, the Court has routinely exercised the power of judicial review to determine the constitutionality of acts of Congress, the executive branch, and the states.

THE FEDERAL COURT SYSTEM

9.2 Describe the structure of the federal judiciary.

The judicial system in the United States can best be described as a dual system consisting of the federal court system and the judicial systems of the fifty states. Cases may arise in either system. Both systems are basically three-tiered. At the bottom of the system are **trial courts**, where litigation begins. In the middle are **appellate courts**; these courts generally review only findings of law made by trial courts. At the top of both the federal and state court systems sits a court of last resort (see Figure 9.1). In the federal court system, trial courts are called district courts, appellate courts are termed courts of appeals, and the Supreme Court is the court of last resort.

The federal district courts, courts of appeals, and the Supreme Court are called **constitutional (or Article III) courts** because Article III of the Constitution either established them or authorized Congress to establish them. The president nominates (with the advice and consent of the Senate) judges who preside over these courts, and they serve lifetime terms, as long as they engage in "good behavior."

In addition to constitutional courts, **legislative courts** are set up by Congress, under its implied powers, generally for special purposes. The U.S. territorial courts (which hear federal cases in the territories) and the U.S. Court of Appeals for Veterans Claims are examples of legislative courts, or what some call Article I courts. The president appoints (subject to Senate confirmation) the judges who preside over these federal courts; they serve fixed, fifteen-year renewable terms.

The District Courts

As we have seen, Congress created U.S. district courts when it enacted the Judiciary Act of 1789. District courts are federal trial courts. Currently, the federal district courts number ninety-four. No district court cuts across state lines. Every state has at least one federal district court, and California, Texas, and New York each have four (see Figure 9.2).[9]

Federal district courts, in which the bulk of the judicial work takes place in the federal system, have original jurisdiction over only specific types of cases. Although rules governing district court jurisdiction can be complex, cases, which are heard in federal district courts by a single judge (with or without a jury), generally fall into one of three categories:

1. They involve the federal government as a party.

2. They present a federal question based on a claim under the U.S. Constitution, a treaty with another nation, or a federal statute. This is called federal question jurisdiction, and it can involve criminal or civil law.

3. They involve civil suits in which citizens are from different states, and the amount of money at issue is more than $75,000.[10]

Each federal judicial district has a U.S. attorney, nominated by the president and confirmed by the Senate. The U.S. attorney in each district is that district's chief law enforcement officer. U.S. attorneys have a considerable amount of discretion

FIGURE 9.1 HOW IS THE AMERICAN JUDICIAL SYSTEM STRUCTURED?

The American judicial system is a dual system consisting of the federal court system and the judicial systems of the fifty states. In both the federal court system and the judiciaries of most states, there are both trial and appellate courts. The U.S. Supreme Court sits at the top of both court systems and has the power to hear appeals from both federal and state courts.

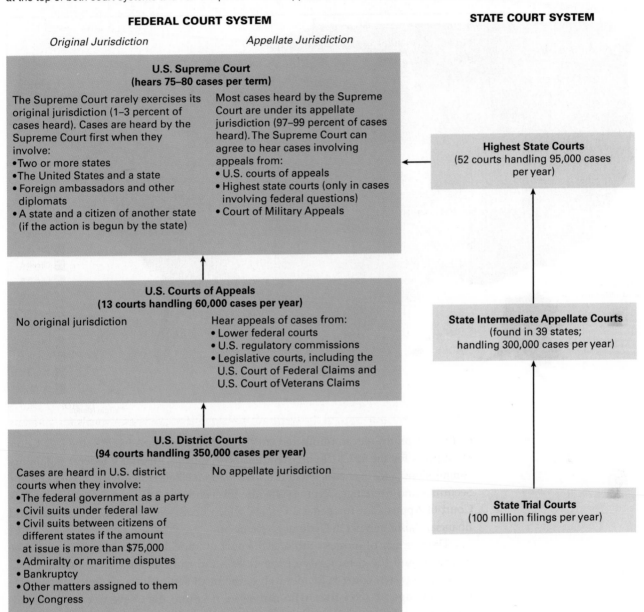

FEDERAL COURT SYSTEM

STATE COURT SYSTEM

Original Jurisdiction   *Appellate Jurisdiction*

U.S. Supreme Court
(hears 75–80 cases per term)

The Supreme Court rarely exercises its original jurisdiction (1–3 percent of cases heard). Cases are heard by the Supreme Court first when they involve:
- Two or more states
- The United States and a state
- Foreign ambassadors and other diplomats
- A state and a citizen of another state (if the action is begun by the state)

Most cases heard by the Supreme Court are under its appellate jurisdiction (97–99 percent of cases heard). The Supreme Court can agree to hear cases involving appeals from:
- U.S. courts of appeals
- Highest state courts (only in cases involving federal questions)
- Court of Military Appeals

Highest State Courts
(52 courts handling 95,000 cases per year)

U.S. Courts of Appeals
(13 courts handling 60,000 cases per year)

No original jurisdiction

Hear appeals of cases from:
- Lower federal courts
- U.S. regulatory commissions
- Legislative courts, including the U.S. Court of Federal Claims and U.S. Court of Veterans Claims

State Intermediate Appellate Courts
(found in 39 states; handling 300,000 cases per year)

U.S. District Courts
(94 courts handling 350,000 cases per year)

Cases are heard in U.S. district courts when they involve:
- The federal government as a party
- Civil suits under federal law
- Civil suits between citizens of different states if the amount at issue is more than $75,000
- Admiralty or maritime disputes
- Bankruptcy
- Other matters assigned to them by Congress

No appellate jurisdiction

State Trial Courts
(100 million filings per year)

regarding whether they pursue criminal or civil investigations or file charges against individuals or corporations. They also have several staff lawyers to help them in their work. The number of assistant U.S. attorneys in each district depends on the amount of litigation each handles.

The Courts of Appeals

The losing party in a case heard and decided in a federal district court can appeal the decision to the appropriate court of appeals. The U.S. courts of appeals (known as the circuit courts of appeals prior to 1948) are the intermediate appellate courts in the federal system and were established in 1789 to hear appeals from federal district

FIGURE 9.2 WHAT ARE THE BOUNDARIES OF FEDERAL DISTRICT COURTS AND COURTS OF APPEALS?

This map shows the location of each U.S. court of appeals and the boundaries of the federal district courts in states with more than one district. Note that there are eleven numbered and two unnumbered courts of appeals. There are also ninety-four district courts. States are divided into between one and four districts; no district court crosses state lines.

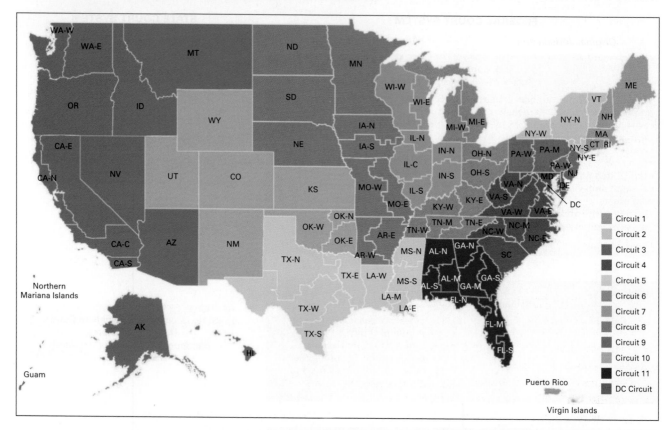

courts. Currently, eleven numbered courts of appeals exist. A twelfth, the U.S. Court of Appeals for the D.C. Circuit, handles most appeals involving federal regulatory commissions and agencies, including the National Labor Relations Board and the Securities and Exchange Commission. The thirteenth federal appeals court is the U.S. Court of Appeals for the Federal Circuit, which deals with patents and contract and financial claims against the federal government.

The number of judges within each court of appeals varies—depending on the workload and the complexity of the cases—and ranges from six to nearly thirty. Supervising each court is a chief judge, the most senior judge in terms of service below the age of sixty-five, who can serve no more than seven years. In deciding cases, judges are divided into rotating three-judge panels, made up of the active judges within the court of appeals, visiting judges (primarily district judges from the same court), and retired judges. In rare cases, all the judges in a court of appeals may choose to sit together (*en banc*) to decide a case of special importance by majority vote.

The courts of appeals have no original jurisdiction. Rather, Congress has granted these courts appellate jurisdiction over two general categories of cases: appeals from criminal and civil cases from the district courts and appeals from administrative agencies. Criminal and civil case appeals constitute about 90 percent of the workload of the courts of appeals; those from administrative agencies constitute about 10 percent.

Once a federal court of appeals makes a decision, a litigant no longer has an automatic right to an appeal. The losing party may submit a petition to the U.S. Supreme Court to hear the case, but the Court grants few of these requests. The courts of appeals, then, are the courts of last resort for almost all federal litigation. Keep in mind, however, that most cases, if they actually go to trial, go no further than the district court level.

In general, courts of appeals try to correct errors of law and procedure that have occurred in lower courts or administrative agencies. Courts of appeals hear no new testimony; instead, lawyers submit written arguments in what is called a **brief** (also submitted in trial courts), and they then appear to present and argue the case orally to the three judge court. Decisions of any court of appeals are binding on only the district courts within its geographic confines.

The Supreme Court

The U.S. Supreme Court is often at the center of highly controversial issues that the political process has yet to resolve successfully. It reviews cases from the U.S. courts of appeals and state supreme courts (as well as other courts of last resort) and acts as the final interpreter of the U.S. Constitution.

Since 1869, the U.S. Supreme Court has consisted of eight associate justices and one chief justice, whom the president nominates specifically for that position. The number nine holds no special significance, and the Constitution does not specify the size of the Court. Between 1789 and 1869, Congress periodically altered the size of the Court. The lowest number of justices on the Court was six; the most, ten. Through January 2017, only seventeen chief justices and 112 justices had served on the Court. President Donald J. Trump is expected to nominate a justice to replace Justice Antonin Scalia soon after his inauguration.

Compared with the president or Congress, the Supreme Court operates with few support staff. Along with the four clerks each justice employs, the Supreme Court has only about 400 staff members.

Decisions of the U.S. Supreme Court, however, are binding throughout the nation and establish national **precedents**, or rules for settling subsequent cases of similar nature. This reliance on past decisions or precedents to formulate decisions in new cases is called *stare decisis* (a Latin phrase meaning "let the decision stand"). The principle of *stare decisis* allows for continuity and predictability in our judicial system. Although *stare decisis* can be helpful in predicting decisions, at times judges carve out new ground and ignore, decline to follow, or even overrule precedents to reach a different conclusion in a case involving similar circumstances. This is a major reason why so much litigation exists in America today. Parties to a suit know that the outcome of a case is not always predictable; if such prediction were possible, there would be little reason to go to court.

HOW FEDERAL COURT JUDGES ARE SELECTED

9.3 Outline the criteria for nominating and the process of approving federal judges and Supreme Court justices.

The selection of federal judges is often a highly political process with important political ramifications because the president must nominate judges and the U.S. Senate must confirm them. Presidents, in general, try to select well-qualified individuals for the bench. But, these appointments also provide presidents with opportunities to shape the federal courts philosophically (see Figure 9.3).

In selecting nominees, the president may look for guidance from members of Congress, advisers, confidantes, or other high-ranking party officials.[11] The U.S. Constitution, for example, mandates that presidents receive advice and consent from the Senate. Historically, presidents have screened their lower court nominees through a process known as **senatorial courtesy**. This is the process by which presidents generally allow senators from the state in which a judicial vacancy occurs to

brief
A document containing the legal written arguments in a case filed with a court by a party prior to a hearing or trial.

precedent
A prior judicial decision that serves as a rule for settling subsequent cases of a similar nature.

stare decisis
In court rulings, a reliance on past decisions or precedents to formulate decisions in new cases.

senatorial courtesy
A process by which presidents generally allow senators from the state in which a judicial vacancy occurs to block a nomination by simply registering their objection.

AMERICAN POLITICS IN COMPARATIVE PERSPECTIVE

Does Democracy Demand Sweeping Powers of Judicial Review?

Nearly all countries of the world have some sort of highest court that is empowered to make final determinations about the rulings made by lower courts. However, in the United States, the judiciary has a much wider scope of authority to conduct judicial review of the constitutionality of laws passed by Congress and state legislatures as well as actions taken by the president. The U.S. Supreme Court is at the pinnacle of the American judicial system, but lower courts also share in this important power. Many other democracies also invest their courts with powers of judicial review, particularly countries that have a separation of powers system. However, other countries, including several close allies of the United States within the English-speaking world, take significantly different approaches.

No Judicial Review: The United Kingdom

Established in 2009, the Supreme Court in the United Kingdom has limited authority. The Court can determine whether a law was incorrectly applied in a particular case, but it cannot strike down laws.

Contingent Judicial Review: Canada

Canada's Supreme Court may strike down laws violating Canada's Charter of Rights and Freedoms. Parliament or the legislative assembly of a province may enforce a law despite Court rulings, however.

Judicial Review by a Constitutional Court: South Africa

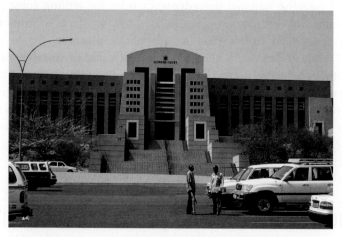

South Africa's Constitutional Court is tasked with defending the integrity of the national constitution, overseeing law in the provinces, and ensuring inclusion of international human rights law.

CRITICAL THINKING QUESTIONS

1. Judicial review has been critical to the expansion of civil liberties and civil rights throughout American history. How might such issues have played out under a different system, such as that in the United Kingdom, Canada, or South Africa?

2. During the Watergate crisis of 1974, the contested presidential election of 2000, and on other occasions, the U.S. Supreme Court stepped into political disputes as a type of "referee." What would it mean for the U.S. political system if the Court were not able to play such a role?

3. A proposed constitutional amendment would allow Congress to have the power to override a Supreme Court ruling by a two-thirds vote of both houses, much as it is able to override a presidential veto. Would you support or oppose such an amendment?

FIGURE 9.3 WHO ARE FEDERAL JUDGES?

Judicial appointments provide presidents with an opportunity to make a lasting impact on public policy. Recent presidents have also used them as an opportunity to increase the gender and racial diversity of the U.S. government and to gain favor with traditionally underrepresented groups. However, on some other measures, such as net worth and previous experience, federal judges continue to be a more homogeneous group.

SOURCE: Federal Judicial Center, Biographical Directory of Federal Judges

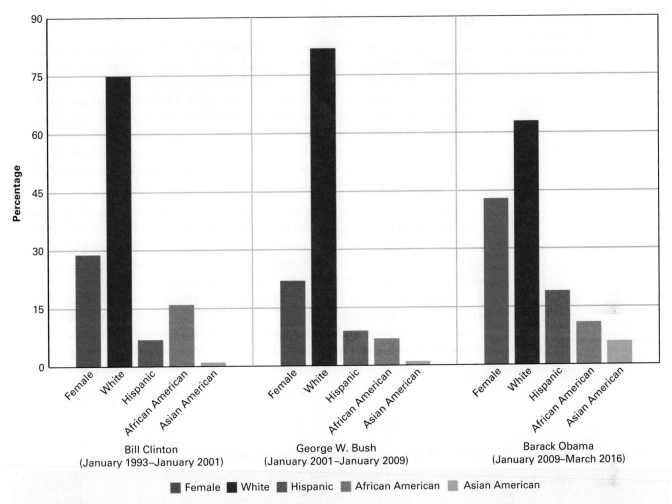

| Female | White | Hispanic | African American | Asian American |

block a nomination by simply registering their objection if they belong to the president's political party. One way senators may voice their opposition is through an informal process known as the "blue slip." When a judicial nomination is forwarded to the Senate Judiciary Committee, senators from the state in which a vacancy occurs are sent a letter, usually printed on light blue paper, asking them to register their support or opposition to a nominee. How seriously senators take the blue slips varies from one Congress to the next.[12] Senators not of the president's party frequently object to nominations on party principles.

Who Are Federal Judges?

Justice Oliver Wendell Holmes once remarked that a justice should be a "combination of Justinian, Jesus Christ and John Marshall."[13] Individuals who serve on judicial tribunals gain this experience through a number of common experiences. Most judges have held other political offices, such as a lower federal or state court judge or prosecutor. Many have been involved in politics, which is what usually brings them into consideration for a position on the federal bench. White males continue to dominate the federal courts, but since the 1970s, most presidents have pledged (with varying degrees of success) to do their best to appoint more African Americans, Hispanics, women, and other

Sandra Day O'Connor
An Associate Justice of the Supreme Court from 1981–2005 who was appointed by President Ronald Reagan as the first woman to serve on the Court.

Elena Kagan
An Associate Justice of the Supreme Court, appointed by President Barack Obama in 2009 while she was serving as solicitor general in his administration.

underrepresented groups to the federal bench. President Obama's appointees to the district courts set new records—41.7 percent of his appointees were from underrepresented groups, more than double that of George W. Bush. Seventy percent of President Barack Obama's nominees were women and minorities, but many of them were not confirmed. As of January 2017, there were 92 vacancies in the federal courts.

Nomination Criteria

Justice **Sandra Day O'Connor** once remarked that "You have to be lucky" to be appointed to the judiciary.[14] Although luck certainly factors in, over the years a variety of reasons have accounted for nominations to the bench. Depending on the timing of a vacancy, a president may or may not have a list of possible candidates or even a specific individual in mind. Until recently, presidents often looked within their circle of friends or their administration to fill a vacancy. Nevertheless, whether the nominee is a friend or someone known to the president only by reputation, at least six criteria are especially important: experience, ideology or policy preferences, rewards, pursuit of political support, religion, and race and gender.

EXPERIENCE Most nominees have had at least some judicial, legal, or governmental experience. For example, John Jay, the first chief justice, was one of the authors of *The Federalist Papers* and was active in New York politics. Similarly, one former federal court of appeals judge once remarked, "For me, becoming a federal judge wasn't very difficult. I managed John F. Kennedy's presidential campaign in Georgia."[15]

Service on a lower federal court has become almost a de facto requirement for nomination to the Supreme Court.[16] Prior to Justice Antonin Scalia's death in mid-February 2016, all nine sitting Supreme Court justices but one—former U.S. Solicitor General **Elena Kagan**—had prior judicial experience (see Table 9.2). Many of the sitting justices also served as law professors; notably, Justice Kagan was past dean of the Harvard Law School.

TABLE 9.2 WHO ARE THE JUSTICES OF THE SUPREME COURT IN JANUARY 2017?*

Name of Justice	Year of Birth	Year Appointed	Political Party	Law School	Appointing President	Religion	Prior Judicial Experience	Prior Government Experience
John Roberts	1955	2005	R	Harvard	G. W. Bush	Roman Catholic	U.S. Court of Appeals	Dept. of Justice, associate White House counsel
Anthony Kennedy	1936	1988	R	Harvard	Reagan	Roman Catholic	U.S. Court of Appeals	None
Clarence Thomas	1948	1991	R	Yale	Bush	Roman Catholic	U.S. Court of Appeals	Chair, Equal Employment Opportunity Commission
Ruth Bader Ginsburg	1933	1993	D	Columbia/Harvard	Clinton	Jewish	U.S. Court of Appeals	None
Stephen Breyer	1938	1994	D	Harvard	Clinton	Jewish	U.S. Court of Appeals	Chief counsel, Senate Judiciary Committee
Samuel Alito	1950	2006	R	Yale	G. W. Bush	Roman Catholic	U.S. Court of Appeals	Dept. of Justice, U.S. attorney
Sonia Sotomayor	1954	2009	D	Yale	Obama	Roman Catholic	U.S. Court of Appeals	Assistant attorney general, City of New York
Elena Kagan	1960	2010	D	Harvard	Obama	Jewish	None	U.S. solicitor general, associate White House counsel

*Justice Antonin Scalia died in February 2016 and was not replaced in 2016.

IDEOLOGY OR POLICY PREFERENCES Most presidents also seek to appoint individuals who share their policy preferences, and almost all have political goals in mind when they appoint a judge or justice. To optimize these goals, most presidents select judges and justices of their own party affiliation and/or who have been active in party politics. Chief Justice John Roberts and Justice Samuel Alito, for example, both Republicans, worked in the Department of Justice during the Reagan and George Bush administrations.

Presidents, however, often have erred in their assumptions about their appointees' ideological or policy preferences. President Dwight D. Eisenhower, a moderate conservative, for example, was appalled by the liberal opinions written by his appointee to chief justice, Earl Warren, concerning criminal defendants' rights.

REWARDS Historically, many of those appointed to the judiciary were personal friends of presidents. Lyndon B. Johnson, for example, appointed his longtime friend Abe Fortas to the bench. Today, this adage no longer holds true. None of the current justices were close friends with their appointing presidents.

PURSUIT OF POLITICAL SUPPORT During Ronald Reagan's successful campaign for the presidency in 1980, some of his advisers feared the gender gap would hurt him. Polls repeatedly showed that he was far less popular with female voters than with men. To gain support from women, Reagan announced during his campaign that should he win, he would appoint a woman to fill the first vacancy on the Supreme Court. When Justice Potter Stewart, a moderate, announced his retirement from the bench, under pressure from women's rights groups, President Reagan nominated Sandra Day O'Connor of the Arizona Court of Appeals to fill the vacancy.

RELIGION Through early 2017, of the more than one hundred justices who have served on the Court, almost all have been members of traditional Protestant faiths. Less than fifteen have been Roman Catholic, and only eight have been Jewish.[17] Today, even after the death of Roman Catholic Justice Antonin Scalia, more Catholics—John Roberts, Anthony Kennedy, Clarence Thomas, Samuel Alito, and Sonia Sotomayor—serve on the Court than at any other point in history. Three Jewish justices—Stephen Breyer, Ruth Bader Ginsburg, and Elena Kagan—round out the Court. At one time, no one could have imagined that Catholics would someday make up a majority of the Court or that no members of any Protestant faiths would serve.

RACE, ETHNICITY, AND GENDER Through January 2017, only two African Americans and four women have served on the Court. Race was undoubtedly a critical issue in the appointment of Clarence Thomas to replace Thurgood Marshall, the first African American justice. But, President George Bush refused to acknowledge his wish to retain a black seat on the Court. Instead, he announced that he was "picking the best man for the job on the merits," a claim that was met with considerable skepticism by many observers.

As the ethnic diversity of the United States increased, presidents also faced greater pressure to nominate a Hispanic justice to the Supreme Court. Early in his presidency, President Barack Obama fulfilled these expectations by nominating Sonia Sotomayor. A Puerto Rican and self-proclaimed "wise Latina woman" who grew up in the Bronx, New York, Sotomayor became the first Hispanic Supreme Court justice at the height of a fierce immigration debate.

As the number of women in the legal profession has grown, presidents have also made conscious efforts to appoint more women to the federal bench. These efforts began in the late 1970s with President Jimmy Carter and have increased over time. Today, more women—three—serve on the Supreme Court than at any other time in history. Significant numbers of female judges serve in the lower federal courts, but their numbers are far from representative in comparison to the overall percentage of women in the legal profession.

The Confirmation Process

The Constitution gives the Senate the authority to approve all nominees to the federal bench. Ordinarily, nominations are referred to the Senate Judiciary Committee. This committee investigates the nominees, holds hearings, and votes on its recommendation for Senate action. At this stage, the committee may reject a nominee or send the nomination to the full Senate for a vote. The full Senate then deliberates on the nominee before voting. A simple majority vote is required for confirmation.

INVESTIGATION   As a president proceeds to narrow the list of possible nominees for a judicial vacancy, White House staff begin an investigation into their personal and professional backgrounds. The Federal Bureau of Investigation also receives names of potential nominees for background checks. In addition, the names are forwarded to the American Bar Association (ABA), the politically powerful organization that represents the interests of the legal profession. After its own investigation, the ABA rates each nominee, based on his or her qualifications, as Well Qualified (previously "Highly Qualified"), Qualified, or Not Qualified.

After a formal nomination is made and sent to the Senate, the Senate Judiciary Committee embarks on its own investigation. To start, the Senate Judiciary Committee asks each nominee to complete a lengthy questionnaire detailing previous work (dating as far back as high school summer jobs), judicial opinions written, judicial philosophy, speeches, and even all interviews ever given to members of the press. Committee staffers also contact potential witnesses who might offer testimony concerning the nominee's fitness for office.

LOBBYING BY INTEREST GROUPS   Many organized interests show keen interest in the nomination process. Interest groups are particularly active in Supreme Court nominations. In 1987, for example, the nomination of Judge Robert H. Bork to the Supreme Court led liberal groups to launch an extensive radio, TV, and print media campaign against the nominee. These interest groups decried Bork's actions as U.S. solicitor general, especially his firing of the Watergate special prosecutor at the request of President Richard M. Nixon, as well as his political beliefs. As a result of this outcry, the Senate rejected Bork's nomination by a 42–58 vote.

WHAT ROLE DOES THE SENATE JUDICIARY COMMITTEEE PLAY IN THE JUDICIAL NOMINATION PROCESS?

Chief Judge Merrick Garland of the U.S. Court of Appeals for the District of Columbia, the nation's second most prestigious court, was President Barack Obama's choice to replace the late Justice Antonin Scalia on the Supreme Court. Here, he arrives on Capitol Hill April 12, 2016, for a breakfast meeting with Senate Judiciary Committee Chairman Sen. Charles Grassley (R–IA). Republican senators, at the insistence of Majority Leader Mitch McConnell (R–KY), remained steadfast in refusing to hold hearings or a confirmation vote on the president's nominee.

More and more, interest groups are also involving themselves in district court and court of appeals nominations. They recognize that these appointments increasingly pave the way for future nominees to the Supreme Court.

THE SENATE COMMITTEE HEARINGS AND SENATE VOTE Not all nominees inspire the kind of intense reaction that kept Bork from the Court. Until 1929, all but one Senate Judiciary Committee hearing on a Supreme Court nominee were conducted in executive session—that is, closed to the public. The 1916 hearings on Louis Brandeis, the first Jewish justice, took place in public and lasted nineteen days, although Brandeis himself never was called to testify. In 1925, Harlan Fiske Stone became the first nominee to testify before the committee.

Since the 1980s, it has become standard for senators to ask the nominees probing questions. Most nominees have declined to answer many of these questions on the grounds that the issues raised ultimately might come before the courts.

After the conclusion of hearings, the Senate Judiciary Committee usually makes a recommendation to the full Senate. Any rejections of presidential nominees to the Supreme Court generally occur only after the Senate Judiciary Committee has recommended against a nominee's appointment. Few recent confirmations have been close, although current Supreme Court Justices Clarence Thomas and Samuel Alito were confirmed by margins of less than ten votes.

HOW THE SUPREME COURT MAKES DECISIONS

9.4 Outline the process by which the Supreme Court makes decisions and the factors that influence judicial decision making.

Given the judicial system's vast size and substantial, although often indirect, power over so many aspects of our lives, it is surprising that so many Americans know very little about the judicial system in general and the U.S. Supreme Court in particular. While the American public's lack of interest can take the blame for much of this ignorance, the Court has also taken great pains to ensure its privacy and sense of decorum. The Court's rites and rituals contribute to its mystique and encourage a "cult of the robe."[18] Consider, for example, the way the Supreme Court conducts its proceedings. Oral arguments are not televised, and utmost secrecy surrounds deliberations concerning the outcome of cases. In contrast, C-SPAN brings us daily coverage of various congressional hearings and floor debate on bills and important national issues, and CNN and other networks provide extensive coverage of many important state court trials. The Supreme Court, however, remains adamant in its refusal to televise its proceedings—including public oral arguments, although it now allows the release of same-day audio recordings of oral arguments.

Deciding to Hear a Case

As many as 8,000 cases are filed at the Supreme Court each term; approximately 75 to 80 cases are orally argued and decided. During its 2015–2016 term, 78 cases were heard, and 82 decisions were issued—some cases are decided without oral arguments. In contrast, from 1790 to 1801, the Court received only 87 total cases under its appellate jurisdiction. In the Court's early years, most of the justices' workload involved their circuit-riding duties.[19] As recently as the 1940s, fewer than 1,000 cases were filed annually. Filings increased at a dramatic rate until the mid-1990s, shot up again in the late 1990s, and generally have now leveled off.

The content of the Court's docket is every bit as significant as its size. During the 1930s, cases requiring the interpretation of constitutional law began to account for a growing portion of the Court's workload, leading the Court to assume a more important role in the policy-making process. At that time, only 5 percent of the Court's cases involved questions concerning the Bill of Rights. By the late 1950s, one-third of filed cases involved such questions; by the 1960s, half did.[20]

writ of *certiorari*
A request for the Supreme Court to order up the records from a lower court to review the case.

WRITS OF *CERTIORARI* AND THE RULE OF FOUR Since 1988, nearly all appellate cases that have gone to the Supreme Court arrived there on a petition for a **writ of *certiorari*** (from the Latin "to be informed"), which is a request for the Supreme Court—at its discretion—to order up the records of the lower courts for purposes of review (see Figure 9.4).

The Supreme Court controls its own caseload through the *certiorari* process, deciding which cases it wants to hear and rejecting most cases that come to it. All petitions, or writs of *certiorari*, must meet two criteria:

1. The case must come from a U.S. court of appeals, a court of military appeals, district court, or a state court of last resort.
2. The case must involve a federal question. Thus, the case must present questions of federal constitutional law or involve a federal statute, action, or treaty. The reasons that the Court should accept the case for review and legal argument supporting that position are set out in the petitioner's writ of *certiorari*.

FIGURE 9.4   HOW DOES A CASE GET TO THE SUPREME COURT?

This figure illustrates both how cases get on the Court's docket and what happens after a case is accepted for review. A case may take several years to wind its way through the federal judiciary and another year or two to be heard and decided by the Supreme Court, if the justices decide to grant *certiorari*.

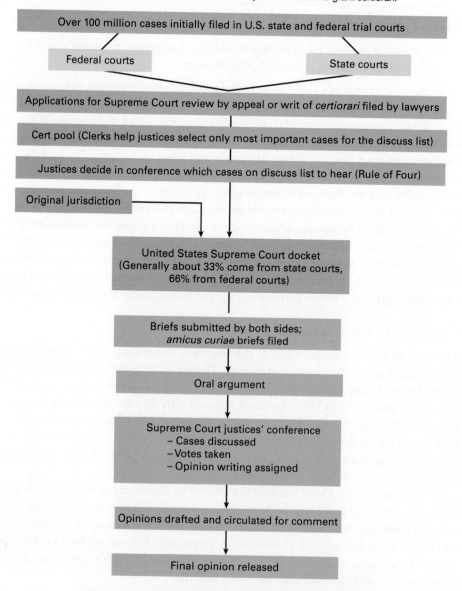

Over 100 million cases initially filed in U.S. state and federal trial courts

Federal courts   State courts

Applications for Supreme Court review by appeal or writ of *certiorari* filed by lawyers

Cert pool (Clerks help justices select only most important cases for the discuss list)

Justices decide in conference which cases on discuss list to hear (Rule of Four)

Original jurisdiction

United States Supreme Court docket
(Generally about 33% come from state courts, 66% from federal courts)

Briefs submitted by both sides; *amicus curiae* briefs filed

Oral argument

Supreme Court justices' conference
– Cases discussed
– Votes taken
– Opinion writing assigned

Opinions drafted and circulated for comment

Final opinion released

The clerk of the Court transmits petitions for writs of *certiorari* first to the chief justice's office, where his clerks review the petitions, and then to the individual justices' offices. On the Roberts Court, all of the justices except Justice Samuel Alito (who allows his clerks great individual authority in selecting the cases for him to review) participate in what is called the *cert* pool. Pool participants review their assigned fraction of petitions and share their notes with each other. Those cases deemed noteworthy by the justices then make it onto the "discuss list" prepared by the chief justice's clerks and are circulated to the chambers of the other justices. All other petitions are dead listed and go no further. Only about 30 percent of submitted petitions make it to the discuss list. During one of their weekly conference meetings, the justices review the cases on the discuss list. The chief justice speaks first, then the rest of the justices, according to seniority. The decision process ends when the justices vote, and by custom, *certiorari* is granted according to the **Rule of Four**—when at least four justices vote to hear a case.

The cases the Court chooses to hear—or not to hear—make a powerful statement about the justices' policy priorities. Cases the Court decides to hear may establish new national policy standards or clarify the decisions of lower courts. When the Court chooses not to hear a case, it allows the decision of the lower court to stand, effectively making another type of statement on public policy.

THE ROLE OF CLERKS   As early as 1850, the justices of the Supreme Court beseeched Congress to approve the hiring of a clerk to assist each justice. Congress denied the request, so when Justice Horace Gray hired the first law clerk in 1882, he paid the clerk himself. Justice Gray's clerk was a top graduate of Harvard Law School whose duties included cutting Justice Gray's hair and running personal errands. Finally, in 1886, Congress authorized each justice to hire a stenographer clerk for $1,600 a year.

Clerks typically are selected from candidates at the top of the graduating classes of prestigious law schools like the justices themselves who all attended Harvard or Yale Law Schools. They perform a variety of tasks, ranging from searching arcane facts to playing tennis or taking walks with the justices. Clerks spend most of their time researching material, reading and summarizing cases, and helping justices

Rule of Four
At least four justices of the Supreme Court must vote to consider a case before it can be heard.

WHY ARE SUPREME COURT CLERKSHIPS IMPORTANT?

Supreme Court clerkships are awarded to a small number of elite law school graduates each year. In addition to providing valuable experience at the Court, clerkships can open doors to opportunities in government and private practice. Justice Elena Kagan (right, seated with former Justice Sandra Day O'Connor) served as a law clerk to Justice Thurgood Marshall. She later went on to serve as White House counsel, Harvard Law School dean, solicitor general, and, ultimately, Supreme Court justice. Chief Justice Roberts and Justice Breyer also served as clerks.

solicitor general
The fourth-ranking member of the Department of Justice; responsible for handling nearly all appeals on behalf of the U.S. government to the Supreme Court.

amicus curiae
"Friend of the court"; amici may file briefs or even appear to argue their interests orally before the court.

write opinions. Clerks also make the first pass through the petitions that come to the Court, undoubtedly influencing which cases get a second look. They often help draft opinions and serve as informal conduits for communication between the justices' chambers. Just how much assistance they provide in the writing of opinions is unknown.[21] However, it is noteworthy that as the number of clerks has grown, so has the length of the Court's written opinions.[22]

Increasing numbers of federal judges are leaving the bench for more lucrative private practice. While a salary of $223,500 (for the chief justice) or $213,900 (for the other justices) may sound like a lot to most people, lawyers in large urban practices routinely earn more than double and triple that amount annually. Supreme Court clerks, moreover, now regularly receive $300,000 signing bonuses (in addition to large salaries) from law firms anxious to pay for their expertise.

How Does a Case Survive the Process?

It can be difficult to determine why the Court decides to hear a particular case. The Court does not offer reasons, and "the standards by which the justices decide to grant or deny review are highly personalized and necessarily discretionary," noted former Chief Justice Earl Warren.[23] Political scientists nonetheless have attempted to determine the characteristics of the cases the Court accepts. Among the cues increasing the odds of the Court hearing a case are the following:

- The federal government is the party asking for review.
- The case involves conflict among the courts of appeals.
- The case presents a civil rights or civil liberties question.
- The case involves the ideological or policy preferences of the justices.
- The case has significant social or political interest, as evidenced by the presence of interest group *amicus curiae* briefs.

FEDERAL GOVERNMENT   One of the most important cues for predicting whether the Court will hear a case is the U.S. solicitor general's position. The **solicitor general**, appointed by the president, is the fourth-ranking member of the Department of Justice and is responsible for handling nearly all appeals on behalf of the U.S. government to the Supreme Court. The solicitor's staff resembles a small, specialized law firm within the Department of Justice. But, because this office has such a special relationship with the Supreme Court, even having a suite of offices within the Supreme Court building, the solicitor general often is called the Court's "ninth and a half member."[24] Moreover, the office of the solicitor general, on behalf of the U.S. government, appears as a party or as an *amicus curiae*, or friend of the court, in more than 50 percent of the cases heard by the Court each term.

This special relationship helps to explain the overwhelming success the solicitor general's office enjoys before the Supreme Court. The Court generally accepts 70 to 80 percent of cases in which the U.S. government is the petitioning party, compared with about 5 percent of all others.[25] But, because of this special relationship, the solicitor general often ends up playing two conflicting roles: representing in Court both the president's policy interests and the broader interests of the United States. At times, solicitors may find these two roles difficult to reconcile.

CONFLICT AMONG THE COURTS OF APPEALS   Conflict among the lower courts is another reason justices take cases. When interpretations of constitutional or federal law are involved, justices seem to want consistency throughout the federal court system. Often these conflicts occur when important civil rights or civil liberties questions arise. Political scientists have noted that justices' ideological leanings play a role.[26] It is not uncommon to see conservative justices voting to hear cases to overrule liberal lower court decisions, or vice versa. Justices also take cases when several circuit courts disagree over a main issue.

INTEREST GROUP PARTICIPATION   A quick way for justices to gauge the ideological ramifications of a particular civil rights or liberties case is by the nature and amount of interest group participation. Richard C. Cortner has noted that "Cases do not arrive on the doorstep of the Supreme Court like orphans in the night."[27] Instead, most cases heard by the Supreme Court involve interest group participation. This participation may come in a number of forms.

Liberal groups, such as the American Civil Liberties Union, People for the American Way, or the NAACP Legal Defense and Educational Fund, and conservative groups, including Americans United for Life, Concerned Women for America, and the American Center for Law and Justice, routinely sponsor cases before the Supreme Court. Sponsorship implies that a group has helped to devise the legal strategy, pay the costs of litigation, and shepherd the case through the court system. It can be very costly and time-consuming.

Other groups participate as *amicus curiae*, or a friend of the Court. *Amicus* participation has increased dramatically since the 1970s. Because litigation is so expensive, few individuals have the money, time, or interest to sponsor a case all the way to the U.S. Supreme Court. All sorts of interest groups, then, find that joining ongoing cases through *amicus* briefs is a useful way to advance their policy preferences. Major cases addressing issues of great national importance, such as campaign finance, health care, or affirmative action attract large numbers of *amicus* briefs as part of interest groups' efforts to lobby the judiciary and bring about desired political objectives.[28] In the 2015 – 2016 term of the high Court, 75 *amicus* briefs were filed in *Zubik* v. *Burwell*, a case involving whether religious institutions should be exempt from Obamacare's contraceptive mandate. In an unsigned opinion, the Court sent the case and six others to their respective lower courts for reconsideration.[29]

The *amicus curiae* briefs filed by interested parties, especially interest groups or other parties potentially affected by the outcome of the case, often echo or expand the positions of both parties in a case and often provide justices with additional information about the potential consequences of a case. Research by political scientists has found that "not only does [an *amicus*] brief in favor of *certiorari* significantly improve the chances of a case being accepted, but two, three, and four briefs improve the chances even more."[30] Clearly, it's the more the merrier, whether the briefs are filed for or against granting review.

Finally, interest groups also support litigants' efforts by holding practice oral arguments during mock court sessions. In these sessions, the lawyer who will argue the case before the justices participates in several complete rehearsals, with prominent lawyers and law professors from various law firms and law schools around Washington, D.C., role-playing the various justices.

Hearing and Deciding the Case

Once the Court accepts a case for review, a flurry of activity begins. Lawyers on both sides of the case prepare their written arguments for submission to the Court. In these briefs, lawyers cite prior case law and make arguments regarding why the Court should find in favor of their client.

ORAL ARGUMENTS   After the Court accepts a case and each side has submitted briefs and *amicus* briefs, oral argument takes place. The Supreme Court's annual term begins the first Monday in October, as it has since the late 1800s, and generally runs through mid-June. Justices hear oral arguments from the beginning of the term until early April. Special cases, such as *U.S.* v. *Nixon* (1974)—which involved President Richard M. Nixon's refusal to turn over tapes of Oval Office conversations to a special prosecutor investigating a break-in at the Democratic Party headquarters in the Watergate complex—have been heard even later in the year.[31] During the term, "sittings," periods of about two weeks in which cases are heard, alternate with "recesses," also about two weeks long. Justices usually hear oral arguments Monday through Wednesday.

Generally, only the immediate parties in the case take part in oral argument, although it is not uncommon for the U.S. solicitor general or one of his or her deputies to make an appearance to argue orally as an *amicus curiae*. Oral argument at the Court is fraught with time-honored tradition and ceremony. At precisely ten o'clock every morning when the Court is in session, the Court marshal, dressed in a formal morning coat, emerges to intone "Oyez! Oyez! Oyez!" as the justices emerge from behind a reddish-purple velvet curtain to take their places on the raised and slightly angled bench. The chief justice sits in the middle. The remaining justices sit to the left and right, alternating in seniority.

Almost all attorneys are allotted one half-hour to present their cases, including the time required to answer questions from the bench. As a lawyer approaches the mahogany lectern, a green light goes on, indicating that the attorney's time has begun. A white light flashes when five minutes remain. When a red light goes on, Court practice mandates that counsel stop immediately. One famous piece of Court lore told to all attorneys concerns a lawyer who continued talking and reading from his prepared argument after the red light went on. When he looked up, he found an empty bench— the justices had risen quietly and departed while he continued to talk.

Although many Court watchers have tried to figure out how a particular justice will vote based on the questioning at oral argument, most researchers find that the

WHY ARE ORAL ARGUMENTS IMPORTANT?

The Supreme Court hears oral argument in most cases in which it reaches a final decision. Scholars have found that oral argument serves a number of important functions. For example, it provides an opportunity for the justices to highlight important case themes and to ask questions about the impact of a case that go beyond what is detailed in the party or *amicus curiae* briefs. Here, an artist's rendering of oral arguments during one of the 2012 cases that decided the constitutionality of the health care reform bill (Obamacare). No cameras are allowed in the courtroom.

nature and number of questions asked do not help much in predicting the outcome of a case. Nevertheless, oral argument has several important functions. First, it is the only opportunity for even a small portion of the public (who may attend the hearings) and the press to observe the workings of the Court. Second, it assures lawyers that the justices have heard the parties' arguments, and it forces lawyers to focus on arguments believed important by the justices. Third, it provides the Court with additional information, especially concerning the Court's broader political role, an issue not usually addressed in written briefs. Finally, Justice Stephen Breyer notes that oral arguments are a good way for the justices to try to highlight certain issues for other justices.

THE CONFERENCE AND THE VOTE   The justices meet in closed conference twice a week when the Court is hearing oral arguments. Since the ascendancy of Chief Justice Roger B. Taney to the Court in 1836, the justices have begun each conference session with a round of handshaking. Once the door to the conference room closes, no others are allowed to enter. The justice with the least seniority acts as the doorkeeper for the other eight, communicating with those waiting outside to fill requests for documents, water, and any other necessities.

Conferences highlight the importance and power of the chief justice, who presides over them and makes the initial presentation of each case. Each individual justice then discusses the case in order of his or her seniority on the Court, with the most senior justice speaking next. Most accounts of the decision-making process reveal that at this point some justices try to change the minds of others, but that most enter the conference room with a clear idea of how they will vote on each case.

During the Rehnquist Court, the justices generally voted at the same time they discussed each case, with each justice speaking only once. Initial conference votes were not final, and justices were allowed to change their minds before final votes were taken later. The Roberts Court is much more informal than the Rehnquist Court. The justices' regular conferences now last longer and, unlike the conferences headed by Rehnquist, Roberts encourages discussion.[32]

WRITING OPINIONS   After the Court has reached a decision in conference, the justices must formulate a formal opinion of the Court. If the chief justice is in the majority, he selects the justice who will write the opinion. This privilege enables him to wield tremendous power and is a very important strategic decision; the author of the decision may determine the tone and content of the Court's opinion. If the chief justice is in the minority, the assignment falls to the most senior justice in the majority.

The opinion of the Court can take several different forms. Most decisions are reached by a majority opinion written by one member of the Court to reflect the views of at least five justices. This opinion usually sets out the legal reasoning justifying the decision, and this legal reasoning becomes a precedent for deciding future cases. The reasoning behind any decision is often as important as the outcome. Under the system of *stare decisis*, both are likely to be relied on as precedent later by lower courts confronted with cases involving similar issues.

In the process of creating the final opinion of the Court, informal caucusing and negotiation often take place, as justices may hold out for word changes or other modifications as a condition of their continued support of the majority opinion. This negotiation process can lead to divisions in the Court's majority. When this occurs, the Court may be forced to decide cases by **plurality opinions**, which attract the support of three or four justices. While these decisions do not have the precedential value of majority opinions, they nonetheless have been used by the Court to decide many major cases. Justices who agree with the outcome of the case, but not with the legal rationale for the decision, may file **concurring opinions** to express their differing approach.

Justices who do not agree with the outcome of a case file **dissenting opinions**. Although these opinions have little direct legal value, they can be an important

plurality opinion
A type of judicial opinion, the reasoning of which is agreed to by fewer than a majority of judges on a court; although it resolves the particular case, the opinion does not establish a binding precedent.

concurring opinion
A type of judicial opinion issued by a minority of judges on a court who agree with the outcome of a case, but wishes to express different legal reasoning.

dissenting opinion
A type of judicial opinion issued by a minority of judges on a court who disagree with the outcome of a case and wish to explain their legal reasoning.

judicial restraint
A philosophy of judicial decision making that posits courts should allow the decisions of other branches of government to stand, even when they offend a judge's own principles.

judicial activism
A philosophy of judicial decision making that posits judges should use their power broadly to further justice.

strict constructionist
An approach to constitutional interpretation that emphasizes interpreting the Constitution as it was originally written and intended by the Framers.

indicator of legal thought on the Court and are an excellent platform for justices to note their personal and legal disagreements with other members of the Court.

Factors Influencing Judicial Decisions

Justices do not make decisions in a vacuum. Principles of *stare decisis* dictate that the justices follow the law of previous cases in deciding cases at hand. But, a variety of legal and extra-legal factors have also been found to affect Supreme Court decision making. These include a judge's view on the role of the courts, ideology, and public opinion

JUDICIAL PHILOSOPHY AND IDEOLOGY One of the primary issues concerning judicial decision making focuses on judicial philosophy, particularly what is called the activism/restraint debate. Advocates of **judicial restraint** argue that courts should allow the decisions of other branches to stand, even when they offend a judge's own principles. Restraintists defend their position by asserting that unelected judges make up the federal courts, which renders the judicial branch the least democratic branch of government. Consequently, the courts should defer policy making to other branches of government as much as possible.

Restraintists refer to *Roe* v. *Wade* (1973), the case that liberalized abortion laws, as a classic example of **judicial activism** run amok. They maintain that the Court should have deferred policy making on this sensitive issue to the states or to the elected branches of the federal government especially because the Court's decision invalidated the abortion laws of forty-seven states.

Advocates of judicial restraint generally agree that judges should be **strict constructionists**; that is, they should interpret the Constitution as the Framers wrote and originally intended it. They argue that in determining the constitutionality of a statute or policy, the Court should rely on the explicit meanings of the clauses in the document, which can be clarified by looking at founding documents.

Advocates of judicial activism contend that judges should use their power broadly to further justice. Activists argue that it is appropriate for courts to correct injustices committed by other branches of government. Implicit in this argument is the notion that courts need to protect oppressed minorities.[33]

Although judicial activists are often considered politically liberal and restraintists politically conservative, in recent years a new brand of conservative judicial activism has become prevalent. Liberal activist decisions often expanded the rights of political and legal minorities. But, conservative activist judges view their positions as an opportunity to issue broad rulings that impose their own political beliefs and policies, such as expanding the rights of corporations.

PUBLIC OPINION Whether or not public opinion directly influences justices, it can act as a check on the power of the courts. To maintain its institutional prestige, the Court must be wary not to make too many decisions that call its authority into question. The Court must also rely on the support of leaders in the other, popularly elected, branches of government to implement its decisions. Thus, many judicial decisions are strategic ones, balancing constitutional and legal interpretation against the court of public opinion. For example, between 1933 and 1936, the Court resisted upholding the constitutionality of President Franklin D. Roosevelt's New Deal programs, viewing them as outside the national powers prescribed by the constitution. However, the justices eventually capitulated to political pressures and public opinion, and after 1936, they reversed many of their earlier decisions. These decisions led to the growth and expansion of many federal programs regulating economic activity, including minimum wage laws.

The courts, especially the Supreme Court, also can be the direct target of public opinion. When *Webster* v. *Reproductive Health Services* (1989) was about to come before

TABLE 9.3   DO SUPREME COURT DECISIONS ALIGN WITH THE VIEWS OF THE AMERICAN PUBLIC?

Issues	Case	Court Decision	Public Opinion Before Decision
Is the death penalty constitutional?	*Gregg* v. *Georgia* (1976)	Yes	Yes (72% favored)
Should homosexual relations between consenting adults be legal?	*Lawrence* v. *Texas* (2003)	Yes	Maybe (50% favored)
Should state and local governments be able to pass laws that ban the possession or sale of handguns?	*McDonald* v. *City of Chicago* (2010)	No	Maybe (50% opposed)
Is donating money a form of free speech protected by the First Amendment?	*Citizens United* v. *FEC* (2010)	Yes	Yes (62% favored)
Is the Patient Protection and Affordable Care Act constitutional?	*National Federation of Independent Businesses* v. *Sebelius* (2012)	Yes	No (48% opposed)

SOURCE: Lexis-Nexis, RPOLL

the Supreme Court, unprecedented lobbying of the Court took place as groups and individuals on both sides of the abortion issue marched and sent appeals to the Court. Mail at the Court, which usually averaged about 1,000 pieces a day, rose to an astronomical 46,000 pieces per day, virtually paralyzing normal lines of communication.

The Supreme Court also appears to affect public opinion. Political scientists have found that the Court's initial rulings on controversial issues such as abortion or capital punishment positively influence public opinion in the direction of the Court's opinion. However, this research also finds that subsequent decisions have little effect.[34]

Public confidence in the Court, as with other institutions of government, has ebbed and flowed. Public support for the Court was highest after the Court issued *U.S. v. Nixon* (1974).[35] At a time when Americans lost faith in the presidency because of the Watergate scandal, they could at least look to the Supreme Court to do the right thing. Although the percentage of Americans with confidence in the courts has fluctuated over time, in 2012, an all-time low of 52 percent of Americans approved of the way the Supreme Court was doing its job.[36] By June 2016, even fewer Americans—36 percent—had a great deal or quite a lot of confidence in the Court.[37]

TOWARD REFORM: POWER, POLICY MAKING, AND THE COURT

9.5 Evaluate the role of the Supreme Court in national policy making.

All judges, whether they recognize it or not, make policy. The decisions of the Supreme Court, in particular, have a tremendous impact on American politics and policy. Over the past 250 years, the justices have helped to codify many of the major rights and liberties guaranteed to the citizens of the United States. Although justices need the cooperation of the executive and legislative branches of the federal and state governments to implement and enforce a good number of their decisions, it is safe to say that many policies we take for granted in the United States would not have come to fruition without support of the Supreme Court.[38] These include the right to privacy and equal rights for African Americans, women, Hispanics, the LGBT community, and other minority groups.

Several Courts have played particularly notable roles in the development of the judiciary's policy-making role. As discussed earlier in the chapter, the Marshall Court played an important role in establishing the role and power of the Supreme Court, including the power of judicial review in *Marbury* v. *Madison* (1803). The Warren Court decided a number of civil rights cases that broadly expanded civil and political rights. These decisions drew a great deal of criticism but played a major role in broadening public understanding of the Court as a policy maker. The Rehnquist Court made numerous decisions related to federalism, which caused observers to take

judicial implementation
How and whether judicial decisions are translated into actual public policies affecting more than the immediate parties to a lawsuit.

note of the Court's ability to referee conflicts between the federal government and the states. And, the Roberts Court reversed the general trend of the Court's agreement with executive actions during times of war by finding in 2008 that the Bush administration's denial of *habeas corpus* rights to prisoners being held at Guantanamo Bay was an unconstitutional exercise of presidential power.[39]

Policy Making

One measure of the power of the courts and their ability to make policy is that more than one hundred federal laws have been declared unconstitutional. Although many of these laws have not been particularly significant, others have. In 2012, for example, the Roberts Court struck down portions of an Arizona state law regulating immigration on the grounds that it violated the Constitution's supremacy clause.[40]

Another measure of the policy-making power of the Supreme Court is its ability to overrule itself. Although the Court generally abides by the informal rule of *stare decisis*, by one count, it has overruled itself in more than 200 cases.[41] *Brown v. Board of Education* (1954), for example, overruled *Plessy v. Ferguson* (1896), thereby reversing years of constitutional interpretation concluding that racial segregation was not a violation of the Constitution. Moreover, in the past few years, the Court repeatedly has reversed earlier decisions in the areas of criminal defendants' rights, reproductive rights, and free speech, revealing its powerful role in determining national policy.

A measure of the growing power of the federal courts is the degree to which they now handle issues that had been considered political questions more appropriately settled by the other branches of government. Prior to 1962, for example, the Court refused to hear cases questioning the size (and population) of congressional districts,

DO UNPOPULAR SUPREME COURT RULINGS THREATEN THE NATION?

The Warren Court's broad expansions of civil and political rights led to a great deal of criticism, including a movement to impeach the chief justice. Here, two California billboards present contrasting views of Warren's performance.

no matter how unequal they were.[42] The boundary of a legislative district was considered a political question. Then, in *Baker v. Carr* (1962), Justice William Brennan, writing for the Court, concluded that simply because a case involved a political issue, it did not necessarily involve a political question. This opened the floodgates to cases involving a variety of issues that the Court formerly had declined to address.[43] In particular, over the last decade at least one voting rights case has appeared on the Court's docket each term.

Implementing Court Decisions

President Andrew Jackson, annoyed about a particular decision handed down by the Marshall Court, is alleged to have said, "John Marshall has made his decision; now let him enforce it." Jackson's statement raises a question: how do Supreme Court rulings translate into public policy? In fact, although judicial decisions carry legal and even moral authority, all courts must rely on other units of government to carry out their directives. If the president or members of Congress, for example, do not like a particular Supreme Court ruling, they can underfund programs needed to implement a decision or seek only lax enforcement. **Judicial implementation** refers to how and whether judicial decisions are translated into actual public policies affecting more than the immediate parties to the lawsuit.

How well a decision is implemented often depends on how well crafted or popular it is. Hostile reaction in the South to *Brown v. Board of Education* (1954) and the absence of precise guidelines to implement the decision meant that the ruling went largely unenforced for years. The *Brown* experience also highlights how much the Supreme Court needs the support of both federal and state courts as well as other governmental agencies to carry out its judgments. For example, you probably graduated from high school after 1992, when the Supreme Court ruled that public middle school and high school graduations could not include a prayer, yet your own commencement ceremony may have included one.[44]

The implementation of judicial decisions involves what political scientists call an implementing population and a consumer population.[45] The implementing population consists of those people responsible for carrying out a decision. Depending on the policy and issues in question, the implementing population can include lawyers, judges, public officials, police officers and police departments, hospital administrators, government agencies, and corporations. In the case of school prayer, the implementing population could include teachers, school administrators, or school boards. The consumer population consists of those people who might be directly affected by a decision—in this case, students and parents.

For effective implementation of a judicial decision, the first requirement is for members of the implementing population to show they understand the original decision. For example, the Supreme Court ruled in *Reynolds* v. *Sims* (1964) that every person should have an equally weighted vote in electing governmental representatives.[46] This "one person, one vote" rule might seem simple enough at first glance, but in practice it can be very difficult to understand. The implementing population in this case consists chiefly of state legislatures and local governments, which determine voting districts for federal, state, and local offices. If a state legislature draws districts in such a way that African American or Hispanic voters are spread thinly across a number of separate constituencies, the chances are slim that any particular district will elect a representative who is especially sensitive to minority concerns. Does that violate "equal representation"? That is often a question for the Court to address given the particular facts of the situation.

The second requirement is that the implementing population actually must follow Court policy. Thus, when the Court ruled that men could not be denied admission to a state-sponsored nursing school, the implementing population—in this case, university administrators and the state board of regents governing the nursing school—had to enroll qualified male students.[47]

Implementation of judicial decisions is most likely to be smooth if a few highly visible public officials, such as the president or a governor, shoulder the responsibility of seeing to the task. By the same token, these officials also can thwart or impede judicial intentions. Recall, for example, the effect of Governor Orval Faubus's initial refusal to allow black children to attend all-white public schools in Little Rock, Arkansas.

The third requirement for implementation is for the consumer population to be aware of the rights that a decision grants or denies them. Teenagers seeking an abortion, for example, are consumers of the Supreme Court's decisions on abortion and contraception. They need to know that most states require them to inform their parents of their intention to have an abortion or to get parental permission to do so. Similarly, criminal defendants and their lawyers are consumers of Court decisions and need to know, for instance, the implications of recent Court decisions for evidence presented at trial, sentencing guidelines, and prison reform.

In 2016, several important questions presented to the Court were left unanswered. The death of extremely conservative Justice Antonin Scalia in February 2016 created a power void on the Court resulting in several 4–4 decisions. In such circumstances, the decision of the lower court is upheld and binding on the jurisdiction (state or federal circuit) below the Supreme Court but holds no precedential value across the rest of the nation.

Roots of the Federal Judiciary

9.1 Describe the constitutional foundations of the federal judiciary and judicial review.

Many Framers viewed the judicial branch of government as little more than a minor check on the other two branches, ignoring Anti-Federalist concerns about an unelected judiciary and its potential for tyranny. The Judiciary Act of 1789 established the basic federal court system we have today. It was the Marshall Court (1801–1835), however, that interpreted the Constitution to include the Court's major power, that of judicial review.

The Federal Court System

9.2 Describe the structure of the federal judiciary.

The federal court system is made up of constitutional and legislative courts. Federal district courts, courts of appeals, and the Supreme Court are constitutional courts.

How Federal Court Judges are Selected

9.3 Outline the criteria for nominating and the process of approving federal judges and Supreme Court justices.

District court, court of appeals, and Supreme Court justices are nominated by the president and must also win Senate confirmation. Important criteria for selection include competence, ideology, rewards, pursuit of political support, religion, race, ethnicity, and gender.

How the Supreme Court Makes Decisions

9.4 Outline the process by which the Supreme Court makes decisions and the factors that influence judicial decision making.

Several factors influence the Court's decision to hear a case. Not only must the Court have jurisdiction, but at least four justices must vote to hear the case. Cases with certain characteristics are most likely to be heard. Once a case is set for review, briefs and *amicus curiae* briefs are filed and oral argument is scheduled. The justices meet in conference after oral argument to discuss the case; votes are taken; and opinions are written, circulated, and then announced.

Judges' decisions are influenced by a number of factors, including the law of previous cases, personal philosophy and ideology, and public opinion.

Toward Reform: Power, Policy Making, and the Court

9.5 Evaluate the role of the Supreme Court in national policy making.

The Supreme Court is an important participant in the policy-making process. The power to interpret laws gives the Court a tremendous policy-making power never envisioned by the Framers. However, if the president or members of Congress oppose a particular Supreme Court ruling, they can underfund programs needed to implement a decision or seek only lax enforcement.

amicus curiae
appellate court
appellate jurisdiction
brief
constitutional (or Article III) courts
dissenting opinions
Chisholm v. *Georgia*
concurring opinions
Elena Kagen
Eleventh Amendment
Federalist No. 78
John Jay

John Marshall
judicial activism
judicial implementation
judicial restraint
judicial review
Judiciary Act of 1789
jurisdiction
lame duck
legislative courts
Marbury v. *Madison* (1803)
original jurisdiction
precedents

plurality opinions
Rule of Four
Sandra Day O'Connor
senatorial courtesy
solicitor general
stare decisis
strict constructionist
trial court
Whiskey Rebellion
writ of *certiorari*

WHY IS PUBLIC OPINION DATA SO IMPORTANT IN A DEMOCRATIC GOVERNMENT?

It is crucial for representative governments to account for citizens' viewpoints. The methodology of collecting public opinion data, however, has evolved over time. Here, a Gallup Poll worker conducts face-to-face interviews before the 1968 presidential election.

PUBLIC OPINION AND POLITICAL SOCIALIZATION

LEARNING OBJECTIVES

10.1 Describe the beginnings of public opinion research.

10.2 Describe the methods for conducting and analyzing different types of public opinion polls.

10.3 Assess the influence of political ideology on political attitudes and behaviors.

10.4 Explain how the agents of socialization influence the development of political attitudes.

10.5 Evaluate the effects of public opinion on policy making.

public opinion
What the public thinks about a particular issue or set of issues at any point in time.

public opinion polls
Interviews or surveys with samples of citizens that are used to estimate the feelings and beliefs of the entire population.

George Gallup
One of the earliest developers of scientific methods for public opinion polling and a proponent for a strong role for the voice of the public in politics and government.

F ree, honest, and open communication from citizens to their governments on matters of public concern has been considered the bedrock of a legitimate government by political philosophers for centuries.[1] Political theorists during the Age of Reason such as John Locke stressed the importance of public opinion in how effective politics works.

The Framers of the United States agreed with this line of argument and addressed it in their writings. The Declaration of Independence, for example, implies that public opinion must be considered and acknowledged by the government since government expressly functions on "the consent of the governed." And, James Madison argued that democratic governments must have knowledgeable citizens with educated opinions to sharpen important political debate. The *Federalist Papers* express the general belief that Americans had more in common than not, which supports its arguments that the U.S. Constitution would succeed as a governing document. In *Federalist No. 2* John Jay wrote that we are "one united people—a people descended from the same ancestors, speaking the same language, professing the same religion, attached to the same principles of government, very similar in manners and customs." Many of those who could vote in Jay's time were of English heritage; almost all were Christian. Moreover, most believed that certain rights—such as freedom of speech, association, and religion—were rights that could not be revoked. Jay also wrote about the importance of shared public opinion and of the need for a national government that reflected American ideals.

In 1863, during another perilous time for the United States, Abraham Lincoln proudly summarized American government as one "of the people, by the people, and for the people." Though this sentiment has always been true to some degree, our modern political landscape has given this old idea new perspective in the midst of a much more diverse population.

● ● ●

Political scientists define **public opinion** as the aggregate of public attitudes or beliefs about government and politics.[2] Today, in an increasingly diverse nation, the growth of modern public opinion research has helped us to better understand Americans' views on political issues and how our varying experiences, values, and heritage shape them. In part, this is attributable to the pervasiveness of polls. Not a day goes by that major cable news networks, newspapers, foundations, or colleges and universities do not poll Americans on something—from views on political issues, such as the environment, race, and health care, to their emotions, including happiness and stress. Polling is so common now that the public needs the ability to interpret often-conflicting poll results. In this chapter, we explore how polls are conducted and analyzed as well as how Americans' beliefs and demographic and cultural experiences shape public opinion.

ROOTS OF PUBLIC OPINION RESEARCH

10.1 Describe the beginnings of public opinion research.

Since the 1930s, governmental decision makers have relied heavily on **public opinion polls**—interviews with samples of citizens that estimate outlook and preferences of larger populations—to gauge the feelings and beliefs of the American public. According to **George Gallup** (1901–1983), considered the founder of modern-day polling, polls have played a key role in defining issues of concern to the public, shaping administrative decisions, and helping "speed up the process of democracy" in the United States.[3]

The Earliest Public Opinion Research

At first glance, public opinion seems to be a straightforward concept: it is what the public thinks about a particular issue or set of issues at any point in time. As early as 1824, one Pennsylvania newspaper tried to predict the winner of that year's presidential contest, showing Andrew Jackson leading over John Quincy Adams. In 1883, the *Boston Globe* sent reporters to selected election precincts to poll voters as they exited voting booths, in an effort to predict the results of key contests. Public opinion polling as we know it today really began to develop in the 1930s, however. Walter Lippmann's seminal work, *Public Opinion* (1922), prompted much of this growth. Lippmann observed that research on public opinion was far too limited, especially in light of its importance. Researchers in a variety of disciplines, including political science, heeded Lippmann's call to learn more about public opinion. Some tried to use scientific methods to measure political thought through the use of surveys or polls. As methods for gathering and interpreting data improved, survey data began to play an increasingly significant role in all walks of life, from politics to retailing.

Literary Digest, a popular magazine that first began national presidential polling in 1916, was a pioneer in the use of the **straw poll**, an unscientific survey used to gauge public opinion, to predict the popular vote, which it did, for Woodrow Wilson. Its polling methods were hailed widely as "amazingly right" and "uncannily accurate."[4] In 1936, however, its luck ran out. *Literary Digest* predicted that Republican Alfred M. Landon would beat incumbent President Franklin D. Roosevelt by a margin of 57 percent to 43 percent of the popular vote. Roosevelt, however, won in a landslide election, receiving 62.5 percent of the popular vote and carrying all but two states.[5]

Literary Digest's 1936 straw poll had three fatal errors. First, it drew its **sample**, a subset of the whole population selected to be questioned for the purposes of prediction or gauging opinion, from telephone directories and lists of automobile owners. This technique oversampled the upper middle class and the wealthy, groups heavily Republican in political orientation. Moreover, in 1936, voting polarized along class lines. Thus, the oversampling of wealthy Republicans was particularly problematic because it severely underestimated working class Democratic voters, who had neither cars nor telephones.

Literary Digest's second problem was timing. The magazine mailed its questionnaires in early September. This did not allow *Literary Digest* to measure the changes in public sentiment that occurred as the election drew closer.

Its third error occurred because of a problem we now call self-selection. Only highly motivated individuals sent back the cards—a mere 22 percent of those surveyed responded. Those who answer mail surveys (or today, online surveys) are quite different from the general electorate; they often care more fervently about the candidate or issues being asked about in the poll. *Literary Digest*, then, failed to observe one of the now well-known cardinal rules of survey sampling: "One cannot allow the respondents to select themselves into the sample."[6]

The Gallup Organization

At least one pollster, however, correctly predicted the results of the 1936 election: George Gallup. Gallup had written his dissertation in psychology at the University of Iowa on how to measure the readership of newspapers. He then expanded his research to study public opinion about politics. He was so confident about his methods that he gave all of his newspaper clients a money-back guarantee: if his poll predictions weren't closer to the actual election outcome than those of *Literary Digest*, he would refund their money. Although Gallup underpredicted Roosevelt's victory by nearly 7 percent, the fact that he got the winner right was what everyone remembered, especially given *Literary Digest*'s dramatic miscalculation.

Through the late 1940s, polling techniques increased in sophistication. The number of private polling firms also dramatically rose, as businesses and politicians began to rely on polling information to market products and candidates. But, in 1948, the polling industry suffered a severe, although fleeting, setback when Gallup and many other pollsters incorrectly predicted that Thomas E. Dewey would defeat President Harry S Truman.

straw poll
Unscientific survey used to gauge public opinion on a variety of issues and policies.

sample
A subset of the whole population selected to be questioned for the purposes of prediction or gauging opinion.

IS POLLING DATA ALWAYS ACCURATE?

Not only did advance polls in 1948 predict that Republican nominee Thomas E. Dewey would defeat Democratic incumbent President Harry S Truman, but on the basis of early and incomplete vote tallies, some newspapers' early editions published the day after the election declared Dewey the winner. Here, a triumphant Truman holds aloft the *Chicago Daily Tribune*.

American National Election Studies (ANES)

Founded in 1952 by researchers at the University of Michigan and Stanford University, ANES collects data on the political attitudes and behavior among voters, such as party affiliation, voting practices, and opinions on parties and candidates.

Nevertheless, as revealed in Figure 10.1, polling organizations continue to predict most presidential popular vote winners successfully. In 2016, however, polling organizations incorrectly called the presidential election for Hillary Clinton. Their miscalculations ranged from assuming Clinton had a lead of 1% to 7% nationally and forecasters generally gave Clinton a better than 70% chance of winning the electoral college and popular vote. Donald J. Trump's electoral college victory in light of these predictions was a major surprise, and political scientists and polling organizations in the wake of the election began analyzing their methods and assumptions in order to prevent similar errors in future elections.

The American National Election Studies

In 1952, researchers at the University of Michigan—later joined by Stanford University researchers—began to conduct the **American National Election Studies (ANES)**. Focusing on the political attitudes and behavior of the electorate, ANES surveys include questions about how respondents voted, their party affiliation, and their opinions of major political parties and candidates. In addition, ANES surveys contain questions about interest in politics and political participation. ANES data are no longer as widely used by academics as was once the case. Additional scientific studies are available now, and as a result election research no longer relies almost exclusively on the ANES.

CONDUCTING AND ANALYZING PUBLIC OPINION POLLS

10.2 Describe the methods for conducting and analyzing different types of public opinion polls.

The polling process most often begins when someone says, "Let's find out about X and Y." Potential candidates for local office may want to know how many people have heard of them (the device used to find out is called a "name recognition survey"). Better-known candidates contemplating a run for higher office might wish to discover how they might fare against an incumbent. Polls also can help gauge the effectiveness of particular ads or how well (or negatively) the public perceives a candidate. Political scientists have found that public opinion polls are critical to successful presidents and

FIGURE 10.1 HOW SUCCESSFUL HAS PRESIDENTIAL ELECTION POLLING BEEN?

As seen in this graph, prominent polling organizations such as Gallup have been able to produce solid, if not perfectly exact, estimations of the popular vote in presidential elections dating back to the 1930s. In each of the years in which a significant discrepancy existed between polling predictions and an election's outcome, a prominent third party candidate played a role. In 1948, Strom Thurmond ran on the Dixiecrat ticket; in 1980, John Anderson ran as the American Independent Party candidate; in 1992, Ross Perot ran as an independent. In 2016, polling organizations underestimated support for Donald J. Trump. As late as Election Day, nearly all polls predicted a narrow win for Democrat Hillary Clinton, but Trump's support turned out to be strong enough in several key swing states to provide him with a winning majority in the Electoral College, though he lost the popular vote.

SOURCES: Data from Gallup (years 1936–2012) and Real Clear Politics (year 2016).

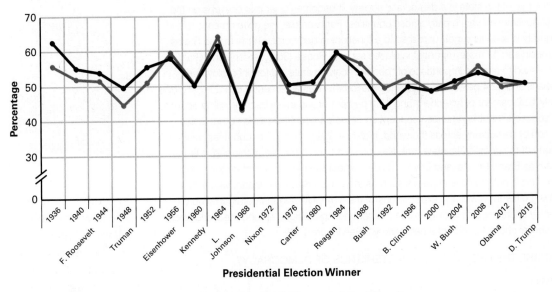

their staffs, who use poll results to "create favorable legislative environment(s) to pass the presidential agenda, to win reelection, and to be judged favorably by history."[7]

Designing the Survey

When deciding to conduct a poll, candidates, political groups, or news organizations must first consider what questions they want answered. Determining the content of a survey is critical to obtaining the desired results; for this reason, candidates, companies, and news organizations generally rely on pollsters. Public opinion polls were even used by the Republican National Committee during the 2016 presidential primary to determine which candidates were allowed to participate in televised debates. Polls may ask, for example, about job performance, demographics, and specific issue areas.

Special care must be taken in constructing the questions. For example, if your professor asked you, "Do you think my grading procedures are fair?" rather than asking, "In general, how fair do you think the grading is in your American Politics course?" you might give a slightly different answer. The wording of the first question tends to put you on the spot and personalize the grading style; the second question is more neutral. Even more obvious differences appear in the real world of polling. Responses to highly emotional issues, such as immigration and affirmative action, often are skewed, depending on the phrasing of a particular question. Even in unbiased polls, how a question is worded can unintentionally skew results.

During a political campaign, strategists will often ask questions that help candidates judge their own strengths and weaknesses as well as those of their opponents. However, sometimes these questions go too far. Questions that cross the line are called **push polls** and often result from ulterior motives.[8] The intent of push polls is to give

push polls
Polls taken for the purpose of providing information on an opponent that would lead respondents to vote against that candidate.

AMERICAN POLITICS IN COMPARATIVE PERSPECTIVE

How Do Global Attitudes Toward Democracy Compare?

Led by a team of international scholars, the World Values Survey (WVS) conducts surveys in more than 100 countries to gain a clearer understanding of the motivations, values, and beliefs of people all across the world. Part of the WVS includes questions about what constitutes "essential characteristics of democracy." What Americans perceive as vital elements of a democracy may not hold true in other parts of the world. It is therefore noteworthy to examine how those in other countries understand what it means to possess "essential characteristics of democracy" and compare these sentiments with American public opinion.

By highlighting the role of the state in a democratic society, it becomes clear that opinions on the scope and function of government vary greatly across countries. For example, the government's role in alleviating income equality is seen as largely unrelated to a functioning democracy in the United States (4.3 percent) but is considered far more important in places such as Russia (30.2 percent) and Brazil (23.3 percent). When asked to rate the importance of "people receiving state aid for unemployment" 40.2 percent of Russians and 42.4 percent of Brazilians believed this was an essential characteristic of a democracy, while only 12.2 percent of Americans and 15.3 percent of Japanese held the same opinion.

The WVS data suggests that the American conception of the democratic ideal is not the sole understanding or notion of democracy across the world. It also suggests that other countries possess views and expectations of the democratic state that differ drastically from the line of thinking in the U.S.. In countries such as Brazil, Russia, and Egypt, citizens expect the democratic state to serve as a provider or caretaker. This is not the case in places such as the United States or Japan, with a majority of those citizens holding different views and expectations of the state. Utilizing the data gathered by the World Values Survey offers important insights into the contrasting opinions around the world about what constitutes "essential characteristics of a democracy." (See Figure 10.2)

FIGURE 10.2 WHAT ARE THE ESSENTIAL CHARACTERISTICS OF DEMOCRACY?

SOURCE: World Values Survey Data.

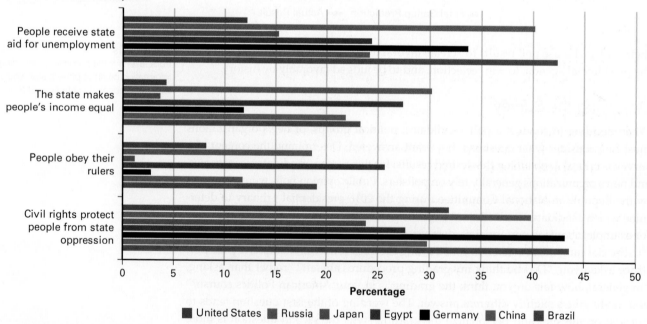

CRITICAL THINKING QUESTIONS

1. What do most people around the world expect from the state in a democracy? Does this differ from how Americans view the state's function in a democracy? How?
2. Do you think there is a connection between the attitudes of some nations' citizens toward their government providing benefits for its people and the belief that people should obey their rulers? If so, why?
3. Do you think these questions asked by the WVS highlight essential characteristics of a democracy? Why, or why not?

respondents some negative or even untruthful information about a candidate's opponent so that they will move away from that candidate and toward the one paying for the poll. A typical push poll might ask a question such as, "If you knew Candidate X beat his wife, would you vote for him?" Push poll takers do not even bother to record the responses because they are irrelevant; the questions are meant to push away as many voters from a candidate as possible. Although campaign organizations generally deny conducting push polls, research shows that this type of polling has targeted more than three-quarters of political candidates.

Selecting the Sample

After deciding to conduct a poll, pollsters must determine the **population**, or the entire group of people whose attitudes a researcher wishes to measure. This universe could be all Americans, all voters, all city residents, all Hispanics, or all Republicans. In a perfect world, the poll would ask every individual to give an opinion, but such comprehensive polling is not practical. Consequently, pollsters take a sample of the population that interests them. One way to obtain this sample is by **random sampling**. This method of selection gives each potential voter or adult approximately the same chance of being selected.

Simple random samples, however, are not very useful for predicting voting because they may undersample or oversample key populations not likely to vote. To avoid such problems, reputable polling organizations use **stratified sampling** (the most rigorous sampling technique) based on U.S. Census data that provide the number of residences in an area and their location. Researchers divide the population into several sampling regions. In each primary sampling unit, pollsters then use demographic characteristics to select a set number of respondents to be interviewed. The typical sample formerly totaled 600 to 1,000 respondents, but now most pollsters make due with smaller numbers. These selected primary sampling units often are used for many years because it is cheaper for polling companies to train interviewers to work in fixed areas.

Contacting Respondents

Most modern polls are conducted using telephone interviews. The most common form of telephone polls is the random-digit dialing survey, in which a computer randomly selects telephone numbers for dialing. Although 47 percent of Americans use cellphones only, most polls done for newspapers and news magazines target those with landlines. In 2016, the PEW Research Center announced that 75 percent of the polling calls it made would be to cellphones.[9] Pollsters are exempt from federal and state do-not-call lists because poll taking is a form of constitutionally protected speech.

During the 1992 presidential elections, the introduction of **tracking polls**, which were taken on a daily basis via phone by some news organizations, allowed presidential candidates to monitor short-term campaign developments and the effects of their campaign strategies. In 2016, presidential tracking polls involved small samples (usually of registered voters contacted at certain times of the day) and took place over three to five day periods (see Figure 10.3).

Some polls, such as the American National Election Studies, continue to perform individual, in-person interviews, which allow surveyors to monitor respondents' body language and to interact on a more personal basis; thus, they may yield higher rates of completion. However, the unintended influence of the questioner or pollster may lead to interviewer bias. How the pollster dresses, relates to the person being interviewed, and asks the questions can affect responses.

Exit polls, a special form of in-person poll, are conducted as voters leave selected polling places on Election Day. Generally, large news organizations send pollsters to selected precincts to sample every tenth voter as he or she emerges from the polling site. The results of these polls help the media predict the outcome of key races, often just a few minutes after the polls close in a particular state and generally before voters

population
The entire group of people whose attitudes a researcher wishes to measure.

random sampling
A method of poll selection that gives each person in a group the same chance of being selected.

stratified sampling
A variation of random sampling; the population is divided into subgroups and weighted based on demographic characteristics of the national population.

tracking polls
Continuous surveys that enable a campaign or news organization to chart a candidate's daily or weekly rise or fall in support.

exit polls
Polls conducted as voters leave selected polling places on Election Day.

FIGURE 10.3 WHAT DOES A TRACKING POLL LOOK LIKE?

Short term fluctuations in public opinion during election contests are often shown through tracking polls. This figure shows the ups and downs of the 2016 presidential election.

SOURCE: Data from Real Clear Politics, www.realclearpolitics.com/epolls/2016/president/us/general_election_trump_vs_clinton-5491.html.

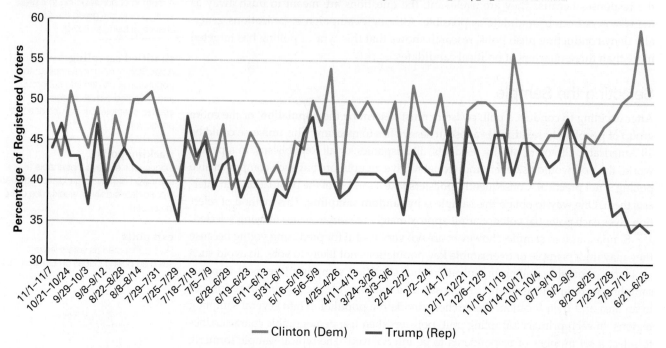

in other areas—sometimes in a later time zone—have cast their ballots. By asking a series of demographic and issue questions, these polls also provide an independent assessment of why voters supported particular candidates.

Finally, survey researchers are increasingly using Internet surveys to predict election outcomes and gauge opinions on numerous issues of importance to the American public. Political scientists, too, use online polling to collect survey research data. The biannual Cooperative Congressional Election Study conducted by political scientists at a consortium of universities is one example of this kind of research.

Contrasting sharply with scientific Internet surveys are unscientific Web polls that allow anyone to weigh in on a topic. Such polls are common on many Web sites, such as CNN.com and ESPN.com. These polls resemble a straw poll in terms of sampling and thus produce results that are largely inconclusive and of interest only to a limited number of people.

Analyzing the Data

Analyzing the collected data is a critical step in the polling process. Analysis reveals the implications of the data for public policy and political campaigns. Data are entered into a computer program, where answers to questions are recorded and analyzed. Often, analysts pay special attention to subgroups within the data, such as Democrats versus Republicans, men versus women, age groups, or political ideology, among others. Reporting the results of this analysis can happen in a variety of ways, such as by news organizations, university research centers, or campaigns.

Shortcomings of Polling

Information derived from public opinion polls has become an important part of governance, as political theorists such as John Locke hoped. When the results of a poll are accurate, they express the attitudes of the electorate and help guide policy makers. However, when the results of a poll are inaccurate, disastrous consequences can result. Polls may

be inaccurate for a number of reasons. These include survey error, limited respondent options, lack of information, difficulty measuring intensity, and lack of interest.

SURVEY ERROR   All polls contain errors. They may come about from natural errors in statistical measurement that arise from using a sample to extrapolate the opinions of the general public, known as the **margin of error**. They may also result from drawing an improper sample, known as **sampling error**.

Margin of Error: Typically, the margin of error in a sample of 1,000 will be about 4 percent. If you ask 1,000 people, "Do you like ice cream?" and 52 percent say yes and 48 percent say no, the results are too close to tell whether more people like ice cream than not. Why? Because the margin of error implies that somewhere between 56 percent (52+4) and 48 percent (5−4) of the people like ice cream, while between 52 percent (48+4) and 44 percent (48−4) do not. The margin of error in a close election makes predictions very difficult, especially when smaller samples with higher margins of error are used. For example, the margin of error for 2016 presidential primary polls that used less than 1,000 respondents was around 3 percent. Some pollsters opted to take their polls over a five- or six-day period. This method usually netted as many as 2,100 to 3,600 respondents with a 2.3 to 4.5 percent margin of error. Thus, while 2016 polling results were off, they nearly always fell within the margin of error.

Sampling Error: Errors may also result from the size or quality of the sample. Small samples, if properly drawn, can be very accurate if each unit in the potential sample universe has an equal opportunity to be sampled. If a pollster fails to sample certain populations, however, his or her results may reflect that shortcoming. Often, polls underrepresent the opinions of the poor and homeless because pollsters give insufficient attention to representatively sampling these groups.

HOW ARE POLLS ANALYZED?
The most common method of conducting a public opinion poll is via telephone. These polls are often administered by survey researchers working at large phone banks, such as the one shown here.

margin of error
A measure of the accuracy of a public opinion poll within statistical parameters.

sampling error
Errors resulting from the size or the quality of a survey sample.

LIMITED RESPONDENT OPTIONS   Famed political scientist V.O. Key Jr. was among the first social scientists to note the problem of limited respondent options. He cautioned students of public opinion to be certain their questions adequately allowed respondents the appropriate range in which they could register their opinions. Simple yes-no (or approve-disapprove) questions may not be sufficient to "take the temperature" of the public. For example, if someone asks you, "How do you like this class?" and then gives only like or dislike options, your full sentiments may not be tapped if you like the class very much or feel only so-so about it. Thus, most polling agencies ask citizens to rank their opinion on five or seven point scales that can better gauge variations in public opinion. Other surveys use "feeling thermometer" questions, wherein respondents provide a response from 0 to 100 measuring how they "feel" about a particular issue.

LACK OF INFORMATION   Public opinion polls may also be inaccurate when they attempt to gauge attitudes toward issues about which the public has little information. Most academic public opinion research organizations use some kind of filter question that first asks respondents whether or not they have thought about the question. These screening procedures generally allow survey researchers to exclude as many as 20 percent of their respondents, especially on complex issues such as the federal budget. Questions on more personal issues, such as moral values, drugs, crime, race, and women's role in society, receive far fewer "no opinion" or "don't know" responses.

DIFFICULTY MEASURING INTENSITY   Another shortcoming of polls concerns their inability to measure intensity of feeling about particular issues. Whereas a respondent might answer affirmatively to any question, it is likely that his or her feelings about issues such as the death penalty, support for the war on terrorism, or a particular candidate are much more intense than questions about the Electoral College or absentee ballot laws. In 2016, the public reported that Hillary Clinton and Donald J. Trump had the highest intensity negatives of any presidential candidates in recent history. This led to greater uncertainty with regard to voter behavior.

LACK OF INTEREST IN POLITICAL ISSUES   When we face policies that do not affect us personally and do not involve moral issues, we often have difficulty forming

CAN POLLS MEASURE INTENSITY OF OPINION?

One of the greatest shortcomings of most public opinion polls is that they measure direction of public opinion, but not intensity. Here, members of the Westboro Baptist Church demonstrate their intense opposition to homosexuality by protesting outside the Supreme Court.

an opinion. This phenomenon is especially true with regard to foreign policy. Most Americans often know little of the world around them. Unless major issues of national importance take center stage, American public opinion on foreign affairs is likely to be volatile in the wake of any new information. In contrast, most Americans are more interested in domestic policy issues, such as health care and employment, which have a greater impact on their daily lives.

POLITICAL IDEOLOGY

10.3 Assess the influence of political ideology on political attitudes and behaviors.

Many of citizens' opinions on political issues are determined by their **political ideology**, or the coherent set of values and beliefs people hold about the purpose and scope of government.[10] Ideologies shape the thinking of individuals and how they view the world, especially in regard to issues of "race, nationality, the role and function of government, the relations between men and women, human responsibility for the natural environment, and many other matters."[11] Observers increasingly have recognized these beliefs as a potent political force. Isaiah Berlin, a noted historian and philosopher, stated that two factors above all others shaped human history in the twentieth century: "one is science and technology; the other is ideological battles—totalitarian tyrannies of both right and left and the explosions of nationalism, racism, and religious bigotry that the most perceptive social thinkers of the nineteenth century failed to predict."[12]

It is easier to understand how ideology affects public opinion when we examine the four functions political scientists attribute to ideologies. These include:

1. *Explanation.* Ideologies can offer reasons why social and political conditions are the way they are, especially in time of crisis.

2. *Evaluation.* Ideologies can provide standards for evaluating social conditions and political institutions and events.

3. *Orientation.* Much like a compass, ideologies provide individuals with an orientation toward issues and a position within the world.

4. *Political Program.* Ideologies help people make political choices and guide their political actions.

Finding Your Political Ideology

The four functions of ideology discussed above clearly have real-world implications. Political ideologies create natural groups within society and can lead to political conflict. In America, we often hear about conservative, liberal, and moderate political ideologies (see Figure 10.4).

CONSERVATIVES According to William Safire's *New Political Dictionary*, a **conservative** "is a defender of the status quo who, when change becomes necessary in tested institutions or practices, prefers that it come slowly, and in moderation."[13] Conservatives tend to believe that limited government is best, especially in terms of regulating the economy. Conservatives favor local and state action over federal intervention, and they emphasize fiscal responsibility. Conservatives are also likely to believe that the private sector is better equipped than the government to address domestic problems such as homelessness, poverty, and discrimination.

Since the 1970s, a growing number of **social conservative** voters (many with ties to the evangelical or Religious Right) increasingly have affected politics and policies in the United States. Social conservatives believe that moral decay must be stemmed and that government should support and further traditional moral teachings. These voters favor government intervention to regulate sexual and social behavior and have led efforts to restrict contraceptives, abortion, and same-sex marriage. While a

political ideology
The coherent set of values and beliefs about the purpose and scope of government held by groups and individuals.

conservative
One who favors limited government intervention, particularly in economic affairs.

social conservative
One who believes that the government should support and further traditional moral teachings.

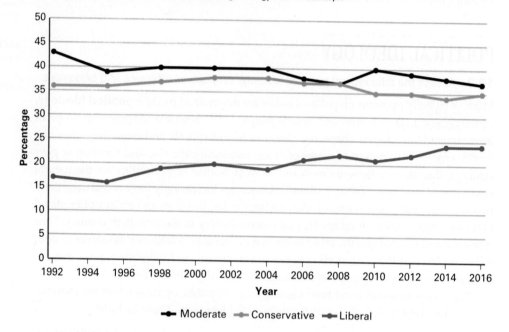

FIGURE 10.4 WHAT ARE AMERICANS' POLITICAL IDEOLOGIES?

Americans' political ideologies have been relatively constant for most of the last twenty years. In 2016, those identifying as moderate and as conservative were almost evenly matched at 35% and 37% respectively. Those identifying as liberals were significantly lower at 24%.

SOURCE: Saad, Lydia. "Conservatives Hang Onto Ideology Lead by a Thread," *Gallup*, Jan. 11, 2016. Accessed at www.gallup.com/poll/188129/conservatives-hang-ideology-lead-thread.aspx

liberal
One who favors greater government intervention, particularly in economic affairs and in the provision of social services.

moderate
A person who takes a relatively centrist or middle-of-the-road view on most political issues.

majority of social conservatives are evangelical Protestants, Mormons, and Roman Catholics, some Jews and many Muslims are also social conservatives. Others are not affiliated with a traditional religion.

LIBERALS   A **liberal** is one who seeks to use the government to change the political, economic, and social status quo and foster the development of equality and the well-being of individuals.[14] The meaning of the word "liberal" has changed over time, but in the modern United States, liberals (who may also refer to themselves as progressives) generally support well-funded government social welfare programs that seek to protect individuals from economic disadvantages or to correct past injustices. In contrast, they generally oppose government efforts to regulate private behavior or infringe on civil rights and liberties.

MODERATES   In general, a **moderate** takes a relatively centrist view on most political issues. Most political philosophers from ancient Greece favored moderate politics, believing a balanced viewpoint was best when it came to managing issues of wealth, poverty, or the role of government.

Problems with Ideological Labels

In a perfect world, liberals would be liberal and conservatives would be conservative. Studies reveal, however, that many people who call themselves conservative actually take fairly liberal positions on many policy issues. In fact, anywhere from 20 percent to 60 percent of people will hold a traditionally conservative view on one issue and a traditionally liberal view on another.[15] People who take conservative stances against "big government," for example, often support increases in spending for the elderly, education, or health care. It is also not unusual to encounter a person who could be considered a liberal on social issues such as abortion and civil rights but a conservative on economic or pocketbook issues.

FIGURE 10.5 HOW DO YOU CLASSIFY IDEOLOGY?

The Nolan Chart, created by Libertarian Party leader David Nolan, is a political ideology chart that helps to classify citizens' political beliefs on two key dimensions—economic and personal freedom. The chart identifies five key political ideologies: left (liberal), centrist or moderate, right (conservative), libertarian, and statist. Where do you believe you fall on this chart?

SOURCE: Advocates for Self Government

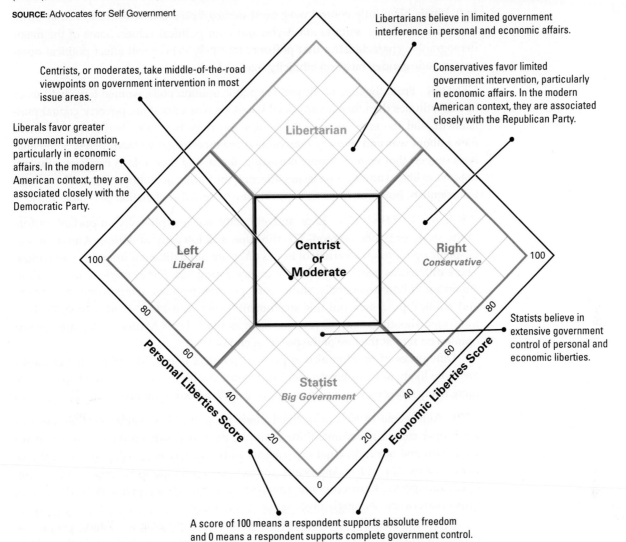

Libertarians believe in limited government interference in personal and economic affairs.

Centrists, or moderates, take middle-of-the-road viewpoints on government intervention in most issue areas.

Conservatives favor limited government intervention, particularly in economic affairs. In the modern American context, they are associated closely with the Republican Party.

Liberals favor greater government intervention, particularly in economic affairs. In the modern American context, they are associated closely with the Democratic Party.

Statists believe in extensive government control of personal and economic liberties.

A score of 100 means a respondent supports absolute freedom and 0 means a respondent supports complete government control.

Some critics also charge that a simple left-to-right continuum cannot capture the full complexity of most citizens' political ideologies (see Figure 10.5). They suggest that the ideologies of most people are better represented by a spectrum measuring individuals' viewpoints on government interference in both economic and personal liberties. This spectrum includes not only liberal, conservative, and moderate ideologies but also **statist** (pro-governmental interference) and **libertarian** (anti-governmental interference) perspectives.

FORMING POLITICAL OPINIONS

10.4 Explain how the agents of socialization influence the development of political attitudes.

Political scientists believe that many of our attitudes about issues are grounded in our political values. The process through which individuals acquire their beliefs is known as **political socialization**.[16] Demographic characteristics, family, school, peers, the

statist
One who believes in extensive government control of personal and economic liberties.

libertarian
One who believes in limited government interference in personal and economic liberties.

political socialization
The process through which individuals acquire their political beliefs and values.

mass media, and political leaders often act as important influences or agents of political socialization.

Demographic Characteristics

Individuals have little control over most demographic characteristics. But, at birth, these characteristics begin to affect you and your political values. Some of the major demographic characteristics that pollsters routinely expect will affect political opinions include gender, race and ethnicity, age, and religion.

GENDER   From the time of the earliest public opinion polls, women have held more liberal attitudes than men about social issues such as education, poverty, capital punishment, and the environment. Public opinion polls have also found that women's views about war and military intervention are more negative than men's. Some analysts suggest that women's more nurturing nature and their role as mothers influence their more liberal attitudes on issues affecting the family or children. Research by political scientists, however, finds no support for a maternal explanation (see Table 10.1).[17]

RACE AND ETHNICITY   Race and ethnicity are exceptionally important factors in the study of public opinion. The direction and intensity of African American and Hispanic opinions on a variety of issues often are quite different from those of whites. These differences generally appear at a very young age. For example, young African American children generally show very positive feelings about American society and political processes, but this attachment lessens considerably over time. Racially motivated shootings and movements such as Black Lives Matter are keeping public opinion on race at the fore of the public agenda.

Differences of opinion also appear on political issues. Minorities, for example, are more likely to favor government-sponsored health insurance. And, Hispanics are more likely than other groups to support liberalized immigration policies.[18]

AGE   Age seems to have a decided effect on political socialization. Our view of the proper role of government, for example, often depends on the era in which we were born and our individual experiences with a variety of social, political, and economic forces. The oldest Americans, for example, continue to be affected by having lived through the hard economic times of the Great Depression and World War II. Millennials overwhelmingly favor same sex marriage.

Age also affects how citizens view government programs.[19] Young people are disproportionately likely to be concerned about student loan debt, while the elderly prioritize the protection of Medicare and Social Security. In states such as Florida, where many northern retirees have flocked to seek relief from cold winters and high taxes, the elderly have voted as a bloc to defeat school tax increases and to pass tax breaks for themselves.

RELIGION   Political scientists have found significant evidence that religion affects the political beliefs and behaviors of the American citizenry. Many American ideals,

TABLE 10.1   DO MEN AND WOMEN THINK DIFFERENTLY ABOUT POLITICAL ISSUES?

	Men Agreeing (%)	Women Agreeing (%)
Labor unions are necessary to protect the working person.	59	68
The best way to ensure peace is through military strength.	57	50
Women get fewer opportunities than men for good jobs.	45	52
Is global climate change a problem?	66	83
Do you support same-sex marriage?	52	58

SOURCE: Pew Research Center

FIGURE 10.6 HOW DO DEMOGRAPHIC CHARACTERISTICS AFFECT PUBLIC OPINION?

Demographic characteristics have a powerful impact on the way citizens view government, political leaders, and public policies. These gaps may be the result of gender, race, age, party, and religion, among other factors. They endure as a result of socialization, cultural norms, and differing value systems. The percentages shown reflect a positive response to the statement "The government should guarantee every citizen enough to eat and a place to sleep."

SOURCE: Pew Center: American Values Survey 2012.

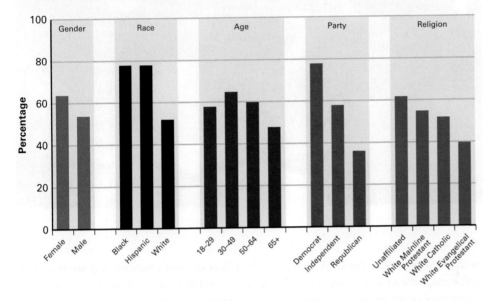

including hard work and personal responsibility, are widely considered to be rooted in our nation's Protestant heritage. These ideals have affected the public policies adopted by government; they may be one reason why the United States has a less developed welfare state than many other industrialized democracies.

Religious beliefs also shape individual attitudes toward political issues. Evangelical Christians and Roman Catholics, for example, may support programs that provide aid to parochial schools, even if it comes at the expense of lowering the wall of separation between church and state. Similarly, Jewish Americans are more likely to favor aid to Israel—a policy at odds with Muslim Americans' support for a Palestinian state. Some Americans have chosen to openly criticize followers of Islam and presidential candidate Donald Trump openly called for a ban on allowing Muslims into the United States during his campaign rallies.

How strictly we practice and follow religious doctrine may also affect political beliefs. For example, strict Roman Catholics, Orthodox Jews, Mormons, and Evangelical Christians believe that abortion should be illegal in all cases; they also believe in more traditional roles for women (See Figure 10.6).

Family, Peers, and School

The influence of the family on political socialization can be traced to two factors: communication and receptivity. Children, especially during their preschool years, spend tremendous amounts of time with their parents; early on, they learn their parents' political values, even though these concepts may be vague. One study of first graders, for example, found that they already had developed political orientations consistent with those of their parents.[20]

A child's peers—that is, children about the same age—also seem to have an important effect on the socialization process. While parental influences are greatest from birth to age five, beyond that point a child's peer group becomes increasingly important, especially as he or she enters middle school or high school. Groups such

HOW DO YOU ENCOURAGE YOUNG WOMEN TO THINK ABOUT CAREERS IN POLITICS?

Researchers find that women are more reluctant than similarly qualified men to think about running for office. In an attempt to change this norm, the Girl Scouts of the USA offer Beyond the Ballot and Public Policy citizenship badges. Farheen Hakeem, shown right, leads a Girl Scout troop in Minneapolis.

as the Girl Scouts of the USA recognize the effect of peer pressure and are trying to influence more young women to participate in, and have a positive view of, politics. Numerous other local, state, and national women's groups work to engage girls to become leaders in the political process.

School age children are also clearly influenced by their daily education. In elementary school, children are taught respect for their nation and its symbols. In many schools, the day begins with the Pledge of Allegiance, and patriotism and respect for country are important components of most school curricula. Support for flag and country creates a foundation for national allegiance that prevails despite the negative views about politicians and government institutions that many Americans develop later in life. High schools continue the elementary school tradition of building good citizens and often reinforce textbook learning with trips to Washington, D.C., or state capitals. They also offer courses on current U.S. affairs and Advanced Placement American Government. Many high schools impose a compulsory service-learning requirement, which some studies report positively affects later political participation.[21]

At the college level, teaching style often changes. Many college courses and texts like this one are designed in part to provide the information necessary for thinking critically about issues of major political consequence. It is common in college for students to be called on to question the appropriateness of certain political actions or to discuss underlying reasons for certain political or policy decisions. Therefore, most researchers believe that college has a liberalizing effect on students. Since the 1920s, studies have shown that students become more liberal each year they are in college.

The Mass Media

Over the years, more and more Americans have turned away from traditional news sources, such as nightly news broadcasts on the major networks and daily newspapers, in favor of different outlets. TV talk shows, talk radio, online magazines, and blogs are important sources of political news for many people. Cable news, the Internet, and social media are almost omnipresent in the lives of modern Americans.

American teenagers, for example, consume almost eleven hours of media content each day.[22]

Cable and Internet news sources are often skewed. Consuming slanted views may affect the way citizens process political information, form opinions on public policy, obtain political knowledge, and receive new ideas. One recent study, for example, revealed that Americans who get most of their news from cable news outlets such as Fox News and MSNBC are even less knowledgeable about political issues than citizens who consume no political news. Individuals who rely on alternative sources such as *The Daily Show*, Sunday morning talk shows, and National Public Radio, are generally more knowledgeable.[23]

Cues from Leaders or Opinion Makers

Political leaders, members of the news media, and a host of other experts have regular opportunities to affect public opinion because of the lack of deep conviction with which most Americans hold many of their political beliefs. The president, especially, is often in a position to mold public opinion through effective use of the bully pulpit. The president derives this power from the majesty of his office and his singular position as head of state. Thus, presidents often take to TV and social media in an effort to drum up support for their programs.[24] President Barack Obama, for example, presented his case for economic reform and job creation directly to the public, urging citizens to support his efforts.

Political Knowledge

Political knowledge and political participation have a reciprocal effect on one another—an increase in one will increase the other. Knowledge about the political system is essential to successful political involvement, which, in turn, teaches citizens about politics and expands their interest in public affairs. And, although few citizens know everything about all of the candidates and issues in a particular election, they can, and often do, know enough to impose their views and values on the general direction the nation should take.

This observation is true despite the fact that most Americans' level of knowledge about history and politics is quite low. According to the U.S. Department of Education, today's college graduates have less civic knowledge than high school graduates did fifty years ago. Americans also do not appear to know much about foreign policy; some critics even argue that many Americans are geographically illiterate (see Table 10.2).[25]

Gender differences in political knowledge are also significant. On many traditional measures of political knowledge, women lag behind their male counterparts. However, on issues of interest to women—such as representation in the legislature—women do as well or better than their male counterparts.[26] The gender gap in political knowledge also appears to be affected by education, age, number of children, and marital status.[27]

TABLE 10.2   WHAT IS THE EXTENT OF AMERICANS' POLITICAL KNOWLEDGE?

Can You Identify the Following?	Percentage Answering Correctly
Photo of Martin Luther King Jr.	91
Majority party in the Senate	52
Pope Francis is from what country? (Argentina)	52
Photo of Senator Elizabeth Warren	51
Number of women on Supreme Court	33

SOURCE: Nick Glass "Americans Bomb Pew Test of Basic Political Knowledge," *Politico*, 4/28/15.

TOWARD REFORM: THE EFFECTS OF PUBLIC OPINION ON POLITICS

10.5 Evaluate the effects of public opinion on policy making.

Public opinion inevitably influences the actions of politicians and public officials. Today, we know more about what "the people" want from their government than ever before. Much of this knowledge comes from our increasing ability to collect representative data on aggregate public opinion. The tools available to pollsters, including the Internet and social media, statistical software, and computerized robocall technology, make data collection, analysis, and dissemination easier than ever.

However, there can be dangerous consequences to having so much data. Just about anything can be proven—or disproven—with a public opinion poll. Moreover, the volume of polls conducted and information available about these studies makes them an attractive topic for news coverage. This phenomenon is especially prevalent during election season. And, while on one hand, it may be interesting to examine the relationship between events and citizens' evaluations of political leaders, on the other hand, constant reports of the results of the latest poll only serve to intensify the horse-race atmosphere of every campaign. More critically, it may also distract from the true issues of the election and obscure citizens' understanding of the political process.

Andrew Kohut, the late president of the Pew Research Center, argued that the public has become more of a critical player in national and international politics in the

HOW DO PUBLIC OPINION POLLS AFFECT POLITICS?

The emergence of a growing number of public opinion research firms means that citizens, the media, and political leaders know more than ever before about how voters perceive political issues and candidates. This information may be useful for promoting a more democratic and representative government. But, it may also be notoriously mercurial, marked by dramatic fluctuations from week to week or even day to day, as illustrated in this political cartoon.

past three decades in large part because of the rise in the number of polls regularly conducted and reported.

According to Kohut, it is impossible to find any major policy proposal for which polling has not "played a significant, even critical role."[28] Another observer of public opinion polls says, "Polls have become more important and necessary in news writing and presentation, to the point that their significance overwhelms the phenomena they are supposed to be measuring or supplementing."[29] Policy makers thus respond intently to the often mercurial changes in citizens' opinion. These opinions also influence the way that political campaigns are run. For example, during the 2016 presidential election, Hillary Clinton deemphasized her vote to go to war in Iraq, in part due to negative public opinion on the military campaigns in Iraq and Afghanistan among Democrats. Examples such as these show how the public's views, registered through public opinion polls, can affect policy.

REVIEW THE CHAPTER

Roots of Public Opinion Research

10.1 Describe the beginnings of public opinion research.

Public opinion is what the public thinks about an issue or a particular set of issues. Polls are used to estimate public opinion. Almost since the beginning of the United States, various attempts have been made to influence public opinion about particular issues or to sway elections. *Literary Digest* first began national presidential polling in 1916, using unscientific straw polls. Modern-day polling did not begin until the 1930s. George Gallup was the first to use scientific polling methods to determine public opinion.

Conducting and Analyzing Public Opinion Polls

10.2 Describe the methods for conducting and analyzing different types of public opinion polls.

Those who conduct polls must follow a careful process: first determining questions, identifying the sample, and selecting the method for contacting respondents. The different types of polls include telephone polls, in-person interviews, and Internet polls. Once the poll results are in, they must be analyzed. Polls, however, may have several shortcomings that create inaccuracies. These include survey errors, limited respondent options, lack of knowledge, inability to measure the intensity of public opinion on an issue, and a lack of interest in political issues.

Political Ideology

10.3 Assess the influence of political ideology on political attitudes and behaviors.

Ideologies, the belief systems that shape the thinking of individuals and how they view the world, affect public opinion. The major categories of political ideology in America are conservative, liberal, and moderate. Critics of this approach believe that statist (pro-governmental interference) and libertarian (anti-governmental interference) perspectives should also be considered when discussing ideology.

Forming Political Opinions

10.4 Explain how the agents of socialization influence the development of political attitudes.

The first step in forming opinions occurs through a process known as political socialization. Demographic characteristics—including gender, race, ethnicity, age, and religion—as well as family, school, and peers all affect how we view political events and issues. The views of leaders and opinion makers as well as the news media also influence our opinions about political matters.

Toward Reform: The Effects of Public Opinion on Politics

10.5 Evaluate the effects of public opinion on policy making.

The prevalence of opinion polling in American culture has a significant impact on media coverage and how individuals view government. Politicians often use knowledge of the public's views on issues to tailor campaigns or to drive policy decisions.

LEARN THE TERMS

American National Election Studies (ANES)
conservative
exit polls
George Gallup
liberal
libertarian
margin of error

moderate
political ideology
political socialization
population
public opinion
public opinion polls
push polls
random sampling

sample
sampling error
social conservative
statist
stratified sampling
straw polls
tracking polls

HOW SHOULD THE NATION BRIDGE ITS PARTISAN DIVIDES?

After a bitterly contested presidential election, political leaders from both parties took a more concil-
iatory tone, even as people marched in the streets to protest the electoral outcome. Just days after the
election, President Barack Obama met with then-President-elect Donald J. Trump in the Oval Office of
the White House to discuss the transition of power. Urging unity, President Obama said, "We are now
all rooting for his success."

POLITICAL PARTIES

LEARNING OBJECTIVES

11.1 Trace the evolution of political parties.

11.2 Describe the structure of political parties at the national, state, and local levels.

11.3 Identify the functions of political parties.

11.4 Describe the forces that create and shape party identification.

11.5 Evaluate the role of minor parties in the U.S. electoral system.

11.6 Assess the reasons for the persistence of the two-party system in American
politics.

political party
An organized group that may include office holders, candidates, activists, and voters who pursue their common interests by gaining and exercising power through the electoral process.

No matter who won on Election Day in 2016, at least forty percent of the electorate was going to be dismayed, despondent or disheartened by the outcome. Because of partisan polarization, there was a closely divided electorate and fierce competition between the parties and candidates to persuade and mobilize different segments of the electorate.

As "historic" or unique as the 2016 election may have seemed, the nation has experienced similar periods of partisan polarization and closely contested elections throughout our history. Like our own time, historical periods of partisan polarization have featured the rise of populist and anti-establishment movements; high levels of social and economic inequality; fierce party competition; shifts in coalitional alignments; and a great deal of negativity in campaigns.

Many analyses of the election suggest that because of partisan polarization, Democrats and Republicans live in separate worlds. The parties tend to speak in their own terms to very different constituencies, and even through different media. In the 2016 election, the parties and the candidates offered completely divergent messages and views of the country, and each camp offered their own set of facts to back these positions. On many issues, Democratic and Republican voters differed on which were most important to them. But the 2016 election also highlighted the weakness of political parties. While they may still vote, the same motivations driving a growing number of people to identify as Independent are also diminishing their willingness to engage in political action, like volunteering for campaigns, thereby diminishing grassroots support and further saturating elections with the voices that are the loudest and most extreme.

Even as there is growing disdain for political parties, they continue to play an important role in organizing coalitions of political leaders, interest groups and voters around ideas and issues about the direction the country should take. With the increasingly negative feelings Americans hold towards members of the opposite party, their candidates in elections and their policy positions, what is perhaps most needed is the opportunity for people of differing world views to listen to one another in order to rehumanize the other side. Even as there are discussions about potential reforms to the parties and the electoral process, we can bridge our partisan divides by working together to revive civic engagement, volunteerism and community service, the pillars of our shared democratic tradition and experiment.

• • •

At the most basic level, a **political party** is an organized effort by office holders, candidates, activists, and voters to pursue their common interests by gaining and exercising power through the electoral process. The goal, of course, is to win office in order to influence public policy. Nominating candidates to run under the party label is, notably, the key differentiating factor between political parties and interest groups. However, as we will discuss later in this text, political parties and interest groups now work together so closely that it may be difficult to tell where one stops and the other begins.

Political scientists sometimes describe political parties as consisting of three separate but related entities: (1) the office holders who organize themselves and pursue policy objectives under a party label (the governmental party); (2) the workers and activists who make up the party's formal organization structure (the organizational party); and, (3) the voters who consider themselves allied or associated with the party (the party in the electorate).[1]

In this chapter, we will address contemporary party politics from each of these vantage points. We will trace parties from their roots in the late 1700s to today and will cover reforms to party politics that have been pursued throughout American history. A discussion of the increasing polarization of American political parties will conclude the chapter.

ROOTS OF THE TWO-PARTY SYSTEM

11.1 Trace the evolution of political parties.

American political parties have been inclusive and pragmatic since the founding of the republic. By tracing the history and development of political parties, we will see that even as dramatic shifts in party coalitions and reforms have taken place to democratize the electoral process, the competitive two-party system has always featured prominently in the United States.

The Development of Political Parties, 1800–1824

Though the Framers warned against a government ruled by permanent political alliances, these alliances actually had their roots in the creation of the U.S. Constitution. Those who supported the stronger central government fashioned in the new Constitution identified with what eventually became the Federalist Party, while the future Democratic-Republicans favored a system of greater state authority similar to that created by the Articles of Confederation. These alliances, however, did not codify into permanent groups until President George Washington stepped off the national stage. To win the presidency in 1796, Washington's vice president, John Adams, narrowly defeated archrival **Thomas Jefferson**. According to the Constitution, Jefferson became vice president. Over the course of Adams's single term, the Federalists and Democratic-Republicans became increasingly organized around these clashing men and their principles. The Federalists were mainly organized around mercantile groups in New England who supported protective tariffs to encourage manufacturing, the assumption of states' Revolutionary War debts, the creation of a national bank, and the resumption of commercial ties to England. On the other hand, the Democratic-Republicans supported free trade, the promotion of agrarian interests, and stronger ties to France. In the presidential election of 1800, the Federalists supported Adams's bid for a second term, but this time the Democratic-Republicans prevailed with their nominee, Jefferson, who became the first U.S. president elected as the nominee of a political party.

Jefferson was deeply committed to the ideas of his party but not nearly as devoted to the idea of a party system. He regarded his party as a temporary measure necessary to defeat Adams, not a long-term political tool or an essential element of democracy. As a result, Jefferson's party never achieved widespread loyalty among the nation; rather, it drew most of its support from the agrarian South. The Federalists, too, remained a regional party, drawing their support from the commercial New England states. No broad-based national party organizations existed to mobilize popular support.[2] Just as the nation was in its infancy, so too was the party system. Nominations of candidates were informal and usually led by local party leaders in meetings called caucuses. Each of the parties organized political clubs and newsletters designed to mobilize elites in society and bring along their followers.

Jacksonian Democracy, 1824–1860

After the spirited confrontations of the republic's early years, political parties faded somewhat in importance for a quarter of a century. By 1820, the Federalist Party dissolved, leaving the nation with only one political party, the Democratic-Republicans, until the 1830s. James Monroe's presidency from 1817 to 1825 produced the so-called Era of Good Feelings, when party competition was nearly nonexistent at the national level (see Figure 11.1). However, there was intense factional fighting within the Democratic-Republican Party during this period, particularly among supporters and opponents of General Andrew Jackson, the military hero of the War of 1812.

Thomas Jefferson
Principle drafter of the Declaration of Independence; second vice president of the United States; third president of the United States from 1801 to 1809. Co-founder of the Democratic-Republican Party.

FIGURE 11.1 HOW HAS THE TWO-PARTY SYSTEM DEVELOPED?

The United States has had two political parties for much of its existence. Though the names of these parties have changed over time, the central controversies over the role of government in citizens' lives have remained constant. The two parties we know today, Democrats and Republicans, have existed since 1856.

SOURCE: Harold W. Stanley and Richard G. Niemi, *Vital Statistics on American Politics, 2007–2008* (Washington, DC: CQ Press, 2007). Updated by the authors.

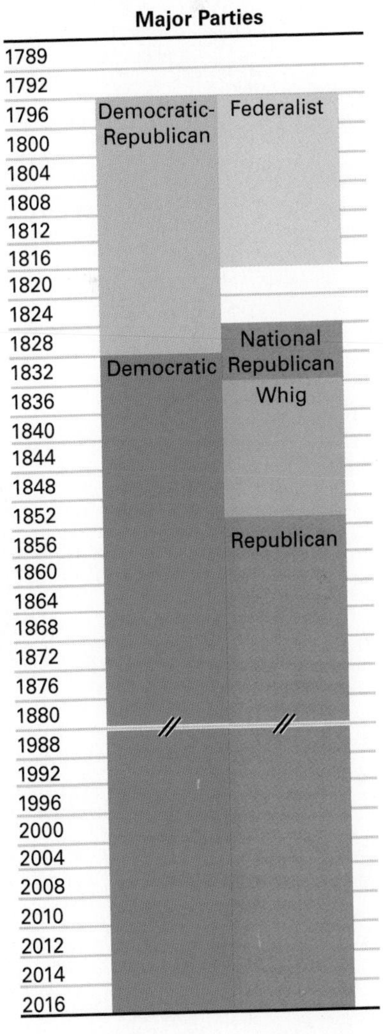

Major Parties

Year	Democratic-Republican	Federalist
1789		
1792		
1796	Democratic-Republican	Federalist
1800		
1804		
1808		
1812		
1816		
1820		
1824		
1828	Democratic	National Republican
1832		
1836		Whig
1840		
1844		
1848		
1852		
1856		Republican
1860		
1864		
1868		
1872		
1876		
1880		
1988		
1992		
1996		
2000		
2004		
2008		
2010		
2012		
2014		
2016		

political machine
A party organization that recruits voter loyalty with tangible incentives and is characterized by a high degree of control over member activity.

Party organizations continued to develop at the state level, fueled in part by the enormous growth in the electorate that took place between 1820 and 1840. During this twenty-year period, the United States expanded westward and most states abolished property requirements as a condition of white male suffrage. The number of votes cast in presidential contests rose from 300,000 to more than 2 million.

Party membership broadened along with the electorate. Formed around President Andrew Jackson's popularity, the Democratic Party, which succeeded the old Jeffersonian Democratic-Republicans, attracted most of the newly enfranchised voters, who were drawn to Jackson's charismatic style. Martin van Buren, Jackson's vice president, was the political organizer behind the movement who established a central party committee, state party organizations, and party newspapers. Jacksonians also established state and national party conventions as the forum for nominating presidential candidates, thus opening the process for greater mass mobilization.

Jackson's strong personality polarized many people, and opposition to the president coalesced into the Whig Party. Among the Whig Party's early leaders was Henry Clay, Speaker of the House from 1811 to 1820. The incumbent Jackson, having won a first term as president in 1828, defeated Clay in the 1832 presidential contest. This election was the first in which the party's nominee was chosen at a large party convention rather than the small undemocratic caucuses popular until that time. Thus, Jackson was the first chief executive to win the White House as the nominee of a truly national, popularly based political party.

The Whigs and the Democrats continued to strengthen after 1832. Their competition usually proved fierce and closely matched, and they brought the United States the first broadly supported two-party system in the Western world.[3] Unfortunately for the Whigs, the issue of slavery sharpened the many divisive tensions within the party, which led to its gradual dissolution and replacement by the new Republican Party. Formed in 1854 by anti-slavery and "free soil" activists, the Republican Party set its sights on the abolition (or at least containment) of slavery. After a losing presidential effort for John C. Frémont in 1856, the party was able to assemble enough support primarily from former Whigs and anti-slavery northern Democrats to win the presidency for Abraham Lincoln in a fragmented 1860 vote. From the presidential election of 1860 to this day, the same two major parties, the Republicans and the Democrats, have dominated elections in the United States, and control of an electoral majority has seesawed between them.

The Golden Age, 1860–1932

Party stability, the dominance of party organizations in local and state governments, and the impact of those organizations on the lives of millions of voters were the central traits of the era called the "Golden Age" of political parties. This era, from the end of post–Civil War Reconstruction until the reforms of the Progressive Era, featured remarkable stability in the identity of both the Republican and Democratic Parties. Such stability has been exceptionally rare in democratic republics around the world.

Political machines, organizations that use tangible incentives such as jobs and favors to win loyalty among voters, were a central element of life for millions of people in the United States during the Golden Age. In fact, for city-dwellers, and particularly immigrants from European countries such as Ireland, Italy, and Germany, party and government were virtually interchangeable during this time. In addition to providing housing, employment, and even food to many voters, parties in most major cities offered entertainment by organizing torchlight parades, weekend picnics, socials, and other community events. Many citizens—even those who were not particularly "political"—attended, thereby forming some allegiance to one party or the other.

The parties also gave citizens the opportunity for upward social mobility as they rose in the organization. As a result, parties generated intense loyalty and devotion among their supporters and office holders, which helped to produce startlingly high levels of voter turnout—75 percent or better in all presidential elections from 1876 to 1900—compared with today's 50–60 percent.[4]

The Modern Era

As a result of one of the great reform movements in American history, the so-called Progressive Era, between 1900 and the 1930s, the government gradually took over a number of important functions previously performed by the parties, such as printing ballots, conducting elections, and providing social welfare services. These changes had a major impact on party loyalty and strength. Beginning in the 1930s with Franklin D. Roosevelt's New Deal, social services began to be regarded as a right of citizenship rather than as a privilege extended in exchange for a person's support of a party. The flow of immigrants also slowed dramatically in the 1920s, causing party machines to lose even greater power in many places.

In the post–World War II era, extensive social changes continued to contribute to the move away from strong parties. A weakening of the party system gave rise to **candidate-centered politics**, which focus on candidates, their particular issues, and character rather than party affiliation. Parties' diminished control over issues and campaigns also has given candidates considerable power in how they conduct themselves during election season and how they seek resources. Interest groups and lobbyists have stepped into the void that weaker parties have left behind. Candidates today compete for endorsements and contributions from a variety of multi- and single-issue organizations.

The population shift from urban to suburban locales has also weakened parties. During the post–World War II era, millions of people moved from the cities to the suburbs, where a sense of privacy and detachment can deter even the most energetic party organizers. In addition, population growth in the last half-century has created legislative districts with far more people, making it less feasible to knock on every door or shake every hand.

Citizen Support and Party Realignment

Periodically, voters make dramatic shifts in partisan preference that drastically alter the political landscape. During these **party realignments**, existing party affiliations are subject to upheaval: many voters may change parties, and the youngest age group of voters may permanently adopt the label of the newly dominant party.[5]

Preceding a major realignment are one or more **critical elections**, which may polarize voters around new issues and personalities in reaction to crucial developments, such as a war or an economic depression. Three tumultuous eras in particular have produced significant critical elections. First, Thomas Jefferson, in reaction against the Federalist Party's agenda of a strong, centralized federal government, formed the Democratic-Republican Party, which won the presidency and Congress in 1800.

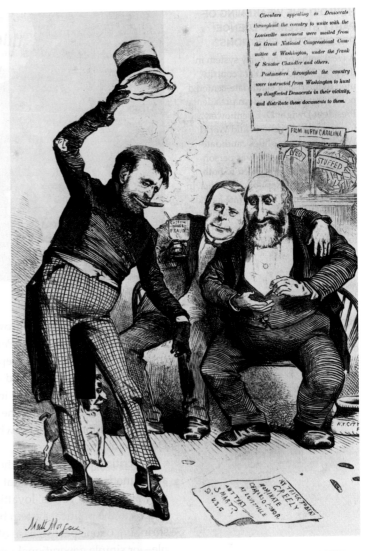

HOW DID POLITICAL MACHINES AFFECT POLITICS?

During the Golden Age of political parties, political machines used tangible incentives to recruit voters and held the functions of government, especially for city-dwellers and immigrants. This satirical cartoon depicts presidential candidate General Ulysses S. Grant as a common minstrel in league with notoriously corrupt New York City politicians, like Boss Tweed, during the election of 1872.

candidate-centered politics
Politics that focus on the candidates, their particular issues, and character rather than party affiliation.

party realignment
Dramatic shifts in partisan preferences that drastically alter the political landscape.

critical election
An election that signals a party realignment through voter polarization around new issues and personalities.

national convention
A party meeting held in the presidential election year for the purposes of nominating a presidential and vice presidential ticket and adopting a platform.

delegate
Role played by representative who votes the way his or her constituents would want, regardless of personal opinions; may refer to an elected representative to Congress or a representative to the party convention.

superdelegate
Delegate to the Democratic Party's national convention that is reserved for a party official and whose vote at the convention is unpledged to a candidate.

The National Party

The national party organization sits at the pinnacle of the party system in the United States. Its primary function is to establish a cohesive vision for partisan identifiers nationwide and to disseminate that vision to party members and voters. A chairperson, who serves as the head of the national committee, leads the national party. Every four years, the national committee organizes a convention designed to reevaluate policies and nominate a candidate for the presidency.

THE NATIONAL CONVENTION   Every four years, each party holds a **national convention** to nominate its presidential and vice presidential candidates. Because the party's chosen candidate is now usually known before the event, organizers of modern party conventions can heavily script the event to present an inclusive and positive image of the party. Modern party conventions, therefore, serve an important role as pep rallies to mobilize supporters and engage more casual observers. The convention also fulfills its function as the ultimate governing body for the party. The rules adopted and the party platform serve as durable guidelines to steer the party until the next convention. In addition, party rules play a role in determining the relative influence of factions within the party and can increase or decrease the party's chances for electoral success.

Delegates, or representatives to the party conventions, do much of the work at the conventions. Delegates are no longer selected by party leaders but by citizens participating in primary elections and grassroots caucuses. The apportionment of delegates to presidential candidates varies by party. A Democratic Party rule decrees that a state's delegates be apportioned in proportion to the votes cast in support of each candidate in the state primary or caucus (so that, for example, a candidate who receives 30 percent of the vote gains about 30 percent of the convention delegates). In contrast, the Republican Party rules require proportionality during a window of primaries and caucuses. After that window closes, states may choose either a proportional or winner-take-all system of delegate allocation.

Who the delegates are, a topic of less importance today than when delegates enjoyed more power in the selection process, still reveals interesting differences between political parties. Both parties draw their delegates from an elite group whose income and educational levels are far above the average American's. About 50 percent of delegates at the 2016 Democratic convention were minorities, and 60 percent were women. Only 6 percent of the delegates to the 2016 Republican convention were racial and ethnic minorities. Just eighteen delegates were black, which, according to one analysis, is the lowest percentage of black delegates at a GOP convention since 1912.

The parties also allow **superdelegates** that are not pledged to a candidate and may support whichever candidate they choose at the convention. Both parties automatically seat superdelegates by virtue of their role in the party, such as current party officials and leaders (for example, party chairs and party committee members) from each state and territory. In addition, the Democratic Party includes former party officials and leaders as superdelegates. Superdelegates allow the party to maintain some level of control over the selection process, while still allowing most delegates to be pledged by the people.

THE NATIONAL COMMITTEE   The first national party committees were skeletal and formed some years after the first presidential nominating conventions in the 1830s. First the Democrats in 1848 and then the Republicans in 1856 established national governing bodies—the Democratic National Committee, or DNC, and the Republican National Committee, or RNC—to make arrangements for the national conventions and to coordinate the subsequent presidential campaigns. Since 1972, the size of staff and the amount of money raised by the national committees has increased substantially. In addition to engaging in general party building activities and aiding presidential campaigns, the committees raise campaign funds primarily for the presidential race, serve to mitigate factional disputes within the parties, and liaise with the media in order to enhance the party's image.

THE NATIONAL CHAIRPERSON A chairperson serves as the key national party official. The chair is usually selected by the sitting president or newly nominated presidential candidate, who is accorded the right to name the individual for at least the duration of his or her campaign. The national committee may also choose the chair when the election has ended and the party has been defeated. The chair is the primary spokesperson and arbitrator for the party during the four years between elections. He or she has the responsibility of damping down factionalism, negotiating candidate disputes, and preparing the machinery for the next presidential election. Perhaps most critically, the chair is called on to raise funds and keep the party financially strong. Balancing the interests of all potential party candidates is a particularly difficult job, and strict neutrality is normally expected from the chair.

Each party has also formed party committees in both chambers of Congress that are loosely allied with the DNC and RNC. The Democratic committees are called the Democratic Congressional Campaign Committee (DCCC) and the Democratic Senatorial Campaign Committee (DSCC). The Republican committees are called the National Republican Campaign Committee (NRCC) and the National Republican Senatorial Committee (NRSC). These organizations raise and distribute campaign funds for House and Senate seats, develop campaign strategies, recruit candidates, and conduct on-the-ground campaigns. In the past two decades, all six national committees have become major players in American campaigns and elections.[8] The congressional committees and the national committees can sometimes be rivals as they seek funds from the same pools of donors but for different candidates.

State and Local Parties

Although national committee activities attract most of the media attention, the roots of the party lie not in Washington, D.C., but in the states and localities. Both of the two major parties have a central committee in each state, and virtually all government regulation of political parties falls to the states. Most importantly, the vast majority of party leadership positions are filled at subnational levels.

The arrangement of party committees provides for a broad base of support. The smallest voting unit, the precinct, usually takes in a few adjacent neighborhoods and is the fundamental building block of the party. The United States has more than

WHAT DOES THE NATIONAL PARTY CHAIRPERSON DO?

The chairperson serves as the key national party official. Among other things, the chairperson is responsible for unifying the party and preparing it for future elections. Donna Brazile (left) served as the interim head of the Democratic National Committee after Debbie Wasserman Schultz was forced to resign over leaked emails showing that the DNC was not a neutral arbiter in the 2016 primary. Chairman of the Republican National Committee Reince Priebus (right) had a challenging but ultimately successful role in 2016 unifying the party behind Donald Trump, and in strategizing and mobilizing party resources to support down-ballot candidates.

100,000 precincts. The precinct committee members are the foot soldiers of any party, and their efforts are supplemented by party committees above them in the wards, cities, counties, towns, villages, and congressional districts.

The state governing body supervising this collection of local party organizations is usually called the state central (or executive) committee. Its members come from all major geographic units, as determined by and selected under state law. Generally, state parties are free to act within the limits set by their state legislatures without interference from the national party. One key exception is the selection and seating of presidential convention delegates. Here, the national committee may establish quotas or mandates regarding type, number, or manner of electing delegates.

State and local parties recruit candidates, conduct voter registration drives, and provide funds to candidates. In contrast to the national party organizations that have enormous fund-raising abilities but are limited by law in the amount of money they can spend on candidates, federal election laws permit state and local parties to spend unlimited amounts of money on party-building activities such as voter registration drives and get-out-the-vote efforts. Thus, the national organizations transfer millions of dollars each year to the state and local organizations to promote national, state, and local candidates. As a result, the parties have become more integrated and nationalized than ever before. In addition, increased fund-raising, campaign events, registration drives, publicity, and distribution of campaign literature have also enabled parties to become more effective political actors over the past three decades.[9]

Informal Groups

Numerous official and semi-official groups also attempt to affect the formal party organizations. Both the DNC and RNC have affiliated organizations of state and local party women (the National Federation of Democratic Women and the National Federation of Republican Women) as well as numerous college campus organizations, including the College Democrats of America and the College Republican National Committee. The youth divisions (the Young Democrats of America and the Young Republican National Federation) have a generous definition of "young," up to and including age thirty-five. State governors in each party have their own party associations, too (the Democratic Governors Association and the Republican Governors Association). Each of these organizations provides loyal and energetic foot soldiers for campaigns and voter mobilization.

Just outside the party orbit are the supportive interest groups and associations that often provide money, labor, or other forms of assistance to the parties. Labor unions, progressive groups, teachers, African American and women's groups, and Americans for Democratic Action are some of the Democratic Party's most important supporters. Businesses, the U.S. Chamber of Commerce, evangelical Christian organizations, and some pro-life groups work closely with the Republicans.

Each party also has several institutionalized sources of policy ideas. Though unconnected to the parties in any official sense, these think tanks—or institutional collections of policy-oriented researchers and academics who are sources of policy ideas—influence party positions and platforms. Republicans have dominated the world of think tanks with prominent conservative groups, including the Hudson Institute, American Enterprise Institute, and Heritage Foundation. And, the libertarian Cato Institute is closely aligned with the Republican Party. While generally fewer in number, prominent think tanks that generally align with the Democratic Party include the Center for American Progress, Center for National Policy, and Open Society Foundations. The Brookings Institution, founded in 1916, prides itself on a scholarly and nonpartisan approach to public policy.

ACTIVITIES OF AMERICAN POLITICAL PARTIES

11.3 Identify the functions of political parties.

For more than 200 years, the two-party system has served as the mechanism American society uses to organize and resolve social and political conflict. Political parties often are the chief agents of change in our political system. They are mainly involved in running candidates for office, getting out the vote, facilitating electoral choice, providing leadership in policy formulation, and organizing institutions of government such as congressional committees.

Running Candidates for Office

Recruiting candidates for local, state, and national office is one of the most important tasks the parties conduct. Party leaders identify strong candidates and interest them in running for the thousands of open or vulnerable state, local, and congressional seats each year.[10] However, it has become increasingly difficult to find and persuade attractive candidates to run for office, particularly in an era when candidates know they will be intensely scrutinized by the press and public.

RAISING MONEY The average cost of winning a seat in Congress has increased some 555 percent since 1984. In 2016, a winning U.S. Senate candidate spent an average of $10.4 million and a winning House of Representatives candidate spent $1.3 million (through October 19, 2016), and these figures do not factor in outside spending. Although candidates must raise substantial funds on their own, political parties, particularly during mid-term and presidential election years, spend a great deal of time raising and disseminating money for candidates. Historically, Republicans enjoyed greater fund-raising success than Democrats, due in large part to a significant number of wealthy identifiers and donors. However, in recent years, Democrats have caught up, even out-raising Republicans since the 2008 presidential election (see Figure 11.4).

The parties can raise so much money because they have developed networks of donors accessed by a variety of methods. The Republican effort to reach donors through the mail dates back to the early 1960s and accelerated in the mid-1970s when postage and production costs were relatively low. Nowadays, both parties have highly successful mail, phone, and e-mail solicitation lists. They also use Internet sites, online advertisements, and social media such as Facebook and Twitter to help reach supporters and raise money for their candidates' electoral pursuits.

MOBILIZING SUPPORT AND GETTING OUT THE VOTE The parties take a number of steps to broaden citizens' knowledge of candidates and campaigns in the days leading up to the election. Parties, for example, spend millions of dollars for national, state, and local public opinion surveys. In important contests, the parties also commission tracking polls to chart the daily rise or fall of public support for a candidate. The information provided in these polls is invaluable to developing campaign strategy in the tense concluding days of an election.

Both parties also operate sophisticated media divisions that specialize in the design and production of TV advertisements for party nominees at all levels. And, both parties train the armies of political volunteers and paid operatives who run the candidates' campaigns. Early in each election cycle, the national parties also help prepare voluminous research reports on opponents, analyzing their public statements, votes, and attendance records.

In addition, the parties, along with civic organizations, register and mobilize large numbers of people to vote. Both parties greatly emphasize their duty to "get out the vote" (GOTV) on Election Day. One tactic used by modern parties is "micro-targeting," a practice derived from the field of consumer behavior. With data obtained from a growing

FIGURE 11.4 HOW MUCH MONEY DO PARTIES RAISE?

Changes in political campaigns and campaign finance laws have allowed both political parties to raise increasing amounts of money over the past twenty years, though fundraising was lower in 2016 than recent presidential elections. Historically, the Republican Party's fund-raising dwarfed that of their Democratic counterparts, but since 2008, the Democratic Party has out-raised the Republican Party.

SOURCES: 2003-2016 from Center for Responsive Politics, www.opensecrets.org, and earlier years from Harold W. Stanley and Richard Niemi, *Vital Statistics on American Politics, 2003–2004* (Washington, DC: CQ Press, 2004). 2016 data as of November 2, 2016.

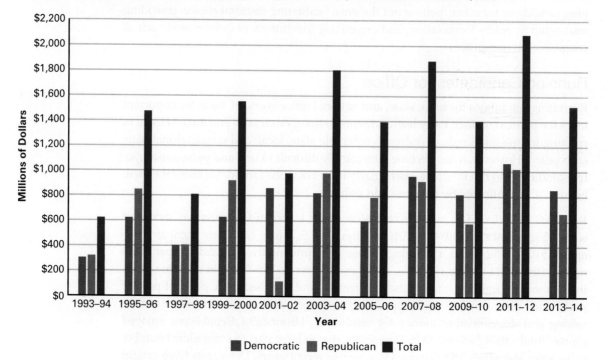

Donald J. Trump
The forty-fifth president, a Republican, elected in 2016; first president elected without prior political or military experience; an experienced businessman.

national party platform
A statement of the general and specific philosophy and policy goals of a political party, usually promulgated at the national convention.

volume of government census records and marketing firms, parties use advanced computer models to identify potential voters based on consumer preferences, personal habits, and past voting behavior. Once identified, these voters' names are stored in a database—Republicans call theirs the GOP Data Center—and shared with individual campaigns, whose volunteers contact voters by phone and personal visits. The detailed information accessed from these databases allows campaigns to carefully tailor their messages to individual voters. Unlike most nominees in recent history, President **Donald J. Trump's** campaign largely ceded the ground game to the Republican Party. And while the GOP said that President Trump's populist message resonated with large swaths of persuadable voters, they also pointed to the party's investments in the ground game, which advocated up and down the ticket, as a major factor in winning the historic 2016 election.

Formulating and Promoting Policy

The **national party platform** is the most visible instrument parties use to formulate, convey, and promote public policy. Every four years, each party writes a lengthy platform explaining its positions on key issues. In a two-party system, a party's platform argues why its preferences are superior to those of the rival party. This is particularly true for contentious social issues, such as abortion and same-sex marriage, which have little room for compromise and divide the electorate.

Scholarship suggests that about two-thirds of the promises in the victorious party's presidential platform are completely or mostly implemented. Moreover, about one-half or more of the pledges of the losing party also tend to find their way into public policy, a trend no doubt reflecting the effort of both parties to support broad policy positions that enjoy widespread support in the general public.[11] For example, in 2016, both party platforms supported prioritizing military readiness and taking care of military veterans,

TABLE 11.1   WHAT DO PARTY PLATFORMS SAY?

Issue	Democratic Platform	Republican Platform
Abortion	Every woman should have access to quality reproductive health care services, including safe and legal abortion	Upholds the "sanctity of human life"; affirms that unborn children have "individual right to life" protected under the 14th amendment of the Constitutio
Defense	Supports a smart, predictable defense budget that meets strategic challenges; would audit the Pentagon	Supports lifting the budget cap for defense; would audit the Pentagon
Healthcare	Healthcare is fundamental human right; Americans should be able to access public coverage through a public option; secure universal healthcare	Would repeal Obamacare
Education	Universal preschool; new investments by the federal government in higher education; relief from student debt	Calls for choice in K-12 education; restoring private sector participation in financing college loans
Same-Sex Marriage	Applauds 2015 Supreme Court decision; will fight for comprehensive federal non-discrimination protections for all LGBT Americans, to guarantee equal rights.	Doesn't accept 2015 Supreme Court decision and urges reversal; laws and government's regulations should recognize marriage as the union of one man and one woman

SOURCES: 2016 Democratic National Platform, https://www.demconvention.com/platform/; Republican National Platform https://www.gop.com/the-2016-republican-party-platform/.

auditing the Pentagon for waste, fraud and abuse, and ending previous cuts to defense spending enacted by Congress as part of sequestration. (see Table 11.1).

Organizing Government

Political parties are able to implement their policy agendas in part because they play such a significant role in organizing the operations of government and providing structure for political conflict within and between the branches. Here, we consider the role of parties in the legislative, executive, and judicial branches at the federal and state levels.

PARTIES IN CONGRESS Nowhere is the party more visible or vital than in the Congress. In this century, political parties have dramatically increased the sophistication and impact of their internal congressional organizations. Prior to the beginning of every session, the parties in both houses of Congress gather (or "caucus") separately to select party leaders and to arrange for the assignment of members of each chamber's committees. In effect, the parties organize and operate Congress.

Congressional party leaders enforce discipline among party members in various ways. These leaders can, for example, award committee assignments and chairs to the loyal or withhold them from the rebellious, regardless of seniority. Pork-barrel projects—government projects yielding rich patronage benefits that sustain many legislators' electoral survival—may be included or deleted during the appropriations process. Small favors and perquisites (such as the allocation of desirable office space or the scheduling of floor votes for the convenience of a member) can also be useful levers.

Perhaps as a response to these increased incentives, party labels have become the most powerful predictor of congressional voting. In the past few years, party-line voting has increased noticeably. Although not invariably predictive, a member's party affiliation has proven to be the best indicator of how he or she votes. In the 113th Congress, which was held from January 2013 to January 2015 under the leadership of former Speaker of the House John Boehner (R-Ohio), Republicans had a Party Unity Score of 94.6 percent, the highest ever for the party, but opposition to Democrats and their policies is what united Republicans.[12]

THE PRESIDENTIAL PARTY The president carries the mantle of leader of his or her party, and he or she is often the public face of his party's agenda. Some presidents have taken their party responsibilities more seriously than others.[13] Democrats

WHAT DOES A PARTISAN PRESIDENT LOOK LIKE?
President Franklin D. Roosevelt dedicated himself to building the Democratic Party both in the electorate and in government. His rise to the presidency and spirited campaigns contributed to the New Deal realignment that drew blue-collar workers, labor union members, white Southerners, and the poor to the Democratic Party. Here, he is greeted by Georgia farmers while en route to Warm Springs, Georgia, just before the 1932 election.

Barack Obama
The first African American president of the United States, a Democrat, who served as forty-fourth president from 2009 to 2017. Senator from Illinois from 2005 to 2008; member of the Illinois Senate from 1997 to 2004.

Woodrow Wilson and Franklin D. Roosevelt dedicated themselves to building their party in both the electorate and in government. Republicans Ronald Reagan and George W. Bush also exemplified the "pro-party" presidency.

With few exceptions, presidents appoint fellow members of their party to key executive departments and other positions. The president and White House also work closely with congressional party leaders to pass legislation. Because the president cannot introduce legislation on his or her own, they nearly always relies on party members in Congress to propose his or her legislative initiatives. Furthermore, the president works with party leaders in Congress to construct a majority to pass White House-backed legislation. Presidents reciprocate the support they receive from members of Congress by appointing many activists to office, recruiting candidates, raising money for the party treasury, and campaigning extensively for party nominees during election seasons. The electoral fortunes of the parties also rise and fall with the success of the president. Even when the president is not on the ballot during mid-term elections, voters will still hold the president's party accountable for current problems.

PARTIES IN THE FEDERAL COURTS Although federal judges do not run for office under a party label, judges are creatures of the political process, and their posts are considered patronage plums. Judges are often chosen not only for their abilities but also as representatives of a certain philosophy or approach to government. Most recent presidents have appointed judges overwhelmingly from their own party. Democratic executives tend to select more liberal judges who are friendly to social programs or labor interests. Republican executives generally lean toward conservatives, hoping they will be tough on criminal defendants, opposed to abortion, and supportive of business interests. These opposing ideals may lead to conflict between the president and the Senate. President **Barack Obama**, for example, saw many of his judicial appointments blocked by Senate Republicans, who refused to allow a vote on the nominations. This tactic is an attempt to forestall ideological changes that can last far beyond the next election cycle.

PARTIES IN STATE GOVERNMENT   Most of the conclusions discussed about the parties' relationships to the national legislative, executive, and judicial branches also apply to those branches at the state level. State legislators, however, depend on their state and local parties for election assistance much more than their congressional counterparts. Whereas members of Congress have significant support from interest groups and large government-provided staffs to assist (directly or indirectly) their reelection efforts, state legislative candidates need party workers and, increasingly, the party's financial support and technological resources at election time.

Governors in many states hold greater influence over their parties' organizations and legislators than do presidents. Many governors have more patronage positions at their command than the president, and these material rewards and incentives give governors added clout with party activists and office holders. In addition, tradition in some states permits the governor to play a part in selecting the legislature's committee chairs and party floor leaders, and some state executives even attend and help direct the party legislative caucuses, activities no president would ever undertake.

The influence of party organizations in state judiciaries varies tremendously. Some states have taken dramatic actions to ensure that their Supreme Court judges can make independent decisions. Many of these states use a selection system called the Missouri Plan, which relies on a nonpartisan judicial nominating commission, to choose appointed state court judges. But, in other states (and in many local judicial elections), Supreme Court judges run as party candidates. These partisan elections have received a great deal of criticism in recent years, as they have become more costly and personal. Many commentators argue that they are contrary to the ideal of blind justice.

Furthering Unity, Linkage, and Accountability

Parties, finally, are the glue that holds together the disparate elements of the U.S. governmental and political apparatus. The Framers designed a system that divides and subdivides power, making it possible to preserve individual liberty but difficult to coordinate and initiate action in a timely fashion. Parties help compensate for this drawback by linking the branches of government. Although rivalry between the branches is inevitable, the partisan and ideological affiliations of the leaders of each branch constitute a common basis for cooperation, as the president and his fellow party members in Congress usually demonstrate daily. Not surprisingly, presidential candidates and presidents are also inclined to push policies similar to those advocated by their party's congressional leaders.

Even within each branch, party affiliation helps bring together members of the House of Representatives and the Senate or the president and the department heads in the bureaucracy. Similarly, the division of national, state, and local governments, while always an invitation to struggle, is made more workable by the intersecting party relationships that exist among office holders at all levels. Party affiliation, in other words, provides a basis for mediation and negotiation laterally among the branches of government and vertically among national, state, and local layers.

The party's linkage function does not end there. Party identification and organization foster communication between the voter and the candidate as well as between the voter and the office holder. The party connection represents one means of increasing accountability in election campaigns and in government. Candidates on the campaign trail and elected party leaders are required from time to time to account for their performance at party-sponsored forums, nominating primaries, and on Election Day.

FIGURE 11.5   HOW MUCH HAS PUBLIC TRUST IN GOVERNMENT DECLINED?

When asked in surveys about their level of trust in the government, Americans are guided by partisanship—Democrats and Republicans each think government runs better when their party is in charge. With public trust in government at historic lows and substantial general dissatisfaction with both major parties, many Americans believe that a third party option is needed in the United States.

SOURCE: Data from Pew Research Center, www.people-press.org/2015/11/23/public-trust-in-government-1958-2015/

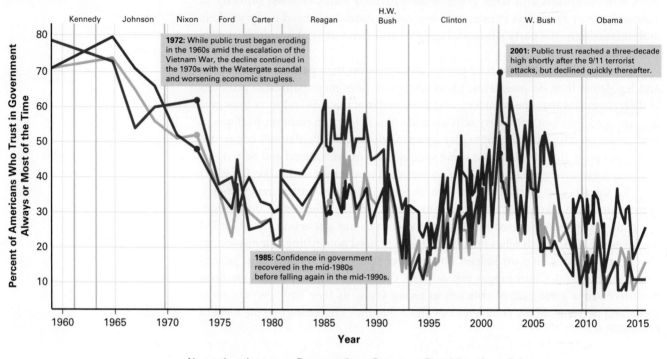

party identification
A citizen's attachment to a political party based on issues, ideology, past experience, or upbringing, which tends to be a reliable indicator of likely voting choices.

PARTY IN THE ELECTORATE

11.4 Describe the forces that create and shape party identification.

The party in the electorate—the mass of potential voters who identify with a party label—is a crucial element of the political party. But, in some respects, it is the weakest component of the U.S. political party system. Although **party identification**, or a citizen's attachment to a political party based on issues, ideology, past experience, or upbringing, tends to be a reliable indicator of likely voting choices, the trend is for fewer voters to declare loyalty to a party; 31 percent of voters called themselves independents on Election Day in 2016, according to exit polls.

For those Americans who do firmly adopt a party label, their attachment is likely to persist and become a central political reference symbol and perceptual screen. Strong party identifiers are more likely than other Americans to turn out on Election Day. Party activists who not only vote, but also contribute time, energy, efforts, and financial support to the party are drawn from the ranks of the strong identifiers.

Political Socialization

Not surprisingly, parents are the single greatest influence in establishing a person's first party identification. Parents who are politically active and share the same party identification raise children who will be strong party identifiers, whereas parents without party affiliations or with mixed affiliations produce offspring more likely to be independents. However, early socialization is hardly the last step in an individual's acquisition and maintenance of a party identity; marriage, economic status, and other aspects of adult life can change one's loyalty. Charismatic political personalities, particularly at the national level (such as Franklin D. Roosevelt and Ronald Reagan), can influence party identification as can cataclysmic events (the Civil War and the Great Depression are the best examples). Hot-button social issues (for instance, abortion and same-sex marriage), sectionalism, and candidate-oriented politics may also influence party ties.

Group Affiliations

Pluralists view political parties as coalitions of many organized groups. Groups try to influence what government does and can offer resources to the parties, such as campaign workers, contributions and votes, in exchange for party support for policies. In the same vein, party leaders build coalitions of groups to win elections and find electoral support for their policies. The challenge for parties is to build winning coalitions that do not create too many conflicting policy demands.

Just as individuals vary in the strength of their partisan choice, so do groups vary in the degree to which they identify with the Democratic Party or the Republican Party. Variations in party identification are particularly noticeable when geography, gender, race and ethnicity, age, social and economic status, and religion are examined (see Figure 11.6). It is important to note, however, that all of the general party identifications discussed below are broad tendencies that reflect and reinforce the issue and policy positions the two parties take.

GEOGRAPHY   While the map has been fairly rigid since 2000 with fewer states changing political sides from one election to the next, there were more competitive states in the 2016 election than in recent previous elections. The 2016 election highlighted divisions between urban and rural communities. While **Hillary Clinton** won almost 90 percent of urban cores, Donald Trump won the vast majority—between 75 and 90 percent—of suburbs, small cities and rural areas.[14]

GENDER   Some political scientists argue that the difference in the way men and women vote first emerged in 1920, when newly enfranchised women registered overwhelmingly as Republicans. Not until the 1980 presidential election, however, did scholars observe a noticeable and possibly significant gender gap—that is, the difference between women's aggregate preferences compared to men's—in party

Hillary Clinton
First female major party candidate for president of the United States, a Democrat, who ran against President Donald J. Trump in 2016. Secretary of State from 2009 to 2013; New York senator from 2001 to 2009; former first lady.

FIGURE 11.6A   HOW DOES GENDER INFLUENCE PARTY IDENTIFICATION?

SOURCE: Data from Pew Research Center, www.people-press.org/2016/09/13/2-party-affiliation-among-voters-1992-2016/

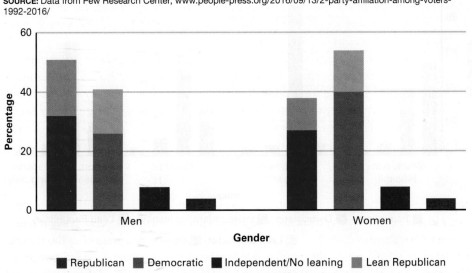

WHICH POLITICAL PARTY DO AFRICAN AMERICANS SUPPORT?

In the decade before 1948, African Americans identified as Democrats about as often as they did Republicans. Two key events increased African American support for the Democratic Party. The first was Democrat Harry Truman's explicit appeal in 1948 for new civil rights measures from Congress, including voter protections, a federal ban on lynching and bolstering existing civil rights laws. The second big jump in Democratic Party support came after the passage of the 1964 Civil Rights Act. In no election since 1936 has the Republican candidate for president gotten more than 40 percent of the black vote. Here, an African American family shows its support for Hillary Clinton.

identification. This pattern continues to play an important role in politics. Today, about 54 percent of women identify as Democrat or lean-Democrat, and 44 percent as Republican or lean Republican.

Most researchers, however, now explain the gender gap by focusing not on the Republican Party's difficulties in attracting female voters, but rather on the Democratic Party's inability to attract the votes of men. As one study notes, the gender gap exists because of the lack of support for the Democratic Party among men and the corresponding male preference for the Republican Party. These differences stem largely from differences in the how the sexes see the size and role of government and divergences of opinions about social welfare and military issues.[15]

FIGURE 11.6B HOW DOES RACE INFLUENCE PARTY IDENTIFICATION?

SOURCE: Data from Pew Research Center, www.people-press.org/2016/09/13/2-party-affiliation-among-voters-1992-2016/

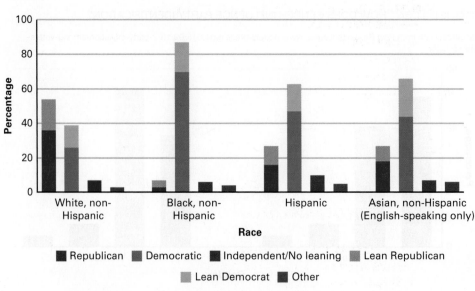

RACE AND ETHNICITY   Race is a significant indicator of party identification. For example, Republicans hold the advantage among white voters, and the party's base of supporters is roughly 90 percent white. Meanwhile, Democrats hold the advantage among minority groups, and people of color are becoming a larger share of the electorate across the country. African Americans are overwhelmingly Democratic in their partisan identification, with some 80 percent describing themselves as Democrats. African Americans provide approximately 25 percent of the Democratic Party's support in presidential elections. The advantage they offer the Democrats in party affiliation dwarfs the edge given to either party by any other significant segment of the electorate, and their proportion of strong Democrats is three times that of whites. Hispanics supplement African Americans as Democratic stalwarts; by about two-thirds, Hispanics prefer the Democratic Party. Some divisions do exist by country of origin. Mexican-Americans, Puerto Ricans, and Central Americans have historically aligned with the Democratic Party. While Cuban Americans have historically identified as Republican, over the last five years, they have shifted toward the Democratic Party. Asian Americans also tend to be divided based on country of origin, but higher income Asian Americans tend to identify as Republican. In the 2016 presidential election, shifting demographics ultimately were not enough to propel Hillary Clinton to the White House as she underperformed among key demographic groups that were central to President Barack Obama's coalition, including young voters, minorities and working class voters who swung to Donald Trump.

AGE   Political socialization creates a strong relationship between age and party identification. Individuals in the same age range are likely to have experienced similar events during the people in which they formed their party loyalties. Today, middle-aged voters tend to favor the Republican Party. These voters, often at the height of their career and, consequently, their earning potential, tend to favor the low taxes championed by Republicans.[16] In contrast, the Democratic Party's more liberal positions on social issues tend to resonate with today's moderate but socially progressive young adults. The nation's oldest voters, who were alive during the Great Depression tend to favor the Republican Party.

FIGURE 11.6C   HOW DOES AGE INFLUENCE PARTY IDENTIFICATION?

SOURCE: Data from Pew Research Center, www.people-press.org/2016/09/13/2-party-affiliation-among-voters-1992-2016/

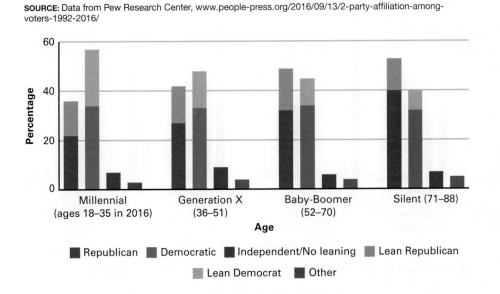

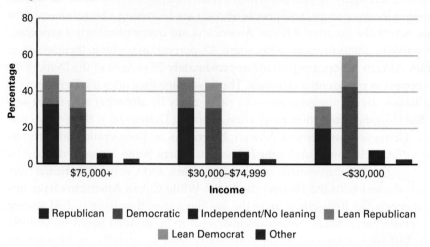

FIGURE 11.6D   HOW DOES INCOME INFLUENCE PARTY IDENTIFICATION?

SOURCE: Data from Pew Research Center, www.people-press.org/2016/09/13/2-party-affiliation-among-voters-1992-2016/

SOCIAL AND ECONOMIC FACTORS Occupation, income, and education are closely related, so many of the same partisan patterns appear in all three classifications. While higher-income Americans are more likely to affiliate with Republicans, middle-class and lower-income Americans are more likely to identify with Democrats. Those with higher levels of education, a college or post-graduate degree, are more likely to identify as Democrat, while those who have some college or less are more likely to identify as Republican.

RELIGION Religion can be evaluated based on both denomination and religiosity, or how frequently an individual engages in activities such as prayer and church attendance. With respect to religious denomination, Jewish and Black Protestant voters tend to favor the Democratic Party, while Mormons and white Protestants—especially Methodists, Presbyterians, and Episcopalians—align with the Republicans. Religiously unaffiliated voters align primarily with the Democratic Party by a more than 40 point gap. The Republican Party has also made gains among the most

FIGURE 11.6E   HOW DOES RELIGION INFLUENCE PARTY IDENTIFICATION?

SOURCE: Data from Pew Research Center, www.people-press.org/2016/09/13/2-party-affiliation-among-voters-1992-2016/

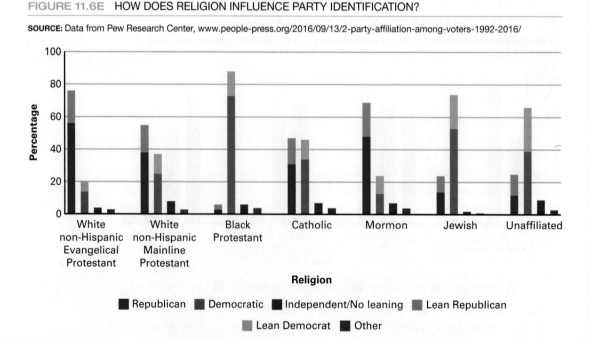

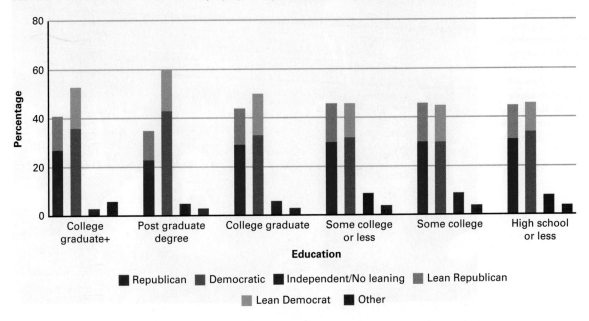

FIGURE 11.6F HOW DOES EDUCATION INFLUENCE PARTY IDENTIFICATION?

SOURCE: Data from Pew Research Center, www.people-press.org/2016/09/13/2-party-affiliation-among-voters-1992-2016/

religious identifiers of all sects; and these increases may reflect the party's visible support for socially conservative viewpoints, including opposition to abortion and contraception.[17]

MINOR PARTIES IN THE AMERICAN TWO-PARTY SYSTEM

11.5 Evaluate the role of minor parties in the U.S. electoral system.

To this point, our discussion has focused largely on the activities of the two major political parties, the Democrats and the Republicans. This is not an entirely complete picture of the political system. Although minor parties face a challenge in surviving and thriving in the American political system, these parties continue to make important contributions to the political process, revealing sectional and political divides and bringing to light new issues and ideas.

The Formation and Role of Minor Parties

The decision to form a political party can be a difficult one. Most parties are rooted in social movements made up of activists and groups whose primary goal is to influence public policy. Parties aim to accomplish the same goal, but they also run candidates for elective office. Making this transition requires a substantial investment of financial and human resources as well as a broad base of political support to compete in elections. Throughout history, therefore, very few social movements have evolved into parties. Those that have succeeded in this mission have had the support of political elites and uninhibited access to the ballot.

For example, during the 1840s and 1850s, the Liberty and Free Soil Parties formed around the abolition of slavery issue. The parties' leaders were well-educated Northerners who accounted for a significant proportion of the electorate. In contrast, when civil rights issues emerged on the agenda again in the early twentieth century, it was through a social movement led by activists in groups such as

**WHAT ROLE DO MINOR PARTIES
PLAY IN THE ELECTORAL
PROCESS?**

As it has been internalized in the
Republican Party, the Tea Party has
played an important role in driving the
ideological trajectory of the party to
the right by emphasizing issues such
as limited government and demanding
budget cuts. It also played an important role in influencing the Republican
presidential nominating contest. Here
Donald Trump joins a Tea Party sponsored rally on Capitol Hill.

the NAACP. One reason why this social movement did not become a party was the
fact that black voters in areas where segregation had the most significant impact
were largely denied the franchise and thus could not have voted for potential party
candidates.

Minor parties based on causes neglected by the major parties have significantly affected American politics (see Table 11.2). These parties find their roots
in sectionalism (as did the Southern states' rights Dixiecrats, who broke away
from the Democrats in 1948); in economic protest (such as the agrarian revolt that
fueled the Populists, an 1892 prairie-states party); in specific issues (such as the
Green Party's support of the environment); in ideology (the Socialist, Communist,
and Libertarian Parties are examples); and in appealing, charismatic personalities
(Theodore Roosevelt's affiliation with the Bull Moose Party in 1912 is perhaps the
best example).

Minor parties achieve their greatest successes when they incorporate new ideas
or alienated groups or nominate attractive candidates as their standard-bearers.
They also thrive when declining trust in the two major political parties plagues the
electorate.

TABLE 11.2 WHAT ARE SOME OF AMERICA'S MINOR PARTIES?

Minor Party	Year Founded	Primary Purpose
Liberty/Free-Soil	1840	Abolition of slavery
Prohibition	1880	Prohibition of alcohol sale and consumption
Progressive/Bull Moose	1912	Factionalism in Republican Party; gave Theodore Roosevelt the platform to run for the presidency
American Independent	1968	States' rights; opposition to desegregation
Libertarian	1971	Opposition to governmental intervention in economic and social policy
Reform	1996	Economic issues: tax reform, national debt, federal deficit
Green	2000	Environmentalism and social justice

Barriers to Minor-Party Success

The ability of the two major parties to evolve and co-opt the ideas and issues of minor parties is one explanation for the short duration of minor parties. The major parties are eager to take the politically popular issue that gave rise to the minor party and make it their own to secure the allegiance of the minor party's supporters. For example, the Republicans of the 1970s absorbed many of the states' rights planks of George Wallace's 1968 presidential bid. Both major parties have also more recently attempted to attract independent voters by sponsoring reforms of the governmental process.

Scholars have also pointed out that third parties are hampered by the single-member-district plurality election system in the United States. Many other countries use **proportional representation**, a voting system that apportions legislative seats according to the percentage of votes a political party receives, giving the candidates of weaker parties a better chance of winning at least some seats. In the American **winner-take-all system**, the party that receives at least one more vote than any other party wins the election. To paraphrase the legendary football coach Vince Lombardi, finishing first is not everything, it is the *only* thing in U.S. politics; placing second, even by one vote, doesn't count. The winner-take-all system encourages the grouping of interests into as few parties as possible (the democratic minimum being two).

The Electoral College system and the rules of public financing for American presidential elections also make it difficult for minor parties to seriously complete. Not only must a candidate win popular votes, but the candidate also must win majorities in states that allow him or her to gain a total of 270 electoral votes.

TOWARD REFORM: UNITED OR DIVIDED?

11.6 Assess the reasons for the persistence of the two-party system in American politics.

In recent years, the existence, consequences, and causes of **partisan polarization**, or the increasingly conflicting and divided viewpoints of the Democratic and Republican Parties, has incited much debate. In this section, we detail each of these factors, making a careful distinction between elite polarization, or divergence among members of the party in government and the most engaged citizens, and mass polarization, or division among members of the general public.[18]

Causes of Polarization

Scholars have noted increasing partisan divisions between members of Congress over the past two decades. As northern liberal Republicans, and particularly, southern conservative Democrats have become increasingly rare, the parties have retreated in two separate directions, with the Republican caucus appearing to move rightward and their Democratic counterparts appearing to shift to the left. These changes have created a Congress with a bimodal distribution of members' ideologies—and fewer members in the center. It is, however, important to note that the parties are not equally polarized—Republicans in Congress are further right and more homogeneous than their Democratic counterparts. While Congress is now more polarized than at any time since the end of Reconstruction, it is also worth noting that hyperpartisanship is not just a current phenomenon. Some scholars argue that every major transformation in American politics, beginning with the contest between Hamilton's Federalists and Jefferson's Republicans, has included intense partisanship.

Recent scholarship also suggests that the American public is becoming more polarized. Scholars have documented a fundamental change in the nature of partisan

proportional representation
A voting system that apportions legislative seats according to the percentage of the vote won by a particular political party.

winner-take-all system
An electoral system in which the party that receives at least one more vote than any other party wins the election.

partisan polarization
The presence of increasingly conflicting and divided viewpoints between the Democratic and Republican Parties.

AMERICAN POLITICS IN COMPARATIVE PERSPECTIVE

How Do Different Electoral Systems Influence Elections?

Electoral systems define and structure the very rules of the political game in a democracy. The design of an electoral system can determine who is elected, how a campaign is fought, and the role of political parties. For example, some encourage or even enforce the formation of strong parties, while others only recognize individual candidates. What's more, electoral systems can provide incentives for parties and groups to be broadly based and accommodating or to rely on narrow appeals to ethnicity or kinship ties. Some systems might encourage factionalism, where groups within a party are constantly at odds with one another, while other systems encourage parties to speak with one voice and suppress dissent. What follows are some comparative examples of electoral systems around the world (see Table 11.3 and Map 11.7).

FIGURE 11.7 WHAT IS THE DISTRIBUTION OF ELECTORAL SYSTEM FAMILIES?

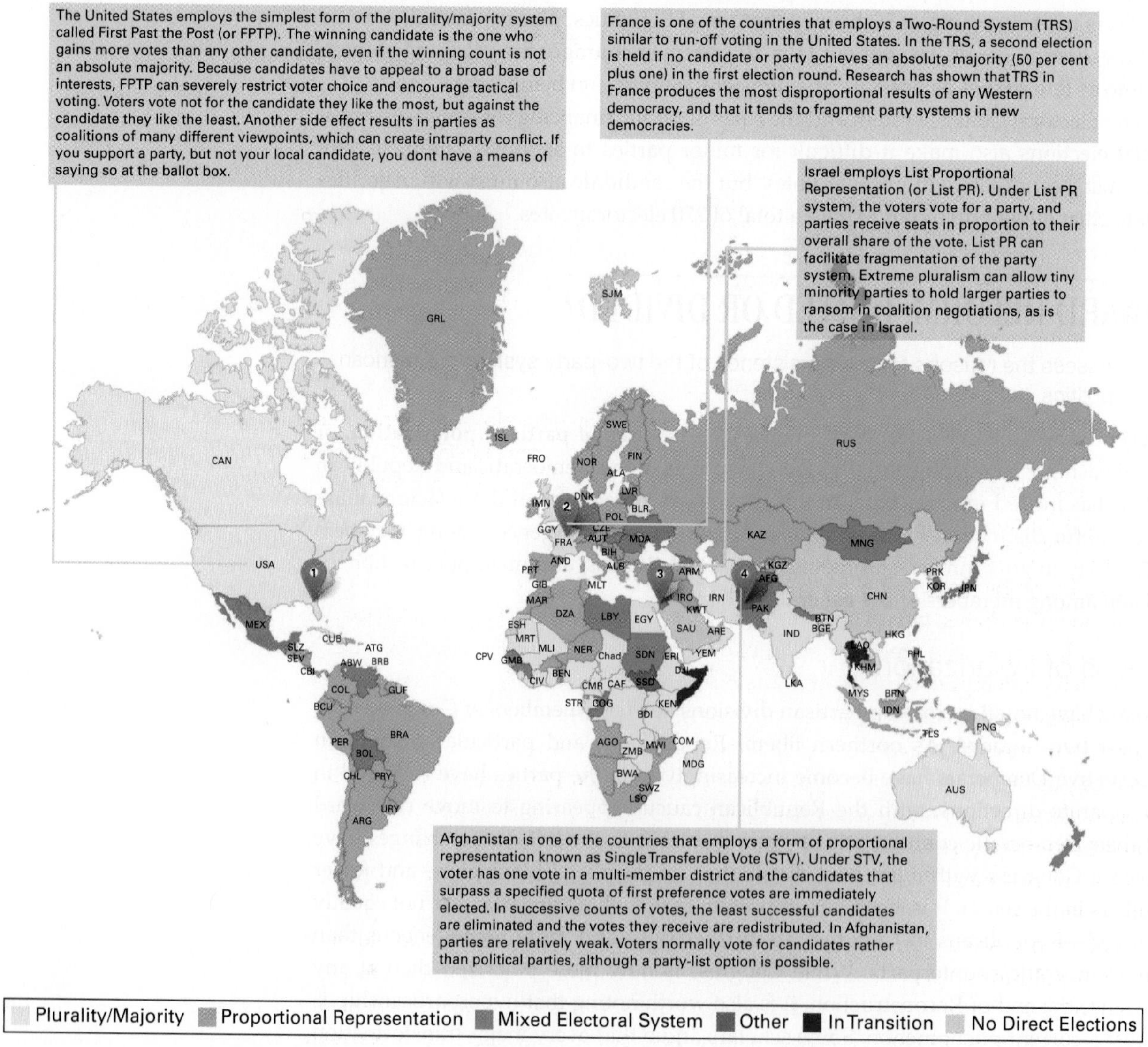
The United States employs the simplest form of the plurality/majority system called First Past the Post (or FPTP). The winning candidate is the one who gains more votes than any other candidate, even if the winning count is not an absolute majority. Because candidates have to appeal to a broad base of interests, FPTP can severely restrict voter choice and encourage tactical voting. Voters vote not for the candidate they like the most, but against the candidate they like the least. Another side effect results in parties as coalitions of many different viewpoints, which can create intraparty conflict. If you support a party, but not your local candidate, you dont have a means of saying so at the ballot box.
France is one of the countries that employs a Two-Round System (TRS) similar to run-off voting in the United States. In the TRS, a second election is held if no candidate or party achieves an absolute majority (50 per cent plus one) in the first election round. Research has shown that TRS in France produces the most disproportional results of any Western democracy, and that it tends to fragment party systems in new democracies.
Israel employs List Proportional Representation (or List PR). Under List PR system, the voters vote for a party, and parties receive seats in proportion to their overall share of the vote. List PR can facilitate fragmentation of the party system. Extreme pluralism can allow tiny minority parties to hold larger parties to ransom in coalition negotiations, as is the case in Israel.
Afghanistan is one of the countries that employs a form of proportional representation known as Single Transferable Vote (STV). Under STV, the voter has one vote in a multi-member district and the candidates that surpass a specified quota of first preference votes are immediately elected. In successive counts of votes, the least successful candidates are eliminated and the votes they receive are redistributed. In Afghanistan, parties are relatively weak. Voters normally vote for candidates rather than political parties, although a party-list option is possible.
1
2
3
4
GRL
SJM
CAN
USA
MEX
ISL
FRO
NOR
SWE
FIN
RUS
KAZ
MNG
CHN
IND
PAK
AFG
IRN
SAU
EGY
LBY
DZA
BRA
ARG
PER
BOL
CHL
AUS
PNG
Plurality/Majority
Proportional Representation
Mixed Electoral System
Other
In Transition
No Direct Elections

TABLE 11.3 WHAT ARE THE SOME OF THE MAJOR ELECTORAL SYSTEMS?

Type of Electoral System	Description	Number of Countries in the World
Plurality/Majority	Also called "first-past-the-post" or "winner-take-all," the candidate who receives the most votes in the electoral district wins the seat, even if that share is less than a majority of 50 percent +1 of the votes.	39% (85 countries)
Proportional Representation	An electoral system that attempts to make the percentage of legislative seats reflect the percentage of votes that parties or candidates received in an election.	39% (84 countries)
Mixed	An electoral system that combines elements of a different system. For example, such systems might combine features of a plurality/majority system with features of proportional system.	14% (31 countries)
Other	Under the Single Non-Transferable Vote system voters cast a single vote in a multi-member district. The candidates with the highest vote totals are declared elected. Voters vote for candidates rather than political parties.	3% (6 countries)
In Transition	Country or territory in transition; new electoral system not decided as of data rendering.	2% (5 countries)
No Election		2% (5 countries)

CRITICAL THINKING QUESTIONS

1. What are the consequences of electoral system design for party development and cohesion?
2. Can an individual's views be adequately represented by the two-party system in the United States?
3. How would partisan politics in the United States change if it adopted a different electoral system?

affect in the American electorate - the rise of negative partisanship, in which voters have formed strong loyalties based more on loathing for the opposing party. [19] Some scholars assert that bipartisanship remains elusive, not because of politicians in the capitol, but because of the American public and their fixation on party membership and loyalty.[20] Other scholars argue that the complex realignment of parties along different demographic and issue dimensions, the decline of civic responsibility and good citizens, and the segregation of citizens into "lifestyle enclaves" where they no longer live around people who share differing views are sources of polarization. But other scholars have attempted to show that the electorate only appears polarized because of the choices they are given in elections. That is, polarization of electoral choices is a result of movement by the candidates.[21] They also question the empirics of geographical sorting in the electorate and argue that even if this type of sorting were proved to occur, the effects would be minimal.[22] Still others take a more middle-of-the-road approach, asserting that polarization has electoral roots, but also that the reactions to members of Congress have amplified the effect of polarization in the electoral environment.[23]

While most Americans still identify overwhelming as politically moderate, that number has shrunk considerably in the last two decades (from 49 percent in 1994 to 39 percent in 2014). Furthermore, the positions of the most politically active citizens seem to suggest a growing division among these members of the electorate. Recent research and polls have found that the level of antipathy that members of each party feel toward the opposing party has surged since 1994.[24] Not only do more partisans have negative views of the other party, it is also more intense, and this is particularly true on the right. In 1994, just 23 percent of consistent liberals expressed a very unfavorable view of the Republican Party. And just 28 percent of consistent conservatives saw the

FIGURE 11.8 ARE AMERICAN POLITICAL PARTIES POLARIZED?

In the past ten years, scholars have hotly debated the question of whether American political parties are polarized. As we have argued in the text, the answer to this question appears to vary based on the definition of political party. The ideological distribution of party in government and the party in the electorate varies dramatically. These differences may have consequences for how Americans view the political parties, the political process, and institutions of government.

SOURCE: Data from Pew Research Center, www.people-press.org/2014/06/12/political-polarization-in-the-american-public/.

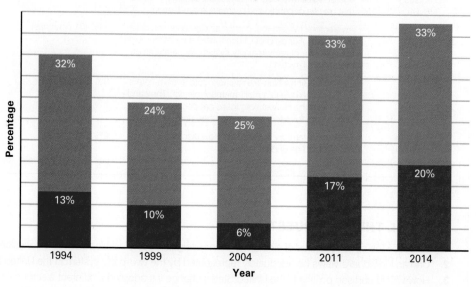

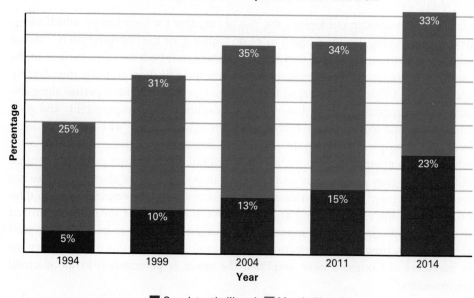

Democratic Party in equally negative terms. Today, 72 percent of consistent conservatives have a very unfavorable opinion of the Democratic Party; 53 percent of consistent liberals have very unfavorable impressions of the GOP. Perhaps not surprisingly, those who are more politically active are more likely to have a more unfavorable view of the opposing party. For example, 54 percent of Republicans and 46 percent of Democrats who have made campaign donations in the past two years describe the other political party as a threat to the nation.

Another cause of polarization is, to some degree, our own belief that we live in a polarized nation. This perception is fed by the 24-hour and Internet news cycles, which constantly need to sell a story to fill the voluminous airtime and attract viewers in a market-driven media environment. The idea that we might live in a world of "red states" and "blue states" is one such story that has provided the media with much fodder for discussion. The perception of deep division not only in Congress but in the mass electorate also has its roots in changing political campaigns. As parties have increasingly used microtargeting to identify and mobilize partisans, we have created stereotypes of party identifiers in our heads.

Finally, polarization between the parties may also be rooted in the clearer articulation of party positions on a range of issues, from national defense and foreign policy to economic affairs to so-called cultural "wedge issues." These cultural issues—summarized by some commentators as "guns, God, and gays"—include such matters as religious freedom, same-sex marriage, and abortion and contraception on which the parties have taken increasingly opposing viewpoints in recent years. Today, for example, being pro-choice on abortion is a litmus test for Democratic candidates in most areas of the country. Some scholars contend that this is not polarization—a term carrying a negative connotation—but, rather, party sorting, which means that parties develop clear issue positions that more efficiently and effectively cue the electorate to identify with a particular label.

Consequences of Polarization

Perhaps just as critical as understanding the sources of partisan rancor are its implications for democratic governance. The consequences of the growing division between the two parties in government have been on clear display in recent Congresses. These Congresses have been among the least productive in history in terms of the number of bills passed. The lack of moderate members, lower incentives to compromise and cross party lines, and the close margins by which the parties have held both the House and the Senate have made it nearly impossible to enact important policy proposals. Furthermore, as some scholars have noted, polarization might also subordinate the integrity of governmental institutions and contribute to a decline in unbiased information.

The consequences of potential polarization in the electorate, however, are less obvious. Some scholars have suggested that forcing the generally moderate American people to choose between two clearly divided political parties will lead to increased political apathy, less trust in government, and lower rates of participation and engagement in politics and government. Other scholars charge that polarization has positive outcomes, including more meaningful choices for the electorate between the parties, parties that are more attentive to their bases, higher voter turnout in elections, and greater engagement in campaign activism. Empirical evidence to date has been mixed. But, as Congress grows increasingly divided, monitoring the electorate for changes in partisan identification, issue positions, and political activity becomes significant for the health of American democracy.

Roots of the Two-Party System

11.1 Trace the evolution of political parties.

Political parties have been a presence in American politics since the nation's infancy. The Federalists and the Democratic-Republicans were the first two parties to emerge in the late 1700s. In 1832, the Democratic Party (which succeeded the Democratic-Republicans) held the first national presidential nomination convention, and the Whig Party formed around opposition to President Andrew Jackson. The Democratic and Whig Parties strengthened for several years until the issue of slavery led to the Whig Party's gradual dissolution and replacement by the Republican Party (formed by anti-slavery activists to push for the containment of slavery). From 1860 to this day, the same two political parties—Democratic and Republican—have dominated elections in the United States.

The Organization of American Political Parties

11.2 Describe the structure of political parties at the national, state, and local levels.

The national party organization sits at the top of the party system. A chairperson leads the national party, and every four years the national committee of each party organizes a national convention to nominate a candidate for the presidency. The state and local parties are the heart of party activism, as virtually all government regulation of political parties falls to the states. The state governing body, generally called the state central or executive committee, supervises the collection of local party organizations.

Activities of American Political Parties

11.3 Identify the functions of political parties.

For more than 200 years, the two-party system has served as the mechanism by which American society organizes and resolves social and political conflict. The two major parties provide vital services to society, including running candidates for office; proposing and formulating policy; organizing government; and furthering unity, linkage, and accountability.

Party Identification

11.4 Describe the forces that create and shape partisan identification.

Most American voters have a personal affinity for a political party, which summarizes their political views and preferences and is expressed by a tendency to vote for the candidates of that party. This party identification begins with political socialization; parents are the single greatest influence on a person's political leanings. However, different group affiliations, including geographic region, gender, race and ethnicity, age, social and economic factors, and religion, also affect individuals' loyalties to political parties, and these may change over the course of a lifetime.

Minor Parties in the American Two-Party System

11.5 Evaluate the role of minor parties in the U.S. electoral system.

Minor parties have often significantly affected American politics. Ideas of minor parties that become popular with the electorate are often co-opted by one of the two major parties eager to secure supporters. Minor parties make progress when the two major parties fail to incorporate new ideas or alienated groups or if they do not nominate attractive candidates for office. However, many of the institutional features of American politics, including the winner-take-all system and the Electoral College, encourage the grouping of interests into as few parties as possible.

Toward Reform: United or Divided?

11.6 Assess the reasons for the persistence of the two-party system in American politics.

In recent years, scholars have debated the presence and origins of growing polarization between the two political parties. Though the cause of these growing divisions can in part be attributed to our own perceptions of polarization and the 24-hour news cycle, clear differences also exist between the parties' positions both in government and in the most active segments of the electorate. The divide between the two parties can make it difficult to create policy in American political institutions.

LEARN THE TERMS

Barack Obama
candidate-centered politics
critical elections
delegate
Donald J. Trump
Hillary R. Clinton

national convention
national party platform
party identification
partisan polarization
party realignment
Political machine

political party
proportional representation
secular realignment
superdelegate
Thomas Jefferson
winner-take-all system

HOW DO PRESIDENTIAL CAMPAIGNS ROUSE THE NATION?

Whistle stop campaigns became prominent with the rise of the modern era of presidential campaigning. Here, Theodore Roosevelt gives a campaign speech from the back of a train in 1912. In similar fashion, Donald Trump rallied supporters throughout the 2016 presidential election in a marathon of campaign events.

CAMPAIGNS, ELECTIONS, AND VOTING

LEARNING OBJECTIVES

12.1 Compare and contrast presidential and congressional elections, and explain the incumbency advantage.

12.2 Outline how campaigns are organized, and evaluate methods for reaching voters.

12.3 Evaluate the influence of money in elections and the main approaches to campaign finance reform.

12.4 Analyze the factors that influence voter turnout and voter choice.

12.5 Evaluate concerns with the electoral process and proposed reforms to address them.

Strategies for campaigning for the White House have changed dramatically since the nation's founding. Because George Washington was the consensus candidate in 1788 and 1792, the first real presidential campaign came in 1796 when Vice President John Adams ran against **Thomas Jefferson**, who had been nominated by the first political opposition party, the Democratic-Republicans. The candidates honored the cultural taboo against direct campaigning and appeals for votes. In 1800, the same two candidates vied for office once again. Jefferson, who had lost in 1796, paid the editor of the *Richmond Examiner* to print anti-Federalist articles and to praise the efforts of the Democratic-Republicans. Jefferson's supporters also accused President Adams of having a "hideous hermaphroditical character, which has neither the force and firmness of a man, nor the gentleness and sensibility of a woman." In response, Adams' campaign distributed a leaflet that called Jefferson "a mean-spirited, low-lived fellow, the son of a half-breed Indian squaw, sired by a Virginia mulatto father."

While there was still largely a taboo on direct appeals throughout the nineteenth century, surrogates campaigned on behalf of candidates at the grassroots level. Negative campaigns also persisted. In 1884, supporters of Republican Party candidate James G. Blaine came up with a campaign jingle alluding to Democratic nominee Grover Cleveland's alleged illegitimate child: "Ma, Ma, where's my Pa?." After Cleveland won the election, his supporters cleverly retorted: "Gone to the White House, ha, ha, ha." Political cartoons also accompanied campaign songs in the 19th century.

Around the turn of the twentieth century, nominees conducted "front porch campaigns," where they received supporters at home and occasionally made statements to the press. Active campaigning became common in the twentieth century. Pre-modern and modern presidents employed "whistle-stop" campaigns, traveling the country by train and delivering speeches from the rear platform. In the election of 1900, vice presidential nominee Theodore Roosevelt conducted a whirlwind whistle-stop tour of an astounding 480 communities across twenty-three states. In 1932, Franklin D. Roosevelt traveled 13,000 miles by train to 36 states, and Harry Truman set the record covering 32,000 miles and averaging ten speeches a day in his successful 1948 presidential bid.

Especially following the first televised debate in 1960, television ushered in a new revolution in the way candidates ran their campaigns, requiring candidates to carefully craft public images and to take advantage of media exposure. Debates play an important role in the campaign process, especially informing voters in the nominating contests. However, in a politically polarized era, general election debates contribute more to reinforcing existing beliefs among supporters than to persuading voters. While advertising has been a central element of campaign strategy in the television age, it was down dramatically in 2016 and **Donald J. Trump** won the election despite airing less than one-third of the ads that **Hillary Clinton** did.

With the Internet and digital media revolution of the twenty-first century, the candidates' digital strategy—which encompasses apps, websites, social media and data research—has become increasingly important. In 2016, the Trump campaign's data-driven digital operation challenged recent campaign orthodoxy, while cultivating fervent supporters, persuading voters, and circumventing traditional political channels. The digital effort augmented President Trump's marathon of cross-country campaign events and the Republican Party's ground game.

From political pamphlets to newspaper smears and catchy slogans, to front porch and whistle stop tours, to televised debates and constant access to candidates in the digital age, the methods for campaigning for the presidency have changed dramatically since the days of Thomas Jefferson. But the central goal of mobilizing voters has remained constant. The most successful candidates harness campaign innovations to reach more voters in the ever-lengthening and costly march to the White House.

Thomas Jefferson
Principle drafter of the Declaration of Independence; second vice president of the United States; third president of the United States from 1801 to 1809. Co-founder of the Democratic-Republican Party.

Donald J. Trump
The forty-fifth president, a Republican, elected in 2016; first president elected without prior political or military experience; an experienced businessman.

Hillary Clinton
First female major party candidate for president of the United States, a Democrat, who ran against President Donald J. Trump in 2016. Secretary of State from 2009 to 2013; New York senator from 2001 to 2009; former first lady.

• • •

electorate
The citizens eligible to vote.

mandate
A command, indicated by an electorate's votes, for the elected officials to carry out a party platform or policy agenda.

primary election
Election in which voters decide which of the candidates within a party will represent the party in the general election.

closed primary
A primary election in which only a party's registered voters are eligible to cast a ballot.

open primary
A primary election in which party members, independents, and sometimes members of the other party are allowed to participate.

In the United States, frequent and regular elections are the means by which the majority of the electorate can hold politicians accountable and keep them attentive to public preferences. Every year, on the Tuesday following the first Monday in November, a plurality of voters, simply by casting ballots peacefully across a continent-sized nation, reelects or replaces politicians at all levels of government—from the president of the United States to members of the U.S. Congress to governors to state legislators to local mayors, councilors and commissioners, and in some states, judges. Americans tend to take this process for granted, but in truth it is a marvel. Many other countries do not enjoy the benefit of competitive elections and the peaceful transition of political power made possible through the electoral process.

By choosing who will govern—not what they should do or what laws should be passed—voters elect politicians to act on their behalf. This chapter focuses on presidential and congressional contests in the United States and examines the range of factors that affect voter choice and voter turnout. We will examine how campaigns try to mobilize supporters and persuade undecided voters. We will also assess the shortcomings of the democratic process in the United States, including low rates of participation in American elections.

ROOTS OF AMERICAN ELECTIONS

12.1 Compare and contrast presidential and congressional elections, and explain the incumbency advantage.

Elections are responsible for most political changes in the United States. At fixed intervals, the **electorate**—citizens eligible to vote—is called on to judge those in power. Elections confirm the concept of popular sovereignty, the idea that legitimate political power derives from the consent of the governed, and they serve as the bedrock for democratic governance. Regular free elections guarantee mass political action, enable citizens to influence the actions of their government, and confer legitimacy on that government. Societies that cannot vote their leaders out of office are left with little choice other than to force them out by means of strikes, riots, or *coups d'état*. Elections are also the primary means to fill public offices and to organize and staff the government. Because candidates advocate certain policies, elections also provide a choice of direction on a wide range of issues, from abortion to civil rights to national defense to the environment, and the winners will claim a **mandate** (a command) from the people to carry out a party platform or policy agenda.

Types of Elections

The United States is almost unrivaled in the variety and number of elections it holds. Under the Constitution, the states hold much of the administrative power over elections, even when national office holders are being elected. Thus, as we will see, states have great latitude to set the date and type of elections, determine the eligibility requirements for candidates and voters, and tabulate the results.

The electoral process has two stages: primary and general elections. In most jurisdictions, candidates for state and national office must compete in both of these races. Some states (but not the national government) also use the electoral process to make public policy and remove office holders. These processes are known as the initiative, referendum, and recall.

PRIMARY ELECTIONS   In **primary elections**, voters decide which candidates within a party will represent the party in the general elections. Primary elections take on a number of different forms, depending on who is allowed to participate. **Closed primaries** allow only a party's registered voters to cast a ballot. In **open primaries**, however, independents and sometimes members of the other party are allowed to

The 2016 Republican presidential nomination contest had the largest primary field in the last 100 years. In primary elections, voters decide which candidates of a party will represent the party in the general election. Primary elections were a Progressive-era reform intended to reduce the potential for mischief in a nomination system controlled by the parties, but they were not widely embraced by states until after the 1968 election. McGovern-Fraser Commission reforms ushered in the modern presidential nomination process by establishing a more direct link between votes cast in primaries and caucuses and the delegates selected to attend the parties' national conventions.

participate. Closed primaries are considered healthier for the party system because they prevent members of one party from influencing the primaries of the opposition party. Studies of open primaries indicate that **crossover voting**—participation in the primary of a party with which the voter is not affiliated—occurs frequently, though little evidence exists for organized attempts by voters of one party to influence the primary results of the other party.[1]

In eleven states, when none of the candidates in the initial primary secures a majority of the votes, there is a **runoff primary**, a contest between the two candidates with the greatest number of votes.[2]

crossover voting
Participation in the primary election of a party with which the voter is not affiliated.

runoff primary
A second primary election between the two candidates receiving the greatest number of votes in the first primary.

GENERAL ELECTIONS   Once the parties have selected their candidates for various offices, each state holds its general election. In the **general election**, voters decide which candidates will actually fill elective public offices. These elections take place at many levels, including municipal, county, state, and national. Whereas primaries are contests between the candidates within each party, general elections are contests between the candidates of opposing parties.

general election
Election in which voters decide which candidates will actually fill elective public offices.

INITIATIVE AND REFERENDUM   Taken together, the initiative and referendum processes are collectively known as ballot measures; both allow voters to enact public policy. They are used by some state and local governments, but not by the national government. Twenty-six states and the District of Columbia offer initiative and referendum rights to their citizens.

An **initiative** is a process that allows *citizens* to propose legislation or state constitutional amendments by submitting them to the electorate for popular vote, provided the initiative supporters receive a certain number of signatures on petitions supporting the placement of the proposal on the ballot. There are two primary types of referenda. In a legislative **referendum**, the *state legislature* submits proposed legislation or state constitutional amendments to the voters for approval. A popular referendum is a measure to approve or repeal an act of the Legislature that appears on the ballot as a result of a voter petition drive.

initiative
An election that allows citizens to propose legislation or state constitutional amendments by submitting them to the electorate for popular vote.

referendum
An election whereby the state legislature submits proposed legislation or state constitutional amendments to the voters for approval.

Ballot measures have been the subject of heated debate in the past decades. Critics charge that ballot measures—intended to give citizens more direct control over policy making—are now unduly influenced by interest groups and "the initiative industry—law firms that draft legislation, petition management firms that guarantee ballot access,

recall
An election in which voters can remove an incumbent from office prior to the next scheduled election.

direct-mail firms, and campaign consultants who specialize in initiative contests."[3] Critics also question the ability of voters to deal with the numerous complex issues that appear on a ballot. In addition, the wording of a ballot measure can have an enormous impact on the outcome. In some cases, a "yes" vote will bring about a policy change; in other cases, a "no" vote will cause a change.[4] Moreover, ballot initiatives are not subject to the same campaign contribution limits applied to donations in candidate campaigns. Consequently, a single wealthy individual can bankroll a ballot measure and influence public policy in a manner that is not available to the individual through the normal policy process.

Supporters of ballot measures argue that critics have overstated their case and that the process has historically been used to champion popular issues that were resisted at the state level by entrenched political interests. Citizens have used initiatives, for example, in popular progressive causes such as banning child labor, expanding suffrage to women, promoting environmental laws, establishing same-sex marriage, and passing campaign finance reform. The process has also been instrumental in passing popular conservative proposals such as tax relief and banning gay marriages.[5] Furthermore, supporters point out that ballot measures can heighten public interest in elections and can increase voter participation.

RECALL **Recall** elections—or deelections—allow voters to remove an incumbent from office prior to the next scheduled election. Recall elections are historically very rare, and sometimes they are thwarted by an official's resignation or impeachment prior to the vote. In recent years, however, recall has become a more popular technique to challenge officials at the state and local levels. In fact, 65 percent of all recalls of state legislators have taken place in the past 30 years, and nearly half have occurred just since 2010.[6] In the first recall election in Colorado's history, voters successfully recalled in 2013 two Democratic state senators who provided crucial support for a package of stricter gun laws. In 2016, there were multiple efforts to recall Governor Rick Snyder in Michigan over the Flint water crisis. Other efforts in 2016 included proposed recalls of seven state legislators, two governors (Bill Walker of Alaska in addition to Rick Snyder of Michigan), twenty-six special districts, six sheriffs, twenty-one school board members, fifty-seven mayors, eight county officials, sixteen county commissioners, ten city officials, and sixty-six city council members. Observers attribute this growing use of recall to the fact that the majority of state legislatures are ruled by a single party and are more politically polarized than ever before. The recall

WHEN DO CITIZENS RECALL THEIR LEADERS?

Although historically rare, recall has become a more popular method to challenge officials at the state and local level. Public furor over Chicago police shootings led Illinois state legislators to introduce legislation in December 2015 that would allow voters to recall Mayor Rahm Emanuel. Illinois state law currently only allows the recall of a governor, a provision voters approved in 2010 after former Illinois Governor Rod Blagojevich was arrested and impeached. Nineteen states and the District of Columbia allow recalls of state and local officials.

provides a solution for minority party legislators and voters to slow down or stop legislation they don't like. In addition, the development of new technologies, such as the Internet, make fund-raising and signature gathering easier. Online news sources, too, may turn local recall elections into national news.[7]

Presidential Elections

No U.S. election can compare to the presidential contest. This quadrennial spectacle brings together all the elements of politics and attracts the most ambitious and energetic politicians to the national stage. Voters in a series of state contests that run through the winter and spring of the election year select delegates who will attend each party's national convention. Following the national convention for each party, a final set of fifty separate state elections to select the president are held on the Tuesday after the first Monday in November. This lengthy process exhausts candidates and voters alike, but it allows the diversity of the United States to be displayed in ways a shorter, more homogeneous presidential election process could not.

THE NOMINATION PROCESS   The state party organizations use several types of methods to elect the national convention delegates who will ultimately select the candidates running against each other in the general election:

1. *Winner-take-all primary.* Under this system, the candidate who wins the most votes in a state secures all of that state's delegates. While Democrats no longer permit its use because they view it as less representative than a proportional system, Republicans generally prefer this process, as it enables a candidate to amass a majority of delegates quickly and shortens the divisive primary season.

2. *Proportional representation primary.* Under this system, candidates who secure a threshold percentage of votes are awarded delegates in proportion to the number of popular votes won. Democrats now use this system in many state primaries, where they award delegates to anyone who wins more than 15 percent of the vote in any congressional district. Although proportional representation is probably the fairest way of allocating delegates to candidates, its downside is that it renders majorities of delegates more difficult to accumulate and thus can lengthen the presidential nomination contest.

3. *Caucus.* The caucus is the oldest, most party-oriented method of choosing delegates to the national conventions. Traditionally, the caucus was a closed meeting of party activists in each state who selected the party's choice for presidential candidate. Today, caucuses (in Iowa, for example) are more open and attract a wider range of the party's membership. Indeed, new participatory caucuses more closely resemble primary elections than they do the old, exclusive party caucuses.[8] At a caucus, participants spend several hours learning about politics and the party. They listen to speeches by candidates or their representatives and receive advice from party leaders and elected officials, then cast a well-informed vote.

The mix of preconvention contests has changed over the years, with the most pronounced trend being the shift from caucuses to primary elections. Only seventeen states held presidential primaries in 1968; in 2016, thirty-eight states chose this method. Many people support the increase in number of primaries because they believe that primaries are more democratic than caucuses because they are accessible to most registered voters. Although both primaries and caucuses attract the most ideologically extreme voters in each party, primaries tend to nominate more moderate and appealing candidates—those that primary voters believe can win in the general election. Primaries are also more similar to the general election and thus constitute a rigorous test for the candidates and a chance to display, under pressure, some of the skills needed to be a successful president.

Critics contend that the qualities tested by the primary system, such as skill at handling national and local media, are by no means a complete list of those needed by

Electoral College
Representatives of each state who cast the final ballots that actually elect a president.

elector
Member of the Electoral College.

reapportionment
The reallocation of the number of seats in the House of Representatives after each decennial census.

a successful president. In addition, primaries may attract more participants than do caucuses, but this quantity does not substitute for the quality of information held by caucus participants.

SELECTING A PRESIDENT: THE ELECTORAL COLLEGE   Given the enormous amount of energy, money, and time expended to nominate two major-party presidential contenders, it is difficult to believe that the general election could be more arduous than the nominating contests, but it usually is. The object of campaigning for the presidency is clear: winning a majority of the **Electoral College**. This uniquely American institution consists of representatives of each state who cast the final ballots that actually elect a president. The total number of **electors**—the members of the Electoral College—for each state is equivalent to the number of senators and representatives that state has in the U.S. Congress. The District of Columbia is accorded three electoral votes, making 538 the total number of votes cast in the Electoral College. Thus, the magic number for winning the presidency is 270 votes.

Through **reapportionment**, representation in the House of Representatives and consequently in the Electoral College is altered every ten years to reflect population shifts. Reapportionment is simply the reallocation of the number of seats in the House of Representatives that takes place after each decennial census. After the 2010 Census, for example, the Electoral College map was redrawn to reflect a sizeable population shift from the Midwest and the Democratic-dominated Northeast to the South and West, where Republicans are much stronger (see Figure 12.1). Texas, for example, gained four congressional districts, and therefore four additional seats in the House of Representatives and four additional votes in the Electoral College. Florida gained two seats and two votes, while six other states gained one. New York and Ohio both lost two seats and two votes, and eight states lost a single seat and electoral vote.

The Electoral College resulted from a compromise among those Framers who argued for selection of the president by the Congress and those who favored selection by direct popular election. Three points are essential to understanding the Framers' design of the Electoral College. The system was constructed to: (1) work without political parties; (2) cover both the nominating and electing phases of presidential selection; and (3) produce a nonpartisan president. Most of the challenges faced by the Electoral College are the result of changes in presidential elections that have occurred over time.

For example, because the Framers expected partisanship to have little influence, they originally designed the Electoral College to elect the president and vice president from the same pool of candidates; the one who received the most votes would become president and the runner-up would become vice president. To accommodate this system, each elector was given two votes. Following the development of the first party system, the republic's fourth presidential election soon revealed a flaw in this plan. Since there was no way under the constitutional arrangements for electors to earmark their votes separately for president and vice president, the presidential election of 1800 resulted in a tie between Thomas Jefferson and Aaron Burr, the presidential and vice presidential candidates advanced by the Democratic-Republican Party. Even though most understood Jefferson to be the actual choice for president, the Constitution mandated that a tie be decided by the House of Representatives, which the Federalists controlled. The controversy was settled in Jefferson's favor, but only after much energy was expended to persuade Federalists not to give Burr the presidency.

The Twelfth Amendment, ratified in 1804 and still the constitutional foundation for presidential elections today, attempted to remedy the confusion between the selection of vice presidents and presidents that beset the election of 1800 by providing for separate elections for each office. In the event of a tie or when no candidate received a majority of the total number of electors, the election still went to the House of Representatives; now, however, each state delegation would have one vote to cast for one of the three

FIGURE 12.1   HOW IS IT POSSIBLE TO WIN THE ELECTION BUT NOT THE POPULAR VOTE?

Donald Trump won the Electoral College in the 2016 presidential election, but Hillary Clinton won the popular vote. This map shows 2016 county-level election results. Democratic voters are often clustered in cities, and Clinton slightly improved upon President Obama's 2012 performance in counties with more than one million people. However, Clinton received less than 30 percent of the vote in counties with less than 20,000 people. It is important to note that in most electoral maps, states are depicted as either blue or red, which masks the fact that large portions of the country are quite evenly divided.

NOTE: Data available as of November 22, 2016.

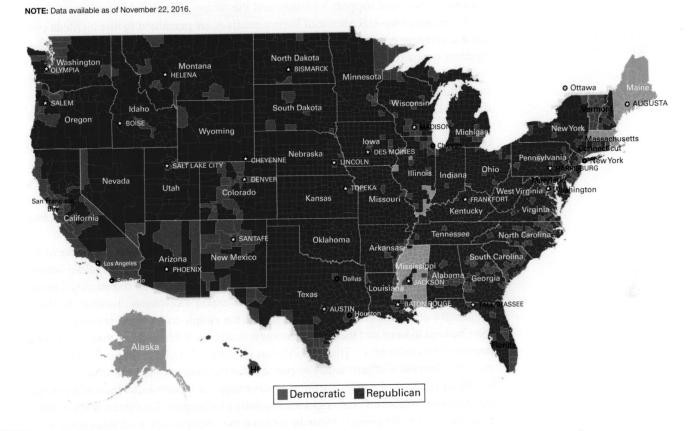

candidates who had received the greatest number of electoral votes. Although the Electoral College modified by the Twelfth Amendment has fared better than the College as originally designed, it has not been problem free. On five occasions—the elections of 1824, 1876, 1888, 2000, and 2016—the electoral process resulted in the selection of a president who received fewer popular votes than his opponent.

Congressional Elections

Compared with presidential elections, congressional elections receive scant national attention. Unlike major-party presidential contenders, most candidates for Congress labor in relative obscurity. Some nominees for Congress are celebrities—television stars, sports heroes, and even local TV news anchors. The vast majority of party nominees for Congress, however, are little-known state legislators and local office holders who receive remarkably limited coverage in many states and communities. For them, just establishing name identification in the electorate is the biggest battle.

THE INCUMBENCY ADVANTAGE   The current system enhances the advantages of **incumbency,** or already holding an office. Those people in office tend to remain in office. In a "bad" year such as the Republican wave of 2010, "only" 87 percent of

incumbancy
Already holding an office.

House incumbents won reelection. Senatorial reelection rates can be much more mercurial. In 2016, 97 percent of House members and 90 percent of senators who sought reelection were successful. To the political novice, these reelection rates might seem surprising, as public trust in government and satisfaction with Congress has remained remarkably low during the very period that reelection rates have been on the rise. To understand the nature of the incumbency advantage, it is necessary to explore its primary causes: staff support, visibility, and the "scare-off" effect.

Members of the U.S. House of Representatives are permitted to hire eighteen permanent and four nonpermanent aides to work in their Washington and district offices. Senators typically enjoy far larger staffs, with the actual size determined by the number of people in the state they represent. Both House and Senate members also enjoy the additional benefits provided by the scores of unpaid interns who assist with office duties. Many activities of staff members directly or indirectly promote the legislator through constituency services, the wide array of assistance provided by members of Congress to voters in need. Constituent service may include tracking a lost Social Security check, helping a veteran receive disputed benefits, or finding a summer internship for a college student. Research has shown that if a House incumbent's staff helped to solve a problem for a constituent, that constituent rated the incumbent more favorably than constituents who were not assisted by the incumbent,[9] therefore providing the incumbent a great advantage over any challenger.

Most incumbents are highly visible in their districts and they enjoy an enormous financial advantage. They have easy access to local media, cut ribbons galore, attend important local funerals, and speak frequently at meetings and community events. Moreover, convenient schedules and generous travel allowances increase the local availability of incumbents. Nearly a fourth of the people in an average congressional district claim to have met their representative, and about half recognize their legislator's name without prompting. This visibility has an electoral payoff, as research shows district attentiveness is at least partly responsible for incumbents' electoral safety.[10]

Research also identifies an indirect advantage of incumbency: the ability of the office holder to fend off challenges from quality challengers, something scholars refer to as the "scare-off" effect.[11] Incumbents have the ability to scare off these opponents because of the institutional advantages of office such as high name recognition, large war chests, free constituent mailings, staffs attached to legislative offices, and overall experience in running a successful campaign. Potential strong challengers facing this initial uphill battle will often wait until the incumbent retires rather than challenge him or her (see Figure 12.2).[12]

WHY INCUMBENTS LOSE While most incumbents win reelection, in every election cycle some members of Congress lose their positions to challengers. Members lose their reelection bids for four major reasons: redistricting, scandals, presidential coattails, and mid-term elections.

At least every ten years, state legislators redraw congressional district lines to reflect population shifts, both in the state and in the nation at large. This political process may be used to secure incumbency advantage by creating "safe" seats for members of the majority party in the state legislature. But, it can also be used to punish incumbents in the out-of-power party. Some incumbents can be put in the same districts as other incumbents, or other representatives' base of political support can be weakened by adding territory favorable to the opposition party. The number of incumbents who actually lose their reelection bids because of redistricting is lessened by the strategic behavior of redistricted members—who often choose to retire rather than wage an expensive reelection battle.[13]

Modern scandals come in many varieties. Incumbents implicated in financial impropriety or by other forms of career-ending incidents typically do not lose reelections—because they simply choose to retire rather than face defeat.[14] For example,

FIGURE 12.2   WHAT ARE REELECTION RATES OVER THE YEARS?

With wide name recognition, and usually an insurmountable advantage in campaign cash, House incumbents typically have little trouble holding onto their seats. While incumbency still benefits Senators, it's not as reliable a margin as House races. Big swings in national mood can sometimes topple long-time office holders, as happened with the Reagan Revolution in 1980.

SOURCE: Data from the Center for Responsives Politics, www.opensecrets.org.

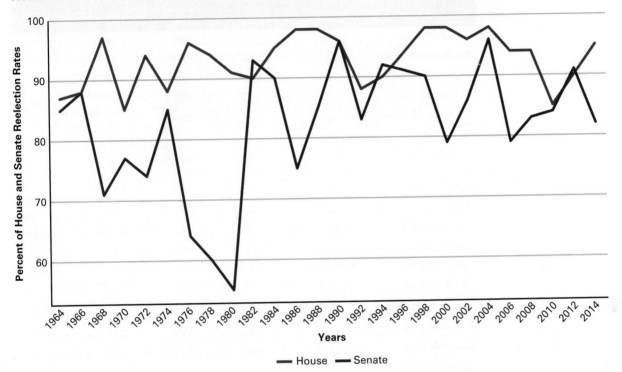

Representative Chaka Fattah (D-PA), resigned in 2016 after a federal jury convicted the 11-term congressman of twenty-two corruption charges related to repayment of an illegal $1 million campaign loan for his unsuccessful run for mayor of Philadelphia in 2007.

The defeat of a congressional incumbent can also occur as a result of **presidential coattails**. Successful presidential candidates usually carry into office congressional candidates of the same party in the year of their election. The strength of the coattail effect has, however, declined in modern times, as party identification has weakened and the powers and perks of incumbency have grown. Whereas Harry S Truman's party gained seventy-six House seats and nine additional Senate seats in 1948, **Barack Obama's** party gained only twenty-one House members and eight senators in 2008. The gains can be minimal, even in presidential landslide reelection years such as 1972 (Nixon) and 1984 (Reagan) (see Table 12.1).

Elections in the middle of presidential terms, called **mid-term elections**, present a threat to incumbents of the president's party. Just as the presidential party usually gains seats in presidential election years, it usually loses seats in off years. The problems and tribulations of governing normally cost a president some popularity, alienate key groups, or cause the public to want to send the president a message of one sort or another. An economic downturn or presidential scandal can underscore and expand this circumstance.

Voters also tend to punish the president's party much more severely in the sixth year of an eight-year presidency. After six years, voters are often restless for change. For example, in what many saw as a repudiation of President Obama's policies, the Republican Party increased its majority in the House of Representatives in the 2014 mid-term election to its highest total since the one it held after the 1928 election, netting at least a dozen additional House seats. Senate elections are less inclined than House elections to follow these off-year patterns. The idiosyncratic nature of Senate contests is due to their intermittent scheduling (only one-third of the seats come up

presidential coattails
When successful presidential candidates carry into office congressional candidates of the same party in the year of their election.

Barack Obama
The first African American president of the United States, a Democrat, who served as forty-fourth president from 2009 to 2017. Senator from Illinois from 2005 to 2008; member of the Illinois Senate from 1997 to 2004.

mid-term election
An election that takes place in the middle of a presidential term.

TABLE 12.1 HOW DOES THE PRESIDENT AFFECT CONGRESSIONAL ELECTIONS?

| Gain (+) or Loss (−) for President's Party | | | | | |
| President/Year | Presidential Election Years | | Mid-Term Election Years | | |
	House	Senate	Year	House	Senate
Truman (D): 1948	+76	+9	1950	−28	−5
Eisenhower (R): 1952	+24	+2	1954	−18	−1
Eisenhower (R): 1956	−2	0	1958	−47	−13
Kennedy (D): 1960	−20	−2	1962	−2	+4
L. Johnson (D): 1964	+38	+2	1966	−47	−3
Nixon (R): 1968	+7	+5	1970	−12	+1
Nixon (R): 1972	+13	−2	Ford (R): 1974	−48	−3
Carter (D): 1976	+2	0	1978	−15	−3
Reagan (R): 1980	+33	+12	1982	−26	−1
Reagan (R): 1984	+15	−2	1986	−5	−8
Bush (R): 1988	−3	−1	1990	−10	−1
Clinton (D): 1992	−10	0	1994	−52	−9[a]
Clinton (D): 1996	+10	−2	1998	+3	0
G. W. Bush (R): 2000	−2	−4	2002	+8	+2
G. W. Bush (R): 2004	+3	+4	2006	−30	−6
Obama (D): 2008	+21	+8	2010	−63	−6
Obama (D): 2012	+5	+2	2014	−9	−13
Trump (R): 2016	−6	−2 or −3			

[a]Includes the switch from Democrat to Republican of Alabama U.S. Senator Richard Shelby—one day after the election.
SOURCE: *Congressional Quarterly Guide to U.S. Elections*, 6th ed. Washington, DC: CQ Press: 2010. Updated by the authors.

for election every two years) and the existence of well-funded, well-known candidates who can sometimes swim against whatever political tide is rising. When you consider all the sixth year mid-term elections of two-term presidencies since World War II, the president's party has lost an average of five seats. However, in the 2014 mid-term election, President Obama's party lost more than the average, making the election look a lot like the sixth year of Ronald Reagan and George W. Bush.

RUNNING FOR OFFICE AND REACHING VOTERS

12.2 Outline how campaigns are organized, and evaluate methods for reaching voters.

Candidates are the center of political campaigns. While a candidate may not make all of the decisions, or even have the expertise or knowledge to handle the wide variety of issues and concerns that affect the campaign, it is ultimately the candidate's name that appears on the ballot. And, on Election Day, voters hold only the candidate truly accountable.

Candidates employ a wide variety of people to help them run an effective campaign. Most candidates for higher offices hire a campaign manager, finance chair, and communications staff. They may also contract the assistance of a variety of political consultants. In addition, candidates rely on networks of grassroots volunteers to spread the campaign's message and to get out the vote.

AMERICAN POLITICS IN COMPARATIVE PERSPECTIVE:

How Are Women Represented in National Legislatures?

Political candidates ultimately become lawmakers and policy makers. As a result, many states around the world have identified a need to make their candidate pools more representative of the country's population at large. One way of achieving this goal is by adopting quotas that mandate a certain percentage of candidates come from traditionally underrepresented groups such as women or ethnic or religious minorities. Examine the data below to consider whether candidate quotas translate into greater representation in government. This example focuses on women as candidates and members of the lower house of each country's legislature. Women still constitute only 22 percent of the members of parliaments around the world, but the use of electoral quotas for women is much more widespread than is commonly held. In fact, half of the countries of the world today use some type of electoral quota for their parliament.

FIGURE 12.3   HOW DOES U.S. GENDER REPRESENTATION COMPARE

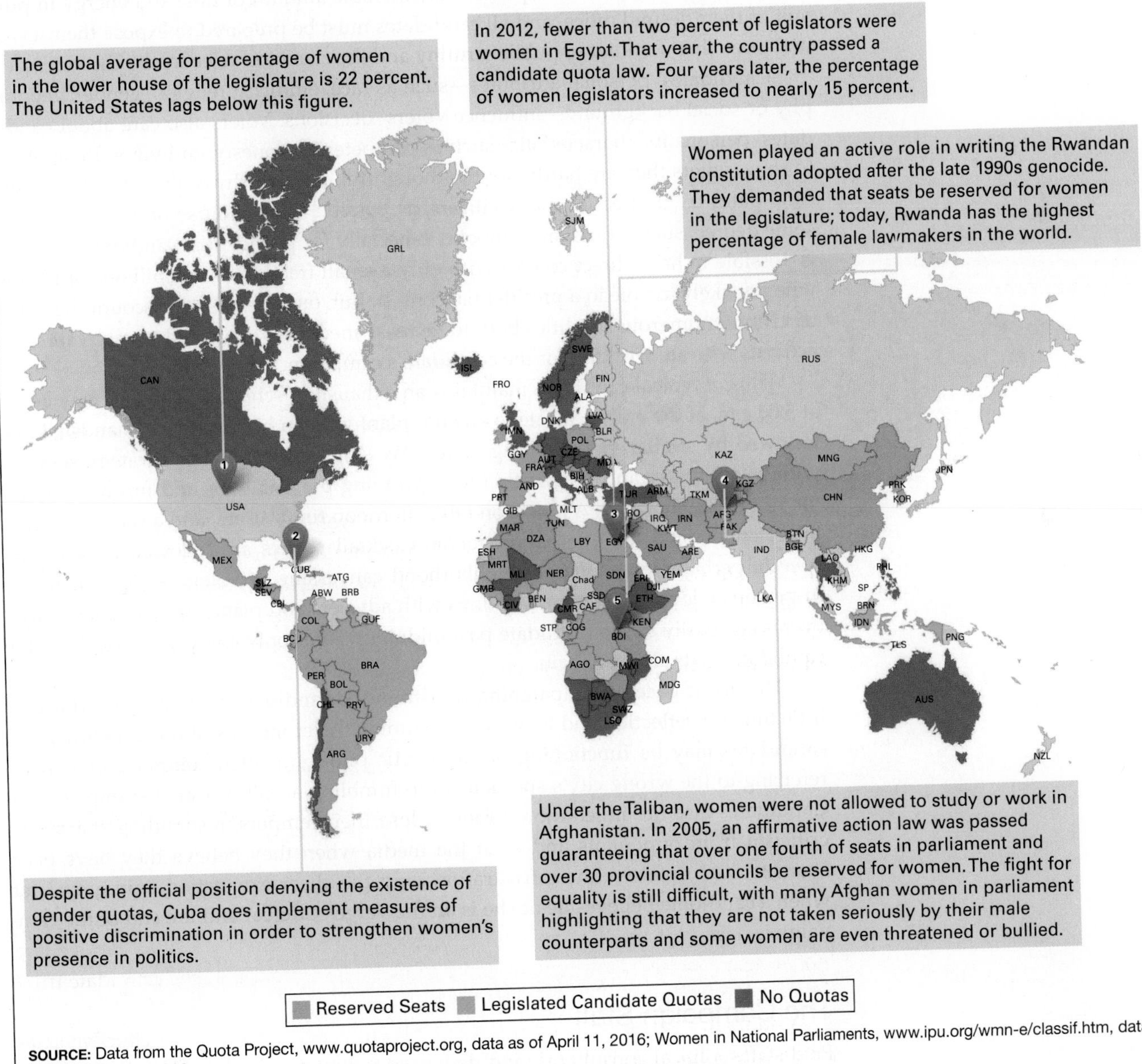

The global average for percentage of women in the lower house of the legislature is 22 percent. The United States lags below this figure.

In 2012, fewer than two percent of legislators were women in Egypt. That year, the country passed a candidate quota law. Four years later, the percentage of women legislators increased to nearly 15 percent.

Women played an active role in writing the Rwandan constitution adopted after the late 1990s genocide. They demanded that seats be reserved for women in the legislature; today, Rwanda has the highest percentage of female lawmakers in the world.

Despite the official position denying the existence of gender quotas, Cuba does implement measures of positive discrimination in order to strengthen women's presence in politics.

Under the Taliban, women were not allowed to study or work in Afghanistan. In 2005, an affirmative action law was passed guaranteeing that over one fourth of seats in parliament and over 30 provincial councils be reserved for women. The fight for equality is still difficult, with many Afghan women in parliament highlighting that they are not taken seriously by their male counterparts and some women are even threatened or bullied.

■ Reserved Seats   ■ Legislated Candidate Quotas   ■ No Quotas

SOURCE: Data from the Quota Project, www.quotaproject.org, data as of April 11, 2016; Women in National Parliaments, www.ipu.org/wmn-e/classif.htm, data as of February 1, 2016.

CRITICAL THINKING QUESTIONS:

1. Does there appear to be a relationship between quota laws and percentages of women in government?

2. In what ways can quotas contribute to the political empowerment of women? Under what conditions might they be effective or ineffective?

3. Should the United States adopt a law requiring that a certain percentage of political candidates be women? Why or why not?

The Candidate

Candidates run for office for any number of reasons, including personal ambition, the desire to promote ideological objectives or pursue specific public policies, or simply because they think they can do a better job than their opponents.[15] In any case, to be successful, candidates must spend a considerable amount of time and energy in pursuit of their desired office, and all candidates must be prepared to expose themselves and often their families to public scrutiny and the chance of rejection by the voters.

Candidates' personal attributes—such as race, ethnicity, religion, gender, geography or social background—influence voters' decisions. Voters also care about candidates' personality characteristics such as competence, honesty, and vigor. In an effort to show voters they are hardworking, thoughtful, and worthy of the office they seek, candidates try to meet as many citizens as possible in the course of a campaign. To some degree, such efforts are symbolic, especially for presidential candidates, since it is possible to have direct contact with only a small fraction of the millions of people who are likely to vote in a presidential contest. But, one should not discount the value of visiting numerous localities both to increase media coverage and to motivate local activists who are working for the candidate's campaign.

Thus, a typical candidate maintains an exhausting schedule. The day may begin at 5:00 a.m. at the entrance gate to an auto plant with an hour or two of handshaking, followed by similar glad-handing at subway stops until 9:00 a.m. Strategy sessions with key advisers and preparation for upcoming presentations and forums may fill the rest of the morning. A luncheon talk, afternoon fundraisers, and a series of media interviews crowd the afternoon agenda. Cocktail parties are followed by a dinner speech, perhaps telephone or neighborhood canvassing of voters, and an online or in-person civic forum or two. Meetings with advisers and planning for the next day's events can easily take a candidate past midnight. After only a few hours of sleep, the candidate starts all over again.

The hectic pace of campaigning can strain the candidate's family life and leaves little time for reflection and long-range planning. After months of this grueling pace, candidates may be functioning on automatic pilot and often commit gaffes, from referring to the wrong city's sports team to fumbling an oft-repeated stump speech. Candidates also are much more prone to lose their tempers, responding sharply to criticism from opponents and even the media when they believe they have been characterized unfairly. These frustrations and the sheer exhaustion only get worse when a candidate believes he or she is on the verge of defeat and the end of the campaign is near.

The Campaign Staff

Paid staff, political consultants, and dedicated volunteers work behind the scenes to support the candidate. Collectively, they plan general strategy, conduct polls, write speeches, craft the campaign's message, and design a communications plan to disseminate that message in the form of TV and digital advertisements, social media posts,

radio spots, Web sites, and direct mail pieces. Others are responsible for organizing fund-raising events, campaign rallies, and direct voter contacts.

It is important to note that the campaign staff varies significantly in size and nature, depending on the type of race. Presidential, senatorial, and gubernatorial races employ large professional staffs and a number of different consultants and pollsters. In contrast, races for state legislatures will likely have only a paid campaign manager and rely heavily on volunteer workers (see Figure 12.2).

A **campaign manager** runs nearly every campaign at the state and national level. The campaign manager travels with the candidate and coordinates the campaign. He or she is the person closest to the candidate who makes the essential day-to-day decisions, such as whom to hire and when to air TV, social media and radio advertisements. The campaign manager also helps to determine the campaign's overall strategy and works to keep the campaign on message throughout the race. Campaign managers can usually run only one campaign during a given election cycle, and he or she may be the only full-time employee of the campaign.

The major role of the **finance chair** is to coordinate the financial efforts of the campaign. This job includes raising money, keeping records of funds received and spent, and filing the required paperwork with the Federal Election Commission, the bureaucratic agency in charge of monitoring campaign activity. As the cost of campaigns has risen and fund-raising has become more important, the finance chair has also grown in prestige and significance. Although a volunteer accountant may fill the role of finance chair in state and local elections, candidates for most federal offices hire someone to fill this position.

A **communications director**, who develops the overall media strategy for the campaign, heads the communications staff. It is the communications director's job to stay apprised of newspaper, TV, radio, and digital coverage as well as supervise media consultants who craft campaign advertisements.

In many campaigns, the communications director works closely with the **press secretary**, who interacts and communicates with journalists on a daily basis and acts as the spokesperson for the campaign. It is the press secretary's job to be quoted in news coverage, to explain the candidate's issue positions, and to react to the actions of opposing candidates. He or she also has the job of delivering bad news and responding to attacks from opponents or interest groups.

campaign manager
The individual who travels with the candidate and coordinates the campaign.

finance chair
The infividual who coordinates the financial business of the campaign.

communications director
The person who develops the overall media strategy for the candidate.

press secretary
The individual charged with interacting and communicating with journalists on a daily basis.

FIGURE 12.4 HOW IS A CAMPAIGN STAFF ORGANIZED?

Presidential candidates have large staffs that help them run the day-to-day operations of their lengthy campaigns to be the chief executive of the United States. Among these officers are the campaign manager, finance chair, communications director, and a large number of professional political consultants.

SOURCES: Eric M. Appleman, Democracy in Action, www.p2016.org/trump/trumporggen.html; Ballotpedia, ballotpedia.org/Donald_Trump_presidential_campaign_key_staff_and_advisors,_2016.

Donald Trump's Campaign Organization

Management and Strategy
Executive Chairman: Steve Bannon
Campaign Manager: Kellyanne Conway
Adviser: Ivanka Trump (daughter)
Adviser: Jared Kushner (son-in-law)
Deputy Campaign Manager: David Bossie
Deputy Campaign Manager: Michael Glassner
National Political Director: Jim Murphy
Policy Director: John Mashburn
Director of Coalitions: Alan Cobb

Communications
Director of Social Media: Daniel Scavino
Digital Director: Brad Parscale
Communications Director: Hope Hicks
Director of New Media: Justin McConney
Senior Communications Adviser: Jason Miller
National Campaign Spokesperson: Katrina Pierson
Surrogate Strategy: Keith Nahigian
Senior Adviser for Battleground Communications: Susie Wiles
Director of Rapid Response: Steven Cheung

Outreach
Battleground States Director: Brian Jack
Director of African American outreach: Omarosa Manigault
Battleground States Coordinator: Molly Michael
National Field Director: Bill Stepien
Midwest Regional Political Director: Stephanie Milligan
Northeast Regional Political Director: Mike Rubino
National Field Coordinator: Matt Mowers
Congressional Liaison: Scott Mason

Finance
National Finance Chairman: Steven Mnuchin

Pollsters
Tony Fabrizio
Kellyanne Conway

Advisors
Informal Adviser: Roger Stone
Adviser: Dr. Ben Carson
Co-Chair and Policy Adviser: Sam Clovis
Senior Adviser: Sarah Huckabee Sanders
Senior Adviser: Michael Biundo
Transition Team Chairman: Gov. Chris Christie
National Security Advisory Council Chairman: U.S. Sen. Jeff Sessions

Data
Director of Data: Camilo Sandoval
Data: Witold Chrabaszcz

An increasingly significant part of the campaign's communications staff is the digital team, which manages the campaign's online communications, outreach, and fundraising. Members of the digital team are responsible for the candidates' social media presence, which is playing an increasingly important role in educating and mobilizing voters. They may organize online town hall forums or real-world meet-ups and grassroots events. They also act as important liaisons with the campaign's volunteers.

Campaign consultants are the private-sector professionals and firms who sell the technologies, services, and strategies many candidates need to get elected. The number of consultants has grown exponentially since they first appeared in the 1930s, and their specialties and responsibilities have increased accordingly.[16] Candidates generally hire specialized consultants who focus on only one or two areas, such as fund-raising, polling, media relations, Internet outreach, and speech writing. Media consultants, for example, design advertisements for distribution on TV, on social media and across the Internet, radio, billboards, and flyers.

Pollsters are campaign consultants who conduct public opinion surveys from a candidate's potential constituents. They are useful because they can tell a candidate where he or she stands relative to opponents or provide useful information about the issues and positions important to voters. Pollsters may also work with the media staff to gauge the potential impact of proposed social media, radio or TV advertisements.

Volunteers are the lifeblood of every national, state, and local campaign. Volunteers answer phone calls, staff candidate booths at festivals and county fairs, copy and distribute campaign literature, and serve as the public face of the campaign. Armed with apps that tell them which voters to target, they go door to door to solicit votes or use computerized telephone banks to call targeted voters with scripted messages, two basic methods of **voter canvass**. Most canvassing, or direct solicitation of support, takes place in the month before the election, when voters are most likely to be paying attention. Closer to Election Day, volunteers begin vital **get-out-the-vote (GOTV)** efforts, contacting supporters to encourage them to vote and arranging for their transportation to the polls if necessary. In recent years, the Internet, digital apps and social networking sites such as Facebook and Twitter have been important tools used by volunteers to get out the vote and energize supporters.

The Role of Conventions and Debates

With the rise of primaries as the means for nominating candidates, the national party conventions are not as important as they once were. However, conventions still serve to formally nominate the parties' candidates for president and vice president of the United States. The gatherings are also designed to engage the party faithful and energize them for the general election campaign.

campaign consultant
A private-sector professional who sells to a candidate the technologies, services, and strategies required to get that candidate elected.

pollster
A campaign consultant who conducts public opinion surveys.

voter canvass
The process by which a campaign reaches individual voters, either by door-to-door solicitation or by telephone.

get-out-the-vote (GOTV)
A push at the end of a political campaign to encourage supporters to go to the polls.

WHAT ROLE DO CAMPAIGN CONSULTANTS PLAY?

Campaign consultants are hired to help candidates focus on areas such as fund-raising, polling, media relations, Internet outreach, and speech writing. Pictured here are Clem Whitaker and Leone Baxter, a husband-and-wife team who together founded Campaigns, Inc., the nation's first public relations agency for political campaigns.

Bernie Sanders
Longest serving independent in the United States Congress. Ran against Hillary Clinton in the 2016 Democratic presidential primary; senator from Vermont since 2007; first elected to the House of Representatives in 1991.

Conventions also attempt to increase voters' interest in the upcoming contest, especially through media coverage of the presidential candidate's acceptance speech on the last night of the convention. The acceptance speech is particularly important because it is the first opportunity for the presidential candidate to address voters in the general electorate and showcase presidential qualities. The speech also outlines policies the candidate will focus on in the general election campaign. Candidates hope the speech will provide a boost, called a "bounce," in their opinion poll ratings. Recent scholarship has shown that it is around convention time when voter preferences are the most volatile and the party conventions play a major role in shuffling the electorate's vote choices. Thus, they do a good job of getting voter's attention sufficiently enough to change minds. But preferences harden nearly every year following the party conventions, with fewer voters changing their minds in the fall general campaign season.[17]

The first face-to-face presidential debate in U.S. history did not occur until 1960, and debates did not become a regular part of presidential campaigns until the 1980s. The last few elections have seen a rise in debates during the nominating process, with a staggering thirteen sanctioned debates among the Republican Party candidates seeking the 2016 nomination. The frequency not only matches a prime-time series, it also shares some of the same elements of a scripted show, including distinct personalities, drama, and in some cases, a dose of vitriol.

Candidates and their staffs recognize the importance of debates as a tool not only for consolidating their voter base but also for correcting misperceptions about the candidate's suitability for office. However, while candidates have complete control over what they say in debates, they cannot control what the news media will highlight and focus on after the debates. Media coverage can benefit some candidates more than others, as it did for Donald Trump and **Bernie Sanders** in during the nominating contest debates. And, even though candidates prepare themselves by rehearsing their responses, they cannot avoid the perils of spontaneity. For example, President Gerald R. Ford's erroneous insistence during an October 1976 debate with Jimmy Carter that Poland was not under Soviet domination (when in fact it was) may have cost him in a close election. In most cases, however, debates do not alter the results of an election, but rather increase knowledge about the candidates and their respective personalities and issue positions, especially among voters who had not previously paid attention to the campaign. Scholars have also shown that presidential debates can polarize partisan attitudes by reinforcing their existing beliefs.

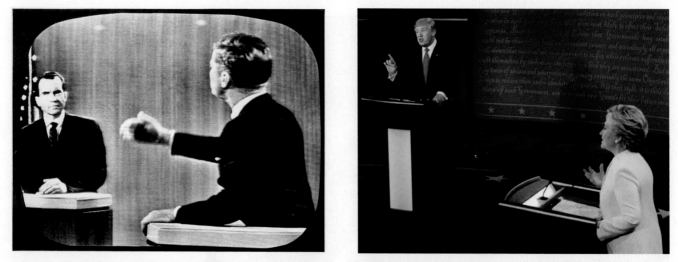

HOW DO PRESIDENTIAL DEBATES MATTER?
We know from extant research and from polling that debates have a limited effect on vote choice and on voting intention. Most people who watch the debates have already made up their mind about the candidates. However, debates do play an important role in providing information on candidates and in rousing citizens to vote. Debates can also have a polarizing effect by reinforcing the existing beliefs of viewers. Pictured left, Richard M. Nixon and John F. Kennedy debate in the first televised debate. Pictured right, Donald J. Trump and Hillary R. Clinton debate in 2016.

The Role of Media

Both traditional news media, including newspapers, magazines, radio and television, and digital media, including content on the Internet, blogs and social media, are central intermediaries between candidates and the public. The media play a large role in determining what voters actually see and hear about the candidate. Both traditional and digital media can be very difficult for a campaign to control. Campaigns, however, have a great deal of control over the content they disseminate directly to followers on social media and include in their campaign advertisements.

In the modern campaign, innovation is the name of the game and candidates are always experimenting with new ways of communicating with the public. The rise of radio advertising in the 1920s replaced handbills and door-to-door canvassing. In the 1960s, television replaced radio. Cable television and new marketing strategies in the 1980s and 1990s (especially the rise of robo-calling and focus groups) allowed candidates to use media to target specific constituencies and demographics. The great innovation of President Obama's campaigns is that they combined digital tools with old-style grassroots organizing, which resulted in a massive communications and fundraising network, in what came to be termed a "netroots campaign."

Contemporary campaigns have an impressive new array of communications weapons at their disposal to gather and disseminate information more quickly and effectively than ever: faster printing technologies, reliable databases, instantaneous digital publishing and mass e-mail, social media sites, autodialed pre-recorded messages, and enhanced telecommunications and teleconferencing. Social media provides constant public access to candidates in a way that dwarfs all previous communications forms between candidates and the public.

During campaign season, the news media constantly report political news. In an age dominated by social media and greater media fragmentation, reporters have less control over setting the agenda of what they report than in previous eras. Reporters are frequently in the position of reacting to what the candidates and campaigns do and say (at all hours of the day). Ultimately, what they report is largely based on news editors' decisions of what is newsworthy or "fit to print." The press often reports what candidates are doing, such as giving speeches, holding fundraisers, meeting with party leaders, or posting and interacting on social media. Reporters may also investigate rumors of a candidate's misdeeds or unflattering personal history, such as run-ins with the law, alleged use of drugs, or alleged sexual improprieties.

Although this free media attention may help candidates increase their name recognition, it may prove frustrating for campaigns, which do not control the content of the coverage. For example, studies have shown that reporters are obsessed with the horse-race aspect of politics—who is ahead, who is behind, and who is gaining—to the detriment of the candidates' issues and ideas. Public opinion polls, especially tracking polls, many of them taken by news outlets, dominate coverage. This horse-race coverage can have an effect on how the public views the candidates. Using poll data, journalists often predict the margins by which they expect contenders to win or lose. A projected margin of victory of 5 percentage points can be judged a setback if the candidate had been expected to win by 12 or 15 points. The tone of the media coverage, that a candidate is either gaining or losing support in polls, can also affect whether people decide to give money and other types of support to a candidate.[18]

Candidates and their media consultants use various strategies in an effort to obtain favorable press coverage. These strategies include seeking to isolate the candidate from the press, staging media events, putting forward the most favorable interpretation for the candidate (and the most negative for their opponent), and circumventing traditional media by appearing on talk shows such as *The Tonight Show with Jimmy Fallon*, *Ellen*, or *Between Two Ferns* with Zach Galifianakis.

positive ad
Advertising on behalf of a candidate that stresses the candidate's qualifications, family, and issue positions, with no direct reference to the opponent.

negative ad
Advertising on behalf of a candidate that attacks the opponent's character or platform.

contrast ad
Ad that compares the records and proposals of the candidates, with a bias toward the candidate sponsoring the ad.

inoculation ad
Advertising that attempts to counteract an anticipated attack from the opposition before the attack is launched.

HOW DO NEGATIVE ADS AFFECT CAMPAIGNS?

Negative attack ads are important part of the rough and tumble of the democratic election process. Recent scholarship has shown that negative ads can stimulate voter interest and enrich the information environment available for voters. Pictured here is an image of then-Senator John Kerry windsurfing during a vacation in 2004, which was used in one of the more memorable attack ads that year. The ad was intended to convey the message that Kerry could not be trusted, that he blew with the political winds. The ad simultaneously showed a lifestyle that was out of touch with regular voters.

As a result of the rise of digital media, candidates have both a greater ability to influence the news cycle and they can employ "rapid-response" techniques, including formulating prompt and informed responses to changing events on the campaign trail. In response to breaking news of a scandal or issue, for example, candidates can conduct background research, implement an opinion poll and tabulate the results, devise a containment strategy and appropriate spin, and deliver a reply. This capability contrasts strongly with techniques used in earlier campaigns, which took much longer to prepare and had little of the flexibility enjoyed by the contemporary digital campaign.[19]

Campaigns also use social media, including Facebook, Twitter, Instagram, Pinterest and Snapchat, as well smartphone technology to target specific demographics who might be sympathetic or engaged constituencies and provide them with appropriate messages and advertisements in the hopes that they might be mobilized to vote. [20] Although these sites have been effective in reaching the politically engaged, how effective they will be in inspiring new demographic groups to become engaged in electoral politics remains to be seen.[21]

CAMPAIGN ADVERTISEMENTS Campaign ads may take a number of different forms and appear in a range of communications platforms - from television to direct mail to digital platforms. While the bulk of paid advertising is still spent on television ads (estimated $2.4 billion in 2016), there is a clear shift toward more targeted digital advertising (as much as $1 billion in 2016, a 576 percent growth over 2012). **Positive ads** stress the candidate's qualifications, family, and issue positions with no direct reference to the opponent. The incumbent candidate usually favors positive ads. **Negative ads** attack the opponent's character or platform. And, with the exception of the candidate's brief, legally required statement that he or she approved the ad, a negative ad may not even mention the candidate who is paying for the airing. **Contrast ads** compare the records and proposals of the candidates, with a bias toward the candidate sponsoring the ad.

Although the number of negative advertisements has increased dramatically during the past two decades, negative advertisements have been a part of American campaigns almost since the nation's founding. In 1796, Federalists portrayed losing presidential candidate Thomas Jefferson as an atheist and a coward. In Jefferson's second bid for the presidency in 1800, Federalists again attacked him, this time spreading a rumor that he was dead. The effects of negative advertising are well documented. Rather than voting *for* a candidate, voters frequently vote *against* a candidate by voting for the opponent, and negative ads can provide the critical justification for such a decision.

Before the 1980s, well-known incumbents usually ignored negative attacks from their challengers, believing that the proper stance was to rise above the fray. But, after some well-publicized defeats of incumbents in the early 1980s in which negative TV advertising played a prominent role,[22] incumbents began attacking their challengers in earnest. The new rule of politics became "An attack unanswered is an attack agreed to." In a further attempt to stave off criticisms from challengers, incumbents began anticipating the substance of their opponents' attacks and airing **inoculation ads** early in the campaign to protect themselves in advance from the other side's spots. Inoculation advertising attempts to counteract an anticipated attack from the opposition before such an attack is launched. For example, a senator who fears a broadside about her voting record on veterans' issues might air advertisements that feature veterans or their families in praise of her support.

CAMPAIGN FINANCE AND REFORM

12.3 Evaluate the influence of money in elections and the main approaches to campaign finance reform.

Successful campaigns require a great deal of money. In 2016, for example, some $1.74 billion was raised by the Democratic and Republican Parties. Presidential candidates raised more than $1.3 billion in additional support for their campaigns. And, candidates for the Senate raised some $684.5 million, while candidates for the House raised nearly $1 billion.[23]

Efforts to regulate campaign spending are nothing new. They are also far from settled. As spending from individuals, political parties, political action committees (PACs) and Super PACs, and other sources continues to rise, it is likely that calls for reform will also continue.

Regulating Campaign Finance

The United States has struggled to regulate campaign spending for well over one hundred years. One early attempt to regulate the way candidates raise campaign resources was enacted in 1883, when Congress passed civil service reform legislation that prohibited solicitation of political funds from federal workers, attempting to halt a corrupt and long-held practice. In 1907, the Tillman Act prohibited corporations from making direct contributions to candidates for federal office. The Corrupt Practices Acts (1910, 1911, and 1925), Hatch Act (1939), and Taft-Hartley Act (1947) all attempted to regulate the manner in which federal candidates finance their campaigns and, to some extent, limit the corrupting influence of campaign spending.

Congress did not enact serious, broad campaign finance regulation, however, until the 1970s, in the wake of the Watergate scandal. The **Federal Election Campaign Act (FECA)** and its amendments established disclosure requirements; the Presidential Public Funding Program provided partial public funding for presidential candidates who meet certain criteria; and the **Federal Election Commission (FEC)**, an independent federal agency, was created to enforce the nation's election laws. Although these provisions altered the campaign landscape, by 2002, it became clear that they were insufficient to regulate ever-increasing campaign expenditures in the United States. Under the leadership of Senators John McCain (R–AZ) and Russell Feingold (D–WI), Congress enacted and President George W. Bush signed into law a new set of campaign finance regulations known as the **Bipartisan Campaign Reform Act (BCRA)** (see Table 12.2).

BCRA regulates political advertising and funding. The act, as it was originally passed, limited the broadcast of issue advocacy ads within thirty days of a primary election and sixty days of a general election, and set hard limits on campaign contributions from a number of sources, including individuals, political parties, political action committees, and members of Congress. Opponents of BCRA, including Senator Mitch McConnell (R–KY) and the National Rifle Association, wasted little time in challenging its limits as an infringement on their right to free speech. In a 2003 decision, the Supreme Court maintained that the government's interest in preventing corruption overrides the free speech rights and upheld restrictions on individual expenditures.[24]

The Supreme Court has, however, declared other sections of BCRA unconstitutional. In 2007, for example, the Court held that the thirty- and sixty-day limits placed on issue advocacy ads were unconstitutional, thus opening the door to these

Federal Election Campaign Act (FECA)
Passed in 1971, this is the primary law that regulates political campaign spending and fundraising. The law originally focused on increased disclosure of contributions for federal campaigns.

Federal Election Commission (FEC)
An independent regulatory agency founded in 1975 by the United States Congress to regulate the campaign finance legislation in the United States.

Bipartisan Campaign Reform Act (BCRA)
Passed in 2002, this act amended the Federal Election Campaign Act of 1971 with several provisions designed to end the use of nonfederal, or "soft money" (money raised outside the limits and prohibitions of federal campaign finance law) for activity affecting federal elections.

TABLE 12.2   WHAT ARE THE CONTRIBUTION LIMITS FOR THE 2015-2016 FEDERAL ELECTIONS?

	To each candidate or candidate committee per election	To each PAC	To state, district & local party committee per calendar year	To national party committee per calendar year	Additional national party committee accounts
Individual may give	$2,700*	$5,000	$10,000 (combined limit)	$33,400* per year	$100,200* per account per year
Authorized Campaign Committee may give	$2,000	$5,000	No limit	No limit	
PAC (multicandidate) may give	$5,000	$5,000	$5,000 (combined limit)	$15,000 per year	$45,000 per account per year
PAC (not multicandidate) may give	$2,700	$5,000	$10,000 (combined limit)	$33,400* per year	$100,200* per account per year
State, District & Local Party Committee may give	$5,000	$5,000	No limit	No limit	
National Party Committee May Give	$5,000 †	$5,000	No limit	No limit	

SOURCE: Federal Election Commission, www.fec.gov. *Indexed for inflation in odd-numbered years. †Additionally, a national party committee and its Senatorial campaign committee may contribute up to $46,800 combined per campaign to each Senate candidate.

Citizens United v. FEC
The 2010 U.S. Supreme Court case that enabled corporations and unions have the same political speech rights as individuals under the First Amendment. As part of this ruling, the Supreme Court found that the government may not prohibit corporations or unions from using their general treasury funds to support or denounce political candidates in elections.

McCutcheon v. FEC
The 2014 Supreme Court ruling that declared Section 441 of the Federal Election Campaign Act (FECA) unconstitutional. Section 441 imposed limits on any individual's total political contributions (to federal candidates, parties, or political action committees) in a two-year period.

electioneering communications throughout the election cycle.[25] And, in 2008, the Court overturned another provision of the act that had attempted to limit the amount of a candidate's own money that could be spent on running for office.[26] More recently, in 2010, the Court handed down a decision in *Citizens United v. FEC* that declared unconstitutional BCRA's ban on electioneering communications made by corporations and unions.[27] This decision struck a significant blow to BCRA's provisions and has had a dramatic effect on the power of interest groups and corporations in campaigns and elections. As a result of these rulings, campaign spending surpassed all recent records, with spending reaching approximately $7 billion on the 2016 election. In *McCutcheon v. FEC* (2014), the Supreme Court struck down the aggregate limits on the amount of money individuals may contribute to all federal candidates, parties, and political action committees combined. Although the ruling maintained the federal campaign limits that restrict how much a donor can give to any one candidate or to any one party committee, it paved the way for increased influence of individual donors in campaigns and elections. It has also allowed candidates and parties to create huge joint fundraising committees.

The cumulative result of these decisions—and the Supreme Court's willingness to equate money with speech—has been to effectively gut campaign finance law in the United States. Though limits still exist on individuals' expenditures to parties and candidates, independent expenditures, or funds spent to advocate for the election of a candidate without coordinating with that candidate's campaign committee, are virtually unlimited. To date, efforts to advance further campaign finance reforms have met with little success in Congress.

Sources of Campaign Funding

As mentioned previously, the Bipartisan Campaign Reform Act regulates campaign contributions from a number of sources, including individuals, political parties, members of Congress, personal savings, and political action committees. The Federal Election Commission regulates, records, and discloses these expenditures. The FEC also monitors infractions of campaign finance rules and acts as a quasi-judicial arbiter of conflicts.

BCRA and more recent judicial interpretations of the law have also opened the door to a number of other actors in political campaigns. Immediately following enactment of the law, 527 political committees became active in the campaign process. Following the Supreme Court's 2007 actions to lift the limits on issue advocacy ads, 501(c) groups increased their role in electoral politics. Since the *Citizens*

WHAT ROLE DO INDIVIDUAL DONORS PLAY IN CAMPAIGN FINANCING?
Although individual contributions are limited under the BCRA, thanks to the rise of Super PACs, unlimited sums can flow from individuals and corporations to the efforts supporting candidates. More than one-fifth of the $1 billion donated to help Hillary Clinton's bid was given by just 100 wealthy individuals, many with a long-history of contributing to the Clintons. The top five donors together contributed one out of every $17 for her 2016 run. Pictured here, billionaire businessman and top contributor Haim Saban hugs Hillary Clinton after the third presidential debate.

United decision, super PACs have become important players in elections, and joint individual-party fundraising committees played a greater role in 2016 following the *McCutcheon* v. *FEC* decision.

INDIVIDUALS   Individual contributions are donations from independent citizens. The maximum allowable contribution under federal law for congressional and presidential elections was $2,700 per election to each candidate in 2015–2016, with primary and general elections considered separately. As previously noted, following the 2014 Supreme Court decision in *McCutcheon* v. *FEC*, individuals were no longer limited in the total amount they could donate to all candidates, political action committees, and parties combined per two-year election cycle. However, individuals still may not write unlimited checks to their favorite candidate. Most candidates receive a majority of all funds directly from individuals. In one recent election, researchers found that individual donors accounted for 60 percent of contributions to candidates for the House of Representatives, 75 percent of contributions to candidates for the Senate, and 85 percent of contributions to presidential candidates.[28] During the 2016 election, Donald Trump raised more than $100 million from nearly two million small-dollar contributions, shattering the small-dollar donation record of previous Republican nominees.[29]

POLITICAL PARTIES   As a result of the 2014 *McCutcheon* v. *FEC* decision and an expansion of party fundraising slipped into an appropriations bill later that year, the parties have been able to vastly increase their top donor levels by pooling numerous accounts and affiliates together into joint fundraising committees. For example, Republicans launched a partnership called the Trump Victory Fund that took donations of up to $449,400 to be split between the Trump campaign, the Republican National Committee (RNC) and 11 state parties. An individual donor who gives the maximum to both the Trump Victory Fund and the RNC's most-elite donor program could contribute as much as $783,400 during the election cycle. A similar partnership was established among Hillary Clinton's campaign, a 32-state joint fundraising committee and the Democratic National Committee. An individual donor giving to the joint fund and a fund for the Democratic National Committee's top-tier convention package could give more than $1.1 million during the election cycle to support Clinton's campaign and the party.[30]

political action committee (PAC)
Officially recognized fund-raising organizations that represent interest groups and are allowed by federal law to make contributions directly to candidates' campaigns.

527 political committee
Organizations created with the primary purpose of influencing electoral outcomes; the term is typically applied only to freestanding interest groups that do not explicitly advocate for the election of a candidate.

In 2016, the Republican and Democratic Parties raised some $1.74 billion. Candidates receive substantial donations from the national and state committees of the Democratic and Republican Parties. Under the current rules, national parties can give up to $5,000 per election to a House candidate and $46,800 to a Senate candidate. In competitive races, the parties may provide almost 20 percent of their candidates' total campaign funds.

PERSONAL SAVINGS   The U.S. Supreme Court ruled in *Buckley* v. *Valeo* (1976) that no limit could be placed on the amount of money candidates can spend from their own families' resources, since such spending is considered a First Amendment right of free speech.[31] For wealthy politicians, this allowance may mean personal spending in the millions. In the 2016 presidential race, Donald Trump personally put more than $56 million in loans and contributions into his campaign. However, Trump sought outside cash for the general election. In 2016, six senate candidates self-funded a primary or general election campaign, though none were successful. All but one of the candidates spent more than $1 million of their personal savings, including Napoleon Harris (D-IL), who spent $2.1 million in a primary election campaign he lost. Nineteen candidates for the House of Representatives self-funded a campaign, including David Trone (D-MD), who spent more than $9.9 million in a primary contest he lost. Nine of the House candidates spent more than $1 million and all of them spent more than $500,000 of their personal savings.

POLITICAL ACTION COMMITTEES (PACS)   **Political action committees (PACs)** are officially recognized fund-raising organizations allowed by federal law to make contributions directly to candidates' campaigns. A wide variety of groups, including labor unions, corporations, trade unions, ideological issue groups, and even members of Congress seeking to build their party's membership in Congress, may create them. Under current rules, a multicandidate PAC can give no more than $5,000 per candidate per election, and $15,000 each year to each of the national party committees.

Although a good number of PACs of all persuasions existed prior to the 1970s, it was during the 1970s—the decade of campaign finance reform—that the modern PAC era began. PACs grew in number from 113 in 1972 to a peak of 4,268 in 1988. Today, approximately 5,800 PACs are registered with the FEC. Since Watergate-era campaign reforms, the number of corporate PACs has increased from 89 in 1974 to 1,677 to July 2015, but union PACs have only grown from 201 to 277 in the same time period. These political committees have historically played a major role, particularly in congressional elections. During the 2016 election, PACs raised some $1.9 billion, and gave some $450.4 million of that to candidates. Approximately $270.3 million of these funds went to Republican candidates, while $179.5 million of these funds went to Democratic candidates. (see Figure 12.6).[32]

PACs remain one of the most controversial parts of the campaign financing process. Some observers claim that PACs are the embodiment of corrupt special interests that use campaign donations to buy the votes of legislators. Studies, in fact, have confirmed this suspicion. PACs effectively use contributions to punish legislators and affect policy, at least in the short run.[33] Legislators who vote contrary to the wishes of a PAC see their donations withheld, but those who are successful in legislating as the PAC wishes gain the reward of even greater donations.[34]

527 POLITICAL COMMITTEES   Named for the section of the tax code from which they draw their name, **527 political committees** are organizations created with the primary purpose of influencing electoral outcomes. Although 527s technically include candidate campaign committees and party committees, the term is typically applied only to freestanding interest groups that do not explicitly advocate for the election of a candidate. Many unions and partisan organizations such as the College Republican National Committee have formed 527s.

527s are subject to very limited government regulation. The Federal Election Commission monitors the contributions given to these groups. However, no limits are

FIGURE 12.5   HOW DO SUPER PACS ALLOCATE THEIR CAMPAIGN CONTRIBUTIONS?

The rise of Super PACs followed the July 2010 federal court decision known as *SpeechNow.org* v. *Federal Election Commission*. Super PACs may raise unlimited sums of money from corporations, unions, associations and individuals. They can also spend unlimited sums to overtly advocate for or against political candidates, though they may not directly donate to candidates and they are not supposed to coordinate efforts with the candidates they support.

SOURCE: Data from the Center for Responsive Politics, www.opensecrets.org/pacs.

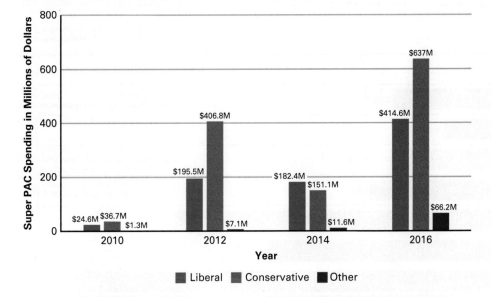

set on how much an individual or other organization may contribute or on how much a group may spend on electoral activities. During the 2016 campaign, 527 groups spent approximately $113.8 million, favoring Democratic candidates two-to-one.[35]

501 (C) GROUPS   **501(c) groups** are interest groups whose primary purpose is not electoral politics. Federal rules, in fact, mandate that no more than half of a 501(c) group's budget be spent on campaign politics. Like 527s, they take their name from the section of the tax code under which they are established. These groups first became significantly involved in electoral politics after the Supreme Court lifted BCRA's ban on issue advocacy. Thus, most of their electoral activity focuses on raising awareness of candidates' positions on issues of interest to the group.

These groups are not required to disclose the source of their donations. However, they spend significant sums of money on campaigns. In the 2016 election cycle, 501(c) groups spent roughly as much as did 527s. Unlike 527s, however, most of these contributions favored Republican candidates. Examples of notable 501(c) groups include American Values Action and the America's Not Stupid both of which lean Republican, and many state chapters of Planned Parenthood, which tend to lean Democratic in their contributions.[36]

SUPER PACS   The fastest-growing and arguably most significant external actor in elections, **super PACs** are a special kind of political action committee established to make **independent expenditures**, or spending for campaign activity that is not coordinated with a candidate's campaign. Unlike traditional PACs, they may not give money directly to candidates or party committees. However, they may advocate on behalf of candidates.

Though Super PACs must disclose the sources of their contributions to the FEC, they may take money from any person or organization interested in influencing the political process. They also are not subject to contribution or expenditure limits, which was abundantly clear in the 2016 elections. Super PACs spent more than $594 million on the 2016 presidential election, with a larger percentage going to Hillary Clinton by a three-to-one ratio. SuperPACs also played an important role during the 2016 presidential primary. Some half of the reported money in the primary elections came from donations

501(c) group
Interest groups whose primary purpose is not electoral politics.

super PAC
Political action committees established to make independent expenditures.

independent expenditures
Spending for campaign activity that is not coordinated with a candidate's campaign.

FIGURE 12.6 HOW HAS CAMPAIGN FINANCING CHANGED OVER TIME?

Campaign financing has changed dramatically in the last ten years. Following the passage of the Bipartisan Campaign Reform Act (BCRA) in 2002, some expenditures traditionally used in political campaigns were outlawed. But subsequent interpretations of BCRA by the Supreme Court opened the door for other forms of money to play increasingly large roles in the political process. The rise of super PACs has been one such change. These political action committees have come under a great deal of fire in the last two presidential elections because of the unlimited sums of money they raised and spent from wealthy donors, potentially silencing the voices of average citizens.

SOURCE: Data from the Center of Responsive Politics, www.opensecrets.org.

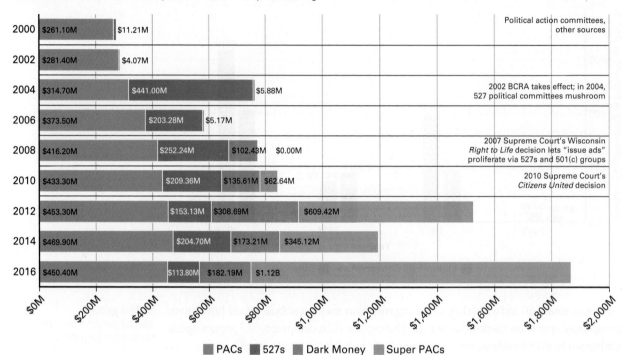

public funds
Donations from general tax revenues to the campaigns of qualifying presidential candidates.

matching funds
Donations to presidential campaigns whereby every dollar raised from individuals in amounts less than $251 is matched by the federal treasury.

to groups outside the candidates' campaigns, like Super PACs, that are not subject to limits. In 2016, groups with a conservative viewpoint outspent groups with a liberal one.

Public Funds

Public funds are donations from general tax revenues to the campaigns of qualifying candidates. On the federal level, only presidential candidates are eligible to receive public funds, although in recent years, few candidates have chosen to accept them. Some states also offer public funds to qualifying individuals running for particular offices, especially within the judiciary.

A candidate for president can become eligible to receive public funds during the nomination campaign by raising at least $5,000 in individual contributions of $250 or less in each of twenty states. The candidate can then apply for federal **matching funds**, whereby every dollar raised from individuals in amounts less than $251 is matched by the federal treasury on a dollar-for-dollar basis. Of course, this assumes the Presidential Election Campaign Fund has enough money to do so. Taxpayers who designate $3 of their taxes for this purpose each year when they send in their federal tax returns provide the money for the fund. (Only about 20 percent of taxpayers check off the appropriate box, even though participation does not increase their tax burden.)

During the general election campaign, the presidential nominee of each major party may become eligible for a public grant of $20 million (plus a cost-of-living adjustment) for campaigning in the general election. To be eligible to receive the public funds, the candidate must limit spending to the amount of the grant and may not accept private contributions for the campaign.[37] A candidate may refuse the money and be free from the spending cap the government attaches to it. In 2008, Barack Obama was the first presidential candidate to opt out of the public financing system. Now, nearly all major-party candidates choose not to accept the public funding in favor of raising unrestricted amounts of private donations. This trend will likely continue into the future.

Minor party candidates are also eligible for public financing in the general election. The amount of public funding to which a minor party candidate is entitled is based on the ratio of the party's popular vote in the preceding presidential election to the average popular vote of the two major party candidates in that election. A new party candidate receives partial public funding after the election if he/she receives 5 percent or more of the vote.

PATTERNS IN VOTER TURNOUT AND CHOICE

12.4 Analyze the factors that influence voter turnout and voter choice.

The act of voting is the most common form of **conventional political participation**, or activism that attempts to influence the political process through commonly accepted forms of persuasion. Other examples of conventional political participation include writing letters and making campaign contributions. Citizens may also engage in **unconventional political participation**, or activism that attempts to influence the political process through unusual or extreme measures. Examples include participating in protests, boycotts, and picketing.

Turnout refers to the proportion of the voting-age public that casts a ballot. Generally, voter turnout is much higher in years of presidential elections, around 50 or 60 percent, than for midterm elections, around 40 to 45 percent of the eligible electorate.

A number of factors influence citizens' choices about which candidate to support and whether or not they will turn out on Election Day. Party affiliation stands at the forefront of predictors for vote choice, but issues and policy preferences and the candidates' personal attributes also influence voters' decisions. Who turns out is important because politicians listen to those who vote. There are some demographic characteristics that are strong predictors of voter turnout, the most important of which are age, residential mobility and education. To a lesser extent, race, ethnicity, gender, civic engagement and interest in politics matter.

Party Identification and Ideology

Party identification remains the most powerful predictor of vote choice. Stated simply, self-described Democrats tend to vote for Democratic candidates and self-described Republicans tend to vote for Republican candidates. This trend is particularly obvious in less visible elections, where voters may not know anything about the candidates and need a cue to help them cast their ballot. However, even in presidential elections, a high correlation exists between voter choice and party affiliation. In 2016, for example, 89 percent of self-identified Democrats voted for Hillary Clinton, and 90 percent of self-identified Republicans voted for Donald Trump.

There are different views about what party identification means, though these different understandings are not necessarily exclusive of each other. One view of party identification can be understood as a psychological attachment to a party. In this view, individuals learn about politics from parents, other adults, peers, and they develop an attachment to a party as part of that socialization process. A second view of party identification is that individuals have a running tally of experience with political leaders and representatives, especially the presidents of each party. As a result of how a president and other members of his party in office performed on issues like the economy or foreign affairs, individuals raise or lower their assessment of the president's party's ability to govern. Individuals

conventional political partici-pation
Activism that attempts to influence the political process through commonly accepted forms of persuasion such as voting or letter writing.

unconventional political participation
Activism that attempts to influence the political process through unusual or extreme measures, such as protests, boycotts, and picketing.

turnout
The proportion of the voting-age public that casts a ballot.

update their beliefs about whether that party can run the government competently or has the right approach to achieve outcomes desired by the public.

A third view of party attachment emphasizes voters' underlying ideologies and policy positions. Ideology represents one of the most significant divisions in contemporary American politics. Liberals, generally speaking, favor government involvement in social programs and are committed to the ideals of tolerance and social justice. Conservatives, on the other hand, are dedicated to the ideals of individualism and market-based competition, and they tend to view government as a necessary evil rather than an agent of social improvement. Moderates lie somewhere between liberals and conservatives on the ideological spectrum; they favor conservative positions on some issues and liberal positions on others.

The ideological alignment of voters and parties has shifted over the last two decades. Not surprisingly, ideology is very closely related to vote choice. Liberals tend to vote for Democrats, and conservatives tend to vote for Republicans. In 2016, 84 percent of self-described liberals voted for Hillary Clinton, whereas only 10 percent voted for Trump. Conservatives, on the other hand, voted for Trump over Clinton at a rate of 81 to 15 percent.[38]

Income and Education

Scholars have found that citizens who vote tend to have higher incomes than non-voters. For example, in 2012, turnout among those making $100,000 or more per year was 77 percent and those making $50,000 to $75,000 was 68 percent, while only about half of those making $30,000 or less turned out to vote. Recent analysis has also shown that the correlation among income and voting is different among liberal and conservative states. In richer, liberal states such as New York and California, there is essentially no correlation between income and voting—rich and poor vote the same way—while in conservative states such as Texas, the rich are much more Republican than the poor. Scholars have also linked higher income inequality within states to lower voter turnout and also to a stronger Democratic vote. Those who are more affluent typically have more education and a professional career in which they have developed skills that are also useful in politics. The more affluent also have social networks that encourage participation and they can be more easily reached by those seeking to mobilize them.

All other things being equal, college graduates are much more likely to vote than those with less education, and people with advanced degrees are the most likely to vote. People with more education tend to learn more about politics, are less hindered by registration requirements, and are more self-confident about their ability to affect public life.[39] Those without a high school degree tend to vote at half the rate of those with a college education.

Although turnout rates are not fully available for 2016, there is some exit polling data about vote choice among groups. Those making *less* than $50,000 per year voted for Clinton by a margin of 52 percent to 41 percent for President Trump, while those making *more* than $50,000 per year voted for Trump by a margin of 49 percent to 47 percent for Clinton. With regard to education, 52 percent of those with at least a college degree voted for Clinton compared to 43 percent for Trump; 52 percent of those without a college degree voted for Trump and 44 percent voted for Clinton.

Race and Ethnicity

Historically, African Americans and other minorities have faced voting barriers in the United States, especially in areas of the Deep South. For example, in the wake of Reconstruction, the southern states made voter registration extremely difficult for African Americans, and only a small percentage of the eligible African American population was registered throughout the South until the 1960s. The Voting Rights Act (VRA) of 1965 helped change this situation by targeting states that once used literacy or morality tests or poll taxes to exclude minorities from the polls. As a result of the VRA and other civil rights reforms, turnout among African Americans has increased

FIGURE 12.7   HOW HAS THE RACIAL AND ETHNIC COMPOSITION OF VOTERS CHANGED?

Although white Americans continue to constitute a majority of the U.S. electorate, black, Hispanic, and Asian voters have accounted for significant percentages of the electorate during recent campaigns. This diversity alters both the voices heard from the voting booth and the demands placed on government.

SOURCE: Data from Pew Research Center and CNN.com.

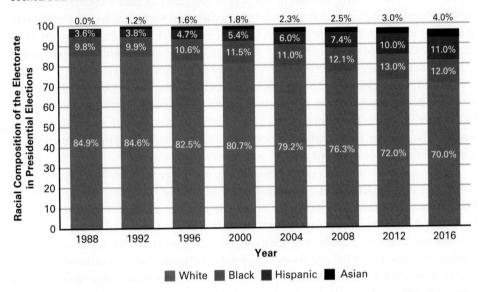

dramatically. Since 2004, Whites and African Americans have turned out at virtually the same rates. However, Hispanics, and other minority groups have turned out at lower rates—by about 20 percentage points lower.

For minorities, there are still many barriers to voting because many such groups tend to be poorer and have less formal education than whites. As a result, one recent survey found, Blacks and Hispanics were three times as likely as whites to not have requisite identification and to have difficulty finding the correct polling place. They were also more than three times as likely as whites to not receive a requested absentee ballots, and roughly twice as likely to be out of town on Election Day or to have to wait in long lines. They were also substantially more likely than whites to report transportation problems, and bad time and location as reasons for not getting to the polls.

While whites have shown an increasing tendency to vote Republican, African American voters remain overwhelmingly Democratic in their voting decisions. Despite the best efforts of the Republican Party to garner African American support, this pattern shows no signs of waning. In 2016, 88 percent of African Americans voted for Hillary Clinton, while Donald Trump received a mere 8 percent of the African American vote.[40]

The Hispanic community in the United States is now slightly larger than the African American community; thus, Hispanics have the potential to wield enormous political power. In California, Texas, Florida, Illinois, and New York, five key electoral states, Hispanic voters have emerged as powerful allies for candidates seeking office. Moreover, their increasing presence in New Mexico, Arizona, Colorado, and Nevada has forced candidates of both parties to place more emphasis on issues that affect Hispanics. Hispanics also are likely to identify with and vote for Democrats, although not as monolithically as African Americans.

Asian and Pacific Island Americans are more variable in their voting than either the Hispanic or the African American community. The considerable political diversity within this group is worth noting: Chinese Americans tend to prefer Democratic candidates, but older Vietnamese Americans, with strong anti-communist leanings, tend to support Republicans. A typical voting split for the Asian and Pacific Island

American community runs about 65 percent Democratic and 35 percent Republican, though it can reach the extreme of a 50–50 split, depending on the election.[41]

Gender and Age

With passage of the Nineteenth Amendment in 1920, women gained the right to vote in the United States. While early polling numbers are not reliable enough to shed light on the voting rate among women in the period immediately following ratification of the Nineteenth Amendment, it is generally accepted that women voted at a lower rate than men. Recent polls suggest that today women vote at a slightly higher rate than their male counterparts. Since women constitute slightly more than 50 percent of the U.S. population, they now account for a majority of the American electorate.

Since 1980, the gender gap—the difference between the voting choices of men and women—has become a staple of American politics. The gender gap (discussed further in Chapter 11) varies considerably from election to election, though normally women support the average Democrat 5 to 7 percent more than men. In 2016, Clinton won 54 percent of the female vote, but only 41 percent of the male vote.[42]

A strong correlation also exists between age and voter turnout. The Twenty-Sixth Amendment to the Constitution, ratified in 1971, lowered the voting age to eighteen. While this amendment obviously increased the number of eligible voters, it did so by enfranchising the group that is least likely to vote. A much higher percentage of citizens age thirty and older vote than citizens younger than thirty, although voter turnout decreases over the age of seventy, primarily due to the difficulties some older voters experience in getting to their polling locations. Regrettably, only about 50 percent of eligible eighteen- to twenty-nine-year-olds are even registered to vote.[43] The most plausible reason is that younger people are more mobile. Because voter registration is not automatic, people who relocate have to make an effort to register. As young people settle down in a community, the likelihood that they will vote increases.[44]

Religious Groups and Civic Organizations

People who frequently attend church or other religious services and individuals who are members of civic organizations, trade and professional organizations, and labor unions are more likely to vote and participate in politics than those who are not members of these or similar types of groups. Many of these organizations emphasize

HOW DOES GENDER INFLUENCE ELECTORAL OUTCOMES?

The gender gap is one of the most powerful and consistent patterns in American elections. While Hillary Clinton held an advantage in support among women, the gender gap was not as wide as many predicted it might be in 2016, and in fact the gender gap was not greater than it was 2012.

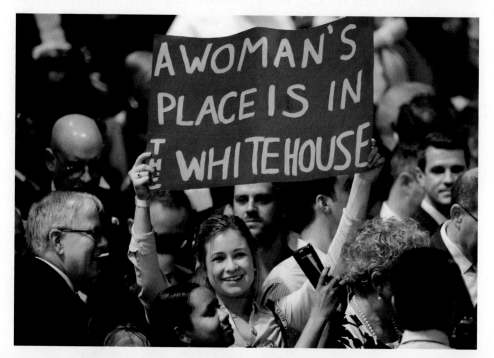

community involvement, which often encourages voting and exposes members to requests for support from political parties and candidates. These groups also encourage participation by providing opportunities for members to develop organizational and communication skills relevant to political activity. Religious groups have tended to vote in distinct patterns, but some of these traditional differences have declined considerably in recent years (see Chapter 11).

A person's reported level of interest in government and public affairs in the single most important individual-factor affecting whether a person participates in the electoral process. Individuals also vary substantially in how much they know about politics and political knowledge is a powerful predictor of voting, on par with formal education.

Issues

Individual issues can have important effects in any given election year. Voters have preferences for the types of policies or outcomes they would like the government to pursue, and they choose the candidates and parties that they think will produce the best results. Candidates seek to make salient certain issues in any given election and to define those issues in ways that will serve their interests. Different issues matter in any given election and voters differ in how they weigh the issues. While the economy tends to be identified by voters as the most important issue, social issues, foreign affairs and national security are also important.

Voters tend to reward the party in government, usually the president's party, during good economic times and punish that party during periods of economic downturn. When this occurs, the electorate is exercising **retrospective judgment**; that is, voters are rendering judgment on the party in power based on past performance on particular issues. At other times, voters might use **prospective judgment**; that is, they vote based on what a candidate pledges to do about an issue if elected. The 2016 election provides an example of how both retrospective and prospective judgments helped voters reach their ballot decisions. Voters who were relatively satisfied with how the Obama administration handled the economy and healthcare, for example, used retrospective judgment to bolster their support for Hillary Clinton, while voters who expressed concern about immigration and trade used prospective judgment to bolster their support for Donald Trump.

The candidates' personal attributes and characteristics also affect voters' decisions. In general, voters prefer candidates who are closer to them on characteristics like race, ethnicity, religion, gender, geography and social background. The candidates' personality and leadership traits also matter, though not as much in an era of partisan polarization. In one Gallup study, the leadership strengths most highly correlated with likely voters were ability to inspire, care for individuals, vision, and courage.

retrospective judgment
A voter's evaluation of a candidate based on past performance on a particular issue.

prospective judgment
A voter's evaluation of a candidate based on what he or she pledges to do about an issue if elected.

TOWARD REFORM: MENDING THE ELECTORAL PROCESS

12.5 Evaluate concerns with the electoral process and proposed reforms to address them.

Political observers and citizens alike have expressed numerous concerns with the electoral process—from the excessive length of campaigns, to the growing costs and ways in which campaigns are financed, to the almost irrational methods we employ to choose presidential nominees and the archaic way in which the Electoral College functions. Inspiring citizens to turn out to vote in this winner-take-all electoral system is particularly challenging. The following sections discuss the concerns with, and potential remedies for, the electoral process.

Frontloading

One of the concerns with the way in which we nominate presidential candidates is the incoherent organization of primaries and caucuses that requires candidates to make

FIGURE 12.8 WHEN DO STATES CHOOSE THEIR NOMINEE FOR PRESIDENT?

These pie graphs show when Republican Party caucuses and primary elections were held in 1976 and 2016. The trend toward front-loading is evident. In 2016, for example, most states held their primaries and caucuses in March; in comparison, in 1976, most states held their nominating contests in May.

SOURCE: Joshua T. Putnam, frontloading.blogspot.com.

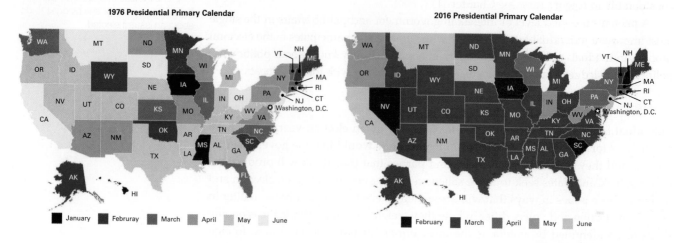

front-loading
The tendency of states to choose an early date on the nomination calendar.

mad-dash attempts to move around the country. The system leaves little time between primaries for midcourse corrections in the selection of nominees. The nominations process has been altered even more in recent times by **front-loading**, the tendency of states to choose an early date on the nomination calendar (see Figure 12.8). This trend is hardly surprising, given the added press emphasis on the first contests and the voters' desire to cast their ballots before the competition is decided. Front-loading has contributed to the elongation of the presidential campaign and a front-loaded schedule generally benefits the front-runner, since opponents have little time to turn the contest around once they fall behind. Furthermore, although online fund-raising has emerged as a means to soften the advantage of a large campaign fund going into a primary battle, front-loading advantages the candidate who wins the "invisible primary," that is, the one who can raise the bulk of the money (as well as also garner party endorsements and respect from various gatekeepers) *before* the nomination season begins, though not the case for Republicans in 2016. Once primaries and caucuses begin, less opportunity is available to raise money to finance campaign efforts simultaneously in many states.

Electoral College

While there hasn't been an Electoral College crisis since 1888, following the 2016 presidential election, many political observers suggested that the system of electing a president be reformed. Similarly, throughout the 2000 presidential campaign, many analysts foresaw that the election would likely be the closest since the 1960 race between John F. Kennedy and Richard M. Nixon. The election was so close that George W. Bush, who lost the popular vote, was not officially declared the Electoral College winner for more than five weeks after Election Day following the Supreme Court's controversial decision in *Bush* v. *Gore* (2000) that stopped a recount of votes cast in Florida.

Some observers have suggested using a national popular vote to choose the president. While this is the most democratic reform, it is least likely to be enacted, given that the U.S. Constitution would have to be amended to abolish the Electoral College. It is unlikely that the Senate, which serves as the bastion of equal representation for all states, regardless of population, would ever pass such an amendment. Another proposed reform is known as the congressional district plan. This plan would retain the Electoral College but give each candidate one electoral vote for each congressional district that he or she wins in a state, and the winner of the overall popular vote in each state would receive two bonus votes (one for each senator) for that state. Maine and Nebraska currently use the congressional district plan.

Although this reform could be adopted without a constitutional amendment, under the congressional district plan, the winner of the popular vote might still lose the presidency. In addition, this reform might further politicize the congressional redistricting process as parties would seek to maximize the number of safe electoral districts for their presidential nominee while minimizing the number of competitive districts. Finally, although candidates might not ignore entire states, they would quickly learn to focus their campaigning on competitive districts while ignoring secure districts, thereby eliminating some of the democratizing effects of such a reform.

Improving Voter Participation

Inspiring citizens to turn out is particularly important because of the winner-take-all electoral system, yet voter turnout is quite low in the United States. Nonparticipation may be rooted in something as complicated as an individual's political philosophy or something as simple as the weather—voter turnout tends to be lower on rainy Election Days. Some voters are alienated, and others are just plain apathetic, possibly because of a lack of pressing issues in a particular year, satisfaction with the status quo, or uncompetitive elections. Furthermore, many citizens may be turned off by the quality of campaigns in a time when petty issues and personal mudslinging are more prevalent than ever.

Reformers have proposed many ideas to increase voter turnout in the United States. Always on the list is raising the political awareness of young citizens, a reform that inevitably must involve our nation's schools. The rise in formal education levels among Americans has had a significant effect on voter turnout.[45] No less important, and perhaps simpler to achieve, are institutional reforms such as making Election Day a national holiday, easing constraints on voter registration, allowing mail and online voting, modernizing the ballot, and strengthening political parties.

REGISTRATION   A major reason for lack of participation in the United States remains the relatively low percentage of the adult population that is registered to vote. Requiring citizens to take the initiative to register is an American invention; nearly every other democratic country places the burden of registration on the government rather than on the individual. Thus, the cost (in terms of time and effort) of registering to vote is higher in the United States than in other industrialized democracies.

Registration laws vary by state, but in most states, people must register prior to Election Day. Thirty one states plus the District of Columbia now allow voters to register online. Although some critics have expressed concerns about the security of this process, it has proved an effective way to increase registration. In Arizona, the first state to implement the online option in 2003, voter registration increased by almost 10 percent as a result of the law.[46] Another way to increase registration would be to allow voters to register on the same day as the election. Among the fourteen states that permit Election Day registration, turnout is generally higher.[47] Better yet, all U.S. citizens could be registered automatically at the age of eighteen. Critics, however, argue that such automatic registration could breed even greater voter apathy and complacency.

VOTING   Stringent ballot access laws are another factor affecting voter turnout in the United States. Voters in thirty-three states, for example, must provide some form of identification to cast a ballot (see Figure 12.9). In thirteen of these states, that identification must include a photo. Though supporters charge that voter identification laws are simply intended to prevent voter fraud, opponents argue that this legislation may disproportionately limit the ballot access of a number of groups, including women, racial and ethnic minorities, the poor, the elderly, and the disabled.[48] As a

TABLE 12.3   HOW DO STATES REGULATE VOTER ELIGIBILITY?

Restrict felons' ability to vote after completion of their sentence	12 states
Allow incarcerated felons to vote from prison	2 states
Require all voters to show some form of identification to vote	32 states
Require all voters to show photo identification to vote	17 states
Require no voter registration	1 state
Allow Election Day registration	13 states and D.C.*
Require voters to register to vote at least 28 days prior to an election	19 states and D.C.
Allow no-excuse absentee balloting	27 states and D.C.
Allow early voting	34 states and D.C.

Although the right to vote is a fundamental right, it is not absolute. States regulate the right to vote and establish criteria that voters must meet before they can participate in elections. Such criteria include residence, age, citizenship, and non-felon status. They also may be able to establish other participation criteria.

SOURCE: Pew Center on the States, www.pewcenteronthestates.org , National Council on State Legislatures, www.ncsl.org, and CIRCLE, www.civicyouth.org. *Hawaii's same day registration will not be implemented until 2018 and Vermont's not until 2017. All numbers as of October 2016.

result of concerns about their constitutionality, courts continue to review these laws in many states.

Citizens who plan to be out of state on Election Day or who are physically unable to go to the polls may also face challenges in casting an absentee ballot. Many states, for instance, require citizens to apply in person for absentee ballots, a burdensome requirement given that a person's inability to be present in his or her home state is often the reason for absentee balloting in the first place. Recent literature in political science links liberalized absentee voting rules and higher turnout.[49]

There are a number of institutional ways by which the barriers to voting might be reduced. Some reformers have proposed that Election Day should be a national holiday to eliminate the busy workday as an obstacle to voting. Early voting is another attempt to make voting more convenient for citizens who may have other commitments on Election Day. Thirty-three states (largely in the West, Midwest, and South) and the District of Columbia currently allow voters to engage in the practice, and several additional states allow voters with a valid excuse to cast a ballot early. Early voting allows citizens to cast their ballot up to a month before the election—the time frame varies by state—either by mail or at a designated polling location. Many citizens have found early voting to be a preferable way to cast their ballot; during the 2016 election, approximately 40 percent of eligible voters took advantage of early voting.

Critics of early voting, however, charge that the method decreases the importance of the campaign. They also fear that voters who cast early ballots may later come to regret their choices. It is possible, for example, that a voter could change his or her mind after hearing new information about candidates just prior to Election Day, or that a voter could cast a ballot for a candidate who subsequently withdraws from the race.

Reformers have also proposed several ways that citizens could vote from their own homes. For example, citizens of Colorado, Oregon, Washington, and some California counties vote almost entirely by mail-in ballots. These systems have been credited with increasing voter turnout rates in those states. But, voting by mail has its downside: concerns about social pressure, decreased ballot security and increased potential for fraud with mail-in elections. Another problem is that it may delay election results as the Board of Elections waits to receive all ballots.

Internet voting may be a more instantaneous way to tally votes. Some states, including Arizona and Michigan, have already experimented with using this method to cast ballots in primary elections. In addition, military members and their families from thirty-two states and Washington, D.C., used Internet voting to cast absentee ballots in the 2012 elections.[50] However, Internet voting booths have been slow to catch on with the general public because many voters are wary of the security of this method and worry about online hackers and an inability to prevent voter fraud. Other observers fear that an all-online system could unintentionally disenfranchise poor voters, who may be less likely to have access to an Internet connection.

As a result of the **Help America Vote Act (HAVA)**, which the federal government enacted in the wake of the 2000 election when the outcome of the presidential election in Florida, and by extension the nation, hinged on "hanging chads," states and localities have made significant upgrades to the types of ballots they use. Traditional, hand-counted, paper ballots are now used in fewer than 10 percent of jurisdictions. In thirty-two states, citizens mark paper ballots, but their votes are computer tabulated. In another eleven states, and large percentages of other states, voting is entirely electronic, often done on touch-screen voting machines.[51] States have also experimented with other new technologies for casting ballots. In Oregon, for example, disabled residents were able to vote with iPads; several other states are exploring expanded use of this technology.[52]

Supporters of electronic voting believe that training poll workers, administrators, and voters on how to effectively use the new equipment is vital. Critics maintain that lack of a paper trail leaves electronic machines vulnerable to fraud and worry that the machines could crash during an election. Still other critics cite the expense of the machines. All, however, agree that updating election equipment and ensuring fair elections across the country should be a legislative priority.

STRENGTHEN POLITICAL PARTIES Political parties today are not as effective as they once were in mobilizing voters, ensuring they are registered, and getting them to the polls. The parties at one time were grassroots organizations that forged strong party–group links with their supporters. Today, candidate- and issue-centered campaigns and the growth of expansive party bureaucracies have resulted in somewhat more distant parties with which fewer people identify very strongly. While efforts have been made in recent elections to bolster the influence of parties—in particular, through sophisticated get-out-the-vote efforts—the parties' modern grassroots activities still pale in comparison to their earlier efforts.

Reformers have long argued that strengthening political parties would increase voter turnout, because parties have historically been the most successful at mobilizing citizens to vote in the United States. During the late 1800s and early 1900s, the country's "Golden Age" of powerful political parties, one of their primary activities was getting out the vote on Election Day. Even today, the parties' Election Day get-out-the-vote drives increase voter turnout by several million people in national contests. The challenge is how to go about enacting reforms that strengthen parties. One way would be to allow political parties to raise and spend greater sums of money during the campaign process. Such a reform, however, raises ethical questions about the role and influence of money in politics. Another potential change would be to enact broader systemic reforms that allow for a multiparty system and facilitate greater party competition. But, these reforms would be very difficult to pass into law.

Ultimately, the solution to ensuring greater voter turnout may lie in encouraging the parties to enhance their get-out-the-vote efforts beyond their existing partisan bases. Additional voter education programs, too, may show voters what is at stake in elections and thereby inspire higher turnout in future elections.

Help America Vote Act (HAVA)
A federal law passed in 2002 that addresses issues of voting systems and voter access that were identified following the 2000 election. It established minimum election administration standards for states and units of local government with responsibility for the administration of federal elections and for other purposes related to the bill.

Roots of American Elections

12.1 Compare and contrast presidential and congressional elections, and explain the incumbency advantage.

Elections in the United States are of four major types: primary elections, general elections, initiatives and referenda, and recall elections. The parties select presidential candidates through either primary elections or caucuses, with the primary process culminating in each party's national convention, after which the general election campaign begins. The American political system uses indirect electoral representation in the form of the Electoral College. In congressional elections, incumbents have a strong advantage over their challengers because of staff support, the visibility they get from being in office, and the "scare-off" effect. Redistricting, scandals, presidential coattails, and mid-term elections serve as countervailing forces to the incumbency advantage and are the main sources of turnover in Congress.

Running for Office and Reaching Voters

12.2 Outline how campaigns are organized, and evaluate methods for reaching voters.

Candidates rely on a campaign manager, professional staff, and political consultants to coordinate the strategy and message of his or her campaign. Volunteer support is also particularly important for mobilizing citizens and getting out the vote. Candidates and campaigns rely on traditional media coverage, news media coverage, and paid campaign advertisements for reaching voters. The national party convention and presidential debates also serve as forums for reaching voters.

Campaign Finance and Reform

12.3 Evaluate the influence of money in elections and the main approaches to campaign finance reform.

Since the 1970s, campaign financing has been governed by the terms of the Federal Election Campaign Act (FECA). This act was amended in 2002 by the Bipartisan Campaign Reform Act (BCRA). BCRA regulates political advertising and funding from a number of sources from which campaigns raise money. In 2010, the Supreme Court, in *Citizens United* v. *FEC* declared unconstitutional BCRA's ban on electioneering communications made by corporations and unions, opening the way for an increase in the power of interest groups and corporations in campaigns and elections. Sources of campaign funding include political parties, individuals, personal savings, Political Action Committees (PACs), 527 Political Committees, 501(c) groups, super PACs, and public funds.

Patterns in Voter Choice

12.4 Analyze the factors that influence voter turnout and voter choice.

A number of factors influence citizens' choices about which candidate to support and whether or not they will turn out on Election Day. Party affiliation, issues and the candidates' characteristics and traits all influence voter choice. Factors that influence voter turnout include age, education, race and ethnicity, gender, civic engagement and interest in politics.

Toward Reform: Mending the Electoral Process

12.5 Evaluate concerns with the electoral process and proposed reforms to address them.

Political observers and citizens alike have expressed numerous concerns with the electoral process. The incoherent organization of primaries and caucuses is compounded by frontloading. Furthermore, the archaic way in which the Electoral College functions might be updated by instituting a national popular vote or a congressional district plan. Inspiring voters is also challenging when they face difficulty registering to vote, difficulty voting, and a weakened connection to the political parties. Suggestions for improving voter turnout include making Election Day a holiday, enabling early voting, allowing for mail and online voting, making the registration process easier, modernizing the ballot, and strengthening political parties. Each of these suggested reforms has both pros and cons.

LEARN THE TERMS

501(c) group
527 political committees
Barack Obama
Bernie Sanders
Bipartisan Campaign Reform Act
  (BCRA)
campaign consultant
campaign manager
Citizens United v. *FEC*
closed primary
communications director
Contrast ad
conventional political participation
crossover voting
Donald J. Trump
elector
electorate
Electorate College

Federal Election Campaign Act (FECA)
Federal Election Commission (FEC)
finance chair
front-loading
general election
get-out-the-vote (GOTV)
Help America Vote Act (HAVA)
Hillary R. Clinton
incumbency
independent expenditures
initiative
inoculation ad
mandate
matching funds
McCutcheon v. *FEC*
mid-term election
Negative ad
open primary

political action committee (PAC)
Pollster
Positive ad
presidential coattails
press secretary
primary election
prospective judgment
public funds
reapportionment
recall
referendum
retrospective judgment
runoff primary
super PAC
turnout
Thomas Jefferson
unconventional political participation
voter canvass

HOW DOES THE MEDIA ACT AS INTERMEDIARY BETWEEN CITIZENS AND GOVERNMENT?

The Internet, smartphones, and social media have transformed many aspects of Americans' lives—and politics is no exception. The newspaper, once the lifeblood of American democracy, was supplanted by TV news in the 1960s. Today, digital media is gaining rapidly, even outpacing TV among the youngest Americans. As former Speaker of the House Newt Gingrich noted, digital media allowed President Donald Trump to bypass the traditional news media and directly reach and engage 13 to 14 million people during his presidential campaign. How have political leaders harnessed digital media for campaign organizing and fundraising, in addition to keeping in touch with their constituents and public opinion?

THE NEWS MEDIA

LEARNING OBJECTIVES

13.1 Describe the structure and the functions of the media, past and present.

13.2 Assess the influence of the media on American politics.

13.3 Analyze the impact of the media on public opinion and political behavior.

13.4 Summarize the ethical standards and federal regulations that govern the news media.

13.5 Describe the effect of recent trends in the news media on political outcomes.

Campaign canvassing and fund-raising? There's an app for that. Counting electoral votes? There's an app for that. Aggregating, sharing, and organizing political news? There's an app for that, too. The Internet, smartphones, and social media have transformed many aspects of Americans' lives—and politics is no exception. Gone are the days of the weekly, and even daily, news cycle. Today, political news is happening—and being reported—almost instantaneously. No longer do newspaper publishers have to typeset every individual letter, as they did in the earliest days of the republic. No longer do journalists file daily reports to be aired on the nightly news, well after a campaign event has occurred. Instead, reporters, not to mention campaign staff, volunteers and supporters, can post live Facebook, Twitter, Snapchat and Instagram updates, complete with photos and video, as a campaign event is occurring.

Even the way citizens consume their news has changed. The newspaper, once the lifeblood of American democracy, was supplanted by TV news in the 1960s. Today, TV is still a popular news source for all Americans, but the majority of Americans across generations now combine a mix of sources and technologies to get their news. Social media is becoming an important tool for people from all generations to get news, but it is not the only one, even for younger generations. Furthermore, social media seems to be adding to, rather than replacing, other ways that people get their news.[1]

These changes in the production and consumption of news have affected the way newsmakers organize their public relations strategies and staffs. From state and local candidates to Congressional candidates to presidential candidates, websites and social media accounts have become a necessity for political leaders to stay in touch with their constituents, to discourse with the media and other political elites, and to monitor public opinion. And, with the advent of narrowcasting and infotainment, political leaders can choose to appear in a greater variety of venues than ever before.

While these changes result in many positives for American democracy and may serve to engage traditionally underserved populations, they also can have negative consequences. The growth of media sources and platforms that cater to partisan audiences may polarize the segment of the population tuning in, contributing to more extreme attitudes among those most engaged in politics. Meanwhile, the growth of choices has allowed broad swaths of the public to avoid political conversations altogether and find something more agreeable, like sports or entertainment. And, moving from professional journalists publishing on clear deadlines to a free-for-all world of nearly constant updates may weaken the media's traditional watchdog role and adherence to journalistic standards.

• • •

The Framers agreed that a free press was necessary to monitor government and ensure the continuation of a democratic society, a tenet they codified in the First Amendment to the U.S. Constitution. Throughout history, the press has fulfilled this watchdog role, acting as an intermediary between citizens and their government. The news media inform the public, giving citizens the information they need to choose their leaders and influence the direction of public policy. As this chapter will discuss, the way the media interact with and report on these political leaders can also significantly influence individuals' views of political issues.

The news media's impact on American politics is so important that it has often been called the "fourth estate," a term harkening back to the British Parliament and implying an integral role for the press in government. This so-called fourth estate comprises a variety of entities, from traditional local news outlets to growing media corporations, and, increasingly, social media and average citizens. It is evident in all facets of American life, from morning newspapers to nightly comedy news shows to Tweets, Snapchats, and Facebook posts.

Though the form of the news media has changed significantly since our nation's founding, the media's informational and watchdog roles remain. This chapter traces

mass media
The entire array of organizations through which information is collected and disseminated to the general public.

news media
Media providing the public with new information about subjects of public interest.

the development of the news media in the United States, explores recent developments affecting the media, and considers how these changes influence politics and government.

ROOTS OF THE NEWS MEDIA IN THE UNITED STATES

13.1 Describe the structure and the functions of the media, past and present.

The **mass media**—the entire array of organizations through which information is collected and disseminated to the general public—have become a colossal enterprise in the United States. The mass media include print sources, movies, TV, radio, and Internet-based material. Collectively, the mass media use broadcast, cable, satellite, and broadband technologies to distribute information that reaches every corner of the United States and the world. A powerful tool for both entertaining and educating the public, they reflect American society but are also the primary lens through which citizens view American culture and politics. The **news media**, one component of the larger mass media, provide new information about subjects of public interest and play a vital role in the political process.[2] Although often referred to as a large, impersonal whole, the media are made up of diverse personalities and institutions, and they form a spectrum of opinion. Through the various outlets composing the news media—from newspapers to social media sites—journalists inform the public, influence public opinion, and affect the direction of public policy in our democratic society.

Throughout American history, technological advances have had a major impact on the way in which Americans receive their news. High-speed presses and more cheaply produced paper made mass-circulation daily newspapers possible. The telegraph and then the telephone enabled easier and much faster newsgathering. When radio became widely available in the 1920s, millions of Americans could hear national politicians instead of merely reading about them. With TV—first introduced in the late 1940s, and nearly a universal fixture in U.S. homes by the early 1960s—citizens could see and hear political candidates and presidents. Now, with the rise of the Internet and mobile digital platforms, access to information has once again changed form. Never before has information been more widely available, and never have the lines between news producer and consumer been less clear.

Print Media

The first example of news media in America took the form of newspapers, which were published in the colonies as early as 1690. The number of newspapers grew throughout the 1700s, as colonists began to realize the value of a press free from government oversight and censorship. The battle between Federalists and Anti-federalists over ratification of the Constitution played out in various partisan newspapers in the late eighteenth century. Thus, it came as no surprise that one of the Anti-federalists' demands was a constitutional amendment guaranteeing freedom of the press.

The partisan press eventually gave way to the penny press. In 1833, Benjamin Day founded the *New York Sun*, which cost a penny at the newsstand. Beyond its low price, the *Sun* sought to expand its audience by freeing itself from the grip of a single political party. Inexpensive and politically independent, the *Sun* was the forerunner of modern newspapers, which relied on mass circulation and commercial advertising to produce profit. By 1861, the penny press had so supplanted partisan papers that President Abraham Lincoln announced his administration would have no favored or sponsored newspaper.

Although the print media were becoming less partisan, they were not necessarily gaining in respectability. Mass-circulation dailies sought wide readership, attracting customers with the sensational and the scandalous. The sordid side of politics became

DID THE PRACTICE OF YELLOW JOURNALISM CONTRIBUTE TO THE RISE OF OBJECTIVE JOURNALISM?

In this 1898 cartoon titled "Uncle Sam's Next Campaign—the War Against the Yellow Press," yellow journalism is attacked for its threats, insults, filth, grime, blood, death, slander, gore, and blackmail. The cartoon was published in the wake of the Spanish-American War, and the cartoonist suggests that, having won the war abroad, the government ought to attack yellow journalists at home.

the entertainment of the times. One of the best-known examples occurred in the presidential campaign of 1884, when the *Buffalo Evening Telegraph* headlined "A Terrible Tale" about Grover Cleveland, the Democratic nominee.[3] The story alleged that Cleveland, an unmarried man, had fathered a child in 1871, while sheriff of Buffalo, New York. Even though paternity was indeterminate because the child's mother had been seeing other men, Cleveland willingly accepted responsibility, since all the other men were married, and he dutifully paid child support for years. The strict Victorian moral code that dominated American values at the time made the story even more shocking than it would be today. Fortunately for Cleveland, another newspaper, the *Democratic Sentinel*, broke a story that helped offset this scandal: The first child of Republican presidential nominee James G. Blaine and his wife had been born just three months after their wedding.

Throughout the nineteenth century, payoffs to the press were common. Andrew Jackson, for instance, gave one in ten of his early appointments to loyal reporters.[4] During the 1872 presidential campaign, the Republicans slipped cash to about 300 newsmen.[5] Wealthy industrialists also sometimes purchased investigative cease-fires for tens of thousands of dollars.

In the late 1800s and early 1900s, prominent publishers such as William Randolph Hearst and Joseph Pulitzer expanded the reach of newspapers in their control by practicing what became pejoratively known as **yellow journalism**, perhaps because both Hearst and Pulitzer published a popular cartoon of the era called "The Yellow Kid." Yellow journalism featured pictures, comics, color, and sensationalized news coverage. These innovations were designed to increase readership and capture a share of the burgeoning immigrant population.

The Progressive movement gave rise to a new type of journalism in the early 1900s. **Muckraking** journalists—so named by President Theodore Roosevelt after a special rake designed to collect manure—devoted themselves to exposing misconduct by government, business, and individual politicians.[6] For Roosevelt, muckraking was a derogatory term used to describe reporters who focused on the carnal underbelly of politics rather than its more lofty pursuits. Nevertheless, much good came from these efforts. Muckrakers stimulated demands for anti-trust regulations—laws that prohibit companies, such as large steel companies, from controlling an entire industry—and exposed deplorable working conditions in factories, as well as outright exploitation of workers by business owners. An unfortunate side effect of this emphasis on crusades and investigations, however, was the frequent publication of gossip and rumor without sufficient proof.

yellow journalism
A form of newspaper publishing in vogue in the late nineteenth century that featured pictures, comics, color, and sensationalized news coverage.

muckraking
A form of journalism, in vogue in the early twentieth century, devoted to exposing misconduct by government, business, and individual politicians.

Reform-minded investigative journalists in the Progressive Era devoted themselves to exposing misconduct by government, business and individual politicians. In a speech in 1906, President Roosevelt called it muckraking journalism, drawing from a character in John Bunyan's 1678 classic, *Pilgrim's Progress*. President Roosevelt tried to steer stories his way by giving journalists, such as Lincoln Steffans, interviews and access to the White House.

A NAUSEATING JOB, BUT IT MUST BE DONE

As the news business grew, so did the focus on increasing its profitability. Newspapers became more careful and less adversarial in their reporting, to avoid alienating the advertisers and readers who produced their revenues. Clearer standards were applied in evaluating the behavior of people in power. Journalism also changed during this period as the industry became more professionalized. Reporters learned to adhere to principles of objectivity and balance and to be motivated by a never-ending quest for the "truth."[7]

More recently, faced by an onslaught of competing forms of media, including radio, TV, and digital media, newspapers have struggled to maintain their circulation. According to a Brookings Institution report, there were 1,749 American newspapers in 1945, but only 1,331 by the end of 2014. Over that same period, circulation per capita declined from 35 percent in the mid-1940s to under 15 percent. Though some print dailies have moved to digital-print hybrids or have created digital versions with pay plans to monetize their content, other papers have failed to adapt to the changing news environment. The full consequences of these changes for citizens' knowledge of politics and public affairs remain to be seen, but preliminary scholarly research of newspaper closures has provoked concerns about falling political participation, increased ideological polarization, and the elimination of a check on government corruption.[8] Whatever the full impact, the laws governing political communication in this country will likely need to be revisited.

Radio News

The advent of radio in the early twentieth century was a media revolution and a revelation to the average American, who rarely, if ever, had heard the voice of a president, governor, or senator. The radio became the center of most homes in the evening, when national networks broadcast the news as well as entertainment shows. Calvin Coolidge was the first president to speak on radio on a regular basis, but President Franklin D. Roosevelt made the radio broadcast a must-listen by presenting "fireside chats" to promote his New Deal.

News radio, which had begun to take a back seat to TV by the mid-1950s, regained popularity with the advent of AM talk radio in the mid-1980s. Controversial radio host Rush Limbaugh began the trend with his unabashedly conservative views, opening the door for other conservative commentators such as Laura Ingraham, Sean Hannity, and Glenn Beck. Statistics show that these conservative radio hosts resurrected the radio as a news medium by giving a strong ideological bent to the information they broadcast. Yet, most truly liberal political talk radio has struggled. Many liberals turn to National Public Radio (NPR), which receives government funding as well as private donations, and does not air solely political content. It also covers a variety of cultural and socially important issues. Studies of the overall political coverage of NPR, moreover, have failed to find any overt liberal bias.[9]

TV News

TV was first demonstrated in the United States at the 1939 World's Fair in New York, but it did not take off as a news source until after World War II. While most homes had TVs by the early 1960s, it took several years more for TV to replace print and radio as the nation's chief news provider. In 1963, most networks provided just fifteen minutes of news per day; only two major networks devoted thirty minutes to news coverage. During this period, a substantial majority of Americans still received most of their news from newspapers. Today, while most Americans get their news from many sources, television is the most common.[10]

Television provides a platform for a range of news outlets, including commercial broadcast network news and cable news. The commercial broadcast networks—ABC, CBS, and NBC—have increased their audience in the last couple of years, with a viewership of 24 million for evening news and around 9.3 million for Sunday morning political talk shows in 2015. The three networks' online presences remain among the top domestic news destinations.[11] Among cable news outlets that provide twenty-four-hour news channels, Fox News is the most prominent, drawing an average of 1.8 million viewers during evening primetime in 2015, followed by CNN with 730,000 viewers and MSNBC with 596,000.[12]

Cable and satellite providers also give consumers access to a less glitzy and more unfiltered source of news. For example, C-SPAN is a basic cable channel that offers gavel-to-gavel coverage of congressional proceedings, as well as major political events when Congress is not in session. It also produces some of its own programming, such as *Washington Journal*, which invites scholars and journalists to speak about topics pertaining to their areas of expertise. Because the content of C-SPAN can be erudite, technical, and sometimes downright tedious (such as the fixed camera shot of the Senate during a roll-call vote), audiences tend to be very small, but they are loyal and give C-SPAN its place as a truly content-driven news source.

Digital Media

Digital media, including Internet news, blogs, and social networking sites, are transforming the relationship between the media and citizens, even challenging our perceptions of what is defined as "media." They also remove many of the traditional filters, such as editors and journalistic standards, which lend credibility to professional news outlets; moreover, they make media more low cost and widely accessible than ever before. The almost instantaneous availability of information through smartphones only enhances these changes. Furthermore, digital media allows individuals to become directly involved in creating and interpreting the news, and in organizing around shared political beliefs. Finally, digital media has become a powerful source for political organizing and fundraising. In 2016, Donald Trump was particularly adept at harnessing digital media to build a base of supporters for an unconventional presidential campaign. The Trump campaign's digital, data-driven effort generated more than 100,000 distinct pieces of creative content, the best of which were displayed to broader audiences, and it generated more than $275 million from 2.5 million small-dollar donors in the general election.[13] Former Breitbart Chairman Stephen K. Bannon, who advised President Trump's campaign and will serve as his Chief Strategist in the White House, noted that he wouldn't have joined

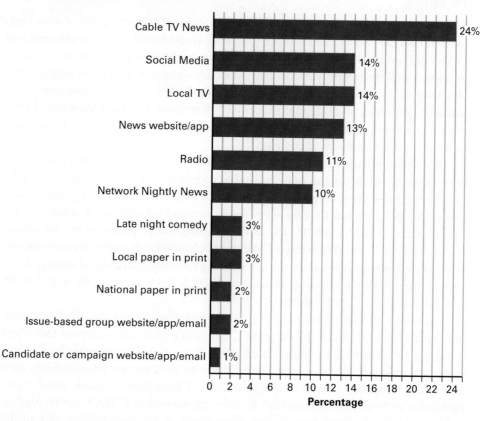

FIGURE 13.1 WHERE DO AMERICANS GET THEIR POLITICAL NEWS?

Americans rely on four main news outlets – television is still the most popular news source, but the Internet, print and radio hold substantial ground. In general, Americans tend to seek information that reinforces their politics. For instance, Fox News' conservative approach attracts more Republicans, while Democrats are twice as likely as Republicans to listen to National Public Radio for news. While both parties are embracing the use of blogs and social media, more Democrats than Republicans have tended to use Facebook to circulate political content.

SOURCE: Data from the Pew Research Center.

the effort if it weren't for the massive Facebook and data engine because that is what "propelled Breitbart to a massive audience. We know its power."

THE INTERNET The Internet, which began as a Department of Defense project named Advanced Research Projects Agency Network (ARPANET) in the late 1960s, has grown into an unprecedented source of public information for people throughout the world. More than half of the American public now sites the Internet as a main source of national and international news. While the percentage is less than television (69 percent), it is far more than print newspapers (28 percent) and radio (twenty-three percent), and it is growing rapidly.[14] Furthermore, Americans now have greater diversity to can access information online—using a range of devices from laptops or computers, smartphones, tablets, gaming consoles and e-readers—and they are doing so throughout the day.[15]

SOCIAL MEDIA Social media is the TV of the Millennial generation. According to a recent Pew report, 61 percent of Americans born between 1981 and 1996 get their political news from Facebook in a given week, while 37 percent of them get political news from TV. Meanwhile, 60 percent of Americans born between 1946 and 1964 get their political information from local TV, and 37 percent from Facebook.[16] Although not their primary purpose, social media sites, such as Facebook, Instagram, YouTube, and Twitter, serve as a resource for political news, information, and finding others who share the same political views. Politicians and candidates have increasingly used these sites to reach citizens and engage them in the political process, for example, by conducting town hall forums or responding to questions from citizens. During 2016, the presidential

FIGURE 13.2   WHERE DO MILLENIALS AND BABY BOOMERS GET THEIR NEWS?

When it comes to political news, Millennials rely more on Facebook than any other source of news. In stark contrast, television tops the list for older Internet-using Americans. But overall, Millennials express less interest in political news (26 percent), compared to Gen Xers (34 percent) and Baby Boomers (45 percent).

SOURCE: Data from the Pew Research Center.

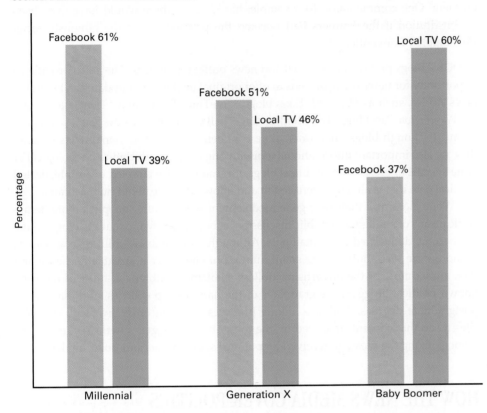

candidates used social media sites to broadcast live events, to organize supporters, to raise money and to attack their opponents. The downside of social media came to the fore in a presidential campaign that turned negative in tone. The majority of users in one Pew survey reported feeling that the political conversations on social media were angrier, less respectful, and less civil than other outlets. One-third of users said they changed their settings to see fewer posts from someone because of political posts, while 27 percent reported blocking or unfriending someone for the same reason.

To discourse with the political class, it is nearly a requirement to have a Twitter account nowadays. Both local and national political leaders have taken to Twitter to make announcements, send messages and respond to breaking political events so their words can be spread even more widely than they would be from a video-taped news conference or written statement. For example, in the 2016 presidential contest, Donald Trump tweeted so often in the presidential campaign that some pundits suggested someone should take his smartphone away. Politicians are also using Twitter to reach out to supporters and to raise money for political campaigns. Average citizens, too, have used Twitter to spread political news. Users have tweeted from political rallies, offered commentary on presidential debates and the president's State of the Union Address, and used hashtags to mark political issues such as health care, jobs, and the economy as trending topics.

Social media sites are fundamentally changing both the media and politics. As CNN political reporter Peter Hamby has commented, Twitter has replaced the campaign bus as the place where political reporters swap information and where media narratives develop.[17] The proportion of journalists on Twitter is roughly three times that of Internet-using adults.[18] Meanwhile, politicians can interact directly with

press release
A document offering an official comment or position.

press briefing
A relatively restricted session between a press secretary or aide and the press.

press conference
An unrestricted session between an elected official and the press.

citizens, without using reporters and editors as intermediaries. Though this may seem more democratic, critics worry that a growing reliance on social networking sites will weaken the media's role as a filter, educator, and watchdog. They also express increasing concerns that politicians may not engage in deliberative democracy, but may instead make policy decisions designed to placate the mobs of citizens that James Madison and the Framers feared would trouble their republican form of government. One commentator, for example, has asked if there would have even been a Constitution if the Framers had tweeted the proceedings of the famously secret Philadelphia Convention.[19]

BLOGS Blogs provide an editorial and news outlet for citizens. They also provide an opportunity for news organizations to offer original analysis and updates on emerging news stories, such as *New York Times* blogs "FiveThirtyEight" and "The Caucus" and the *Washington Post* blog, "The Monkey Cage," all of which focus on politics and government. Though blogs often offer more commentary than traditional news sources, they are also important informational tools, linking people with common ideological or issue-specific interests. Most political blogs, for example, are targeted to a sophisticated political elite that is already interested in and knowledgeable about public affairs.

While blogs and their user-generated content seem to offer people a more democratic means of engaging in public discussion, concern is growing that the blogosphere has become dominated by a small elite. Although more than 173 million blogs can be found on the Web, only a very small number of sites have a sizeable audience and thus attract most of the advertising dollars available.[20] Moreover, most of the best-known political bloggers are graduates of the nation's top colleges, and many have postgraduate degrees. And, the linking practices common on many blogs and Web sites mean that content produced by the top political bloggers often rises to the top, homogenizing the message received by political sophisticates and policy makers.[21]

HOW THE NEWS MEDIA COVER POLITICS

13.2 Assess the influence of the media on American politics.

The news media focus an extraordinary amount of attention on politicians and the day-to-day operations of government. With more than 3,600 members, the Radio and Television Correspondents Association, the major organization of reporters covering Congress, in theory outnumber members of Congress nearly six-to-one.[22] The media have a visible presence at the White House as well; these reporters come from traditional and online media outlets and hail from across the country and, increasingly, around the world. Consequently, the media report, then intensively scrutinize and interpret, a politician's every public utterance.

How the Press and Public Figures Interact

Communication between elected officials or public figures and the media takes a number of different forms. A **press release**, also called a news release, is a written document offering an official comment or position on an issue or news event; it is usually faxed, e-mailed, or handed directly to reporters. A **press briefing** is a relatively restricted live engagement with the press, with the range of questions limited to one or two specific topics. In a press briefing, a press secretary or aide represents the elected official or public figure, who does not appear in person. In a full-blown **press conference**, an elected official appears in person to talk with the press at great length about an unrestricted range of topics. Press conferences provide a field on which reporters struggle to obtain the answers they need and public figures attempt to retain control of their message and spin the news and issues in ways favorable to them. Recent presidents, including Barack Obama, have also pursued a strategy of giving exclusive access

WHY DID PRESIDENT OBAMA GO ALL THE WAY TO ALASKA FOR AN INTERVIEW?

Presidents are always trying to control press coverage so it is favorable to them and their policy agenda. With the proliferation of media outlets, one tack the Obama administration pursued was to grant exclusive access to news outlets deemed sympathetic to the president's message on a particular topic. In an attempt to highlight climate change, for example, President Obama went to the Arctic and spent a quarter of his time there with *Rolling Stone* magazine in an exclusive interview and private photo shoot.

to news outlets deemed sympathetic to the president's message on a particular topic, in a dramatic setting that showcases and reinforces that message.

Politicians and media interact in a variety of other ways as well. Politicians hire campaign consultants who use focus groups and polling in an attempt to gauge how to present the candidate to the media and to the public. In addition, politicians can attempt to bypass the national news media through social media, paid advertising and by appearing on talk shows and local news programs. Politicians also use the media to attempt to retain a high level of name recognition and to build support for their ideological and policy ideas.

Covering the Presidency

The three branches of the U.S. government—the executive, the legislative, and the judicial—are roughly equal in power and authority. But, in the world of media coverage, the president stands first among equals. The White House beat is one of the most prestigious posts a political reporter can hold. The careers of many of the most famous network news journalists, including CBS's John Dickerson, were launched by covering the presidency.

The attention of the press to the White House enables a president to appear even on very short notice and to televise live, interrupting regular programming. The White House's press briefing room is a familiar sight on the evening news, not just because presidents use it fairly often but also because the presidential press secretary has almost daily question and answer sessions there.

The post of press secretary to the president has existed only since Herbert Hoover's administration (1929–1933). The power of this position, however, has grown tremendously over time. Presidents increasingly resist facing the media on their own and leave this task to their press secretary. As a result, press secretaries have a difficult job; they must convince the media of the importance of the president's policy decisions as well as defend any actions taken by the executive branch. In many ways, the prestige and power of the presidency depend on the "spin" of the press secretary and his or her ability to win over the media. Thus, many presidents choose close aides with whom they have worked previously and who are familiar with their thinking. For example, President Barack Obama's third press secretary, Josh Earnest, has worked with President Obama since March 2007 in various communications roles before being appointed press secretary in May 2014.

FIGURE 13.3 WHERE DO REPORTERS SIT IN THE WHITE HOUSE BRIEFING ROOM?

There are 49 assigned seats in the James S. Brady briefing room in the White House. In addition, there are typically another 30–60 people standing in the U-shaped ring around the seating perimeter during briefings. The White House Correspondents Association determines seat assignments, not the White House Press Office, though the WHCA doesn't determine who has access to the briefing room. Where reporters sit is important because those who sit closer to the front have a better chance of getting their question answered.

The front row, center seat, long reserved for UPI reporter Helen Thomas, is considered the "best seat in the house" because of its proximity to the press secretary. Today, the Associated Press takes this seat.

The press secretary stands at a podium in the front of the room, facing reporters. Shown here is President Obama's second press secretary, Jay Carney.

Brady Briefing Room Seating Chart As of March 2015

Podium

1 National Broadcasting Company	Fox News	Columbia Broadcasting System	Associated Press	American Broadcasting Company	Reuters	Cable News Network
2 Wall Street Journal	Columbia Broadcasting System Radio	Bloomberg	National Public Radio	Washington Post	New York Times	Associated Press Radio
3 Agence France Presse	USA Today	McClatchy	American Urban Radio Networks	Politico	Tribune	ABC Radio
4 Foreign Pool	Microsoft and the National Broadcasting System	Washington Times	The Hill	Fox News Radio	Voice of America	National Journal
5 Bloomberg BNA	Time	New York Daily News	Hearst, S.F. Chronicle, Baltimore Sun	New York Post	Real Clear Politics	Chicago Sun-Times, Al Jazeera
6 Washington Examiner	Yahoo! News	Salem Radio Network	Media News Group, The Daily Beast	Christian Science Monitor	Sirius XM	Dow Jones
7 Talk Radio Service	Dallas Morning News	Roll Call	Christian Broadcasting Network News	BBC, The Boston Globe	Scripps BuzzFeed	Financial Times, The Guardian

Occupying seats farther from the press secretary are foreign news outlets, such as the BBC, and comparatively small daily newspapers, such as the *Dallas Morning News*.

Covering Congress

With 535 voting members representing distinct geographic areas, covering Congress poses a difficult challenge for the media. Most news organizations solve the size and decentralization problems by concentrating coverage on three groups of individuals. First, the leaders of both parties in both chambers receive the lion's share of attention because only they can speak for a majority of their party's members. Usually, the majority and minority leaders in each house and the Speaker of the House are the preferred spokespersons, but the whips also receive a substantial share of air time and column inches. Second, key committee chairs command center stage when subjects in their domain are newsworthy. Heads of the most prominent committees (such as Appropriations or Judiciary) are guaranteed frequent coverage, but even the chairs and members of minor committees or subcommittees can achieve fame when the time and issue are right. For example, a sensational scandal may lead to congressional committee hearings that receive extensive media coverage. Third, local newspapers and broadcast stations normally devote some resources to covering local senators and representatives, even when these legislators are junior and relatively lacking in influence.

As with coverage of the president, media coverage of Congress is disproportionately negative. A significant segment of media attention given to the House and Senate focuses on conflict among members. Some political scientists believe that such reporting is at least partially responsible for the public's negative perceptions of Congress.[23]

Covering the Supreme Court

While the president and Congress interact with the media on a regular basis, the Supreme Court remains a virtual media vacuum. TV cameras have never been permitted to record Supreme Court proceedings. Print and broadcast reporters, however, are granted access to the Court. Still, fewer than a dozen full-time reporters cover the Supreme Court, and the amount of space dedicated to Court-related news has continued to shrink. Stories involving complex legal issues are not as easy to sell as well-illustrated stories dealing with the Congress or president.[24]

HOW DOES THE MEDIA COVER THE SUPREME COURT?

TV cameras are not allowed inside the Supreme Court. As a result, when the Court hands down an important opinion, such as its health care decision in 2012, it is not uncommon to see journalists sprinting from the courtroom with draft opinions in hand, hoping to be the first news agency to report the Court's decision.

media effects
The influence of news sources on public opinion.

agenda setting
The process of forming the list of issues to be addressed by government.

framing
The process by which a news organization defines a political issue and consequently affects opinion about the issue.

The justices, citing the need to protect the public's perception of the Supreme Court as a nonpolitical and autonomous entity, have given little evidence to suggest they are eager to become more media friendly. Many veteran reporters have criticized this decision. As longtime Court reporter Tony Mauro noted, "Of course we don't want the Supreme Court playing to the crowd, ruling to please the majority. But that does not mean the [C]ourt should be invisible and unaccountable. Clarence Thomas on *Face the Nation*? John Roberts taking questions posted on YouTube? Sam Alito blogging? Why not? Really, why not?"[25]

NEWS MEDIA INFLUENCE, NEWS MEDIA BIAS, AND PUBLIC CONFIDENCE

13.3 Analyze the impact of the media on public opinion and political behavior.

Many important questions pertain to the news media's relationship with the public. For instance, how much influence do the media actually have on the public's understanding of political issues? Do the media have a discernible ideological bent or bias, as some people suggest? Are people able to resist information that is inconsistent with their preexisting beliefs? And, how much confidence does the public have in the news media?

News Media Influence

Some political scientists argue that the content of news coverage accounts for a large portion of the volatility and changes in public opinion and voting preferences of Americans, when measured over relatively short periods of time.[26] These changes are called **media effects**. These effects may be visible in a number of ways.

First, the media can influence the list of issues to be addressed by government through a process known as **agenda setting**. Significant media attention to an issue often increases the salience of that issue with average citizens. These citizens then pressure the government to take action. For example, media coverage of an immigration law enacted by the state of Arizona in 2010 ignited citizens' passions about the matter and made it a hot topic in many congressional campaigns. The media's agenda-setting role also came to the fore in the 2016 presidential election. Analysis of television mentions of presidential candidates showed that Donald Trump dominated coverage and President Trump himself wasn't shy in boasting about his ability to drive media coverage.

Second, the media influence public opinion through **framing**—the process by which a news organization defines a political issue and consequently affects opinion about the issue. For example, an experiment conducted by one group of scholars found that if a news story about a Ku Klux Klan rally was framed as a civil rights story (i.e., a story about the right of a group to express its ideas, even if they are unpopular), viewers were generally tolerant of the rally. However, if the story was framed as a law and order issue (i.e., a story about how the actions of one group disrupted a community and threatened public safety), public tolerance for the rally decreased. In either case, the media exert subtle influence over the way people respond to the same information.[27]

Third, the media have the power to indirectly influence the way the public views politicians and government. For example, voters' choices in presidential elections often relate to their assessments of the economy. In general, a healthy economy motivates voters to reelect the incumbent president or their party, whereas a weak economy impels them to choose the challenger. Hence, if the media paint a consistently dismal picture of the economy, that picture may well hurt the incumbent president or the incumbent party seeking reelection.

FIGURE 13.4 HOW DID MEDIA COVERAGE OF THE 2016 PRESIDENTIAL CANDIDATES INFLUENCE THE ELECTION?

The media possess a powerful influence called agenda setting, which is the ability to tell us which issues are important. The data displayed here are from the Television News Archive and shows how many times each U.S. presidential candidate was mentioned on each of the major television news networks monitored by the Archive. What influence do you think media coverage of Donald Trump and Hillary Clinton had in the election outcomes?

SOURCE: Data from Internet Archive TV News Archive, as of May 2016.

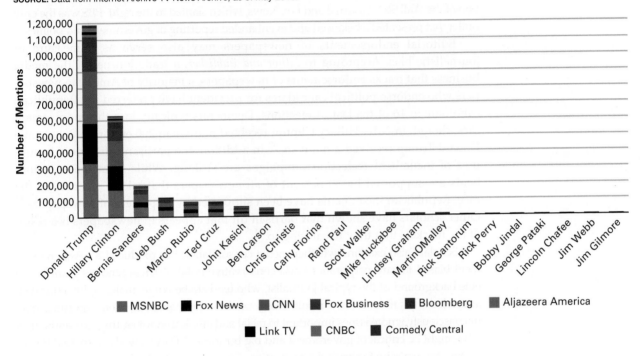

Fourth, reporting can sway the public opinion and votes of people who lack strong political beliefs. So, for example, the media have a greater influence on political independents than on strong partisans.[28] That said, the sort of politically unmotivated individual who is subject to media effects may be less likely to engage in political affairs, in which case the media's influence may be more limited.

Finally, the media likely have a greater impact on topics far removed from the lives and experiences of readers and viewers. News reports can probably shape public opinion about events in foreign countries somewhat easily. Yet, what the media say about domestic issues, such as rising food or gas prices, neighborhood crime, or child rearing, may have relatively little effect, because most citizens have personal experience of, and well-formed ideas about, these subjects.

News Media Bias

Are journalists biased? The answer is simple and unavoidable. Of course they are. Journalists, like all human beings, have values, preferences, and attitudes galore—some conscious, others subconscious, but all reflected at one time or another in the subjects covered or the portrayal of events or content communicated. Given that the press is biased, in what ways is it biased, and when and how are the biases shown?

Much of the debate over media bias in contemporary politics has centered on the ideological bias of the people who report the news. Surveys conducted by the Pew Center for Excellence and the Knight Foundation have found that about twice as many journalists self-identify as liberal or Democratic than as conservative or Republican.[29] However, several studies have shown that there is little evidence of political favoritism or bias in coverage.[30]

One of the ways in which bias does appear in news stories is in the language journalists use to describe politicians. In a 2005 study, Timothy Groseclose and Jeffrey Milyo found that reporters uses ideological terms to describe some politicians, but not others. For example, journalists might editorialize by referring to a politician as a *radical* or *extreme conservative*. When taking into account this more subtle measure of bias, they found that the reporting of most media organizations slanted to the left, with the exception of the Wall Street Journal and Fox News, which slanted to the right. PBS was the only outlet that presented a balanced and evenhanded reporting of government and politics.[31]

Editorial endorsements of newspapers may also serve as a measure of journalistic bias. According to *Editor and Publisher*, a trade journal of the media business that tracks endorsements of newspapers, a majority of American newspapers who endorse political candidates for president have preferred the Republican candidate in 16 of the last 21 elections. Democrats typically lose the endorsement race, though in 2016, Hillary Clinton received more than 200 endorsements, while Donald Trump received a mere six.[32] In addition, the partisan differences in support of incumbent reelection campaigns are striking. While Democratic incumbents are supported by 30 percent of all newspapers that take a position on the race, Republican incumbents have been supported by 70 percent of newspapers.[33] Other scholars have shown that partisan tilt that appears in newspapers is a result of the markets that they're catering to.[34]

Scholars also examine whether media consolidation has produced a news environment biased toward corporations and conservative politics. These scholars point to the elite background of the typical journalist, who tends to be white, male, highly educated, and relatively affluent. As a result, many of these journalists, in their reporting, may unconsciously ignore issues important to racial and ethnic minorities, the poor, and others who might be critical of government and big business.[35] They may also look to different sources for expertise to enrich their reporting. One study of the 2012 election, for example, revealed that, even on issues of concern to women, male pundits were four to seven times more likely to be quoted by the news media than their female counterparts.[36]

Perhaps the deepest bias among political journalists is the desire to grab a good story. News people know that if they report news with spice and drama, they will increase their audience. The fear of missing a good story shapes how media outlets develop headlines and frame their stories.

In the absence of an intriguing story, news people may attempt to create a horse race where none exists. While the horse-race components of elections are intrinsically interesting, the limited time that TV devotes to politics is disproportionately given to electoral competition, leaving less time for adequate discussion of public policy.[37] One study of media coverage of the 2016 national party conventions, found that policies and issues comprised only eight percent of media coverage and that tone of coverage was overwhelmingly negative for both candidates.[38]

One other source of bias, or at least of nonobjectivity, is the increasing celebrity status of many people who report the news. In an age of media stardom and blurring boundaries between entertainment and news, journalists in prominent media positions have unprecedented opportunities to attain fame and fortune. And, especially in the case of journalists with highly ideological perspectives, close involvement with wealthy or powerful special-interest groups can blur the line between reporting on policy issues and influencing them. Some journalists find work as political consultants or members of government—which seems reasonable, given their prominence, abilities, and expertise, but which can become problematic when they attempt to straddle both spheres. A good example of this phenomenon is Donna Brazile, who served both as interim chair of the Democratic National Committee and as a political contributor on CNN. When hacked emails revealed that she had passed along questions to the Clinton campaign in advance of CNN debates during the Democratic primary, she resigned from her network role.

Public Confidence

Americans' general assessment of the news media is considerably unfavorable and has trended downward since the 1980s. According to recent Gallup polls, American trust in media are at historic lows and only three in 10 say they have "a great deal" or "a fair amount" of trust and confidence in the mass media to report the news fully, accurately, and fairly.[39] The Pew Research Center also found that only two in ten Americans trust the information they get from news organizations and only 4 percent of web-using adults have a lot of trust in the information they find on social media. Furthermore, 74 percent believe that news organizations tend to favor one side, with conservative Republicans most likely to think this.[40]

Despite the increasing displeasure expressed by most Americans about these and other shortcomings, the media have managed to maintain higher approval ratings than other political institutions. Americans also continue to value the media's watchdog role, with the three-quarters of Americans believing that press scrutiny keeps political leaders from wrongdoing.[41] Thus, while public confidence in media organizations has declined and reforms are certainly warranted, Americans have not wavered in their support for a vigorous free press and for the role of the media in a democratic society.

RULES GOVERNING THE NEWS MEDIA

13.4 Summarize the ethical standards and federal regulations that govern the news media.

Professional journalists may obtain and publish information in a number of ways. They are, however, subject to boundaries in this pursuit. Journalists are primarily limited by the ethical standards of their profession. In some cases, additional governmental regulations may apply.

Journalistic Standards

The heaviest restrictions placed on reporters come from the industry's own professional norms and each journalist's level of integrity, as well as from oversight by editors who are ultimately responsible for the accuracy of the news they produce. To guide the ethical behavior of journalists, the Society of Professional Journalists publishes a detailed "Code of Ethics" that includes principles and standards governing issues such as avoiding conflicts of interest and verifying the information being reported.

One dilemma faced by reporters is how to deal ethically with sources. Informants may speak to reporters in a number of ways. If a session is **on the record**, as in a formal press conference, every word an official utters can be printed. In contrast, a journalist may obtain information **off the record**, which means that nothing the official says may be printed. Reporters may also obtain information **on background**, meaning that none of the information can be attributed to the source by name. Whereas background talks can be euphemistically attributed to sources, such as "unnamed senior officials," information on **deep background** must be completely unsourced, with the reporter giving the reader no hint about the origin. When reporters obtain information in any of these ways, they must take care to respect their source's wishes. Otherwise, not only might that person refuse to talk to them in the future, but other potential sources may do the same.

Journalists also grapple with the competitive nature of the news business. The pressure to get the story right is often weighed against the pressure to get the story first, or at the very least to get it finished before the next deadline. The twenty-four-hour news cycle, brought to life by cable news stations and nourished by the

on the record
Information provided to a journalist that can be released and attributed by name to the source.

off the record
Information provided to a journalist that will not be released to the public.

on background
Information provided to a journalist that will not be attributed to a named source.

deep background
Information provided to a journalist that will not be attributed to any source.

HOW HAS THE DIGITAL AGE CHANGED JOURNALISM?

During a bitterly fought election campaign, the whistleblowing organization WikiLeaks released more than one hundred thousand election-related documents, including a series of emails from the Democratic National Committee and Hillary Clinton's campaign chairman John Podesta. WikiLeaks founder Julian Assange, who has been holed up in the Ecuador Embassy in London for more than four years, defended their release, saying the right to "receive and impart true information" was the guiding principle of WikiLeaks, and he hailed "an open model of journalism that gatekeepers are uncomfortable with, but which is perfectly harmonious with the First Amendment."

prior restraint
Constitutional doctrine that prevents the government from prohibiting speech or publication before the fact; generally held to be in violation of the First Amendment.

expansion of digital media, has heightened the pressure to produce interesting copy in a timely manner.

To ensure professional integrity, several major newspapers and magazines, including the *Washington Post* and the *New York Times*, have hired internal media critics, or ombudsmen, who assess how well their newspaper and its reporters are performing their duties. Some nonprofits, such as Media Matters and the Project for Excellence in Journalism at the Pew Research Center in Washington, D.C., conduct scientific studies of the news and entertainment media. Other groups, including the conservative watchdog group Accuracy in Media (AIM) and its liberal counterpart Fairness and Accuracy in Reporting (FAIR), critique news stories and attempt to set the record straight on important issues they believe have received biased coverage. All of these organizations have a role in making sure the media treat topics important to citizens in a fair and objective manner.

Government Regulations

The U.S. government regulates media in a number of ways. Some regulations apply to all forms of media. Libel and slander, for example, are illegal in all cases. Beginning with the landmark case in 1931 of *Near* v. *Minnesota*, the Supreme Court has upheld that, except under the most extraordinary circumstances, the Constitution also places a limit on **prior restraint**—that is, the government may not limit any speech or publications before they actually occur. This principle was clearly affirmed in *New York Times Co.* v. *U.S.* (1971).[42] In this case, the Supreme Court ruled that the government could not prevent publication by the *New York Times* of the Pentagon Papers, classified government documents about the Vietnam War that had been photocopied and sent to the *Times* and the *Washington Post* by Daniel Ellsberg, a government employee. "Only a free and unrestrained press can effectively expose deception in the government," Justice Hugo Black wrote in a concurring opinion for the Court. "To find that the President has 'inherent power' to halt the publication of news by resort to the courts would wipe out the First Amendment."

Government can, however, regulate electronic media such as radio or TV more heavily than print content. Two reasons account for this unequal treatment. First, the airwaves used by the electronic media are considered public property and are leased by the federal government to private broadcasters. Second, those airwaves are in limited supply; without some regulation, the nation's many radio and TV stations would interfere with one another's frequency signals. The scope of government regulation of the Internet remains unclear and has been debated hotly in recent years. Government regulations of electronic media apply in two major areas: ownership and content.

MEDIA OWNERSHIP In 1996, Congress passed the sweeping Telecommunications Act, deregulating whole segments of the electronic media. The Telecommunications Act sought to provide an optimal balance of competing corporate interests, technological innovations, and consumer needs. It appeared to offer limitless opportunities for entrepreneurial companies to give consumers enhanced services. This deregulation, however, resulted in the sudden merger of previously distinct kinds of media in order to create a more "multimedia" approach to communicating information and entertainment. This merger paved the way for the formation of multimedia corporations such as Viacom, Time Warner, and Comcast and the media consolidation discussed later in this chapter.

Since the initial passage of this act, the Federal Communications Commission (FCC) has continued to relax ownership standards, leading to even greater media consolidation. Today, a single company may own up to 45 percent of media in a given market. Whether a media conglomerate may own both a newspaper and a TV station in a single market, however, continues to be fiercely debated.

CONTENT The government also subjects the electronic media to substantial **content regulations**, or limitations on the substance of the mass media. To ensure that the airwaves "serve the public interest, convenience, and necessity," the FCC has attempted to promote equity in broadcasting. For example, the **equal time rule** requires that broadcast stations sell air time equally to all candidates in a political campaign if they choose to sell it to any, which they are under no obligation to do. An exception to this rule is a political debate: stations may exclude from this event less well known and minor-party candidates. Another regulation is the **right of rebuttal**, which requires

content regulations
Limitations on the substance of the mass media.

equal time rule
The rule that requires broadcast stations to sell air time equally to all candidates in a political campaign if they choose to sell it to any.

right of rebuttal
The rule that requires broadcast stations to give individuals the right to have the opportunity to respond to personal attacks made on a radio or TV broadcast.

HOW DOES THE GOVERNMENT REGULATE THE INTERNET?
The emergence of the Internet has presented a regulatory challenge for the U.S. government. On the one hand, there is a need to protect intellectual property and ensure the Internet can profitably distribute content. On the other hand, consumers and businesses alike are concerned that Internet Service Providers and the government should treat all data on the Internet equally. Here, Apple co-founder Steve Wozniak, left, stands up and joins others in the audience applauding the Federal Communications Commission (FCC) vote to impose new regulations on Internet service providers like Comcast, Verizon, and AT&T, in favour of "net neutrality".

AMERICAN POLITICS IN COMPARATIVE PERSPECTIVE:

What Is the Role of Media in a Democracy?

The media play an important role in democracy. Media outlets increasingly determine the political agenda, even in less technologically developed countries. Through unfettered scrutiny and discussion of the successes and failures of candidates, governments and electoral management bodies, the media informs the public and helps to hold them accountable. Among other roles, the media also enable public participation in elections by allowing parties and candidates to debate with each other and by providing a platform for the political parties and candidates to communicate their message to the public. Review the graphs below for information on how different countries around the world allow the media to serve as a campaign platform and as an open forum for debate and discussion.

FIGURE 13.5 IS THERE A MAXIMUM AMOUNT THAT A POLITICAL PARTY IS PERMITTED TO SPEND ON PAID ADVERTISING DURING A CAMPAIGN PERIOD?

SOURCE: The Electoral Knowledge Network; http://aceproject.org/

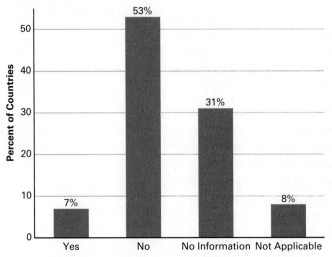

FIGURE 13.6 WHAT ARE THE CRITERIA FOR ALLOCATING FREE BROADCAST TIME AND/OR FREE PRINTED ADVERTISEMENT SPACE TO POLITICAL PARTIES?

SOURCE: The Electoral Knowledge Network; http://aceproject.org/

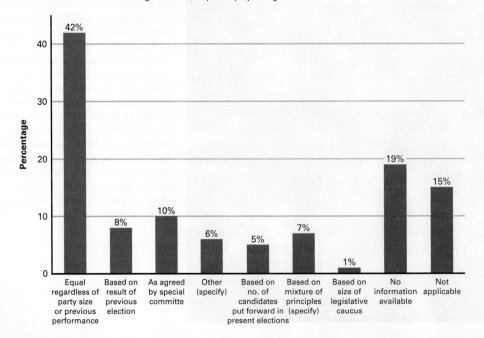

FIGURE 13.7 ARE TELEVISED DEBATES BETWEEN CANDIDATES OR PARTY REPRESENTATIVES NORMALLY CONDUCTED?

SOURCE: The Electoral Knowledge Network; http://aceproject.org/.

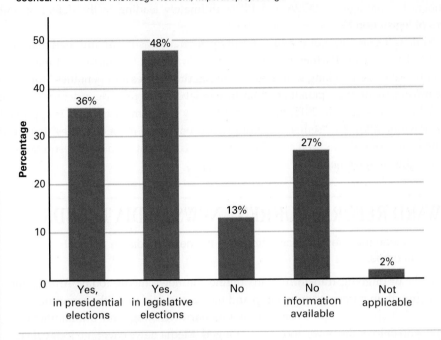

CRITICAL THINKING QUESTIONS

1. How might political and cultural viewpoints of countries contribute to different roles for the media?
2. How might the variance in how freely the media can broadcast political messages affect public opinion in different countries?
3. If candidates had greater access to media, would it make them less beholden to interests who fund their campaigns?

that individuals be given the opportunity to respond to personal attacks made on a radio or television broadcast.

The emergence of the Internet has posed new regulatory challenges. One of the foremost concerns has centered on protecting intellectual property and making the Internet a profitable means for distributing content. Preventing free distribution of copyrighted content, especially music and movies, has been the locus of concern. In *A&M Records* v. *Napster* (2001), the Ninth Circuit court ruled against the file-sharing service arguing that it had infringed the copyrights of the record companies.

Internet service providers (ISPs) have also attempted to limit users' access to pirated movies and music, slowing the network connections of those suspected of using illegal file-sharing programs. But, following more than a decade of controversy, the FCC approved along partisan lines the Open Internet Order in 2015, which bans ISPs from blocking, throttling, and paid-prioritization fast lanes. The so-called "net neutrality" rule, was a victory for Web-based companies such as Google and Yahoo, which argued that any other ruling would infringe on users' First Amendment rights.

Congress has attempted to take actions to limit online piracy. In early 2012, controversy arose over two similar pieces of legislation—the Stop Online Piracy Act (SOPA) and the PROTECT IP Act (PIPA). These acts, which were supported by content producers such as the Recording Industry Association of America and the Motion Picture Association of America, would have given officials the power to shutter entire Internet domains if federal law enforcement officers suspected they were infringing on copyright laws. Opponents of the law, concerned that the government could potentially have the power to shut down any Web site at will, feared the consequences of such a mandate. An Internet "blackout" led by online content providers such as Wikipedia and Google raised citizens' awareness of these bills. During early January 2012, Google estimates that more than 7 million people petitioned Congress, asking members to vote against SOPA and PIPA, ultimately leading to the defeat of both pieces of legislation.[43]

While Congress has not yet successfully passed a measure, an international trade deal, the Trans-Pacific Partnership (TPP), may provide just the means that major corporations have been seeking to impose "criminal procedures and penalties" for copyright infringement and "penalties of sufficient severity to provide a deterrent." The deal, which was signed in 2015, must be ratified by the member nations. If approved, the TPP would allow for "sentences of imprisonment" and "monetary fines" for doing the dirty on copyright, as well as allow for longer copyright terms and restrictions on digital rights management.

TOWARD REFORM: CURRENT NEWS MEDIA TRENDS

13.5 Describe the effect of recent trends in the news media on political outcomes.

A number of ongoing transformations define the news media today. Among these are the growth in corporate ownership and media consolidation; the targeting of programming at specific populations, known as narrowcasting; and infotainment. The people who deliver the news, too, have changed. Media news coverage today increasingly relies both on subject-matter experts and on average citizens.

Taken together, these changes create a news environment in which the boundaries between producers and consumers of news are increasingly blurred. Without the traditional lines of demarcation between news owners and objects of the news, and consumers and producers, the media's informational and watchdog roles are at risk of compromise.

Corporate Ownership and Media Consolidation

Private ownership of the media in the United States has proved to be a mixed blessing. While private ownership ensures media independence, something that cannot be said about state-controlled media in countries such as China, it also brings market pressures to journalism that do not exist in state-run systems. The news media in the United States are multi-billion-dollar, for-profit businesses that ultimately are driven by the bottom line. As with all free market enterprises, the pressure in privately owned media is to increasingly consolidate media ownership, to reap the benefits that come from larger market shares and fewer large-scale competitors.

Consequently, the top six media chains—Viacom, News Corporation, Comcast, CBS, Time Warner and Disney—account for more than 90 percent of news media content. Large media conglomerates such as Gannett, Media News Group, and News Corporation own most daily newspapers; fewer than 300 of the approximately 1,400 daily newspapers are independently owned. AT&T's recently proposed acquisition of Time Warner has set off alarm bells regarding consolidation over control of both the pipes of distribution and much of content that travels through the pipes. In addition, media companies are also seeking to commodify and privatize the internet, which some view as the next great media battle.

Unlike traditional industries, in which the primary concern associated with consolidation is price manipulation, consolidation of the media poses far greater potential risks. As the media have increasingly become dominated by a few mega-corporations, observers have grown fearful that these groups could limit the flow of information and ideas that define the essence of a free society and that make democracy possible. These profit-driven media chains, aimed at expanding market shares and pleasing advertisers, may overwhelmingly focus on sensational issues and avoid those that could alienate their audiences, anger executives, or compromise relationships with government regulators. Former *CBS Evening News* anchor Dan Rather, for example, summarizes media consolidation's threat to democracy by saying, to put it bluntly, "very big business is in bed with very big government in Washington, and has more to do with what the average person sees, hears, and reads than most people know."[44]

narrowcasting
Targeting media programming at specific populations within society.

Narrowcasting

In recent years, fierce competition to attract viewers and the availability of additional TV channels made possible by cable and satellite TV have led media outlets to move toward **narrowcasting**—targeting media programming at specific populations within society. Within the realm of cable news, MSNBC and Fox News are most notable for engaging in this form of niche journalism. The two stations divide audiences by ideology. Fox News emphasizes a conservative viewpoint, and MSNBC stresses a more liberal perspective.

Audiences also divide along partisan lines over other news sources. Republicans, for example, are more likely than Democrats and Independents to listen to AM talk radio.[45] And, while only a small disparity in newspaper reading exists between Republicans and Democrats, newspapers can be categorized by ideology; for instance, the *Washington Times* offers more conservative fare than its rival, the *Washington Post* (see Figure 13.8). As a result, political scientists have

---

FIGURE 13.8 WHERE DO NEWS AUDIENCES FIT ON THE POLITICAL SPECTRUM?

When it comes to getting news about government and politics, there are stark ideological differences in the sources that online Americans use. Those with consistently conservative political values are oriented around a single outlet—Fox News—to a much greater degree than those in any other ideological group. On the left of the political spectrum, no single outlet predominates. Among consistent liberals, CNN (15%), NPR (13%), MSNBC (12%) and the New York Times (10%) all rank near the top of the list.

SOURCE: Data from the Pew Research Center.

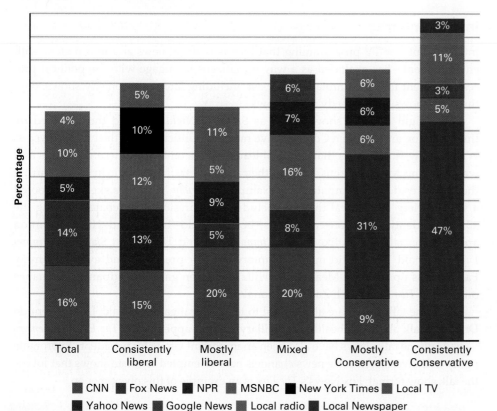

found that simply knowing where someone gets his or her news can predict party affiliation.[46]

Other narrowcasting targets specific racial, ethnic, or religious groups. Examples include Spanish-language news programs on stations such as Univision and Telemundo as well as news programming geared toward African American viewers on cable's Black Entertainment Television (BET). For evangelical Christians, Pat Robertson's Christian Broadcasting Network (CBN), with its flagship *700 Club*, has been narrowcasting news for over forty years. The rising use of smartphones and mobile apps, too, has helped narrowcasting to grow.

While narrowcasting can promote the interests specific to segments of the population, especially racial and ethnic minorities who may ordinarily be left out of mainstream media coverage, it comes with a social cost. Narrowcasting increases the chance that group members will rely on news that appeals to their preexisting views. By limiting one's exposure to a broad range of information or competing views, narrowcasting could result in further polarization of public opinion. The polarization made possible by narrowcasting is particularly problematic when it comes to programs that are narrowcasted in a specific ideological direction.[47] These broadcasts may result in what has been called the "Fox effect" or the "CNN effect." These effects result when a network chooses an ideologically favorable storyline—true or untrue—to cover almost *ad nauseam*. In so doing, the network sets the agenda both for partisans, who adopt the storyline being sold, and for other news networks, who feel compelled to address the issue.[48]

Narrowcasting also enables political leaders to exercise extraordinary levels of message control as they can choose on which shows to appear and custom tailor a message for that audience. In addition, recent trends toward "hyperpersonalization" afforded by digital networked media may also have important political and social consequences. As companies like Google, Microsoft, Apple and Facebook have begun directing personalized searches and news feeds, users have been categorized into neatly defined clusters that may create "walls" between them and may contribute to social fragmentation.[49]

Infotainment

Infotainment—or TV programming that blends political news and information with entertainment—has exploded as a way for citizens to engage with the political process. Different forms of infotainment exist, including late night comedy shows, daytime talk shows, and comedy news shows.

Late night comedy shows, such as *Saturday Night Live* and those hosted by Jimmy Fallon and Stephen Colbert, have mocked politicians and the news for years. What is new, however, is that political leaders have embraced these programs as a way to connect with citizens, both on the campaign trail and while in office. During the 2016 presidential campaign, for example, *Saturday Night Live* sketches spoofed a wide variety of political themes, including the presidential debates. During the 2016 presidential election campaigns, both Donald Trump and Hillary Clinton appeared on talk shows like *Jimmy Kimmel Live!* and *The Tonight Show with Jimmy Fallon*. Donald Trump did mock job interviews for president and even let Jimmy Fallon mess up his hair. Meanwhile, Hillary Clinton gave a deadpan performance on *Between Two Ferns* with Zach Galifianakis.

Daytime talk shows are also central to the political game. Donald Trump went on Dr. Oz to talk about his health, and Hillary Clinton appeared on *The Ellen DeGeneres Show*. Daytime talk shows have also been an important venue for presidents to promote policy initiatives. Even cable news channels have attempted to create shows that follow the talk show format; Fox News's *The Five* is an example of this phenomenon.

Political leaders see many advantages to appearing on infotainment programs, including connecting with citizens. Infotainment makes political news and events more accessible to Americans. However, research has shown that the effects of infotainment may be clearest for those citizens who are already the most politically knowledgeable.

Political leaders see many advantages to appearing on late night and talk shows. These soft news programs give politicians an opportunity to reach much larger and more diverse audiences than do Sunday morning talk shows or cable news channels. In addition, the questions asked by hosts of *Live! With Kelly* or *The Today Show* are often less technical and hard-hitting than those asked by the traditional news media. And, infotainment programs may also provide a venue to humanize the politician and make viewers connect with him or her on a more personal level.

In addition, the emergence of comedy news shows such as *Last Week Tonight with John Oliver, Real Time with Bill Maher*, or *The Daily Show* has also changed the way Americans receive their political news. These shows present news "freed from the media's preoccupation with balance, the fixation with fairness. They have no obligation to deliver the day's most important news, if that news is too depressing, too complicated or too boring. Their sole allegiance is to comedy."[50] As a result, many viewers find news presented by comedy shows to be more palatable, and more entertaining, than what they might view on a nightly network news show. The shows are especially popular news sources among younger Americans, who are often jaded by the conventions of traditional journalism and politics.

Infotainment, overall, makes political news and events more accessible to Americans. But, research has shown that the effects of infotainment may be clearest for highly attentive citizens. Watching soft news about politics makes sophisticates' political behavior more consistent. In essence, for these people, infotainment acts as an information shortcut that helps them to better remember facts and figures about the governmental process.[51] The effects of infotainment on less sophisticated audiences, however, are not as clear. Some less politically engaged citizens may also fail to find humor in shows like *Saturday Night Live*'s political coverage or *Last Week Tonight* because they lack the context in which to process the information provided by the programming; these citizens, however, may connect with a show like *The View*.

Increasing Use of Experts

Most journalists know a little bit about many subjects but do not specialize in any one area and certainly do not possess enough knowledge to fill the hours of airtime made possible by cable TV's twenty-four-hour news cycle. Therefore, especially on

citizen journalists
Ordinary individuals who collect, report, and analyze news content.

cable stations, the news media employ expert consultants from a number of different disciplines ranging from medical ethics to political campaigning. These experts, also referred to as pundits, or the more derogatory term "talking heads," are hired to discuss the dominant issues of the day. For example, during the 2016 presidential campaign, one could not turn on the TV or read a newspaper without encountering a stable full of government officials, campaign consultants, former candidates, academics, and other experts giving their thoughts about the election.

Experts have a significant impact on how we view political news stories. One study, for example, finds that "news from experts or research studies is estimated to have almost as great an impact" as anchorpersons, reporters in the field, or special commentators. These "strong effects by commentators and experts are compatible with a picture of a public that engages in collective deliberation and takes expertise seriously."[52]

However, two main concerns arise about the increasing use of experts in news reporting. First, it is unclear how objective these experts are. Many of the pundits on air during the presidential campaign, for example, had ties to one of the two major candidates. Others were political operatives closely connected to the Democratic and Republican parties and to members of Congress. Second, so-called experts may weaken democratic deliberation, even though they are not particularly accurate in their predictions. But, because many pundits have official-sounding titles such as "strategist" or "former administration official," viewers assign privilege to experts' beliefs and do not take time to form their own political opinions. In many cases, the educated evaluations of citizens would be as accurate as the "expert" opinions they hear on TV or read in newspapers.[53]

Citizen Journalists

In the past, only professionals whose occupation was to cover current events filed news reports. Today, however, much of what we call "news" content is written and filmed by amateur **citizen journalists**, ordinary individuals who collect, report, and analyze news content.

Many citizen journalists use the Internet as a way to reach an interested news audience. Some sites cover a broad range of issues. Other sites, such as local news and politics blogs, focus on niche issues and local events, such as town meetings, school closings, and recycling initiatives, that often are left out of larger publications.

HOW HAVE CITIZEN JOURNALISTS CHANGED JOURNALISM?

Following the unrest in Ferguson, Missouri after a white police officer killed Michael Brown, an unarmed black teenager, This Week in Blackness (TWiB!) livestreamed police sweeping neighborhoods, showering black residents with tear gas, while CNN reported that everything was quiet in the streets. Citizen journalism has harnessed a broad set of tools, from podcasts to social media, to show the disconnect between mass media coverage and the reality on the ground.

Uploading videos to Twitter, Snapchat, and YouTube may also allow citizens to show-case content not covered by traditional news outlets or provide a location to share common experiences, such as natural disasters. Citizens may also use social media to highlight narratives or opinions about newsworthy occurrences.

Many traditional news organizations have embraced the value of citizen journalism. In addition to bringing new perspectives—and perhaps new readers and viewers—into the fold, citizen journalists may reach the scene of important events before news crews. Citizen journalism also has financial benefits for traditional news outlets: using citizen coverage and footage is far cheaper than hiring reporters. This can be a way for news outlets to continue offering coverage of a broad range of issues in an era of decreasing budgets.

Media scholars have hotly debated the value of citizen journalism. On one hand, citizen journalism can act as a democratizing force, allowing more people to participate in setting agendas and framing issues. It can also give more instantaneous coverage than traditional media. On the other hand, citizen journalists are often not trained in the rules and standards of journalism. They may not treat their sources with the same respect or fact-check as thoroughly as professional reporters. Perhaps as a result, research has shown that consumers of citizen journalism score lower on political knowledge than those who rely on professional news organizations.[54] Finally, and perhaps most importantly, citizen journalists once again blur the line between producers and consumers of news, compromising the objectivity of news coverage.

REVIEW THE CHAPTER

Roots of the News Media in the United States

13.1 Describe the structure and the functions of the media, past and present.

News media, a component of the larger mass media, provide the public with key information about subjects of public interest and play a crucial role in the political process. The news media consist of print, broadcast, and new media. The nation's first newspaper was published in 1690. Until the mid- to late 1800s, when independent papers first appeared, newspapers were partisan; that is, they openly supported a particular party. In the twentieth century, first radio in the late 1920s and then TV in the late 1940s revolutionized the transmission of political information. The growth of digital media, such as the Internet, blogs, and social media sites, continues to transform the relationship between media and citizens.

How the News Media Cover Politics

13.2 Assess the influence of the media on American politics.

The news media cover every aspect of the political process, including the executive, legislative, and judicial branches of government, though the bulk of attention focuses on the president. Congress, with its 535 members and complex committee system, poses a challenge to the modern media, as does the Supreme Court, with its legal rulings and aversion to media attention. Politicians have developed a symbiotic relationship with the media, both feeding the media a steady supply of news and occasionally being devoured by the latest media feeding frenzy.

News Media Influence, News Media Bias, and Public Confidence

13.3 Analyze the impact of the media on public opinion and political behavior.

By controlling the flow of information, framing issues in a particular manner, and setting the agenda, the media have the potential to exert influence over the public, though generally they have far less effect than people believe. While the media do possess biases, a wide variety of news options are available in the United States, providing news consumers with an unprecedented amount of information from which to choose. Public opinion regarding the media is largely critical, although Americans continue to value the news media's watchdog role.

Rules Governing the News Media

13.4 Summarize the ethical standards and federal regulations that govern the news media.

Journalists are guided in ethical behavior by a detailed "Code of Ethics" published by the Society of Professional Journalists, which includes principles and standards concerning issues such as avoiding conflicts of interest, verifying the information being reported, and dealing ethically with sources. In addition, the U.S. government regulates both media ownership and content. The Telecommunications Act of 1996 deregulated whole segments of the electronic media, paving the way for greater media consolidation. Content regulation such as network neutrality has also been a subject of significant government attention.

Toward Reform: Current News Media Trends

13.5 Describe the effect of recent trends in the news media on political outcomes.

Five trends affecting the modern media are: (1) corporate ownership and increasing consolidation of media outlets; (2) narrowcasting in order to capture particular segments of the population; (3) the growth of infotainment; (4) the increasing use of experts; and, (5) the rise of citizen journalists—ordinary individuals who collect, report, and analyze news content. These trends have all altered the news content citizens receive.

LEARN THE TERMS

agenda setting
citizen journalists
content regulations
deep background
equal time rule
framing
mass media

muckraking
media effects
news media
narrowcasting
off the record
on background
on the record

press briefing
press conference
press release
prior restraint
right of rebuttal
yellow journalism

The FŒDERALIST, No. 10.

To the People of the State of New-York.

AMONG the numerous advantages promised by a well constructed Union, none deserves to be more accurately developed than its tendency to break and control the violence of faction. The friend of popular governments, never finds himself so much alarmed for their character and fate, as when he contemplates their propensity to this dangerous vice. He will not fail therefore to set a due value on any plan which, without violating the principles to which he is attached, provides a proper cure for it. The instability, injustice and confusion introduced into the public councils, have in truth been the mortal diseases under which popular governments have every where perished; as they continue to be the favorite and fruitful topics from which the adversaries to liberty derive their most specious declamations. The valuable improvements made by the American Constitutions on the popular models, both ancient and modern cannot certainly

The influence of factious leaders may kindle a flame within their particular States, but will be unable to spread a general conflagration through the other States: A religious sect, may degenerate into a political faction in a part of the confederacy; but the variety of sects dispersed over the entire face of it, must secure the national Councils against any danger from that source: A rage for paper money, for an abolition of debts, for an equal division of property, or for any other improper or wicked project, will be less apt to pervade the whole body of the Union, than a particular member of it; in the same proportion as such a malady is more likely to taint a particular county or district, than an entire State.

In the extent and proper structure of the Union, therefore, we behold a republican remedy for the diseases most incident to republican Government. And according to the degree of pleasure and pride, we feel in being Republicans, ought to be our zeal in cherishing the spirit and supporting the character of Fœderalists.

PUBLIUS.

WHY DID JAMES MADISON OPPOSE "FACTION"?

In *Federalist No. 10*, pictured above, James Madison famously warned that the "mischiefs of faction," or what we would today call interest groups, needed to be curbed and controlled. Later generations of American political observers, however, have come to see interest groups as essential to the functioning of democracy.

INTEREST GROUPS

LEARNING OBJECTIVES

14.1 Explain the origins of interest groups in America.

14.2 Describe the genesis of modern American interest groups.

14.3 Describe how interest groups form and identify different types of interest groups.

14.4 Analyze the methods and activities that interest groups use to influence political outcomes.

14.5 Evaluate the factors that affect the relative success of interest groups.

14.6 Assess the effectiveness of regulations designed to control interest groups.

t is ironic that James Madison in *Federalist No. 10* cautioned about the mischief of factions. Indeed, placating existing factions was key to the ratification of the U.S. Constitution. Before and during the Revolutionary War, Federalists and Anti-Federalists argued passionately over whether or not the new nation required a strong national government. Anti-Federalists, those favoring a decentralized political structure in which states (the former colonies) largely were free to act as independent nations, won this initial round of the debate with ratification of the Articles of Confederation. While the government created under the Articles successfully managed to conduct and win the war with Great Britain, problems soon arose as a weak national government attempted to repay its war-created debts without any means of raising funds other than appealing to the thirteen member states.

The heated disagreements among Federalists, arguing for a stronger national government, and Anti-Federalists, arguing that a strong national government could lead to tyranny of the kind practiced by the British, ultimately led to the ratification of the Constitution and the Bill of Rights. This outcome suggests that interest groups (factions, in eighteenth-century parlance) have placed an indelible stamp on our nation from the beginning.

● ● ●

Interest groups are organized collections of people or organizations that try to influence public policy; they have various modern names: special interests, pressure groups, organized interests, nongovernmental organizations (NGOs), political groups, lobby groups, and public interest groups. Interest groups are differentiated from political parties largely by the fact that interest groups do not run candidates for office.

The face of interest group politics in the United States is constantly changing. In the wake of Supreme Court decisions that equate money with speech, a protected right under the First Amendment, big business and trade groups are increasing their activities and engagement in the political system. At the same time, evidence concerning whether ordinary citizens join political groups is conflicting. Political scientist Robert Putnam, for example, has argued that fewer Americans are joining groups of all kinds, a phenomenon he labeled "bowling alone."[1] Other observers disagree, concluding that America is in the midst of an "explosion of voluntary groups, activities and charitable donations [that] is transforming our towns and cities."[2]

interest group
A collection of people or organizations
that tries to influence public policy.

ROOTS OF AMERICAN INTEREST GROUPS

14.1 Explain the origins of interest groups in America.

Their experiences as British colonists led the Framers to tailor a governmental system of multiple pressure points to check and balance political factions. It was their belief that the division of power between national and state governments and across the three branches would prevent any one individual or group of individuals from becoming too influential. They also believed that decentralizing power would neutralize the effect of special interests, who would find it impossible to spread their efforts with any effectiveness throughout so many different levels of government. But, as farsighted as they were, the Framers could not have envisioned the vast sums of money and political influence interest groups would wield as the nature of these groups evolved over time.

National Groups Emerge (1830–1889)

The Constitution, or, more specifically the Bill of Rights, directly aided the development of interest groups. The First Amendment not only secures the right to peaceable assembly but also free speech and the right to petition the government directly. It was almost as though those in the First Congress foresaw the eventual development of interest groups of all kinds.

American Anti-Slavery Society
A major interest group, founded in 1833, to advocate for the abolition of the institution of slavery throughout the United States.

Women's Christian Temperance Union (WCTU)
A public interest group created in 1874 with the goal of outlawing the sale of liquor. Its activities included prayer groups, protest marches, lobbying, and the destruction of saloons.

The Grange
Founded in 1867 as an educational organization for farmers, The Grange evolved into the first truly national interest group by working to protect the political and economic concerns of farming communities and rural areas.

lobbyist
Interest group representative who seeks to influence legislation that will benefit his or her organization or client through political and/or financial persuasion.

Although all kinds of local groups proliferated throughout the colonies and in the new states, the first national groups did not emerge until the 1830s when communication networks improved. Many were single-issue groups deeply rooted in the Christian religious revivalism sweeping the nation. Concern with humanitarian causes such as temperance, peace, education, abolition of slavery, and women's rights led to the founding of numerous associations dedicated to addressing these issues. Among the first of these groups was the **American Anti-Slavery Society**, founded in 1833 by William Lloyd Garrison. By 1838, it had about 250,000 members.

After the Civil War, more groups were founded. For example, the **Women's Christian Temperance Union (WCTU)** was created in 1874 with the goal of outlawing the sale of liquor. Its members, many of them quite religious, believed that alcohol consumption was an evil injurious to family life because many men drank away their paychecks, leaving no money to feed or clothe their families. The WCTU's activities took conventional and unconventional forms, which included organizing prayer groups, lobbying for prohibition legislation, conducting peaceful marches, and engaging in more violent protests such as the destruction of saloons.

The Grange also was formed during the period after the Civil War. Created with help from the federal government as an educational society for farmers, it taught them about the latest agricultural developments. Although its charter formally stated that the Grange was not to involve itself in politics, in 1876 it formulated a detailed plan to pressure Congress into enacting legislation favorable to farmers.

Business interests also began to figure even more prominently in both state and national politics during the late 1800s. A popular saying of the day noted that the Standard Oil Company did everything to the Pennsylvania legislature except refine it. Increasingly large trusts, monopolies, business partnerships, and corporate conglomerations in the oil, steel, and sugar industries became sufficiently powerful to control the votes of many representatives in state and the national legislatures.

Perhaps the most effective organized interest of the day was the railroad industry. In a move that could not take place today because of its clear impropriety, the Central Pacific Railroad sent its own **lobbyist** to Washington, D.C., in 1861, where he eventually became the clerk (staff administrator) of the committees of both houses of Congress that were charged with overseeing regulation of the railroad industry. Subsequently, Congress awarded the Central Pacific Railroad (later called the Southern Pacific) vast grants of lands along its route and large subsidized loans.

WHAT WERE THE FIRST NATIONAL GROUPS TO EMERGE FOLLOWING THE CIVIL WAR?

One of the first truly national groups was The National Grange of the Order of Patrons of Husbandry or, more simply, The Grange. Established in 1867 to educate and disseminate knowledge to farmers, the group also lobbied for farmers' interests.

The Progressive Era (1890–1920)

By the 1890s, a profound change had occurred in the nation's political and social outlook. A host of problems, including crime, poverty, squalid and unsafe working conditions, and widespread political corruption were created by rapid industrialization, an influx of immigrants, and monopolistic business practices. Many Americans began to believe that new measures would be necessary to impose order on this growing chaos and to curb some of the more glaring problems in society. The political and social movement that grew out of these concerns was called the **Progressive movement**.

Progressive era groups ranged from those rallying for public libraries and kindergartens to those seeking better labor conditions for workers—especially for women and children. Other groups, including the National Association for the Advancement of Colored People (NAACP), were dedicated to ending racial discrimination. Groups seeking women's suffrage also were active during this time.

Not even the Progressives could agree on what the term "progressive" actually meant, but their desire for reform led to an explosion of all types of interest groups, including single-issue, trade, labor, and the first **public interest groups**. Politically, the movement took the form of the Progressive Party, which sought on many fronts to limit or end the power of the industrialists' near-total control of the steel, oil, railroad, and other key industries.

In response to the pressure applied by Progressive era groups, the national government began to regulate business. Because businesses had a vested interest in keeping wages low and costs down, more business groups organized to consolidate their strength and to counter Progressive moves. Not only did governments have to mediate Progressive and business demands, but they also had to accommodate the role of organized labor, which often allied itself with Progressive groups against big business.

ORGANIZED LABOR   Until creation of the **American Federation of Labor (AFL)** in 1886, no real national union activity had taken place. The AFL brought skilled workers from several trades together into one stronger national organization for the first time. As the AFL grew in power, many business owners began to press individually or collectively to quash the unions. As business interests pushed states for what are called open shop laws to outlaw unions from organizing workers in their factories, the AFL became increasingly political. It also was forced to react to the success of big businesses' use of legal injunctions to prohibit union organization. In 1914, massive lobbying by the AFL and its members led to passage of the Clayton Act, which labor leader Samuel Gompers hailed as the Magna Carta of the labor movement. This law allowed unions to organize free from prosecution and guaranteed their members' right to strike—a powerful weapon against employers.

BUSINESS GROUPS AND TRADE ASSOCIATIONS   The **National Association of Manufacturers (NAM)** was founded in 1895 by manufacturers who had suffered business losses in the economic panic of 1893 and who believed they were being affected adversely by the growth of organized labor. NAM first became active politically in 1913 when a major tariff bill was under congressional consideration. NAM's tactics were "so insistent and abrasive" and its expenditures so lavish that President Woodrow Wilson was forced to denounce its lobbying tactics as an "unbearable situation."[3] Congress immediately called for an investigation of NAM's activities but found no member of Congress willing to testify that he had ever even encountered a member of NAM (probably because many members of Congress had received illegal contributions and gifts).

The second major business organization, the **U.S. Chamber of Commerce**, came into being in 1912, with the assistance of the federal government. NAM, the Chamber of Commerce, and other **trade associations**, groups representing specific industries, were effective spokespersons for their member companies. They planned elaborate and successful litigation campaigns to overturn key regulations affecting business.[4]

Progressive movement
A broad group of political and social activists from the 1890s to the 1920s who opposed corruption in government, supported regulation of monopolies, and sought improvement of socioeconomic conditions.

public interest group
An organization that seeks a collective good that if achieved will not selectively and materially benefit group members.

American Federation of Labor (AFL)
Founded in 1886, the AFL brought skilled workers from several trades together into one stronger national organization for the first time. It merged in 1955 with the Congress of Industrial Organizations to form the AFL-CIO.

National Association of Manufacturers (NAM)
An organization founded in 1895 by manufacturers to combat the growth of organized labor.

U.S. Chamber of Commerce
A major pro-business lobbying group founded in 1912.

trade association
A group that represents a specific industry.

Jerry Falwell
A Southern Baptist minister who, in 1978, founded the conservative religious interest group the Moral Majority.

Moral Majority
A conservative religious interest group credited with helping to mobilize conservative Evangelical Christian voters from its founding in 1978 through the presidency of Ronald Reagan (1981-1989).

Pat Robertson
A Southern Baptist minister and television evangelist who ran for president in 1988 and in 1989 founded the conservative religious interest group the Christian Coalition.

Christian Coalition
A religious interest group founded in 1989 to advance conservative Christian principles and traditional values in American politics.

WHAT PUBLIC INTEREST GROUPS FORMED IN THE 1960S AND 1970S?

The 1960s brought a revitalization of groups formed in the public interest. One of the most notable of these groups was Public Citizen. The group was founded in 1971 by Ralph Nader, who attained fame and notoriety for pointing out safety concerns with the Chevrolet Corvair. In 2000 Nader ran as the Green Party's candidate for U.S. president.

THE RISE OF THE INTEREST GROUP STATE

14.2 Describe the genesis of modern American interest groups.

Whether you realize it or not, you have probably encountered many interest groups in your daily life. For example, the American Civil Liberties Union lobbies for the protection of individuals' rights as citizens. The NAACP Legal Defense and Educational Fund (LDF) litigates for equality for African Americans. And, labor unions work to assure workplace safety and fair compensation for employees in a variety of fields, including manufacturing, education, and service industries. Modern interest groups are more numerous and just as ideologically divided as they were at the Founding.

The Rise of Public Interest Groups

During the 1960s and 1970s, the Progressive spirit reappeared in the rise of public interest groups. Generally, these groups devoted themselves to representing the interests of African Americans, women, the elderly, the poor, and consumers, or to working on behalf of the environment. Many of their leaders and members had been active in the civil rights and anti–Vietnam War movements of the 1960s. Other groups formed during the Progressive era, such as the American Civil Liberties Union (ACLU) and the NAACP, gained renewed vigor. Many of them had as their patron the liberal Ford Foundation, which helped to bankroll numerous groups, including the Women's Rights Project of the ACLU, the Mexican American Legal Defense and Educational Fund, the Puerto Rican Legal Defense and Education Fund (now called Latino Justice PRLDEF), and the Native American Rights Fund.[5] The American Association of Retired Persons, now simply called AARP, also came to prominence in this era.

The civil rights and anti-war struggles left many Americans feeling cynical about a government that, in their eyes, failed to respond to the will of the majority. They also believed that if citizens banded together, they could make a difference. Thus, two major new public interest groups—Common Cause and Public Citizen—were founded during this time. Common Cause, a good-government group that acts as a watchdog over the federal government, is similar to some of the early Progressive movement's public interest groups. Public Citizen is a group that advocates for consumer safety and awareness.

CONSERVATIVE RESPONSE: RELIGIOUS AND IDEOLOGICAL GROUPS Conservatives, concerned by the activities of these liberal public interest groups, responded by forming religious and ideological groups that became a potent force in U.S. politics in the late 1970s and early 1980s. In 1978, the Reverend **Jerry Falwell** founded the first major new religious interest group, the **Moral Majority**. The Moral Majority was widely credited with assisting in the election of Ronald Reagan as president in 1980.[6] However, the group dissolved in the late 1980s. To fill this void, **Pat Robertson**, a televangelist, formed the **Christian Coalition** in 1989. Since then, it has grown in power and influence. Each election cycle, the group distributes tens of millions of voter guides in evangelical churches throughout the United States. Although these guides do not explicitly advocate for the selection of a particular candidate, they do highlight party nominees' stances on a number of key issues—ranging from abortion to taxation to health care—and it is not unusual for candidates to be endorsed from the pulpit.

The Christian Coalition is not the only conservative interest group to play an important role in the policy process as well as in elections at the state and national level. The **National Rifle Association (NRA)**, an opponent of gun control legislation, remains a potent player in the political process. And, groups such as the Young America's Foundation have made special efforts to reach conservative high school and college students through its young American's for Freedom program.

BUSINESS GROUPS, CORPORATIONS, AND ASSOCIATIONS Business leaders, unsatisfied with the work of the National Association of Manufacturers and the U.S. Chamber of Commerce, decided during the 1970s to start new organizations to advance their political and financial interests in Washington, D.C. The Business Roundtable, for example, was created in 1972. The Roundtable is "an association of chief executive officers of leading U.S. companies working to promote sound public policy and a thriving U.S. economy."[7] It urges its members to engage in direct lobbying to influence the course of policy formation.

Most large corporations, in addition to having their own governmental affairs departments, employ D.C.-based lobbyists to keep them apprised of legislation that may affect them, or to lobby bureaucrats for government contracts. Large corporations also channel significant sums of money to favored politicians or political candidates.

ORGANIZED LABOR Membership in labor unions held steady throughout the early twentieth century and then skyrocketed toward the end of the Depression. Labor became a stronger force in U.S. politics when the American Federation of Labor (AFL) merged with the Congress of Industrial Organizations (CIO) in 1955. Concentrating its efforts largely on the national level, the new **AFL-CIO** immediately channeled its

National Rifle Association (NRA)
The major gun-rights lobbying group in the United States, which opposes gun control and advances an expansive interpretation of the Second Amendment.

AFL-CIO
A large labor union founded in 1955 by the merging of the American Federation of Labor (AFL) and its one-time rival the Congress of Industrial Organizations (CIO).

FIGURE 14.1 WHERE IS UNION MEMBERSHIP HIGHEST?

During the peak of union membership in the 1950s, nearly 30 percent of working Americans were members of a union. However, union membership, especially among private sector employees, has declined in recent years. It also varies dramatically by region, with southern states having much lower rates of union membership than other parts of the country.

SOURCE: Data from Bureau of Labor Statistics

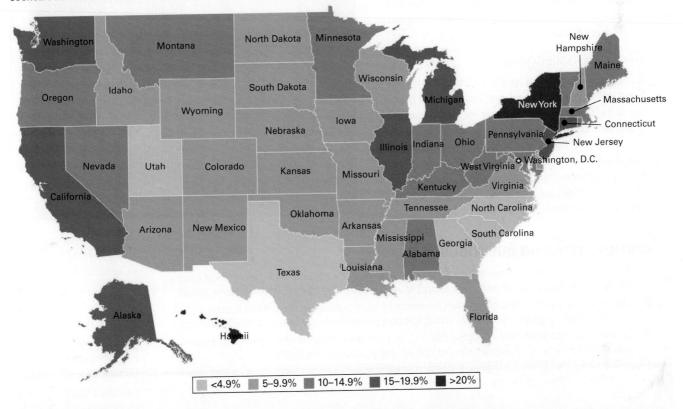

<4.9%   5–9.9%   10–14.9%   15–19.9%   >20%

AMERICAN POLITICS IN COMPARATIVE PERSPECTIVE

How Does the Role of Organized Labor Vary From Nation to Nation?

Within the scope of interest groups around the world, organized labor – usually called "unions" in the United States – plays a distinctive role. Membership in unions varies widely across the countries within the Organization for Co-Operation and Development (OECD), whose 34 members comprise the most economically advanced democracies. Unionization varies from a high in Nordic countries, such as 85.5 percent in Iceland and 69 percent in Finland, to lows of 6 percent in Turkey and 5.7 percent in Estonia in 2013; in the same year, the U.S. unionization rate was at 10.8 percent. Though overall unionization rates have been declining for decades, organized labor still has a powerful role in many democracies.

Labor Parties

In many countries, there are political parties whose membership base is derived directly from trade unions. The UK Labour Party has become more centrist in the past two decades but still has an official Trade Union and Labour Party Liaison Organisation that represents the interests of workers directly to the party leadership. In the U.S., labor unions have generally been allied with the Democratic Party but without having such direct institutional ties.

Labor Days

Many countries designate a special holiday to highlight the role of workers in society, often marking it with large-scale celebratory parades. These holidays are often held on May 1, which is the socialist-oriented International Workers Day. In the U.S., Labor Day is held on the first Monday in September, partly to avoid association with socialism, and is not so much celebrated in itself as it is considered a long weekend marking the unofficial end of summer.

Centralized Bargaining

Some countries treat labor unions as official partners who are authorized to provide direct input into the making of government policy with regard to issues such as wages and working conditions. For instance, the Swedish Trade Union Confederation, an umbrella organization for workers, holds seats on a number of influential government boards. In the U.S., labor unions often try to influence policy, but they must compete with many other contending interests.

Regime Challengers

Some labor organizations have been critical to changes in the very regime of their nations. The organized opposition of the Solidarity trade union movement in Poland was critical to the downfall of that country's Communist regime in 1989. The Congress of South African Trade Unions was part of a "tripartite alliance" that brought down the racist *apartheid* regime there in 1994. Labor in the United States has rarely played such an openly confrontational role with the U.S. government itself.

WHAT CAN ORGANIZED LABOR ACCOMPLISH?
Phillippe Martinez, secretary general of the General Confederation of Labor or C.G.T., leads the largest and oldest union in France. C.G.T. and other union groups went on strike in the spring and summer of 2016 to protest a new labor law.

CRITICAL THINKING QUESTIONS:

1. To what extent do labor unions influence political ideology, and to what extent does political ideology influence the place of unions within a country? In what ways might this influence be bidirectional?

2. How would U.S. politics and government be affected if labor unions had more direct access and input into the making of government policy? Would this be a positive or negative development, and why?

3. Should organized labor have a "special role" in U.S. politics as it does in other countries? How would this affect the competitive nature of interest group activity in the U.S.?

energies into pressuring the government to protect concessions won from employers at the bargaining table and to other issues of concern to its members, including minimum wage laws, workplace safety, civil rights, medical insurance, and health care. Organized labor began to wield potent political power, as it was able to turn out its members in support of particular political candidates, many of whom were Democrats.

More recently, the political clout of organized labor has waned at the national level (see Figure 14.1). Membership peaked at about 30 percent of the workforce in the late 1940s. Since that time, union membership has plummeted as the nation changed from a land of manufacturing workers and farmers to a nation of white-collar professionals and service workers.

WHY DO INTEREST GROUPS FORM, AND WHAT TYPES OF GROUPS EXIST?

14.3 Describe how interest groups form, and identify different types of interest groups.

Interest group formation, development, and maintenance have many significant implications for the American political system. Political scientists believe that involvement in community groups and activities with others of like interests enhances the level of **social capital**, "the web of cooperative relationships between citizens that facilitates resolution of collective action problems."[8] The more social capital that exists in a given community, the more citizens are engaged in its governance and well-being, and the more likely they are to work for the collective good.[9] This tendency to form small-scale associations for the public good, or **civic virtue**, creates fertile ground within communities for improved political and economic development.[10] Interest groups may give the unrepresented or underrepresented an opportunity to have their voices heard, thereby making the government and its policy-making process more representative of diverse populations and perspectives. In addition, interest groups offer powerful and wealthy interests even greater access to, or influence on, policy makers at all levels of government.

Theories of Interest Group Formation

Interest groups may form in society for a variety of reasons. Political scientists have posited several theories to explain this phenomenon. **Pluralist theory** argues that political power is distributed among a wide range of diverse and competing interest groups. Pluralist theorists such as David B. Truman explain the formation of interest groups through **disturbance theory**. According to this approach, groups form as a result of changes in the political system. Moreover, one wave of groups will give way to another wave representing a contrary perspective (a countermovement). Thus, Truman argues, all salient issues will be represented in government. The government, in turn, should provide a forum in which the competing demands of groups and the majority of the U.S. population can be heard and balanced.[11]

Transactions theory arose out of criticisms of the pluralist approach. Transactions theory argues that public policies are the result of narrowly defined exchanges or transactions among political actors. Transactions theorists offer two main contentions: it is not rational for people to mobilize into groups, and therefore, the groups that do mobilize will represent elites. This idea arises from economist Mancur Olson's *The Logic of Collective Action*.[12] In this work, Olson assumes that individuals are rational and have perfect information on which to make informed decisions. He uses these assumptions to argue that, especially in the case of **collective goods**, or things of value that may not be withheld from nonmembers, such as a better environment, it makes little sense for individuals to join a group if they can gain the benefits secured by others at no cost and become "free riders." (The problem of free riders is discussed later in this chapter.)

social capital
Cooperative relationships that facilitate the resolution of collective problems.

civic virtue
The tendency to form small-scale associations for the public good.

pluralist theory
The theory that political power is distributed among a wide array of diverse and competing interest groups.

disturbance theory
The theory that interest groups form as a result of changes in the political system.

transactions theory
The theory that public policies are the result of narrowly defined exchanges or transactions among political actors.

collective good
Something of value that cannot be withheld from a nonmember of a group, for example, a tax write-off or a better environment.

economic interest group
A group with the primary purpose of promoting the financial interests of its members.

The elite bias that transactionists expect in the interest group system is the result of differences in the relative cost of mobilization for elite and nonelite citizens. Individuals who have greater amounts of time or money available simply have lower transaction costs. Thus, according to one political scientist, "The flaw in the pluralist heaven is that the heavenly chorus sings with a strong upper-class bias."[13] Still, social media is now challenging this assumption as people are able to organize meet ups online such as was the case with several "impromptu" protests by anti-Trump activists in 2016.

Types of Interest Groups

Interest groups take many forms. Several major categories of groups include public interest groups, business and economic groups, governmental units such as state and local governments, and political action committees (PACs).

PUBLIC INTEREST GROUPS   One political scientist defines public interest groups as organizations "that seek a collective good, the achievement of which will not selectively and materially benefit the membership or activists of the organization."[14] For example, upper- and middle-class women created many Progressive era groups in an attempt to solve the varied problems of new immigrants and the poor. Today, civil liberties groups, environmental groups, good government groups, peace groups, church groups, and groups that speak out for those who cannot (such as children, the mentally ill, or animals) are examples of public interest groups. Ironically, even though many of these groups are not well funded, they are highly visible and can actually wield more political clout than other better-funded groups.

ECONOMIC INTEREST GROUPS   **Economic interest groups** are groups whose primary purpose is to promote the financial interests of their members. Historically, the three largest categories of economic interest groups were business groups (including trade and professional groups, such as the American Medical Association), labor organizations (such as the AFL-CIO), and organizations representing the interests of farmers. The influence of farmers and labor unions is on the decline, but big businesses such as General Electric and AT&T are spending increasingly large amounts contributing to campaigns and hiring lobbyists. This trend intensified after the Supreme

Court's 2010 *Citizen's United* v. *Federal Election Commission* ruling. In it, the Court decided that corporations have the same free speech rights as individuals and thus cannot be banned from making independent political expenditures to fund political broadcasts in campaigns and elections under the First Amendment's free speech protections. This decision was a huge blow to the McCain/Feingold Campaign Finance Act, a notable attempt to limit the influence of big money in elections.

Groups that mobilize to protect particular economic interests generally are the most fully and effectively organized of all interest group types.[15] They exist to make profits and to obtain economic benefits for their members. To achieve these goals, however, they often find they must resort to political means rather than trust the operation of economic markets to produce favorable outcomes.

GOVERNMENTAL UNITS   State and local governments—as well as intergovernmental associations, such as the Council of Local Governments—are becoming strong organized interests as they lobby the federal government to make certain they get their fair share of federal dollars in the form of block grants or pork projects. Most states, large cities, and even public universities retain lobbyists in Washington, D.C., to advance their interests or to keep them informed about relevant legislation. States seek to influence the amount of money allotted to them in the federal budget for projects such as building roads and schools, enhancing parks or waterways, or other public works projects.

POLITICAL ACTION COMMITTEES   In 1974, amendments to the Federal Election Campaign Act made it legal for businesses, labor unions, and interest groups to form **political action committees (PACs)**, officially registered fund-raising organizations that represent interest groups in the political process. Many elected officials also have leadership PACs to help raise money for themselves and other candidates. Unlike many other types of interest groups, PACs do not have formal members; they simply have contributors (which since *Citizens United* v. *FEC* can include unions and nonprofit and for-profit corporations) who seek to influence public policy by electing legislators sympathetic to their aims.

political action committee (PAC)

Officially recognized fund-raising organization that represents interest groups and is allowed by federal law to make contributions directly to candidates' campaigns.

WHAT DO INTEREST GROUPS DO?

14.4   Analyze the methods and activities that interest groups use to influence political outcomes.

Just as members of Congress are assumed to represent the interests of their constituents in Washington, D.C., interest groups are assumed to represent the interests of their members to policy makers at all levels of government. In the 1950s, for example, the NAACP was able to articulate the interests of African Americans to national decision makers, even though as a group they had little or no electoral clout, especially in the South. Without the efforts of civil rights groups, it is unlikely that either the courts or Congress would have acted as quickly to make race discrimination illegal. By banding together with others who have similar interests at a particular time, all sorts of individuals—from railroad workers to women to physical therapists to concerned parents to members of the LGBT community to mushroom growers—can advance their collective interests in Congress, statehouses, communities, and school districts. Gaining celebrity support or hiring a lobbyist to advocate those interests also increases the likelihood that issues of concern will be addressed and acted on favorably.

Interest groups, however, do have a downside. Because groups make claims on society, they can increase the cost of public policies. The elderly can push for more costly health care and Social Security programs; people with disabilities, for improved access to public buildings and accommodations at work; industry, for tax loopholes; and veterans, for improved access to medical care and benefits that may take funds usually appropriated for other social programs. Many Americans believe that interest groups

HOW DO INTEREST GROUPS INCREASE AWARENESS OF SOCIAL ISSUES?

Over the past decade, activism regarding the stagnation of working-class wages alongside the concentration of both new income and cumulative wealth among a small sliver of the highest earners has emerged in the United States. Labor unions have had an integral role in raising awareness of this issue. Above, members of the the Service Employees International Union (SEIU), 2 million workers strong, which broke from the AFL-CIO in 2005, frame the issue as between the "99%" and the "1%."

lobbying
The activities of a group or organization that seek to persuade political leaders to support the group's position.

exist simply to advance their own selfish interests, with little regard for the rights of other groups or, more importantly, of people not represented by any organized group.

Whether good or bad, interest groups play an important role in U.S. politics. In addition to enhancing the democratic process by providing increased representation and participation, they raise public awareness about important issues, help frame the public agenda, and often monitor programs to guarantee effective implementation. Most often, they accomplish these goals through lobbying, electoral activities, or educational campaigns. The push for a national minimum wage of $15 is one such example.

Lobbying

Lobbying is at the top of most interest groups' agendas because it allows groups to effectively pursue their policy agendas by seeking to persuade political leaders to support the group's position. The exact origin of the term is disputed. In mid-seventeenth-century England, there was a room located near the floor of the House of Commons where members of Parliament would congregate and could be approached by their constituents and others who wanted to plead a particular cause. Similarly, in the United States, people often waited outside the chambers of the House and Senate to speak to members of Congress as they emerged. Because they waited in the lobbies to argue their cases, by the nineteenth century they were commonly referred to as lobbyists. An alternate piece of folklore explains that when Ulysses S. Grant was president, he would frequently walk from the White House to the Willard Hotel on Pennsylvania Avenue just to relax in its comfortable and attractive lobby. Interest group representatives and those seeking favors from Grant would crowd into that lobby and try to press their claims. Soon they were nicknamed lobbyists (see Figure 14.2).

FIGURE 14.2   HOW MANY LOBBYISTS ARE THERE? HOW MUCH DO THEY SPEND?

In 2016, 9,700 registered lobbyists attempted to influence public policy in Congress and the federal agencies. While this number represented a record low since 1998, this large-scale lobbying effort is an expensive industry, costing 3.1 billion dollars.

SOURCE: Center for Responsive Politics.

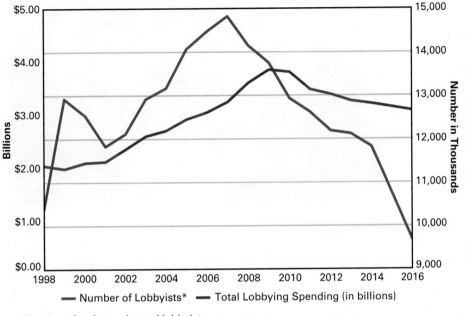

*Number of active registered lobbyists

Most politically active groups use lobbying to make their interests heard and understood by those in a position to influence or change governmental policies. Depending on the type of group and on the role it aims to play, lobbying can take many forms. You probably have never thought of the Boy Scouts or Girl Scouts as political. Yet, when Congress began debating the passage of legislation dealing with discrimination in private clubs, representatives of both organizations testified in the hope of persuading Congress to allow them to remain single-sex organizations.

LOBBYING CONGRESS   A wide variety of lobbying activities target members of Congress: congressional testimony on behalf of a group, individual letters or e-mails from interested constituents, campaign contributions, or the outright payment of money for votes. Of course, the last activity is illegal, but there exist numerous documented instances of money changing hands for votes.

Lobbying Congress and issue advocacy are skills that many people have developed over the years. In 1869, for example, women gathered in Washington, D.C., for the second annual meeting of the National Woman Suffrage Association and marched to Capitol Hill to hear one of their members (unsuccessfully) ask Congress to pass legislation that would enfranchise women under the terms of the Fourteenth Amendment. Practices such as these floor speeches are no longer permitted.

Today, many effective lobbyists are former members of Congress, staff aides, or other Washington insiders. These connections help them develop close relationships with senators and House members in an effort to enhance their access to the policy-making process. A symbiotic relationship between members of Congress, interest group representatives, and affected bureaucratic agencies often develops. Congressional representatives and their staff members, who face an exhausting workload and legislation they frequently know little about, often look to lobbyists for information. "Information is the currency on Capitol Hill, not dollars," said one lobbyist.[16] One aide reports: "My boss demands a speech and a statement for the *Congressional Record* for every bill we introduce or co-sponsor—and we have a lot of bills. I just can't

WHAT ROLE DO LOBBYISTS PLAY IN CONGRESS?

This cartoon presents one popular view of how legislation gets enacted on Capitol Hill. Political science research, however, reveals that interest groups do not directly "buy" members' votes in a quid pro quo. They do, however, reward loyal supporters in Congress with campaign contributions and other incentives.

do it all myself. The better lobbyists, when they have a proposal they are pushing, bring it to me along with a couple of speeches, a *Record* insert, and a fact sheet."[17]

Not surprisingly, lobbyists work most closely with representatives who share their interests.[18] A lobbyist from the National Rifle Association (NRA), for example, would be unlikely to try influencing a liberal representative who, on record, was strongly in favor of gun control. It is much more effective for a group such as the NRA to provide useful information for its supporters and to those who are undecided. Good lobbyists also can encourage members to file amendments to bills favorable to their interests. They also can urge their supporters in Congress to make speeches (often written by the group) and to pressure their colleagues in the chamber.

A lobbyist's effectiveness depends largely on his or her reputation for fair play and provision of accurate information. No member of Congress wants to look uninformed. As one member noted: "It doesn't take very long to figure out which lobbyists are straightforward and which ones are trying to snow you. The good ones will give you the weak points as well as the strong points of their case. If anyone ever gives me false or misleading information, that's it—I'll never see him again."[19]

LOBBYING THE EXECUTIVE BRANCH As the executive branch has increasingly concerned itself with shaping legislation, lobbying efforts directed toward the president and the bureaucracy have gained in frequency and importance. Groups often target one or more levels of the executive branch because so many potential access points exist, including the president, White House staff, and numerous levels of the executive branch bureaucracy. Groups try to work closely with the administration to influence policy decisions at their formulation and later implementation stages as well as to obtain appropriations from various departments and government entities. Bureaucrats often look to organized interests to help them implement rules, while interest groups may pressure bureaucrats to approach regulation with caution.

As with congressional lobbying, the effectiveness of a group often depends on its ability to provide decision makers with important information and a sense of where the public stands on the issue. The National Women's Law Center, for example, has been instrumental in seeing that Title IX, which Congress passed to mandate educational equity for women and girls, is always on the agenda of the Department of Education, which is charged with its enforcement.

LOBBYING THE COURTS   The courts, too, have proved a useful target for interest groups.[20] Although you might think the courts decide cases affecting only the parties involved or they should be immune from political pressures, interest groups for years have recognized the value of lobbying the courts, especially the U.S. Supreme Court, and many political scientists view it as a form of political participation.[21]

Generally, interest group lobbying of the courts takes two forms: (1) direct sponsorship, or (2) the filing of *amicus curiae* briefs. Sponsorship involves providing resources (financial, human, or otherwise) to shepherd a case through the judicial system, and the group may even become a named party, as in *Planned Parenthood of Southeastern Pennsylvania* v. *Casey* (1992). Interest groups may be parties to a case even when they are not named as the lead party. In *Zubik* v. *Burwell*, a 2016 Supreme Court decision, seven cases from different lower courts were consolidated under one name. Little Sisters of the Poor and Priests for Life, lead parties in two of the seven cases, were not named.

When a case that a group is interested in, but not actually sponsoring, comes before a court, the organization often will file an *amicus* brief—either alone or with other like-minded groups—to inform the justices of the group's policy preferences, generally offered in the guise of legal arguments. Over the years, as the number of both liberal and conservative groups viewing litigation as a useful tactic has increased, so has the number of briefs submitted to the courts. An interest group has sponsored or filed an *amicus curiae* brief in most of the major U.S. Supreme Court cases noted in this text.[22] Interest groups also file *amicus* briefs in lower federal and state supreme courts.

In addition to litigating, interest groups try to influence nominations to the federal courts. For example, they play an important part in judicial nominees' Senate confirmation hearings. In 2009, for example, 218 groups testified or prepared statements for or against the nomination of Sonia Sotomayor to the Supreme Court. The diversity of groups was astounding, from gun rights groups to pro-choice groups, women's groups, and Hispanic advocacy organizations.[23]

GRASSROOTS LOBBYING   Interest groups regularly try to inspire their members to engage in grassroots lobbying, hoping that lawmakers will respond to those pressures and the attendant publicity.[24] In essence, the goal of many organizations is to persuade ordinary voters to serve as their advocates. In the world of lobbying, few things are more useful than a list of committed supporters. Radio and TV talk-show hosts such as conservative Rush Limbaugh and liberal Rachel Maddow try to stir up their listeners by urging them to contact their representatives in Washington, D.C. Other interest groups use petition drives and carefully targeted and costly TV advertisements pitching one side of an argument. It is also routine for interest groups to e-mail or text message their members and provide a direct Web link as well as suggested text that citizens can use to lobby their legislators.

PROTESTS AND RADICAL ACTIVISM   A highly visible tactic used by some groups is nonviolent protest activity such as that once used by the Southern Christian Leadership Council and also by the Black Lives Matter movement today. Although most groups opt for more conventional forms of lobbying and seek to influence policy through the electoral process, when these forms of interest group activities are unsuccessful, some groups (or individuals within groups) resort to more forceful measures to attract attention to their cause.

Legal, peaceful protests are now the norm among interest groups in the United States, but a minority of participants and groups within larger movements may rely on illegal protest activities and tactics that range from intimidation to terrorist violence. Intimidation tactics include publishing the names, contact information, and addresses of those groups or individuals believed to be engaging in wrongful activity and urging supporters to phone, e-mail, or protest outside of their homes. Some groups have faced federal terrorism charges for their illegal actions. In other situations, overreaction by members of the police or individual protesters may result in violence and injuries at the site of an otherwise peaceful protest.

Election Activities

In addition to trying to achieve their goals (or at least draw attention to them) by lobbying, many interest groups also become involved more directly in the electoral process. Interest groups recruit and endorse candidates, aid in get out the vote campaigns, and rate officeholders. The recent midterm and presidential elections, for example, were the targets of significant fund raising of more than one billion dollars by organized interests.

CANDIDATE RECRUITMENT AND ENDORSEMENTS Interest groups play an important role in helping to identify potential candidates for political office. Involvement in an interest group helps citizens to develop the skills necessary to be effective leaders, fundraisers, and communicators. Organized interests may also believe that activists and members will be particularly effective advocates for their causes as candidates or elected officials. To further this goal, many groups also provide candidate training, make direct and indirect contributions to campaigns, help to hire campaign consultants, and fund some print and digital media.

Interest groups may also choose to endorse candidates who express views consistent with their policy positions. Candidate endorsements play a prominent role in focusing voters' attention on candidates who share their beliefs. Endorsements may also help to mobilize group members and provide much needed volunteers and enthusiasm. They may also provide voters with reasons not to vote for a particular candidate. An NRA endorsement, for example, may lead gun control advocates to vote against an NRA supported candidate.

GETTING OUT THE VOTE Many interest groups believe they can influence public policy by putting like-minded representatives in office. To that end, many groups across the ideological spectrum launch massive get-out-the-vote (GOTV) efforts. These include identifying prospective voters and transporting them to the polls. Well-financed interest groups often cast a wider net, producing issue-oriented ads for newspapers, radio, TV, and social media designed to educate the public as well as increase voter interest in election outcomes. Planned Parenthood and the NRA did so in 2016, for example.

RATING THE CANDIDATES OR OFFICE HOLDERS Many ideological groups rate candidates to help their members (and the general public) evaluate the voting records of members of Congress. They use these ratings to help their members and other voters make informed voting decisions. The American Conservative Union (conservative) and Americans for Democratic Action (liberal)—two groups at ideological polar extremes—are just two examples of groups that routinely rate candidates and members of Congress based on their votes on key issues.

CAMPAIGN CONTRIBUTIONS Corporations, labor unions, and interest groups may give money to political candidates in a number of ways. Organized interests are allowed to form political action committees (PACs) to raise money for direct contributions to political candidates in national elections. PAC money plays a significant role in the campaigns of many congressional incumbents, often averaging more than half a House candidate's total spending (see Figure 14.3). PACs generally contribute to those who have helped them before and who serve on committees or subcommittees that routinely consider legislation of concern to that group.

Some organized interests may also prefer to make campaign expenditures through industry PACs, leadership PACs, and Super PACs, among others. Based on

FIGURE 14.3 HOW MUCH MONEY DO TOP PACS SPEND ON NATIONAL
ELECTIONS?

Political action committees play an important role in national elections. The amount of money they spend
and how it is allocated between Democrats and Republicans varies widely over interest group sectors,
as shown in this illustration of spending through October 28 during the 2015–2016 election cycle.

SOURCE: Center for Responsive Politics, www.opensecrets.org.

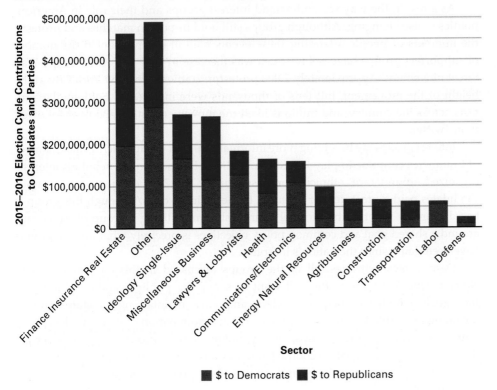

federal court decisions starting in 2010, Super PACs may raise unlimited funds since
political speech is considered protected speech, but such funds may not be given to or
spent in coordination with a candidate's campaign. This money may be used for issue
advocacy, however, which may help a group's preferred candidate indirectly. These
groups have been major players in recent elections.

Educational Campaigns

Interest groups may choose to raise awareness and sway voters to their viewpoints
on key issues—especially when voters have a choice between a candidate sympathetic to a group's views and a candidate who is not. In these circumstances, interest
groups often try to simplify or even oversimplify the issue with a slogan or biting
campaign ad. Groups also identify issues that they believe are of particular interest
to certain groups of voters. The American Association of University Women is one
such group.

WHAT MAKES INTEREST GROUPS SUCCESSFUL?

14.5 Evaluate the factors that affect the relative success of interest groups.

In early America, interest groups were largely ad hoc organizations formed in local
communities. Following the advent of television, the first national political organizations began to take shape. Today, smartphones and social media platforms such

Marian Wright Edelman
A lawyer who in 1973 founded the Children's Defense Fund to protect the rights of children, particularly those who are members of disadvantaged groups.

as Facebook and Twitter have once again contributed to changes in the interest group system.

No longer does joining a group imply attending physical meetings or becoming a dues-paying or card-carrying member. Today, joining an interest group or participating in a social movement may be as simple as clicking a "like" button, signing an online petition, sharing on Facebook or signing up for an e-mail listserv.

As a result, the way we understand interest groups and their role in American politics is also changing. Although groups still hold in-person marches and protests, the numbers of people attending these events pale in comparison to the number of supporters groups have online. Such was the case in 2011 with the Occupy Wall Street movement. Approximately 2,000 protestors gathered in New York City at the height of the movement, but tens of thousands were inspired to hold similar protests across the country, and millions liked the movement on Facebook or followed it on Twitter.

Interest groups are becoming more informal. Stalwart groups such as the Chamber of Commerce continue to play key roles in politics. But, so, too, do nebulous interests organized around race, ethnicity, or class. During the 2016 elections, for example, candidates paid a great deal of attention to the "middle class." Though this group is based more on identity than formal membership, mobilizing a group of Americans around a shared goal and common policy objectives is precisely what interest groups have been doing since the nation's inception.

Despite these changes, all of the groups discussed in this chapter have one characteristic in common: they all want to shape the public agenda and advance their goals, whether by helping to elect candidates, maintaining the status quo, or obtaining favorable legislation or judicial rulings from national, state, and local governments.[25] For powerful groups, simply making sure that certain issues never get discussed may be the goal. In contrast, other groups succeed when an issue they care about becomes front-page news and citizens place pressure on government leaders to address it.

Groups succeed when they win legislation, court cases, or even elections individually or in coalition with other groups.[26] They also are successful when their leaders become elected officials or policy makers in any of the three branches of the government. For example, Representative Rosa DeLauro (D–CT) was a former political director of EMILY's List. And, President Barack Obama worked as a grassroots community organizer for a variety of Chicago-based groups before being elected a senator from Illinois.

Political scientists have studied several phenomena that contribute in varying degrees—individually and collectively—to particular groups' successes. These include leaders, funding and patrons, and a solid membership base.

Leaders

Interest group theorists frequently acknowledge the role of leaders in the formation, viability, and success of interest groups while noting that leaders often vary from rank-and-file members on various policies.[27] Without the powerful pen of William Lloyd Garrison in the 1830s, who knows whether the abolition movement would have been as successful? Other notable leaders include Frances Willard of the WCTU; **Marian Wright Edelman**, who founded the Children's Defense Fund; and Jerry Falwell Jr., who has continued his father's work as president of Liberty University.

The role of an interest group leader is similar to that of an entrepreneur in the business world. Leaders of groups must find ways to attract members. As in the marketing of a new product, an interest-group leader must offer something attractive to entice members to join. Potential members of the group must be convinced that the

benefits of joining outweigh the costs. Union members, for example, must be persuaded that the union's winning higher wages and concessions for them will offset the cost of their union dues.

patron
A person who finances a group or individual activity.

Funding and Patrons

Advertising, litigating, and lobbying are expensive. Without financiers, few public interest groups could survive their initial start-up periods. To remain in business, many interest groups rely on membership dues, direct-mail solicitations, special events, and patrons. Charismatic leaders often are especially effective fundraisers and recruiters of new members. In addition, governments, foundations, and wealthy individuals can serve as **patrons**, providing crucial start-up funds for groups, especially public interest groups.[28]

Members

Organizations usually comprise three kinds of members. At the top are a relatively small number of leaders who devote most of their energies to the single group. The second tier of members generally is involved psychologically as well as organizationally. They are the workers of the group—they attend meetings, pay dues, and chair committees to see that things get done. In the bottom tier are the rank-and-file members who don't actively participate. They pay their dues and call themselves group members, but they do little more. Most group members fall into this last category. Their reasons for joining may be varied; some choose to participate because they feel a particular right is threatened, while others, such as lawyers who join the American Bar Association, do so in part for professional credibility.

Survey data have consistently revealed that group membership is drawn primarily from people with higher income and education levels.[29] Individuals who are wealthier can afford to belong to more organizations because they have more money and, often, more leisure time. Money and education also are associated with greater confidence that one's actions will bring results, a further incentive to devote time to organizing or supporting interest groups. These elites also are often more involved in politics and hold stronger opinions on many political issues.

HOW DO INTEREST GROUPS CONVINCE POTENTIAL MEMBERS TO BECOME DUES-PAYING MEMBERS?

AARP has been particularly successful at motivating its pool of potential members to join, in large part because it offers a variety of material benefits. Here, AARP members in Michigan hold a rally advocating the importation of cheaper prescription drugs from Canada, just across the bridge shown in the background.

free rider problem
Potential members who fail to join a group because they can get the benefit, or collective good, sought by the group without contributing the effort.

People who do belong to groups often join more than one. Overlapping memberships can affect the cohesiveness of a group. Imagine, for example, that you are an officer in the College Republicans. If you call a meeting, people may not attend because they have academic, athletic, or social obligations. Divided loyalties and multiple group memberships frequently affect the success of a group, especially if any one group has too many members who simply fall into the dues-paying category.

Groups vary tremendously in their ability to enroll what are called potential members. As noted earlier, according to Mancur Olson, all groups provide a collective good.[30] If one union member at a factory gets a raise, for example, all other workers at that factory will, too. Therefore, those who don't join or work for the benefit of the group still reap the rewards of the group's activity. The downside of this phenomenon is called the **free rider problem**. As Olson asserts, potential members may be unlikely to join a group because they realize that they will receive many of the benefits the group achieves, regardless of their participation. Not only is it irrational for free riders to join any group, but the bigger the group, the greater the free rider problem. In a small group such as the National Governors Association, any individual's share of the collective good may be great enough to make it rational for him or her to join.

Groups attempt to overcome the free rider problem in numerous ways. One method used by many groups is providing a variety of material benefits to convince potential members to join. The American Automobile Association (better known as AAA), for example, offers roadside assistance and trip-planning services to its members. Similarly, AARP offers a wide range of discount programs to its members over the age of fifty. Many of those members do not necessarily support all of the group's positions but simply want to take advantage of its discounts. Other groups may overcome this problem by forming alliances that allow interests to work together to solve problems. Finally, patrons, be they large foundations such as the Koch Family Foundation or individuals such as wealthy financier George Soros, may also help to alleviate the free rider problem for public interest groups.[31] They make the costs of joining minimal because they contribute much of the group's necessary financial support.[32]

TOWARD REFORM: REGULATING INTEREST GROUPS AND LOBBYISTS

14.6 Assess the effectiveness of regulations designed to control interest groups.

For the first 150 years of our nation's history, federal lobbying practices went unregulated. While the courts remain largely free of lobbying regulations, reforms have altered the state of affairs in Congress and the executive branch.

Regulating Congressional Lobbyists

In 1946, in an effort to limit the power of lobbyists, Congress passed the Federal Regulation of Lobbying Act, which required anyone hired to lobby any member of Congress to register and file quarterly financial reports. For years, few lobbyists actually filed these reports and numerous good-government groups continued to argue for the strengthening of lobbying laws.

By 1995, public opinion polls began to show that Americans believed the votes of members of Congress were available to the highest bidder. Thus, in late 1995, Congress passed the first effort to regulate lobbying since the 1946 act. The **Lobbying Disclosure Act** employed a strict definition of lobbyist (one who devotes at least 20 percent of a client's or employer's time to lobbying activities). It also required lobbyists to: (1) register with the clerk of the House and the secretary of the Senate; (2) report their clients and issues and the agency or house they lobbied; and (3) estimate the amount they are paid by each client. These reporting requirements made it easier for watchdog groups or the media to monitor lobbying activities, but they did little to reduce the influence of pressure groups in the Congress, where it is believed that some lobbyists are no longer registering.

In the wake of a variety of lobbying scandals, Congress attempted to remedy this problem by passing the **Honest Leadership and Open Government Act of 2007**. Among the act's key provisions were a ban on gifts and honoraria worth over fifty dollars to members of Congress and their staffs, tougher disclosure requirements, and longer time limits on moving from the federal government to the private lobbying sector. Many observers complained, however, that the law did not go far enough. In particular, many commentators were critical of the fact that the ban on gifts applied only to private lobbyists. Thus, state and local agencies and public universities, for example, are still free to offer tickets for football and basketball games, as well as to provide meals and travel.[33] And, spending on lobbying has not abated; in one recent Congress, nearly $6 million was spent on lobbying for every member.[34]

Regulating Executive Branch Lobbyists

Formal lobbying of the executive branch is governed by some restrictions in the 1995 Lobbying Disclosure Act as well as updates contained in the Honest Leadership and Open Government Act. Executive branch employees are also constrained by the 1978 Ethics in Government Act. Enacted in the wake of the Watergate scandal, this legislation attempted to curtail questionable moves by barring members of the executive branch from representing any clients before their agency for two years after leaving governmental service. Thus, someone who worked in air pollution policy for the Environmental Protection Agency and then went to work for the Environmental Defense Fund would have to wait two years before lobbying his or her old agency.

More recently, the Obama administration has implemented reforms that bring congressional-style lobbying regulation to the executive branch. In regulations put into place on his first day on the job, Barack Obama limited aides leaving the White

Lobbying Disclosure Act
A 1995 federal law that employed a strict definition of lobbyist and established strict reporting requirements on the activities of lobbyists.

Honest Leadership and Open Government Act of 2007
Lobbying reform banning gifts to members of Congress and their staffs, toughening disclosure requirements, and increasing time limits on moving from the federal government to the private sector.

House from lobbying executive agencies within two years. He also banned members of the administration from accepting gifts from lobbyists.

Regulating Judicial Branch Lobbyists

There are few formal regulations on interest group participation before the Supreme Court. Though interested parties must ask the Court for permission to file an *amicus curiae* brief, in practice, the great majority of these petitions are granted. In recent years, activists have called for reform to the case sponsorship and oral advocacy processes before the Court, but to no avail. Similarly, a number of nonprofit and good government groups have suggested that additional restrictions are needed on groups' access to judges in "legal education" sessions—many of which are held at fancy resorts at little to no cost to the judges. Congress and the judiciary have also failed to put these regulations in place.

REVIEW THE CHAPTER

Roots of American Interest Groups

14.1 Explain the origins of interest groups in America.

An organized interest is a collection of people or groups with shared attitudes who make claims on government. Interest groups did not begin to emerge in the United States until the 1830s. From 1890 to 1920, the Progressive movement dominated.

The Rise of the Interest Group State

14.2 Describe the genesis of modern American interest groups.

The 1960s saw the rise of a wide variety of liberal interest groups. During the 1970s and 1980s, conservatives formed new groups to counteract those efforts. Business groups, corporations, and unions also established their presence in Washington, D.C., during this time.

Why Do Interest Groups Form, and What Types of Groups Exist?

14.3 Describe how interest groups form, and identify different types of interest groups.

Political scientists approach the development of interest groups from a number of theoretical perspectives, including pluralist theory and the transactions approach. Interest groups can be classified in a variety of ways, based on their functions and membership. Several major categories of groups include public interest groups, business and economic groups, governmental units such as state and local governments, and political action committees (PACs).

What Do Interest Groups Do?

14.4 Analyze the methods and activities that interest groups use to influence political outcomes.

Interest groups often fill voids left by the major political parties and give Americans opportunities to make organized claims on government. The most common activity of interest groups is lobbying, which takes many forms. Groups routinely pressure members of Congress and their staffs, the president and the bureaucracy, and the courts; they use a variety of techniques to educate and stimulate the public to pressure key governmental decision makers. Interest groups also attempt to influence the outcome of elections. They may run their own candidates for office, rate elected officials, or form political action committees (PACs).

What Makes Interest Groups Successful?

14.5 Evaluate the factors that affect the relative success of interest groups.

Interest group success can be measured in a variety of ways, including a group's ability to get its issues on the public agenda, winning key pieces of legislation in Congress or executive branch or judicial rulings, or backing successful candidates. Several factors contribute to interest group success, including leaders and patrons, funding, and committed members.

Toward Reform: Regulating Interest Groups and Lobbyists

14.6 Assess the effectiveness of regulations designed to control interest groups.

In 1995, Congress passed the Lobbying Disclosure Act, which required lobbyists to register with both houses of Congress. By 2007, a rash of scandals resulted in sweeping reforms called the Honest Leadership and Open Government Act, which dramatically limited what lobbyists can do. The executive branch is regulated by the 1978 Ethics in Government Act. Lobbying the judiciary is largely unregulated.

LEARN THE TERMS

AFL-CIO
American Anti-Slavery Society
American Federation of Labor
    (AFL)
Christian Coalition
civic virtue
collective good
disturbance theory
economic interest group
free rider problem
Honest Leadership and Open
    Government Act of 2007

interest group
Jerry Falwell
lobbying
Lobbying Disclosure Act
lobbyist
Marian Wright Edelman
Moral Majority
National Association of
    Manufacturers (NAM)
National Rifle Association (NRA)
Pat Robertson
patron

pluralist theory
Progressive movement
political action committee (PAC)
public interest group
social capital
The Grange
trade association
transactions theory
U.S. Chamber of Commerce
Women's Christian Temperance
    Union (WCTU)

WHY DOES THE AFFORDABLE CARE ACT PROVOKE SUCH STRONG REACTIONS?
The Affordable Care Act (ACA) dramatically expanded the role of the federal government in health insurance. Above, anti-ACA protesters from the Tea Party movement at the Supreme Court in 2012 decried "Obamacare" as a move toward socialism.

SOCIAL AND ECONOMIC POLICY

LEARNING OBJECTIVES

15.1 Trace the stages of the policy-making process.

15.2 Describe the scope of the federal budget and analyze problems associated with the national deficit and debt.

15.3 Assess the effectiveness of the monetary policy tools used by the federal government to manage the economy.

15.4 Describe current U.S. policy in health care.

15.5 Describe current U.S. policy in primary, secondary, and higher education.

15.6 Describe U.S. social welfare policy and programs.

15.7 Review ongoing challenges in U.S. social and economic policy making.

Affordable Care Act (ACA)
A 2010 law designed to ensure that nearly all Americans would have access to health care coverage, including those living in poverty.

public policy
An intentional course of action or inaction followed by government in dealing with some problem or matter of concern.

The **Affordable Care Act**—also known as the ACA or "Obamacare"—was the signature domestic policy achievement of the Obama Administration. Enacted in 2010, the ACA largely accomplished what Democrats had sought since the days of President Harry Truman in the mid-twentieth century: the near-universal availability of health care throughout the country. Yet, the enactment of the ACA is a story of many challenges, compromises, and even near-death experiences.

Even with a staunchly committed president, House Speaker, and Senate majority leader, as well as substantial majorities in both houses of Congress, enactment of the ACA during the period 2009–2010 was far from assured. Some on the left advocated for a UK-style, government-run national health service; others preferred a "single-payer" system like that in Canada, where the government pays for all insurance costs. Many on the right saw the ACA as yet another example of overreach, overregulation, and excessive spending by "big government."

Among fierce and unified opposition by Republicans and intense, self-interested lobbying by entrenched insurance, health care, pharmaceutical, and other interest groups, the ACA barely made it through Congress. The law was also more modest in scope than some Democrats had desired—its major innovations were all incremental reforms. But still, the ACA prompted a potent backlash. Republicans recaptured control of the House in 2010 and sponsored a series of votes to repeal the law. Some Republican governors refused to create insurance exchanges or to accept federal funding to expand Medicaid programs in their states. A disastrously inept rollout of the healthcare.gov Web site further soured opinions among an already skeptical public. And then two potent legal challenges began making their way up to the Supreme Court.

However, the Supreme Court twice upheld the law, and after its second ruling in June 2015, President Obama argued that "the Affordable Care Act is here to stay"; and he might be right. Once a major new public program becomes established—whether it be Social Security, Medicare, the Environmental Protection Agency, or the expansion of national security powers after the September 11th attacks—it eventually becomes understood to be part of the expected scope of government.

Donald Trump and the Republican majorities in both houses of Congress have committed themselves to "repeal and replace" Obamacare. Despite this rhetoric, many of their proposals would amend the existing law rather than to abolish it. For example, insurance companies would still be required to provide coverage for pre-existing conditions and children could remain on their parents' insurance policies until age 26. Many Americans, including supporters of the Republican Party, have already come to reply on provisions such as these.

• • •

Public policy is an intentional course of action (or, sometimes, inaction) followed by government in dealing with some problem or matter of concern.[1] Individuals, groups, and even government agencies that do not comply with policies can face penalties of fines, loss of benefits, or even jail terms. The phrase "course of action" implies that policies develop or unfold over time. They involve more than a legislative decision to enact a law or a presidential decision to issue an executive order. Also important is how the law or executive order is carried out. The impact or meaning of a policy depends on whether it is vigorously enforced, enforced only in some instances, or not enforced at all. Government inaction, or the decision not to make policy, also defines public policy.

This chapter begins by discussing the policy-making process and examines how it has played out in five major areas of social and economic policy: monetary policy, fiscal policy, health, education, and social welfare. While myriad other policy areas exist, these five broad issue areas provide an overview of both the roots and reform of social and economic policy.

ROOTS OF PUBLIC POLICY: THE POLICY-MAKING PROCESS

15.1 Trace the stages of the policy-making process.

The Framers of the Constitution created a decentralized policy-making process with powers shared by Congress, the president, the courts, and the states. In addition, social forces, including public opinion toward the role and size of government, constrain the development of government policies. In some areas, such as fiscal and monetary policy, the initiative usually takes place at the federal level. In areas such as health, education, and social welfare, policy making often begins at the state and local levels, where these "laboratories for democracy" set the stage for federal governmental action. The bureaucracy is also an important policy maker. Through a quasi-legislative process known as rule making, executive branch agencies formulate and implement policies in nearly every imaginable issue area. Rules, in fact, are the largest source of policy decisions made by the national government. Even the judicial branch, which the Framers thought would be largely powerless, has evolved into an important source of policy decisions. In recent years, the Supreme Court has made policy prescriptions in each of the domestic policy issue areas discussed in this chapter as well as in criminal justice, civil liberties, civil rights, and many other areas.

As issues evolve, which branch and level of government dominates can change over time. During the nineteenth century, the national government defined its economic role narrowly, although it did collect tariffs, fund public improvements, and encourage private development. Later, the federal government's involvement in domestic policy making shifted to include improvement of social and working conditions created by industrialization and an expanded focus on issues such as health care, welfare, education, and public safety. The Great Depression sparked clear changes in the federal government's role in fiscal, monetary, and other domestic policy making, specifically in the president's role in dominating that process. President Franklin Roosevelt's New Deal created the modern welfare state and the first entitlement programs: Social Security and Aid to Families with Dependent Children. From that point, the federal government, under the direction of strong presidential advocates, continued to expand its role in domestic policy.

Theories of the Policy-Making Process

Political scientists and other social scientists have developed many theories and models to explain the formation of public policies. These theories include elite theory, bureaucratic theory, special interest theory, and pluralist theory. According to elite theory, all societies are divided into elites and masses. The elites have power to make and implement policy, while the masses simply respond to the desires of the elites. Elite theorists believe an unequal distribution of power in society is normal and inevitable.[2] Elites, however, are not immune from public opinion nor do they necessarily oppress the masses.

Bureaucratic theory dictates that all institutions, governmental and nongovernmental, have fallen under the control of a large and ever-growing bureaucracy that carries out policy using standardized procedures. This growing complexity of modern organizations has empowered bureaucrats, who become dominant as a consequence of their expertise and competence. Eventually, the bureaucrats wrest power from others, especially elected officials.

In contrast, according to special interest theory, narrow, specialized groups—not elites or bureaucrats—control the governmental process. Interest group theorists believe there are so many potential pressure points in the three branches of the

distributive policies
Public policies that provide benefits to individuals, groups, communities, or corporations.

regulatory policies
Public policies that limit the activities of individuals and corporations or prohibit certain types of unacceptable behavior.

redistributive policies
Public policies that transfer resources from one group to assist another group.

systemic agenda
A set of of issues to be discussed or given attention; it consists of all public issues viewed as requiring governmental attention.

governmental (institutional) agenda
Problems to which public officials feel obliged to devote active and serious attention.

national government, as well as at the state level, that interest groups can step in on narrow issues of particular concern to them.[3]

Finally, many political scientists subscribe to the pluralist perspective. This theory argues that political resources in the United States are scattered so widely that no single group or interest could ever gain monopoly control over any substantial area of policy.[4] Participants in every political controversy have the ability to weigh in; thus, each has some impact on how political decisions are made.

Which theory applies depends, in part, on the type of policy. Some policies are procedural in nature, incrementally changing existing policy, while others are substantive, involving bold revisions or innovation to change a policy outcome. Policy types can also be categorized as distributive, regulatory, or redistributive.[5] **Distributive policies** provide benefits to individuals, groups, communities, or corporations. These policies are the most common and, typically, the least controversial form of federal action to solve public problems, providing tangible benefits to the recipient while costs are shared widely and not necessarily viewed as competitive. Examples include student loans, farm subsidies, and water projects. **Regulatory policies** limit the activities of individuals and corporations or prohibit certain types of unacceptable behavior. Land use regulations, for example, limit how property can be developed in order to protect the environment. These policies are typically more controversial because the costs are concentrated, in this case on developers, while the benefits are diffused, or shared by the larger community. **Redistributive policy** involves transferring resources from one group to assist another group. Most social welfare programs are intrinsically redistributive in nature, which is partly why they face considerable political opposition.

Although the policy-making process is often described in terms of stages or functional activities, the process is not necessarily sequential. One illustration of such a model is shown in Figure 15.1. This model can be used to analyze any of the issues discussed in this book. Although models such as these can be useful, it is important to remember that they simplify the actual process. Moreover, models for analyzing the policy-making process do not always explain why public policies take the specific forms they do. Nor do models necessarily tell us who dominates or controls the formation of public policy.

Policy making typically can be regarded as a process of sequential steps:

1. *Agenda setting.* Government recognition that a problem is worthy of consideration for governmental intervention.
2. *Policy formulation.* Identification of alternative approaches to addressing the problems placed on the government's agenda.
3. *Policy adoption.* The formal selection of public policies through legislative, executive, judicial, and bureaucratic means.
4. *Policy implementation.* The actual funding and administration or application of public policies to their targets.
5. *Policy evaluation.* The determination of a policy's accomplishments, consequences, or shortcomings.

With this overview in mind, the chapter examines the various stages of the policy process or cycle.

The Policy-Making Cycle

An agenda is the set of issues to be discussed or given attention. Every political community—national, state, and local—has a **systemic agenda**. The systemic agenda is essentially a discussion agenda; it consists of all issues viewed as requiring public attention and as involving matters within the legitimate jurisdiction of governments.[6] A **governmental or institutional agenda**, in contrast, is much narrower.

FIGURE 15.1   WHAT ARE THE STAGES OF THE PUBLIC POLICY PROCESS?

One of the best ways to understand public policy is to examine the process by which policies are made. In the figure, the general process of policy making is broken down into five steps. Each step has distinguishing features, but it is important to remember that the steps often merge into one another in a less distinct manner.

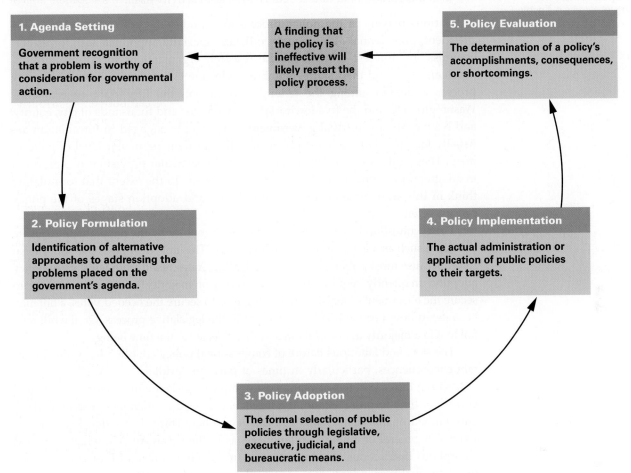

1. Agenda Setting

Government recognition that a problem is worthy of consideration for governmental action.

A finding that the policy is ineffective will likely restart the policy process.

5. Policy Evaluation

The determination of a policy's accomplishments, consequences, or shortcomings.

2. Policy Formulation

Identification of alternative approaches to addressing the problems placed on the government's agenda.

4. Policy Implementation

The actual administration or application of public policies to their targets.

3. Policy Adoption

The formal selection of public policies through legislative, executive, judicial, and bureaucratic means.

It includes only problems to which public officials feel obliged to devote active and serious attention. The movement of an issue from the systemic to the institutional agenda is known as **agenda setting**. John Kingdon has described this process as three streams—problems, policies, and politics—that must converge to create a policy window, or opportunity, for government action.[7]

Policy formulation is the crafting of proposed courses of action to resolve public problems. It has both political and technical components.[8] The political aspect of policy formulation involves determining generally what should be done to address a problem. The technical facet involves correctly stating in specific language what one wants to authorize or accomplish, to adequately guide those who must implement policy and to prevent distortion of legislative intent.

Policy formulation may take many forms:

1. *Routine formulation* is the process of altering existing policy proposals or creating new proposals within an issue area the government has previously addressed. For instance, the formulation of policy government retirees is routine.

2. *Analogous formulation* handles new problems by drawing on experience with similar problems in the past or in other jurisdictions. What has been done in the past to cope with economic recession? How have other states dealt with child abuse or divorce law reform?

agenda setting
The process of forming the list of issues to be addressed by government.

policy formulation
The crafting of proposed courses of action to resolve public problems.

policy adoption
The approval of a policy proposal by people with the requisite authority, such as a legislature.

policy implementation
The process of carrying out public policy.

3. *Creative formulation* involves attempts to develop new or unprecedented proposals that represent a departure from existing practices and that will better resolve a problem. For example, plans to develop systems that capture and store carbon dioxide emissions represent a different approach to combating climate change than more traditional calls to reduce industrial activity itself.

Various players in the policy process may undertake policy formulation: the president, presidential aides, agency officials, specially appointed task forces and commissions, interest groups, private research organizations (or "think tanks"), and legislators and their staffs. Notably, under the U.S. federal system, the policy process is shared among the federal government, the fifty state governments; Washington DC and the five territorial governments; and thousands of city, county, and Native American tribal governments. The people engaged in formulation are usually looking ahead toward policy adoption at their particular level of government. These individuals may include or exclude particular provisions of a proposal in an attempt to enhance its likelihood of adoption. To the extent that formulators think in this strategic manner, the formulation and adoption stages of the policy process often overlap.

Policy adoption is the approval of a policy proposal by the people with requisite authority, such as a legislature or chief executive. This approval gives the policy legal force. Because most public policies in the United States result from legislation, policy adoption frequently requires building a series of majority coalitions necessary to secure the enactment of legislation in Congress. To secure the needed votes, a bill may be watered down or modified at any point in the legislative process. Or, the bill may fail to win a majority at one of them and die, at least for the time being.

The slow and laborious nature of congressional policy adoption has some important consequences, particularly in times of partisan "gridlock" in Washington D.C., as has been the case in recent years. First, complex legislation may require substantial periods of time to pass. Second, the legislation passed is often incremental, making only limited or marginal changes in existing policy. Third, legislation is frequently written in general or ambiguous language, as in the Clean Air Act, which provided amorphous instructions to administrators in the Environmental Protection Agency to set air quality standards that would allow for an "adequate margin of safety" to protect the public health. Phrases such as "adequate margin" are highly subjective and open to a wide range of interpretations.[9] Language such as this may provide considerable discretion to the people who implement the law and leave them doubting its intended purposes.

Policy implementation is the process of carrying out public policies, most of which are implemented by administrative agencies. Some policies, however, are enforced in other ways. Voluntary compliance by businesses and individuals is one such technique. When grocers take out-of-date products off their shelves or when consumers choose not to buy food products after their expiration dates, voluntary compliance is at work. Implementation also involves the courts when they are called on to interpret the meaning of legislation, review the legality of agency rules and actions, and determine whether institutions such as prisons and mental hospitals conform to legal and constitutional standards.

Administrative agencies may be authorized to use a number of techniques to implement public policies within their jurisdictions. These techniques can be categorized as authoritative, incentive, capacity, or hortatory, depending on the behavioral assumptions on which they are based.[10]

1. *Authoritative techniques* for policy implementation rest on the notion that people's actions must be directed or restrained by government enforcement in order to prevent or eliminate activities or products that are unsafe, unfair, evil, or immoral.

2. *Incentive techniques* for policy implementation encourage people to act in their own best interest by offering payoffs or financial inducements for compliance with public policies. Such policies may provide tax deductions to encourage charitable giving or the purchase of alternative fuel vehicles, such as hybrid automobiles. Conversely, sanctions, such as high taxes, may discourage the purchase and use of products such as tobacco and liquor, and pollution fees may reduce the discharge of pollutants by making this action more costly to businesses.

3. *Capacity techniques* provide people with information, education, training, or resources that enable them to participate in desired activities. The assumption underlying these techniques is that people have an incentive or desire to do what is right but sometimes lack the capacity to act accordingly.

4. *Hortatory techniques* encourage people to comply with policy by appealing to their "better instincts" and thereby directing them to act in desired ways. In this instance, policy implementers assume that people decide how to act according to their personal values and beliefs.

Often, government will turn to a combination of authoritative, incentive, capacity, and hortatory approaches to reach its goals. For example, public health officials use all of these tools in their efforts to reduce tobacco use. These techniques include laws prohibiting smoking in public places, taxes on the sales of tobacco products, warning labels on packs of cigarettes, and anti-smoking commercials on TV. There is no easy formula that will guarantee successful policy implementation; in practice, many policies only partially achieve their goals.

Budgeting also influences policy implementation. When a policy is adopted, funding levels are recommended but must be finalized by another set of policy makers. Congress often separates the authorizations of new policies from the appropriations of funds so that debates over new policies do not delay or derail the national budgetary process. Whether a policy is well funded, poorly funded, or funded at all has a significant effect on its scope, impact, and effectiveness.

Practitioners of **policy evaluation** seek to determine whether a course of action is achieving its intended goals. They may also try to determine whether a policy is being fairly or efficiently administered. Policy evaluation may be conducted by a variety of players, including congressional committees, presidential commissions, administrative agencies, the courts, university researchers, private research organizations, and the Government Accountability Office (GAO). The GAO, created in 1921, conducts hundreds of studies of government agencies and programs each year, either at the request of members of Congress or on its own initiative.

Evaluation research and studies can stimulate attempts to modify or terminate policies and thus restart the policy process. Legislators and administrators may formulate and advocate for amendments designed to correct problems or shortcomings in a policy. The evaluation process may also result in the termination of policies. Policies may also be terminated automatically through sunset provisions, or "expiration dates," that Congress can add to legislation.

The budgetary process also gives the president and the Congress an opportunity to review the government's many policies and programs, to inquire into their administration, to appraise their value and effectiveness, and to exercise some influence on their conduct.

Not all of the government's thousands of programs undergo full examination every year. But, over a period of several years, most programs come under scrutiny. The demise of programs is relatively rare; more often, a troubled program is modified or allowed to limp along because it provides a popular service or is supported by a powerful organized interest group.

policy evaluation
The process of determining whether a course of action is achieving its intended goals.

fiscal policy
The deliberate use of the national government's taxing and spending policies to maintain economic stability.

national debt
The total amount owed by the federal government to its creditors, both domestic and international.

laissez-faire
Economic philosophy that endorses a very limited role for government in the economy.

FISCAL POLICY

15.2 Describe the scope of the federal budget, and analyze problems associated with the national deficit and debt.

Fiscal policy is the deliberate use of the national government's taxing and spending policies to maintain economic growth and stability (see Figure 15.2 for breakdowns of federal spending for fiscal year 2017). Government spending, taxing, and borrowing are the principal tools used to expand or contract the economy as needed. Deficits or surpluses are the outcomes of these policy decisions. When government spending is not offset by tax revenue, the result is a deficit at the end of the fiscal year. If, however, tax revenue exceeds spending, the result is a government surplus.

Economists argue that increased government spending stimulates economic growth, which can help the economy rebound from a recession. However, it also means that government is likely to run a deficit. The continuation of deficits long term, especially after the economy has recovered, can have adverse effects, including inflation and increased **national debt**. The national debt is the total amount owed by the federal government to its creditors, both domestic and international. Financing a large national debt reduces government savings and the amount of capital available for investment. As the debt grows, interest payments increase and must be offset by tax increases or spending cuts. If investor confidence in the government's ability to manage its finances weakens, lenders will charge the government higher interest rates. High debt also reduces the government's ability to use taxes and spending to address fiscal crises in the future. The right combination of government spending and taxes is a constant source of debate, influenced by economic theory, history, politics, and public opinion.

The Foundations of Fiscal Policy

Prior to the 1930s, the U.S. government largely subscribed to a *laissez faire* (literally "to allow to do" or "to leave alone") economic philosophy, which endorses a

FIGURE 15.2 HOW DOES THE FEDERAL GOVERNMENT RAISE AND SPEND MONEY?

The federal government budget outlines how taxpayer revenues are raised and spent, summarizing the priorities of federal government policy making.

SOURCES: Data from the National Priorities Project, www.nationalpriorities.org/budget-basics/federal-budget-101/revenues/and www.nationalpriorities.org/budget-basics/federal-budget-101/spending/

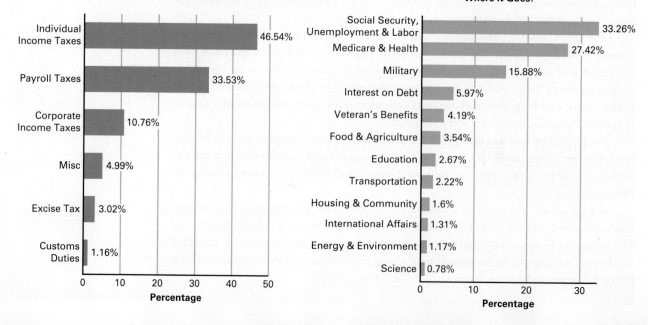

very limited role for government in the economy. In the late nineteenth and early twentieth century, Congress began to expand its oversight of new economic developments such as railroads and telecommunications. It also enacted antitrust laws to prevent large-scale monopolistic practices. But it was not until the New Deal—and President Franklin D. Roosevelt's response to the Great Depression—that the federal government played an increasingly interventionist role through financial reforms, agricultural policy, protection of laborers, and regulation of industry.

In the era of the Great Depression, British economist John Maynard Keynes revolutionized economic policy theory by arguing that spending by governments could prevent the worst impacts of **recession** and **depression** through increasing people's disposable income to encourage economic activity, even at the risk of running government deficits. This view represented a departure from *laissez-faire*, which suggested that if left alone, a free market would regulate itself. In contrast, proponents of **Keynesian economics** maintained that increasing demand would increase employment, stimulating a cycle of economic growth much faster than a free market would accomplish on its own.

The benefits of more immediate economic growth, they believed, outweighed the costs of government deficits in the short run. Governments could increase demand through increased government spending, tax cuts, or a combination of the two. Economists argued, however, that government spending would increase consumption and demand more directly than tax cuts. This is the case because people do not always spend their tax cuts; they often save the money or use it to pay down existing debt. The precise mix of government spending and taxes, however, is often dictated more by politics than economics.

In the short term, budget deficits may have positive economic benefits. However, in the long term, running deficits year after year can have negative consequences. A high national debt such as this can stifle economic growth and cause **inflation**, a rise

recession
A decline in the economy that occurs as investment sags, production falls off, and unemployment increases.

depression
A severe and long lasting decline in the economy that occurs as investment sags, production falls off, and unemployment increases.

Keynesian economics
An economic approach first championed by economist John Maynard Keynes in the 1930s, who maintained that spending by government can stimulate economic growth much faster than a free market could on its own.

inflation
A rise in the general price levels of goods and services within an economy.

WHO WAS JOHN MAYNARD KEYNES?

Often referred to as the father of modern macroeconomic theory, the British economist John Maynard Keynes is shown here addressing a conference in the 1940s. In the context of the Great Depression, he introduced theories favoring government spending to promote economic growth.

budget deficit
The economic condition that occurs when expenditures exceed revenues.

in the general price levels of an economy. The national debt—as with personal debt in the form of credit cards and student loans—must also be paid back with interest. This repayment can be a costly proposition that diverts attention and money from other governmental programs for years to come.

In the early 1960s, Democratic President John F. Kennedy, committed to getting the country moving again through the use of fiscal policy, brought economists to Washington, D.C. to study the issue. There emerged a consensus that greater government spending, even at the expense of an increase in the **budget deficit**, was needed to achieve full employment. This thinking is consistent with Keynesian economics; however, many conservatives opposed budget deficits as bad public policy. To appease these critics, the president's advisers decided that many Americans would find deficits less objectionable if they were achieved by cutting taxes rather than by increasing government spending. This decision resulted in adoption of the Revenue Act of 1964, which President Lyndon B. Johnson signed into law. The act reduced personal and corporate income tax rates. The tax-cut stimulus contributed to the expansion of the economy throughout the remainder of the 1960s and reduced the unemployment rate to less than 4 percent, its lowest peacetime rate and what many people then considered essentially full employment.[11] The 1970s, however, were marred by the experience of so-called "stagflation" in which wages are stagnant but inflation is increasing due to outside factors, in this case the global price of oil.

During the 1980s when President Ronald Reagan introduced "supply-side economics," which advanced the idea that deep cuts in the tax rates paid by high earners would stimulate new investment and economic growth. Therefore, *lower* tax rates would ultimately result in *higher* overall tax revenues by expanding the size of the economy. Likewise, under a theory of "trickle-down economics," tax cuts targeted at the wealthy would create opportunities throughout the entire economy because the wealthy would then cause the private sector to grow and to create new and better-paying jobs. Reagan also endorsed cuts in spending on most nonmilitary programs and promoted an ideology of rolling back the level of government regulation of the economy. Despite the theory of supply-side economics, however, in practice the federal deficit expanded considerably during the Reagan era, due partly to lower tax revenues and partly to increased spending on defense.

The National Deficit and Debt

While most of the fifty states are required by their state constitutions or laws to have a balanced budget—revenues must meet or exceed expenditures—this is not the norm for the federal government. The Constitution does not limit the annual deficit nor the overall level of debt for the federal government. For most of the first 200 years of U.S. history, the federal government usually ran annual budget deficits only in times of war or economic downturns. This pattern was broken in the 1980s, with peacetime deficits averaging $206 billion between 1983 and 1992. This increased the level of government debt from $789 billion in 1981 to $3 trillion in 1992.[12]

The federal government briefly ran surpluses again in the late 1990s, when the economy was experiencing an expansion due to the widespread use of the Internet and budget deals cut between Democratic President Bill Clinton and a Congress fully controlled by Republicans for the first time since the 1950s. However, a new pattern of extraordinary annual deficits resulted during the George W. Bush administration due to such factors as tax cuts, the wars in Iraq and Afghanistan, and expanded spending on homeland security.

In the fall of 2008, an economic recession and the collapse of the mortgage industry led to a cascading crisis that threatened the world's financial system. As the risk of a global economic depression grew, the federal government acted repeatedly to stimulate the economy and reinvigorate consumer spending through fiscal policy. Under both Presidents George W. Bush and Barack Obama, Congress enacted various "bailout packages" for distressed banks, extended unemployment insurance, cut taxes, and raised spending. Prominent among these programs were the Troubled Assets Relief Program (TARP), which helped to stabilize American banks, and the American Recovery and Reinvestment Act (ARRA), which authorized the more than $787 billion in spending on a variety of tax cuts and public works programs designed to stimulate the economy and to maintain and create jobs. In response to stubborn rates of unemployment, the federal government also extended and expanded unemployment benefits. The government's response to the economy—increased government spending plus tax cuts—fits the Keynesian model, and labor market indicators began to improve. The economy started to grow steadily by the third quarter of 2009, and employment increased. From a peak of 10.0 percent in October 2009, unemployment decreased to 8.1 percent by 2012 and to 5 percent in 2016.[13]

As a consequence, however, in 2008 the federal government's debt exceeded $10 trillion for the first time and in 2011 reached $14.2 trillion, which Congress had established by law as the limit on how much the U.S. government can borrow. This breaching of the so-called "debt ceiling" forced President Barack Obama and congressional leaders to struggle to reach a compromise that linked an increase in the debt ceiling to long-term spending cuts. The Budget Control Act of 2011 authorized a short-term increase in the debt ceiling but also led to a policy of automatic across-the-board budget cuts known as "sequestration." The inability of Congress and the president to agree on spending levels or tax rates means that the country faces a potential crisis every time the debt limit is reached. In 2013, this impasse reached a low point when the federal government was briefly forced to shut down nonessential services and even ran the risk of defaulting on its loan payments, which could have had catastrophic effects in the United States and worldwide.[14]

Since then, some of the political brinksmanship has subsided. In November 2015, Congress voted to set a budget, ease sequestration, and at least postpone the risk of debt default in the near future. However, the ideological polarization of the two major parties has continued to block agreement on a so-called "grand bargain" in which Democrats would concede some domestic spending cuts and Republicans would accept some higher tax rates. By 2016, the national debt increased to $19.2 trillion, over 100 percent of **gross domestic product (GDP)**, or the total market value of all goods and services produced in a country during a year. The federal government budget included a projected $503 billion deficit for fiscal year 2017.[15]

MONETARY POLICY

15.3 Assess the effectiveness of the monetary policy tools used by the federal government to manage the economy.

Economic stability is also promoted through **monetary policy**, by regulating the nation's supply of money and influencing interest rates. The **Federal Reserve System** (informally, "the Fed"), especially its Board of Governors, handles much of the day-to-day management of monetary policy and is given a number of tools to aid its efforts.

The Federal Reserve System

Created in 1913 to adjust the money supply to the needs of agriculture, commerce, and industry, the Federal Reserve System comprises the Federal Reserve Board, the Federal Open Market Committee (FOMC), the twelve Federal Reserve Banks in regions throughout the country, and other member banks.[16] Typically, the **Board of Governors** of the Federal Reserve System, a seven-member board that makes most economic decisions regarding interest rates and the supply of money, dominates this process. The board is designed to be politically independent.

gross domestic product (GDP)
The total market value of all goods and services produced in a country during a year.

monetary policy
A form of government regulation in which the nation's money supply and interest rates are controlled.

Federal Reserve System
The organization in the United States tasked with such responsibilities as managing the money supply, stabilizing prices, moderating interest rates, and reducing unemployment.

Board of Governors
In the Federal Reserve System, a seven-member board that makes most economic decisions regarding interest rates and the supply of money; it is led by the Federal Reserve chair.

open market operations
The buying and selling of government securities by the Federal Reserve Bank.

discount rate
The rate of interest at which the Federal Reserve Board lends money to member banks.

reserve requirements
Government requirements that a portion of member banks' deposits be retained as backing for their loans.

The president appoints (subject to Senate confirmation) the seven members of the Board of Governors, who serve fourteen-year, overlapping terms. The president can remove a member who commits illegal activities, but this has never occurred. The president designates one board member to serve as chair for a four-year term, which runs from the midpoint of one presidential term to the midpoint of the next to ensure economic stability during a change of administrations. It also insulates monetary policy from being excessively influenced by political considerations. Federal Reserve Chairs are among the most high-profile and powerful appointed officials in the nation, with wide-ranging influence over the U.S. economy.

The Tools of Monetary Policy

The primary monetary policy tools used by the Fed are open market operations, control of the discount rate, and the setting of reserve requirements for member banks. **Open market operations** are the buying and selling of government securities, or debt, by the Federal Reserve Bank. The Federal Open Market Committee meets periodically to decide on purchases or sale of government securities to member banks. When member banks buy long-term government bonds, they make dollar payments to the Fed and reduce the amount of money available for loans.

The Fed also influences interest rates through the **discount rate**, or the rate of interest at which it lends money to member banks. Lowering the discount rate encourages member banks to increase their borrowing from the Fed and extend more loans at lower rates. This practice expands economic activity, since more people should be able to qualify for car loans or mortgages if rates are lower. As a consequence of cheaper interest rates, more large durable goods (such as houses and cars) can be produced and sold.

Reserve requirements set by the Federal Reserve designate the portion of deposits that member banks must retain on hand. The reserves determine how much or how little banks can lend to businesses and consumers. For example, if the Fed changed the reserve requirements and allowed banks to keep $10 on hand rather than $15 for every $100 in deposits it held, it would free up additional money for loans.

In addition to these formal tools, the Fed can also use "moral suasion" to influence the actions of banks and other members of the financial community by

AMERICAN POLITICS IN COMPARATIVE PERSPECTIVE

How Does the Federal Reserve Compare with Other Central Banks?

Throughout the world, institutions known as central banks are tasked with managing currencies, establishing monetary policies, and setting interest rates. Since the financial crisis of 2008, central banks have played an increased role in stabilizing national economies and preventing recessions. In the United States, the Federal Reserve has two principal mandates: controlling inflation and limiting unemployment. The Bank of Japan has been focused mainly on maintaining price stability. Less than twenty years old, the European Central Bank has faced severe challenges due to recurrent economic crises within some member states of the European Union (EU).

The Federal Reserve was created in 1913 to prevent and contain economic crises. It consists of the Federal Reserve Board and its chair in Washington, D.C., and twelve regional Federal Reserve Banks.

The European Central Bank, based in Frankfurt, Germany, was created in 1998 to promote financial integration among the states of the current twenty-eight-member EU. The bank plays a particularly important role in regulation of the euro, the currency shared by nineteen EU member states.

The Bank of Japan was established in 1882 to regulate monetary policy, to control inflation, and to promote stable economic growth. Currently, the bank is controlled by a policy board, including a governor, deputy governor, and six executive directors.

CRITICAL THINKING QUESTIONS

1. Is it the government's responsibility to minimize the economic impact of recessions, or to prevent depressions?

2. What should a government do when economic goals come into conflict? If, for example, combating inflation increases unemployment, which goal should be prioritized?

3. Should there be more global economic regulation?

Medicare
The federal program established during Lyndon B. Johnson's administration that provides medical care to elderly Social Security recipients.

suggestion, exhortation, and informal agreement. Because of its commanding position as a monetary policy maker, the media, economists, and market observers pay attention to verbal signals sent by the Fed and its chair with regard to economic trends and conditions.

During the economic crisis that began in 2008, monetary policy played a critically important function, in part because it can be easily implemented and has fewer long-term financial consequences than the deficit spending typified by fiscal policy. In early 2008, the Federal Reserve Board responded quickly to the economic slowdown, taking extraordinary action to lower interest rates and engaging in large open market operations and discount rate reductions to increase liquidity in the markets. The Fed also injected large-scale funds into the U.S. banking system by offering banks low-interest, one-month loans to ease the tightening credit conditions. It later took action to adjust mortgage lending rules and expand the commodities that U.S. markets could borrow against in order to increase the money supply in the market.

In addition to these traditional tools of monetary policy, the Fed has taken extraordinary measures designed to stimulate bank lending, including the purchase of mortgage-backed securities, credit easing, and quantitative easing (i.e., increasing the amount of money in circulation). New regulations on capital leverage, risk management, and liquidity passed in the Dodd-Frank Wall Street Reform and Consumer Protection Act of 2011 attempt to reduce the risks associated with the international interconnectedness of large financial institutions.

Despite signs of an ongoing economic recovery, the Fed has continued to keep interest rates low in the hope of attracting borrowers who will inject money into the market. Among the factors the Fed considers are the interrelated variables of the unemployment rate, which has been gradually decreasing since the crisis, and the inflation rate, which remains low but is expected to slowly rise back toward the Fed's preferred target of about 2 percent per year. (the "American Government in Comparative Perspective" highlights the Fed and two other central banks outside the United States.)

HEALTH POLICY

15.4 Describe current U.S. policy in health care.

Under the U.S. system of federalism, states and localities traditionally had primary responsibility for public health issues, including public sanitation, clean water programs, immunization programs, and other activities designed to reduce the incidence of infectious and communicable diseases. However, the national government's involvement in health policy also extends to a range of policy areas. Many millions of people receive medical care through the medical branches of the armed forces, the hospitals, and medical programs of the Department of Veterans Affairs and the Indian Health Service. In the 1960s, the government began funding health programs for senior citizens and the poor and disabled, known as Medicare and Medicaid, respectively. In a major expansion of the program, Medicare began to cover many costs of prescription drugs beginning in 2006. In 2010, the Democratic Congress passed, and President Barack Obama signed into law, the Affordable Care Act, which expanded the federal government's role in providing health insurance and in ensuring access to quality care. The federal government is also critical to the nation's response to public health challenges, including basic research, prevention of disease, and control of chronic illnesses.

Medicare and Medicaid

Medicare, which was created by Congress and Democratic President Lyndon B. Johnson in 1965, covers persons over age 65 without regard to income, medical history, or health status, as well as some younger people with disabilities. The program is administered by the Centers for Medicare and Medicaid Services in the **Department of Health and Human Services**. Today, Medicare provides health insurance coverage for more than 55 million Americans. Coverage includes many medical care services, including hospitalizations, doctor visits, prescription drugs, and other specialized care.

Medicare is financed by general revenues (41 percent in 2015), payroll tax contributions (38 percent), beneficiary premiums (13 percent), and other sources. Employees and employers share the cost of a 2.9 percent tax on the total amount of wages and salaries, with individuals earning over $200,000 a year paying slightly more. In 2015, Medicare spending accounted for 14 percent of total federal spending and 20 percent of national personal health spending. In 2015, Medicare benefit payments totaled $632 billion; due to the aging of the population, spending is projected to grow to $1.085 trillion in 2026.[17]

Medicaid, a government program that subsidizes health insurance for the poor and disabled, was enacted in 1965, at the same time as Medicare. It provides health insurance coverage for low-income Americans who meet a set of eligibility requirements. To receive Medicaid benefits, citizens must meet minimum-income thresholds, be disabled, or be pregnant. In 2015, Medicaid program provided health and long-term care coverage to nearly 70 million low-income Americans.

Unlike Medicare, which is financed and administered by the national government, Medicaid is a joint venture between the national and state governments. The hybrid nature of the program has caused tensions between federal- and state-level priorities and led to substantial state variation across states for the level of access to coverage and care for low-income Americans. The national government provides between 50 and 75 percent of the funding necessary to administer Medicaid programs (depending on state per capita income). This money is given to the states in the form of block grants. States then supplement the national funds with money from their own treasuries. They also are given the latitude to establish eligibility thresholds and the level of benefits available to citizens. The Affordable Care Act (ACA) included provisions of a significant expansion of Medicaid to include all citizens and legal residents earning up to 133 percent of the poverty line; however, not all state governments chose to participate.[18]

The Affordable Care Act

The Affordable Care Act (ACA) of 2010 marked the first major change in national health policy since the adoption of Medicare and Medicaid in 1965. A major priority of the Obama administration—to the point that its critic dubbed it "Obamacare"—the primary purpose of the ACA was to ensure that nearly all Americans would have access to health care coverage. This includes those living in poverty, who are eligible for special government subsidies. Other major features included allowing children to remain under their parents' health insurance coverage until age 26 and disallowing the long-standing practice of denying insurance coverage to individuals with pre-existing conditions.

The ACA established government-run health insurance exchanges financed by a number of taxes and fees, most notably an increase in the Medicare tax for individuals earning more than $200,000 per year. Americans had the option to buy into one of these exchanges or simply to retain their existing private health insurance. However, in one of its more controversial provisions, the ACA requires by law that every American have some form of health insurance or else pay a fine. This "individual mandate" was necessary so that the overall pool of those purchasing health insurance would be large enough that the premiums of healthy people help to underwrite the costs of care to the smaller proportion of more seriously ill people.

In 2016, nine out of ten Americans were estimated to have access to health insurance, closing one of the major gaps in health policy between the United States

Department of Health and Human Services (HHS)
The cabinet-level department administering most federal social welfare and health-related policies and programs; it includes the National Institutes for Health (NIH), the Centers for Disease Control and Prevention (CDC), and the Food and Drug Administration (FDA).

Medicaid
A government program that subsidizes medical care for the poor.

and other wealthy countries. However, many elements of the ACA have proven highly controversial. Some criticisms are ideologically based, arguing that the ACA was tantamount to a "government takeover" of the health care system and took control from the private sector. Others were practical, including higher than anticipated premiums and co-pays for some and the cost burdens placed on smaller businesses. Still other concerns were religious in nature, particularly objections by employers over requirements to provide access to birth control. Public confidence and support was also undermined by a very badly managed "roll-out" in the fall of 2013, in which the Healthcare.gov Web site was unable to manage the sudden influx of applicants.

The ACA has been especially unpopular with state governments led by Republican governors and legislatures. These states believed that the act is an infringement on states' reserved powers, and more than half of the states sued to block implementation of the policy. However, in 2012, the Supreme Court upheld the constitutionality of the individual mandate and, again in 2015, upheld the legal status of the health-insurance exchanges. The new Republican majorities in Congress and the Trump Administration vow to "repeal and replace" the ACA but, as with many government programs, the longer it is in place and the more people use its provisions, the harder it will be to completely eliminate.

Public Health

Government also plays a major role in curbing the spread of infectious disease and managing increases in chronic conditions. From HIV/AIDS and tuberculosis to drug abuse and obesity, public policy makers have attempted to use government power to fight threats to the nation's health. Among the government's tools are immunizations, education, advertisements, and regulations. For many contagious diseases such as polio, measles, and chickenpox, the government requires immunization of young children if they are enrolled in day care, preschool, or elementary school. Public health officials also use vaccines in the adult population to manage the spread of diseases such as influenza (the flu). While not requiring citizens to receive flu shots, the government recommends that high-risk groups (infants, senior citizens) receive immunizations and subsidizes vaccines for low-income populations.

The national government also finances medical research, primarily through the National Institutes of Health (NIH). The National Cancer Institute, the National Heart, Lung, and Blood Institute, the National Institute of Allergy and Infectious Diseases, and the other NIH institutes and centers spend more than $30 billion annually on biomedical research.[19] NIH scientists and scientists at universities, medical schools, and other research facilities receiving NIH research grants conduct the research. Another leading agency is the Centers for Disease Control and Prevention (CDC), which are tasked with prevention and management of infectious disease, food and water-borne pathogens, environmental health, occupational safety, injury prevention and conditions such as as obesity and diabetes. Likewise, the Food and Drug Administration (FDA) plays an important regulatory role with regard to such substances as tobacco products, dietary supplements, pharmaceutical drugs, vaccines, food, cosmetics, and veterinary products.

An increasingly important area of public health involves interactions between humans and the environment. In response to alarm among scientists and an outcry by the public, governments have increasingly taken steps to reduce the health problems associated with pollution by regulating the industry. Starting in the 1970s, the United States initiated a large number of programs intended to stave off the harmful effects that pollution has on health and created the Environmental Protection Agency, which now serves as the primary environmental regulator in the country. These legislative accomplishments addressed myriad environmental concerns, most significantly water and air pollution. In this era of government action, the use of harmful

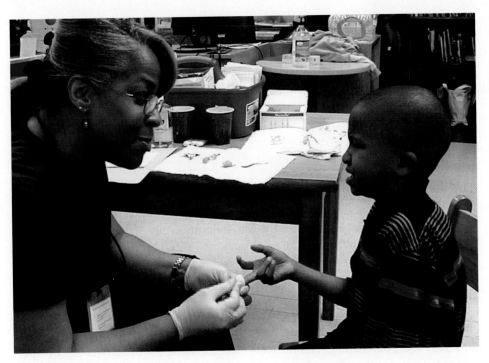

A child has blood drawn during a lead-testing clinic in Flint, Michigan. Thousands of Flint parents have had their children tested since residents became aware that their water had become contaminated with lead after the city began drawing water from the Flint River to save money. Nationwide, an estimated 4 million households include children who are being exposed to high levels of lead, which can adversely affect nearly every system in the body.

chlorofluorocarbons (CFCs) was also successfully restricted, protecting humans from increased ultraviolet radiation associated with the depletion of the ozone layer.

However, there persist many health threats related to the environment. Most recently in 2016, discovery of dangerously elevated levels of lead in the water supply of the city of Flint, Michigan, has raised questions about the efficacy of environmental policy. The crisis erupted after, as a cost-saving measure, the city government switched the water supply from Lake Huron to the polluted Flint River. Even after the discovery of elevated levels of lead, which is especially harmful to children and can cause irreversible organ damage, the response of governments at several levels was sluggish at best and perhaps criminally negligent at worst. The event spurred renewed focus on questions of "environmental justice," particularly considering that the residents of Flint were disproportionately low-income people of color.

EDUCATION POLICY

15.5 Describe current U.S. policy in primary, secondary, and higher education.

Historically, the states have taken the lead in the field of public education. Following the Revolutionary War, reformers of that era, such as Benjamin Franklin, began to see education as a means of legitimizing democratic institutions in the minds of young people and of establishing social and political order in the United States. In 1852, Massachusetts passed the first compulsory education law, and by 1918 all states had similar laws. In the late nineteenth and early twentieth century, when immigration was at high levels, education again emerged on the governmental agenda as a tool for assimilating immigrants and for protecting social and political order. By the mid-twentieth century, the Cold War between the United States and the Soviet Union sparked new curriculum reforms focused on enhancing math and science programs.

At the same time, education policy making at the federal level shifted toward access and equality. The Supreme Court's landmark decision in *Brown* v. *Board of Education* (1954) ruled that separate educational facilities for black and white students were inherently unequal. *Brown* established both the road map for racial desegregation in American schools and a national standard for equality of educational

No Child Left Behind Act (NCLB)
Bipartisan education reform bill that employed high standards and measurable goals as a method of improving American education across states; in 2016, it was largely replaced by the Every Student Succeeds Act (ESSA).

Common Core
A voluntarily adopted multi-state approach to setting standards that all students should achieve up through the high-school level.

opportunity. As part of President Lyndon Johnson's War on Poverty, Head Start was initiated in 1964 to provide preschool to at-risk low-income children, and the Elementary and Secondary Education Act of 1965 created Title I programs to improve educational opportunities for low-income K–12 students. These policies marked an important turning point in education policy. Enforcement of civil rights legislation—related to both race and gender, such as Title IX of the Education Amendments of 1972—required the national government to increasingly involve itself in directly in education.

Primary and Secondary Education

Policy making with regard to primary and secondary education in the United States represents an important example of the intertwining nature of American federalism, involving the active participation of the federal, state, and local governments, as well as many counties, Native American tribal governments, and neighborhood school districts. As such, it highlights both the strengths of federalism, such as flexibility and grassroots participation, and the controversies, including the appropriate level of federal involvement and the allocation of a fair share of resources across lines of race, ethnicity, and socioeconomic status. Primary and secondary education also accounts for a large share of federal government spending, totaling $40 billion in 2015, or 4 percent of federal spending.[20]

In recent years, the largest shift toward the federal government in educational policy making came with the 2002 bipartisan education reform bill supported by the late Democratic Senator Edward M. Kennedy (D–MA) and Republican President George W. Bush, commonly referred to as the **No Child Left Behind Act (NCLB)**. The legislation was designed to monitor student achievement in schools, paying special attention to disadvantaged student populations. The aim was to set high standards and establish measurable goals as a method of improving American education across states.

However, disillusionment grew over time with NCLB, including among many parents of school-age children. Critics argued that it set unrealistic and overly broad standards, to the particular detriment of already-challenged populations such as low-income families, students with disabilities, English learners, Native American students, foster and homeless youth, and migrant and seasonal farmworker children. They also claimed that it relied too heavily on the use of standardized tests, which had begun to drive the content of school curricula rather than reflect it—a phenomenon sometimes called "teaching to the test." This meant that subjects not covered on the tests, such as arts, music, or civics, could be discounted or even eliminated from schools. In a rare show of bipartisan support in Congress, the law was replaced at the end of 2015 with the Every Student Succeeds Act (ESSA), which restores greater control to states over issues of accountability, teacher quality, and school improvement.[21]

ESSA also largely withdrew federal support for the **Common Core** State Standards Initiative. Common Core is jointly sponsored by the National Governors Association and the Council of Chief State School Officers to establish a set of clear college- and career-ready standards for kindergarten through twelfth grade in language and mathematics. The goal is to define expectations for what every child should know, and be able to do academically, when they graduate from high school and then to establish corresponding educational standards. The program was introduced in 2010 and by 2016, forty-two states and the District of Columbia had voluntarily adopted and implemented the standards.[22] However, a backlash quickly built in the years since the program's roll-out in 2010 from parents, teachers, administrators. They argue that the pedagogical approaches applied are confusing, reinforce a one-size-fits-all approach, and overemphasize rote learning over true comprehension.

Another area of controversy in educational policy has been the question of "school choice," which argues that if a child is attending a failing school, students and their parents should have the option to enroll at a more successful institution. In some cases, this may mean sending a child to another public school in the district or to a private school. One way to implement a school choice policy is through the use of **vouchers**, or certificates issued by the government that may be applied toward the cost of attending private or other public schools. The monetary value of these certificates usually correlates with the cost of educating a student in his or her local public school. Supporters of vouchers believe that if parents remove their students from failing schools, these schools will quickly learn that they have to take steps to improve educational quality, or they will no longer have a reason to exist. Opponents, however, contend that allowing students to take money away from failing schools is counterintuitive and actually makes it harder for failing schools to improve.

Parents may also choose to send their children to **charter schools**. Charter schools are semipublic schools founded by universities, corporations, or concerned parents. They have open admission and receive some support from the government; they may also receive private donations to increase the quality of education. When the number of students interested in attending a school exceeds the openings available, students are usually selected by means of a random lottery. Charter schools are rapidly increasing in popularity in the United States. In some jurisdictions, such as New Orleans, charter schools are consistently among the highest performing institutions in the city. Critics, however, charge that it is difficult to ensure that charter schools are meeting educational standards and that a system that cannot accommodate all students interested in attending is inherently flawed. Because charter schools are semi-private, they do not have the same controls on curriculum—and the fact that there are not enough slots for all those who want to attend creates inequality in access to good education.

Higher Education

Federal governmental policies toward higher education provide indirect support through funding of research grants and financial assistance to students. The federal government also funds academies for the U.S. army, navy, air force, coast guard,

vouchers
Certificates issued by the government that may be applied toward the cost of attending private or other public schools.

charter schools
Semi-public schools that have open admission and receive some support from the government and may also receive private donations to increase the quality of education.

HOW DID TITLE IX CHANGE EDUCATION?

Title IX of the education amendments of 1972 greatly expanded educational and athletic opportunities for women. As a result of gender equity requirements, women's basketball programs have gained more prominence in recent years.

and merchant marine. Any school that receives federal funding (K–12 or higher education) must comply with Title IX of the Educational Amendment Acts of 1972, barring any discrimination on the basis of sex in admissions, student financial aid, or athletics.

The most prominent higher education policy focus in recent years has been on improving access to affordable higher education. In 2015, students graduated from higher education with an average debt of $35,000, yet the federal government spends more than $130 billion each year in grants and loans. Grants, based on financial need, do not require repayment. The Federal Direct Student Loan Program allows students and families to borrow money to pay for college, with repayment (with interest) deferred until a student graduates or leaves college. College Work Study programs, providing part-time jobs to college students while enrolled in school, also rely on federal funding. Loans from private sources are also available to some students and families.

Over the past two decades, the overall level of higher education debt taken on by American students and their families has been rapidly increasing. Since 1989, inflation-adjusted tuition and fees more than doubled at four-year public institutions and increased by more than 50 percent at private four-year and public two-year colleges. Further, Americans on the whole have steadily been increasing the number of years of education that they complete. As a result, since 1989 the average debt levels of borrowers with a graduate degree more than quadrupled, from just under $10,000 to more than $40,000; for those with a bachelor's degree, average debt increased from $6,000 to $16,000. In 2012, outstanding student debt passed $1 trillion; it should be noted, however, that this was the nationwide cumulative total, and only 4 percent of student loan balances were greater than $100,000.[23]

Education increases average lifetime incomes and contributes to the overall economy by increasing the level of job skills and, later, enhancing collection of tax revenue. All of this makes it a sound investment at both the personal and societal levels. However, high unemployment rates following the 2008–2009 recession meant that the economy has not always created enough new jobs to keep pace with well-educated job seekers. Following on the heels of the mortgage crisis of the mid-2000s, some public policy analysts fear that a bubble in student debt could lead to wide-scale defaults and the need for a taxpayer bailout. A range of public policy responses have been considered, including expanding access to educational grants, cutting interest rates, and easing repayment terms. For example, in 2015 the Department of Education expanded Pay As You Earn loan repayment plans (PAYE) so that student loan repayments would be capped at 10 percent of current monthly income.

SOCIAL WELFARE POLICY

15.6 Describe current U.S. social welfare policy and programs.

Social welfare programs protect people against loss of income because of retirement, disability, unemployment, death, or absence of the family breadwinner. In 1780, for example, national legislation was passed to provide a pension to the widows of sailors. These programs, however, like many of the other issues discussed in this chapter, were not a priority for the federal government during much of its first 150 years. Beginning with the passage of the Social Security Act as a part of the 1930s New Deal, the government began to pay greater attention to this policy area. Today, the federal government administers a range of social welfare programs, so termed because they fall under the Constitution's goal to "promote the general welfare." These policies fall into two major areas—non–means-tested programs (in which benefits are provided regardless of income) and means-tested programs (in which benefits are provided to those whose incomes fall below a designated level).

The Foundations of Social Welfare Policy

With the election of President Franklin D. Roosevelt in 1932, the federal government began to play a more active role in addressing the hardships and turmoil that grew out of the Great Depression. An immediate challenge facing the Roosevelt administration was massive unemployment, viewed as having a corrosive effect on the economic well-being and moral character of American citizens. An array of programs to put people back to work would, in Roosevelt's words, "eliminate the threat that enforced idleness brings to spiritual and moral stability."[24]

A major legacy of the New Deal was the creation of the Social Security program. The intent of Social Security was to go beyond various "emergency" programs such as the Works Projects Administration (WPA) and provide at least a minimum of economic security for all Americans. Passage of the **Social Security Act** in 1935 thus represented the beginning of a permanent welfare state in America and a dedication to the ideal of greater equity. The act consisted of three major components: (1) old-age insurance (what we now call Social Security); (2) public assistance for the needy, aged, blind, and families with dependent children (known as SSI); and (3) unemployment insurance and compensation. Since that time, the program has expanded to include a much greater percentage of American workers. It has also become one of the most successful government programs. In the 1930s, poverty rates were highest among the elderly. Today, seniors age sixty-five or older have the lowest rate of poverty among any age group in the United States.

Social Welfare Programs Today

Modern social welfare programs help a wide variety of citizens to survive in cases of unintentional loss of income. They also help disabled, elderly, and low-income citizens to make ends meet and provide a minimally decent standard of living for themselves and their families. In 2016, the poverty threshold for a four-person family unit was $24,300.

Social Security Act
A 1935 law that established old age insurance; assistance for the needy, aged, blind, and families with dependent children; and unemployment insurance.

OF COURSE WE MAY HAVE TO CHANGE REMEDIES IF WE DONT GET RESULTS

HOW DID THE NEW DEAL ADVANCE SOCIAL WELFARE?

President Franklin Delano Roosevelt is portrayed as Dr. New Deal trying several remedies for an ailing Uncle Sam; Congress is portrayed as a nurse following the doctor's orders. The role of the federal government in domestic policy making was revolutionized during the 1930s in response to the social dislocations of the Great Depression.

entitlement programs
Government benefits that all citizens meeting eligibility criteria—such as age, income level, or unemployment—are legally "entitled" to receive.

non–means-tested programs
Programs that provide cash assistance to qualified beneficiaries, regardless of income; among these are Social Security and unemployment insurance.

means-tested programs
Programs requiring beneficiaries to have incomes below specified levels to be eligible for benefits; among these are Social Security Insurance (SSI), Temporary Aid to Needy Families, (TANF), and the Supplemental Nutrition Assissance Program (SNAP), formerly called "food stamps."

Many social welfare programs are **entitlement programs**, government benefits which all citizens meeting eligibility criteria—such as age, income level, or unemployment—are legally entitled to receive. Unlike programs such as public housing, military construction, and space exploration, spending for entitlement programs is mandatory and places a substantial ongoing obligation on the federal budget.

Some of these are **non–means-tested programs** that provide cash assistance to qualified beneficiaries, regardless of income. Contributions are made by or on behalf of the prospective beneficiaries, their employers, or both. When a person becomes eligible for benefits, he or she is paid as a matter of right, regardless of wealth or unearned income. Sometime referred to as "social insurance" programs, these include programs for old-age, survivors, and disability insurance (Social Security) and unemployment insurance. In contrast, **means-tested programs** require people to have incomes below specified levels to be eligible for benefits. Benefits of means-tested programs may come either as cash or in-kind benefits, such as help with finding employment or child care. Included in the means-tested category are the Supplemental Security Income (SSI) program and the Supplemental Nutrition Assistance Program (SNAP, also known as food stamps). Temporary Assistance for Needy Families (TANF) is also means-tested, but the program is not an entitlement. States are given discretion to determine TANF eligibility and benefits.

OLD AGE, SURVIVORS, AND DISABILITY INSURANCE As mentioned earlier, the Social Security program is a non–means-tested program that began as old-age insurance, providing benefits only to retired workers. Its coverage was extended to survivors of covered workers in 1939 and to the permanently disabled in 1956. Nearly all employees and most of the self-employed are now covered by Social Security. Americans born before 1938 are eligible to receive full retirement benefits at age sixty-five. The full retirement age gradually rises until it reaches sixty-seven for persons born in 1960 or later. In 2016, the average monthly Social Security benefit for retired workers was $1,346.72, with the maximum monthly benefit set at $2,639.00.

Social Security is not, as many people believe, a pension program that collects contributions from workers, invests them, and then returns them with interest to beneficiaries. Instead, current workers pay employment taxes that go directly toward providing benefits for retirees. In 2016, for example, a tax of 6.2 percent was levied on the first $118,500 of an employee's wages and placed into the Social Security Trust Fund. An additional 6.2 percent tax was levied on employers.

As a result of this system, in recent years, it has become increasingly apparent that the current Social Security system is on a collision course with itself. Americans are living longer and having fewer children. And, beginning in 2010, the exceptionally large age cohort of the Baby Boom generation (roughly speaking, those born in the two decades immediately following World War II) began to retire. These factors, taken together, skew the number of working Americans per retiree, and lead the Social Security system toward financial insolvency. The trustees of the Social Security Trust Fund have estimated that—barring major policy changes—by about 2030, payments to beneficiaries will exceed revenues collected from employees.

UNEMPLOYMENT INSURANCE Unemployment insurance is a social insurance program financed by a payroll tax paid by employers. The program benefits full-time employees of companies of four or more people who become unemployed through no fault of their own. Unemployed workers who have been fired for professional faults or who have quit their jobs, or those who are unwilling to accept suitable employment, do not receive benefits.

State governments administer unemployment insurance programs. As a result, unemployment programs differ a great deal in levels of benefits, length of benefit payment, and eligibility for benefits. For example in 2015, average weekly benefit payments ranged from $215 in Mississippi to just over $698 in Massachusetts. In

FIGURE 15.3   HOW DO STATE UNEMPLOYMENT RATES VARY?

Rates of unemployment vary considerably across states, as does the duration of temporary unemployment insurance. This graphic shows the unemployment rate in each state (and Washington D.C.) in early 2016, along with the number of weeks that the unemployed are provided with benefits.

SOURCE: Data from Bureau of Labor Statistics, www.bls.gov/web/laus/laumstrk.htm; and Center on Budget and Policy Priorities, http://www.cbpp.org/research/economy/policy-basics-how-many-weeks-of-unemployment-compensation-are-available

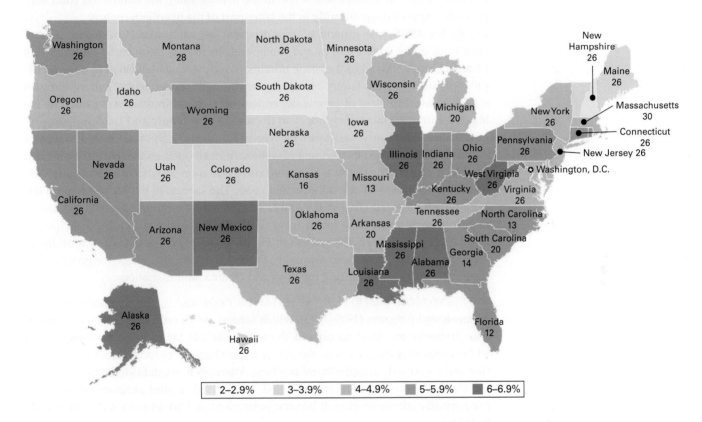

general, less generous programs exist in southern states, where labor unions are less powerful. Nationwide, only about 27 percent who are counted as unemployed at any given time are receiving benefits.

In April 2016, the national unemployment rate stood at 5 percent, but differences were considerable across the country. In North Dakota and New Hampshire, the unemployment rate was about 2.5 percent, Oregon and Tennessee were at about 4.5 percent, and Illinois and West Virginia had some of the highest rates at about 6.5 percent. Unemployment rates also varied quite a bit across races and by age. For example, the level of unemployment for African Americans was more than 50 percent above the national average and nearly twice that of whites.[25]

SUPPLEMENTAL SECURITY INCOME   The Supplemental Security Income (SSI) program is a means-tested program that began under the Social Security Act as a government benefit for needy elderly or blind citizens. In 1950, Congress extended coverage to needy people who were permanently and totally disabled. The federal government, which provides primary funding for SSI, prescribes minimum national benefit levels. The states may also choose to supplement national benefits, and forty-six states take advantage of this option.

To be eligible for SSI, beneficiaries can have only a very limited income; the lower an individual's income, the higher the SSI payment. SSI beneficiaries may also have only a limited number of possessions. The total of an individual's personal resources, including bank accounts, vehicles, and personal property, cannot exceed $733.00. In 2016, monthly payments to eligible beneficiaries were about $2000 per person.

FAMILY AND CHILD SUPPORT The Aid to Dependent Children program is a means-tested program first established as part of the Social Security Act in 1935. In 1950, it was broadened to include not only dependent children without fathers but also the mothers or other adults with whom dependent children were living. At this time, it was retitled the Aid to Families and Dependent Children (AFDC) program. As a result of this change and changes in the American family (including a rise in the birthrate to unwed mothers and a rise in the divorce rate), the family and child support rolls expanded significantly in the latter part of the twentieth century.

By the 1990s, the growth of this program began to attract widespread criticism from many conservatives and moderates, including Democratic President Bill Clinton. Critics pointed to the rising number of recipients and claimed that the AFDC program undermined family structures, encouraged dependency, and resulted in a semi-permanent class of people dependent on welfare. In what is regarded as the biggest shift in social welfare policy in decades, a new family and child support program called Temporary Assistance for Needy Families (TANF) was created to replace AFDC. TANF switched the funding of welfare from an open-ended matching program to a block grant to the states, which were also given more flexibility in reforming their welfare programs toward work-oriented goals. The success of the TANF program has been widely debated. The total number of Americans receiving benefits has fallen, in part because states have found ways to minimize the number of TANF recipients. Little evidence supports the success of the program in job training or as a means of reducing economic and social inequality. Despite these shortcomings, the program has continued to be funded during the Bush and Obama administrations.

SUPPLEMENTAL NUTRITION ASSISTANCE PROGRAM The first attempt at this means-tested program (1939–1943), which is more commonly known as food stamps, was primarily an effort to expand domestic markets for farm commodities. Food stamps provided the poor with the ability to purchase more food, thus increasing the demand for American agricultural produce. Attempts to reestablish the program during the Eisenhower administration failed, but in 1961, a pilot program began under the Kennedy administration. It became permanent in 1964 and extended nationwide in 1974.

The method of delivering the food stamp benefit has changed dramatically over time. For much of the program's history, the benefit was administered as actual paper coupons—quite literally, food "stamps"—given to citizens who were eligible for relief. Today, the program is administered entirely using an electronic debt program, much like an ATM card. This change in administration necessitated a formal name change for the program—from food stamps to the **Supplemental Nutrition Assistance Program (SNAP)**—in 2008. Still, this benefit continues to be an important means of ensuring income security. In 2016, more than 45 million Americans received SNAP aid. The average participant received $125.78 worth of assistance per month. In addition to SNAP, the national government operates several other food programs for the needy. These programs include a special nutritional program for women, infants, and children, known as WIC; a school breakfast and lunch program; and an emergency food assistance program.

TOWARD REFORM: ONGOING CHALLENGES IN SOCIAL AND ECONOMIC POLICY MAKING

15.7 Review ongoing challenges in U.S. social and economic policy making.

Social and economic policy has a long and complex history in the United States, as has been discussed in this chapter. However, in each of the issue areas considered, public policy challenges have yet to be solved. Some Americans are not yet covered by health insurance, implementation of education reforms has not met goals for standards and performance, and income inequality remains at historically high levels. Innovative, bold solutions to problems, however, are difficult to achieve in a decentralized policy-making process. Ultimately, which group dominates the process varies by issue. The elite theory, bureaucratic theory, special interest theory, and pluralist theory are useful models for understanding the politics of domestic policy making. It is also important to understand that each stage of the policy-making process presents both opportunities and barriers to change.

At the agenda-setting stage, rarely do all three streams—problems, policies, and politics—converge to open a policy window. In addressing education reform, for example, the competing values of local control versus national standards makes it difficult to gain consensus on a solution. Policy often is formulated in the context of uncertainty. The actual results of the enormous bailout and stimulus bills of 2008–2009 were very hard to predict: Could the banking system be protected? Would these actions stave off a full-scale economic depression? Policy makers do not always have complete information on the long-term costs and benefits of proposed policy solutions. As a result, incrementalism often describes the policy adoption stage.

At the implementation stage, policies can change shape as they are carried out day to day by the bureaucracy. As schools implemented No Child Left Behind and the Common Core, new standards and teaching to the test changed the content and delivery of information to K–12 students—and then feedback from parents, teachers, and others led to calls for further reform. Policies also are constantly subject to challenge, in routine evaluations and budget allocations, or in constitutional challenges in the courts. Challenges to the Patient Protection and Affordable Care Act jeopardized full implementation of Obama's health care initiative.

As new policy concerns rise, the policy-making cycle starts over again. At the same time, this process has limits. Political scientists have described an issue attention cycle in which problems are easier to address when a crisis or critical mobilizing event captures the public's attention. As the problem is addressed, or the shocking nature of the crisis fades, the public loses interest. Sometimes, realization dawns that no easy solution is possible, or that the costs outweigh benefits. Incremental steps toward solving the problem, or just the perception that something is going to be done, can also shift the public's attention to another issue. Once the intensity of public interest fades, comprehensive policy making is much more difficult to achieve.

The year 2017 is poised to begin a new era in policy making in the United States, with the presidency and both houses of Congress all under the control of the Republican Party again for the first time since 2006. Pent-up demand for policy changes in a rightward direction is certain to draw renewed attention to many public policy issues that had either moved in a more liberal direction or else been "gridlocked" over the past decade. It seems likely that the cycle of public policy making will begin anew with regard to fiscal policy, monetary policy, health care, education and many other issues.

REVIEW THE CHAPTER

Roots of Public Policy: The Policy-making Process

15.1 Trace the stages of the policy-making process.

Public policy is an intentional course of action or inaction followed by government in dealing with some problem or matter of concern. A popular model used to describe the policy-making process views it as a sequence of stages that include agenda setting, policy formulation, policy adoption, policy implementation, and policy evaluation. Although this model can be useful, it is a simplification of the actual process, and it does not always explain why policies take the forms they do or who controls the formation of public policy. Approaches to explaining policy-making outcomes include elite, bureaucratic, special interest, and pluralist theories.

Fiscal Policy

15.2 Describe the scope of the federal budget, and analyze the problems associated with the federal deficit and debt.

Fiscal policy is the deliberate use of the national government's taxing and spending policies to maintain economic stability and promote prosperity. Many factors influence fiscal policy, including concerns about unemployment, inflation, and the risk of recession or depression. The federal government has generally run a budget deficit, which can have negative consequences for the economy over the long term. The overall national debt has also been rising for more than three decades, which has been exacerbated in recent years due to the combined effects of tax cuts, increased military and national security spending, and the bailout and stimulus bills passed in response to the recession of 2008–2009.

Monetary Policy

15.3 Assess the effectiveness of the monetary policy tools used by the federal government to manage the economy.

Monetary policy is a form of government regulation through which the nation's money supply and interest rates are controlled. In 1913, the federal government created the Federal Reserve System ("the Fed"), which handles much of the day-to-day management of monetary policy. It has a number of tools to aid its efforts, including open market operations, which involve the buying and selling of government securities by the Federal Reserve Bank in the securities market; control of the discount rate, or the rate of interest at which the Federal Reserve Board lends money to member banks; and the ability to set reserve requirements, or government requirements that a portion of member banks' deposits be retained as backing for their loans.

Health Policy

15.4 Describe current U.S. policy in health.

Government in the United States has a long history of involvement in the health of Americans. Beginning in the 1960s, the government began to fund health programs for senior citizens and the poor, known as Medicare and Medicaid, respectively. In 2010, after several failed attempts by prior administrations, the Democratic Congress passed and President Barack Obama signed the Affordable Care Act, expanding the national government's role in providing health insurance. The U.S. government also plays a prominent role in public health through agencies such as the National Institutes of Health (NIH), the Centers for Disease Control and Prevention (CDC), and the Food and Drug Administration (FDA).

Education Policy

15.5 Describe current U.S. policy in primary, secondary, and higher education.

Education policy in the United States has been a work in progress for more than two centuries, and reform has focused on social and political order, individual liberty, and social and political equality. In 2002, President George W. Bush signed into law a bipartisan bill commonly referred to as No Child Left Behind (NCLB) to set high standards and measurable goals as a method of improving American education. By 2016, however, NCLB had been largely dismantled and a related initiative, Common Core, was also under attack. Higher education is supported by the federal government in the form of grants and low-interest student loans. Due to rising costs, reforms have been made to limit the amount of debt students must repay.

Social Welfare Policy

15.6 Describe current U.S. social welfare policy in the United States.

Social welfare programs protect people against loss of income. These programs also serve as automatic stabilizers, increasing government spending during economic crises. Social welfare policy was not a priority for the federal government until the 1930s, when it passed the Social Security Act. Today, the federal government administers a range of social welfare programs that fall into two major areas: non–means-tested and means-tested programs. Non–means-tested programs provide cash assistance to qualified beneficiaries regardless of income; they include old age, survivors, and disability insurance; and unemployment insurance. Means-tested programs require that people have incomes below specified levels to be eligible for benefits; they include Supplemental Security Income (SSI), family and child support, and the Supplemental Nutrition Assistance Program (food stamps).

Toward Reform: Ongoing Challenges in Domestic Policy

15.7 Assess the ongoing challenges in U.S. social and economic policy.

Policy making in the United States is a decentralized process that makes it difficult to pass comprehensive reform.

Each of the domestic policy areas highlighted in this chapter illustrate the forces that create opportunities for and constraints on change. Each of the five stages of policy making—agenda setting, policy formulation, policy adoption, implementation, and evaluation—presents an additional hurdle for policies to survive. Often, it takes policy entrepreneurs or crises to elevate an issue to national attention and force governmental action. Still, most policy making takes place in a context of uncertainty. The nature of problems also constantly evolves, and the policy cycle repeats itself continuously. The issue attention cycle suggests, however, is that the country's attention does not stay focused on any one problem for very long.

LEARN THE TERMS

Affordable Care Act (ACA)
agenda setting
Board of Governors
budget deficit
charter school
Common Core
Department of Health and Human Services
depression
discount rate
distributive policies
entitlement programs
Federal Reserve System

fiscal policy
governmental (institutional) agenda
gross domestic product (GDP)
inflation
Keynesian economics
laissez-faire
means-tested programs
Medicaid
Medicare
monetary policy
national debt
No Child Left Behind Act (NCLB)
non–means-tested programs

open market operations
policy adoption
policy evaluation
policy formulation
policy implementation
public policy
recession
redistributive policies
regulatory policies
reserve requirements
Social Security Act
systemic agenda
vouchers

HOW DOES THE PRESIDENT LEAD ON FOREIGN POLICY?

President Ronald Reagan speaks at the Brandenburg Gate in Berlin, near the Berlin Wall, issuing a challenge to Soviet leader Mikhail Gorbachev to "tear down this wall." Presidents have numerous powers that enable them to play the lead role on relations with other nations.

FOREIGN AND DEFENSE POLICY

LEARNING OBJECTIVES

16.1 Outline the major events and issues in the development of U.S. foreign and defense policy.

16.2 Describe the roles of government officials and of other influences in U.S. foreign and defense policy.

16.3 Evaluate major foreign and defense policy challenges now facing the United States.

16.4 Understand emerging challenges that are shaping U.S. foreign and defense policies in four critical regions.

For the dozen years from 1991 to 2001, the United States experienced a unique "unipolar moment" in which it was the world's sole superpower. This era was a time in which it seemed possible that the major remaining challenges to capitalism, Western democracy, and America's global leadership role had been swept aside. One essayist famously even termed it "the end of history" in the sense that the major ideological and political disagreements dividing the globe had been essentially resolved.[1]

This unipolar moment had been nearly a half century in the making. Since the end of World War II, the U.S. had led the democratic West in the long, tense stand-off known as the Cold War. Its principal adversary was the Union of Soviet Socialist Republics (also called the USSR or simply the Soviet Union) and its bloc of allies. For decades, there was deep uncertainty about which side would prevail – or even whether both sides, and much of the rest of the world, would be reduced to rubble in an exchange of nuclear weapons.

Then in November 1989, authorities in Communist-controlled East Germany permitted the opening of the Berlin Wall, which had long divided the two halves of Germany and was the ultimate symbol of the post-WWII division of the European continent. The removal of the wall had been called for by U.S. President Ronald Reagan the prior year, and marked the culmination of a reform process in the USSR and its satellite states. Within a year, the two halves of Germany would go on to be reunified; just over two years later, the Soviet Union itself ceased to exist.

Much of the democratic world felt a wave of both euphoria and relief that the Cold War was over.

The 1990s were a time of triumph for U.S. foreign and defense policy. The Soviet Union's principal successor state, Russia, sought integration rather than confrontation with the rest of the world. The NATO military alliance expanded into the former Soviet sphere of influence and other smaller-scale conflicts began to be resolved in places such as South Africa, Nicaragua, and Northern Ireland. The United Nations authorized coordinated worldwide military action to reverse the occupation of the nation of Kuwait by neighboring Iraq. Globalization of trade relations expanded and the then-nascent World Wide Web promised to bring the world closer, with English increasingly serving as a worldwide lingua franca.

But the unipolar moment would prove short-lived. The devastating terrorist attacks of September 11, 2001 jolted the United States into an awareness that it still had many ideological enemies and military threats from abroad. The subsequent American-led invasions of Iraq and Afghanistan proved both the ability of the U.S. to topple enemy regimes but also revealed its inability to "win the peace" that followed such incursions. Challengers old and new, such as Russia, China, and North Korea, became increasingly assertive on the world stage, even as U.S. allies in Europe and Japan struggled with their own economic and social problems. It soon became clear that while the twenty-first century challenges facing U.S. foreign and defense policy would look quite different from those of the twentieth century, but the world was not in fact any closer to the "end of history."

• • •

Although popular and governmental opinions on the role of the United States in the world have changed dramatically in the past 225 years, many fundamental challenges remain the same. Should the United States, for example, isolate itself from other nations or become engaged in international conflicts? When do diplomatic solutions fall short, necessitating warfare? And, how do economic policies at home and abroad affect these relationships?

Evaluating the potential strengths and weaknesses of U.S. foreign policy today starts with acquiring a broad understanding of the roots of past foreign and defense policies and the political forces that have shaped them. We must also look closely at

foreign policy
Area of policy making that encompasses how one country builds relationships with other countries in order to safeguard its national interest.

defense policy
Area of policy making that focuses on the strategies that a country uses to protect itself from its enemies.

isolationism
The U.S. policy of avoiding entangling alliances with foreign powers.

Farewell Address
When President George Washington left office, he wrote a letter, addressed to the People of the United States, warning them of the dangers to avoid in order to preserve the republic.

the key issues confronting the United States as it attempts to address emerging issues in foreign and defense policy.

ROOTS OF U.S. FOREIGN AND DEFENSE POLICY

16.1 Outline the major events and issues in the development of U.S. foreign and defense policy.

Foreign and defense policy are two separate areas of policy making. **Foreign policy** relates to how one country (referred to as a state by political scientists) builds relationships with other countries to safeguard its national interests. **Defense policy** comprises the strategies a country uses to protect itself from its enemies. However, foreign policy and defense policy are interrelated. Countries use defense policy for many problems that are better addressed by well-planned foreign policy, and a failure to make good foreign policy can require the use of defense policy.

Like domestic social and economic policies, U.S. foreign and defense policies have evolved. Today, the United States is a powerful and influential presence on the world stage, but it was not always this way. Upon its founding, the United States was a weak country on the margins of world affairs, with an uncertain future. The historical roots of American foreign and defense policy are found in the period from the founding of the republic to the period leading up to its leadership in World War II and the Cold War. The importance of these early experiences comes into clearer focus when we consider three distinct pre-World War II periods: (1) isolation in the early republic; (2) the United States as an emerging power; and (3) World War I (1917–1918), and the interwar years (between World Wars I and II).

Isolationism in the Early Republic

Independence did not change the fundamental foreign policy problem faced by colonial America: steering a safe course between Great Britain and France, the two feuding giants of world politics in the late 1700s. For some Framers, the best course of action was to maintain a close relationship with one of these two powers. Alexander Hamilton, for example, became a champion of a pro-British foreign policy, whereas Thomas Jefferson was an early supporter of a pro-French foreign policy.

For other early political leaders, the best course of action was one of neutrality and relative **isolationism**, a national policy that did not mean avoiding participation in foreign affairs but, instead, sidestepping "entangling alliances" with the major European powers. President George Washington articulated this neutrality position most forcefully. In his **Farewell Address**, he called for a policy that would "steer clear of permanent alliances with any portion of the foreign world."

The dual goals of isolationism and neutrality, however, did not guarantee the ability of the United States to always stay out of international conflicts. The United States fought an undeclared naval war in the 1790s with France because France was seizing U.S. ships that were trading with its enemies. Shortly thereafter, the United States fought the Barbary Wars against North African Barbary States, which had captured ships and held sailors for ransom.

Nor was conflict with the British resolved after the American Revolution. In the early 1800s, the ongoing wars between France and Great Britain, British support for American Indian tribes opposing U.S. westward expansion, and the British naval practice of impressment (stopping U.S. ships to seize suspected deserters of the British Royal Navy, and sometimes seizing ships and cargo while forcing American sailors to serve on British ships) led to the War of 1812 between the U.S. and Great Britain.

After the 1815 defeat of French leader Napoleon Bonaparte at Waterloo, Europe was at peace for the first time in almost two decades. Europeans celebrated, but the United States feared that European powers would try to reestablish control in the

Western Hemisphere. To prevent this, President James Monroe issued the **Monroe Doctrine** in 1823. It warned European countries that the United States would view "any attempt on their part to extend their system to any portion of this hemisphere as dangerous to our peace and safety." It also promised to continue the American policy of noninterference in the internal concerns of European powers.

The United States as an Emerging Power

Throughout most of the nineteenth century, the United States gained territory, developed economically, and emerged as a world power. This process centered on four areas: (1) trade policy and commerce, (2) continental expansion and manifest destiny, (3) dominance over the Western Hemisphere, and (4) interests in Asia.

TRADE POLICY AND COMMERCE   The neutrality articulated in Washington's Farewell Address made free trade a cornerstone of early American foreign policy. Reciprocity and most favored nation status were its guiding principles. Reciprocity meant that the U.S. government treated foreign traders in the same way that foreign countries treated American traders. Most favored nation status guaranteed that a country's imports into the United States would be given the lowest possible **tariffs**, or taxes on imported goods.

Increased global trade and competition following the end of the Napoleonic Wars led the United States to abandon the policies of reciprocity and most favored nation status. Beginning in 1816, Congress adopted the "American System" of trade protection by adding increasingly higher tariffs, sometimes as high as 100 percent of the value of the goods being imported.[2] High tariffs remained the American norm well into the twentieth century.

CONTINENTAL EXPANSION AND MANIFEST DESTINY   During the nineteenth century, the United States acquired immense quantities of land in various ways. It took land from American Indians in wars against the Creek, Seminole, Sioux, Comanche, Apache, and other tribes. It bought territory from the French (the Louisiana Territory), Spanish (Florida), and Russians (Alaska). It also fought the 1846 Mexican War, acquiring a large expanse of Mexican territory in the American Southwest and California.

Manifest destiny is the summary phrase used to capture the logic behind American continental expansionism. According to this idea, the United States had a divinely supported obligation to expand across North America to the Pacific and "overspread the continent allotted by Providence for the free development of our multiplying millions."[3] Manifest destiny was viewed as natural and inevitable, far different from the colonial expansion of European states.

DOMINANCE OVER THE WESTERN HEMISPHERE   The twentieth century began with a revision of the Monroe Doctrine. In what came to be known as the **Roosevelt Corollary** to the Monroe Doctrine, President Theodore Roosevelt asserted in 1904 that it was the responsibility of the United States to ensure stability in Latin America and the Caribbean. In accordance with this role, the United States would intervene with military force to punish wrongdoing and establish order in these nations when their own governments were incapable of doing so.

Roosevelt was particularly concerned with the Dominican Republic. It was deeply in debt, plagued by growing domestic unrest, and faced the threat of hostile military action by

Monroe Doctrine
President James Monroe's 1823 pledge that the United States would oppose attempts by European states to reestablish their political control in the Western Hemisphere.

tariffs
Taxes on imported goods.

manifest destiny
Theory that the United States was divinely supported to expand across North America to the Pacific Ocean.

Roosevelt Corollary
Concept developed by President Theodore Roosevelt early in the twentieth century declaring that it was the responsibility of the United States to ensure stability in Latin America and the Caribbean.

HOW DID THE ROOSEVELT COROLLARY AFFECT AMERICAN FOREIGN POLICY?

In this political cartoon, President Theodore Roosevelt is shown policing Panama, carrying the "big stick" of military intervention proposed by the Roosevelt Corollary.

World War I
A global military conflict from 1914–1918 across Europe and its overseas territories, into which the United States militarily intervened in 1917–1918.

League of Nations
A multilateral diplomatic organization that existed from 1920–1946 that sought, unsuccessfully, to prevent future wars; the United States never joined.

collective security
The idea that an attack on one country is an attack on all countries.

France. Roosevelt blocked French action by taking over customs collection there in 1906. Later, the United States sent troops to other countries in the Americas, including Cuba, Haiti, Nicaragua, Panama, and Mexico.

Although these exercises of military power were significant in establishing regional dominance, the signature event of this period for American foreign policy was the acquisition of the Panama Canal Zone. The United States wished to build a canal through Panama, which was then part of Colombia, but when the Colombian government refused to approve the necessary treaty, the Roosevelt administration supported a Panamanian independence movement. When this movement achieved success, the U.S. government quickly recognized the independent state and signed an agreement granting the United States rights to a ten-mile strip of land connecting the Atlantic and Pacific Oceans. Construction of the Panama Canal began in 1904 and was completed in 1914, providing a way for ships to avoid the long and dangerous trip around South America in reaching western U.S. territories.

Supporting Panamanian independence was not the only way the United States established its influence in Central America and the Caribbean. Beginning with the William H. Taft administration, the United States also began to use its economic power through so-called "dollar diplomacy." Dollar diplomacy was designed to make the United States the banker of the region, and to open up countries throughout all of Latin America to American investment.

INTERESTS IN ASIA   The 1898 Spanish-American War, fought between the United States and Spain over Spanish policies and presence in Cuba, gave the United States control over Cuba as well as other Spanish colonies such as Puerto Rico and the Philippines. As a result, the United States now had an overseas colony and a major stake in Asian affairs. The major problems confronting the United States in Asia were the disintegration of China and the rising power of Japan.

In 1898 and 1899, as European powers were extending their influence in China, the United States called on Russia, Germany, France, and Great Britain not to discriminate against other investors in their spheres of influence. While the United States could not force other countries to agree, the logic behind this Open Door Policy was consistent with long-standing American support for opening up foreign markets to U.S. investment.

In sharp contrast to the unilateral action taken on China, President Theodore Roosevelt sought to contain Japan through a series of international agreements. The most notable of these was the Taft-Katsura Agreement of 1905. This act recognized Japanese preeminence over Korea in return for a Japanese agreement to respect American control over the Philippines and Hawaii.

World War I and the Interwar Years

When **World War I** broke out in Europe in 1914, the United States remained neutral at first. It was a European war, and no U.S. interests were directly involved. In addition, the United States population was largely composed of immigrants from many countries in Europe, and Americans were deeply divided about whom to support. As the war progressed, however, it became increasingly difficult to remain neutral. Under Germany's policy of unrestricted submarine warfare, German subs sank U.S. ships carrying cargo to Great Britain and France as well as a passenger-liner called the *Lusitania*.

Finally, declaring that the United States was fighting "to make the world safe for democracy," President Woodrow Wilson led the nation into the war in 1917. Wilson also put forward a statement of American aims, the Fourteen Points. The Fourteenth Point called for the creation of a **League of Nations**, which was established at the Paris Peace Conference at the conclusion of the war. Its guiding principle was **collective security**, the idea that an attack on one country is an attack on all countries. Wilson failed, however, to build support at home and the Senate voted against joining the League of Nations.

The period between the two world wars saw U.S. foreign policy was dominated by isolationist sentiment. In 1928, support for disarmament led to the signing of the Kellogg-Briand Pact in which the United States, Japan, and the European powers (including Great Britain, France, and Germany) agreed to renounce war "as an instrument of national policy" and to resolve their disputes "by pacific means." In 1930, Congress passed the Smoot-Hawley Tariff Act, and other countries responded by raising their tariffs. By 1932, these higher tariffs, in conjunction with the Great Depression, caused world trade to drop to about one-third its former level.[4]

Belief in isolationism also led to the passage of four neutrality acts in the 1930s. Among their core provisions were arms embargoes and a prohibition on loans to countries involved in international conflicts. After Great Britain and France declared war on Nazi Germany in the late 1930s, however, President Franklin D. Roosevelt was able to soften these bans to enacting a "lend-lease" policy to allow Great Britain to obtain American weapons in return for allowing the United States to lease British military bases.

World War II and Its Aftermath

The United States entered **World War II** in response to the Japanese bombing of Pearl Harbor in Hawaii on December 7, 1941. For the first time since the War of 1812, the United States was attacked on its own territory, and began an unprecedented "total war mobilization" in which all sectors of the American economy and society were primed for battle. The war was fought by the Allied Powers (including the United States, the Soviet Union, Great Britain, and France) against the Axis Powers (including Nazi Germany, Italy, and Japan) in Europe, North Africa, Asia, and the Pacific. World War II was the most extensive and destructive conflict in all of human history. It brought about the mass death not only of military but also civilian populations caught in war zones and also those targeted for genocide as part of the Holocaust and other crimes against humanity. It has shaped much of the subsequent course of human history.

World War II concluded in Europe first, in May 1945 with the unconditional surrender of the Nazis to the United States, Great Britain, the Soviet Union, and its Allies. World War II ended in the Pacific in August 1945, following the still debated U.S. decision to destroy the Japanese cities of Hiroshima and Nagasaki using the unprecedented power of the newly developed atomic bomb.

World War II was a watershed in U.S. foreign policy. Prior to the war, isolationist sentiment dominated American thinking on world politics, but after it, internationalism emerged triumphant. In contrast to its earlier rejection of the League of Nations, the United States enthusiastically led in the creation of the **United Nations (UN)**, establishing itself as a permanent member of the **UN Security Council**, along with Great Britain, France, China, and the Soviet Union. It also entered into security alliances with countries around the globe, with an implicit understanding that America's role was to be "the leader of the free world."

President Franklin D. Roosevelt took an activist role in World War II diplomacy, holding or attending several major conferences until he died in April 1945. The most consequential of these was the Yalta Conference, held in the Soviet Union in February 1945, to decide the future of Germany and Eastern Europe, and to discuss the development of the UN. The Yalta agreement opened the way for the Soviet Union to continue to occupy the eastern half of Europe, bringing down what British Prime Minister Winston Churchill later termed an **Iron Curtain** across the center of the continent.

In the belief that protectionist trade policies had led to the rise of dictators and the beginning of World War II, the United States moved to create a set of

World War II
A global military conflict from 1939–1945 in Europe, Africa, Asia, and the Pacific region, in which the United States was engaged from 1941–1945.

United Nations
A multilateral diplomatic organization founded in 1945 and continuing today that is intended to promote peaceful resolution of international disputes and advance human development worldwide; the United States is a founding member.

UN Security Council
A principal part of the United Nations, charged with authorizing peacekeeping operations, international sanctions, and military action in order to maintain global peace and security.

Iron Curtain
A term used during the Cold War to describe the divide between the capitalist West and communist East.

HOW DID WORLD WAR II CHANGE U.S. FOREIGN POLICY?
World War II cemented America's role as a world power. Here President Franklin D. Roosevelt meets with British Prime Minister Winston Churchill and Soviet Premier Josef Stalin at Yalta in 1945 to plan the postwar settlement.

Bretton Woods System
International financial system devised shortly before the end of World War II that created the World Bank and the International Monetary Fund.

International Monetary Fund (IMF)
International governmental organization designed to stabilize international currency transactions.

World Bank
International governmental organization created to provide loans for large economic development projects.

General Agreement on Tariffs and Trade (GATT)
Post–World War II economic development treaty designed to help facilitate international trade negotiations and promote free trade.

World Trade Organization (WTO)
An international organization that replaced GATT in 1995 to supervise and expand international trade.

Cold War
The period of superpower rivalry and confrontation between the United States and the Soviet Union, lasting from the end of World War II to 1991.

containment
U.S. policy of opposing Soviet expansion and communist revolutions around the world with military forces, economic assistance, and political influence.

international economic organizations to encourage and manage global trade and finance. Collectively, they came to be known as the **Bretton Woods System**, which remain a powerful influence on the global economy. The **International Monetary Fund (IMF)** was established to stabilize international currency transactions. In addition, the International Bank for Reconstruction and Development, also called the **World Bank**, was set up to help the world recover from the destruction of World War II and to help poorer countries prosper by providing loans for large economic development projects. Created in 1947, the **General Agreement on Tariffs and Trade (GATT)** had as its mission the facilitation of international trade negotiations and promotion of free trade; in 1995, it evolved into the **World Trade Organization(WTO)**. This process occurred through negotiating "rounds" or multiyear international conferences.

The Cold War: Containment and Deterrence

The **Cold War** was the defining feature of the international system from the end of World War II in 1945 until the collapse of communism in Eastern Europe and the Soviet Union in the late 1980s and early 1990s. It was a period of intense competition, hostility, tension, and the near outbreak of direct conflict between the Western powers (the United States, Great Britain, and Western Europe) and the communist bloc states (Eastern Europe and the Soviet Union). However, the Cold War never escalated into direct and open warfare between the U.S. and the Soviet Union, which came to be known as the two "superpowers."

American foreign policy during the Cold War was organized around two key concepts. The first was **containment**, which held that the "the main element of any United States policy toward the Soviet Union must be that of a long-term, patient but firm and vigilant containment of Russian expansionist tendencies."[5] This meant that the United States would oppose Soviet expansion with military forces, economic assistance, and political influence.

The second concept was nuclear **deterrence**. From the 1950s through the 1980s, the United States and the Soviet Union developed large arsenals of nuclear weapons, which it was believed would prevent both sides from ever actually using them. This drastically altered the traditional calculus of warfare by making it clear that neither side in an all-out nuclear exchange could prevail at a bearable cost, a condition referred to as "mutually assured destruction" or MAD. This reality kept the cold war from ever turning fully "hot."

March 1947 brought the enunciation of the **Truman Doctrine**, stating that the United States will provide economic assistance and military aid to countries fighting against communist revolutions or political pressure. Three months later, the United States took a major action consistent with this political worldview. Secretary of State George Marshall announced that the United States would help finance Europe's economic recovery. All European states were invited to participate in the drafting of a European collective recovery plan known as the **Marshall Plan**. Importantly, the Soviet Union chose not to participate in this program and prevented its Eastern European "satellite states" from participating as well.

In 1949, the economic division of Europe was reinforced by its military partition with the establishment of the **North Atlantic Treaty Organization (NATO)**. This alliance, the first peacetime military treaty joined by the United States, was a collective security pact among the United States, Canada, and parts of Europe. In retaliation, the Soviet Union organized its Eastern European allies into the Warsaw Pact. This division of Europe was further established by the **Berlin Wall**, built by East Germany in 1961 to cut off democratic West Berlin from communist East Berlin. The Warsaw Pact was disbanded by its members in 1991, but the NATO alliance continues as a significant force to the current day.

MILITARY CONFLICTS OF THE COLD WAR   Cold War competition between the United States and the Soviet Union moved to Latin America in the late 1950s and early 1960s. The most intense confrontation involved the Communist regime installed in 1959 by the revolutionary Fidel Castro in Cuba, which was intensively opposed by Presidents Dwight D. Eisenhower and John F. Kennedy. In October 1962, the United States and Soviet Union directly confronted one another over the deployment of nuclear missiles in Cuba. Perhaps at no time was the world closer to a nuclear war than it was during this event, known as the **Cuban Missile Crisis**. In response, President Kennedy established a "quarantine" on Cuba, a naval blockade that prevented Soviet ships from landing in Cuba. The crisis ended after two weeks, when Soviet Premier Nikita Khrushchev agreed to remove the Soviet missiles. However, the incident provoked a half-century of tension between the United States and Cuba which only began to abate with the reestablishment of diplomatic relations in 2015.

The Cold War also reached into Asia, anchored by the victory of Communists in 1949 after a long-running civil war in China. In the early 1950s, the United States fought the inconclusive **Korean War**, which left the Korean peninsula divided between a communist regime in the North and a capitalist regime in the South down the current day. Likewise, the United States became embroiled in a civil war in the Southeast Asian country of Vietnam. The **Vietnam War** escalated in the 1960s under President Lyndon B. Johnson. American forces carried out sustained and massive bombing campaigns against the North, and U.S. ground troops began fighting in the South. The Vietnam War was an especially difficult one, fought in unfamiliar terrain with little chance of success. Casualties escalated quickly, and the American public soon turned against the war. The peace movement that emerged at this time in response to the war and the military draft significantly influenced public opinion, helping to bring about America's withdrawal from the war and the collapse of its South Vietnamese allies.

DÉTENTE   When Richard M. Nixon became president in 1969, he declared it was time to move from "an era of confrontation" to "an era of negotiation" in relations with the Soviet Union.[6] The improvement in U.S.–Soviet relations was called **détente**. At its core was a series of negotiations that aimed to use linked rewards and punishments (rather than military power) to contain the Soviet Union. The greatest success of détente was in the area of arms control, most notably with the signing of the Strategic Arms Limitation Treaties (SALT I and SALT II), which limited the deployment of

deterrence
The military strategy of employing enormous force, including nuclear weapons, in order to prevent the outbreak or escalation of armed conflicts.

Truman Doctrine
U.S. anti-communist policy initiated in 1947 that became the basis of U.S. foreign policy throughout the Cold War.

Marshall Plan
European collective recovery program, named after Secretary of State George C. Marshall, that provided extensive American aid to Western Europe after World War II.

North Atlantic Treaty Organization (NATO)
The first peacetime military treaty joined by the United States; NATO is a collective security pact that includes the United States, Canada, and parts of Europe.

Berlin Wall
A barrier built by East Germany in 1961 to cut off democratic West Berlin from communist East Berlin.

Cuban Missile Crisis
The 1962 confrontation over the deployment of ballistic missiles in Cuba that nearly escalated into nuclear war between the United States and the Soviet Union.

Korean War
A civil war from 1950-1953 in which the United States supported the South Korean regime against Communist forces in North Korea.

Vietnam War
A civil war in which the United States supported the South Vietnamese regime against Communist forces in North Vietnam, which escalated through the 1960s before ending in 1975.

détente
The improvement in relations between the United States and the Soviet Union that occurred during the 1970s.

human rights
The protection of people's basic freedoms and needs.

Reagan Doctrine
The Reagan administration's commitment to ending communism by providing military assistance to anti-communist groups.

nuclear weapons. Another key element of détente was improved relations with China, which Nixon cemented by seeking the normalization of relations and visiting Beijing in 1972.

The greatest failure of détente, however, was an inability to establish agreed-upon rules to govern competition in the developing world. In Africa, Asia, and Latin America, the United States and Soviet Union each armed and supported competing sides in many civil wars. In Chile, Nixon used covert action to undermine the government of President Salvador Allende and reestablish a strong pro-American regime. In many places, the United States subsequently experienced so-called "blowback" from its activities, most notably in Iran where in 1979 the U.S.-supported ruling monarch, the Shah, was overthrown by a radical Islamist revolution. The new regime held 52 American hostages for over a year and began sponsoring terrorist activities in the Middle East and beyond.

THE END OF THE COLD WAR   During his one term as president (1977–1981), Jimmy Carter reoriented American foreign policy from the management of the Cold War to the promotion of **human rights**, the protection of people's basic freedoms and needs. This new emphasis began to slowly undermine the credibility of the Communist nations, who were only able to maintain control by ruthlessly suppressing all domestic dissent.

Republican President Ronald Reagan replaced Carter in the White House in January 1981, and took a more assertive stance, promising to reestablish American credibility and restore American military strength. The Reagan administration's commitment to combating communism by providing military assistance to anti-communist groups, such as in Nicaragua and El Salvador, became known as the **Reagan Doctrine**. In the Central Asian country of Afghanistan, the United States vehemently opposed the Soviet Union's 1979 invasion of that country, which supported a pro-communist government in power. The Soviet occupation army grew but could never defeat the guerrilla forces, known as the mujahideen. American military aid contributed to the defeat of the Soviet Union and its eventual withdrawal (but also sowed seeds of later conflict with terrorists based in Afghanistan).

The Soviet retreat from Afghanistan was part of a larger change in Soviet policy in the mid-1980s. After nearly two decades of economic and social stagnation within the Soviet Union, a new generation of leaders saw that the country's path was unsustainable. A new, more pragmatic Soviet leader, Mikhail Gorbachev, entered into nuclear arms control agreements with the United States, and reduced foreign aid to Soviet allies. At home, Gorbachev also implemented a program of political openness and economic reform that were meant to strengthen communism, but instead undermined the control of the Communist Party.

Once it became clear that the Gorbachev government would not intervene militarily, one communist regime after another in Eastern Europe collapsed in the fall of 1989, with the most potent symbol being the opening of the Berlin Wall. Two years later, the Soviet Union itself collapsed and broke apart into 15 separate countries. These developments left only the People's Republic of China as a major power under the control of a communist party. The China regime ruthlessly reasserted its claim to power by massacring student democracy protestors in Tiananmen Square in Beijing in the spring of 1989.

The Post–Cold War World

In a period of barely two years, the long-standing "bipolar" world split between the influence of the two superpowers was transformed. In the 1990s, it seemed for a time that the United States might lead the world in a unilateral and unchallenged way. George H.W. Bush, who became president in 1989, sought to navigate through this new, post–Cold War world. In 1990-91, Bush was able to assemble a unified and overwhelmingly effective response to the invasion by Iraq of neighboring country Kuwait. Proclaiming that the end of the Cold War was ushering in a "new world order" unaffected by the superpower rivalry, Bush turned to the United Nations, whose members voted to impose economic sanctions and authorized the use of force. During the ensuing **Gulf War** the U.S.-led coalition was victorious in removing Iraqi forces from Kuwait after just six weeks.

Bush's successor in office, Bill Clinton, sought to define a clear role for the United States in world affairs now that a dismantled Soviet Union no longer posed a clear and present danger. The president chose to actively promote the expansion of democracy, open markets, and free trade throughout the world. Clinton secured Senate approval for the North American Free Trade Agreement (NAFTA), an agreement promoting free movement of goods and services among Canada, Mexico, and the United States. The United States also brought former Soviet allies into the NATO military alliance, while supporting their integration with Western Europe. Even in the 1990s, however, it became clear that there were limits to American power. In Somalia and Rwanda, the United States was unable to resolve civil conflicts which resulted in mass casualties, including a brutal genocide in Rwanda. Even on the continent of Europe, the United States and its allies were only belatedly able to halt "ethnic cleansing" amidst the collapse of the formerly communist country of Yugoslavia.

In the late 1990s, a little-known radical Islamic terrorist group known as **al-Qaeda** began to attack vulnerable American targets overseas. The group vehemently objected to the intrusion of U.S. troops into Arab and Muslim countries. Its leadership, including founder Osama bin Laden, operated from safe havens in the wartorn nation of Afghanistan and neighboring Pakistan. The group adopted a decentralized organization with a range of affiliates and associates, making it difficult for the United States to counter and giving it wide latitude to carry out its operations.

September 11, 2001, and the War on Terror

On **September 11**, 2001, the vulnerability of even the American homeland was demonstrated to devastating effect. That morning, 19 members of al-Qaeda simultaneously hijacked four U.S. commercial airliners and crashed two of them into the World Trade Center in New York City and one into the Pentagon near Washington, D.C, with

Gulf War
A military conflict from 1990-1991 in which a U.S.-led international coalition reversed the occupation of Kuwait by the armed forces of Iraq.

al-Qaeda
The Islamic terrorist organization responsible for the 9/11 terrorist attacks and numerous other actions against U.S. overseas interests.

September 11
A terrorist plot carried out on September 11, 2001 that used hijacked civilian aircraft to attack the World Trade Center in New York and the Pentagon near Washington D.C.

HOW DID THE SEPTEMBER 11 TERRORIST ATTACKS AFFECT AMERICAN FOREIGN POLICY

The twin towers of the World Trade Center collapsed September 11, 2001 after they were struck by hijacked airplanes. The attacks caused thousands of deaths and injuries and resulted in the beginning of an ongoing war on terrorism.

global war on terror
An international action, initiated by President George W. Bush after the 9/11 terrorist attacks, to weed out terrorist operatives throughout the world.

Afghanistan War
A military conflict begun in 2002 in which a U.S.-led international coalition invaded Afghanistan in order to depose the government and deny a safe haven to terrorists.

Iraq War
A military conflict from 2003–2011 in which a U.S.-led international coalition invaded Iraq and deposed its regime but proved unable to establish a stable new government.

the fourth crashing in an open field in Pennsylvania. Nearly 3,000 people lost their lives that day, the first time since Pearl Harbor that U.S. territory had been directly attacked. This shocking event challenged Americans' longstanding belief in their security at home and reinforced the reality that the world had never been as unipolar as some had hoped.

THE WAR IN AFGHANISTAN   In response, President George W. Bush declared a **global war on terror** to weed out terrorist operatives throughout the world. It demanded that the government of Afghanistan, which was led by an extremist group called the Taliban, expel Osama bin Laden and al-Qaeda and sever its ties with international terrorist groups. When this did not occur, the United States and its NATO allies in October 2001 began aerial strikes and, subsequently, ground assaults against terrorist facilities and Taliban military targets inside Afghanistan. The Taliban proved no match for this combination of air and ground power, and its last stronghold fell before the end of the year. However, the Taliban and al-Qaeda soon pursued a sustained insurgency against American troops and the new Afghan government. The **Afghanistan War** eventually became America's military conflict, continuing through the tenure of President Barack Obama. The leader of al-Qaeda, Osama bin Laden eluded capture until May 2011, when he was killed in Pakistan by U.S. special forces.

THE WAR IN IRAQ   A broader foreign policy agenda emerged in President Bush's 2002 State of the Union Address. In this speech, Bush identified Iraq, North Korea, and Iran as an "axis of evil" that threatened American security interests. Claiming that Iraqi dictator Saddam Hussein was actively pursuing nuclear and other weapons of mass destruction, the administration moved toward war with Iraq. It also enunciated a new doctrine of "preemption," in which threats to American interests would not be allowed to grow, as had al-Qaeda, but proactively attacked by whatever means necessary. The **Iraq War** was also justified in terms of the need to secure access to oil supplies and the desire to topple dictatorships and foster democracy in the region.

Following a series of authorization negotiations with Congress, Operation Iraqi Freedom began on March 19, 2003, with a decapitation strike aimed at targets in Baghdad, Iraq's capital city. On April 9, Baghdad fell, and one month later, Bush declared the "mission accomplished." However, the Bush administration did not prepare for a long or contested occupation of Iraq and forces opposing the new government and the presence of American troops launched a guerrilla war. By mid-2008, more than 4,000 U.S. military personnel and Department of Defense civilians had died in Iraq, and 30,000 had been wounded, prompting increased calls for an end to the war. Barack Obama came into the presidency in 2009 pledging to end the war in Iraq. An end to formal U.S. combat operations was announced in 2010, and the last U.S. combat forces left Iraq in December 2011.

However, internal violence in Iraq continued and, indeed, the larger Middle East entered a period of severe turmoil and strife which left the United States with little opportunity to act unilaterally, as it often had over prior decades. Supported by airstrikes by American and other NATO forces, rebels in Libya overthrew and killed its longtime dictator Moamar Quadafi in 2011. However, Libya thereafter fell into civil strife, which included the murder of four Americans at the U.S. consulate in Benghazi the following year. Several other countries in the region, including Tunisia, Yemen, and Egypt have likewise experienced uprisings, chaos, and military crackdowns.

Most devastating has been the protracted civil war in Syria in which some half million people are believed to have lost their lives, with millions more being displaced and seeking refuge throughout the Middle East, North Africa, and Europe. The unprecedented outflows of population from Syria, Afghanistan, Libya, and elsewhere caused a humanitarian disaster and raised serious political tensions within the United States, the European Union, and other nations about how to address the refugee crisis.

Likewise, the vacuum created by civil war and insurgency in Syria and Iraq has allowed the proliferation of a virulent new terrorist threat to face the United States since al-Qaeda—the Islamic State in Iraq and Greater Syria, commonly known by the initials **ISIS** or, sometimes, ISIL. ISIS poses a major challenge to U.S. foreign and defense policies on at least three fronts. First, its presence destabilizes Syria, Iraq, and their immediate neighbors; second, it promotes the proliferation of other terrorist groups from Libya, to Nigeria, to Somalia; and third, it directs, or indirectly inspires, supporters to mount attacks in the United States and other Western nations. For example, in 2015 and 2016 violent mass-casualty massacres were carried out by followers of ISIS in California, Florida, France, Belgium, and other places beyond the Middle East. It was partly on the strength of public sentiment for a stronger U.S. response to global terrorism that Donald Trump won the presidency in 2016.

ISIS
A terrorist organization that calls itself an Islamic State, controls parts of Syria and Iraq and uses that as a base to direct and inspire terrorist attacks abroad.

FOREIGN AND DEFENSE POLICY DECISION MAKING

16.2 Describe the roles of the government and of other influences on U.S. foreign and defense policy.

The basic structure of foreign and defense policy decision making is laid out in the Constitution. The executive branch is the most powerful branch of government in the formulation and implementation of U.S. foreign and defense policy. Congress also influences and shapes policy through oversight, treaty ratification, appointments, appropriations, and war powers. The judiciary has a more limited role in foreign and defense affairs, usually addressing questions of executive authority. In addition, public opinion, political parties, and interest groups have important forms of influence.

The Constitution

When the Framers of the U.S. Constitution met in Philadelphia in 1787, they wanted a stronger national government to keep the United States out of European affairs and to keep Europe out of American affairs. As a result, they bequeathed the power to formulate and implement foreign policy to the national government rather than the states. In addition, many foreign and military powers not specified in the Constitution were, over time, asserted by the national government.

The Framers of the Constitution divided national authority for foreign and military policy functions between the president and Congress. The Framers named the president commander in chief of the armed forces but gave Congress power to fund the army and navy and to declare war. The president has authority to negotiate and sign treaties, but these take effect only after the Senate ratifies them by a two-thirds majority. Similarly, the president appoints ambassadors and other key foreign and military affairs officials, but the Senate grants advice and a majority of senators must give their consent to nominees. Ultimately, all such actions are subject to judicial review, although the judiciary tends to provide the elected branches with a great deal of latitude on foreign and military affairs.

The Executive Branch

The executive branch is the central place for creating and implementing U.S. foreign and defense policy, and within the executive branch, the president is the most important individual. Among executive departments, the Department of State is primarily responsible for diplomatic activity and the Department of Defense for military policy. Other parts of the executive branch, such as the National Security Council and the Central Intelligence Agency (CIA), provide additional resources for the president. The Department of Homeland Security focuses on the territory of the U.S. itself but also influences foreign and defense policy making.

National Security Council
The agency within the White House, led by the national security advisor, which brings together key foreign policy actors to advise the president.

Department of State
Chief executive branch department responsible for formulation and implementation of U.S. foreign policy.

THE PRESIDENT The president is preeminent in foreign and defense policy. As the Framers intended, presidents have greater access to and control over information than any other government official or agency, and presidents alone can act with little fear that their actions will be countermanded. As such, we tend to discuss U.S. foreign policy in terms of presidential action.

However, presidents have also come to rely increasingly on organizations and individuals located within the White House to help them make foreign policy. The most notable of these organizations is the **National Security Council**, led by the national security advisor, which brings together key foreign policy actors, including the vice president, the secretaries of state and of defense, intelligence officials, military leaders, and other presidential advisors. The organization's primary goal is to advise and assist the president on foreign and defense policy, particularly in crisis situations when speed in decision making is essential. Originally, the national security advisor was a neutral voice in the decision-making process, but today can be a significant player in foreign policy. Prominent former national security advisors include Henry Kissinger, Colin Powell, and Condoleezza Rice, all of whom went on to become Secretary of State.

THE DEPARTMENTS OF STATE, DEFENSE, AND HOMELAND SECURITY According to tradition, the **Department of State**, the oldest of all Cabinet agencies, is the leading executive branch department responsible for formulation and implementation of U.S. foreign policy. The Department of State serves as a link between foreign governments and U.S. policy makers and as a source of advice on how to deal with problems. The Secretary of State is one of the most prominent figures in any administration, and has most recently been held by two prominent former U.S. senators who had themselves been presidential contenders, Hillary Clinton and John Kerry. The State Department includes a large bureaucracy in Washington D.C., as well as a sprawling diplomatic corps composed of ambassadors and lower level officials in every country with which the U.S. has diplomatic relations.

Today, the Department of State's position of prominence has been challenged from many directions. Within the White House, the national security advisor may have competing views. Within each foreign country, the U.S. ambassador is often described as head of the "country team" that operates inside a U.S. embassy. In the U.S. Embassy in Mexico, for example, this means not only coordinating Department of State officials

WHO ARE THE KEY PLAYERS IN NATIONAL SECURITY POLICY?

As part of the core foreign and defense policy team for this second term, President Obama appointed Susan Rice (at podium) as National Security Advisor and Samantha Power as U.S. ambassador to the United Nations in 2013.

but also individuals from the Departments of Defense, Agriculture, Commerce, Labor, and Homeland Security, as well as the Federal Bureau of Investigation, the Drug Enforcement Agency, and the U.S. Trade Representative.

The **Department of Defense** is the chief executive branch department responsible for formulation and implementation of U.S. military policy. It came into existence after World War II, when the War Department and the Navy Department were combined into a single agency for military affairs. The Secretary of Defense is the nation's chief civilian military official, subordinate only to the president. Still, within the department, numerous lines of potential disagreement exist. Among the most prominent are those between professional military officers and civilians working in the Office of the Secretary of Defense, and between the separate branches of the armed services (Army, Navy, Air Force, and Marines) over missions, weapons, and priorities. To overcome these differences in outlook, the president relies on the **Joint Chiefs of Staff**, the military advisory body that includes the Army chief of staff, the Air Force chief of staff, the chief of naval operations, and the Marine commandant.

The **Department of Homeland Security**, the Cabinet department created after the 9/11 terrorist attacks in order to coordinate domestic security efforts, straddles the line between foreign and domestic policy making. The department brought together twenty-two existing agencies, approximately thirty newly created agencies or offices, and 180,000 employees into a single agency. Among its key units are the Transportation Security Administration (TSA), the organization responsible for aviation security; the Federal Emergency Management Agency (FEMA), the primary federal disaster relief organization; Customs and Border Protection; the U.S. Coast Guard; the Secret Service; and Immigration and Customs Enforcement (ICE).[7]

In addition to State, Defense, and Homeland Security, the complexity of contemporary foreign policy problems has increased the importance of views held by other Cabinet-level departments such as Treasury, Justice, and Commerce. In an interdependent global economy, these can also play critical roles, for example in the enforcement of economic sanctions against foreign countries.

THE INTELLIGENCE COMMUNITY The intelligence community is a term used to describe the agencies of the U.S. government that are involved in the collection and analysis of information, counterintelligence (the protection of U.S. intelligence), and covert action. The head of the intelligence community is the Director of National Intelligence (DNI), but its most prominent branch is the **Central Intelligence Agency (CIA)**, which gathers and analyzes information about the activities of foreign countries and nonstate actors. Perhaps more famously, the CIA also carries out covert operations to advance American strategic interests – which has included even the toppling of foreign governments.

Beyond the CIA, other key members of the intelligence community include the Bureau of Intelligence and Research in the Department of State; the Defense Intelligence Agency; the military service intelligence agencies; the National Security Agency in the Department of Defense; the Federal Bureau of Investigation in the Department of Justice; and the Department of Homeland Security. Coordinating these units can be difficult, since each has control over its own budget and they do not always share intelligence information with each other. Some branches have come under significant scrutiny and criticism for overstepping their established boundaries, such as regarding the use of extreme interrogation measures by the CIA and by the extensive and invasive monitoring of electronic communications by the NSA.

Congress

While the U.S. Constitution specifies several responsibilities for Congress, in practice it has much less influence over foreign and defense policy than does the president. Congress particularly tends to be deferential to the executive in times of war or threats

Department of Defense
Chief executive branch department responsible for formulation and implementation of U.S. defense and military policy.

Joint Chiefs of Staff
Military advisory body that includes the Army chief of staff, the Air Force chief of staff, the chief of naval operations, and the Marine commandant.

Department of Homeland Security
Cabinet department created after the 9/11 terrorist attacks to coordinate domestic security efforts.

Central Intelligence Agency (CIA)
A U.S. government agency dedicated to intelligence gathering and covert operations.

to national security. For example, the attacks on September 11, 2001, prompted adoption of the USA PATRIOT Act, a law proposed by the Department of Justice and passed by Congress in October 2001. The law gave the government greater law enforcement authority to gather intelligence domestically, detain and deport immigrants, search business and personal records, and conduct wiretaps. There is usually greater agreement on foreign and military affairs in the United States than on most domestic issues. Nevertheless, the legislative branch does plays a significant role in the policy process.

OVERSIGHT   Congress conducts oversight by holding hearings that monitor agency activities, as well as the content and conduct of U.S. policy. Congress may also establish reporting requirements; for instance, the State Department must submit annual evaluations of other nations' human rights practices and the president must notify Congress "in a timely fashion" of CIA covert actions. Members of Congress also engage in oversight of foreign and defense policy by visiting other countries, where they conduct "fact finding" missions and meet with political leaders, businesspeople, and even dissidents.

TREATIES AND EXECUTIVE AGREEMENTS   Additionally, the Constitution gives the Senate explicit power to approve treaties, although the Senate has rejected treaties only twenty times in U.S. history.[8] The most famous of these unapproved treaties was the international agreement to establish the League of Nations, which the Senate refused to approve in 1919. More recently, in 1999, the Senate rejected the Comprehensive Test Ban Treaty, which would prohibit testing of nuclear weapons among the countries that approve it.

On many issues, presidents can avoid the treaty process by drawing on their inherent constitutional authority to enter in to "executive agreements" with other countries. Unlike treaties, these do not require Senate approval. Prior to 1972, the president did not have to inform Congress of the text of these accords. Although many executive agreements deal with routine foreign policy matters, a great many also involve major military commitments on the part of the United States. Among them are agreements allowing for military bases in the Philippines and defense in Saudi Arabia.

This remains an evolving area of constitutional practice. For example, in 2015 the Obama Administration agreed to a novel arrangement in which both houses of Congress would have the opportunity to vote on whether to uphold a multilateral agreement with Iran regarding the dismantling of its nuclear weapons program in exchange for the cessation of economic sanctions. Due to a Democratic filibuster in the Senate, no action was taken by Congress in this case and the deal moved forward.

APPOINTMENTS AND APPROPRIATIONS   Another significant power wielded by Congress involve the Senate's authority to reject the president's nominees to high military and diplomatic offices. Although this power is rarely exercised in practice, the potential for rejection by the Senate can influence the nominations made by presidents. For example, due to Senate opposition in 2013, President Obama changed his plans to appoint Susan Rice as secretary of state, naming her instead to be national security advisor a role that does not require confirmation.

Congress also influences foreign and defense policy through its power to appropriate funds, and it can influence when and where the United States fights through its control of the budget. Although the power to go to war is shared by the executive and legislative branches of government, the power to appropriate funds belongs to the legislature alone. A significant problem faced by Congress in using budgetary powers to set the foreign policy agenda is that after the president publicly commits the United States to a high-profile course of action, it is very hard for Congress to intervene. For example, nothing came of discussion among Democrats in 2007 to halt the war in Iraq

FIGURE 16.1   HOW HAS DEFENSE SPENDING CHANGED OVER TIME?

This chart shows U.S. spending on national defense since 1940. Defense spending was at its highest levels during World War II and at its second highest in the post-9/11 period. Dollar amounts were adjusted for inflation to 2015 dollars.

SOURCE: U.S. Office of Management and Budget, Table 3.1—Outlays by Superfunction and Function: 1940–2021.

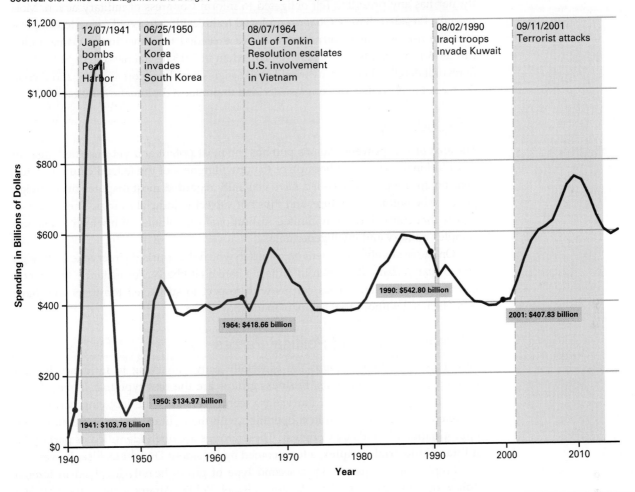

by cutting appropriations. Once U.S. troops were already involved in combat, any effort to cut funding was seen as a lack of support for American troops, who could be endangered by budget shortfalls.

WAR POWERS   Under the Constitution, the president is commander-in-chief of the armed forces, but it is reserved to Congress to make a formal declaration of war. During most of American history, it did so for all major international hostilities, including the War of 1812, the Spanish-American War, the Mexican-American War, and the two World Wars. However, as the nature of war has evolved since World War II, this practice has lapsed – even though the United States has pursued sustained military engagements in Korea, Vietnam, the Persian Gulf, Afghanistan, and Iraq.

In 1973, Congress enacted the **War Powers Resolution**. This articulated a new norm that, absent a declaration of war, military actions by the president would need a vote of approval from both houses of Congress. Under the resolution, the president is required to consult with Congress before deploying American troops into hostile situations. Under certain conditions, the president is required to report to Congress within forty-eight hours of the deployment. A presidential report can trigger a sixty-day clock that requires congressional approval for any continued military involvement past the sixty-day window. If Congress does not give explicit approval within sixty days, the president then has thirty days to withdraw the troops. Under the resolution,

War Powers Resolution
Passed by Congress in 1973; the president is limited in the deployment of troops overseas to a sixty-day period in peacetime (which can be extended for an extra thirty days to permit withdrawal) unless Congress explicitly gives its approval for a longer period.

military-industrial complex
The network of political and financial relations formed by defense industries, the U.S. armed forces, and Congress.

the president can respond to an emergency such as rescuing endangered Americans but cannot engage in a prolonged struggle without congressional approval.

The War Powers Resolution is controversial and has not been an effective restraint on presidential military authority. No president has recognized its constitutionality, nor has any president felt obligated to inform Congress of military action. Most recently, President Barack Obama employed technicalities to avoid going to Congress after the use of military airpower in Libya exceeded the time limit. Obama added further confusion into this area of the law when in 2013 he claimed the right to attack Syria unilaterally, then said he would seek congressional support anyway, and then in the face of likely defeat in Congress decided to pursue a diplomatic solution.

The Judiciary

The area of war powers remains perhaps the most potent and yet unsettled areas of constitutional law, in part because of the unwillingness of the federal courts to intervene on such topics. The courts have generally regarded most disputes over foreign policy to be political in nature, and thus not subject to judicial rulings. They also recognize that courts have only limited institutional capabilities with which to analyze complex military and intelligence data.

On the relatively infrequent occasions in which the courts do intervene on foreign and military affairs, it is often to protect a core civil liberty. For instance, the federal courts have ruled on habeas corpus with respect to suspected terrorists who have been detained without trial at Guantanamo Bay, Cuba.

Interest Groups and Political Parties

Four types of interest groups are especially active in trying to influence foreign and defense policy decisions. Business groups are the first type that lobbies heavily on foreign policy issues. Particularly controversial is the lobbying carried out by defense industries, often in cooperation with the military, to try to maximize the appropriation of funds by Congress. These groups are often identified as part of the **military-industrial complex**, a term coined by President Dwight D. Eisenhower.

Ethnic interest groups are a second type of group heavily involved in foreign policy decision making. The American-Israel Public Affairs Committee (AIPAC)

WHAT ARE THE INFLUENCES ON FOREIGN AND DEFENSE POLICYMAKING?

The U.S. military prison in Guantanamo Bay, Cuba, where since 2002 suspected terrorists have been held indefinitely, reflects the range of influences on U.S. policymaking: Congress, the Supreme Court, and the President have all taken different positions. Public opinion can also have a powerful influence, as reflected above in a protest at the White House in 2016.

and the Cuban-American National Foundation (CANF) are generally the two most influential groups. Periodically, Trans Africa has also emerged as an important foreign policy lobbying force for the African-American community. Among the most significant new ethnic lobbying groups are ones centered on Indian Americans and Pakistani Americans.

Foreign governments and companies are a third type of organized lobbying interest. The most common concerns of foreign governments are acquiring foreign aid and preventing hostile legislation from being passed. Turkey, for example, has lobbied extensively to prevent Congress from passing resolutions labeling as genocide the deaths of Armenians at the hands of the Ottoman Empire around the time of World War I. Foreign companies also actively lobby to gain access to the American market and improve the terms under which their investments in the United States are made.

Ideological-public interest groups are the final type of group active in foreign policy lobbying. This broad category encompasses think tanks such as the left-leaning Brookings Institution and the conservative Heritage Foundation, activist nongovernmental organizations such as Amnesty International and Greenpeace, and religious organizations. Opinions on major foreign policy issues such as military interventionism, free trade, and environmental agreements often vary widely on the basis of the political ideology held by these organizations.

Foreign and military policy are also the subject of disagreement across party lines, with Republicans typically assuming a more assertive, unilateral, and at times belligerent approach and Democrats often are more inclined toward diplomacy and the use of multilateral institutions. In recent years, a major source of frustration for Republicans had been the unwillingness of President Obama to take decisive military action to intervene in the civil war in Syria or to confront ISIS in its strongholds in Iraq and Syria. On the other hand, Republicans have generally approved of Obama's extensive use of unmanned military drones to attack potential terrorists, while the main critics of this policy have come from the left wing of the Democratic Party.

Another factor complicating the conduct of American foreign and defense policy is public opinion which is often deeply divided over how to proceed on different issues. It can also be difficult to get citizens to devote attention to foreign policy. This is known as the "guns and butter" theory. Generally speaking, most citizens are more interested in domestic policy issues ("butter") because they have a greater impact on their everyday lives. Only in case of emergency or times of crisis do citizens express significant concern over foreign policy issues ("guns"). This tendency complicates foreign policy making, and can make it difficult for foreign policy issues to occupy space on the policy agenda. When they do, public opinion can often tilt in the direction of favoring harsh and excessive action, such as in support voiced for taking extreme actions against ISIS.

CONTEMPORARY CHALLENGES IN FOREIGN AND DEFENSE POLICY

16.3 Evaluate major foreign and defense policy challenges now facing the United States.

Under the direction of the president and other government leaders, the foreign policy and military establishments must address a multitude of contemporary challenges in foreign and defense policy. This section begins by framing the international context within which the United States operates. Then, it highlights four specific issue areas: trade, terrorism, nuclear weapons, and global climate change. The evolving position of the U.S. on many of these issues seems likely to change significantly as part of the shift from the Obama administration to the Trump administration.

AMERICAN POLITICS IN COMPARATIVE PERSPECTIVE

How Does U.S. Military Spending Compare With Other Nations?

All countries spend some proportion of their national budget on military and defense expenditures, but no country spends as much as the United States. In 2015, the United States spent $596 billion, accounting for 36 percent of the world's total military spending ($1.635 trillion). The next highest spender, China, accounts for only about one-third of the U.S. total.

The United States spends far more on its military than any other country. This is reflected in U.S. bases around the world, military operations in places like Iraq and Afghanistan, and the significant foreign policy role that the United States plays involving issues and problems around the world.

In spite of the close economic ties that the United States and China maintain, many in the United States believe that China represents a rising threat and is likely to become a significant strategic competitor to the United States in the coming decades.

Historically, countries with the strongest economies have enjoyed the greatest military power. The table demonstrates that today, this is still the case, as countries that currently have large and/or rapidly growing economies top the list of military spending.

TABLE 16.1

Country	Dollars (billions)	% of World Total
1. United States	596	36.5
2. China	215	13.1
3. Saudi Arabia	87	5.3
4. Russia	66	4.1
5. United Kingdom	55	3.4
6. India	51	3.1
7. France	51	3.1
8. Japan	41	2.5
9. Germany	39	2.4
10. South Korea	36	2.2
11. Brazil	25	1.5
12. Italy	24	1.5
13. Australia	24	1.4
14. Israel	16	1.0
15. Turkey	15	0.9
Total	1635	

SOURCE: Stockholm International Peace Research Institute Military Expenditure Database, www.sipri.org/research/armaments/milex/milex_database/milex_database.

CRITICAL THINKING QUESTIONS

1. Are these numbers surprising? Why or why not?
2. What do you think accounts for the high level of U.S. military spending?
3. In 2004, China spent $57.5 billion on defense, representing 4 percent of the world's total military spending. Now it spends far more. How might China's rapid increase in military spending impact its relations with the United States?

The International Context

In the making of foreign and defense policy, the international context is crucially important—U.S. domestic laws and institutions do not extend beyond its borders, and so American policymakers must contend with the leaders of other countries, the realities of power rivalries among global competitors, and the role of nonstate actors, including multinational corporations, transnational nongovernmental organizations, political and religious social movements, organized crime, and terrorist groups.

The field of international relations is a complex one, but two main theories are usually applied to explain the behavior of countries and their foreign and defense policies. One perspective, known as **foreign-policy realism**, argues that nations first and foremost act is to protect their core national interests, including the integrity of their territory, the safety of their citizens, the prosperity of their economies, and the welfare of their key allies. Realist approaches typically emphasize the role of force, including nuclear deterrence, conventional military power, coercive economic pressure, covert intelligence capabilities, and, increasingly, the threat of cyberattacks.

An alternate view, known as **foreign-policy idealism**, contends that the behavior of countries in the international arena is mainly intended to advance the values and principles that motivate them, such as advancement of free-market capitalism, protection of human rights, and propagation of democratic norms. Idealists emphasize the skillful use of diplomacy, promote peaceful economic interdependence, and make use of multilateral international institutions such as the United Nations, the World Bank, and the International Monetary Fund.

Often, both realism and idealism can simultaneously motivate national behavior. For instance, the Iraq War was partly motivated by classic realist aims to eliminate a potential terrorist threat, to protect regional allies, and to secure access to supplies of oil from the Middle East. But the war was also framed as an opportunity to rid Iraq of a violent dictator, protect the human rights of Iraqis, and advance democratic goals throughout the larger Middle East. Although the United States was unable to secure a U.N. Security Council resolution authorizing the use of force, it did its best to assemble a multinational coalition and worked toward the return of sovereignty to the Iraqi people via free elections rather than attempting an open-ended occupation. Exactly what balance between realism and idealism is applied by the Trump administration remains to be seen.

Trade

Trade among nations has been a priority in international relations since antiquity. It can be a source of cooperation, competition, or conflict among countries. In the modern world, countries adopt one of three basic approaches in constructing their international trade policy: (1) protectionism; (2) strategic trade; and, (3) free trade. In practice, most countries use some elements of each approach.

TYPES OF TRADE POLICY First, countries may engage in **protectionism**. In this trade policy, a country takes steps to limit the import of foreign goods. It may also provide domestic producers with subsidies to help them compete against foreign imports. The early American system was rooted in protectionist thinking, including during the Great Depression in the 1930s.

Second, countries may embrace a **strategic trade policy**. Under such a policy, governments identify key industries that they want to see grow. They then provide those industries with economic support through tax breaks, low-interest loans, and other benefits. In the United States, computers, aerospace, and biotechnology are sectors that have often been singled out for support.

Finally, countries may choose to participate in an international **free trade system**. The hallmark of such a system is limited government involvement in international trade. Instead, goods and services cross borders according to supply and demand, as well as the principle of comparative advantage, in which countries sell goods they can produce most efficiently and buy from countries what they cannot. Creating and supporting a free trade system has been a major goal of U.S. trade policy since World War II.

Currently, the United States has trade relations with most countries in the world, but much of U.S. trade policy is defined by its relationship with China, with

foreign-policy realism
A perspective contending that the behavior of countries in the international arena is mainly intended to protect their economic and security interests.

foreign-policy idealism
A perspective contending that the behavior of countries in the international arena is mainly intended to advance their values and principles.

protectionism
A trade policy wherein a country takes steps to limit the import of foreign goods through tariffs and subsidies to domestic firms.

strategic trade policy
A trade policy wherein governments identify key industries that they wish to see grow and enact policies to support their development and success.

free trade system
A system of international trade that limits government interference on the sale of goods and services among countries.

North American Free Trade Agreement (NAFTA)
Agreement that promotes free movement of goods and services among Canada, Mexico, and the United States.

which trade has increased dramatically over the past three decades. In 1980, the year after the first U.S.-China bilateral trade agreement was signed, total trade (the value of imports and exports) was valued at $5 billion, but by 2015, it was $598 billion. That same year, the United States continued its longstanding and severe trade deficit with China, importing $482 billion from the Chinese while exporting only $116 million in goods to the Chinese.[9] This imbalance has been widely criticized within the United States, partly because some deem it responsible for the loss of domestic manufacturing jobs. Further, China has pledged to reduce tariffs on agricultural and industrial products, limit agricultural subsidies, open its banking system to foreign banks, halt manipulations of the value of its currency, permit full trading rights to foreign firms, and respect intellectual property rights. The country's failure to fully meet these conditions has been a repeated source of conflict with the United States and others.

MAKING TRADE POLICY   Three broad policy options exist for the United States under a free trade approach. The first is to emphasize bilateral trade, or that between two nations. Bilateral agreements have a rich history in the United States and continue to be used today. President George W. Bush was able to gain congressional approval for bilateral trade agreements with Australia, Chile, and Singapore. Under President Obama, Congress approved long-stalled trade agreements with South Korea, Colombia, and Panama.

In an attempt to adapt to globalization and incorporate a greater number of trading partners, presidents have increasingly turned to regional trade agreements. Such agreements involve more than two but as few as three states. This was the case with the 1994 **North American Free Trade Agreement (NAFTA)**, which further unites the economies of Mexico, Canada, and the United States. NAFTA created

FIGURE 16.2   WHAT ARE THE MAJOR MARKETS FOR U.S. EXPORTS?

The United States exports more goods to Canada than any other country. China, Mexico, and Japan also account for large shares of U.S. exports. Above are U.S. exports, in billions of dollars, to key trading partners in 2015.

SOURCE: U.S. Census Bureau, Foreign Trade Statistics.

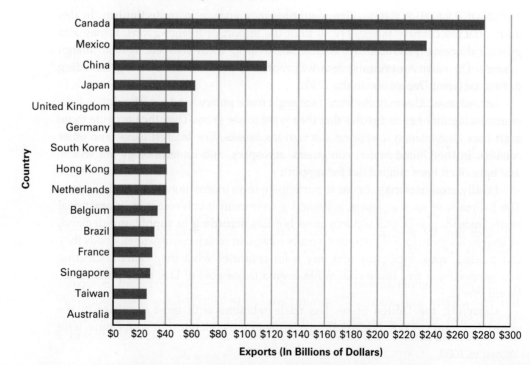

the world's largest regional free trade area with a market, but has been criticized for moving manufacturing jobs from the United States to Mexico, where labor is much cheaper. More recently, the Obama administration led negotiations for the **Trans-Pacific Partnership (TPP)** an agreement between the United States and eleven other nations on the Pacific Rim intended to substantially lower tariffs and protect intellectual property. The TPP received mixed reception from the American public, with critics citing a lack of transparency in the negotiations and stronger provisions allowing corporations to directly sue governments. However, as of the end of 2016, Congress had not approved the TPP, and the election of the avowedly protectionist Donald Trump as president seems certain to further dim its prospects.

A wide variety of concerns produce congressional opposition to bilateral and regional trade agreements. Among the most frequent are concerns for workers' rights, labor standards, environmental protection policies, and the health and safety of imports from other countries. Presidents have sought to overcome congressional opposition and tried to stop legislators from inserting amendments to these agreements by obtaining what is known as fast-track authority. Congress has the option to give this power to the president for a specific period of time. It requires that Congress may vote on—but not amend—trade agreements concluded by the president, such as NAFTA and TPP.

Most modern trade agreements are concluded under a global free trade system. The best known (but not always the most successful) example of this system is the WTO, the international organization created in 1995 to replace the General Agreement on Tariffs and Trade (GATT) and to supervise and expand international trade. Like its predecessor, GATT, the WTO reaches agreements through negotiating rounds. The latest round of WTO talks began in 2001 and has involved more than 150 countries. It quickly stalled as rich and poor countries found themselves in deep disagreement over free trade in agricultural products and clothing, protecting the environment, and intellectual property rights. Most recently, the WTO agreed in 2013 on a "Bali Package" to enable developing countries to trade with the developed world in global markets, but the agreement has not yet been ratified by all member states.

Terrorism

Terrorism is violence designed to achieve political intimidation and instill fear and panic in a population. It is generally pursued for ideological, political, or religious goals, and deliberately disregards or directly targets the safety of noncombatants. Terrorism is usually regarded as a tactic pursued by nongovernmental organizations, but governments may also engage in or support terrorism against either domestic or foreign enemies. Over time and in many different settings, terrorist activities have been used by insurgents against their own governments, by colonized peoples against their occupiers, and by people with grievances against outside countries, including the United States. Terrorism attacks the enemy through a series of largely independent and episodic strikes that, when added together, have an effect far greater than the sum of the individual actions.

TERRORISM AGAINST THE UNITED STATES   In recent years, most terrorist activities directly affecting the United States has been conducted by groups and individuals inspired by the Islamic concept of *jihad*, or holy war. A major goal has been to drive the United States out of the Middle East, and to return this region to Muslim rule. Even before the devastating attacks of September 11, 2001, this wave of terrorist activity had produced a steady flow of assaults. These included bombings of the United States marine barracks in Lebanon in 1983, the World Trade Center in 1993, American embassies in Kenya and Tanzania in 1998, and the *USS Cole* in port in Yemen in 2000.

Trans-Pacific Partnership (TPP)
A proposed agreement between the U. S. and eleven other nations on the Pacific Rim intended to substantially lower tariffs and protect intellectual property.

ديفيد كاوثورن هاينز

David Cawthorne Haines

أريد ان اقول اني أحمّلك يا ديفيد كاميرون المسؤولية الكاملة عن إعدامي

HOW DOES ISIS CHALLENGE THE CIVILIZED WORLD?

With highly publicized beheadings and mass killings, the Islamic State in Syria and Iraq (ISIS) terrorist group has reached every greater heights of barbarity. The group has destabilized the Middle East, threatened other nations, spawned copycat groups, and inspired "lone wolf" actors in the U.S. and other countries. Above, a screen-shot of the infamous ISIS terrorist nicknamed "Jihadi John" preparing to murder captured American journalist David Cawthorne Haines in 2014.

Since 9/11, *jihad*-related terrorist activities within the United States have been limited but still have resulted in number of civilian casualties. Prominent examples have included a massacre at an army base in Fort Hood, Texas in 2009, the bombing of the Boston marathon in 2013, and shootings at a party in San Bernardino, California in 2015. A number of other attempted attacks have been prevented, such as the so-called "underwear bomber" who was thwarted by other passengers aboard an airplane on Christmas Day 2009, and the attempted detonation of a car bomb in Times Square in 2010, which was spotted by onlookers and defused by police. Some other unknowable number of other potential attacks have been detected, deterred, and defended against by vigilance among citizens, by effective law enforcement techniques, and by U.S. intelligence and military capabilities abroad.

COUNTERTERRORISM POLICY   Terrorist activity is difficult to combat because it is planned and conducted with stealth and has a broad base of support in many parts of the world. Unlike in traditional warfare, it can also be difficult to define victory against nebulous groups and unknown individual who harbor terrorist inclinations and intentions. Some actors may have direct links to known organizations such as al-Qaeda or ISIS and can be detected through surveillance programs; others may be so-called "lone wolves" who are inspired by terrorist organizations but act on their own initiative.

After 9/11, the National Strategy for Combating Terrorism, prepared by the U.S. National Security Council, broadly defined victory over terrorism in terms of a world in which terrorism does not define the daily lives of Americans. To that end, it put forward a "4D strategy." The United States will: (1) defeat terrorist organizations; (2) deny them support from rogue states; (3) work to diminish the conditions that give rise to terrorism; and, (4) defend the United States, its citizens, and foreign interests from attack.[10] American policy makers have a number of policy instruments to choose from in designing strategies to combat terrorism. Diplomacy may be used to persuade other states to assist the United States, such as by sharing intelligence about potentially violent radicals. Military power, such as operations by U.S. Special Forces or strikes by aerial drones, can also be used to deny safe havens for the leadership of terrorist groups. Likewise, economic power may also be used through the imposition of economic sanctions in order to force states to stop supporting terrorists.

Critics of President Barack Obama have argued that he often seemed too dispassionate in his reaction to terrorist incidents and too mild in his military response. The president defended himself by arguing that a measured, reasoned response was the best way to minimize disruption to the "American way of life," which was itself a primary goal of terrorists. Rather than posing an existential threat to the United States and its allies, he argued, terrorism is a problem to be managed by a slow and steady approach to degrading ultimately defeating ISIS, al-Qaeda, and their supporters.

Nuclear Weapons

Since the American bombings of the Japanese cities of Hiroshima and Nagasaki in 1945, the existence, proliferation, and potential use of nuclear weapons has been a central concern of U.S. foreign policy. The potential for a catastrophic exchange of nuclear weapons between the United States and the Soviet Union was the defining fear of the Cold War. However, nuclear weapons were never again used after 1945, and the overall number of operational warheads has declined since its peak during the late Cold War. Still, there are estimated to be more than 10,000 warheads remaining under the control of nine countries.[11] In addition to the five UN Security Council members (the United States, Russia, Britain, France, and China), the less stable and more conflict-prone countries of India, Pakistan, North Korea, and Israel, also possess nuclear arms.

This proliferation raises the ongoing risk not only of direct military confrontation, but also that warheads or other nuclear materials could come under the control of terrorist groups. Their mere existence also adds anxiety and uncertainty to international relations, such as when the unstable and unpredictable North Korea periodically threatens to use nuclear weapons against its regional neighbors and even against Washington, D.C. Other countries, most notably Iran, have created global tensions merely through their pursuit of nuclear capabilities. All of these concerns have posed major ongoing challenges for U.S. foreign and defense policy. Several strategies traditionally have been in place to limit arms proliferation: disarmament, arms control, defense, and counterproliferation.

DISARMAMENT   Disarmament takes the very existence of weapons as a cause for conflict and hopes to secure peace through eliminating them. The earliest nuclear disarmament proposals, following World War II, aimed to place all aspects of nuclear energy production and use under international control but such aspirations foundered under the pressure of the Cold War. In the 1990s, a number of countries unilaterally chose to pursue disarmament, including the former Soviet countries of Belarus, Kazakhstan, and Ukraine as well as South Africa. Likewise, the vision of a world without weapons does remain alive today. President Barack Obama endorsed disarmament in a July 2009 speech in Moscow. He thereafter co-founded a biennial Nuclear Security Summit, and in March 2016 hosted a meeting of the group that included the leaders of 29 countries. However, the current prospects for moving toward abolition of nuclear weapons seem very slim.

ARMS CONTROL   A second strategy is arms control. This approach takes the existence of conflict between countries as a given in world politics and attempts to find ways of reducing the chances that those conflicts will become deadly. Decreasing the numbers and types of weapons at the disposal of policy makers is one approach. All but one of the world's major nuclear arms control agreements have been made between the United States and the Soviet Union (and its principal successor state, Russia), as they have possessed the largest numbers of these weapons. This regime of arms control has achieved considerable success, considering that stockpiles of operational nuclear warheads have declined more than six-fold since the mid-1980s. Also significant is the Nuclear Nonproliferation Treaty (NPT) of 1968, which has been joined by nearly every member of the United Nations. The NPT commits those countries that do not already have nuclear weapons not to develop them, while those that do have them commit to pursuing disarmament and to sharing technologies for the use of nuclear energy for peaceful purposes. However, the limits of the NPT were made evident when North Korea withdrew in 2003 and then, despite multiple rounds of diplomatic negotiations, went on to test both nuclear weapons and long-range missiles.

DEFENSE   A third strategy is defense. Essentially, this goal encourages the creation of a system to block or intercept attacks from other countries, particularly by developing the capability to strike down nuclear-armed missiles. Such a system was the animating vision of the Strategic Defense Initiative (SDI), introduced by the Reagan administration in 1983. Although SDI was actually far beyond what was technologically possible at the time, or even today, it is credited by some for increasing pressure on the Soviet Union and hastening the end of the Cold War. More recently, the United States has begun to deploy a limited system of long-range missile interceptors positioned within U.S. territory, on navy vessels, and most recently in NATO ally Romania.

COUNTERPROLIFERATION   A final strategy embraced by many countries today is counterproliferation. This involves the use, or at least threat, of preemptive military action against a threatening country or terrorist group. One of the major rationales for the 2003 invasion of Iraq by a U.S.-led multinational coalition was to eliminate the nuclear and other weapons of mass destruction alleged to exist there. More recently, the threat of such a preemptive attack—combined with crippling economic sanctions—led to a diplomatic breakthrough with Iran in 2015. Under the terms of a wide-ranging "nuclear deal," the Iranian regime agreed to dismantle its existing nuclear facilities and submit to invasive international inspections for at least a decade in exchange for reintegration in to the world economy.

Global Climate Change

The issue of global climate change has been on the global political agenda since at least 1994, with the establishment of the United Nations Framework Convention on Climate (UNFCCC). In 1997 President Bill Clinton signed the Kyoto Protocol. This landmark multilateral agreement codified an international consensus that rising levels of "greenhouse gas emissions" are causing a dangerous increase in the Earth's temperature. Some remaining skeptics, particularly among conservatives in the United States, argue either that climate change is not serious threat or that it is simply a naturally occurring phenomenon. However, over the past two decades, a robust body of scientific evidence has demonstrated that climate-warming trends over the last century have been caused primarily by human industrial activities.

One report by the U.S. National Aeronautics and Space Administration (NASA) identified a range of potentially disastrous effects from global temperature increases, including warming oceans and sea level rise, shrinking ice sheets and glacial retreat, decreased snow cover, and ocean acidification.[12] Such changes could increase the incidence of catastrophic droughts, floods, hurricanes, heatwaves, crop failures, and health problems among both human and animal populations. These impacts are likely to be greatest on the poorest countries with the fewest resources—ironically, the very ones that have benefitted the least from the mass industrialization in wealthier countries that led to climate change. According to the Intergovernmental Panel on Climate Change, some risks of damaging climate change occur at just 1 or 2°C above preindustrial levels; an increase of global mean temperature of 4°C or more above preindustrial levels could cause disastrous consequences.[13] The submersion of highly-populated coastal areas, mass flows of refugees, increased border conflict, widespread starvation, and even the disappearance of several small island nations are all among the potential politically destabilizing impacts of global climate change.

In response to such threats, the Obama administration released a Climate Action Plan in 2013 that consisting of three main pillars: (1) cut carbon pollution in America; (2) prepare the United States for impacts of climate change; and (3) lead international efforts in terms of climate change.[14] Domestically, this led to calls for the United States to cut carbon pollution from power plants, accelerate the use of "clean" energy sources, modernize the electricity grid, and address the impacts of environmental change. On the international front, the battle against global climate change has called on all U.S. resources and tools in foreign and defense policy making, in both bilateral and multilateral forums. In 2009, the United States launched the Major Economies Forum on Energy and Climate, a high-level forum that brings together 17 countries that account for approximately 75 percent of global greenhouse gas emissions, in order to support the international climate negotiations and spur cooperative action to combat climate change. In 2010, a Presidential Policy Directive on Global Development identified the Global Climate Change Initiative as one of three priority U.S. development initiatives. The administration has also expanded bilateral cooperation with key major emerging economies, through initiatives including the U.S.-China Clean Energy Research Center, the U.S.-India Partnership to Advance Clean Energy, and the Strategic Energy Dialogue with Brazil.

In November 2015, President Obama and President Xi Jinping of China reached an agreement to collaborate on phasing out of hydrofluorocarbons, a major form of greenhouse gas emission. The two countries also pledged to collaborate on developing carbon dioxide "capture and storage systems" that could provide clean coal-burning for power plants, steel manufacturers, cement-making factories, and other heavy emitters. The deal also had a trade component, by potentially reducing tariffs on "green goods" such as more energy-efficient and resilient building materials.

This bilateral cooperation between the world's two largest "emitters" provided momentum for further multilateral diplomatic agreement the following month. The Paris Climate Agreement brought together 196 developed and developing countries to resolve to bring down global greenhouse gas emissions "as soon as possible," to retain an existing target of keeping global warming below 2°C while aspiring to 1.5°C, and to aim for no further net increases in emissions from human activities after 2050. Critics of the Paris agreement condemned it for a lack of urgency, noting that its goals were too incremental, that many provisions were not legally binding, and that commitments for new funding were too vague. Nonetheless, in a fractured and contentious world, the fact that nearly all of the countries on the planet met in the single forum of the UNFCCC and managed to reach an agreement was a major achievement for global cooperation.[15]

TOWARD REFORM: EMERGING CHALLENGES

16.4 Understand emerging challenges that are shaping U.S. foreign and defense policies.

The United States remains a dominant power in world politics, with the world's largest economy and its strongest military. It has many allies and provides economic and military aid to many countries around the globe. At the same time, however, the lengthy wars in Iraq and Afghanistan, the ongoing challenges posed by al-Qaeda and ISIS, domestic political gridlock, and other social, political, and economic factors have demonstrated some of the limits of American power. This concluding section considers emerging challenges facing the United States and the Trump administration with regard to four critical world regions: China, Russia, Europe, and the Middle East and North Africa (MENA) region.

China

The tremendous economic growth and global influence of China is leading it to
become both a challenger to the United States in some areas, but also its most logi-
cal partner in others. Both countries benefit from trade and globalization; both want
to limit the spread of nuclear weapons; and both are served by reining in countries
such as Iran and North Korea that threaten peace and stability. There is still considerable tension and mistrust as well. China depends on the U.S. market to sell exports
and fuel its economic growth. The United States borrows heavily from China, which
finances growing U.S. budget deficits by purchasing American Treasury bonds. This
type of interaction creates a potentially unhealthy mutual dependency for economic
prosperity, especially as China's rate of growth has slowed in recent years.

At the same time, China is modernizing its navy, missiles, aircraft, cyber warfare
capabilities, and anti-satellite weapons. In a move deemed provocative by many of its
neighbors, China has even constructed artificial islands in the South China Sea and
claimed sovereignty over them—giving it a stronger foothold for military action and
a tighter grip on a major transit route for global trade. In response, the United States
has begun deploying more military forces in the Pacific, including a new deployment
of 2,500 Marines in Australia. It has also strengthened and even expanded its partnership with India, Japan, South Korea, and other Asian countries who serve as regional
counterweights to China in the Asia-Pacific region. In all, the relationship between the
United States and China will increasingly determine how peaceful or dangerous the
world becomes, and quite possibly also how prosperous it is.

Russia

Russia has begun to aggressively reassert the great-power status that it lost in the
early 1990s with the collapse of the Soviet Union. Strongman President Vladimir
Putin has consolidated power domestically by crushing terrorist threats from the
Caucasus region, taking control of Russian television and some other media, and
by using heavy-handed tactics to suppress political dissent. Long propelled by high
oil prices, Putin has cannily used his leverage to attempt to reestablish a zone of
influence in neighboring countries that had been part of the Russian Empire and the
Soviet Union.

Where possible, Putin has used economic means, including promotion of a "Eurasian Economic Community" as a counterweight to the European Union. But Putin has also not hesitated to use military means, including outright invasions of former Soviet countries Georgia and Ukraine and an intervention in Syria to prop up his ally Bashar al-Assad. A global decline in the price of oil has curtailed Putin's latitude for action, but Russia remains a continuing geopolitical rival for the United States.

European Union
An organization with political institutions that join 28 countries in Europe into a union that promotes free trade, a central bank, flow of labor and capital, and a common currency among most members.

Europe

At the same time that China and Russia have been strengthening, America's strongest allies in Europe have lately lurched from crisis to crisis in both the political and economic realms. This has also posed a challenge for the United States, whose global standing is tied to that of Europe, which forms the core of the NATO military alliance, constitutes the world's largest economic bloc, and is a key U.S. trading partner. A cornerstone of European peace, prosperity, and democracy has been the 28-member **European Union (EU)**, which promotes cooperation rather than conflict among the nations on the once-wartorn continent.

In recent years, however, the EU has faced severe challenges. Several countries, including Greece, Spain, Portugal, Italy, and Ireland, have run the risk of defaulting on their loans. This has undermined the Euro, the common currency shared by 17 EU nations, and required numerous bailouts by Europe's richer countries, whose citizens are often resentful. At the same time, a crisis caused by massive flows of refugees from Syria, Iraq, and other conflict zones has escalated tensions within the EU and threatened the viability of its much-valued open borders and free flow of populations. Even worse has been a series of terrorist attacks, especially in France and Belgium, against which police and intelligence communities were unable to respond in an effective or coordinated fashion. Then on June 23, 2016, voters in the United Kingdom, who had long been ambivalent about EU membership, approved a referendum to begin the country's withdrawal from the union. Cumulatively, these crises have emboldened anti-EU political parties across the continent, laid bare the limits of the EU's ability to govern collectively, and even threatened the viability of the EU itself.

The Middle East and North Africa (MENA) Region

The United States also faces myriad foreign and defense policy challenges created by rapidly unfolding events in the world's most volatile area: the Middle East and North Africa (MENA) region. Following the U.S.-led invasions of Afghanistan in 2002 and Iraq in 2003, and a series of popular uprisings in several Arab countries beginning in 2010, the entire MENA region has become destabilized. Certainly, hopes of a democratic awakening have been mostly dashed: some MENA countries have devolved into chaos and civil war, such as Libya, Yemen and Syria, while others have undergone harsh military crackdowns, such as Egypt and Bahrain.

The United States has numerous key interests in the MENA region, including support for allies such as Turkey and Israel, protection of the global supply of oil, and the need to thwart terrorist forces originating in the region. For every step forward for U.S. policy, such as the nuclear deal with Iran and efforts to bring peace to Syria, new threats emerge, such as the proliferation of ISIS and escalating tensions between the Sunni and Shia sects of Islam. Indeed, no other region of the world exemplifies both the continuing power of the United States and its sharp limitations as an actor in the world. On the one hand, the country faces no serious existential threats such as those posed by the Soviet Union during the Cold War. The United States retains the planet's most potent military power, backed by the world's largest economy, and has no single serious rival for global leadership. At the same time, the United States faces turbulence and conflict in nearly every corner of the world and a range of persistent threats requiring ongoing vigilance and determination.

REVIEW THE CHAPTER

Roots of U.S. Foreign and Defense Policy

16.1 Outline the major events and issues in the development of U.S. foreign and defense policy.

For most of the nation's first century, foreign and defense policy largely involved trade and commerce, isolationism with regard to Europe, and expansion across North America. As U.S. economic interests expanded, the United States intervened more and more overseas, especially in Latin America and Asia. The United States' status as a world power was cemented by its entry into, and subsequent victory in, World Wars I and II. During the Cold War, U.S. foreign and defense policy was focused on its confrontation with the Soviet Union. The September 11, 2001, terrorist attacks marked a new direction in American foreign policy, as the United States pursued a war on terrorism both at home and overseas.

Foreign and Defense Policy Decision Making

16.2 Describe the roles of government officials and of other influences in U.S. foreign and defense policy.

The basic structure of foreign and defense policy decision making is laid out in the Constitution. The executive branch of government dominates foreign and defense policy. The president is preeminent, with the Departments of State, Defense, and Homeland Security also playing important roles, along with the intelligence community. Congress also influences and shapes policy through oversight, approval of treaties and appointments, appropriations, and the War Powers Resolution. Four types of interest groups are also especially active in trying to influence foreign and defense policy decisions; these groups include the military-industrial complex, ethnic interest groups, foreign governments and companies, and ideological-public interest groups. Political parties and public opinion also influence the shape of U.S. foreign and defense policies.

Contemporary Challenges in Foreign and Defense Policy

16.3 Evaluate foreign and defense policy challenges now facing the United States.

The United States faces major challenges in foreign and defense policy during the twenty-first century. These include trade, terrorism, nuclear weapons, and global climate change. In terms of trade, the United States operates within a global free trade system but runs an overall trade imbalance of more imports than exports. The biggest threat related to terrorism comes from ISIS, the self-styled Islamic State, and al-Qaeda, the perpetrators of the September 11, 2001 terrorist attacks. The threat of nuclear weapons has receded somewhat since the end of the Cold War, but rogue nations and terrorist organization still raise serious concerns. Global climate change poses a potential threat to political, economic, and social stability around the globe, yet the world's leaders have been hard-pressed to find effective collective solutions.

Toward Reform: Emerging Challenges

16.4 Understand emerging challenges that are shaping U.S. foreign and defense policies in four key regions.

The United States remains a dominant power in world politics, with the world's largest economy and its largest military, but faces challenge on many fronts. China has emerged as the most important partner, rival, but also potential threat to U.S. global supremacy, and Russia has also reasserted itself on the world stage. At the same time, Europe and the European Union are under growing duress, and the Middle East and North Africa (MENA) region is embroiled in conflict and turmoil. These and other emerging challenges pose threats, and in some cases also opportunities, for the United States today and in the years ahead.

LEARN THE TERMS

Afghanistan War
al-Qaeda
Berlin Wall

Bretton Woods System
Central Intelligence Agency (CIA)
Cold War

collective security
containment
Cuban Missile Crisis

defense policy
Department of Defense
Department of Homeland Security
Department of State
détente
deterrence
European Union
Farewell Address
foreign policy
foreign-policy idealism
foreign-policy realism
free trade system
General Agreement on Tariffs and
    Trade (GATT)
global war on terror
Gulf War
human rights

International Monetary Fund (IMF)
Iraq War
Iron Curtain
ISIS
isolationism
Joint Chiefs of Staff
Korean War
League of Nations
manifest destiny
Marshall Plan
military-industrial complex
Monroe Doctrine
National Security Council
North American Free Trade
    Agreement (NAFTA)
North Atlantic Treaty Organization
    (NATO)

protectionism
Reagan Doctrine
Roosevelt Corollary
September 11
strategic trade policy
tariffs
Trans-Pacific Partnership (TPP)
Truman Doctrine
UN Security Council
United Nations
Vietnam War
War Powers Resolution
World Bank
World Trade Organization
    (WTO)
World War I
World War II

THE DECLARATION OF INDEPENDENCE

In Congress, July 4, 1776
The Unanimous Declaration
of the Thirteen United States of America

When in the Course of human events it becomes necessary for one people to dissolve the political bands which have connected them with another, and to assume, among the powers of the earth, the separate and equal station to which the Laws of Nature and of Nature's God entitle them, a decent respect to the opinions of mankind requires that they should declare the causes which impel them to the separation.

We hold these truths to be self-evident, that all men are created equal, that they are endowed by their Creator with certain unalienable Rights, that among these are Life, Liberty and the pursuit of Happiness. That to secure these rights, Governments are instituted among Men, deriving their just powers from the consent of the governed. That whenever any Form of Government becomes destructive of these ends, it is the Right of the People to alter or to abolish it, and to institute new Government, laying its foundation on such principles and organizing its powers in such form, as to them shall seem most likely to effect their Safety and Happiness. Prudence, indeed, will dictate that Governments long established should not be changed for light and transient causes; and accordingly all experience hath shewn that mankind are more disposed to suffer, while evils are sufferable, than to right themselves by abolishing the forms to which they are accustomed. But when a long train of abuses and usurpations, pursuing invariably the same Object evinces a design to reduce them under absolute Despotism, it is their right, it is their duty, to throw off such Government, and to provide new Guards for their future security. —Such has been the patient sufferance of these Colonies; and such is now the necessity which constrains them to alter their former Systems of Government. The history of the present King of Great Britain is a history of repeated injuries and usurpations, all having in direct object the establishment of an absolute Tyranny over these States. To prove this, let Facts be submitted to a candid world.

He has refused his Assent to Laws, the most wholesome and necessary for the public good.

He has forbidden his Governors to pass Laws of immediate and pressing importance, unless suspended in their operation till his Assent should be obtained; and when so suspended, he has utterly neglected to attend to them.

He has refused to pass other Laws for the accommodation of large districts of people, unless those people would relinquish the right of Representation in the Legislature, a right inestimable to them and formidable to tyrants only.

He has called together legislative bodies at places unusual, uncomfortable, and distant from the depository of their Public Records, for the sole purpose of fatiguing them into compliance with his measures.

He has dissolved Representative Houses repeatedly, for opposing with manly firmness his invasions on the rights of the people.

He has refused for a long time, after such dissolutions, to cause others to be elected; whereby the Legislative Powers, incapable of Annihilation, have returned to the People at large for their exercise, the State remaining in the mean time exposed to all the dangers of invasion from without, and convulsions within.

He has endeavored to prevent the population of these States; for that purpose obstructing the Laws of Naturalization of Foreigners; refusing to pass others to encourage their migration hither, and raising the conditions of new Appropriations of Lands.

He has obstructed the Administration of Justice, by refusing his Assent to Laws for establishing Judiciary powers.

He has made Judges dependent on his Will alone, for the tenure of their offices, and the amount and payment of their salaries.

He has erected a multitude of New Offices, and sent hither swarms of Officers to harass our people, and eat out their substance.

He has kept among us, in times of peace, Standing Armies without the Consent of our legislatures.

He has affected to render the Military independent of and superior to the Civil power.

He has combined with others to subject us to a jurisdiction foreign to our constitution, and unacknowledged by our laws, giving his Assent to their Acts of pretended Legislation:

For quartering large bodies of armed troops among us:

For protecting them, by a mock Trial, from punishment for any Murders which they should commit on the Inhabitants of these States:

For cutting off our Trade with all parts of the world:

For imposing Taxes on us without our Consent:

For depriving us in many cases, of the benefits of Trial by Jury:

For transporting us beyond Seas to be tried for pretended offences:

For abolishing the free System of English Laws in a neighboring Province, establishing therein an Arbitrary government, and enlarging its Boundaries so as to render it at once an example and fit instrument for introducing the same absolute rule into these Colonies:

For taking away our Charters, abolishing our most valuable Laws, and altering fundamentally the Forms of our Governments:

For suspending our own Legislatures, and declaring themselves invested with power to legislate for us in all cases whatsoever.

He has abdicated Government here, by declaring us out of his Protection and waging War against us.

He has plundered our seas, ravaged our Coasts, burnt our towns, and destroyed the lives of our people.

He is at this time transporting large Armies of foreign Mercenaries to compleat the works of death, desolation and tyranny, already begun with circumstances of Cruelty and perfidy scarcely paralleled in the most barbarous ages, and totally unworthy the Head of a civilized nation.

He has constrained our fellow Citizens taken Captive on the high Seas to bear Arms against their Country, to become the executioners of their friends and Brethren, or to fall themselves by their Hands.

He has excited domestic insurrections amongst us, and has endeavored to bring on the inhabitants of our frontiers, the merciless Indian Savages, whose known rule of warfare, is an undistinguished destruction of all ages, sexes and conditions.

In every stage of these Oppressions We have Petitioned for Redress in the most humble terms: Our repeated Petitions have been answered only by repeated injury: A Prince, whose character is thus marked by every act which may define a Tyrant, is unfit to be the ruler of a free people.

Nor have We been wanting in attention to our British brethren. We have warned them from time to time of attempts by their legislature to extend an unwarrantable jurisdiction over us. We have reminded them of the circumstances of our emigration and settlement here. We have appealed to their native justice and magnanimity; and we have conjured them by the ties of our common kindred to disavow these usurpations, which would inevitably interrupt our connections and correspondence. They too have been deaf to the voice of justice and consanguinity. We must, therefore, acquiesce in the necessity, which denounces our Separation, and hold them, as we hold the rest of mankind, Enemies in War, in Peace Friends.

We, therefore, the Representatives of the United States of America, in General Congress, Assembled, appealing to the Supreme Judge of the world for the rectitude of our intentions, do, in the Name, and by Authority of the good People of these Colonies, solemnly publish and declare, That these United Colonies are, and of Right ought to be Free and Independent States; that they are Absolved from all Allegiance to the British Crown, and that all political connection between them and the State of Great Britain, is and ought to be totally dissolved: and that as Free and Independent States, they have full power to levy War, conclude Peace, contract Alliances, establish Commerce, and to do all other Acts and Things which Independent States may of right do. And for the support of this Declaration, with a firm reliance on the protection of Divine Providence, we mutually pledge to each other our Lives, our Fortunes and our sacred Honor.

JOHN HANCOCK

NEW HAMPSHIRE
Josiah Bartlett
William Whipple
Matthew Thornton

MASSACHUSETTS
Samuel Adams
John Adams
Robert Treat Paine
Elbridge Gerry

RHODE ISLAND AND
PROVIDENCE PLANTATIONS
Stephen Hopkins
William Ellery

CONNECTICUT
Roger Sherman
Samuel Huntington
William Williams
Oliver Wolcott

NEW YORK
William Floyd
Philip Livingston
Francis Lewis
Lewis Morris

NEW JERSEY
Richard Stockton
John Witherspoon
Francis Hopkinson
John Hart
Abraham Clark

PENNSYLVANIA
Robert Morris
Benjamin Rush
Benjamin Franklin
John Morton
George Clymer
James Smith
George Taylor
James Wilson
George Ross

DELAWARE
Caesar Rodney
George Read
Thomas McKean

MARYLAND
Samuel Chase
William Paca

Thomas Stone
Charles Carroll

VIRGINIA
George Wythe
Richard Henry Lee
Thomas Jefferson
Benjamin Harrison
Thomas Nelson, Jr.
Francis Lightfoot Lee
Carter Braxton

NORTH CAROLINA
William Hooper
Joseph Hewes
John Penn

SOUTH CAROLINA
Edward Rutledge
Thomas Heyward, Jr.
Thomas Lynch, Jr.
Arthur Middleton

GEORGIA
Button Gwinnett
Lyman Hall
George Walton

THE CONSTITUTION OF THE UNITED STATES OF AMERICA

We the People of the United States, in Order to form a more perfect Union, establish Justice, insure domestic Tranquility, provide for the common defence, promote the general Welfare, and secure the Blessings of Liberty to ourselves and our Posterity, do ordain and establish this Constitution for the United States of America.

ARTICLE I

Section 1

All legislative Powers herein granted shall be vested in a Congress of the United States, which shall consist of a Senate and House of Representatives.

Section 2

The House of Representatives shall be composed of Members chosen every second Year by the People of the several States, and the Electors in each State shall have the Qualifications requisite for Electors of the most numerous Branch of the State Legislature.

No person shall be a Representative who shall not have attained to the Age of twenty five Years, and been seven Years a Citizen of the United States, and who shall not, when elected, be an Inhabitant of that State in which he shall be chosen.

Representatives and direct Taxes shall be apportioned among the several States which may be included within this Union, according to their respective Numbers which shall be determined by adding to the whole Number of free Persons, including those bound to Service for a Term of Years, and excluding Indians not taxed, three fifths of all other Persons. The actual Enumeration shall be made within three Years after the first Meeting of the Congress of the United States, and within every subsequent Term ten Years, in such Manner as they shall by Law direct. The Number of Representatives shall not exceed one for every thirty Thousand, but each State shall have at Least one Representative; and until such enumerations shall be made, the State of New Hampshire shall be entitled to chuse three, Massachusetts eight, Rhode-Island and Providence Plantations one, Connecticut five, New-York six, New Jersey four, Pennsylvania eight, Delaware one, Maryland six, Virginia ten, North Carolina five, South Carolina five, and Georgia three.

When vacancies happen in the Representation from any State, the Executive Authority thereof shall issue Writs of Election to fill such Vacancies.

The House of Representatives shall chuse their speaker and other Officers; and shall have the sole Power of Impeachment.

Section 3

The Senate of the United States shall be composed of two Senators from each State chosen by the Legislature thereof, for six Years; and each Senator shall have one Vote.

Immediately after they shall be assembled in Consequence of the first Election, they shall be divided as equally as may be into three Classes. The Seats of the Senators of the first Class shall be vacated at the Expiration of the second year, of the second Class at the Expiration of the fourth Year, and of the third Class at the Expiration of the sixth Year, so that one third may be chosen every second Year and if Vacancies happen by Resignation, or otherwise, during the Recess of the Legislature of any State, the Executive thereof may make temporary Appointments until the next Meeting of the Legislature, which shall then fill such Vacancies.

No Person shall be a Senator who shall not have attained to the Age of thirty Years, and been nine Years a Citizen of the United States, and who shall not, when elected, be an Inhabitant of that State for which he shall be chosen.

The Vice President of the United States shall be President of the Senate, but shall have no Vote, unless they be equally divided.

The Senate shall chuse their other Officers, and also a President pro tempore, in the Absence of the Vice President, or when he shall exercise the Office of President of the United States.

The Senate shall have the sole Power to try all Impeachments. When sitting for that Purpose, they shall be on Oath or Affirmation. When the President of the United States is tried, the Chief Justice shall preside: And no Person shall be convicted without the Concurrence of two thirds of the Members present.

Judgment in Cases of Impeachment shall not extend further than to removal from Office, and disqualification to hold and enjoy any Office of honor, Trust or Profit under the United States; but the Party convicted shall nevertheless be liable and subject to Indictment, Trial, Judgment and Punishment, according to law.

Section 4

The Times, Places and Manner of holding Elections for Senators and Representatives, shall be prescribed in each State by the Legislature thereof; but the Congress may at any time by Law make or alter such Regulations, except as to the Places of chusing Senators.

The Congress shall assemble at least once in every Year, and such Meeting shall be on the first Monday in December, unless they shall by Law appoint a different Day.

Section 5

Each House shall be the Judge of the Elections, Returns and Qualifications of its own Members, and a Majority of each shall constitute a Quorum to do business; but a smaller Number may adjourn from day to day, and may be authorized to compel the Attendance of absent Members, in such Manner, and under such Penalties as each House may provide.

Each House may determine the Rules of its Proceedings, punish its Members for disorderly Behaviour, and with the Concurrence of two thirds, expel a Member.

Each House shall keep a Journal of its Proceedings, and from time to time publish the same, excepting such Parts as may in their judgment require Secrecy; and the Yeas and Nays of the Members of either House on any question shall, at the Desire of one fifth of those present, be entered on the Journal.

Neither House, during the Session of Congress, shall, without the Consent of the other, adjourn for more than three days, nor to any other Place than that in which the two Houses shall be sitting.

Section 6

The Senators and Representatives shall receive a Compensation for their Services, to be ascertained by Law, and paid out of the Treasury of the United States. They shall in all Cases, except Treason, Felony and Breach of the Peace, be privileged from Arrest during their Attendance at the Session of their respective Houses, and in going to and returning from the same; and for any Speech or Debate in either House, they shall not be questioned in any other Place.

No Senator or Representative shall, during the Time for which he was elected, be appointed to any civil Office under the Authority of the United States, which shall have been created, or the Emoluments whereof shall have been encreased during such time; and no Person holding any Office under the United States, shall be a Member of either House during his Continuance in Office.

Section 7

All Bills for raising Revenue shall originate in the House of Representatives; but the Senate may propose or concur with Amendments as on other Bills.

Every Bill which shall have passed the House of Representatives and the Senate, shall, before it become a Law, be presented to the President of the United States; If he approve he shall sign it, but if not he shall return it, with his Objections to that House in which it shall have originated, who shall enter the Objections at large on their Journal, and proceed to reconsider it. If after such Reconsideration two thirds of that House shall agree to pass the Bill, it shall be sent, together with the Objections, to the other House, by which it shall likewise be reconsidered, and if approved by two thirds of that House, it shall become a Law. But in all such Cases the Votes of both Houses shall be determined by Yeas and Nays, and the Names of the Persons voting for and against the Bill shall be entered on the Journal of each House respectively. If any Bill shall not be returned by the President within ten Days (Sundays excepted) after it shall have been presented to him, the Same shall be a Law, in like Manner as if he had signed it, unless the Congress by their Adjournment prevent its Return, in which Case it shall not be a Law.

Every Order, Resolution, or Vote to which the Concurrence of the Senate and House of Representatives may be necessary (except on a question of Adjournment) shall be presented to the President of the United States; and before the Same shall take Effect, shall be approved by him, or being disapproved by him, shall be repassed by two thirds of the Senate and House of Representatives, according to the Rules and Limitations prescribed in the Case of a Bill.

Section 8

The Congress shall have Power To lay and collect Taxes, Duties, Imposts and Excises, to pay the Debts and provide for the common Defence and general Welfare of the United States; but all Duties, Imposts and Excises shall be uniform throughout the United States;

To borrow Money on the credit of the United States;

To regulate Commerce with foreign Nations, and among the several States, and with the Indian Tribes;

To establish a uniform Rule of Naturalization, and uniform Laws on the subject of Bankruptcies throughout the United States;

To coin Money, regulate the Value thereof, and of foreign Coin, and fix the Standard of Weights and Measures;

To provide for the Punishment of counterfeiting the Securities and current Coin of the United States;

To establish Post Offices and post Roads;

To promote the Progress of Science and useful Arts, by securing for limited Times to Authors and Inventors exclusive Right to their respective Writings and Discoveries;

To constitute Tribunals inferior to the supreme Court;

To define and punish Piracies and Felonies committed on the high Seas, and Offences against the Law of Nations;

To declare War, grant Letters of Marque and Reprisal, and make rules concerning Captures on Land and Water;

To raise and support Armies, but no Appropriation of Money to that Use shall be for a longer Term than two Years;

To provide and maintain a Navy;

To make Rules for the Government and Regulation of the land and naval Forces;

To provide for calling forth the Militia to execute the Laws of the Union, suppress Insurrections and repel Invasions;

To provide for organizing, arming, and disciplining, the Militia, and for governing such Part of them as may be employed in the Service of the United States, reserving to the States respectively, the Appointment of the Officers, and the Authority of training the Militia according to the discipline prescribed by Congress;

To exercise exclusive Legislation in all Cases whatsoever, over such District (not exceeding ten Miles square) as may, by Cession of particular States, and the Acceptance of Congress, become the Seat of the Government of the United States, and to exercise like Authority over all Places purchased by the Consent of the Legislature of the State in which the Same shall be for the Erection of Forts, Magazines, Arsenals, dock-Yards, and other needful Buildings;

—And To make all Laws which shall be necessary and proper for carrying into Execution the foregoing Powers, and all other Powers vested by this Constitution in the Government of the United States, or in any Department or Officer thereof.

Section 9

The Migration or Importation of such Persons as any of the States now existing shall think proper to admit, shall not be prohibited by the Congress prior to the Year one thousand eight hundred and eight, but a Tax or duty may be imposed on such Importation, not exceeding ten dollars for each Person.

The Privilege of the Writ of *Habeas Corpus* shall not be suspended, unless when in Cases of Rebellion or Invasion the public Safety may require it.

No Bill of Attainder or *ex post facto* Law shall be passed.

No Capitation, or other direct, Tax shall be laid, unless in Proportion to the Census or Enumeration herein before directed to be taken.

No Tax or Duty shall be laid on Articles exported from any State.

No Preference shall be given by any Regulation of Commerce or Revenue to the Ports of one State over those of another: nor shall Vessels bound to, or from, one State, be obliged to enter, clear, or pay Duties in another.

No money shall be drawn from the Treasury, but in Consequence of Appropriations made by Law; and a regular Statement and Account of the Receipts and Expenditures of all public Money shall be published from time to time.

No Title of Nobility shall be granted by the United States: And no Person holding any Office of Profit or Trust under them, shall, without the Consent of the Congress, accept of any present, Emolument, Office, or Title, of any kind whatever, from any King, Prince, or foreign State.

Section 10

No state shall enter into any Treaty, Alliance, or Confederation; grant Letters of Marque and Reprisal; coin Money; emit Bills of Credit; make any Thing but gold and silver Coin a Tender in Payment of Debts; pass any Bill of Attainder, *ex post facto* Law, or Law impairing the Obligation of Contracts, or grant any Title of Nobility.

No State shall, without the Consent of the Congress, lay any Imposts or Duties on Imports or Exports, except what may be absolutely necessary for executing its inspection Laws: and the net Produce of all Duties and Imposts, laid by any State on Imports or Exports, shall be for the Use of the Treasury of the United States, and all such Laws shall be subject to the Revision and Controul of the Congress.

No State shall, without the Consent of Congress, lay any Duty of Tonnage, keep Troops, or Ships of War in time of Peace, enter into any Agreement or Compact with another State, or with a foreign Power, or engage in War, unless actually invaded, or in such imminent Danger as will not admit of delay.

ARTICLE II
Section 1

The executive Power shall be vested in a President of the United States of America. He shall hold his Office during the Term of four Years, and, together with the Vice President, chosen for the same Term, be elected as follows.

Each State shall appoint, in such Manner as the Legislature thereof may direct, a Number of Electors, equal to the whole Number of Senators and Representatives to which the State may be entitled in the Congress; but no Senator or Representative, or Person holding an Office of Trust of Profit under the United States, shall be appointed an Elector.

The Electors shall meet in their respective States, and vote by Ballot for two Persons, of whom one at least shall not be an Inhabitant of the same State with themselves. And they shall make a List of all the Persons voted for, and, of the Number of Votes for each; which List they shall sign and certify, and transmit sealed to the Seat of the Government of the United States, directed to the President of the Senate. The President of the Senate shall, in the Presence of the Senate and House of Representatives, open all the Certificates, and the Votes shall then be counted. The Person having the greatest Number of Votes shall be the President, if such Number be a Majority of the whole Number of Electors appointed; and if there be more than one who have such Majority, and have an equal Number of Votes, then the House of Representatives shall immediately chuse by Ballot one of them for President; and if no Person have a Majority, then from the five highest on the List the said House shall in like Manner chuse the President. But in chusing the President, the Votes shall be taken by States, the Representation from each State having one Vote; A quorum for this Purpose shall consist of a Member or Members from two thirds of the States, and a Majority of all the States shall be necessary to a Choice. In every Case, after the Choice of the President, the Person having the greatest Number of Votes of the Electors shall be the Vice President. But if there should remain two or more who have equal Votes, the Senate shall chuse from them by Ballot the Vice President.

The Congress may determine the Time of chusing the Electors, and the Day on which they shall give their Votes; which Day shall be the same throughout the United States.

No Person except a natural born Citizen, or a Citizen of the United States, at the time of the Adoption of this Constitution, shall be eligible to the Office of President; neither shall any Person be eligible to that Office who shall not have attained to the Age of thirty five Years, and been fourteen Years a Resident within the United States.

In Case of the Removal of the President from Office, or of his Death, Resignation, or Inability to discharge the Powers and Duties of the said Office, the Same shall devolve on the Vice President, and the Congress may by Law provide for the Case of Removal, Death, Resignation or Inability, both of the President and Vice President, declaring what Officer shall then act as President, and such Officer shall act accordingly, until the Disability be removed, or a President shall be elected.

The President shall, at stated Times, receive for his Services, a Compensation, which shall neither be encreased nor diminished during the Period for which he shall have been elected, and he shall not receive within that Period any other Emolument from the United States, or any of them.

Before he enter on the Execution of his Office, he shall take the following Oath or Affirmation:— "I do solemnly swear (or affirm) that I will faithfully execute the Office of President of the United States, and will to the best of my Ability, preserve, protect and defend the Constitution of the United States."

Section 2

The President shall be Commander in Chief of the Army and Navy of the United States, and of the Militia of the several States, when called into the actual Service of the United States; he may require the Opinion, in writing, of the principal Officer in each of the executive Departments, upon any Subject relating to the Duties of their respective Offices, and he shall have Power to grant Reprieves and Pardons for Offences against the United States, except in Cases of Impeachment.

He shall have Power, by and with the Advice and Consent of the Senate, to make Treaties, provided two thirds of the Senators present concur; and he shall nominate, and by and with the Advice and Consent of the Senate, shall appoint Ambassadors, other public Ministers and Consuls, Judges of the supreme Court, and all other Officers of the United States, whose Appointments are not herein otherwise provided for, and which shall be established by Law: but the Congress may by Law vest the Appointment of such inferior Officers, as they think proper, in the President alone, in the Courts of Law, or in the Heads of Departments.

The President shall have Power to fill up all Vacancies that may happen during the Recess of the Senate, by granting Commissions which shall expire at the End of their next Session.

Section 3

He shall from time to time give to the Congress Information of the State of the Union, and recommend to their Consideration such Measures as he shall judge necessary and expedient; he may, on extraordinary Occasions, convene both Houses, or either of them, and in Case of Disagreement between them, with Respect to the Time of Adjournment, he may adjourn them to such Time as he shall think proper; he shall receive Ambassadors and other public Ministers; he shall take Care that the Laws be faithfully executed, and shall Commission all the Officers of the United States.

Section 4

The President, Vice President and all civil Officers of the United States, shall be removed from Office on Impeachment for, and Conviction of, Treason, Bribery, or other High Crimes and Misdemeanors.

ARTICLE III
Section 1

The judicial Power of the United States, shall be vested in one supreme Court, and in such inferior Courts as the Congress may from time to time ordain and establish. The Judges, both of the supreme and inferior Courts, shall hold their Offices during good Behaviour, and shall, at stated Times, receive for their Services, a Compensation, which shall not be diminished during their Continuance in Office.

Section 2

The judicial Power shall extend to all Cases, in Law and Equity, arising under this Constitution, the Laws of the United States, and Treaties made, or which shall be made, under their Authority;—to all Cases affecting Ambassadors, other public Ministers and Consuls;—to all Cases of admiralty and maritime Jurisdiction;—to Controversies to which the United States shall be a Party;—to Controversies between two or more States;—between a State and Citizens of another State;—between Citizens of different States;—between Citizens of the same State claiming Lands under Grants of different States,—and between a State, or the Citizens thereof, and foreign States, Citizens or Subjects.

In all Cases affecting Ambassadors, other public Ministers and Consuls, and those in which a State shall be Party, the supreme Court shall have original Jurisdiction. In all the other Cases before mentioned, the supreme Court shall have appellate Jurisdiction, both as to Law and Fact, with such Exceptions, and under such Regulations as the Congress shall make.

The Trial of all Crimes, except in Cases of Impeachment, shall be by Jury; and such Trial shall be held in the State where the said Crimes shall have been committed; but when not committed within any State, the Trial shall be at such Place or Places as the Congress may by Law have directed.

Section 3

Treason against the United States, shall consist only in levying War against them, or in adhering to their Enemies, giving them Aid and Comfort. No Person shall be convicted of Treason unless on the Testimony of two Witnesses to the same overt Act, or on Confession in open Court.

The Congress shall have Power to declare the Punishment of Treason, but no Attainder of Treason shall work Corruption of Blood, or Forfeiture except during the Life of the Person attainted.

ARTICLE IV

Section 1

Full Faith and Credit shall be given in each State to the public Acts, Records, and judicial Proceedings of every other State. And the Congress may by general Laws prescribe the Manner in which such Acts, Records and Proceedings shall be proved, and the Effect thereof.

Section 2

The Citizens of each State shall be entitled to all Privileges and Immunities of Citizens in the several States.

A Person charged in any State with Treason, Felony, or other Crime, who shall flee from Justice, and be found in another State, shall on Demand of the executive Authority of the State from which he fled, be delivered up, to be removed to the State having Jurisdiction of the Crime.

No Person held to Service or Labour in one State under the Laws thereof, escaping into another, shall, in Consequence of any Law or Regulation therein, be discharged from such Service or Labour, but shall be delivered up on Claim of the Party to whom such Service or Labour maybe due.

Section 3

New States may be admitted by the Congress into this Union; but no new State shall be formed or erected within the Jurisdiction of any other State; nor any State be formed by the Junction of two or more States, or Parts of States, without the Consent of the Legislatures of the States concerned as well as of the Congress.

The Congress shall have Power to dispose of and make all needful Rules and Regulations respecting the Territory or other Property belonging to the United States; and nothing in this Constitution shall be so construed as to Prejudice any Claims of the United States, or of any particular State.

Section 4

The United States shall guarantee to every State in this Union a Republican Form of Government, and shall protect each of them against Invasion; and on Application of the Legislature, or of the Executive (when the Legislature cannot be convened) against domestic Violence.

ARTICLE V

The Congress, whenever two thirds of both Houses shall deem it necessary, shall propose Amendments to this Constitution, or, on the Application of the Legislatures of two thirds of the several States, shall call a Convention for proposing Amendments, which, in either Case, shall be valid to all Intents and Purposes, as Part of this Constitution, when ratified by the Legislatures of three fourths of the several States, or by Conventions in three fourths thereof, as the one or the other Mode of Ratification may be proposed by the Congress; Provided that no Amendment which may be made prior to the Year One thousand eight hundred and eight shall in any Manner affect the first and fourth Clauses in the Ninth Section of the first Article; and that no State, without its Consent, shall be deprived of its equal Suffrage in the Senate.

ARTICLE VI

All Debts contracted and Engagements entered into, before the Adoption of this Constitution, shall be as valid against the United States under this Constitution, as under the Confederation.

This Constitution, and the Laws of the United States which shall be made in Pursuance thereof; and all Treaties made, or which shall be made, under the Authority of the United States, shall be the supreme Law of the Land; and the Judges in every State shall be bound thereby, any Thing in the Constitution or Laws of any State to the Contrary notwithstanding.

The Senators and Representatives before mentioned, and the Members of the several State Legislatures, and all executive and judicial Officers, both of the United States and of the several States, shall be bound by Oath or Affirmation, to support this Constitution; but no religious Test shall ever be required as a Qualification to any Office or public Trust under the United States.

ARTICLE VII

The Ratification of the Conventions of nine States, shall be sufficient for the Establishment of this Constitution between the States so ratifying the Same.

Done in Convention by the Unanimous Consent of the States present the Seventeenth Day of September in the Year of our Lord one thousand seven hundred and Eighty seven and of the Independence of the United States of America the Twelfth. IN WITNESS whereof We have hereunto subscribed our Names,

G. WASHINGTON,
Presid't. and deputy from Virginia

Attest
WILLIAM JACKSON,
Secretary

Articles in addition to, and amendment of the Constitution of the United States of America, proposed by Congress and ratified by the Legislatures of the several states, pursuant to the Fifth Article of the original Constitution.

(The first ten amendments were passed by Congress on September 25, 1789, and were ratified on December 15, 1791.)

DELAWARE
George Read
Gunning Bedford, Jr.
John Dickinson
Richard Basset
Jacob Broom

MASSACHUSETTS BAY
Nathaniel Gorham
Rufus King

CONNECTICUT
William Samuel Johnson
Roger Sherman

NEW YORK
Alexander Hamilton

NEW JERSEY
William Livingston
David Brearley

William Paterson
Jonathan Dayton

PENNSYLVANIA
Benjamin Franklin
Thomas Mifflin
Robert Morris
George Clymer
Thomas FitzSimons
Jared Ingersoll
James Wilson
Gouverneur Morris

NEW HAMPSHIRE
John Langdon
Nicholas Gilman

MARYLAND
James McHenry
Daniel of St. Thomas Jenifer
Daniel Carroll

VIRGINIA
John Blair
James Madison, Jr.

NORTH CAROLINA
William Blount
Richard Dobbs Spaight
Hugh Williamson

SOUTH CAROLINA
John Rutledge
Charles Cotesworth Pinckney
Charles Pinckney
Pierce Butler

GEORGIA
William Few
Abraham Baldwin

AMENDMENT I

Congress shall make no law respecting an establishment of religion, or prohibiting the free exercise thereof; or abridging the freedom of speech, or of the press; or the right of the people peaceably to assemble, and to petition the Government for a redress of grievances.

AMENDMENT II

A well regulated Militia, being necessary to the security of a free State, the right of the people to keep and bear Arms, shall not be infringed.

AMENDMENT III

No Soldier shall, in time of peace be quartered in any house, without the consent of the Owner, nor in time of war, but in a manner to be prescribed by law.

AMENDMENT IV

The right of the people to be secure in their persons, houses, papers, and effects, against unreasonable searches and seizures, shall not be violated, and no warrants shall issue, but upon probable cause, supported by Oath or affirmation, and particularly describing the place to be searched, and the persons or things to be seized.

AMENDMENT V

No person shall be held to answer for a capital, or otherwise infamous crime, unless on a presentment or indictment of a Grand Jury, except in cases arising in the land or naval forces, or in the Militia, when in actual service in time of War or public danger; nor shall any person be subject for the same offence to be twice put in jeopardy of life or limb; nor shall be compelled in any criminal case to be a witness against himself, nor be deprived of life, liberty, or property, without due process of law; nor shall private property be taken for public use, without just compensation.

AMENDMENT VI

In all criminal prosecutions, the accused shall enjoy the right to a speedy and public trial, by an impartial jury of the State and district wherein the crime shall have been committed, which district shall have been previously ascertained by law, and to be informed of the nature and cause of the accusation; to be confronted with the witnesses against him; to have compulsory process for obtaining witnesses in his favor, and to have the assistance of counsel for his defence.

AMENDMENT VII

In Suits at common law, where the value in controversy shall exceed twenty dollars, the right of trial by jury shall be preserved, and no fact tried by a jury, shall be otherwise re-examined in any Court of the United States, than according to the rules of the common law.

AMENDMENT VIII

Excessive bail shall not be required, nor excessive fines imposed, nor cruel and unusual punishments inflicted.

AMENDMENT IX

The enumeration in the Constitution, of certain rights, shall not be construed to deny or disparage others retained by the people.

AMENDMENT X

The powers not delegated to the United States by the Constitution, nor prohibited by it to the States, are reserved to the States respectively, or to the people.

AMENDMENT XI

(Ratified on February 7, 1795)

The Judicial power of the United States shall not be construed to extend to any suit in law or equity, commenced or prosecuted against one of the United States by Citizens of another State, or by Citizens or Subjects of any Foreign State.

AMENDMENT XII

(Ratified on June 15,1804)

The Electors shall meet in their respective states, and vote by ballot for President and Vice-President, one of whom, at least, shall not be an inhabitant of the same state with themselves; they shall name in their ballots the person voted for as President, and in distinct ballots the person voted for as Vice-President, and they shall make distinct lists of all persons voted for as President, and of all persons voted for as Vice-President, and of the number of votes for each, which lists they shall sign and certify, and transmit sealed to the seat of the government of the United States, directed to the President of the Senate;

The President of the Senate shall, in the presence of the Senate and House of Representatives, open all the certificates and the votes shall then be counted;

The person having the greatest number of votes for President, shall be the President, if such number be a majority of the whole number of Electors appointed; and if no person have such majority; then from the persons having the highest numbers not exceeding three on the list of those voted for as President, the House of Representatives shall choose immediately, by ballot, the President. But in choosing the President, the votes shall be taken by states, the representation from each state having one vote; a quorum for this purpose shall consist of a member or members from two-thirds of the states, and a majority of all the states shall be necessary to a choice. And if the House of Representatives shall not choose a President whenever the right of choice shall devolve upon them, before the fourth day of March next following, then the Vice-President shall act as President, as in the case of the death or other constitutional disability of the President.

The person having the greatest number of votes as Vice-President, shall be the Vice-President, if such number be a majority of the whole number of Electors appointed, and if no person have a majority, then from the two highest numbers on the list, the Senate shall choose the Vice-President; a quorum for the purpose shall consist of two-thirds of the whole number of Senators, and a majority of the whole number shall be necessary to a choice. But no person constitutionally ineligible to the office of President shall be eligible to that of Vice-President of the United States.

AMENDMENT XIII

(Ratified on December 6,1865)
Section 1

Neither slavery nor involuntary servitude, except as a punishment for crime whereof the party shall have been duly convicted, shall exist within the United States, or any place subject to their jurisdiction.

Section 2

Congress shall have power to enforce this article by appropriate legislation.

AMENDMENT XIV

(Ratified on July 9,1868)
Section 1

All persons born or naturalized in the United States, and subject to the jurisdiction thereof, are citizens of the United States and of the State wherein they reside. No State shall make or enforce any law which shall abridge the privileges or immunities of citizens of the United States; nor shall any State deprive any person of life, liberty, or property, without due process of law; nor deny to any person within its jurisdiction the equal protection of the laws.

Section 2

Representatives shall be apportioned among the several States according to their respective numbers, counting the whole number of persons in each State, excluding Indians not taxed. But when the right to vote at any election for the choice of electors for President and Vice President of the United States, Representatives in Congress, the Executive and Judicial officers of a State, or the members of the Legislature thereof, is denied to any of the male inhabitants of such State, being twenty-one years of age, and citizens of the United States, or in anyway abridged, except for participation in rebellion, or other crime, the basis of representation therein shall be reduced in the proportion which the number of such male citizens shall bear to the whole number of male citizens twenty-one years of age in such State.

Section 3

No person shall be a Senator or Representative in Congress, or elector of President and Vice President, or hold any office, civil or military, under the United States, or under any State, who, having previously taken an oath, as a member of Congress, or as an officer of the United States, or as a member of any State legislature, or as an executive or judicial officer of any State, to support the Constitution of the United States, shall have engaged in insurrection or rebellion against the same, or given aid or comfort to the enemies thereof. But Congress may by a vote of two-thirds of each House, remove such disability.

Section 4

The validity of the public debt of the United States, authorized by law, including debts incurred for payment of pensions and bounties for services in suppressing insurrection or rebellion, shall not be questioned. But neither the United States nor any State shall assume or pay any debt or obligation incurred in aid of insurrection or rebellion against the United States, or any claim for the loss or emancipation of any slave, but all such debts, obligations and claims shall be held illegal and void.

Section 5

The Congress shall have power to enforce, by appropriate legislation, the provisions of this article.

AMENDMENT XV

(Ratified on February 3,1870)
Section 1

The right of citizens of the United States to vote shall not be denied or abridged by the United States or by any State on account of race, color, or previous condition of servitude.

Section 2

The Congress shall have power to enforce this article by appropriate legislation.

AMENDMENT XVI

(Ratified on February 3,1913)

AMENDMENT XVII

(Ratified on April 8,1913)

The Senate of the United States shall be composed of two Senators from each State, elected by the people thereof, for six years; and each Senator shall have one vote. The electors in each State shall have the qualifications requisite for electors of the most numerous branch of the State legislatures.

When vacancies happen in the representation of any State in the Senate, the executive authority of such State shall issue writs of election to fill such vacancies: Provided, That the legislature of any State may empower the executive thereof to make temporary appointments until the people fill the vacancies by election as the legislature may direct.

This amendment shall not be so construed as to affect the election or term of any Senator chosen before it becomes valid as part of the Constitution.

AMENDMENT XVIII

(Ratified on January 16,1919)
Section 1

After one year from the ratification of this article the manufacture, sale, or transportation of intoxicating liquors within, the importation thereof into, or the exportation thereof from the United States and all territory subject to the jurisdiction thereof for beverage purposes is hereby prohibited.

Section 2

The Congress and the several States shall have concurrent power to enforce this article by appropriate legislation.

Section 3

This article shall be inoperative unless it shall have been ratified as an amendment to the Constitution by the legislatures of the several States, as provided in the Constitution, within seven years from the date of the submission hereof to the States by the Congress.

AMENDMENT XIX

(Ratified on August 18,1920)

The right of citizens of the United States to vote shall not be denied or abridged by the United States or by any State on account of sex.

Congress shall have power to enforce this article by appropriate legislation.

AMENDMENT XX

(Ratified on February 6,1933)
Section 1

The terms of the President and Vice President shall end at noon on the 20th day of January, and the terms of Senators and Representatives at noon on the 3d day of January, of the years in which such terms would have ended if this article had not been ratified; and the terms of their successors shall then begin.

Section 2

The Congress shall assemble at least once in every year, and such meeting shall begin at noon on the 3d day of January, unless they shall by law appoint a different day.

Section 3

If, at the time fixed for the beginning of the term of the President, the President elect shall have died, the Vice President elect shall become President. If a President shall not have been chosen before the time fixed for the beginning of his term, or if the President elect shall have failed to qualify, then the Vice President elect shall act as President until a President shall have qualified; and the Congress may by law provide for the case wherein neither a President elect nor a Vice President elect shall have qualified, declaring who shall then act as President, or the manner in which one who is to act shall be selected, and such person shall act accordingly until a President or Vice President shall have qualified.

Section 4

The Congress may by law provide for the case of the death of any of the persons from whom the House of Representatives may choose a President whenever the rights of choice shall have devolved upon them, and for the case of the death of any of the persons from whom the Senate may choose a Vice President whenever the right of choice shall have devolved upon them.

Section 5

Sections 1 and 2 shall take effect on the 15th day of October following the ratification of this article.

Section 6

This article shall be inoperative unless it shall have been ratified as an amendment to the Constitution by the legislatures of three-fourths of the several States within seven years from the date of its submission.

AMENDMENT XXI

(Ratified on December 5,1933)
Section 1

The eighteenth article of amendment to the Constitution of the United States is hereby repealed.

Section 2

The transportation or importation into any State, Territory, or possession of the United States for delivery or use therein of intoxicating liquors, in violation of the laws thereof, is hereby prohibited.

Section 3

This article shall be inoperative unless it shall have been ratified as an amendment to the Constitution by conventions in the several States, as provided in the Constitution, within seven years from the date of the submission hereof to the States by the Congress.

AMENDMENT XXII

(Ratified on February 27,1951)
Section 1

No person shall be elected to the office of the President more than twice, and no person who has held the office of President, or acted as President, for more than two years of a term to which some other person was elected President shall be elected to the office of the President more than once. But this Article shall not apply to any person holding the office of President when this Article was proposed by the Congress, and shall not prevent any person who may be holding the office of President, or acting as President, during the term within which this Article becomes operative from holding the office of President or acting as President during the remainder of such term.

Section 2

This article shall be inoperative unless it shall have been ratified as an amendment to the Constitution by the legislatures of three-fourths of the several States within seven years from the date of its submission to the States by the Congress.

AMENDMENT XXIII

(Ratified on March 29,1961)
Section 1

The District constituting the seat of Government of the United States shall appoint in such manner as the Congress may direct:

A number of electors of President and Vice President equal to the whole number of Senators and Representatives in Congress to which the District would be entitled if it were a State, but in no event more than the least populous State; they shall be in addition to those appointed by the States, but they shall be considered, for the purposes of the election of President and Vice President, to be electors appointed by a State; and they shall meet in the District and perform such duties as provided by the twelfth article of amendment.

Section 2

The Congress shall have power to enforce this article by appropriate legislation.

AMENDMENT XXIV

(Ratified on January 23,1964)
Section 1

The right of citizens of the United States to vote in any primary or other election for President or Vice President, for electors for President or Vice President, or for Senator or Representative in Congress, shall not be denied or abridged by the United States or any State by reason of failure to pay any poll tax or other tax.

Section 2

The Congress shall have power to enforce this article by appropriate legislation.

AMENDMENT XXV

(Ratified on February 10,1967)
Section 1

In case of the removal of the President from office or of his death or resignation, the Vice President shall become President.

Section 2

Whenever there is a vacancy in the office of the Vice President, the President shall nominate a Vice President who shall take office upon confirmation by a majority vote of both Houses of Congress.

Section 3

Whenever the President transmits to the President pro tempore of the Senate and the Speaker of the House of Representatives his written declaration that he is unable to discharge the powers and duties of his office, and until he transmits to them a written declaration to the contrary, such powers and duties shall be discharged by the Vice President as Acting President.

Section 4

Whenever the Vice President and a majority of either the principal officers of the executive departments or of such other body as Congress may by law provide, transmit to the President pro tempore of the Senate and the Speaker of the House of Representatives their written declaration that the President is unable to discharge the powers and duties of his office, the Vice President shall immediately assume the powers and duties of the office as Acting President.

Thereafter, when the President transmits to the President pro tempore of the Senate and the Speaker of the House of Representatives his written declaration that no inability exists, he shall resume the powers and duties of his office unless the Vice President and a majority of either the principal officers of the executive department or of such other body as Congress may by law provide, transmit within four days to the President pro tempore of the Senate and the Speaker of the House of Representatives their written declaration that the President is unable to discharge the powers and duties of his office. Thereupon Congress shall decide the issue, assembling within forty-eight hours for that purpose if not in session. If the Congress, within twenty-one days after receipt of the latter written declaration, or, if Congress is not in session, within twenty-one days after Congress is required to assemble, determines by two-thirds vote of both Houses that the President is unable to discharge the powers and duties of his office, the Vice President shall continue to discharge the same as Acting President; otherwise, the President shall resume the powers and duties of his office.

AMENDMENT XXVI

(Ratified on July 1,1971)

Section 1

The right of citizens of the United States, who are eighteen years of age or older, to vote shall not be denied or abridged by the United States or by any State on account of age.

Section 2

The Congress shall have power to enforce this article by appropriate legislation.

AMENDMENT XXVII

(Ratified on May 7,1992)

No law, varying the compensation for the services of the Senators and Representatives, shall take effect until an election of Representatives shall have intervened.

THE FEDERALIST PAPERS

The Federalist Papers, essays initially released alone and serially by proponents of the U.S. Constitution, provide us with firsthand views of the Framers' intentions. John Jay, James Madison, and Alexander Hamilton were engaged in the writing of the Constitution, and they used *The Federalist Papers* to help persuade citizens to support ratification of that document. Jay was later named the first chief justice of the Supreme Court of the United States, Madison served as the nation's fourth president, and Hamilton (prevented from seeking the presidency by his birth in the British West Indies) was the first secretary of the treasury. Annotated below are three of the most often read and cited of the essays.

FEDERALIST NO. 10

November 22, 1787

James Madison

To the People of the State of New York:

Controlling factions, or groups of like-minded citizens united in a common interest adverse to the interests of the community, was a major concern of the Framers. In *Federalist No. 10*, James Madison argues that one of the best ways to check the power of faction is to create a republican form of government.

Among the numerous advantages promised by a well constructed Union, none deserves to be more accurately developed than its tendency to break and control the violence of faction. The friend of popular governments, never finds himself so much alarmed for their character and fate, as when he contemplates their propensity to this dangerous vice.

He will not fail therefore to set a due value on any plan which, without violating the principles to which he is attached, provides a proper cure for it. The instability, injustice and confusion introduced into the public councils, have in truth been the mortal diseases under which popular governments have every where perished; as they continue to be the favorite and fruitful topics from which the adversaries to liberty derive their most specious. The valuable improvements made by the American Constitutions on the popular models, both ancient and modern, cannot certainly be too much admired; but it would be an unwarrantable partiality, to contend that they have as effectually obviated the danger on this side as was wished and expected.

Complaints are every where heard from our most considerate and virtuous citizens, equally the friends of public and private faith, and of public and personal liberty, that our governments are too unstable; that the public good is disregarded in the conflicts of rival parties; and that measures are too often decided, not according to the rules of justice, and the rights of the minor party, but by the superior force of an interested and over-bearing majority. However anxiously we may wish that these complaints had no foundation, the evidence of known facts will not permit us to deny that they are in some degree true. It will be found indeed, on a candid review of our situation, that some of the distresses under which we labor, have been erroneously charged on the operation of our governments; but it will be found, at the same time, that other causes will not alone account for many of our heaviest misfortunes; and particularly, for that prevailing and increasing distrust of public engagements, and alarm for private rights, which are echoed from one end of the continent to the other. These must be chiefly, if not wholly, effects of the unsteadiness and injustice, with which a factious spirit has tainted our public administrations.

By a faction I understand a number of citizens, whether amounting to a majority or minority of the whole, who are united and actuated by some common impulse of passion, or of interest, adverse to the rights of other citizens, or to the permanent and aggregate interests of the community.

There are two methods of curing the mischiefs of faction: the one, by removing its causes; the other, by controlling its effects.

There are again two methods of removing the causes of faction: the one by destroying the liberty which is essential to its existence; the other, by giving to every citizen the same opinions, the same passions, and the same interests.

It could never be more truly said than of the first remedy, that it is worse than the disease. Liberty is to faction, what air is to fire, an aliment without which it instantly expires. But it could not be a less folly to abolish liberty, which is essential to political life, because it nourishes faction, than it would be to wish the annihilation of air, which is essential to animal life, because it imparts to fire its destructive agency.

The second expedient is as impracticable, as the first would be unwise. As long as the reason of man continues fallible, and he is at liberty to exercise it, different opinions will be formed. As long as the connection subsists between his reason and his self-love, his opinions and his passions will have a reciprocal influence on each other; and the former will be objects to which the latter will attach themselves.

The diversity in the faculties of men from which the rights of property originate, is not less an insuperable obstacle to a uniformity of interests. The protection of these faculties is the first object of Government. From the protection of different and unequal faculties of acquiring property, the possession of different degrees and kinds of property immediately results: and from the influence of these on the sentiments and views of the respective proprietors, ensues a division of the society into different interests and parties.

The latent causes of faction are thus sown in the nature of man; and we see them everywhere brought into different degrees of activity, according to the different circumstances of civil society. A zeal for different opinions concerning religion, concerning Government and many other points, as well of speculation as of practice; an attachment to different leaders ambitiously contending for pre-eminence and power; or to persons of other descriptions whose fortunes have been interesting to the human passions, have in turn divided mankind into parties, inflamed them with mutual animosity, and rendered them much more disposed to vex and oppress each other, than to cooperate for their common good. So strong is this propensity of mankind to fall into mutual animosities, that where no substantial occasion presents itself, the most frivolous and fanciful distinctions have been sufficient to kindle their unfriendly passions, and excite their most violent conflicts. But the most common and durable source of factions, has been the various and unequal distribution of property. Those who hold, and those who are without property, have ever formed distinct interests in society. Those who are creditors, and those who are debtors, fall under a like discrimination. A landed interest, a manufacturing interest, a mercantile interest, a monied interest, with many lesser interests, grow up of necessity in civilized nations, and divide them into different classes, actuated by different sentiments and views. The regulation of these various and interfering interests forms the principal task of modern Legislation, and involves the spirit of party and faction in the necessary and ordinary operations of Government.

No man is allowed to be a judge in his own cause, because his interest would certainly bias his judgment, and, not improbably, corrupt his integrity. With equal, nay with greater reason, a body of men, are unfit to be both judges and parties, at the same time; yet, what are many of the most important acts of legislation, but so many judicial determinations, not indeed concerning the rights of single persons, but concerning the rights of large bodies of citizens, and what are the different classes of legislators, but advocates and parties to the causes which they determine? Is a law proposed concerning private debts? It is a question to which the creditors are parties on one side, and the debtors on the other. Justice ought to hold the balance between them. Yet the parties are and must be themselves the judges; and the most numerous party, or, in other words, the most powerful

faction, must be expected to prevail. Shall domestic manufactures be encouraged, and in what degree, by restrictions on foreign manufactures? are questions which would be differently decided by the landed and the manufacturing classes; and probably by neither, with a sole regard to justice and the public good. The apportionment of taxes on the various descriptions of property, is an act which seems to require the most exact impartiality; yet, there is perhaps no legislative act in which greater opportunity and temptation are given to a predominant party, to trample on the rules of justice. Every shilling with which they over-burden the inferior number, is a shilling saved to their own pockets.

It is in vain to say, that enlightened statesmen will be able to adjust these clashing interests, and render them all subservient to the public good. Enlightened statesmen will not always be at the helm. Nor, in many cases, can such an adjustment be made at all, without taking into view indirect and remote considerations, which will rarely prevail over the immediate interest which one party may find in disregarding the rights of another, or the good of the whole.

The inference to which we are brought, is, that the *causes* of faction cannot be removed; and that relief is only to be sought in the means of controlling its *effects*.

If a faction consists of less than a majority, relief is supplied by the republican principle, which enables the majority to defeat its sinister views by regular vote. It may clog the administration, it may convulse the society, but it will be unable to execute and mask its violence under the forms of the Constitution. When a majority is included in a faction, the form of popular government on the other hand enables it to sacrifice to its ruling passion or interest, both the public good and the rights of other citizens. To secure the public good, and private rights, against the danger of such a faction, and at the same time to preserve the spirit and the form of popular government, is then the great object to which our enquiries are directed. Let me add that it is the great desideratum, by which alone this form of government can be rescued from the opprobrium under which it has so long labored, and be recommended to the esteem and adoption of mankind.

By what means is this object attainable? Evidently by one of two only. Either the existence of the same passion or interest in a majority at the same time, must be prevented; or the majority, having such co-existent passion or interest, must be rendered, by their number and local situation, unable to concert and carry into effect schemes of oppression. If the impulse and the opportunity be suffered to coincide, we well know that neither moral nor religious motives can be relied on as an adequate control. They are not found to be such on the injustice and violence of individuals, and lose their efficacy in proportion to the number combined together; that is, in proportion as their efficacy becomes needful.

From this view of the subject, it may be concluded, that a pure Democracy, by which I mean, a Society, consisting of a small number of citizens, who assemble and administer the Government in person, can admit of no cure for the mischiefs of faction. A common passion or interest will, in almost every case, be felt by a majority of the whole; a communication and concert results from the form of Government itself; and there is nothing to check the inducements to sacrifice the weaker party, or an obnoxious individual. Hence it is, that such Democracies have ever been spectacles of turbulence and contention; have ever been found incompatible with personal security, or the rights of property; and have in general been as short in their lives, as they have been violent in their deaths. Theoretic politicians, who have patronized this species of Government, have erroneously supposed, that by reducing mankind to a perfect equality in their political rights, they would, at the same time, be perfectly equalized and assimilated in their possessions, their opinions, and their passions.

A republic, by which I mean a government in which the scheme of representation takes place, opens a different prospect, and promises the cure for which we are seeking. Let us examine the points in which it varies from pure democracy, and we shall comprehend both the nature of the cure and the efficacy which it must derive from the union.

The two great points of difference, between a democracy and a republic, are, first, the delegation of the government, in the latter, to a small number of citizens, elected by the rest; secondly, the greater number of citizens, and greater sphere of country, over which the latter may be extended.

The effect of the first difference is, on the one hand, to refine and enlarge the public views, by passing them through the medium of a chosen body of citizens, whose wisdom may best discern the true interest of their country, and whose patriotism and love of justice, will be least likely to sacrifice it to temporary or partial considerations. Under such a regulation, it may well happen, that the public voice, pronounced by the representatives of the people, will be more consonant to the public good, than if pronounced by the people themselves, convened for the purpose. On the other hand the effect may be inverted. Men of factious tempers, of local prejudices, or of sinister designs, may by intrigue, by corruption, or by other means, first obtain the suffrages, and then betray the interest of the people. The question resulting is, whether small or extensive republics are most favorable to the election of proper guardians of the public weal, and it is clearly decided in favor of the latter by two obvious considerations.

In the first place, it is to be remarked that, however small the republic may be, the representatives must be raised to a certain number, in order to guard against the cabals of a few; and that however large it may be, they must be limited to a certain number, in order to guard against the confusion of a multitude. Hence, the number of representatives in the two cases not being in proportion to that of the constituents, and being proportionally greatest in the small republic, it

follows, that if the proportion of fit characters be not less in the large than in the small republic, the former will present a greater option, and consequently a greater probability of a fit choice.

In the next place, as each Representative will be chosen by a greater number of citizens in the large than in the small Republic, it will be more difficult for unworthy candidates to practise with success the vicious arts, by which elections are too often carried; and the suffrages of the people being more free, will be more likely to center on men who possess the most attractive merit, and the most diffusive and established characters.

It must be confessed, that in this, as in most other cases, there is a mean, on both sides of which inconveniences will be found to lie. By enlarging too much the number of electors, you render the representatives too little acquainted with all their local circumstances and lesser interests; as by reducing it too much, you render him unduly attached to these, and too little fit to comprehend and pursue great and national objects. The Federal Constitution forms a happy combination in this respect; the great and aggregate interests being referred to the national, the local and particular, to the state legislatures.

The other point of difference is, the greater number of citizens and extent of territory which may be brought within the compass of Republican, than of Democratic Government; and it is this circumstance principally which renders factious combinations less to be dreaded in the former, than in the latter. The smaller the society, the fewer probably will be the distinct parties and interests composing it; the fewer the distinct parties and interests, the more frequently will a majority be found of the same party; and the smaller the number of individuals composing a majority, and the smaller the compass within which they are placed, the more easily will they concert and execute their plans of oppression. Extend the sphere, and you take in a greater variety of parties and interests; you make it less probable that a majority of the whole will have a common motive to invade the rights of other citizens; or if such a common motive exists, it will be more difficult for all who feel it to discover their own strength, and to act in unison with each other. Besides other impediments, it may be remarked, that where there is a consciousness of unjust or dishonorable purposes, communication is always checked by distrust, in proportion to the number whose concurrence is necessary.

Hence it clearly appears, that the same advantage, which a Republic has over a Democracy, in controlling the effects of faction, is enjoyed by a large over a small Republic—is enjoyed by the Union over the States composing it. Does this advantage consist in the substitution of Representatives, whose enlightened views and virtuous sentiments render them superior to local prejudices, and to schemes of injustice? It will not be denied, that the Representation of the Union will be most likely to possess these requisite endowments. Does it consist in the greater security afforded by a greater variety of parties, against the event of any one party being able to outnumber and oppress the rest? In an equal degree does the increased variety of parties, comprised within the Union, increase this security? Does it, in fine, consist in the greater obstacles opposed to the concert and accomplishment of the secret wishes of an unjust and interested majority? Here, again, the extent of the Union gives it the most palpable advantage.

The influence of factious leaders may kindle a flame within their particular States, but will be unable to spread a general conflagration through the other States: a religious sect, may degenerate into a political faction in a part of the Confederacy but the variety of sects dispersed over the entire face of it, must secure the national Councils against any danger from that source: a rage for paper money, for an abolition of debts, for an equal division of property, or for any other improper or wicked project, will be less apt to pervade the whole body of the Union, than a particular member of it; in the same proportion as such a malady is more likely to taint a particular county or district, than an entire State.

In the extent and proper structure of the Union, therefore, we behold a Republican remedy for the diseases most incident to Republican Government. And according to the degree of pleasure and pride, we feel in being Republicans, ought to be our zeal in cherishing the spirit, and supporting the character of Federalists.

PUBLIUS

FEDERALIST NO. 51

February 6, 1788

James Madison

To the People of the State of New York:

Federalist No. 51 is one of the most widely cited of all *The Federalist Papers*. In it, James Madison carefully explains how the structure of the new government helps to protect citizens' individual liberties. He contends that the Constitution contains two main protections: a system of checks and balances, and a federal system of government that divides power between state and national governments. Perhaps the most famous line of this paper is "Ambition must be made to counteract ambition."

To what expedient then shall we finally resort for maintaining in practice the necessary partition of power among the several departments, as laid down in the Constitution? The only answer that can be given is, that as all these exterior provisions are found to be inadequate, the defect must be supplied, by so contriving the interior structure of the government, as that its several constituent parts may, by their mutual relations, be the means of keeping each other in their proper places. Without presuming to undertake a full development of this important idea, I will hazard a few general observations, which may perhaps place it in a clearer light, and enable us to form a more correct judgment of the principles and structure of the government planned by the convention.

In order to lay a due foundation for that separate and distinct exercise of the different powers of government, which to a certain extent, is admitted on all hands to be essential to the preservation of liberty, it is evident that each department should have a will of its own; and consequently should be so constituted, that the members of each should have as little agency as possible in the appointment of the members of the others. Were this principle rigorously adhered to, it would require that all the appointments for the supreme executive, legislative, and judiciary magistracies, should be drawn from the same fountain of authority, the people, through channels, having no communication whatever with one another. Perhaps such a plan of constructing the several departments would be less difficult in practice than it may in contemplation appear.

Some difficulties however, and some additional expense, would attend the execution of it. Some deviations therefore from the principle must be admitted. In the constitution of the judiciary department in particular, it might be inexpedient to insist rigorously on the principle; first, because peculiar qualifications being essential in the members, the primary consideration ought to be to select that mode of choice, which best secures these qualifications; secondly, because the permanent tenure by which the appointments are held in that department, must soon destroy all sense of dependence on the authority conferring them.

It is equally evident that the members of each department should be as little dependent as possible on those of the others, for the emoluments annexed to their offices. Were the executive magistrate, or the judges, not independent of the legislature in this particular, their independence in every other would be merely nominal.

But the great security against a gradual concentration of the several powers in the same department, consists in giving to those who administer each department, the necessary constitutional means, and personal motives, to resist encroachments of the others. The provision for defense must in this, as in all other cases, be made commensurate to the danger of attack. Ambition must be made to counteract ambition. The interest of the man must be connected with the constitutional right of the place. It may be a reflection on human nature, that such devices should be necessary to control the abuses of government. But what is government itself but the greatest of all reflections on human nature? If men were angels, no government would be necessary. If angels were to govern men, neither external nor internal controls on government would be necessary. In framing a government which is to be administered by men over men, the great difficulty lies in this: you must first enable the government to control the governed; and in the next place, oblige it to control itself. A dependence on the people is no doubt the primary control on the government; but experience has taught mankind the necessity of auxiliary precautions.

This policy of supplying by opposite and rival interests, the defect of better motives, might be traced through the whole system of human affairs, private as well as public. We see it particularly displayed in all the subordinate distributions of power; where the constant aim is to divide and arrange the several offices in such a manner as that each may be a check on the other; that the private interest of every individual, may be a sentinel over the public rights. These inventions of prudence cannot be less requisite in the distribution of the supreme powers of the state.

But it is not possible to give to each department an equal power of self defense. In republican government the legislative authority, necessarily, predominates. The remedy for this inconveniency is, to divide the legislature into different branches; and to render them by different modes of election, and different principles of action, as little connected with each other, as the nature of their common functions, and their common dependence on the society, will admit. It may even be necessary to guard against dangerous encroachments by still further precautions. As the weight of the legislative authority requires that it should be thus divided, the weakness of the executive may require, on the other hand, that it should be fortified. An absolute negative, on the legislature, appears at first view to be the natural defense with which the executive magistrate should be armed. But perhaps it would be neither altogether safe, nor alone sufficient. On ordinary occasions, it might not be exerted with the requisite firmness; and on extraordinary occasions, it might be prefidiously abused.

May not this defect of an absolute negative be supplied, by some qualified connection between this weaker department, and the weaker branch of the stronger department, by which the latter may be led to support the constitutional rights of the former, without being too much detached from the rights of its own department? If the principles on which these observations are founded be just, as I persuade myself they are, and they be applied as a criterion, to the several state constitutions, and to the federal constitution, it will be found, that if the latter does not perfectly correspond with them, the former are infinitely less able to bear such a test.

There are moreover two considerations particularly applicable to the federal system of America, which place that system in a very interesting point of view.

First. In a single republic, all the power surrendered by the people, is submitted to the administration of a single government; and usurpations are guarded against by a division of the government into distinct and separate departments. In the compound republic of America, the power surrendered by the people, is first divided between two distinct governments, and then the portion allotted to each, subdivided among distinct and separate departments. Hence a double security arises to the rights of the people.

The different governments will control each other; at the same time that each will be controlled by itself.

Second. It is of great importance in a republic, not only to guard the society against the oppression of its rulers; but to guard one part of the society against the injustice of the other part. Different interests necessarily exist in different classes of citizens.

If a majority be united by a common interest, the rights of the minority will be insecure. There are but two methods of providing against this evil: the one by creating a will in the community independent of the majority, that is, of the society itself; the other by comprehending in the society so many separate descriptions of citizens, as will render an unjust combination of a majority of the whole, very improbable, if not impracticable. The first method prevails in all governments possessing an hereditary or self appointed authority. This at best is but a precarious security; because a power independent of the society may as well espouse the unjust views of the major, as the rightful interests, of the minor party, and may possibly be turned against both parties. The second method will be exemplified in the federal republic of the United States. While all authority in it will be derived from and dependent on the society, the society itself will be broken into so many parts, interests and classes of citizens, that the rights of individuals or of the minority, will be in little danger from interested combinations of the majority. In a free government, the security for civil rights must be the same as for religious rights. It consists in the one case in the multiplicity of interests, and in the other, in the multiplicity of sects. The degree of security in both cases will depend on the number of interests and sects; and this may be presumed to depend on the extent of country and number of people comprehended under the same government.

This view of the subject must particularly recommend a proper federal system to all the sincere and considerate friends of republican government. Since it shows that in exact proportion as the territory of the union may be formed into more circumscribed confederacies or states, oppressive combinations of a majority will be facilitated, the best security under the republican form, for the rights of every class of citizens, will be diminished; and consequently, the stability and independence of some member of the government, the only other security, must be proportionally increased. Justice is the end of government. It is the end of civil society.

It ever has been, and ever will be pursued, until it be obtained, or until liberty be lost in the pursuit. In a society under the forms of which the stronger faction can readily unite and oppress the weaker, anarchy may as truly be said to reign, as in a state of nature where the weaker individual is not secured against the violence of the stronger; and as in the latter state even the stronger individuals are prompted by the uncertainty of their condition, to submit to a government which may protect the weak as well as themselves; so, in the former state, will the more powerful factions or parties be gradually induced by a like motive, to wish for a government which will protect all parties, the weaker as well as the more powerful. It can be little doubted, that if the state of Rhode Island was separated from the confederacy, and left to itself, the insecurity of rights under the popular form of government within such narrow limits, would be displayed by such reiterated oppressions of factious majorities, that some power altogether independent of the people would soon be called for by the voice of the very factions whose misrule had proved the necessity of it. In the extended republic of the United States, and among the great variety of interests, parties and sects which it embraces, a coalition of a majority of the whole society could seldom take place on any other principles than those of justice and the general good; and there being thus less danger to a minor from the will of the major party, there must be less pretext also, to provide for the security of the former, by introducing into the government a will not dependent on the latter; or in other words, a will independent of the society itself. It is no less certain than it is important, notwithstanding the contrary opinions which have been entertained, that the larger the society, provided it lie within a practicable sphere, the more duly capable it will be of self government. And happily for the *republican cause*, the practicable sphere may be carried to a very great extent, by a judicious modification and mixture of the *federal principle*.

PUBLIUS

FEDERALIST NO. 78

May 28, 1788

Alexander Hamilton

To the People of the State of New York:

Federalist No. 78 is the first of six *Federalist Papers* that discuss the judicial branch. Alexander Hamilton's analysis focuses on several points. Among these are the method of judicial selection, tenure in office, and the scope of judicial authority. This piece is perhaps best known for its defense of lifetime terms for judges, as well as its declaration that the judiciary would be the "least dangerous branch."

We proceed now to an examination of the judiciary department of the proposed government.

In unfolding the defects of the existing Confederation, the utility and necessity of a federal judicature have been clearly pointed out. It is the less necessary to recapitulate the considerations there urged, as the propriety of the institution in the abstract is not disputed; the only questions which have been raised being relative to the manner of constituting it, and to its extent. To these points, therefore, our observations shall be confined.

The manner of constituting it seems to embrace these several objects: 1st. The mode of appointing the judges. 2d.

The tenure by which they are to hold their places. 3d. The partition of the judiciary authority between different courts, and their relations to each other.

First. As to the mode of appointing the judges; this is the same with that of appointing the officers of the Union in general, and has been so fully discussed in the two last numbers, that nothing can be said here which would not be useless repetition.

Second. As to the tenure by which the judges are to hold their places: this chiefly concerns their duration in office; the provisions for their support; the precautions for their responsibility.

According to the plan of the convention, all judges who may be appointed by the United States are to hold their offices *during good behavior*; which is conformable to the most approved of the State constitutions and among the rest, to that of this State. Its propriety having been drawn into question by the adversaries of that plan, is no light symptom of the rage for objection, which disorders their imaginations and judgments. The standard of good behavior for the continuance in office of the judicial magistracy, is certainly one of the most valuable of the modern improvements in the practice of government. In a monarchy it is an excellent barrier to the despotism of the prince; in a republic it is a no less excellent barrier to the encroachments and oppressions of the representative body. And it is the best expedient which can be devised in any government, to secure a steady, upright, and impartial administration of the laws.

Whoever attentively considers the different departments of power must perceive, that, in a government in which they are separated from each other, the judiciary, from the nature of its functions, will always be the least dangerous to the political rights of the Constitution; because it will be least in a capacity to annoy or injure them. The Executive not only dispenses the honors, but holds the sword of the community. The legislature not only commands the purse, but prescribes the rules by which the duties and rights of every citizen are to be regulated. The judiciary, on the contrary, has no influence over either the sword or the purse; no direction either of the strength or of the wealth of the society; and can take no active resolution whatever. It may truly be said to have neither *force* nor *will*, but merely judgment; and must ultimately depend upon the aid of the executive arm even for the efficacy of its judgments.

This simple view of the matter suggests several important consequences. It proves incontestably, that the judiciary is beyond comparison the weakest of the three departments of power[1]; that it can never attack with success either of the other two; and that all possible care is requisite to enable it to defend itself against their attacks. It equally proves, that

---

[1]The celebrated Montesquieu, speaking of them, says: "Of the three powers above mentioned, the judiciary is next to nothing."—"Spirit of Laws," vol. 1, page 186.

though individual oppression may now and then proceed from the courts of justice, the general liberty of the people can never be endangered from that quarter; I mean so long as the judiciary remains truly distinct from both the legislature and the Executive. For I agree, that "there is no liberty, if the power of judging be not separated from the legislative and executive powers."[2] And it proves, in the last place, that as liberty can have nothing to fear from the judiciary alone, but would have every thing to fear from its union with either of the other departments; that as all the effects of such a union must ensue from a dependence of the former on the latter, notwithstanding a nominal and apparent separation; that as, from the natural feebleness of the judiciary, it is in continual jeopardy of being overpowered, awed, or influenced by its co-ordinate branches; and that as nothing can contribute so much to its firmness and independence as permanency in office, this quality may therefore be justly regarded as an indispensable ingredient in its constitution, and, in a great measure, as the citadel of the public justice and the public security.

The complete independence of the courts of justice is peculiarly essential in a limited Constitution. By a limited Constitution, I understand one which contains certain specified exceptions to the legislative authority; such, for instance, as that it shall pass no bills of attainder, no ex-post-facto laws, and the like. Limitations of this kind can be preserved in practice no other way than through the medium of courts of justice, whose duty it must be to declare all acts contrary to the manifest tenor of the Constitution void. Without this, all the reservations of particular rights or privileges would amount to nothing.

Some perplexity respecting the rights of the courts to pronounce legislative acts void, because contrary to the Constitution, has arisen from an imagination that the doctrine would imply a superiority of the judiciary to the legislative power. It is urged that the authority which can declare the acts of another void, must necessarily be superior to the one whose acts may be declared void. As this doctrine is of great importance in all the American constitutions, a brief discussion of the ground on which it rests cannot be unacceptable.

There is no position which depends on clearer principles, than that every act of a delegated authority, contrary to the tenor of the commission under which it is exercised, is void. No legislative act, therefore, contrary to the Constitution, can be valid. To deny this, would be to affirm, that the deputy is greater than his principal; that the servant is above his master; that the representatives of the people are superior to the people themselves; that men acting by virtue of powers, may do not only what their powers do not authorize, but what they forbid.

If it be said that the legislative body are themselves the constitutional judges of their own powers, and that the construction they put upon them is conclusive upon the other departments, it may be answered, that this cannot be the natural presumption, where it is not to be collected from any particular provisions in the Constitution. It is not otherwise to be supposed, that the Constitution could intend to enable the representatives of the people to substitute their *will* to that of their constituents. It is far more rational to suppose, that the courts were designed to be an intermediate body between the people and the legislature, in order, among other things, to keep the latter within the limits assigned to their authority. The interpretation of the laws is the proper and peculiar province of the courts. A constitution is, in fact, and must be regarded by the judges, as a fundamental law. It therefore belongs to them to ascertain its meaning, as well as the meaning of any particular act proceeding from the legislative body. If there should happen to be an irreconcilable variance between the two, that which has the superior obligation and validity ought, of course, to be preferred; or, in other words, the Constitution ought to be preferred to the statute, the intention of the people to the intention of their agents.

Nor does this conclusion by any means suppose a superiority of the judicial to the legislative power. It only supposes that the power of the people is superior to both; and that where the will of the legislature, declared in its statutes, stands in opposition to that of the people, declared in the Constitution, the judges ought to be governed by the latter rather than the former. They ought to regulate their decisions by the fundamental laws, rather than by those which are not fundamental.

This exercise of judicial discretion, in determining between two contradictory laws, is exemplified in a familiar instance. It not uncommonly happens, that there are two statutes existing at one time, clashing in whole or in part with each other, and neither of them containing any repealing clause or expression. In such a case, it is the province of the courts to liquidate and fix their meaning and operation. So far as they can, by any fair construction, be reconciled to each other, reason and law conspire to dictate that this should be done; where this is impracticable, it becomes a matter of necessity to give effect to one, in exclusion of the other. The rule which has obtained in the courts for determining their relative validity is, that the last in order of time shall be preferred to the first. But this is a mere rule of construction, not derived from any positive law, but from the nature and reason of the thing. It is a rule not enjoined upon the courts by legislative provision, but adopted by themselves, as consonant to truth and propriety, for the direction of their conduct as interpreters of the law. They thought it reasonable, that between the interfering acts of an *equal* authority, that which was the last indication of its will should have the preference.

---

[2]Idem, page 181.

But in regard to the interfering acts of a superior and subordinate authority, of an original and derivative power, the nature and reason of the thing indicate the converse of that rule as proper to be followed. They teach us that the prior act of a superior ought to be preferred to the subsequent act of an inferior and subordinate authority; and that accordingly, whenever a particular statute contravenes the Constitution, it will be the duty of the judicial tribunals to adhere to the latter and disregard the former.

It can be of no weight to say that the courts, on the pretense of a repugnancy, may substitute their own pleasure to the constitutional intentions of the legislature. This might as well happen in the case of two contradictory statutes; or it might as well happen in every adjudication upon any single statute. The courts must declare the sense of the law; and if they should be disposed to exercise *will* instead of *judgment*, the consequence would equally be the substitution of their pleasure to that of the legislative body. The observation, if it prove any thing, would prove that there ought to be no judges distinct from that body.

If, then, the courts of justice are to be considered as the bulwarks of a limited Constitution against legislative encroachments, this consideration will afford a strong argument for the permanent tenure of judicial offices, since nothing will contribute so much as this to that independent spirit in the judges which must be essential to the faithful performance of so arduous a duty.

This independence of the judges is equally requisite to guard the Constitution and the rights of individuals from the effects of those ill humors, which the arts of designing men, or the influence of particular conjunctures, sometimes disseminate among the people themselves, and which, though they speedily give place to better information, and more deliberate reflection, have a tendency, in the meantime, to occasion dangerous innovations in the government, and serious oppressions of the minor party in the community. Though I trust the friends of the proposed Constitution will never concur with its enemies,[3] in questioning that fundamental principle of republican government, which admits the right of the people to alter or abolish the established Constitution, whenever they find it inconsistent with their happiness, yet it is not to be inferred from this principle, that the representatives of the people, whenever a momentary inclination happens to lay hold of a majority of their constituents, incompatible with the provisions in the existing Constitution, would, on that account, be justifiable in a violation of those provisions; or that the courts would be under a greater obligation to connive at infractions in this shape, than when they had proceeded wholly from the cabals of the representative body. Until the people have, by some solemn and authoritative act, annulled or changed the established form, it is binding upon themselves collectively, as well as individually; and no presumption, or even knowledge, of their sentiments, can warrant their representatives in a departure from it, prior to such an act. But it is easy to see, that it would require an uncommon portion of fortitude in the judges to do their duty as faithful guardians of the Constitution, where legislative invasions of it had been instigated by the major voice of the community.

But it is not with a view to infractions of the Constitution only, that the independence of the judges may be an essential safeguard against the effects of occasional ill humors in the society. These sometimes extend no farther than to the injury of the private rights of particular classes of citizens, by unjust and partial laws. Here also the firmness of the judicial magistracy is of vast importance in mitigating the severity and confining the operation of such laws. It not only serves to moderate the immediate mischiefs of those which may have been passed, but it operates as a check upon the legislative body in passing them; who, perceiving that obstacles to the success of iniquitous intention are to be expected from the scruples of the courts, are in a manner compelled, by the very motives of the injustice they meditate, to qualify their attempts. This is a circumstance calculated to have more influence upon the character of our governments, than but few may be aware of. The benefits of the integrity and moderation of the judiciary have already been felt in more States than one; and though they may have displeased those whose sinister expectations they may have disappointed, they must have commanded the esteem and applause of all the virtuous and disinterested. Considerate men, of every description, ought to prize whatever will tend to beget or fortify that temper in the courts: as no man can be sure that he may not be to-morrow the victim of a spirit of injustice, by which he may be a gainer to-day. And every man must now feel, that the inevitable tendency of such a spirit is to sap the foundations of public and private confidence, and to introduce in its stead universal distrust and distress.

That inflexible and uniform adherence to the rights of the Constitution, and of individuals, which we perceive to be indispensable in the courts of justice, can certainly not be expected from judges who hold their offices by a temporary commission. Periodical appointments, however regulated, or by whomsoever made, would, in some way or other, be fatal to their necessary independence. If the power of making them was committed either to the Executive or legislature, there would be danger of an improper complaisance to the branch which possessed it; if to both, there would be an unwillingness to hazard the displeasure of either; if to the people, or to persons chosen by them for the special purpose, there would be too great a disposition to consult popularity, to justify a reliance that nothing would be consulted but the Constitution and the laws.

---

[3]Vide "Protest of the Minority of the Convention of Pennsylvania," Martin's Speech, etc.

There is yet a further and a weightier reason for the permanency of the judicial offices, which is deducible from the nature of the qualifications they require. It has been frequently remarked, with great propriety, that a voluminous code of laws is one of the inconveniences necessarily connected with the advantages of a free government. To avoid an arbitrary discretion in the courts, it is indispensable that they should be bound down by strict rules and precedents, which serve to define and point out their duty in every particular case that comes before them; and it will readily be conceived from the variety of controversies which grow out of the folly and wickedness of mankind, that the records of those precedents must unavoidably swell to a very considerable bulk, and must demand long and laborious study to acquire a competent knowledge of them. Hence it is, that there can be but few men in the society who will have sufficient skill in the laws to qualify them for the stations of judges. And making the proper deductions for the ordinary depravity of human nature, the number must be still smaller of those who unite the requisite integrity with the requisite knowledge. These considerations apprise us, that the government can have no great option between fit character; and that a temporary duration in office, which would naturally discourage such characters from quitting a lucrative line of practice to accept a seat on the bench, would have a tendency to throw the administration of justice into hands less able, and less well qualified, to conduct it with utility and dignity. In the present circumstances of this country, and in those in which it is likely to be for a long time to come, the disadvantages on this score would be greater than they may at first sight appear; but it must be confessed, that they are far inferior to those which present themselves under the other aspects of the subject.

Upon the whole, there can be no room to doubt that the convention acted wisely in copying from the models of those constitutions which have established *good behavior* as the tenure of their judicial offices, in point of duration; and that so far from being blamable on this account, their plan would have been inexcusably defective, if it had wanted this important feature of good government. The experience of Great Britain affords an illustrious comment on the excellence of the institution.

PUBLIUS

501(c) group   Interest groups whose primary purpose is not electoral politics.

527 political committee   Organizations created with the primary purpose of influencing electoral outcomes; the term is typically applied only to freestanding interest groups that do not explicitly advocate for the election of a candidate.

abolitionist   A supporter, especially in the early nineteenth century, of ending the institution of slavery.

Abraham Lincoln   Sixteenth president of the United States, the first elected Republican president, who served from 1861–65. Lincoln, who led the Union during the Civil War, was assassinated in 1865 by a Confederate sympathizer, John Wilkes Booth.

administrative adjudication   A quasi-judicial process in which a bureaucratic agency settles disputes between two parties similar to the way courts resolve disputes.

administrative discretion   The ability of bureaucrats to make choices concerning the best way to implement congressional or executive intentions.

affirmative action   Policies designed to give special attention or compensatory treatment to members of a previously disadvantaged group.

Affordable Care Act (ACA)   A 2010 law designed to ensure that nearly all Americans would have access to health care coverage, including those living in poverty.

Afghanistan War   A military conflict begun in 2002 in which a U.S.-led international coalition invaded Afghanistan in order to depose the government and deny a safe haven to terrorists.

AFL-CIO   A large labor union founded in 1955 by the merging of the American Federation of Labor (AFL) and its one-time rival the Congress of Industrial Organizations (CIO).

agenda setting   The process of forming the list of issues to be addressed by government.

Alexander Hamilton   A key Framer who envisioned a powerful central government, co-authored *The Federalist Papers*, and served as the first secretary of the treasury.

al-Qaeda   The Islamic terrorist organization responsible for the 9/11 terrorist attacks and numerous other actions against U.S. overseas interests.

Alien and Sedition Acts   Laws passed in 1798 that allowed the imprisonment and deportation of aliens considered dangerous and criminalized false statements against the government.

American Anti-Slavery Society   A major interest group, founded in 1835, to advocate for the abolition of the institution f slavery throughout the United States.

American Dream   An American ideal of a happy, successful life, which often assumes wealth, a house, and a better life for one's children.

American Federation of Labor (AFL)   Founded in 1886, the AFL brought skilled workers from several trades together into one stronger national organization for the first time. It merged in 1955 with the Congress of Industrial Organizations to form the AFL-CIO.

American National Election Studies (ANES)   Founded in 1952 by researchers at the University of Michigan and Stanford University, ANES collects data on the political attitudes and behavior among voters, such as party affiliation, voting practices, and opinions on parties and candidates.

Americans with Disabilities Act (ADA)   A law enacted by Congress in 1990 designed to guarantee accommodation and access for people with a wide range of disabilities.

amicus curiae   "Friend of the court"; *amici* may file briefs or even appear to argue their interests orally before the court.

Andrew Jackson   The seventh president, a Democrat, who served from 1829 to 1837. Jackson strengthened the office of the president by aggressively wielding his veto power against Congress and asserting the authority of the national government over state government.

Andrew Johnson   Seventeenth president of the United States, a Republican, who served from 1865 to 1869. Johnson had served as Abraham Lincoln's vice president and became president after Lincoln's assassination.

Anne Hutchinson   Seventeenth century political leader and thinker who supported religious liberty.

Anti-Federalists   Those who favored strong state governments and a weak national government; opposed ratification of the U.S. Constitution.

appellate court   Court that generally reviews only findings of law made by lower courts.

appellate jurisdiction The power vested in particular courts to review and/or revise the decision of a lower court.

apportionment The process of allotting congressional seats to each state according to its proportion of the population, following the decennial census.

Article I Vests all legislative powers in the Congress and establishes a bicameral legislature, consisting of the Senate and the House of Representatives; it also sets out the qualifications for holding office in each house, the terms of office, the methods of selection of representatives and senators, and the system of apportionment among the states to determine membership in the House of Representatives.

Article II Vests the executive power, that is, the authority to execute the laws of the nation, in a president of the United States; section 1 sets the president's term of office at four years and explains the Electoral College and states the qualifications for office and describes a mechanism to replace the president in case of death, disability, or removal from office.

Article III Establishes a Supreme Court and defines its jurisdiction.

Article IV Mandates that states honor the laws and judicial proceedings of other states. Article IV also includes the mechanisms for admitting new states to the union. *See also* "full faith and credit clause."

Article V Specifies how amendments can be added to the Constitution.

Article VI Contains the supremacy clause, which asserts the basic primacy of the Constitution and national law over state laws and constitutions. *See also* "supremacy clause."

Articles of Confederation The compact between the thirteen original colonies that created a loose league of friendship, with the national government drawing its powers from the states.

Barack Obama The first African American president of the United States, a Democrat, who served as forty-fourth president from 2009 to 2017. Senator from Illinois from 2005 to 2008; member of the Illinois Senate from 1997 to 2004.

Barron v. *Baltimore* **(1833)** Supreme Court ruling that, before the Civil War, limited the applicability of the Bill of Rights to the federal government and not to the states.

Benjamin Franklin A brilliant inventor and senior statesman at the Constitutional Convention who urged colonial unity as early as 1754, twenty-two years before the Declaration of Independence.

Berlin Wall A barrier built by East Germany in 1961 to cut off democratic West Berlin from communist East Berlin.

Bernie Sanders Longest serving independent in the United States Congress. Ran against Hillary Clinton in the 2016 Democratic presidential primary; senator from Vermont since 2007; first elected to the House of Representatives in 1991.

bicameral legislature A two-house legislature.

bill of attainder A law declaring an act illegal without a judicial trial.

Bill of Rights The first ten amendments to the U.S. Constitution, which largely guarantee specific rights and liberties.

bill A proposed law.

Bipartisan Campaign Reform Act (BCRA) Passed in 2002, this act amended the Federal Election Campaign Act of 1971 with several provisions designed to end the use of nonfederal, or "soft money" (money raised outside the limits and prohibitions of federal *campaign* finance law) for activity affecting federal elections.

Black Lives Matter (BLM) A recent social movement focused on direct protest and political activism against police brutality, mass incarceration, and related offenses against African Americans.

block grant A large grant given to a state by the federal government with only general spending guidelines.

Board of Governors In the Federal Reserve System, a seven-member board that makes most economic decisions regarding interest rates and the supply of money; it is led by the Federal Reserve chair.

Bretton Woods System International financial system devised shortly before the end of World War II that created the World Bank and the International Monetary Fund.

brief A document containing the legal written arguments in a case filed with a court by a party prior to a hearing or trial.

Brown v. *Board of Education* **(1954)** U.S. Supreme Court decision holding that school segregation is inherently unconstitutional because it violates the Fourteenth Amendment's guarantee of equal protection of the law.

budget deficit The economic condition that occurs when expenditures exceed revenues.

bully pulpit The view that a major power of the presidency, albeit not one prescribed by the Constitution, is to draw attention to and generate support for particular positions.

Burger Court The period in Supreme Court history during which Warren Burger served as Chief Justice (1969–1986).

Cabinet departments   Major administrative units with responsibility for a broad area of government operations. Departmental status usually indicates a permanent national interest in a particular governmental function, such as defense, commerce, or agriculture.

Cabinet   The formal body of presidential advisers who head the fifteen executive departments. Presidents often add others to this body of formal advisers.

Calvin Coolidge   Thirtieth president of the United States, a Republican, who served from 1923 to 1929.

campaign consultant   A private-sector professional who sells to a candidate the technologies, services, and strategies required to get that candidate elected.

campaign manager   The individual who travels with the candidate and coordinates the campaign.

candidate-centered politics   Politics that focus on the candidates, their particular issues, and character rather than party affiliation.

capital cases   Court cases in which a conviction may result in the application of the death penalty.

categorical grants   Grants that appropriate federal funds to states for a specific purpose.

Central Intelligence Agency (CIA)   A U.S. government agency dedicated to intelligence gathering and covert operations.

Cesar Chavez   Labor organizer who, with Dolores Huerta, founded the United Farm Workers Union (UFW) in the 1960s.

charter schools   Semi-public schools that have open admission and receive some support from the government and may also receive private donations to increase the quality of education.

charter   A document that, like a constitution, specifies the basic policies, procedures, and institutions of local government. Charters for local governments must be approved by state legislatures.

checks and balances   A constitutionally mandated structure that gives each of the three branches of government some degree of oversight and control over the actions of the others.

Chinese Exclusion Act   A law passed by Congress in 1882 that prohibited all new immigration into the U.S. from China.

Chisholm v. Georgia (1793)   A Supreme Court case that allowed U.S. citizens to bring a lawsuit against states in which they did not reside; overturned by the Eleventh Amendment in 1789.

Christian Coalition   A religious interest group founded in 1989 to advance conservative Christian principles and traditional values in American politics.

citizen journalists   Ordinary individuals who collect, report, and analyze news content.

Citizens United v. FEC (2010)   The 2010 U.S. Supreme Court case that enabled corporations and unions have the same political speech rights as individuals under the First Amendment. As part of this ruling, the Supreme Court found that the government may not prohibit corporations or unions from using their general treasury funds to support or denounce political candidates in elections.

civic virtue   The tendency to form small-scale associations for the public good.

civil liberties   The personal guarantees and freedoms that the government cannot abridge by law, constitution, or judicial interpretation.

Civil Rights Act of 1875   Passed by Congress to enforce the Fourteenth Amendment's guarantees of equal protection to African Americans. Granted equal access to public accommodations among other provisions.

Civil Rights Act of 1964   Wide-ranging legislation passed by Congress to outlaw segregation in public facilities and discrimination in employment, education, and voting; created the Equal Employment Opportunity Commission.

civil rights   The government-protected rights of individuals against arbitrary or discriminatory treatment by governments or individuals.

civil service system   The merit system by which many federal bureaucrats are selected.

Civil War   The military conflict from 1861 to 1865 in the United States between the Northern forces of the Union and the Southern forces of the Confederacy. Over 600,000 Americans lost their lives during this war.

clear and present danger test   Test articulated by the Supreme Court in *Schenck v. U.S.* (1919) to draw the line between protected and unprotected speech; the Court looks to see "whether the words used" could "create a clear and present danger that they will bring about substantive evils" that Congress seeks "to prevent."

closed primary   A primary election in which only a party's registered voters are eligible to cast a ballot.

cloture   Mechanism requiring the vote of sixty senators to cut off debate.

Cold War   The period of superpower rivalry and confrontation between the United States and the Soviet Union, lasting from the end of World War II to 1991.

collective good   Something of value that cannot be withheld from a nonmember of a group; for example, a tax write-off or a better environment.

collective security   The idea that an attack on one country is an attack on all countries.

Committee of the Whole   A procedure that allows the House of Representatives to deliberate with a lower quorum and to expedite consideration and amendment of a bill.

Common Core   A voluntarily adopted multi-state approach to setting standards that all students should achieve up through the high-school level.

Common Sense   A pamphlet written by Thomas Paine that challenged the authority of the British government to govern the colonies.

communications director   The person who develops the overall media strategy for the candidate.

concurrent powers   Powers shared by the national and state governments.

concurring opinion   A type of judicial opinion issued by a minority of judges on a court who agree with the outcome of a case, but wishes to express different legal reasoning.

Confederate States of America   The political system created by the eleven states that seceded from the Union during the Civil War, which ceased to exist upon the Union victory.

confederation   Type of government in which the national government derives its powers from the states; a league of independent states.

conference committee   Special joint committee created to reconcile differences in bills passed by the House and Senate.

Congressional Budget Act of 1974   Act that established the congressional budgetary process by laying out a plan for congressional action on the annual budget resolution, appropriations, reconciliation, and any other revenue bills.

Congressional Budget Office (CBO)   Created in 1974, the CBO provides Congress with evaluations of the potential economic effects of proposed spending policies and also analyzes the president's budget and economic projections.

Congressional Research Service (CRS)   Created in 1914, the non-partisan CRS provides information, studies, and research in support of the work of Congress, and prepares summaries and tracks the progress of all bill.

congressional review   A process whereby Congress can nullify agency regulations within a 60-day window by passing a joint resolution of legislative disapproval. The president's approval of the resolution or a two-thirds majority vote in both houses to overrule a presidential veto is also required.

conservative   One who favors limited government intervention, particularly in economic affairs.

constitution   A document establishing the structure, functions, and limitations of a government.

Constitutional Convention   The meeting in Philadelphia in 1787 that was first intended to revise the Articles of Confederation but produced an entirely new document, the U.S. Constitution.

constitutional (or Article III) courts   Federal courts specifically created by the U.S. Constitution or by Congress pursuant to its authority in Article III.

containment   U.S. policy of opposing Soviet expansion and communist revolutions around the world with military forces, economic assistance, and political influence.

content regulations   Limitations on the substance of the mass media.

contrast ad   Ad that compares the records and proposals of the candidates, with a bias toward the candidate sponsoring the ad.

conventional political participation   Activism that attempts to influence the political process through commonly accepted forms of persuasion such as voting or letter writing.

cooperative federalism   The intertwined relationship between national, state, and local governments that began with the New Deal; often referred to as marble-cake federalism.

counties   The basic administrative units of local government.

Crispus Attucks   An African American and first American to die in what became known as the Boston Massacre in 1770.

critical election   An election that signals a party realignment through voter polarization around new issues and personalities.

Critical Period   The chaotic period from 1781 to 1789 after the American Revolution during which the former colonies were governed under the Articles of Confederation.

crossover voting   Participation in the primary election of a party with which the voter is not affiliated.

Cuban Missile Crisis   The 1962 confrontation over the deployment of ballistic missiles in Cuba that nearly escalated into nuclear war between the United States and the Soviet Union.

Declaration of Independence   Document drafted largely by Thomas Jefferson in 1776 that proclaimed the right of the American colonies to separate from Great Britain.

deep background   Information provided to a journalist that will not be attributed to any source.

defense policy   Area of policy making that focuses on the strategies that a country uses to protect itself from its enemies.

DeJonge v. *Oregon* (1937)   Supreme Court case that applied the First Amendment's protections of freedom of assembly to the states.

delegate   Role played by representative who votes the way his or her constituents would want, regardless of personal opinions; may refer to an elected representative to Congress or a representative to the party convention.

democracy   A system of government that gives power to the people, whether directly or through elected representatives.

Department of Defense   Chief executive branch department responsible for formulation and implementation of U.S. defense and military policy.

Department of Health and Human Services (HHS)   The cabinet-level department administering most federal social welfare and health-related policies and programs; it includes the National Institutes for Health (NIH), the Centers for Disease Control and Prevention (CDC), and the Food and Drug Administration (FDA).

Department of Homeland Security   Cabinet department created after the 9/11 terrorist attacks to coordinate domestic security efforts.

Department of State   Chief executive branch department responsible for formulation and implementation of U.S. foreign policy.

depression   A severe and long lasting decline in the economy that occurs as investment sags, production falls off, and unemployment increases.

détente   The improvement in relations between the United States and the Soviet Union that occurred during the 1970s.

deterrence   The military strategy of employing enormous force, including nuclear weapons, in order to prevent the outbreak or escalation of armed conflicts.

Dillon's Rule   A premise articulated by Judge John F. Dillon in 1868 that states that local governments do not have any inherent sovereignty and instead must be authorized by state governments that can create or abolish them.

direct incitement test   Test articulated by the Supreme Court in *Brandenburg* v. *Ohio* (1969) holding that the First Amendment protects advocacy of illegal action unless imminent lawless action is intended and likely to occur.

discharge petition   Petition that gives a majority of the House of Representatives the authority to bring an issue to the floor in the face of committee inaction.

discount rate   The rate of interest at which the Federal Reserve Board lends money to member banks.

dissenting opinion   A type of judicial opinion issued by a minority of judges on a court who disagree with the outcome of a case and wish to explain their legal reasoning.

distributive policies   Public policies that provide benefits to individuals, groups, communities, or corporations.

disturbance theory   The theory that interest groups form as a result of changes in the political system.

divided government   The political condition in which different political parties control the presidency and at least one house of Congress.

Dolores Huerta   Labor organizer who, with Cesar Chavez, founded the United Farm Workers Union (UFW) in the 1960s.

Donald J. Trump   The forty-fifth president, a Republican, elected in 2016; first president elected without prior political or military experience; an experienced businessman.

double jeopardy clause   Part of the Fifth Amendment that protects individuals from being tried twice for the same offense in the same jurisdiction.

Dred Scott v. *Sandford* (1857)   A Supreme Court decision that ruled the Missouri Compromise unconstitutional and denied citizenship rights to enslaved African Americans. *Dred Scott* heightened tensions between the pro-slavery South and the abolitionist North in the run up to the Civil War.

dual federalism   The belief that having separate and equally powerful levels of government is the best arrangement, often referred to as layer-cake federalism.

due process clause   Clause contained in the Fifth and Fourteenth Amendments; over the years, it has been construed to guarantee a variety of rights to individuals.

due process rights   Protections drawn from the Fourth Amendment and the Bill of Rights. Due process may be procedural, ensuring fair treatment, or substantive, protecting fundamental rights.

Dwight D. Eisenhower   The thirty-fourth president, a Republican, who served from 1953 to 1961. Eisenhower commanded Allied Forces during World War II.

Earl Warren   The fourteenth Chief Justice of the United States who served from 1953 to 1969 and led the Court through an important liberal phase; previously a Republican governor and vice presidential nominee.

economic interest group   A group with the primary purpose of promoting the financial interests of its members.

Edmund Burke   Conservative British political philosopher of the eighteenth century who articulated the view that elected representatives should act as "trustees" and use their own best judgment when voting.

Eighteenth Amendment A 1913 amendment that created the nationwide prohibition on alcoholic beverages; it was repealed in 1933 by the Twentieth Amendment.

Eighth Amendment Part of the Bill of Rights that states: "Excessive bail shall not be required, nor excessive fines imposed, nor cruel and unusual punishments inflicted."

Eleanor Roosevelt First Lady of the United States from 1933 to 1945. Roosevelt championed human rights throughout her life and served as the U.S.'s first delegate to the United Nations General Assembly and later chaired the UN's Commission on Human Rights.

elector Member of the Electoral College.

Electoral College The system established by the Constitution through which the president is chosen by electors from each state, which has as many electoral votes as it has members of Congress.

electorate The citizens eligible to vote.

Elena Kagan An Associate Justice of the Supreme Court, appointed by President Barack Obama in 2009 while she was serving as solicitor general in his administration.

Eleventh Amendment An amendment adopted in 1789 protecting states from being sued in federal court by a citizen of a different state or country.

Elizabeth Cady Stanton Leading nineteenth century feminist, suffragist, and abolitionist who, along with Lucretia Mott, organized the Seneca Falls Convention. Stanton later founded the National Woman Suffrage Association (NWSA) with Susan B. Anthony.

Emancipation Proclamation President Abraham Lincoln issued this proclamation on January 1, 1863, in the third year of the Civil War. It freed all slaves in states that were in active rebellion against the United States.

Enlightenment A philosophical movement in eighteenth-century Europe; its adherents advocated liberty and tolerance of individual differences, decried religious and political abuses, and rejected the notion of an absolute monarch.

entitlement programs Government benefits that all citizens meeting eligibility criteria—such as age, income level, or unemployment—are legally "entitled" to receive.

enumerated powers The powers of the national government specifically granted to Congress in Article I, section 8 of the Constitution.

Equal Pay Act of 1963 Legislation that requires employers to pay men and women equal pay for equal work.

equal protection clause Section of the Fourteenth Amendment that guarantees that all citizens receive "equal protection of the laws."

Equal Rights Amendment (ERA) Proposed amendment to the Constitution that states "Equality of rights under the law shall not be denied or abridged by the United States or any state on account of sex."

equal time rule The rule that requires broadcast stations to sell air time equally to all candidates in a political campaign if they choose to sell it to any.

Espionage Act A 1917 law that prohibited urging resistance to the draft or distributing anti-war leaflets; upheld by the Supreme Court in *Schenck* v. *U.S.*

establishment clause The first clause of the First Amendment; it directs the national government not to sanction an official religion.

European Union An organization with political institutions that join 28 countries in Europe into a union that promotes free trade, a central bank, flow of labor and capital, and a common currency among most members.

ex post facto **law** Law that makes an act punishable as a crime, even if the action was legal at the time it was committed.

exclusionary rule Judicially created rule that prohibits police from using illegally seized evidence at trial.

executive agreements Formal international agreements entered into by the president that do not require the advice and consent of the U.S. Senate.

Executive Office of the President (EOP) A mini-bureaucracy created in 1939 to help the president oversee the executive branch bureaucracy.

executive order Rule or regulation issued by the president that has the effect of law. All executive orders must be published in the *Federal Register*.

executive privilege An implied presidential power that allows the president to refuse to disclose information regarding confidential conversations or national security to Congress or the judiciary.

exit polls Polls conducted as voters leave selected polling places on Election Day.

extradition clause Part of Article IV of the Constitution that requires states to extradite, or return, criminals to states where they have been convicted or are to stand trial.

Farewell Address When President George Washington left office, he wrote a letter, addressed to the People of the United States, warning them of the dangers to avoid in order to preserve the republic.

federal bureaucracy The thousands of federal government agencies and institutions that implement and administer federal laws and programs.

Federal Election Campaign Act (FECA) Passed in 1971, this is the primary law that regulates political campaign spending and fundraising. The law originally focused on increased disclosure of contributions for federal campaigns.

Federal Election Commission (FEC) An independent regulatory agency founded in 1975 by the United States Congress to regulate the campaign finance legislation in the United States.

Federal Register The official journal of the U.S. government, including all federal rules and public notices so that citizens and organization can follow proposed changes and comply with rule changes.

Federal Reserve System The organization in the United States tasked with such responsibilities as managing the money supply, stabilizing prices, moderating interest rates, and reducing unemployment.

federal system System of government in which the national government and state governments share power and derive all authority from the people.

federalism The distribution of constitutional authority between state governments and the national government, with different powers and functions exercised by both.

Federalist No. 78 A *Federalist Papers* essay authored by Alexander Hamilton that covers the role of the federal judiciary, including the power of judicial review.

Federalists Those who favored a stronger national government and supported the proposed U.S. Constitution; later became the first U.S. political party.

Fifteenth Amendment One of three major amendments ratified after the Civil War; specifically enfranchised newly freed male slaves.

Fifth Amendment Part of the Bill of Rights that imposes a number of restrictions on the federal government with respect to the rights of persons suspected of committing a crime. It provides for indictment by a grand jury and protection against self-incrimination, and prevents the national government from denying a person life, liberty, or property without the due process of law. It also prevents the national government from taking property without just compensation.

fighting words Words that "by their very utterance inflict injury or tend to incite an immediate breach of peace." Fighting words are not subject to the restrictions of the First Amendment.

filibuster A formal way of halting Senate action on a bill by means of long speeches or unlimited debate.

finance chair The individual who coordinates the financial business of the campaign.

First Amendment Part of the Bill of Rights that imposes a number of restrictions on the federal government with respect to civil liberties, including freedom of religion, speech, press, assembly, and petition.

First Continental Congress Meeting held in Philadelphia from September 5 to October 26, 1774, in which fifty-six delegates (from every colony except Georgia) adopted a resolution in opposition to the Coercive Acts.

first lady The designation provided to the wife of a president or, at the state level, of a governor; no specific analogue exists for a male spouse.

fiscal policy The deliberate use of the national government's taxing and spending policies to maintain economic stability.

foreign policy Area of policy making that encompasses how one country builds relationships with other countries in order to safeguard its national interest.

foreign-policy idealism A perspective contending that the behavior of countries in the international arena is mainly intended to advance their values and principles.

foreign-policy realism A perspective contending that the behavior of countries in the international arena is mainly intended to protect their economic and security interests.

Fourteenth Amendment One of three major amendments ratified after the Civil War; guarantees equal protection and due process of the law to all U.S. citizens.

Fourth Amendment Part of the Bill of Rights that protects people from unreasonable searches and seizures of their persons, houses, papers, and effects without a warrant from a judge.

framing The process by which a news organization defines a political issue and consequently affects opinion about the issue.

Franklin D. Roosevelt (FDR) Thirty-second president, a Democrat, who served from 1933 to 1945. FDR's leadership took the United States through the Great Depression and World War II.

Frederick Douglass A former slave born in the early 1800s who became a leading abolitionist, writer, and suffragist.

free exercise clause The second clause of the First Amendment; it prohibits the U.S. government from interfering with a citizen's right to practice his or her religion.

free rider problem Potential members fail to join a group because they can get the benefit, or collective good, sought by the group without contributing the effort.

free trade system A system of international trade that limits government interference on the sale of goods and services among countries.

French and Indian War The American phase of what was called the Seven Years War, fought from 1754 to 1763 between Britain and France with Indian allies.

front-loading The tendency of states to choose an early date on the nomination calendar.

full faith and credit clause Section of Article IV of the Constitution that ensures judicial decrees and contracts made in one state will be binding and enforceable in any other state.

fundamental freedoms Those rights defined by the Court as essential to order, liberty, and justice and therefore entitled to the highest standard of review.

G.I. (Government Issue) Bill Federal legislation enacted in 1944 that provided college loans for returning veterans and reduced mortgage rates to enable them to buy homes.

General Agreement on Tariffs and Trade (GATT) Post–World War II economic development treaty designed to help facilitate international trade negotiations and promote free trade.

general election Election in which voters decide which candidates will actually fill elective public offices.

George Gallup One of the earliest developers of scientific methods for public opinion polling and a proponent for a strong role for the voice of the public in politics and government.

George Washington Widely considered the "Father of the Nation," he was the commander of the revolutionary armies; served as the presiding officer of the Constitutional Convention, and as the United States' first president from 1789 to 1797.

gerrymandering The drawing of congressional districts to produce a particular electoral outcome without regard to the shape of the district.

get-out-the-vote (GOTV) A push at the end of a political campaign to encourage supporters to go to the polls.

Gibbons v. *Ogden* **(1824)** The Supreme Court upheld broad congressional power to regulate interstate commerce. The Court's broad interpretation of the Constitution's commerce clause paved the way for later rulings upholding expansive federal powers.

Gitlow v. *New York* **(1925)** A Supreme Court case that extended the First Amendment's protections of freedom of speech and of the press to the state governments.

global war on terror An international action, initiated by President George W. Bush after the 9/11 terrorist attacks, to weed out terrorist operatives throughout the world.

Government Accountability Office (GAO) Established in 1921, the GAO is an independent regulatory agency for the purpose of auditing the financial expenditures of the executive branch and federal agencies; until 2004, the GAO was known as the General Accounting Office.

government corporations Businesses established by Congress to perform functions that private businesses could provide, such as the U.S. Postal Service and Amtrak. Often established when the financial incentives for private industry to provide services are minimal.

government The formal vehicle through which policies are made and affairs of state are conducted.

governmental (institutional) agenda Problems to which public officials feel obliged to devote active and serious attention.

grand jury A group of citizens charged with determining whether enough evidence exists for a case to go to trial. Guaranteed by the Fifth Amendment.

grandfather clause Voter qualification provision in many southern states that allowed only those citizens whose grandfathers had voted before Reconstruction to vote unless they passed a wealth or literacy test.

Great Compromise The final decision of the Constitutional Convention to create a two-house legislature, with the lower house elected by the people and powers divided between the two houses; also made national law supreme.

Great Depression A severe global economic downturn marked by mass unemployment and poverty that began in the United States in 1929 and persisted to some degree until the end of the 1930s.

Great Society Reform program begun in 1964 by President Lyndon B. Johnson that was a broad attempt to combat poverty and discrimination through urban renewal, education reform, and unemployment relief.

gross domestic product (GDP) The total market value of all goods and services produced in a country during a year.

Gulf War A military conflict from 1990-1991 in which a U.S.-led international coalition reversed the occupation of Kuwait by the armed forces of Iraq.

Harriet Tubman Born a slave in Maryland in the early 1820s, Tubman escaped to freedom and became a conductor on the Underground Railroad. She led more than seventy people to freedom in the North, served in the Union during the Civil War, and championed women's suffrage.

Harry S Truman The thirty-third president, a Democrat, who served from 1945 until 1953. Truman became president when Franklin D. Roosevelt died in office; he led the United States through the end of World War II and the start of the Cold War.

Hatch Act The 1939 act to prohibit civil servants from taking activist roles in partisan campaigns. This act prohibited federal employees from making political contributions, working for a particular party, or campaigning for a particular candidate.

hate speech Communication that belittles a person or group on the basis of race, gender, ethnicity, or other characteristics.

Help America Vote Act (HAVA) A federal law passed in 2002 that addresses issues of voting systems and voter access that were identified following the 2000 election. It established minimum election administration standards for states and units of local government with responsibility for the administration of federal elections and for other purposes related to the act.

Herbert Hoover Thirty-first president of the United States, a Republican, who served from 1929 to 1933 during the start of the Great Depression.

Hillary Clinton First female major party candidate for president of the United States, a Democrat, who ran against President Donald J. Trump in 2016. Secretary of State from 2009 to 2013; New York senator from 2001 to 2009; former first lady.

hold A procedure by which a senator asks to be informed before a particular bill or nomination is brought to the floor. This request signals leadership that a member may have objections to the bill (or nomination) and should be consulted before further action is taken.

Honest Leadership and Open Government Act of 2007 Lobbying reform banning gifts to members of Congress and their staffs, toughening disclosure requirements, and increasing time limits on moving from the federal government to the private sector.

House Committee on Rules The influential "Rules Committee" determines the scheduling and conditions, such as length of debate and type of allowable amendments, for all bills in the House of Representatives (but not in the Senate, where debate is less regulated).

human rights The protection of people's basic freedoms and needs.

impeachment The power delegated to the House of Representatives in the Constitution to charge the president, vice president, or other "civil officers," including federal judges, with "Treason, Bribery, or other high Crimes and Misdemeanors." This is the first step in the constitutional process of removing government officials from office.

implementation The process by which a law or policy is put into operation.

implied powers The powers of the national government derived from the enumerated powers and the necessary and proper clause.

incorporation doctrine An interpretation of the Constitution holding that the due process clause of the Fourteenth Amendment requires state and local governments to guarantee the rights stated in the Bill of Rights.

incumbency Already holding an office.

independent executive agencies Governmental units that closely resemble a Cabinet department but have narrower areas of responsibility and perform services rather than regulatory functions.

independent expenditures Spending for campaign activity that is not coordinated with a candidate's campaign.

independent regulatory commission An entity created by Congress outside a major executive department that regulates a specified interest or economic activity.

inflation A rise in the general price levels of goods and services within an economy.

inherent powers Powers that belong to the president because they can be inferred from the Constitution.

initiative An election that allows citizens to propose legislation or state constitutional amendments by submitting them to the electorate for popular vote.

inoculation ad Advertising that attempts to counteract an anticipated attack from the opposition before the attack is launched.

interagency councils Working groups created to facilitate coordination of policy making and implementation across a host of governmental agencies.

interest group A collection of people or organizations that tries to influence public policy.

intermediate standard of review A standard of review in which the Court determines whether classifications serve an important governmental objective and are substantially related to serving that objective. Gender-related legislation automatically accorded this level of review.

International Monetary Fund (IMF) International governmental organization designed to stabilize international currency transactions.

interstate compacts Contracts between states that carry the force of law; generally now used as a tool to address multistate policy concerns.

Iraq War A military conflict from 2003–2011 in which a U.S.-led international coalition invaded Iraq and deposed its regime but proved unable to establish a stable new government.

Iron Curtain A term used during the Cold War to describe the divide between the capitalist West and communist East.

iron triangles The relatively ironclad relationships and patterns of interaction that occur among agencies, interest groups, and congressional committees or subcommittees.

Iroquois Confederacy A political alliance of American Indian tribes established in the seventeenth century that featured aspects of the federal system of government adapted by the Framers.

ISIS A terrorist organization that calls itself an Islamic State, controls parts of Syria and Iraq and uses that as a base to direct and inspire terrorist attacks abroad.

isolationism The U.S. policy of avoiding entangling alliances with foreign powers.

issue networks The loose and informal relationships that exist among a large number of actors who work in broad policy areas.

James Madison A key Framer often called the "Father of the Constitution" for his role in conceptualizing the federal government. Co-authored *The Federalist Papers*; served as secretary of state; served as the fourth U.S. president from 1809 to 1817.

Jerry Falwell A Southern Baptist minister who, in 1978, founded the conservative religious interest group the Moral Majority.

Jim Crow laws Laws enacted by southern states that required segregation in public schools, theaters, hotels, and other public accommodations.

John C. Calhoun A politician and political theorist from South Carolina who supported slavery and states' rights in the pre-Civil War era and served as vice president from 1825 to 1832.

John F. Kennedy The thirty-fourth president, a Democrat, who served from 1961 to 1963 and marked a generational shift in U.S. politics at the height of the Cold War. He was assassinated November 22, 1963.

John Jay A member of the Founding generation who was the first Chief Justice of the United States. A diplomat and a co-author of *The Federalist Papers*.

John Marshall The longest-serving Supreme Court chief justice, Marshall served from 1801 to 1835. Marshall's decision in *Marbury* v. *Madison* (1803) established the principle of judicial review in the United States.

Joint Chiefs of Staff Military advisory body that includes the Army chief of staff, the Air Force chief of staff, the chief of naval operations, and the Marine commandant.

joint committee Standing committee that includes members from both houses of Congress set up to conduct investigations or special studies.

judicial activism A philosophy of judicial decision making that posits judges should use their power broadly to further justice.

judicial implementation How and whether judicial decisions are translated into actual public policies affecting more than the immediate parties to a lawsuit.

judicial restraint A philosophy of judicial decision making that posits courts should allow the decisions of other branches of government to stand, even when they offend a judge's own principles.

judicial review Power of the courts to review acts of other branches of government and the states.

Judiciary Act of 1789 Legislative act that established the basic three-tiered structure of the federal court system.

jurisdiction Authority vested in a particular court to hear and decide the issues in a particular case.

Keynesian economics An economic approach first championed by economist John Maynard Keynes in the 1930s, who maintained that spending by government can stimulate economic growth much faster than a free market could on its own.

Korean War A civil war from 1950-1953 in which the United States supported the South Korean regime against Communist forces in North Korea.

***Korematsu* v. *U.S.* (1944)** A Supreme Court ruling that upheld the authority of the U.S. government to require mass interment of people of Japanese ancestry in the U.S. during World War II.

laissez-faire Economic philosophy that endorses a very limited role for government in the economy.

lame duck An executive or legislature during the period just before the end of a term of office, when its power and influence are considered to be diminished.

***Lawrence* v. *Texas* (2003)** A 2003 Supreme Court ruling that anti-sodomy laws violated the constitutional right to privacy.

League of Nations A multilateral diplomatic organization that existed from 1920–1946 that sought, unsuccessfully, to prevent future wars; the United States never joined.

League of United Latin American Citizens (LULAC) An activist group founded in 1929 to combat discrimination against, and promote assimilation among, Americans of Hispanic origin.

legislative courts Courts established by Congress for specialized purposes, such as the Court of Appeals for Veterans Claims.

***Lemon* test** Three-part test created by the Supreme Court for examining the constitutionality of religious establishment issues.

Lexington and Concord   The first sites of armed conflict between revolutionaries and British soldiers; remembered for the "shot heard 'round the world" in 1775.

LGBT Community   A minority group based on sexual orientation and gender identity that includes lesbian, gay, bisexual, and transgender (LGBT) people.

libel   False written statement that defames a person's character.

liberal   One who favors greater government intervention, particularly in economic affairs and in the provision of social services.

libertarian   One who believes in limited government interference in personal and economic liberties.

lobbying   The activities of a group or organization that seek to persuade political leaders to support the group's position.

Lobbying Disclosure Act   A 1995 federal law that employed a strict definition of lobbyist and established strict reporting requirements on the activities of lobbyists.

lobbyist   Interest group representative who seeks to influence legislation that will benefit his or her organization or client through political and/or financial persuasion.

logrolling   Vote trading; voting to support a colleague's bill in return for a promise of future support.

Lucretia Mott   Leading nineteenth century feminist, suffragist, and abolitionist who, along with Elizabeth Cady Stanton, organized the Seneca Falls Convention.

Lyndon B. Johnson (LBJ)   Thirty-sixth president of the United States, a Democrat, who served from 1963 to 1969. LBJ led the nation during the civil rights era and the Vietnam War.

majority leader   The head of the party controlling the most seats in the House of Representatives or the Senate; is second in authority to the Speaker of the House and in the Senate is regarded as its most powerful member.

majority party   The political party in each house of Congress with the most members.

mandate   A command, indicated by an electorate's votes, for the elected officials to carry out a party platform or policy agenda.

manifest destiny   Theory that the United States was divinely supported to expand across North America to the Pacific Ocean.

Marbury v. Madison (1803)   Case in which the Supreme Court first asserted the power of judicial review by finding that part of the congressional statute extending the Court's original jurisdiction was unconstitutional.

margin of error   A measure of the accuracy of a public opinion poll within statistical parameters.

Marian Wright Edelman   A lawyer who in 1973 founded the Children's Defense Fund to protect the rights of children, particularly those who are members of disadvantaged groups.

markup   A session in which committee members offer changes to a bill before it goes to the floor.

Marshall Plan   European collective recovery program, named after Secretary of State George C. Marshall, that provided extensive American aid to Western Europe after World War II.

Martin Luther King Jr.   A Baptist minister, proponent of non-violence, and the most prominent leader of the civil rights movement of the 1950s and 1960s. He was assassinated on April 4, 1968.

mass media   The entire array of organizations through which information is collected and disseminated to the general public.

matching funds   Donations to presidential campaigns whereby every dollar raised from individuals in amounts less than $251 is matched by the federal treasury.

Max Weber   German sociologist active in the late nineteenth and early twentieth centuries who articulated the hierarchical structure and near-mechanical functioning of bureaucracies in complex societies.

Mayflower   The ship carrying Pilgrim settlers from England whose arrival in Massachusetts in 1620 is considering a founding moment for the nation.

McCulloch v. Maryland (1819)   The Supreme Court upheld the power of the national government and denied the right of a state to tax the federal bank, using the Constitution's supremacy clause. The Court's broad interpretation of the necessary and proper clause paved the way for later rulings upholding expansive federal powers.

McCutcheon v. FEC (2014)   The 2014 Supreme Court ruling that declared Section 441 of the Federal Election Campaign Act (FECA) unconstitutional. Section 441 imposed limits on any individual's total political contributions (to federal candidates, parties, or political action committees) in a two-year period.

means-tested programs   Programs requiring beneficiaries to have incomes below specified levels to be eligible for benefits; among these are Social Security Insurance (SSI), Temporary Aid to Needy Families, (TANF), and the Supplemental Nutrition Assistance Program (SNAP), formerly called "food stamps."

media effects   The influence of news sources on public opinion.

Medicaid A government program that subsidizes medical care for the poor.

Medicare The federal program established during Lyndon B. Johnson's administration that provides medical care to elderly Social Security recipients.

mercantilism An economic theory designed to increase a nation's wealth through the development of commercial industry and a favorable balance of trade.

merit system A system of employment based on qualifications, test scores, and ability, rather than party loyalty.

Mexican American Legal Defense and Educational Fund (MALDEF) An organization modeled on the NAACP Legal Defense and Educational Fund that works to protect the civil rights of Americans of Mexican and other Hispanic heritage.

mid-term election An election that takes place in the middle of a presidential term.

military-industrial complex The network of political and financial relations formed by defense industries, the U.S. armed forces, and Congress.

Miller **v.** *California* **(1973)** Supreme Court case that created the "Miller test" to determine when sexually-explicit expression was obscene and therefore beyond the protection of the First Amendment.

minority leader The head of the party with the second highest number of elected representatives in the House of Representatives or the Senate.

minority party The political party in each house of Congress with the second most members.

Miranda **rights** Statements required of police that inform a suspect of his or her constitutional rights protected by the Fifth Amendment, including the right to an attorney provided by a court if the suspect cannot afford one.

Miranda **v.** *Arizona* **(1966)** A landmark Supreme Court ruling holding that the Fifth Amendment requires individuals arrested for a crime to be advised of their right to remain silent and to have counsel present.

moderate A person who takes a relatively centrist or middle-of-the-road view on most political issues.

monarchy A form of government in which power is vested in hereditary kings and queens who govern the entire society.

monetary policy A form of government regulation in which the nation's money supply and interest rates are controlled.

Monroe Doctrine President James Monroe's 1823 pledge that the United States would oppose attempts by European states to reestablish their political control in the Western Hemisphere.

Montesquieu The French baron and political theorist who first articulated the concept of separation of powers with checks and balances.

Moral Majority A conservative religious interest group credited with helping to mobilize conservative Evangelical Christian voters from its founding in 1978 through the presidency of Ronald Reagan (1981–89).

muckraking A form of journalism, in vogue in the early twentieth century, devoted to exposing misconduct by government, business, and individual politicians.

municipalities City governments created in response to the emergence of relatively densely populated areas.

NAACP Legal Defense and Educational Fund (LDF) The legal arm of the NAACP that successfully litigated the landmark case of *Brown* v. *Board of Education* and a host of other key civil rights cases.

narrowcasting Targeting media programming at specific populations within society.

National American Woman Suffrage Association (NAWSA) Organization created by joining the National and American Woman Suffrage Associations.

National Association for the Advancement of Colored People (NAACP) An important rights organization founded in 1909 to oppose segregation, racism, and voting rights violations targeted against African Americans.

National Association of Manufacturers (NAM) An organization founded in 1895 by manufacturers to combat the growth of organized labor.

national convention A party meeting held in the presidential election year for the purposes of nominating a presidential and vice presidential ticket and adopting a platform.

national debt The total amount owed by the federal government to its creditors, both domestic and international.

National Organization for Women (NOW) The leading activist group of the women's rights movement, especially in the 1960s and 1970s.

national party platform A statement of the general and specific philosophy and policy goals of a political party, usually promulgated at the national convention.

National Rifle Association (NRA) The major gun-rights lobbying group in the United States, which opposes gun control and advances an expansive interpretation of the Second Amendment.

National Security Council The agency within the White House, led by the national security adviser, which brings together key foreign policy actors to advise the president.

National Woman's Party (NWP) A militant suffrage organization founded in the early twentieth century. Members of the NWP were arrested, jailed, and even force-fed by authorities when they went on hunger strikes to secure voting rights for women.

necessary and proper clause   The final paragraph of Article I, section 8, of the Constitution, which gives Congress the authority to pass all laws "necessary and proper" to carry out the enumerated powers specified in the Constitution; also called the elastic clause.

negative ad   Advertising on behalf of a candidate that attacks the opponent's character or platform.

New Deal   The political program enacted by President Franklin D. Roosevelt in the 1930s that greatly expanded the role of the federal government in order to combat the effects of the Great Depression.

New Federalism   Federal–state relationship proposed by the Reagan administration during the 1980s; hallmark is returning administrative powers to the state governments.

New Jersey Plan   A framework for the Constitution proposed by a group of small states; it called for a one-house legislature with one vote for each state, a Congress with the ability to raise revenue, and a Supreme Court appointed for life.

New World   The Western hemisphere of Earth, also called The Americas, which was unknown to Europeans before 1492.

New York Times Co. v. Sullivan **(1964)**   Case in which the Supreme Court concluded that "actual malice" must be proven to support a finding of libel against a public figure.

New York Times Co. v. U.S. **(1971)**   The case in which the Supreme Court ruled that the U.S. government could not block the publication of secret Department of Defense documents illegally furnished to the *Times* by anti-war activists. Also called the *Pentagon Papers* case.

news media   Media providing the public with new information about subjects of public interest.

Nineteenth Amendment   Amendment to the Constitution passed in 1920 that guaranteed women the right to vote.

Ninth Amendment   Part of the Bill of Rights that makes it clear that enumerating rights in the Constitution or Bill of Rights does not mean that others do not exist.

No Child Left Behind Act (NCLB)   Bipartisan education reform bill that employed high standards and measurable goals as a method of improving American education across states; in 2016, it was largely replaced by the Every Student Succeeds Act (ESSA).

non–means-tested programs   Programs that provide cash assistance to qualified beneficiaries, regardless of income;

among these are Social Security and unemployment insurance.

North American Free Trade Agreement (NAFTA)   Agreement that promotes free movement of goods and services among Canada, Mexico, and the United States.

North Atlantic Treaty Organization (NATO)   The first peacetime military treaty joined by the United States; NATO is a collective security pact that includes the United States, Canada, and parts of Europe.

nullification   The believe in the right of a state to declare void a federal law.

Obergefell v. *Hodges* **(2015)**   Supreme Court ruling that held that same-sex couples have a fundamental right to marry under the Constitution.

Occupy Wall Street   A recent social movement that promotes protests and political activism against income inequality and corporate greed.

off the record   Information provided to a journalist that will not be released to the public.

Office of Management and Budget (OMB)   The office that prepares the president's annual budget proposal, reviews the budget and programs of the executive departments, supplies economic forecasts, and conducts detailed analyses of proposed bills and agency rules.

oligarchy   A form of government in which the right to participate depends on the possession of wealth, social status, military position, or achievement.

on background   Information provided to a journalist that will not be attributed to a named source.

on the record   Information provided to a journalist that can be released and attributed by name to the source.

open market operations   The buying and selling of government securities by the Federal Reserve Bank.

open primary   A primary election in which party members, independents, and sometimes members of the other party are allowed to participate.

original jurisdiction   The jurisdiction of courts that hear a case first, usually in a trial. These courts determine the facts of a case.

pardon   An executive grant providing restoration of all rights and privileges of citizenship to a specific individual charged with or convicted of a crime.

partisan polarization   The presence of increasingly conflicting and divided viewpoints between the Democratic and Republican Parties.

party caucus (or conference)   A formal gathering of all party members.

party identification Citizen's attachment to a political party based on issues, ideology, past experience, or upbringing, which tends to be a reliable indicator of likely voting choices.

party realignment Dramatic shifts in partisan preferences that drastically alter the political landscape.

Pat Robertson A Southern Baptist minister and television evangelist who ran for president in 1988 and in 1989 founded the conservative religious interest group the Christian Coalition.

patron A person who finances a group or individual activity.

patronage Jobs, grants, or other special favors that are given as rewards to friends and political allies for their support.

Pendleton Act Reform measure that established the principle of federal employment on the basis of open, competitive exams and created the Civil Service Commission.

***Planned Parenthood of Southeastern Pennsylvania* v. *Casey* (1992)** The Supreme Court's decision in this abortion case replaced the strict scrutiny standard of *Roe* with the less stringent undue burden standard.

***Plessy* v. *Ferguson* (1896)** Supreme Court case that challenged a Louisiana statute requiring that railroads provide separate accommodations for blacks and whites; the Court found that separate-but-equal accommodations did not violate the equal protection clause of the Fourteenth Amendment.

pluralist theory The theory that political power is distributed among a wide array of diverse and competing interest groups.

plurality opinion A type of judicial opinion, the reasoning of which is agreed to by fewer than a majority of judges on a court; although it resolves the particular case, the opinion does not establish a binding precedent.

pocket veto If Congress adjourns during the ten days the president has to consider a bill passed by both houses of Congress, the bill is considered vetoed without the president's signature.

policy adoption The approval of a policy proposal by people with the requisite authority, such as a legislature.

policy coordinating committees (PCCs) Committees created at the sub-Cabinet level to facilitate interactions between agencies and departments to handle complex policy problems.

policy evaluation The process of determining whether a course of action is achieving its intended goals.

policy formulation The crafting of proposed courses of action to resolve public problems.

policy implementation The process of carrying out public policy.

political action committee (PAC) Officially recognized fundraising organization that represents interest groups and is allowed by federal law to make contributions directly to candidates' campaigns.

political culture Commonly shared attitudes, behaviors, and core values about how government should operate.

political ideology The coherent set of values and beliefs about the purpose and scope of government held by groups and individuals.

political machine An organized group that may include office holders, candidates, activists, and voters who pursue their common interests by gaining and exercising power through the electoral process.

political party An organized group that may include office holders, candidates, activists, and voters who pursue their common interests by gaining and exercising power through the electoral process.

political socialization The process through which individuals acquire their political beliefs and values.

politico An elected representative who acts as a trustee or as a delegate, depending on the issue.

politics The study of who gets what, when, and how—or how policy decisions are made.

poll taxes Taxes levied in many southern states and localities that had to be paid before an eligible voter could cast a ballot.

pollster A campaign consultant who conducts public opinion surveys.

population The entire group of people whose attitudes a researcher wishes to measure.

pork Legislation that allows representatives to bring money and jobs to their districts in the form of public works programs, military bases, or other programs.

positive ad Advertising on behalf of a candidate that stresses the candidate's qualifications, family, and issue positions, with no direct reference to the opponent.

precedent A prior judicial decision that serves as a rule for settling subsequent cases of a similar nature.

president pro tempore The official chair of the Senate; usually the most senior member of the majority party.

president The chief executive officer of the United States, as established by Article II of the U.S. Constitution.

presidential coattails When successful presidential candidates carry into office congressional candidates of the same party in the year of their election.

Presidential Succession Act A 1947 law enacted by Congress that provides for the filling of any simultaneous vacancy of the presidency and vice presidency.

press briefing A relatively restricted session between a press secretary or aide and the press.

press conference An unrestricted session between an elected official and the press.

press release A document offering an official comment or position.

press secretary The individual charged with interacting and communicating with journalists on a daily basis.

primary election Election in which voters decide which of the candidates within a party will represent the party in the general election.

prior restraint Constitutional doctrine that prevents the government from prohibiting speech or publication before the fact; generally held to be in violation of the First Amendment.

privileges and immunities clause Part of Article IV of the Constitution guaranteeing that the citizens of each state are afforded the same rights as citizens of all other states.

programmatic requests Federal funds designated for special projects within a state or congressional district. Also referred to as earmarks.

Progressive Era (1890–1920) A period of widespread activism to reform political, economic, and social ills in the United States.

progressive federalism A pragmatic approach to federalism that views relations between national and state governments as both coercive and cooperative.

Progressive movement A broad group of political and social activists from the 1890s to the 1920s who opposed corruption in government, supported regulation of monopolies, and sought improvement of socioeconomic conditions.

proportional representation A voting system that apportions legislative seats according to the percentage of the vote won by a particular political party.

prospective judgment A voter's evaluation of a candidate based on what he or she pledges to do about an issue if elected.

protectionism A trade policy wherein a country takes steps to limit the import of foreign goods through tariffs and subsidies to domestic firms.

public funds Donations from general tax revenues to the campaigns of qualifying presidential candidates.

public interest group An organization that seeks a collective good that if achieved will not selectively and materially benefit group members.

public opinion polls Interviews or surveys with samples of citizens that are used to estimate the feelings and beliefs of the entire population.

public opinion What the public thinks about a particular issue or set of issues at any point in time.

public policy An intentional course of action or inaction followed by government in dealing with some problem or matter of concern.

push polls Polls taken for the purpose of providing information on an opponent that would lead respondents to vote against that candidate.

random sampling A method of poll selection that gives each person in a group the same chance of being selected.

rational basis standard of review A standard of review in which the Court determines whether any rational foundation for the discrimination exists. Legislation affecting individuals based on age, wealth, or mental capacity is generally given this level of review.

Reagan Doctrine The Reagan administration's commitment to ending communism by providing military assistance to anti-communist groups.

reapportionment The reallocation of the number of seats in the House of Representatives after each decennial census.

recall An election in which voters can remove an incumbent from office prior to the next scheduled election.

recession A decline in the economy that occurs as investment sags, production falls off, and unemployment increases.

reconciliation A procedure that allows consideration of controversial issues affecting the budget by limiting debate to twenty hours, thereby ending threat of a filibuster.

Reconstruction The period from 1865–1877 after the Civil War in which the U.S. militarily occupied and dominated the eleven former states of the Confederacy.

redistributive policies Public policies that transfer resources from one group to assist another group.

redistricting The process of redrawing congressional districts to reflect increases or decreases in seats allotted to the states, as well as population shifts within a state.

referendum An election whereby the state legislature submits proposed legislation or state constitutional amendments to the voters for approval.

regulations Rules governing the operation of all government programs that have the force of law.

regulatory policies Public policies that limit the activities of individuals and corporations or prohibit certain types of unacceptable behavior.

republic A government rooted in the consent of the governed; a representative or indirect democracy.

reserve requirements Government requirements that a portion of member banks' deposits be retained as backing for their loans.

reserved powers Powers reserved to the states by the Tenth Amendment that lie at the foundation of a state's right to legislate for the public health and welfare of its citizens.

retrospective judgment A voter's evaluation of a candidate based on past performance on a particular issue.

Richard M. Nixon The thirty-seventh president, a Republican, who served from 1969 to 1974. Nixon advocated détente during the Cold War and resigned rather than face impeachment and likely removal from office due to the Watergate scandal.

right of rebuttal The rule that requires broadcast stations to give individuals the right to have the opportunity to respond to personal attacks made on a radio or TV broadcast.

right to privacy The right to be left alone; a judicially created principle encompassing a variety of individual actions protected by the penumbras cast by several constitutional amendments, including the First, Third, Fourth, Ninth, and Fourteenth Amendments.

Roe v. Wade (1973) A case where the Supreme Court found that a woman's right to an abortion was protected by the right to privacy that could be implied from specific guarantees found in the Bill of Rights applied to the states through the Fourteenth Amendment.

Roger B. Taney Supreme Court Chief Justice who served from 1835–1864. Taney supported slavery and states' rights in the pre-Civil War era.

Roger Williams Seventeenth century religious and political leader who was expelled by Puritans in Massachusetts and then established the colony of Providence Plantations that later became Rhode Island.

Ronald Reagan Fortieth president of the United States, a Republican, who served from 1981 to 1989. Reagan led the nation through the end of the Cold War and his leadership led to a national shift toward political conservatism.

Roosevelt Corollary Concept developed by President Theodore Roosevelt early in the twentieth century declaring that it was the responsibility of the United States to ensure stability in Latin America and the Caribbean.

Rosa Parks A leading civil rights activist of the twentieth century. Parks was most notably involved with the Montgomery Bus Boycott.

rule making A quasi-legislative process resulting in regulations that have the characteristics of a legislative act.

Rule of Four At least four justices of the Supreme Court must vote to consider a case before it can be heard.

runoff primary A second primary election between the two candidates receiving the greatest number of votes in the first primary.

sample A subset of the whole population selected to be questioned for the purposes of prediction or gauging opinion.

sampling error Errors resulting from the size or the quality of a survey sample.

Samuel Adams Cousin of President John Adams and an early leader against the British and loyalist oppressors; he played a key role in developing the Committees of Correspondence and was active in Massachusetts and colonial politics.

Sandra Day O'Connor An Associate Justice of the Supreme Court from 1981–2005 who was appointed by President Ronald Reagan as the first woman to serve on the Court.

secession A unilateral assertion of independence by a geographic region within a country. The eleven Southern states making up the Confederacy during the Civil War seceded from the United States.

Second Continental Congress Meeting that convened in Philadelphia on May 10, 1775, at which it was decided that an army should be raised and George Washington of Virginia was named commander in chief.

secular realignment The gradual rearrangement of party coalitions, based more on demographic shifts than on shocks to the political system.

sedition laws Laws that make it illegal to speak or write any political criticism that threaten to diminish respect for the government, its laws, or public officials. State sedition laws were overturned as a result of the 1925 *Gitlow* Supreme Court decision.

select (or special) committee Temporary committee appointed for a specific purpose.

selective incorporation   A judicial doctrine whereby most, but not all, protections found in the Bill of Rights are made applicable to the states via the Fourteenth Amendment.

senatorial courtesy   A process by which presidents generally allow senators from the state in which a judicial vacancy occurs to block a nomination by simply registering their objection.

Seneca Falls Convention   The first major feminist meeting, held in New York State in 1848, which produced the historic "Declaration of Sentiments" calling for voting rights for women.

seniority   Time of continuous service on a committee.

separate-but-equal doctrine   The central tenet of the *Plessy v. Ferguson* decision that claimed that separate accommodations for blacks and whites did not violate the Constitution. This doctrine was used by Southern states to pass widespread discriminatory legislation at the end of the nineteenth century.

separation of powers   A way of dividing the power of government among the legislative, executive, and judicial branches, each staffed separately, with equality and independence of each branch ensured by the Constitution.

September 11th   A terrorist plot carried out on September 11, 2001 that used hijacked civilian aircraft to attack the World Trade Center in New York and the Pentagon near Washington, D.C.

Seventeenth Amendment   Amendment to the U.S. Constitution that made senators directly elected by the people, removing their selection by state legislatures.

Shays's Rebellion   A rebellion in which an army of 1,500 disgruntled and angry farmers led by Daniel Shays marched to Springfield, Massachusetts, and forcibly restrained the state court from foreclosing mortgages on their farms.

signing statements   Occasional written comments attached to a bill signed by the president.

Sixteenth Amendment   Amendment to the U.S. Constitution that authorized Congress to enact a national income tax.

Sixth Amendment   Part of the Bill of Rights that sets out the basic requirements of procedural due process for federal courts to follow in criminal trials. These include speedy and public trials, impartial juries, trials in the state where the crime was committed, notice of the charges, the right to confront and obtain favorable witnesses, and the right to counsel.

slander   Untrue spoken statements that defame the character of a person.

social capital   Cooperative relationships that facilitate the resolution of collective problems.

social conservative   One who believes that the government should support and further traditional moral teachings.

social contract theory   The belief that governments exist based on the consent of the governed.

Social Security Act   A 1935 law that established old age insurance; assistance for the needy, aged, blind, and families with dependent children; and unemployment insurance.

solicitor general   The fourth-ranking member of the Department of Justice; responsible for handling nearly all appeals on behalf of the U.S. government to the Supreme Court.

Sons and Daughters of Liberty   Loosely organized groups of patriotic American colonists who were forerunners of the revolutionaries.

Speaker of the House   The only officer of the House of Representatives specifically mentioned in the Constitution; the chamber's most powerful position; traditionally a member of the majority party.

special district   A local government that is restricted to a particular function.

spoils system   The firing of public-office holders of a defeated political party to replace them with loyalists of the newly elected party.

Stamp Act Congress   A gathering of nine colonial representatives in 1765 in New York City where a detailed list of Crown violations was drafted; first official meeting of the colonies and the first official step toward creating a unified nation.

standards of review   The levels of deference the Court gives governments to craft policies that make distinctions on the basis of personal characteristics. These standards stem from the Court's need to ensure that laws do not undermine the Fourteenth Amendment's equal protection clause.

standing committee   Committee to which proposed bills are referred; continues from one Congress to the next.

stare decisis   In court rulings, a reliance on past decisions or precedents to formulate decisions in new cases.

statist   One who believes in extensive government control of personal and economic liberties.

strategic trade policy   A trade policy wherein governments identify key industries that they wish to see grow and enact policies to support their development and success.

stratified sampling   A variation of random sampling; the population is divided into subgroups and weighted based on demographic characteristics of the national population.

straw poll   Unscientific survey used to gauge public opinion on a variety of issues and policies.

strict constructionist   An approach to constitutional interpretation that emphasizes interpreting the Constitution as it was originally written and intended by the Framers.

strict scrutiny   A heightened standard of review used by the Supreme Court to determine the constitutional validity of a challenged practice. Legislation affecting the fundamental freedoms of speech, assembly, religion, and the press as well as suspect classifications are automatically accorded this level of review.

substantive due process   Judicial interpretation of the Fifth and Fourteenth Amendments' due process clauses. Protects citizens from arbitrary or unjust state or federal laws.

suffrage movement   The drive for voting rights for women that took place in the United States in the nineteenth and early twentieth centuries until ratification of the Nineteenth Amendment in 1920.

super PAC   Political action committees established to make independent expenditures.

superdelegate   Delegate to the Democratic Party's national convention that is reserved for a party official and whose vote at the convention is unpledged to a candidate.

supremacy clause   Portion of Article VI of the Constitution mandating that national law is supreme over (that is, supersedes) all other laws passed by the states or by any other subdivision of government.

Susan B. Anthony   Nineteenth century feminist, suffragist, and founder of the National Woman Suffrage Association with Elizabeth Cady Stanton. Anthony later formed the National American Woman Suffrage Association (NAWSA) which along with the National Woman's Party (NWP) helped to ensure ratification of the Nineteenth Amendment.

suspect classifications   Category or class, such as race or a fundamental freedom, that triggers the highest standard of scrutiny from the Supreme Court.

symbolic speech   Symbols, signs, and other methods of expression generally considered to be protected by the First Amendment.

systemic agenda   A set of of issues to be discussed or given attention; it consists of all public issues viewed as requiring governmental attention.

tariffs   Taxes on imported goods.

Tenth Amendment   The final part of the Bill of Rights that defines the basic principle of American federalism in

stating that the powers not delegated to the national government are reserved to the states or to the people.

The Crown v. Zenger **(1735)**   Legal case in the colony of New York that is considered a precursor to free press provisions in the Constitution. The case did not set legal precedent, but did reflect a difference between British authorities and colonists with regard to press freedoms.

The Federalist Papers   A series of eighty-five political essays written by Alexander Hamilton, James Madison, and John Jay in support of ratification of the U.S. Constitution.

The Grange   Founded in 1867 as an educational organization for farmers, The Grange evolved into the first truly national interest group by working to protect the political and economic concerns of farming communities and rural areas.

Thirteenth Amendment   One of three major amendments ratified after the Civil War; specifically bans slavery in the United States.

Thomas Hooker   Colonial-era politician who supported expanded voting rights.

Thomas Jefferson   Principle drafter of the Declaration of Independence; second vice president of the United States; third president of the United States from 1801 to 1809. Co-founder of the Democratic-Republican Party created to oppose Federalists.

Thomas Paine   The influential writer of *Common Sense*, a pamphlet that advocated for independence from Great Britain.

Three-Fifths Compromise   Agreement reached at the Constitutional Convention stipulating that three-fifths of the total slave population of each state was to be for purposes of determining population for representation in the U.S. House of Representatives.

Thurgood Marshall   A leading civil rights lawyer and the first head of the NAACP's Legal Defense and Educational Fund. Marshall was the first African American appointed to the Supreme Court and served on the Court from 1967 until 1991.

Title IX   Provision of the Education Amendments of 1972 that bars educational institutions that receive federal funds from discriminating against female students.

totalitarianism   A form of government in which power resides in leaders who rule by force in their own self-interest and without regard to rights and liberties.

tracking polls   Continuous surveys that enable a campaign or news organization to chart a candidate's daily or weekly rise or fall in support.

trade association   A group that represents a specific industry.

Trans-Pacific Partnership (TPP)   A proposed agreement between the U.S. and eleven other nations on the Pacific Rim intended to substantially lower tariffs and protect intellectual property.

transactions theory   The theory that public policies are the result of narrowly defined exchanges or transactions among political actors.

trial court   Court of original jurisdiction where cases begin.

Truman Doctrine   U.S. anti-communist policy initiated in 1947 that became the basis of U.S. foreign policy throughout the Cold War.

trustee   Role played by an elected representative who listens to constituents' opinions and then uses his or her best judgment to make a final decision.

turnout   The proportion of the voting-age public that casts a ballot.

Twenty-Fifth Amendment   Adopted in 1967 to establish procedures for filling vacancies in the office of president and vice president as well as providing for procedures to deal with the disability of a president.

Twenty-Second Amendment   Adopted in 1951; prevents presidents from serving more than two terms, or more than ten years if they attain office via the death, resignation, or removal of their predecessor.

U.S. Chamber of Commerce   A major pro-business lobbying group founded in 1912.

***U.S. v. Nixon* (1974)**   Supreme Court ruling on power of the president, holding that no absolute constitutional executive privilege allows a president to refuse to comply with a court order to produce information needed in a criminal trial.

UN Security Council   A principal part of the United Nations, charged with authorizing peacekeeping operations, international sanctions, and military action in order to maintain global peace and security.

unconventional political participation   Activism that attempts to influence the political process through unusual or extreme measures, such as protests, boycotts, and picketing.

undue burden test   A standard set by the Supreme Court, in the *Casey* case in 1992 that narrowed *Roe* v. *Wade* and allowed for greater regulation of abortion by the states.

unified government   The political condition in which the same political party controls the presidency and Congress.

unitary system   System of government in which the local and regional governments derive all authority from a strong national government.

United Nations   A multilateral diplomatic organization founded in 1945 and continuing today that is intended to promote peaceful resolution of international disputes and advance human development worldwide; the United States is a founding member.

***United States* v. *Windsor* (2013)**   A Supreme Court ruling striking down the 1996 Defense of Marriage Act (DOMA), which prohibited federal recognition of same-sex marriages.

veto   The formal, constitutional authority of the president to reject bills passed by both houses of Congress, thus preventing them from becoming law without further congressional action.

vice president   An officer created by Article II of the U.S. Constitution to preside over the U.S. Senate and to fill any vacancy in the office of president due to death, resignation, removal, or (since 1967) disability.

Vietnam War   A civil war in which the United States supported the South Vietnamese regime against Communist forces in North Vietnam, which escalated through the 1960s before ending in 1975.

Virginia Plan   A proposed framework for the Constitution favoring large states. It called for a bicameral legislature, which would appoint executive and judicial officers.

voter canvass   The process by which a campaign reaches individual voters, either by door-to-door solicitation or by telephone.

vouchers   Certificates issued by the government that may be applied toward the cost of attending private or other public schools.

War Powers Resolution   Passed by Congress in 1973; requires the authorization of Congress to deploy troops overseas and limits the time of their deployment.

Warren Court   The period in Supreme Court history during which Earl Warren served as Chief Justice (1953–1969), noted for its many rulings expanding civil liberties and civil rights.

Warren E. Burger   The fifteenth Chief Justice of the United States who served from 1969 to 1986 and who led the Court in an increasingly conservative direction.

Watergate   A scandal in the early 1970s involving a break-in at the Democratic National Committee offices in the Watergate office complex. The involvement of members of the Nixon administration and subsequent cover-up attempts led to President Richard Nixon's resignation from office and jail sentences for some members of his administration.

whip   Party leader who keeps close contact with all members of his or her party, takes vote counts on key legislation, prepares summaries of bills, and acts as a communications link within a party.

Whiskey Rebellion A civil insurrection in 1794 that was put down by military forces led by President George Washington, thereby confirming the power of the new national government.

Whole Woman's Health **v.** *Hellerstedt* **(2016)** Supreme Court abortion ruling that struck down state law provisions in Texas as presenting an undue burden on women seeking abortions. This decision invalidated numerous state and local laws that imposed similar limitations on clinics.

William Penn Quaker leader and supporter of religious tolerance who founded Pennsylvania.

winner-take-all system An electoral system in which the party that receives at least one more vote than any other party wins the election.

Women's Christian Temperance Union (WCTU) A public interest group created in 1874 with the goal of outlawing the sale of liquor. Its activities included prayer groups, protest marches, lobbying, and the destruction of saloons.

World Bank International governmental organization created to provide loans for large economic development projects.

World Trade Organization (WTO) An international organization that replaced GATT in 1995 to supervise and expand international trade.

World War I A global military conflict that took place from 1914–1918 across Europe and its overseas territories. The United States militarily intervened from 1917–1918.

World War II A global military conflict from 1939–1945 in Europe, Africa, Asia, and the Pacific region, in which the United States was engaged from 1941–1945.

writ of *certiorari* A request for the Supreme Court to order up the records from a lower court to review the case.

writ of *habeas corpus* Petition requesting that a judge order authorities to prove that a prisoner is being held lawfully and that allows the prisoner to be freed if the government's case does not persuade the judge. *Habeas corpus* rights imply that prisoners have a right to know what charges are being made against them.

yellow journalism A form of newspaper publishing in vogue in the late nineteenth century that featured pictures, comics, color, and sensationalized news coverage.

Chapter 1

1. Susan A. MacManus, *Young v. Old: Generational Combat in the 21st Century* (Boulder, CO: Westview, 1995), 3.

2. Gina Kolata, "Rise in Deaths for U.S. Whites in Middle Age," *New York Times* (November 3, 2015): A1; Sabrina Tavernise, "Sweeping Pain as Suicides Hit a 30-Year High," *New York Times* (April 22, 2016): A1.

3. Peter Monseau, "The Muslims of Early America," New York Times (February 9, 2015): A17.

4. James B. Gimpel and Kimberly A. Karnes, "The Rural Side of the Urban-Rural Gap," *PS: Political Science and Politics* (July 2006): 467–72.

5. CNN Exit Polls, http://www.cnn.com/election/2012/results/race/president#exit-polls.

6. U.S. Census Bureau, *2014 Statistical Abstract of the United States.*

7. *Obergefell* v. *Hodges*, 576 U.S.____ (2015).

Chapter 2

1. See Richard B. Bernstein with Jerome Agel, *Amending America* (New York: New York Times Books, 1993), 138–40.

2. *Oregon* v. *Mitchell*, 400 U.S. 112 (1970).

3. Bernstein with Agel, *Amending America*, 139.

4. For an account of the early development of the colonies, see D. W. Meining, *The Shaping of America*, vol. 1: *Atlantic America, 1492–1800* (New Haven, CT: Yale University Press, 1986).

5. For an excellent chronology of the events leading up to the writing of the Declaration of Independence and the colonists' break with Great Britain, see Calvin D. Lonton, ed., *The Bicentennial Almanac* (Nashville, TN: Thomas Nelson, 1975).

6. See Garry Wills, *Inventing America: Jefferson's Declaration of Independence* (New York: Random House, 1978). Wills argues that the Declaration was signed solely to secure foreign aid for the ongoing war effort.

7. See Gordon S. Wood, *The Creation of the American Republic, 1776–1787*, reissue ed. (New York: Norton, 1993).

8. John Fiske, *The Critical Period of American History* (Boston: Houghton Mifflin, 1988).

9. Charles A. Beard, *An Economic Interpretation of the Constitution of the United States*, reissue ed. (Mineola, NY: Dover, 2004).

10. Quoted in Richard N. Current, et al., *American History: A Survey*, 6th ed. (New York: Knopf, 1983), 170.

11. John Patrick Diggins, "Power and Authority in American History: The Case of Charles A. Beard and His Critics," *American Historical Review* 86 (October 1981): 701–30; and Robert Brown, *Charles Beard and the Constitution: A Critical Analysis of An Economic Interpretation of the Constitution* (Princeton, NJ: Princeton University Press, 1956).

12. Wood, *The Creation of the American Republic.*

13. For more on the political nature of compromise at the convention, see Calvin C. Jillson, *Constitution Making: Conflict and Consensus in the Federal Constitution of 1787* (New York: Agathon, 1988).

14. Quoted in Current, et al., *American History*, 168.

15. Bernard Bailyn, *The Ideological Origins of the American Revolution* (Cambridge, MA: Belknap Press, 1967).

16. Richard E. Neustadt, *Presidential Power: The Politics of Leadership from FDR to Carter* (New York: Macmillan, 1980), 26.

17. Federal Republicans favored a republican or representative form of government (do not confuse this term with the modern Republican Party, which came into being in 1854). Ultimately, the word federal referred to the form of government embodied in the new Constitution, and confederation referred to a "league of states," as under the Articles, and later was applied in the "Confederacy" of 1861–1865 that governed the southern states.

18. See Ralph Ketcham, ed., *The Anti-Federalist Papers and the Constitutional Debates* (New York: New American Library, 1986).

19. See Herbert J. Storing, *What the Anti-Federalists Were For* (Chicago: University of Chicago Press, 1981), for a fuller discussion of Anti-Federalist views.

20. See Jane J. Mansbridge, *Why We Lost the ERA* (Chicago: University of Chicago Press, 1986).

21. *Marbury* v. *Madison*, 5 U.S. 137 (1803).

22. See, for example, the speech by Attorney General Edwin Meese III before the American Bar Association, July 9, 1985, Washington, DC. See also Antonin Scalia and Amy Gutman, eds., *A Matter of Interpretation: Federal Courts and the Law* (Princeton, NJ: Princeton University Press, 1998).

23. See, for example, the speech by Associate Justice William J. Brennan Jr. at Georgetown University Text and Teaching Symposium, October 10, 1985, Washington, DC.

24. *Riley* v. *California*, ____ U.S. ____ (2014).

Chapter 3

1. *Missouri* v. *Holland*, 252 U.S. 416 (1920).
2. John Mountjoy, "Interstate Cooperation: Interstate Compacts Make a Comeback," Council of State Governments, www.csg.org.
3. *McCulloch* v. *Maryland*, 17 U.S. 316 (1819).
4. *Gibbons* v. *Ogden*, 22 U.S. 1 (1824).
5. For more on *Gibbons*, see Thomas H. Cox, Gibbons *v.* Ogden: *Law and Society in the Early Republic* (Athens, OH: Ohio University Press, 2010).
6. *Barron* v. *Baltimore*, 32 U.S. 243 (1833).
7. For more on *Barron*, see Brendan J. Doherty, "Interpreting the Bill of Rights and the Nature of Federalism: *Barron* v. *City of Baltimore*." *Journal of Supreme Court History* 32 (2007): 211–28.
8. *Dred Scott* v. *Sandford*, 60 U.S. 393 (1857).
9. *Pensacola Telegraph* v. *Western Union*, 96 U.S. 1 (1877).
10. John O. McGinnis, "The State of Federalism," Testimony before the Senate Government Affairs Committee, May 5, 1999.
11. Jeff Shesol, *Supreme Power: Franklin Roosevelt* vs. *the Supreme Court* (New York: W.W. Norton, 2010).
12. *NLRB* v. *Jones and Laughlin Steel Co.*, 301 U.S. 1 (1937).
13. *Wickard* v. *Filburn*, 317 U.S. 111 (1942).
14. Peter Harkness, "What Brand of Federalism Is Next?" *Governing* (January 2012): http://www.governing.com/columns/potomac-chronicle/gov-col-what-brand-of-federalism-is-next.html.
15. *New State Ice Co.* v. *Liebmann*, 285 U.S. 262 (1932).
16. Richard P. Nathan, Fred C. Doolittle, and Associates, *Reagan and the States* (Princeton, NJ: Princeton University Press, 1987), 4.
17. Citizens Against Government Waste, *2016 Congressional Pig Book* (cagw.org)
18. Linda Greenhouse, "The Rehnquist Court and Its Imperiled States' Rights Legacy," *New York Times* (June 12, 2005): A3.
19. *Arizona* v. *United States*, 567 U.S. ____ (2012) and *National Federation of Independent Business* v. *Sebelius*, 567 U.S.____ (2012).

Chapter 4

1. The absence of a bill of rights led Mason to refuse to sign the proposed Constitution, noting that he "would sooner chop off his right hand than put it to the Constitution as it now stands." Quoted in Eric Black, *Our Constitution: The Myth That Binds Us* (Boulder, CO: Westview, 1988), 75.
2. Quoted in Jack N. Rakove, "Madison Won Passage of the Bill of Rights but Remained a Skeptic," *Public Affairs Report* (March 1991): 6.

3. *Barron* v. *Baltimore*, 32 U.S. 243 (1833).
4. *Allgeyer* v. *Louisiana*, 165 U.S. 578 (1897).
5. *Gitlow* v. *New York*, 268 U.S. 652 (1925).
6. *Near* v. *Minnesota*, 283 U.S. 697 (1931). For more about *Near*, see Fred W. Friendly, *Minnesota Rag: The Dramatic Story of the Landmark Case That Gave New Meaning to Freedom of the Press* (New York: Random House, 1981).
7. *Palko* v. *Connecticut*, 302 U.S. 319 (1937).
8. *Benton* v. *Maryland*, 395 U.S. 784 (1969).
9. *Cantwell* v. *Connecticut*, 310 U.S. 296 (1940).
10. *Lemon* v. *Kurtzman*, 403 U.S. 602 (1971).
11. *Engel* v. *Vitale*, 370 U.S. 421 (1962).
12. *Abington School District* v. *Schempp*, 374 U.S. 203 (1963).
13. *Lee* v. *Weisman*, 505 U.S. 577 (1992).
14. *Widmar* v. *Vincent*, 454 U.S. 263 (1981).
15. *Mitchell* v. *Helms*, 530 U.S. 793 (2000).
16. *Zelman* v. *Simmons-Harris*, 536 U.S. 639 (2002).
17. *Rosenberger* v. *University of Virginia*, 515 U.S. 819 (1995) and *Christian Legal Society* v. *Martinez*, 561 U.S. ____ (2010).
18. *McCreary County* v. *ACLU of Kentucky*, 545 U.S. 844 (2005).
19. *Salazar* v. *Buono*, 559 U.S. ____ (2010).
20. *U.S.* v. *Seeger*, 380 U.S. 163 (1965).
21. *O'Lone* v. *Estate of Shabazz*, 482 U.S. 342 (1987).
22. The Religious Freedom Restoration Act (RFRA) of 1993 and the Religious Land Use and Institutionalized Persons Act (RLUIPA) of 2000 are two noteworthy examples.
23. *Gonzales* v. *O Centro Espirita Beneficente Unia˜o do Vegetal*, 546 U.S. 418 (2006).
24. *Ex parte Merryman*, 17 F. Cas. 144 (C.C.D. Md. 1861)
25. *Schenck* v. *U.S.*, 249 U.S. 47 (1919).
26. *Brandenburg* v. *Ohio*, 395 U.S. 444 (1969).
27. *New York Times Co.* v. *U.S.*, 403 U.S. 713 (1971).
28. *Nebraska Press Association* v. *Stuart*, 427 U.S. 539 (1976).
29. *Abrams* v. *U.S.*, 250 U.S. 616 (1919).
30. *Stromberg* v. *California*, 283 U.S. 359 (1931).
31. *Tinker* v. *Des Moines Independent Community School District*, 393 U.S. 503 (1969).
32. *Morse* v. *Frederick*, 551 U.S. 393 (2007).
33. *R.A.V.* v. *City of St. Paul*, 505 U.S. 377 (1992).
34. *Virginia* v. *Black*, 538 U.S. 343 (2003).
35. Nina Burleigh "Fightin' Words," *Newsweek* (June 3, 2016): pp. 24–33.
36. *Chaplinsky* v. *New Hampshire*, 315 U.S. 568 (1942).
37. *New York Times Co.* v. *Sullivan*, 376 U.S. 254 (1964).
38. *Hustler Magazine* v. *Falwell*, 485 U.S. 46 (1988).
39. *Chaplinsky* v. *New Hampshire*, 315 U.S. 568 (1942).
40. *Miller* v. *California*, 413 U.S. 15 (1973).
41. *Barnes* v. *Glen Theater*, 501 U.S. 560 (1991).
42. *U.S.* v. *Williams*, 553 U.S. 285 (2008).
43. *DeJonge* v. *Oregon*, 229 U.S. 353 (1937).
44. *John Doe #1* v. *Reed*, 561 U.S. ____ (2010).

45. *U.S. v. Miller*, 307 U.S. 174 (1939).
46. *D.C. v. Heller*, 554 U.S. 290 (2008).
47. *Heller v. District of Columbia*, civil action 08-1289 (2010).
48. *McDonald v. City of Chicago*, 561 U.S. ____ (2010).
49. *Johnson v. U.S.*, 333 U.S. 10 (1948).
50. *Fernandez v. California*, ____ U.S.____ (2014).
51. *Carroll v. U.S.*, 267 U.S. 132 (1925).
52. *U.S. v. Arvizu*, 534 U.S. 266 (2002).
53. *South Dakota v. Neville*, 459 U.S. 553 (1983).
54. *Arizona v. Gant*, 556 U.S. 332 (2009).
55. *United States v. Jones*, 564 U.S. ____ (2012).
56. *U.S. v. Sokolov*, 490 U.S. 1 (1989).
57. *Hester v. U.S.*, 265 U.S. 57 (1924).
58. *Michigan v. Tyler*, 436 U.S. 499 (1978).
59. *Counselman v. Hitchcock*, 142 U.S. 547 (1892).
60. *Brown v. Mississippi*, 297 U.S. 278 (1936).
61. *Lynum v. Illinois*, 372 U.S. 528 (1963).
62. *Miranda v. Arizona*, 384 U.S. 436 (1966).
63. *Rhode Island v. Innis*, 446 U.S. 291 (1980).
64. *Arizona v. Fulminante*, 499 U.S. 279 (1991).
65. *Weeks v. U.S.*, 232 U.S. 383 (1914).
66. *Mapp v. Ohio*, 367 U.S. 643 (1961).
67. *Stone v. Powell*, 428 U.S. 465 (1976).
68. *Powell v. Alabama*, 287 U.S. 45 (1932).
69. *Johnson v. Zerbst*, 304 U.S. 458 (1938).
70. *Gideon v. Wainwright*, 372 U.S. 335 (1963).
71. *Argersinger v. Hamlin*, 407 U.S. 25 (1972).
72. *Rothgery v. Gillespie County*, 554 U.S. 191 (2008).
73. *Rompilla v. Beard*, 545 U.S. 374 (2005).
74. *Hernandez v. Texas*, 347 U.S. 475 (1954).
75. *Batson v. Kentucky*, 476 U.S. 79 (1986).
76. *J.E.B. v. Alabama*, 511 U.S. 127 (1994).
77. *Maryland v. Craig*, 497 U.S. 836 (1990).
78. *Hallinger v. Davis*, 146 U.S. 314 (1892).
79. *O'Neil v. Vermont*, 144 U.S. 323 (1892).
80. *Montgomery v. Louisiana*, Docket No. 14-280, __U.S.__ (2016).
81. See Michael Meltsner, *Cruel and Unusual: The Supreme Court and Capital Punishment* (New York: Random House, 1973).
82. *Furman v. Georgia*, 408 U.S. 238 (1972).
83. *Gregg v. Georgia*, 428 U.S. 153 (1976).
84. *McCleskey v. Kemp*, 481 U.S. 279 (1987).
85. *McCleskey v. Zant*, 499 U.S. 467 (1991).
86. *Baze v. Rees*, 553 U.S. 35 (2008).
87. *Atkins v. Virginia*, 536 U.S. 304 (2002); and *Roper v. Simmons*, 543 U.S. 551 (2005).
88. *Skinner v. Switzer*, 562 U.S. ____ (2011).
89. *House v. Bell*, 547 U.S. 518 (2006).
90. *Olmstead v. U.S.*, 277 U.S. 438 (1928).
91. *Griswold v. Connecticut*, 381 U.S. 481 (1965).
92. *Eisenstadt v. Baird*, 410 U.S. 113 (1972).
93. *Roe v. Wade*, 410 U.S. 113 (1973).
94. *Beal v. Doe*, 432 U.S. 438 (1977); and *Harris v. McRae*, 448 U.S. 297 (1980).
95. *Webster v. Reproductive Health Services*, 492 U.S. 490 (1989).
96. *Planned Parenthood of Southeastern Pennsylvania v. Casey*, 505 U.S. 833 (1992).
97. *Whole Woman's Health v. Hellerstedt* ____ U.S. ____ (2016).
98. *Bowers v. Hardwick*, 478 U.S. 186 (1986); and *Lawrence v. Texas*, 539 U.S. 558 (2003).
99. Jennifer Levin, "Alternative Reality About Public War," *Associated Press* (May 29, 2007).
100. "Surveillance Under the USA Patriot Act," American Civil Liberties Union, April 3, 2003.
101. *Boumediene v. Bush*, 553 U.S. 723 (2008).
102. *Hamdan v. Rumsfeld*, 548 U.S. 557 (2006).
103. Charlie Savage, "Appeals Court Allows Challenges by Inmates at Guantanamo Prison," *New York Times* (February 11, 2014): A15.
104. Shane Scott, David Johnston, and James Risen, "Secret U.S. Endorsement of Severe Interrogations," *New York Times* (October 7, 2007): A1.
105. Jennifer Loven and Devlin Barrett, "CIA Officials Won't Be Prosecuted for Waterboarding, Obama Admin Says," *Huffington Post* (April 16, 2009), www.huffingtonpost.com.
106. "Donald Trump Renews Support for Waterboarding at Ohio Rally: 'I like it a lot'," *The Guardian* (June 28, 2016).
107. "Donald Trump on Terrorists: 'Take out their families.'" CNN Politics.com; CNN.com 12/2/2015; "Donald Trump 2016: We to take out ISIL members' families." *POLITICO*, Dec. 2, 2015.
108. Jackobson, Louis. "Geneva Conventions bar Donald Trump's idea of killing terrorists' families, as Rand Paul says." *POLITIFACT*, Dec. 17, 2015.

Chapter 5

1. Civil Rights Cases, 109 U.S. 3 (1883).
2. *Plessy v. Ferguson*, 163 U.S. 537 (1896).
3. Jack Greenberg, *Judicial Process and Social Change: Constitutional Litigation* (St. Paul, MN: West, 1976), 583–86.
4. *Williams v. Mississippi*, 170 U.S. 213 (1898); and *Cummins v. Richmond County Board of Education*, 175 U.S. 528 (1899).
5. *Missouri* ex rel. *Gaines v. Canada*, 305 U.S. 337 (1938).
6. *McLaurin v. Oklahoma State Regents*, 339 U.S. 637 (1950).
7. *Sweatt v. Painter*, 339 U.S. 629 (1950); and *McLaurin v. Oklahoma*, 339 U.S. 637 (1950).
8. *Sweatt v. Painter*, 339 U.S. 629 (1950).
9. *Brown v. Board of Education*, 347 U.S. 483 (1954).
10. But see Gerald Rosenberg, *The Hollow Hope: Can Courts Bring About Social Change?* (Chicago: University of Chicago Press, 1991).

11. Quoted in Williams, *Eyes on the Prize*, 10.

12. Michael McCann, "Reform Litigation on Trial." *Law and Social Inquiry* 17(1992): 715–43.

13. *Brown v. Board of Education II*, 349 U.S. 294 (1955).

14. Quoted in Williams, *Eyes on the Prize*, 37.

15. *Cooper v. Aaron*, 358 U.S. 1 (1958).

16. *Heart of Atlanta Motel v. U.S.*, 379 U.S. 241 (1964).

17. Jo Freeman, *The Politics of Women's Liberation* (New York: Longman, 1975), 57.

18. Betty Friedan, *The Feminine Mystique* (New York: Dell, 1963).

19. *Meritor Savings Bank v. Vinson*, 477 U.S. 57 (1986).

20. *Oncale v. Sundowner Offshore Services, Inc.*, 523 U.S. 75 (1998).

21. *Hishon v. King & Spalding*, 467 U.S. 69 (1984).

22. *Johnson v. Transportation Agency*, 480 U.S. 616 (1987).

23. Danielle Paquette, "Male-female Wage Gap Significantly Widening for Young Workers, Study Shows," *Washington Post* (April 29, 2016): A14.

24. Joyce Gelb and Marian Lief Palley, *Women and Public Policies* (Charlottesville: University of Virginia Press, 1996).

25. *Davis v. Monroe County Board of Education*, 526 U.S. 629 (1999).

26. *Jackson v. Birmingham Board of Education*, 544 U.S. 167 (2005).

27. Alixandra B. Yanus and Karen O'Connor, "To Comply or Not to Comply: Evaluating Compliance with Title IX of the Educational Amendments of 1972," *Journal of Women, Politics & Policy* 37 (2016): 341–358.

28. *Hernandez v. Texas*, 347 U.S. 475 (1954).

29. *White v. Register*, 412 U.S. 755 (1973).

30. *San Antonio Independent School District v. Rodriguez*, 411 U.S. 1 (1973).

31. *Edgewood Independent School District v. Kirby*, 777 S.W.2d 391 Texas 1989.

32. "MALDEF Pleased with Settlement of California Public Schools Inequity Case, *Williams v. California*," August 13, 2004: www.maldef.org.

33. Roger Daniels, *Asian America: Chinese and Japanese in the United States Since 1850* (Seattle: University of Washington Press, 1988).

34. *Yick Wo v. Hopkins*, 118 U.S. 356 (1886).

35. *Ozawa v. U.S.*, 260 U.S. 178 (1922).

36. Diane Helene Miller, *Freedom to Differ: The Shaping of the Gay and Lesbian Struggle for Civil Rights* (New York: New York University Press, 1998).

37. Sarah Brewer et al., "Sex and the Supreme Court: Gays, Lesbians, and Justice," in Craig A. Rimmerman, Kenneth D. Wald, and Clyde Wilcox, eds., *The Politics of Gay Rights* (Chicago: University of Chicago Press, 2000): 377–408.

38. Evan Gerstmann, *The Constitutional Underclass: Gays, Lesbians, and the Failure of Class-Based Equal Protection* (Chicago: University of Chicago Press, 1999).

39. *Romer v. Evans*, 517 U.S. 620 (1996).

40. Joan Biskupic, "Court's Opinion on Gay Rights Reflects Trends," *USA Today* (July 18, 2003): 2A.

41. *United States v. Windsor*, 570 U.S. 12 (2013).

42. David Pfeiffer, "Overview of the Disability Movement: History, Legislative Record and Political Implications," *Policy Studies Journal* (Winter 1993): 724–42; and "Understanding Disability Policy," *Policy Studies Journal* (Spring 1996): 157–74.

43. American Association of People with Disabilities, www.aapd.com.

44. *Korematsu v. U.S.*, 323 U.S. 214 (1944). This is the only case involving race-based distinctions applying the strict scrutiny standard where the Court has upheld the restrictive law.

45. *Grutter v. Bollinger*, 539 U.S. 306 (2003).

46. *Gratz v. Bollinger*, 539 U.S. 244 (2003).

47. *Fisher v. University of Texas*, No. 14–981 (2016).

48. *Reed v. Reed*, 404 U.S. 71 (1971).

49. *Craig v. Boren*, 429 U.S. 190 (1976).

50. *Rostker v. Goldberg*, 453 U.S. 57 (1981).

51. *Nebbia v. New York*, 291 U.S. 502 (1934).

Chapter 6

1. Charles S. Bullock III, "House Careerists: Changing Patterns of Longevity and Attrition," *American Political Science Review* 66 (December 1972): 1295–1300.

2. Richard F. Fenno Jr., "U.S. House Members in Their Constituencies: An Exploration," *American Political Science Review* 71 (September 1977): 883–917.

3. Richard F. Fenno Jr., *Home Style: House Members in Their Districts* (New York: Longman, 2009), 32; and Judy Schneider and Michael L. Koempel, *Congressional Deskbook 2005–2007: 109th Congress* (Alexandria, VA: Capital Net, 2005).

4. Conversation with Karen O'Connor, July 2015.

5. Hedrick Smith, *The Power Game* (New York: Ballantine Books, 1989), 108.

6. "Life in Congress: The Member Perspective, A Joint Research Report by the Congressional Management Foundation and the Society for Human Resource Management," accessed May 30, 2016 at: http://www.congressfoundation.org/storage/documents/CMF_Pubs/life-in-congress-the-member-perspective.pdf.

7. Ryan Grim and Sabrina Siddiqui, "Call Time for Congress Shows How Fundraising Dominates Bleak Work Life" *The Huffington Post*, January 9, 2013, accessed May 30, 2016 at: http://www.huffingtonpost.com/2013/01/08/call-time-congressional-fundraising_n_2427291.html.

8. Jennifer E. Manning, "Membership of the 113th Congress: A Profile," *Congressional Research Service Report for Congress* (January 31, 2014): http://opencrs.com.

9. Warren E. Miller and Donald Stokes, "Constituency Influence in Congress," *American Political Science Review* 57 (March 1963): 45–57.

10. Gary W. Cox and Jonathan N. Katz, "Why Did the Incumbency Advantage in U.S. House Elections Grow?" *American Journal of Political Science* 40 (May 1996): 478–97; Kenneth N. Bickers and Robert M. Stein, "The Electoral Dynamics of the Federal Pork Barrel," *American Journal of Political Science* 40 (November 1996): 1300–26; "2010 Overview: Incumbent Advantage," www.opensecrets.org; and Scott Ashworth and Ethan Bueno de Mesquita, "Electoral Selection, Strategic Challenger Entry, and the Incumbency Advantage," *Journal of Politics* 70 (October 2008): 1006–25.

11. Marjorie Randon Hershey, "Congressional Elections," in Gerald M. Pomper, et al., *The Election of 1992: Reports and Interpretations* (Chatham, NJ: Chatham House, 1993), 159.

12. "How to Rig an Election," *Economist* (April 25, 2002) 51–54.

13. *Bethune-Hill* v. *Virginia State Board of Elections*, Docket no. 15-680.

14. In *Davis* v. *Bandemer*, 478 U.S. 109 (1986), the Court found that gerrymandering was not a political question but was unable to determine a standard by which to judge constitutionality.

15. *Harris* v. *Arizona Independent Redistricting Commission*, Docket No. 14-232 (April 20, 2016).

16. *Reynolds* v. *Sims*, 377 U.S. 533 (1964).

17. *Thornburg* v. *Gingles*, 478 U.S. 30 (1986).

18. *Shaw* v. *Reno*, 509 U.S. 630 (1993).

19. *LULAC* v. *Perry*, 548 U.S. 399 (2006).

20. "What Is the Democratic Caucus?" www.dcaucusweb. house.gov.

21. Barbara Hinckley, *Stability and Change in Congress*, 3rd ed. (New York: Harper and Row, 1983), 166.

22. David R. Mayhew, "Supermajority Rule in the U.S. Senate," *PS: Political Science and Politics* 36 (January 2003): 31–36.

23. Barbara Sinclair, "The Struggle over Representation and Law-making in Congress: Leadership Reforms in the 1990s," in James A. Thurber and Roger H. Davidson, eds., *Remaking Congress: Change and Stability in the 1990s* (Washington, DC: CQ Press, 1995), 105.

24. Woodrow Wilson, *Congressional Government: A Study in American Politics* (Cambridge, MA: Riverside Press, 1885).

25. Roger H. Davidson, "Congressional Committees in the New Reform Era: From Combat to the Contract," in Thurber and Davidson, eds. *Remaking Congress*, 28.

26. Christopher Deering and Steven S. Smith, *Committees in Congress*, 3rd ed. (Washington, DC: CQ Press, 1997).

27. Wilson, *Congressional Government*.

28. "The Mysteries of the Congressional Review Act," *Harvard Law Review* 122 (June 2009): 2163–83.

29. Cindy Skrzycki, "Reform's Knockout Act, Kept Out of the Ring," *Washington Post* (April 18, 2006): D1.

30. Stuart Shapiro, "The Congressional Review Act, Rarely Used and (Almost Always) Unsuccessful," *The Hill* (April 17, 2015).

31. Quoted in Stewart M. Powell, "Lee Fight Signals Tougher Battles Ahead on Nomination," *Commercial Appeal* (December 21, 1997): A15.

32. John W. Kingdon, Congressmen's Voting Decisions, 3rd ed. (Ann Arbor: University of Michigan Press, 1989). See also Lee Sigelman, Paul J. Wahlbeck, and Emmett H. Buell Jr., "Vote Choice and the Preference for Divided Government: Lessons of 1992," *American Journal of Political Science* 41 (July 1997): 879–94.

33. Barbara S. Romzek and Jennifer A. Utter, "Congressional Legislative Staff: Political Professionals or Clerks?" *American Journal of Political Science* 41 (October 1997): 1251–79; and Michael T. Heaney, "Brokering Health Policy: Coalitions, Parties, and Interest Group Influence," *Journal of Health Politics, Policy, and Law* 31 (October 2006): 887–944.

Chapter 7

1. "Two Hundred Years of Presidential Funerals," *Washington Post* (June 10, 2004): C14.

2. Gail Russell Chaddock, "The Rise of Mourning in America," *Christian Science Monitor* (June 11, 2004): 1.

3. Richard E. Neustadt, *Presidential Power and the Modern Presidency* (New York: Free Press, 1991).

4. Edward S. Corwin, *The President: Office and Powers, 1787–1957*, 4th ed. (New York: New York University Press, 1957), 5.

5. Quoted in Corwin, *The President*, 11.

6. Reynolds Holding, "Executive Privilege Showdown," *Time* (March 21, 2007): 21–24.

7. Craig Whitlock, "Gates Says Pentagon Faces Spending 'Crisis' over Congressional Inaction," *Washington Post* (January 28, 2011): A1.

8. Benjamin I. Page and Mark P. Petracca, *The American Presidency* (New York: McGraw-Hill, 1983), 262.

9. "Treaties," United States Senate Web site, www.senate. gov.

10. D. Roderick Kiewiet and Mathew D. McCubbins, "Presidential Influence on Congressional Appropriations Decisions," *American Journal of Political Science* 32 (August 1988): 713-36.

11. Julie Hirschfeld Davis and Gardiner Harris, "Obama Issues Reductions of Sentences in Drug Cases" *New York Times* (July 14, 2015): A11.

12. Quoted in Neustadt, *Presidential Power*, 9.

13. Quoted in Paul F. Boller Jr., *Presidential Anecdotes* (New York: Penguin Books, 1981), 78.

14. Lyn Ragsdale and John Theis III, "The Institutionalization of the American Presidency, 1924–1992," *American Journal of Political Science* 41 (October 1997): 1280–1318.

15. Quoted in Page and Petracca, *The American Presidency*, 57.

16. Alfred Steinberg, *The First Ten: The Founding Presidents and Their Administrations* (New York: Doubleday, 1967), 59.

17. George Reedy, *The Twilight of the Presidency* (New York: New American Library, 1971), 38–39.

18. Neustadt, *Presidential Power*, 1–10.

19. Kernell, *Going Public*.

20. Tom Rosenstiel, *Strange Bedfellows: How Television and Presidential Candidates Changed American Politics* (New York: Hyperion Books, 1992).

21. Brandice Canes-Wrone and Kenneth W. Shotts, "The Conditional Nature of Presidential Responsiveness to Public Opinion," *American Journal of Political Science* 48 (October 2004): 690–706.

22. See Louis Fisher, *Constitutional Conflicts Between Congress and the President*, 7th ed. (Lawrence: University Press of Kansas, 2007).

23. Franklin D. Roosevelt, Press Conference, July 23, 1937.

24. Lyndon B. Johnson, *The Vantage Point* (New York: Holt, Rinehart and Winston, 1971), 448.

25. See Cary Covington, J. Mark Wrighton, and Rhonda Kinney, "A 'Presidency-Augmented' Model of Presidential Success on House Roll Call Votes," *American Journal of Political Science* 39 (November 1995): 1001–24; and Wayne P. Steger, "Presidential Policy Initiation and the Politics of Agenda Control," *Congress & the Presidency* 24 (Spring 1997): 102–14.

26. Quoted in Thomas E. Cronin, *The State of the Presidency*, 2nd ed. (Boston: Little, Brown, 1980), 169.

27. *Youngstown Sheet and Tube v. Sawyer*, 343 U.S. 579 (1952).

28. Charlie Savage, "Are Signing Statements Constitutional?" *Boston Globe* (April 30, 2006): A4.

Chapter 8

1. Gallup Poll, July 10–12, 2009.

2. Harold D. Lasswell, *Politics: Who Gets What, When and How* (New York: McGraw-Hill, 1938).

3. "A Century of Government Growth," *Washington Post* (January 3, 2000): A17. On the difficulty of counting the exact number of government agencies, see David Nachmias and David H. Rosenbloom, *Bureaucratic Government: U.S.A.* (New York: St. Martin's Press, 1980).

4. Mark Landler, *Alter Egos: Hillary Clinton, Barack Obama, and the Twilight Struggle Over America* (New York: Random House, 2016).

5. The classic work on regulatory commissions is Marver Bernstein, *Regulating Business by Independent Commission* (Princeton, NJ: Princeton University Press, 1955).

6. *Humphrey's Executor v. U.S.*, 295 U.S. 602 (1935).

7. John F. Duffy, "The Death of the Independent Regulatory Commission and the Birth of a New Independence," www.law.georgetown.edu/faculty/documents/duffy_paper.pdf.

8. Joe Davidson, "Details of Hatch Act Difficult to Enforce," *Washington Post* (June 28, 2011): B4.

9. David Osborne and Ted Gaebler, *Reinventing Government* (Reading, MA: Addison-Wesley, 1992), 20–21.

10. Al Kamen, "Feingold, McCain Try to Trim Appointees," *Washington Post* (March 9, 2010): B3.

11. Office of Personnel Management, *The Fact Book* (February 8, 2014), http://www.opm.gov/policy-data-oversight/data-analysis-documentation/federal-employment-reports/reports-publications/the-fact-book/.

12. Barbara Slavin, "State Department Having Staffing Trouble," *USA Today* (November 30, 2005): 10A.

13. USASpending.Gov (May 12, 2012), www.usaspending.gov.

14. Patricia Niehaus, "Statement on State of the Civil Service" (April 22, 2009), www.fedmanagers.org.

15. Niehaus, "Statement on the State of the Civil Service."

16. H. H. Gerth and C. Wright Mills, *From Max Weber* (New York: Oxford University Press, 1958).

17. Michael Lipsky, *Street-Level Bureaucracy: Dilemmas of the Individual in Public Services*, (New York: Russell Sage Foundation, 1980).

18. Cornelius M. Kerwin, *Rulemaking: How Government Agencies Write Law and Make Policy*, 2nd ed. (Washington, DC: CQ Press, 1999), xv.

19. Quoted in Arthur Schlesinger Jr., *A Thousand Days* (Greenwich, CT: Fawcett Books, 1967), 377.

20. Thomas V. DiBacco, "Veep Gore Reinventing Government—Again!" *USA Today* (September 9, 1993): 13A.

21. George A. Krause, "Presidential Use of Executive Orders, 1953–1994," *American Politics Quarterly* 25 (October 1997): 458–81.

22. Irene Murphy, *Public Policy on the Status of Women* (Lexington, MA: Lexington Books, 1974).

23. Rosemary O'Leary, *Environmental Change: Federal Courts and the EPA* (Philadelphia: Temple University Press, 1995).

Chapter 9

1. Bernard Schwartz, *The Law in America* (New York: American Heritage, 1974), 48.

2. Julius Goebel Jr., *History of the Supreme Court of the United States, vol. 1: Antecedents and Beginnings to 1801* (New York: Macmillan, 1971), 206.

3. Quoted in Goebel, *History of the Supreme Court*, 280.

4. *Chisholm v. Georgia*, 2 U.S. 419 (1793).

5. *Fletcher v. Peck*, 10 U.S. 87 (1810); *Martin v. Hunter's Lessee*, 14 U.S. 304 (1816); and *Cohens v. Virginia*, 19 U.S. 264 (1821).

6. *McCulloch v. Maryland*, 17 U.S. 316 (1819).

7. *Marbury v. Madison*, 5 U.S. 137 (1803).

8. *Marbury v. Madison*, 5 U.S. 137 (1803).

9. David W. Neubauer, *Judicial Process: Law, Courts, and Politics* (Pacific Grove, CA: Brooks/Cole, 1991), 57.

10. Cases involving citizens from different states can be filed in state or federal court.

11. Sheldon Goldman and Elliot E. Slotnick, "Clinton's First Term Judiciary: Many Bridges to Cross," *Judicature* (May/June 1997): 254–5.

12. Betsy Palmer, "Evolution of the Senate's Role in the Nomination and Confirmation Process." *CRS Report RL 31498* (March 29, 2005).

13. Quoted in Judge Irving R. Kaufman, "Charting a Judicial Pedigree," *New York Times* (January 24, 1981): A23.

14. Quoted in Lawrence Baum, *The Supreme Court*, 3rd ed. (Washington, DC: CQ Press, 1989), 108.

15. Quoted in Nina Totenberg, "Will Judges Be Chosen Rationally?" *Judicature* (August/September 1976): 93.

16. Lee Epstein, Andrew D. Martin, Kevin M. Quinn, and Jeffrey A. Segal. "Circuit Effects: How the Norm of Federal Judicial Experience Biases the Supreme Court." *University of Pennsylvania Law Review* 157 (2008): 833–80.

17. See Barbara A. Perry, *A Representative Supreme Court? The Impact of Race, Religion, and Gender on Appointments* (New York: Greenwood, 1991). Clarence Thomas was raised a Catholic but attended an Episcopalian church at the time of his appointment, having been barred from Catholic sacraments because of his remarriage. He again, however, is attending Roman Catholic services.

18. John Brigham, *The Cult of the Court* (Philadelphia: Temple University Press, 1987).

19. Stephen L. Wasby, *The Supreme Court in the Federal Judicial System*, 4th ed. (Chicago: Nelson-Hall, 1988), 194.

20. Wasby, *The Supreme Court in the Federal Judicial System*, 199. Much of this change occurred as the result of an increase in state criminal cases, of which nearly 100 percent concerned constitutional questions.

21. Paul Wahlbeck, et al., "Ghostwriters on the Court? A Stylistic Analysis of U.S. Supreme Court Opinion Drafts," *American Politics Research* 30 (March 2002): 166–92. Wahlbeck et al. note that "between 1969 and 1972—the period during which the justices each became entitled to a third law clerk … the number of opinions increased by about 50 percent and the number of words tripled."

22. Richard A. Posner, *The Federal Courts: Crisis and Reform* (Cambridge, MA: Harvard University Press, 1985), 114; Todd Peppers and Clare Cushman, eds. *Of Courtiers and Kings: More Stories of Supreme Court Law Clerks and Their Justices* (Charlottesville: University of Virginia Press, 2016).

23. "Retired Chief Justice Warren Attacks Freund Study Group's Composition and Proposal," *American Bar Association Journal* 59 (July 1973): 728.

24. Kathleen Werdegar, "The Solicitor General and Administrative Due Process," *George Washington Law Review* (1967–1968): 482.

25. Rebecca Mae Salokar, *The Solicitor General: The Politics of Law* (Philadelphia: Temple University Press, 1992), 3.

26. See, for example, Lawrence Baum, *The Supreme Court*, 4th ed. (Washington, DC: CQ Press, 1992), 106.

27. Richard C. Cortner, *The Supreme Court and Civil Liberties* (Palo Alto, CA: Mayfield, 1975), vi.

28. *Brown v. Board of Education*, 347 U.S. 483 (1954); *Planned Parenthood of Southeastern Pennsylvania v. Casey*, 585 U.S. 833 (1992); and *Grutter v. Bollinger*, 539 U.S. 306 (2003).

29. *Zubick v. Burwell* 578 U.S. __(2016).

30. Gregory A. Caldeira and John R. Wright, "Amicus Curiae Before the Supreme Court: Who Participates, When and How Much?" *Journal of Politics* 52 (August 1990): 803.

31. *U.S. v. Nixon*, 418 U.S. 683 (1974).

32. Linda Greenhouse, "With O'Connor Retirement and a New Chief Justice Comes an Awareness of Change," *New York Times* (January 28, 2006): A10.

33. Donald L. Horowitz, *The Courts and Social Policy* (Washington, DC: Brookings Institution, 1977), 538.

34. Timothy R. Johnson and Andrew D. Martin, "The Public's Conditional Response to Supreme Court Decisions," *American Political Science Review* 92 (June 1998): 299–309.

35. *U.S. v. Nixon*, 418 U.S. 683 (1974).

36. Pew Research Center for People and the Press, "Supreme Court Favorability Reaches New Low" (May 1, 2012).

37. Gallup, *Supreme Court In Depth: Topics A to Z. N.D.*

38. Alixandra B. Yanus, "Neither Force Nor Will: A Theory of Judicial Power," doctoral dissertation, University of North Carolina, 2010.

39. *Boumediene v. Bush*, 553 U.S. 723 (2008).

40. *Arizona v. United States*, 567 U.S. (2012).

41. "Supreme Court Cases Overruled by Subsequent Decision," www.gpoaccess.gov/constitution/pdf/con041.pdf.

42. See, for example, *Colegrove v. Green*, 328 U.S. 549 (1946).

43. *Baker v. Carr*, 369 U.S. 186 (1962).

44. Kevin T. McGuire, "Public Schools, Religious Establishments, and the U.S. Supreme Court: An Examination of Policy Compliance," *American Politics Research*, 37 (2009): 50–74.

45. Charles Johnson and Bradley C. Canon, *Judicial Policies: Implementation and Impact*, 2nd ed. (Washington, DC: CQ Press, 1998), ch. 1.

46. *Reynolds v. Sims*, 377 U.S. 533 (1964).

47. *Mississippi University for Women v. Hogan*, 458 U.S. 718 (1982).

Chapter 10

1. Spier, Hans, "Historical Development of Public Opinion," *American Journal of Sociology* 55(4) (Jan. 1950), 376.

2. Bianco, William T. and David T. Canon, "Public Opinion" in *American Politics Today* 3rd ed. (New York: Norton, 2013).

3. Alan M. Winkler, "Public Opinion," in Jack Greene, ed., *The Encyclopedia of American Political History* (New York: Charles Scribner's Sons, 1988).

4. *Literary Digest* 125 (November 14, 1936): 1.

5. Walker, Don D. "Woodrow Wilson and Walter Lippman: A Narrative Historical Imagery" *Western Political Quarterly* 12(4 Dec. 1959): 939-947; Turner, Henry A. "Woodrow Wilson and Public Opinion," *Public Opinion Quarterly*, 21 4 (Winter, 1957 – 1958):506-520.

6. Robert S. Erikson, Norman R. Luttbeg, and Kent L. Tedin, *American Public Opinion: Its Origin, Contents, and Impact* (New York: Wiley, 1980), 28.

7. Diane J. Heith, "Staffing the White House Public Opinion Apparatus 1969–1988," *Public Opinion Quarterly* 62 (Summer 1998): 165.

8. Francis J. Connolly and Charley Manning, "What 'Push Polling' Is and What It Isn't," *Boston Globe* (August 16, 2001): A21.

9. McGeeny, Kyley. "PEW Research Center will call 75% cellphones for surveys in 2016." PEW Research Center, January 5, 2016.

10. This discussion draws heavily from Terence Ball and Richard Dagger, *Political Ideologies and the Democratic Ideal*, 5th ed. (New York: Longman, 2004).

11. Ball and Dagger, *Political Ideologies and the Democratic Ideal*, 2.

12. Isaiah Berlin, *The Crooked Timber of Humanity: Chapters in the History of Ideas* (New York: Vintage, 1992), 1.

13. William Safire, *Safire's New Political Dictionary* (New York: Random House, 1993), 144–5.

14. Jack C. Plano and Milton Greenberg, *The American Political Dictionary*, 9th ed. (Fort Worth, TX: Harcourt Brace, 1993), 16.

15. Philip E. Converse, "The Nature of Belief Systems in Mass Publics," in David E. Apter, ed., *Ideology and Discontent* (New York: Free Press, 1964), 206–21.

16. Richard Dawson and Kenneth Prewitt, *Political Socialization*, 2nd ed. (Boston: Little, Brown, 1977), 33.

17. Nicholas J. G. Winter, *Dangerous Frames: How Ideas About Race and Gender Shape Public Opinion* (Chicago: University of Chicago Press, 2008).

18. Pew Research Center, 2012 American Values Survey, www.people-press.org/values-questions/.

19. Susan A. MacManus, *Young v. Old: Generational Combat in the 21st Century* (Boulder, CO: Westview, 1995).

20. Jan W. van Deth, Simone Abendschon, and Meike Vollmar, "Children and Politics: An Empirical Reassessment of Early Political Socialization," *Political Psychology* 32 (2011): 147–74.

21. James Simon and Bruce D. Merrill, "Political Socialization in the Classroom Revisited: The Kids Voting Program," *Social Science Journal* 35 (1998): 29–42.

22. Kaiser Family Foundation, "Daily Media Use Among Children and Teens Up Dramatically from Five Years Ago," (January 21, 2010): www.kff.org/entmedia/entmedia012010nr.cfm.

23. Fairleigh Dickinson University Public Mind Poll, May 3, 2012, http://publicmind.fdu.edu/2012/confirmed/.

24. Roderick P. Hart, *The Sound of Leadership: Presidential Communication in the Modern Age* (Chicago: University of Chicago Press, 1989).

25. National Geographic-Roper Public Affairs Poll, December 17, 2005–January 20, 2006, www.nationalgeographic.com.

26. Kathleen Dolan, "Do Women and Men Know Different Things? Measuring Gender Differences in Political Knowledge," *Journal of Politics* 73 (2011): 97–107.

27. Joy K. Dow, "Gender Differences in Political Knowledge: Distinguishing Characteristics-Based and Returns-Based Differences," *Political Behavior* 31 (2009): 117–36.

28. Andrew Kohut, "But What Do the Polls Show? How Public Opinion Surveys Came to Play a Major Role in Policymaking and Politics," Pew Research Center Publications, (October 14, 2009): http://pewresearch.org/pubs/.

29. Quoted in Kohut, "But What Do the Polls Show?"

Chapter 11

1. This conception of a political party was originally put forth by V. O. Key Jr. in *Politics, Parties, and Pressure Groups* (New York: Crowell, 1958).

2. John H. Aldrich, *Why Parties? The Origin and Transformation of Party Politics in America* (Chicago: University of Chicago Press, 1995).

3. By contrast, Great Britain did not develop truly national, broad-based parties until the 1870s.

4. See *Historical Statistics of the United States: Colonial Times to 1970*, part 2, series Y-27-28 (Washington, DC: Government Printing Office, 1975), based on unpublished data prepared by Walter Dean Burnham. See also Harold W. Stanley and Richard G. Niemi, *Vital Statistics on American Politics 2009–2010* (Washington, DC: CQ Press, 2009), for contemporary turnout figures.

5. On the subject of party realignment, see Walter Dean Burnham, *Critical Elections and the Mainsprings of American Politics* (New York: Norton, 1970); Kristi Andersen, *The Creation of a Democratic Majority* (Chicago: University of Chicago Press, 1979); and John R. Petrocik, "Realignment: New Party Coalitions and the Nationalization of the South," *Journal of Politics* 49 (May 1987): 347–75.

6. See, for example, V. O. Key Jr., "A Theory of Critical Elections," *Journal of Politics* 17 (February 1955): 3–18.

7. For a discussion of secular realignment in the South, see Jeffrey M. Stonecash, "Class and Party: Secular Realignment and the Survival of Democrats Outside the South," *Political Research Quarterly* 53:4 (2000): 731–52.

8. John Green and Paul S. Herrnson, eds., *Responsible Partisanship: The Evolution of American Political Parties Since the 1950s* (Lawrence: University Press of Kansas, 2003).

9. Cornelius P. Cotter, et al., *Party Organizations in American Politics* (Pittsburgh: University of Pittsburgh Press, 1989).

10. For an analysis of the parties' role in recruiting candidates, see Paul S. Herrnson, *Congressional Elections: Campaigning at Home and in Washington* (Washington, DC: CQ Press, 1995).

11. See David E. Price, *Bringing Back the Parties* (Washington, DC: CQ Press, 1984), 284–88.

12. Nate Silver, "Republicans Were More United Than Ever Under John Boehner," *FiveThirtyEight*, September 28, 2015, http://fivethirtyeight.com/datalab/republicans-were-more-united-than-ever-under-john-boehner/.

13. Sidney M. Milkis, *The President and the Parties: The Transformation of the American Party System Since the New Deal* (New York: Oxford University Press, 1993).

14. Lazaro Gamio and Dan Keating, "How Trump redrew the electoral map, from sea to shining sea," *Washington Post*, November 9, 2016, https://www.washingtonpost.com/graphics/politics/2016-election/election-results-from-coast-to-coast/.

15. Karen M. Kaufmann and John R. Petrocik, "The Changing Politics of American Men: Understanding the Sources of the Gender Gap," *American Journal of Political Science* 43 (July 1999): 864–87.

16. William H. Flanigan and Nancy H. Zingale, *Political Behavior of the American Electorate*, 12th ed. (Washington, DC: CQ Press, 2010).

17. The Pew Forum on Religion and Public Life, "Trends in Party Identification of Religious Groups," (February 2, 2012): http://www.pewforum.org/Politics-and-Elections/Trends-in-Party-Identification-of-Religious-Groups.aspx.

18. This section draws on Morris Fiorina, *Culture War? The Myth of a Polarized America* (New York: Longman, 2011); Morris P. Fiorina and Samuel J. Abrams, "Political Polarization in the American Public," *Annual Review of Political Science* 11 (2008): 563–88; and Alan I. Abramowitz and Kyle L. Saunders, "Is Polarization a Myth?" *Journal of Politics* 70 (2008): 542–55.

19. Alan I. Abramowitz and Steven Webster, "The rise of negative partisanship and the nationalization of U.S. elections in the 21st century," *Electoral Studies* 41 (2016), 12–22.

20. Alan Abramowitz, *The Polarized Public? Why American Government Is So Dysfunctional*, Pearson, 2012.

21. Samuel J. Abrams and Morris P. Fiorina, *Disconnect: The Breakdown of Representation in American Politics* (University of Oklahoma Press, 2009).

22. Samuel J. Abrams and Morris P. Fiorina, "'The Big Sort' That Wasn't: A Skeptical Reexamination," *PS: Political Science and Politics*, Volume 45, Issue 02, April 2012: 203–10.

23. Barbara Sinclair, *Party Wars: Polarization and the Politics of National Policy Making* (University of Oklahoma Press, 2006).

24. Pew Research Center, "A Deep Dive Into Party Affiliation," April 7, 2015, http://www.people-press.org/2015/04/07/a-deep-dive-into-party-affiliation/.

Chapter 12

1. Paul Allen Beck, *Party Politics in America*, 8th ed. (New York: Longman, 1998); David Adamany, "Cross-Over Voting and the Democratic Party's Reform Rules," *American Political Science Review* 70 (1976): 536–41; Ronald Hedlund and Meredith W. Watts, "The Wisconsin Open Primary: 1968 to 1984," *American Politics Quarterly* 14 (1986): 55–74; Gary D. Wekkin, "The Conceptualization and Measurement of Crossover Voting," *Western Political Quarterly* 41 (1988): 105–14; Gary D. Wekken, "Why Crossover Voters Are Not 'Mischievous' Voters," *American Politics Quarterly* 19 (1991): 229–47; and Todd L. Cherry and Stephan Kroll, "Crashing the Party: An Experimental Investigation of Strategic Voting in Primary Elections," *Public Choice* 114 (2003): 387–420.

2. Of these ten states, South Dakota is the only state outside the South to hold a runoff primary. A runoff is held only if no candidate receives at least 35 percent of the vote. See "Statutory Election Information of the Several States," *The Green Papers*, www.thegreenpapers.com/slg/sei.phtml?format=sta.

3. Shaun Bowler, et al., eds., *Citizens as Legislators: Direct Democracy in the United States* (Columbus: Ohio State University Press, 1998).

4. For a more in-depth discussion of initiative, referendum, and recall voting, see Larry J. Sabato, Howard R. Ernst, and Bruce Larson, *Dangerous Democracy? The Battle over Ballot Initiatives in America* (Lanham, MD: Rowman and Littlefield, 2001); and David S. Broder, *Democracy Derailed: Initiative Campaigns and the Power of Money* (New York: Harcourt, 2000).

5. Howard R. Ernst, "The Historical Role of Narrow-Material Interests in Initiative Politics," in Larry J. Sabato, Howard R. Ernst, and Bruce Larson, eds., *Dangerous Democracy?*

6. Seth Masket, "The Recall Is the New Normal," *Pacific Standard Magazine*, September 17, 2013, http://www.psmag.com/politics-and-law/recall-election-now-thing-permanent-campaign-election-66344.

7. Joshua Spivak, "The 21st Century Recall—Cheaper, Faster, Easier," *Politico* (March 18, 2011): 19.

8. Elaine Ciulla Kamarck and Kenneth M. Goldstein, "The Rules Matter: Post-Reform Presidential Nominating Politics," in L. Sandy Maisel, ed., *The Parties Respond: Changes in American Parties and Campaigns* (Boulder, CO: Westview, 1994), 174.

9. George Serra, "What's in It for Me? The Impact of Congressional Casework on Incumbent Evaluation," *American Politics Quarterly* 22 (1994): 403–20.

10. Glenn R. Parker and Suzanne L. Parker, "Correlates and Effects of Attention to District by U.S. House Members," *Legislative Studies Quarterly* 10 (May 1985): 223–42.

11. Jamie L. Carson, "Strategy, Selection, and Candidate Competition in U.S. House and Senate Elections," *Journal of Politics* 67 (2005): 1–28.

12. Gary W. Cox and Jonathan N. Katz, "Why Did the Incumbency Advantage in U.S. House Elections Grow?" *American Journal of Political Science* 40 (May 1996): 478–97.

13. Sunhil Ahuja, et al., "Modern Congressional Election Theory Meets the 1992 House Elections," *Political Research Quarterly* 47 (1994): 909–21; and Paul S. Herrnson, *Congressional Elections: Campaigning at Home and in Washington,* 2nd ed. (Washington, DC: CQ Press, 1998).

14. Gary C. Jacobson and Michael A. Dimock, "Checking Out: The Effects of Bank Overdrafts on the 1992 House Elections," *American Journal of Political Science* 38 (1994): 601–24; and Herrnson, *Congressional Elections.*

15. See "Candidates and Nominations," in Paul S. Herrnson, *Congressional Elections: Campaigning at Home and in Washington,* 4th ed. (Washington, DC: CQ Press, 2004), 35–68.

16. Dennis W. Johnson, *No Place for Amateurs: How Political Consultants Are Reshaping American Democracy* (New York: Routledge, 2001).

17. Robert S. Erikson and Christopher Wlezien, *The Timeline of Presidential Elections: How Campaigns Do and Do Not Matter* (Chicago: University of Chicago Press, 2012).

18. Diana C. Mutz, "Effects of Horse-Race Coverage on Campaign Coffers: Strategic Contributing in Presidential Primaries," *Journal of Politics* 57 (November 1995): 1015–42.

19. See "Media, Old and New," in Johnson, *No Place for Amateurs,* 115–47.

20. Emily Schultheis, "Campaigns Picking Up on Mobile Ads," *Politico* (November 29, 2011): 21–22.

21. Jody C. Baumgartner and Jonathan S. Morris, "My-FaceTube Politics: Social Networking Sites and Political Engagement of Young Adults," *Social Science Computer Review* 28 (2010): 24–44.

22. Five liberal Democratic U.S. senators, including George McGovern of South Dakota, were defeated in this way in 1980, for example.

23. Center for Responsive Politics, www.opensecrets.org/.

24. *McConnell* v. *FEC,* 540 U.S. 93 (2003).

25. *FEC* v. *Wisconsin Right to Life, Inc.,* 551 U.S. 449 (2007).

26. *Davis* v. *FEC,* 554 U.S. 729 (2008).

27. *Citizens United* v. *FEC,* 558 U.S. 50 (2010).

28. Herrnson, *Congressional Elections,* 133.

29. Center for Responsive Politics, www.opensecrets.org/.

30. Matea Gold, "Trump's deal with the RNC shows how big money is flowing back to the parties," Washington Post, May 18, 2016, https://www.washingtonpost.com/politics/trumps-deal-with-the-rnc-shows-how-big-money-is-flowing-back-to-the-parties/2016/05/18/4d84e14a-1d11-11e6-b6e0-c53b7ef63b45_story.html.

31. *Buckley* v. *Valeo,* 424 U.S. 1 (1976).

32. Center for Responsive Politics, www.opensecrets.org/.

33. Steven T. Engel and David J. Jackson, "Wielding the Stick Instead of Its Carrot: Labor PAC Punishment of Pro-NAFTA Democrats," *Political Research Quarterly* 51 (September 1998): 813–28.

34. Janet M. Box-Steffensmeier and J. Tobin Grant, "All in a Day's Work: The Financial Rewards of Legislative Effectiveness," *Legislative Studies Quarterly* 24 (November 1999): 511–23.

35. Campaign Finance Institute, "501(c) Groups Emerge as Big Players Alongside 527s," www.cfinst.org. Information also drawn from www.opensecrets.org/527s/types.php.

36. Campaign Finance Institute, "501(c) Groups Emerge."

37. Federal Election Commission, "Public Funding of Presidential Elections," Published in August 1996 (updated February 2016, www.fec.gov/pages/brochures/pubfund.shtml#anchor688095.

38. CNN, 2016 election results, www.cnn.com/election/results/exit-polls.

39. Steven J. Rosenstone and John Mark Hanson, *Mobilization, Participation, and Democracy in America* (New York: Macmillan, 1993).

40. CNN, 2016 election results, www.cnn.com/election/results/exit-polls.

41. CNN, 2016 election results, www.cnn.com/election/results/exit-polls

42. CNN, 2016 election results, www.cnn.com/election/results/exit-polls

43. Karlo Bakkios Marcelo, et al., "Young Voter Registration and Turnout Trends," www.civicyouth.org. Estimates of young voter registration vary widely in large part because they are often based on polling numbers, and these numbers are subject to overreporting as well as difficulties in reaching and surveying this demographic group.

44. Squire, P., Wolfinger, R.E. and Glass, D.P. (1987) 'Residential Mobility and Voter Turnout', *American Political Science Review,* 81(1), pp. 45–65. doi: 10.2307/1960778.

45. Adam J. Berinsky and Gabriel S. Lenz, Education and Political Participation: Exploring the Causal Link, Polit Behav (2011) 33:357–373, web.mit.edu/berinsky/www/files/edu.pdf.

46. See, for example, Brennan Center for Justice, "Automatic Voter Registration and Modernization in the States," July 12, 2016, www.brennancenter.org/analysis/voter-registration-modernization-states.

47. See, for example, Barry C. Burden, et al. "Election laws, mobilization, and turnout: The unanticipated consequences of election reform." *American Journal of Political Science* 58.1 (2014): 95–109.

48. See for example, David C. Wilson and Paul R. Brewer, "The Foundations of Public Opinion on Voter ID Laws: Political Predispositions, Racial Resentment, and Information Effects *Public Opinion Quarterly* first published online October 4, 2013 doi:10.1093/poq/nft026.

49. See for example, Paul Gronke, Paul, et al. "Convenience voting." *Annual Review of Political Science* 11 (2008): 437–455.

50. See for example, U.S. Vote Foundation, "The Future of Voting: End-to-End Verifiable Internet Voting," 2015, www.usvotefoundation.org/sites/default/files/E2EVIV_full_report.pdf.

51. Verified Voting, www.verifiedvoting.org.

52. Beyond Chads: Voting technology catches up," Washington Post, November 2, 2016, www.washingtonpost.com/sf/brand-connect/beyond-chads-voting-technology-catches-up/.

Chapter 13

1. American Press Institute, "The Personal News Cycle: How Americans Choose to Get Their News," accessed March 17, 2014, https://www.americanpressinstitute.org/ publications/reports/survey-research/personal-news- cycle/single-page/.

2. See Mitchell Stephens, *A History of News: From the Drum to the Satellite* (New York: Viking, 1989).

3. See Shelley Ross, *Fall from Grace* (New York: Ballantine, 1988), Chapter 12.

4. Richard L. Rubin, *Press, Party, and Presidency* (New York: Norton, 1981), 38–39.

5. Stephen Bates, *If No News, Send Rumors* (New York: St. Martin's, 1989), 185.

6. See Doris A. Graber, *Mass Media and American Politics*, 3rd ed. (Washington, DC: CQ Press, 1989), 12; and Thomas C. Leonard, *The Power of the Press: The Birth of American Political Reporting* (New York: Oxford University Press, 1986), chapter 7.

7. Darrell M. West, *The Rise and Fall of the Media Establishment* (Boston: Bedford/St. Martin's, 2001).

8. See, for example: Matthew Gentzkow, Jesse M. Shapiro, and Michael Sinkinso, "The Effect of Newspaper Entry and Exit on Electoral Politics," *American Economic Review* 101 (December 2011): 2980–3018, http://www.aeaweb.org/articles.php?doi.

9. Fairness and Accuracy in Reporting, "How Public Is Public Radio?" www.fair.org.

10. American Press Institute, "The Personal News Cycle," March 2014, http://www.americanpressinstitute.org/wp-content/uploads/2014/03/AP_NORC_API-Personal-News-Cycle_Topline_March-18-Release.pdf.

11. Pew Research Center, State of the Media 2015: Network News Fact Sheet, April 29, 2015, www.journalism.org/2015/04/29/network-news-fact-sheet/.

12. Rick Kissell, "Cable News Ratings: CNN on the Rise in 2015; Fox News Channel Remains Dominant," *Variety*, http://variety.com/2015/tv/news/cable-news-ratings-cnn-top-gainer-fox-news-channel-dominant-1201666151/. See also: Pew Research Center, "State of the News Media 2015," www.journalism.org/2015/04/29/cable-news-fact-sheet/.

13. Joshua Green and Sasha Issenberg, "Inside the Trump Bunker, With Days to Go," Bloomberg, October 27, 2016, www.bloomberg.com/news/articles/2016-10-27/inside-the-trump-bunker-with-12-days-to-go.

14. Pew Research Center, "12 Trends Shaping Digital News," (October 13, 2013): www.pewresearch.org/fact-tank/2013/10/16/12-trends-shaping-digital-news/.

15. American Press Institute, "How Americans Get Their News," March 17, 2014, www.americanpressinstitute.org/publications/reports/survey-research/how-americans-get-news/.

16. Pew Research Center, "Millennials and Political News," June 1, 2015, www.journalism.org/2015/06/01/millennials-political-news/.

17. Peter Hamby, "Did Twitter Replace the Boys on the Bus?" Joan Shorenstein Center on the Press, Politics and Public Policy Discussion Paper Series #D-80, September 2013, shorensteincenter.org/wp-content/uploads/2013/08/d80_hamby.pdf.

18. Ann Friedman, "Should All Journalists Be on Twitter," Columbia Journalism Review, October 9, 2014, www.cjr.org/realtalk/journalists_using_twitter.php?page=all.

19. Wesley Donehue, "The Danger of Twitter, Facebook Politics," CNN.com (April 24, 2012): www.cnn.com/2012/04/24/opinion/donehue-social-media-politics/index.html.

20. Nielsen Media Research, "Buzz in the Blogosphere: Millions More Bloggers and Blog Readers," (March 8, 2012): blog.nielsen.com/nielsenwire/online_mobile/buzz-in-the-blogosphere-millions-more-bloggers-and-blog-readers/.

21. Henry Farrell and Daniel W. Drezner, "The Power and Politics of Blogs," *Public Choice* 134 (2008): 15–30.

22. Radio and Television Correspondents Association, rtcacaphill.org/board/.

23. John R. Hibbing and Elizabeth Theiss-Morse, *Congress as Public Enemy: Political Attitudes Toward American Political Institutions* (New York: Cambridge University Press, 1995).

24. Karen Aho, "Broadcasters Want Access, but Will They Deliver Serious Coverage?" *Columbia Journalism Review* 5 (September/October 2003): www.cjr.org.

25. Tony Mauro, "A Gun Case in Need of Some Explaining: But Because of Our Reclusive Court, Today's Argument Is All We'll Get," *USA Today* (March 2, 2010): www.usatoday.com.

26. Benjamin I. Page, et al., "What Moves Public Opinion?" *American Political Science Review* 81 (March 1987): 23–44.

27. Thomas E. Nelson, et al., "Media Framing of a Civil Liberties Conflict and Its Effect on Tolerance," *American Political Science Review* 92 (September 1997): 567–83.

28. Shanto Iyengar and Donald R. Kinder, *News That Matters*, reprint ed. (Chicago: University of Chicago Press, 1989).

29. The Knight Foundation survey conducted by Dan Weaver of Indiana University found that 36 percent of journalists identify as Democrats, while 18 percent identify as Republicans, 33 percent say they do not identify with any party, and 13 percent identify with another party. The Pew Center found that most journalists self-identify as moderates (54 percent), but 34 percent say they are liberal and 7 percent say they are conservative. Dan Weaver, *The American Journalist of the 21st Century: U.S. News People at the Dawn of a New Millennium* (Mahwah, NJ: Erlbaum, 2007); Pew Center on Press and Politics, "How Journalists See Journalists," Washington, DC, 2004, people-press.org/files/legacy-pdf/214.pdf.

30. See for example the classic study by CBS and the New York Times in the 1980s: Michael J. Robinson and Margaret A. Sheehan, *Over the Wire and on TV: CBS and UPI in Campaign '80* (New York: Russell Sage Foundation, 1983). In a comparison of press coverage of the first 100 days of the presidencies of Bill Clinton and George W. Bush, the pew Project for Excellence in Journalism found that coverage was nearly identical—about half of printed stories were neutral, a quarter were positive, and a quarter negative. In comparison, 42 percent of stories were positive toward President Obama during his first 100 days, 38 percent were neutral, and 20 percent were negative. Pew Research Center's Project for Excellence in Journalism, "Obama's first 100 Days: How the President Fared in the Press vs. Clinton and Bush," April 28, 2009, www.journalism.org/2009/04/28/obamas-first-100-days/.

31. Timothy Groseclose and Tom Milyo, "A Measure of Media Bias," *Quarterly Journal of Economics* 120 (2005): 1191–1237.

32. John McIver, "Shoptalk/Commentary: How Incumbent Presidents Fare in Newspaper Endorsements," *Editor and Publisher*, November 6, 2012, www.editorandpublisher .com/Columns/Article/Shoptalk-Commentary–How- Incumbent-Presidents-Fare-in-Newspaper-Endorsements# sthash.jkcAwjYj.dpuf.

33. See for example, Stephen Ansolabehere, Rebecca Lessem, and James M. Snyder, Jr., "The Orientation of Newspaper Endorsements 1940-2002," Quarterly Journal of Political Science 1, no. 4 (October 2006): 393–404.

34. See for example, Matthew Gentzkow and Jesse M. Shapiro, "Political Slant of United States Daily Newspapers, 2005 (ICPSR 26242), www.icpsr.umich.edu/icpsr-web/ICPSR/studies/26242

35. Eric Alterman, *What Liberal Media? The Truth About Bias and the News* (New York: Basic Books, 2003).

36. The Fourth Estate, "Silenced: Gender Gap in the 2012 Election Coverage," www.4thestate.net/female-voices-in-media/infographic.

37. Girish Gulati, et al., "News Coverage of Political Campaigns," in Lynda Kaid, ed., *The Handbook of Political Communication Research* (New York: Lawrence Erlbaum, 2004).

38. Thomas E. Patterson, "News Coverage of the 2016 National Conventions: Negative News, Lacking Context," Shorenstein Center on Media, Politics and Public Policy, September 21, 2016, www.shorensteincenter.org/news-coverage-2016-national-conventions/.

39. Gallup, "Americans' Trust in Mass Media Sinks to New Low," September 14, 2016, www.gallup.com/poll/195542/americans-trust-mass-media-sinks-new-low.aspx.

40. Amy Mitchell, Jeffrey Gottfried, Michael Barthel and Elisa Shearer, "The Modern News Consumer: New Attitudes and Practices in the Digital Era," Pew Research Center, July 7, 2016, www.journalism.org/2016/07/07/the-modern-news-consumer/.

41. Pew Research Center, "The Modern News Consumer: New Attitudes and Practices in the Digital Era."

42. *New York Times Co.* v. *U.S.*, 403 U.S. 713 (1971).

43. Vivek Wadhwa, "Social Media's Role in Politics," *Washington Post* (January 25, 2012): www.washingtonpost.com/national/on-innovations/social-media-as-role-in-politics/2012/01/25/gIQAQvZgdQ_story.html; Google, "Take Action," https://www.google.com/takeaction/.

44. "Dan Rather: Corporate Media Is 'in Bed' with Washington," *Huffington Post* (May 20, 2012): www.huffingtonpost.com/2012/05/20/dan-rather-cbs-news-corporate-media_n _1531121.html?ref=fb&src=sp&comm_ref=false.

45. Pew Research Center for the People and the Press, "Partisanship and Cable News Audiences," (October 30, 2009): www.pewresearch.org/.

46. Shanto Iyengar and Kyu S. Hahn, "Red Media, Blue Media: Evidence of Ideological Selectivity in Media Bias," *Journal of Communication* 59 (2009): 19–39.

47. Cass R. Sunstein, Republic.com *2.0* (Princeton, NJ: Princeton University Press, 2009).

48. David Brock and Ari Rabin-Havit, *The Fox Effect: How Roger Ailes Turned a Network into a Propaganda Machine* (New York: Anchor Books, 2012).

49. Preetam Kaushik, "Tomorrow's Internet: A World of Hyper-Personalized Tribes?," *Wired*, www.wired.com/insights/2014/03/todays-internet-world-hyper- personalized-tribes/.

50. Rachel Smolkin, "What the Mainstream Media Can Learn from Jon Stewart," *American Journalism Review* (June/July 2007): http://www.ajr.org/article.asp?id=4329.

51. Matthew A. Baum and Angela Jamison, "The Oprah Effect: How Soft News Helps Inattentive Citizens Vote Consistently," *Journal of Politics* 68 (2008): 946–59.

52. Donald L. Jorand and Benjamin I. Page, "Shaping Foreign Policy Opinions: The Role of TV News," *Journal of Conflict Resolution* 36 (June 1992): 227–41.

53. Philip E. Tetlock, *Expert Political Judgment: How Good Is It? How Can We Know?* (Princeton, NJ: Princeton University Press, 2006).

54. Kelly Kaufhold, Sebastian Valenzuela, and Homero Gil de Zuniga, "Citizen Journalism and Democracy: How User-Generated News Use Relates to Political Knowledge and Participation," *Journalism and Mass Communication Quarterly* 87 (2010): 515–29.

Chapter 14

1. Robert D. Putnam, "Bowling Alone: America's Declining Social Capital," *Journal of Democracy* 6 (1995): 650–65; and Putnam, *Bowling Alone: The Collapse and Revival of American Community* (New York: Simon and Schuster, 2000).

2. Everett Carll Ladd, quoted in Richard Morin, "Who Says We're Not Joiners," *Washington Post* (May 2, 1999): B5.

3. Quoted in Grant McConnell, "Lobbies and Pressure Groups," in Jack Greene, ed., *Encyclopedia of American Political History*, vol. 2 (New York: Macmillan, 1984), 768.

4. Lee Epstein, *Conservatives in Court* (Knoxville: University of Tennessee Press, 1985).

5. Jack L. Walker, "The Origins and Maintenance of Interest Groups in America," *American Political Science Review* 77 (June 1983): 390–406.

6. Peter Steinfels, "Moral Majority to Dissolve: Says Mission Accomplished," *New York Times* (June 12, 1989): A14.

7. "Business Roundtable: About Us," (January 2014): http://businessroundtable.org/about.

8. John Brehm and Wendy Rahn, "Individual-Level Evidence for the Causes and Consequences of Social Capital," *American Journal of Political Science* 41 (July 1997): 999.

9. Mark Schneider, et al., "Institutional Arrangements and the Creation of Social Capital: The Effects of Public School Choice," *American Political Science Review* 91 (March 1997): 82–93.

10. Nicholas Lemann, "Kicking in Groups," *Atlantic Monthly* (April 1996), NEXIS.

11. David B. Truman, *The Governmental Process: Political Interests and Public Opinion* (New York: Knopf, 1951), ch. 16.

12. Mancur Olson, *The Logic of Collective Action: Public Goods and the Theory of Groups* (Cambridge, MA: Harvard University Press, 1965).

13. E. E. Schattschneider, *The Semisovereign People* (New York: Holt, Rinehart and Winston, 1960), 35.

14. Jeffrey M. Berry, *Lobbying for the People: The Political Behavior of Public Interest Groups* (Princeton, NJ: Princeton University Press, 1977), 7.

15. Berry, *Lobbying for the People*, 7.

16. Michael Wines, "For New Lobbyists, It's What They Know," *New York Times* (November 3, 1993): B14.

17. Quoted in Kay Lehman Schlozman and John T. Tierney, *Organized Interests and American Democracy* (New York: Harper and Row, 1986), 85.

18. Ken Kollman, "Inviting Friends to Lobby: Interest Groups, Ideological Bias, and Congressional Committees," *American Journal of Political Science* 41 (April 1997): 519–44.

19. Quoted in Norman J. Ornstein and Shirley Elder, Interest Groups, Lobbying and Policy Making (Washington, DC: CQ Press, 1978), 77.

20. Some political scientists speak of "iron rectangles," reflecting the growing importance of a fourth party, the courts, in the lobbying process.

21. Clement E. Vose, "Litigation as a Form of Pressure Group Activity," *Annals* 319 (September 1958): 20–31.

22. Paul M. Collins Jr., *Friends of the Supreme Court* (New York: Oxford University Press, 2008).

23. Amy Harder and Charlie Szymanski, "Sotomayor in Context: Unprecedented Input from Interest Groups," *National Review* (August 5, 2009): www.nationaljournal.com.

24. Robert A. Goldberg, *Grassroots Resistance: Social Movements in Twentieth Century America* (Belmont, CA: Wadsworth, 1991).

25. Ken Kollman, *Outside Lobbyists: Public Opinion and Interest Group Strategies* (Princeton, NJ: Princeton University Press, 1998); and Karen O'Connor, *Women's Organizations' Use of the Courts* (Lexington, MA: 1980).

26. Marie Hojnacki, "Interest Groups' Decisions to Join Alliances or Work Alone," *American Journal of Political Science* 41 (January 1997): 61–87.

27. Lee Ann Banaszak, *Why Movements Succeed or Fail: Opportunity, Culture, and the Struggle for Woman Suffrage* (Princeton, NJ: Princeton University Press, 1996); Frank R. Baumgartner and Beth L. Leech, *Basic Interests: The Importance of Groups in Politics and in Political Science* (Princeton, NJ: Princeton University Press, 1990); Nancy E. McGlen, et al., *Women, Politics, and American Society*, 5th ed. (New York: Longman, 2010); Robert H. Salisbury, "An Exchange Theory of Interest Groups," *Midwest Journal of Political Science* 13 (1969): 1–32; and Jack Walker, *Mobilizing Interest Groups in America: Patrons, Professions, and Social Movements* (Ann Arbor: University of Michigan Press, 1991).

28. Walker, *Mobilizing Interest Groups in America*.

29. Schattschneider, *The Semisovereign People*, 35.

30. Olson, *The Logic of Collective Action*.

31. Leslie Wayne, "And for His Next Feat, Billionaire Sets Sights on Bush," *New York Times* (May 31, 2004): A14.

32. Walker, "The Origins and Maintenance of Interest Groups," 390–406.

33. Richard Simons, "Bush Signs Bill to Tighten Lobbying Rules," *Los Angeles Times* (September 15, 2007): A13.

34. Center for Responsive Politics, www.opensecrets.org.

Chapter 15

1. This discussion draws on James E. Anderson, *Public Policy-making: An Introduction,* 2nd ed. (Boston: Houghton Mifflin, 1994), 5.

2. Thomas R. Dye, *Who's Running America?* (Englewood Cliffs, NJ: Prentice Hall, 1976).

3. David B. Truman, *The Governmental Process* (New York: Knopf, 1951).

4. Robert Dahl, *Who Governs?* (New Haven, CT: Yale University Press, 1961).

5. Theodore J. Lowi, "American Business, Public Policy Case Studies, and Political Theory," *World Politics,* XVI (July 1964): 677–715.

6. Roger W. Cobb and Charles D. Elder, *Participation in American Politics: The Dynamics of Agenda-Building,* 2nd ed. (Baltimore, MD: Johns Hopkins University Press, 1983), 85.

7. John W. Kingdon, *Agendas, Alternatives, and Public Policies,* 2nd ed. (New York: Harper Collins, 1995).

8. Charles O. Jones, *An Introduction to the Study of Public Policy,* 3rd ed. (Monterey, CA: Brooks/Cole, 1984), 87–89.

9. R. Frank, "Health Issues in the Clean Air Act," Environmental Health Perspectives 53 (1983): 241–246.

10. This discussion draws on Anne Schneider and Helen Ingram, "Behavioral Assumptions of Policy Tools," *Journal of Politics* 52 (May 1990): 510–29.

11. James D. Savage, *Balanced Budgets and American Politics* (Ithaca, NY: Cornell University Press, 1988), 176–79.

12. Budget of the United States Government, Fiscal Year 2017, www.whitehouse.gov/sites/default/files/omb/budget/fy2017/assets/hist_intro.pdf

13. U.S. Department of Labor, Bureau of Labor Statistics, "Labor Force Statistics from the Current Population Survey," www.data.bls.gov/timeseries/LNS14000000.

14. Congressional Research Service, *The Debt Limit: History and Recent Increases,* www.senate.gov/CRSReports/crs-publish.cfm?pid='0E%2C*P%5C%3F%3D%23%20%20%20%0A

15. Budget of the United States Government, Fiscal Year 2017 Summary Tables, www.whitehouse.gov/sites/default/files/omb/budget/fy2017/assets/tables.pdf.

16. About 38 percent of the nation's commercial banks are members of the Federal Reserve System. See www.richmondfed.org.

17. Kaiser Family Foundation, "An Overview of Medicare" (April 1, 2016), www.kff.org/medicare/issue-brief/an-overview-of-medicare/

18. Kaiser Family Foundation, "Status of State Action on the Medicaid Expansion Decision" (October 14, 2016), www.kff.org/health-reform/state-indicator/state-activity-around-expanding-medicaid-under-the-affordable-care-act/

19. HHS FY 2017 Budget in Brief www.hhs.gov/about/budget/budget-in-brief/nih/index.html

20. Office of Management and Budget, "Budget of the United States Government Fiscal Year 2017," www.gpo.gov/fdsys/pkg/BUDGET-2017-BUD/pdf/BUDGET-2017-BUD.pdf

21. Jennevieve Fong, "Lawmmkers push officials on No Child Left Behind rewrite" *The Hill,* www.thehill.com/blogs/blog-briefing-room/270795-lawmakers-push-officials-to-implement-education-reform-law

22. Common Core State Standards Initiative, "About the Standards," www.corestandards.org/about-the-standards/

23. Matthew M. Chingos and Beth Akers, "Is a Student Loan Crisis on the Horizon?" Brookings Institution (June 24, 2014), www.brookings.edu/research/is-a-student-loan-crisis-on-the-horizon/

24. Ronald Edsforth, *The New Deal: America's Response to the Great Depression* (Boston: Blackwell, 2000), 137.

25. Bureau of Labor Statistics, "Labor Force Statistics from the Current Population Survey" (October 7, 2016), www.bls .gov/web/empsit/cpsee_e16.htm

Chapter 16

1. Francis Fukuyama, *The End of History and the Last Man.* (New York: Free Press, 1992).

2. Alfred E. Eckes Jr., *Opening America's Market: U.S. Foreign Trade Policy Since 1776* (Chapel Hill: University of North Carolina Press, 1995).

3. John L. O'Sullivan, writing in 1845, quoted in Julius W. Pratt, "The Ideology of American Expansion," in Avery Craven, ed., *Essays in Honor of William E. Dodd* (Chicago: University of Chicago Press, 1935), 343–44.

4. Charles P. Kindleberger, *The World in Depression, 1929–1939* (Berkeley: University of California Press, 1986).

5. Mr. X., "The Sources of Soviet Conduct," *Foreign Affairs* (July 1947): 566–82. Mr. X. was later revealed to be U.S. ambassador and diplomat George Kennan.

6. Richard M. Nixon, Inaugural Address, January 20, 1969, Public Papers of the Presidents of the United States (Washington, DC: Government Printing Office).

7. Department of Homeland Security, "History," www.dhs.gov/history

8. *Congress A to Z,* 4th ed. (Washington, DC: CQ Press, 2003).

9. United States Census Bureau, www.census.gov/foreign-trade/balance/c5700.html] .

10. National Strategy for Combating Terrorism, www.globalsecurity.org/security/library/policy/national/nsct_sep2006.htm.

11. Doomsday and the history of nuclear weapons, *The Economist*, Jan 28, 2016. www.economist.com/blogs/graphicdetail/2016/01/daily-chart-21

12. NASA Global Climate Change: Climate change, "How Do We Know?" www.climate.nasa.gov/evidence/

13. IPCC (Intergovernmental Panel on Climate Change), Climate Change 2014: Impacts, Adaptation, and Vulnerability, www.ipcc.ch/report/ar5/wg2/

14. White House: The President's Climate Action Plan, www.whitehouse.gov/sites/default/files/image/president27sclimateactionplan.pdf

15. FFiona Harvey, "Paris Climate Change Agreement: The World's Greatest Diplomatic Success," *The Guardian* (December 14, 2015), www.theguardian.com/environment/2015/dec/13/paris-climate-deal-cop-diplomacy-developing-united-nations.

Index